RELIGIOUS TRENDS
IN ENGLISH POETRY

RELIGIOUS TRENDS
IN ENGLISH POETRY

By HOXIE NEALE FAIRCHILD

PROFESSOR OF ENGLISH

HUNTER COLLEGE OF THE CITY OF NEW YORK

VOLUME I: 1700-1740

PROTESTANTISM AND THE

CULT OF SENTIMENT

IN LITTERIS
LIBERTAS

1754·1893

NEW YORK: MORNINGSIDE HEIGHTS

COLUMBIA UNIVERSITY PRESS

Copyright 1939
COLUMBIA UNIVERSITY PRESS, NEW YORK

First printing 1939
Second printing 1949

PUBLISHED IN GREAT BRITAIN, CANADA, AND INDIA
BY GEOFFREY CUMBERLEGE, OXFORD UNIVERSITY PRESS,
LONDON, TORONTO, AND BOMBAY

Manufactured in the United States of America

TO THE MEMORY OF MY MOTHER

PREFACE

IF THE NEEDFUL YEARS AND HEALTH ARE GRANTED ME, I SHALL DEVOTE A SERIES of studies to religious thought and feeling as reflected in English poetry from the eighteenth century to the twentieth. The first of these books is here presented to my fellow-students. My files contain practically all of the material for a closely related sequel covering the period from 1740 to 1780. It should be ready for the press in two or three years. Three other volumes, dealing respectively with religious trends in romantic, Victorian, and contemporary poetry, will appear at much longer intervals.

Though this project will hardly arouse much popular enthusiasm, for various reasons it seems worth carrying out. It is generally recognized that there is a large poetic element in religion and a large religious element in poetry. A juxtaposition of the two may shed some light upon each. Though I shall not often theorize about the subject, I shall provide a body of material on which speculations may be based. I prefer, however, to stress the historical rather than the æsthetic or metaphysical uses of my theme. The student of the history of religion may wish to know what certain intelligent and imaginative Englishmen have thought and felt and said about religion from the eighteenth century to his own day. The student of the history of literature may wish to know how changing trends in religion have conditioned the poetry of various periods. More particularly, he may turn to these volumes for facts and ideas about such topics as the relations between Christianity and romanticism and the influence of modern science upon the basically religious art of the poet. In order to make my treatment of the subject as broadly useful as possible, I shall adopt a very loose and hospitable conception of the term "religion." Any idea or sentiment which a poet seems to regard as religious is grist for my mill, and I shall include poetic responses to philosophical and scientific trends which have significant religious implications.

In the present study, the first of the series, the method of investigation is strictly inductive. The sub-title hints at a theme which emerges only gradually, and at a conclusion which is not explicitly argued for until the final chapter. I merely ask the reader to examine with me the work of certain eighteenth-century poets with a view to determining the quantity and quality of religious thought and feeling which it displays. Despite my strong interest in the history of ideas, I have not classified my material according to topics. The frigid unreality of some recent studies in intellectual historiography perhaps arises from forgetfulness of the fact that books are written by men, not by abstractions floating about in the air. In the history of human thought, an idea cannot profitably be detached from the minds of the individuals who receive it, steep it in their personal temperament, combine it with other ideas and feelings, and give it a particular mode of expression. While I study the poets in the ultimate hope of arriving at historical generalizations, my basic units are individual writers and their works.

Thus the reader is invited to move down a long gallery hung with the self-portraits of eighteenth-century souls. To some the patient inspection of one poet after another may prove wearisome; I can only say that in my own case it has resulted in a more intimate understanding of the spirit of the period. Whether my general interpretation be right or wrong, I have learned to know a good many eighteenth-century men. The objection that only a few of them are *worth* knowing does not commend itself to a realistic historian of religious thought or of its literary expression. The obscurest scribbler may be interestingly symptomatic in himself and may increase our understanding of more important figures. But students who shrink from traversing the whole picture-gallery may refer to the Index of Names; or, if they do not wish to concern themselves with individual writers, to the Index of Topics.

But what, after all, can such an investigation tell us about the actual feelings of men? The pressure of literary tradition and fashion, the desire to imitate more successful writers, the temptation to say what one does not mean in order to be thought witty or edifying or sublime—these remind us of the inevitable differences between art and life. A study of what certain poets have *said* must not too confidently be used in estimating the actual state of religious thought in eighteenth-century England.

For the student of literature, of course, the history of what has been said in poetry on any important subject is worth knowing for its own sake. Other values, however, may be claimed for such a book as the present one. Though literary history and social history are by no means identical, the fact remains that in a general way poetry does reflect the real feelings of the more intelligent and articulate persons of the age in which it is produced. A small group of peculiar and distinguished writers will not, of course, convey a faithful impression of the *Zeitgeist;* but a large group representing various social classes, intellectual traditions, temperamental qualities, and degrees of literary skill may provide evidence of objective value. For the purposes of realistic literary history, one must examine not only many writers, but many poems by each writer. While a single poem will seldom justify any statement as to the author's customary views on the subject with which it deals, the whole mass of his work often gives a reliable insight into the workings of his mind.

The value of such evidence can often be judged by measuring the writer's poetic utterances against the known facts of his life. It has been no part of my task to make original researches into the lives of my poets. I have, however, used such biographical knowledge as could be gathered from scholarly books and articles, prefatory memoirs, the *Dictionary of National Biography,* and other easily accessible sources. It has been assumed that the reader is acquainted with the main features of the lives of the major writers. When pertinent biographical facts about minor figures were obtainable without labors of a kind which would have led away from, rather than toward, the heart of my subject, they have either been woven into the text or supplied in footnotes.

Always, however, the poet's work has been regarded as much more important than the details of his life. In gathering material I have concentrated on poets whose work falls wholly or chiefly between 1700 and 1740 and has been published in collected form, either in the eighteenth century or later. Incomplete eighteenth-century collections of a writer's poems have often been supplemented by his more important separately published but uncollected pieces. I find that I have read the work of 118 poets either completely or so nearly completely that I can hardly have missed in them anything of value for my subject. Ten poets whose work has never been collected were recognized as too important to be ignored— Richard Blackmore, for example, could not be passed over in a study of this kind. Of these writers I speak less confidently, but I have read their chief poems and feel entitled to generalize about them.

I am therefore acquainted with the religious ideas and feelings expressed by 128 poets concentrated within a span of about forty years. The list is very far from exhaustive, but it is plentiful, representative, and well-balanced. It covers, I believe, all varieties of religious feeling to be found in the period selected. It includes all the most famous poets, all the more familiar minor figures, and many writers who have received little or no scholarly attention from any viewpoint. Some students have ransacked a larger number of volumes, drawn from a longer section of the eighteenth century, in search of Miltonic blank verse, melancholy, loco-descriptive poems, or signs of the influence of the *Georgics;* but I am not aware that so many eighteenth-century poets of so brief a period have previously been studied as individual writers whose views on an important subject were to be chewed and digested.

For strict consistency I should have been content with my basic list of 128 poets. My reading in the British Museum, however, brought to light other material which I could not allow myself to omit. Twenty-one additional poets, therefore, are represented by one, two, or three substantial pieces. I also make use of eight separately published anonymous poems and seven miscellanies.

As a rough but workable means of showing the historical movement of religious feeling I have divided my poets into two main groups: those who flourished between 1700 and 1720, and those who flourished between 1720 and 1740. The artificiality of this arrangement is obvious in the case of poets whose careers occupy part of both periods, but I believe that the scheme is justified in its fruits. If a writer produced a substantial amount of characteristic poetry before 1720, all of his work, of whatever date, is considered in Part I; otherwise all of his work, of whatever date, is considered in Part II. Exceptional and doubtful cases are pointed out in footnotes. Wishing to achieve a compromise between the absurdity of beginning such a book with any particular year and the necessity of beginning it somewhere, I have included in Part I a few late-seventeenth-century poets whose careers form a bridge between the Restoration and the Queen Anne periods. I have avoided including in Part II poets who, though they begin to write before 1740, are more active after than before that date and may hence be treated more profitably in the next volume of this series. The omission of Edward Young demands some explanation. He is active in both the 1700-1720 and 1720-1740 periods; but his masterpiece does not begin to appear until after 1740, his long career runs into the 1760's, and by saving him for my next volume I obtain a useful link between it and the present study.

I have almost always suppressed the desire to draw corroborative material from the prose literature of the eighteenth century. Sporadic raids into drama, novel, and essay would have been misleading, and a careful study of these types in relation to religious thought would have swelled a lengthy book to impossible proportions. I regret the limitation of my field chiefly in discussing such writers as Defoe, Swift, and Addison, who express their religious views so much more fully and effectively in their prose than in their verse. Even here, however, I have clung to my rule. I make exception only of prefaces and critical treatises included in volumes of poetry; these are drawn upon freely. The exclusion of dramatic poetry applies also to prologues and epilogues. I do not concern myself with writers whose religious verse consists wholly of hymns or psalm-paraphrases for congregational singing; but the hymns of men like Watts, who also compose other forms of religious poetry, receive some attention with the rest of their work.

Whatever its shortcomings in other respects may be, my study does not exemplify the type of literary history which is all background and no literature. Perhaps, indeed, it goes too far in the opposite direction. The emphasis has been placed squarely upon the thought of poets, not upon the thought of philosophers and divines. When it is certain or clearly probable that a poet is indebted to another poet or to a more technically philosophical or theological prose writer, the fact enters into the discussion of his work; but I have not attempted to discover specific sources for the ideas and feelings of the writers examined. I have, however, suggested their relationship to general religious and philosophical tendencies, and in the last chapter I interpret my findings in terms of the history of religious thought.

I have not aspired to be read with equal pleasure by the man in the street, the busy housewife, the college freshman, and the seasoned scholar. I have addressed myself to readers who, though not necessarily specialists in the eighteenth century, are familiar with at least the principal roads which traverse that province of learning. Hence in the discussion of well-

known poets a good deal is taken for granted, while more obscure figures
receive what may seem to be a disproportionate amount of elaboration.
It should also be remembered that from the viewpoint of this study
eminent writers may be of negligible importance, while poets unknown
to fame may provide a wealth of material which deserves analysis.

Some readers will feel that my quoted passages are too numerous and
too long. On this point, however, I am incurably stubborn. I like very
copious quotation in a study of this kind. For our purposes, these individual writers are important; what they say is important; their way of
saying it is important. Whatever their faults in other respects may be,
eighteenth-century poets express themselves with considerable clarity.
Their own words are generally good enough for me. I have deliberately
assembled a large body of passages which reveal the religious temper of
the period more vividly than my own words could possibly do.

In the choice of texts for reading and quotation no great bibliographical
finesse has been practised. In general I have given preference to modern
scholarly editions, but for the great majority of the poets no such editions
exist. Alexander Chalmers's collection, very rich in eighteenth-century
poetry, has been freely used. When a poet has neither been edited by a
modern scholar nor printed in "Chalmers" I have used an eighteenth-
century edition of his works—by no means always the first, for later
eighteenth-century editions often contain additional poems or useful
memoirs. Any imperfections in the texts selected would hardly be such
as to affect our understanding of the writer's religious thought. In quoting
passages of poetry it seemed best to follow the eighteenth-century or
modern text exactly despite resultant inconsistencies of spelling, punctuation, and capitalization in my book. I have, however, sometimes
altered definitely bad eighteenth-century punctuation which might con-
fuse the most experienced reader; and especially in texts of the 1700-1720
period I have romanized a good many needless italics. Unless otherwise
stated, all italics remaining in quotations are those of the writer quoted.

I considered it an absurd waste of time and space to provide volume-
and-page references for the hundreds of quotations drawn from eighteenth-century poetry. On the other hand, I have been anxious to respect
not only the individuality of the author but the individuality of the poem.
The very title of a poem is often revelatory of taste and feeling. The
reader, too, would frequently find it difficult to follow my discussion of

a poet unless he understood that I had ceased to speak of one poem and
had begun to speak of another. Hence the titles of all poems which I
quote or to which I refer are supplied either in footnotes or in my text.
Since Appendix I lists all volumes of eighteenth-century poetry from
which material has been drawn, an exceptionally curious reader could
trace my quotations to their sources. References to eighteenth-century
prose works and to modern books and articles are supplied in the conventional way, and all such sources are listed in Appendix II. My examination of secondary sources has by no means been exhaustive, but I trust
I have neglected no important scholarly work which would illumine my
subject. If I have sometimes asked questions which more minute research
might have answered, I beg the reader to consider that time flies, and that
other books lie ahead of me.

The composition of this volume has been a rather lonely task. To
several friends I am grateful for interest and encouragement rather than
for actual assistance. My views as to the historical relationship between
Protestantism and sentimentalism, though independently arrived at, have
been confirmed and clarified by conversations with my colleague, Professor William Haller, and more recently by his new book, *The Rise of
Puritanism,* the proofsheets of which he kindly allowed me to read.
Professor George Sherburn and Professor Ernest Hunter Wright examined portions of the manuscript and made helpful comments. Dr. Maynard Mack of Yale University placed me in his debt by lending me a
copy of his unpublished dissertation, *The Intellectual Background of
Alexander Pope's "Essay on Man."* I am also greatly obliged to Miss Elizabeth Sherwood of the Columbia University Press for her careful editorial
services.

In these days of psychological analysis one seldom opens a book without asking what emotional drives the author is attempting to rationalize,
and what "real" reasons lurk behind his "apparent" reasons. Such questions would be easier to answer if authors would frankly disclose any
peculiarities which their critics might interpret as sources of "wishful-
ness." To make guesswork unnecessary, let me say that I am an Anglo-
Catholic in theory and in practise. That is the bias which the reader
must temper with his own prejudices as he scans the following pages.

                                                          H. N. F.

Barnard College
Columbia University
October, 1938

CONTENTS

Part I. 1700–1720

   I. Indifference, Negation, Scepticism   3

  II. Poets of Controversy   41

 III. Divine Poets   98

 IV. Middle-Classicists   155

  V. The Beginnings of Sentimentalism   205

Part II. 1720–1740

  VI. Neither Christian Nor Very Sentimental   265

 VII. Divine Poets   282

VIII. Non-Sentimental Christians   315

 IX. Sentimentalism—Mild Cases   361

  X. Sentimentalism—Severer Cases   424

 XI. Pope and Thomson   488

 XII. Protestantism and Sentimentalism   535

Appendix I. Primary Sources   577

Appendix II. Secondary Sources   586

Index of Names   593

Index of Topics   601

PART ONE: 1700–1720

Chapter I

INDIFFERENCE, NEGATION, SCEPTICISM

"THERE IS NO PROFUSION OF THE ETHEREAL SPIRIT AMONG US," BOLINGBROKE said.[1] Few students of the age of Queen Anne would dispute the accuracy of that statement. Religion—especially religion of that emotional and imaginative sort which inspires poetic expression—was at low tide. Large numbers of intelligent and cultivated men were at best indifferent, at worst hostile, to faith in the supernatural. We may therefore begin by examining poets of the 1700-1720 period whose verses suggest indifference, hostility, or an ambiguously sceptical attitude toward religion.

First let us summon up the shades of three noblemen. The first, the Earl of Halifax (1661-1715), can be dismissed in a single sentence. His cool, empty verses do not reveal the fact that he was a notorious free-thinker and libertine, but they contain not the faintest glimmer of religious feeling.

More outspoken than Montagu, at least on some occasions, is John Sheffield, Earl of Mulgrave and Duke of Buckingham (1648-1721), who left behind him an epitaph expressing doubt of his immortality. This dissipated infidel was a warm supporter of the High Church party and an intimate friend of Bishop Atterbury. Earlier in life, as a means of winning the favor of James II, he encouraged the report that he had strong leanings toward Roman Catholicism. Nothing could have been further from the truth. "His religion," says Dr. Johnson, "he may be supposed to have learned from Hobbes." In a poem *On Mr. Hobbes, and His Writings,* he praises the philosopher as the great liberator of the human mind from superstitious fears:

> While in dark ignorance we lay, afraid
> Of fancies, ghosts, and every empty shade,
> Great Hobbes appear'd, and by plain reason's light
> Put such fantastic forms to shameful flight.

[1] Walter Sichel, *Bolingbroke and His Times,* I, 93.

This freedom from superstition, the noble rake hastens to add, does not imply immorality:

> Fond is their fear, who think men needs must be
> To vice enslav'd, if from vain terrours free;
> The wise and good morality will guide,
> And superstition all the world beside.

It is at first rather surprising to read in Buckingham's short poem *On the Deity* that God is too lofty a subject for a human poet:

> While others vainly strive to know thee more,
> Let me in silent reverence adore;
> Wishing that human power were higher rais'd,
> Only that thine might be more nobly prais'd!
> Thrice happy angels in their high degree,
> Created worthy of extolling thee!

But is the inconsistency after all so very glaring? Since God is beyond the reach of human thought, let us cease to think about Him. Leaving to the angels the task of extolling Him, and casting off superstitious fears, let us lead rational Hobbistic lives in the material world which obviously surrounds us. Of the two poems, *On Mr. Hobbes* is by far the more honest and characteristic. There was not much silently reverent adoration in John Sheffield.

Lord Lansdowne, Pope's "Granville the polite" (1667-1735), was a Tory, a Jacobite, and a High Churchman of a better type than Buckingham. With his friend St. John, he supported the bill to prevent Occasional Conformity and later opposed its repeal, protesting against " 'sacrificing the Body and Blood of our Saviour to worldly and sinister purposes.' " [2] To quote a contemporary election slogan, he was

> ". . . sound as a bell
> For the Queen and the Church and Sacheverell." [3]

Whether his loyalty to the Church arose from any source deeper than Tory partisanship is an uncertain question. For an aristocrat of this period he led a decent life. Miss Handasyde, his modern biographer, asserts that "he had a deep sense of religion, a sincere love of the historic ritual of his Church, and an almost physical horror of Dissent." [4] The

[2] Elizabeth Handasyde, *Granville the Polite,* p. 167.
[3] *Ibid.,* p. 109.   [4] *Ibid.,* p. 168.

second and third clauses of this statement need not be quarreled with, but the first is unsupported by any evidence. Granville was primarily a Tory, though we may grant that his politics were suffused with an emotional and quasi-religious veneration for the Church which the Royal Martyr had died to defend.

However this may be, there is little or no religion in Granville's smooth, elegant verses. His comparison of James II's victory over Monmouth to the Resurrection of our Lord [5] indicates deep Toryism rather than "a deep sense of religion." *Meditation on Death,* one of a very few serious poems, is similar in theme to Shirley's famous *memento mori*:

> One destined period men in common have,
> The great, the base, the coward, and the brave,
> All food alike for worms, companions in the grave.

But there is no element of consolation, for we hear nothing of the immortality conferred upon "the actions of the just."

The poem on the death of his hero Waller is completely pagan: in Olympus, the dead poet has supplanted Apollo as "God of Verse." To the great majority of Granville's poems, indeed, Dr. Johnson's words are applicable: "He is forever amusing himself with the puerilities of mythology." Poetry for him was an aristocratic pastime presided over—before the apotheosis of Waller—by Apollo and the Muses. There may have been, there probably was, a little religion in his heart, but the author of the *Essay upon Unnatural Flights in Poetry* was not the man to set it down on paper.

Despite numerous exceptions, the female aristocrats of the period are likely to be somewhat more pious than the males, but two of them must be included in this chapter. The Honorable Mary Monck is one of those women who carry the tradition of the "learned lady" [6] from the seventeenth century into the eighteenth. In 1716, the year following her death,[7] her father, Viscount Molesworth, published her verses under the title, *Marinda. Poems and Translations upon Several Occasions.*

In his dedication to Princess Caroline, Molesworth lauds his daughter's moral principles, and for all I know she was no less religious than

---

[5] *To the King, In the First Year of His Majesty's Reign.*
[6] Cf. Myra Reynolds, *The Learned Lady in England.*
[7] The date of her birth is unknown.

learned. Her poems, however, furnish but little evidence on this point. Most of them are translations, chiefly from Italian and Spanish. Two or three of these, such as Filicaja's *Providenza,* are on religious themes, but one doubts whether this fact was an important motive in her choice of material. None of the original pieces in *Marinda* is religious at all. She wanders in the fading twilight of the Renaissance, translating or composing pastorals, elegant chatter about love, and such trifles as *A Dialogue between Lucinda and Strephon, on a Butter-fly that reviv'd before the Fire, and afterwards flew into it and was burnt.*

Marinda does not contain Mrs. Monck's least worthless poem, the *Verses Wrote on her Death-Bed at Bath, to her Husband in London.*[8] Death, she assures her husband, is not to be dreaded:

> Th' eternal scenes of heav'n he sets in view,
> And tells me that no other joys are true.
> But love, fond love, would yet resist his pow'r;
> Would fain awhile defer the parting hour:
> He brings thy mourning image to my eyes,
> And would obstruct my journey to the skies.
> But say, thou dearest, thou unwearied friend,
> Say, shoulds't thou grieve to see my sorrows end?
> Thou know'st a painful pilgrimage I've past,
> But should'st thou grieve that rest is come at last?
> Rather rejoice to see me shake off life,
> And die as I have liv'd, thy faithful wife.

"She died not only like a *Christian* but a *Roman* lady," says her father in the dedication of *Marinda,* arranging his adjectives in climactic order. These lines, despite the allusion to "scenes of heav'n," are more Roman than Christian in atmosphere. Even on her deathbed at Bath, Mary Monck is still the virtuous *précieuse* who can read Latin.

According to her biographer, Lady Mary Wortley Montagu (1689-1762)[9] "seems to have held the same religious views as the 'sensible men' of her period, which is not crediting her with any exceptional piety. She thought that 'religion' was a useful instrument for keeping the mob in order, and in consequence she considered it incumbent upon the upper classes to patronise the established church, and to refrain, at any rate in

---

[8] It may be found in *Poems by Eminent Ladies* (1755), II, 196.

[9] Somewhat hesitantly I assign her to the 1700-1720 period because her *Town Eclogues* were published in 1716 and because by that date her poems already filled a manuscript volume.

public, from expressing doubts on the subject of divine revelation." [10] In private, she regarded herself as a stoic,[11] but her stoicism was little more than a rationalization of her aversion to whatever lay beyond the scope of her keen but limited mind.

Lady Mary's poems do not, to any important extent, reflect either her personal scepticism or the more orthodox façade which protected that scepticism from the public gaze. In *The Court of Dullness* she is very severe against the irreligion of Swift and Bolingbroke, but in the first of her *Town Eclogues,* for equally personal reasons, she satirizes the piety of Lady Roxburgh. Two epistles, *To a Friend on His Travels* and *To the Same,* voice not only disillusionment at the emptiness of her own life, but indignation at the viciousness and impiety which lie all about her:

> Worse than the iron age, our impious times
> Have learned to laugh at most flagitious crimes.
> Are you to know that 'tis a jest to find
> Unthinking honesty pervade the mind?
> At best, they say, the man is strangely odd
> Who keeps his oath, and can believe a God.

And yet even the worst of men is not exempt from the pangs of remorse, for

> There is a time when conscience shakes the soul,
> When Toland's tenets cannot fear controul,
> When secret anguish fills the anxious breast,
> Vacant from business, nor compos'd by rest;
>
> .   .   .   .
>
> The wretch will start at every flash that flies,
> Grows pale at the first murmur of the skies;
> Then, if a fever fires corrupted blood,
> In every fit he feels the hand of God.

This tone, however, is exceptional in Lady Mary's poems. They are full of a restless desire to possess something that the world of wits and fops and rakes does not provide, but they never suggest that she has found in any sort of religion a solution of her problem. Once, to be sure, the spectacle of doves billing in her garden raises the question,

[10] George Paston, *Lady Mary Wortley Montagu and Her Times,* p. 541. The author goes on to say that "a long residence in Italy rendered Lady Mary more orthodox in her later days," but the fact is not important in the interpretation of her poems.

[11] *Ibid.,* p. 543. In early life she translated the *Enchiridion* of Epictetus.

Can all the doctrines of our schools,
Our maxims, our religious rules,
Can learning to our lives ensure
Virtue so bright, or bliss so pure?
The great Creator's happy ends
Virtue and pleasure ever blends:
In vain the church and court have try'd
Th' united essence to divide.
Alike they find their wild mistake,
The pedant priest, and giddy rake.[12]

A few more such utterances would disqualify Lady Mary for her position in this chapter, placing her instead among the sentimentalists. For better or worse, however, her mind is usually too hard and sharp to permit her to derive spiritual lessons from the sexual play of birds. She falls below common sense quite as rarely as she rises above it. In her old age, stoicism is wholly unable to bring her peace, but there seems to be nothing else to take its place. She writes:

Wisdom, slow product of laborious years,
The only fruit that life's cold winter bears;
Thy sacred seeds in vain in youth we lay,
By the fierce storm of passion torn away.

Should some remain in a rich gen'rous soil,
They long lie hid, and must be rais'd with toil;
Faintly they struggle with inclement skies,
No sooner born than the poor planter dies.[13]

We shall not expect to find much religion in the poems of those comic dramatists who inflamed the virtuous wrath of Collier and Blackmore. The poems of Congreve (1670-1729) are less obviously unreligious than his plays, precisely because they are much less genuine expressions of his personality; nevertheless they contain almost nothing to the present purpose. His "irregular ode" On Mrs. Arabella Hunt, Singing, refers warmly to the songs of the angels, but only by way of compliment to Arabella; and when, in A Hymn to Harmony, in Honour of St. Cecilia's Day, 1701, he associates harmony with the divine creative act, he is merely imitating Dryden. His verses do not reveal, though they do not deny, those classical standards of measure and prudence by which he regulated his private life.

[12] Verses Written in a Garden.   [13] Written at Lovere, 1755.

We do Farquhar (1678-1707), like Congreve, injustice in considering him from the unilluminating viewpoint provided by his poems. For him verse-writing is a trivial pastime almost wholly unrelated to his real thoughts and feelings. He can use scriptural allusions for purposes of eulogy,[14] or to give point to the epigram *On the Riding-House in Dublin, made into a Chapel:*

> A Chappel of the Riding-House is made;
> We thus once more see Christ in Manger laid,
> Where still we find the Jocky Trade supply'd;
> The Laymen bridled, and the Clergy ride.

In somewhat the same vein is a passage in his long battle-piece, *Barcellona,* satirizing the political contentiousness of the clergy. Except for this faint aroma of anti-clericalism, nothing significant for us emerges from Farquhar's poems. He was, we recall, the son of a clergyman.

The case of William Wycherley (1640?-1716) is much more complex, and it will be necessary to examine with some care his harsh, contorted, and often incoherent verses. He will undertake to write a poem about anything, from *To a Lady, who wore Drawers in an Ill Hour* to *The Good Conscience, the only Certain, Lasting Good.* He takes pleasure in writing on opposite sides of the same subject: two of his poems are respectively entitled *For the Publick Active Life, against Solitude* and *For Solitude and Retirement against the Publick Active Life.* Poetry is for him chiefly a means of displaying his paradoxical smartness in casuistry.

His favorite paradox is summed up in the title, *Upon the Impertinence of Knowledge, the Unreasonableness of Reason, and the Brutality of Humanity; proving the Animal Life the most Reasonable Life, since the most Natural, and most Innocent.* More than once, evidently with Erasmus' *Praise of Folly* in mind,[15] he reverts to this theme. Elsewhere, to be sure, he can advise a youth to subject his "brutish passions" to the curb of reason;[16] but on the whole Wycherley is, for him, unusually consistent in his anti-intellectualism.

This distrust of reason is not enlisted in the defense of religion, though it was probably a main element in the modicum of personal faith that

---

[14] Cf. *On the Death of General Schomberg* and *On the Death of the Late Queen.*
[15] Cf. *Upon the Discretion of Folly.*   [16] *Against Pride and Ambition.*

Wycherley possessed. In *The Intellectual Milieu of John Dryden,* Professor Bredvold has shown how large a part was played by fideistic scepticism in the Roman Catholicism of the seventeenth century. During his stay in France, Wycherley adopted the Roman creed, only to be reconverted to Protestantism soon after the Restoration. In the reign of James, however, he found it convenient to slip over to Rome once more. There is no evidence that he ever took the trouble of going through a second reconversion to Protestantism; indeed, there seems to be no doubt that shortly before his miserable death he received the *viaticum* as a Roman Catholic.[17]

These spiritual experiences—if they deserve that epithet—are not explicitly reflected in Wycherley's verse. He is not, however, without ethical and even religious interests. In snarling, crabbed satires which remind one of Oldham, this friend of Charles II and of his mistresses can be very severe against the vices of the age.[18] He can assert that atheists are more bigoted than Christians, since they cling to the one inconceivable miracle—

> That Motion is without a Mover wrought,
> That Reason's no Result of Sense or Thought;
> That Method is the blind Effect of Chance,
> And Order is without an Ordinance.[19]

If a man like Wycherley believes in a God at all, he had best believe in an extremely amiable one. Against "an ill-natur'd Lady, who said Good Nature was Folly, and the Disgrace of Good Sense," he defends the slandered virtue. Where would mankind be now, he asks, were not God eminently good-natured? [20] In the same spirit he addresses a clumsy but apparently sincere rhapsody *To Love:*

> Thou the Great Law of Nature art, O Love!
> By whom, Man first was made, does live, and move;
> Great Law of Nature! but for which, in vain,
> Religion, Justice could their own maintain.

Yet Wycherley loves to sneer at pious folk as conceited and hypocritical. Religious enthusiasm and poetical sublimity are both nonsense, and he scornfully compares them in these lines:

[17] H. P. Vincent, "The Death of William Wycherley," *Harvard Studies and Notes in Philology and Literature,* XV, 235.   [18] Cf. *The World Unmask'd.*   [19] *Against Atheism.*   [20] *In Vindication of Simplicity, and Good Nature.*

> As Quakers on the Spirit lay
> The Nonsense, which they preach, or pray;
> Make their dark senseless Fustian-Stuff,
> Their sole Illumination's Proof,
> So Bards of old, and present Time,
> Their Sense i' th' Clouds, will call Sublime.[21]

This is just the tone of Samuel Butler. Again Wycherley is typically the Cavalier when he writes, in an *Epistle to the King:*

> And Zeal is oft the Pious Fool's Excuse,
> Whose rude Pray'r is the Deity's Abuse.

In the same poem he insists that the nonconformist preachers who attack the stage are swayed by professional jealousy; for they themselves are actors, and very bad ones, who

> Against the Play-houses so much declare,
> Cause such their Meeting-houses only are.

Scorn of dissenters is to be expected from a Restoration loyalist. Wycherley, however, delivers similar thrusts even against the Establishment in *To an University-Wit, or Poet; who had written some ill Verses, with an ill Play or two; which, not succeeding, he resolv'd to turn Parson.* The poetaster has chosen to

> ... damn Your Age, not to be damn'd by it.
> You'd leave Prophane and witty Poetry,
> To lie o' God's-Name, more ingeniously.

Now that he has changed his "poetic sock" for "canonical galloshes" he will fare better, since

> ... Nonsense, Sacred, in the Pulpit is,
> Where Clergy-Fictions, Lay-men dare not hiss,
> Railing or Damning, dare not take amiss;
> Nonsense is safe still, in the House of Pray'r,
> Since there are none, who to refute it dare.

Not only dislike of Nonconformity but a more general anticlericalism and scorn of zeal are evidently strong in Wycherley.

His poems convey no inkling of his attitude toward Roman Catholicism except for *A Disswasive to his Mistress on her resolving to turn Nun.* He insists that the vow was

---

[21] *The Dedication to the Greatest Friend of the Muses, Vanity.*

> Made in the Weakness of your falt'ring Soul,
> When Superstition did its Pow'rs controul.

But the poem should not be taken very seriously: he concludes it by saying that if she wishes to lead a truly penitential life she had better marry *him*.

Wycherley's inconsistency, combined with his readiness to say whatever will impress the reader with his ingenuity, makes it difficult to place him in relation to our subject. One may at least be grateful to him for speaking boldly on topics not even glanced at by the poets hitherto considered. In a few scattered pieces, too, he shows a little more religious sense than our knowledge of his life and of his comedies would suggest. To put it very mildly, however, his poems taken as a whole are not rich in spiritual values.

Not only writers of racy comedies but divines of the Church of England must be included in this chapter. Richard Duke (1658-1711) was dissolute as a young man, but mended his ways and took holy orders soon after receiving his M.A. from Cambridge in 1682.[22] His poems, most of which were written before he donned his "canonical galloshes," consist of translations and miscellaneous trifles of no great merit. Southey regarded him as indecent—a judgment probably based on his fondness for translating sensuous passages from Ovid. His original poems as printed in Volume IX of "Chalmers" are inoffensive, but wholly nonreligious. He uses the scriptural-background device of *Absalom and Achitophel* in a fragment entitled *The Review,* paraphrases Hamlet's "To be or not to be" soliloquy, and refers to Charles I as a saint. Duke was just a mediocre Age-of-Dryden wit who sensibly abandoned his scribbling soon after he entered the Church.

On the other hand, scribbling of a more amusing kind was at no time abandoned by the Rabelaisian gourmet and wit, the Reverend William King (1663-1712). This Vicar General to the Lord Primate of Ireland produced a lively modernized translation of Ovid's *Ars Amatoria* in hudibrastic verse. This, and his more characteristic pieces such as *The*

---

[22] He rose to be a prebendary of Gloucester and chaplain to Queen Anne, but died before he could enjoy the fruits of a rich Oxfordshire living which had recently been presented to him.

Art of Cookery, Mully of Mountoun, The Fairy Feast, and the short—and broad—verse-tales, lie beyond the farthest bourn of our subject. Even when he attacks Marlborough, as in *Rufinus,* or lauds Bolingbroke and Oxford, as in *Britain's Palladium,* he seems to avoid the ecclesiastical side of political questions. We know, however, that he was a strong High Churchman, a supporter of Sacheverell, and a friend of the great Tory Dean.

Chaucer would at once recognize King as a lineal descendent of his monk, but he would be puzzled by the figure who next advances. In the Middle Ages there was nobody like Bishop Thomas Sprat (1636-1713). Not only in science but also in religion would the historian of the Royal Society "separate the knowledge of Nature, from the colours of Rhetoric, the devices of Fancy, or the delightful conceit of Fables." [23] Since the Church of England is a perfectly reasonable church, it "can never be præjudic'd by the light of Reason." Conversely the Royal Society should not be attacked by the Church, since "we [of the Church] cannot make war against Reason, without undermining our own strength, seeing it is the constant weapon we ought to employ" against the dangers of Popery and Nonconformity. The spirit of the Royal Society and the spirit of the Church of England are the same, in that both are hostile to the "implicit Faith" of the Romanists and the "Enthusiasm" of the Dissenters.[24]

Most of Sprat's poems were written early in his career, before such ideas as these had fully crystallized in his mind, but not before the temperament which produced those ideas had taken form.[25] Religion, with a trifling exception soon to be noted, is completely absent from his poems. The High Churchmanship which he cultivated after the Restoration was merely a complex of political, social, and economic prejudices without any effect upon his imagination.

Sprat may briefly be characterized as a bad imitator of the pseudo-Pindarics of Cowley, of whom he was also the friend, biographer, and editor; and it is Cowley who on one occasion stirs a little religious feeling in his admirer:

[23] *History of the Royal Society* (1667), p. 62.
[24] *Ibid.,* p. 370.
[25] His scientific interests date from his college days at Wadham.

> Cowley! What God did fill thy breast,
>   And taught thy hand t'endite?
>   (For God's a poet too,
>   He doth create, and so do you.)
>   Or else at least
> What angel sat upon thy pen when thou didst write? [26]

This implicit recognition of the creative power of imagination, and of its essentially divine nature, falls strangely from Sprat's lips. He goes on to praise Cowley for showing that poets are not necessarily corrupters of mankind:

> You first the Muses to the Christians brought,
> And you them first the holy language taught:
> In you good poetry and divinity meet,
> You are the first bird of Paradise with feet.

Sprat had feet, but he was no bird of paradise. Apparently he never emulated Cowley in uniting divinity and poetry. For him the essence of divinity was empirical reason, opposition to superstition and enthusiasm, and judicious compromise with science. Except perhaps in the hands of a rare genius like Cowley, it could only be perverted by "the colours of Rhetorick, the devices of Fancy, or the delightful conceit of Fables." As for poetry, it was after all only a bedizened kind of nonsense, and he soon forsook it for more important matters.

The next division in this parade of poets is a miscellaneous one. By far the ablest of the group is Sir Samuel Garth (1661-1719), whom Pope declared to be an excellent Christian without knowing it [27] and whom Bolingbroke described as "the best wild man I ever knew." [28] He enjoyed a reputation for kindness, generosity, fast living, and free thinking. One is not sure whether, according to Pope, he died a Romanist, or whether, according to Addison, he died convinced that Christianity was an imposture.[29] Whatever light may or may not have dawned upon the dying Garth, in poetry his scepticism is not searching enough to suggest the fideism of a Pascal. He goes no deeper than the observation that

[26] *Upon the Poems of ... Abraham Cowley.*
[27] *A Farewell to London.*
[28] Walter Sichel, *Bolingbroke and His Times,* I, 46.
[29] John Dennis, *The Age of Pope,* p. 98.

> From stratagem to stratagem we run,
> And he knows most, who latest is undone.

The Dispensary, in which this couplet occurs, makes incidental use of the timeworn devices of the Christian epic. In Canto II the fury Envy recalls Tasso, and in Canto III the council of plotting apothecaries is obviously Miltonic.

Garth's satire in this poem is of course not primarily directed against the clergy, but he takes a casual fling at slothful divines:

> How sleek their looks, how goodly is their mien,
> When big they strut behind a double chin.
> Each faculty in blandishments they lull,
> Aspiring to be venerably dull.
> No learn'd debates molest their downy trance,
> Or discompose their pompous ignorance.

But The Dispensary has nothing to do with religion. The same may be said of Garth's other poems, though the topographical piece Claremont has conventional passages praising the Druids and the blessings of nature. There is no real faith in the witty Garth, and he is honest enough not to assume any in his poetry.

Pope's early mentor, William Walsh (1663-1708), wit, critic, philanderer, and man-about-town, need not long detain us. The Golden Age Restored, 1703 is a fairly clever modernized imitation of Virgil's Fourth Eclogue. The work of a staunch Whig, it ironically expresses rapture at the prospect of the Tories' coming into power. The High Church doctrines of the Tories, especially that of non-resistance, are ridiculed.

Walsh sometimes rather neatly voices a humorous cynicism which is, however, too superficial to be very meaningful. He has a perverse way of treating sentimental themes in a non-sentimental manner—the jolly little anthology-piece, The Dispairing Lover, is a case in point. The Retirement, written in the stanza of Gray's Elegy, is a curiously ironic variant of its type. In these "sacred solitary groves," he says, he can escape the world, but not the pangs of love. It is better to spend one's youth in folly and thus become thoroughly disillusioned about women "while there's time to mend." In his sonnet, Death, he asserts that death is not to be dreaded, since it "only gives us quiet at the last." He fears death only because it will entail his losing Caelia. Here what we expect to be a serious poem is twisted into a smirking compliment in a way characteristic of this thoroughly non-religious, though not avowedly anti-religious, cynic.

George Stepney (1663-1707),[30] the rakish and unbelieving friend of Halifax and Prior, occasionally uses Biblical allusions to spice a bit of flattery; otherwise he is from our viewpoint, if not from any viewpoint, a zero.

Equally unfruitful for us are the trivial but not unamusing earlier poems of that bibulous parson Laurence Eusden (1688-1730). After he won the laureateship in 1718 he became much duller, confining himself to birthday odes and other official assignments. I have read only a few of these dreary effusions, but one may safely assume that they occasionally refer to the House of Hanover as the bulwark of Protestantism.

Another barren fig tree is *Poems on Several Occasions* (1696) by John Oldmixon (1673-1742). It grows only translations, anacreontics, poems of gallantry, and light familiar epistles. *To the Bath, and Zelinda in it* will sufficiently characterize the collection. Though Oldmixon lived on until 1742, he soon became a mere party scribbler, writer of "secret histories," and Grub Street dunce. A few of his poems published after 1700 I have left unread with no sense of guilt.

Bezaleel Morrice, with startling originality, believes that poetry must instruct as well as delight, and must avoid anything "offensive to Truth, Decency, or those Things which justly claim the Regard of the more rational Part of Mankind." [31] The passions, he further insists in a poem called *The Request,* should be controlled by reason, and reason by experience. In agreement with these views, the moral tone of his verses is unexceptionable. True, he favors us with love songs, anacreontics, the Venus and Adonis story, a poem in praise of Ovid, and a translation from that poet; but these are not so written as to offend the more rational part of mankind. Yet despite his general sobriety, and despite the expectations raised by his puritan-sounding Christian name, there is nothing definitely religious in Morrice's poems.

[30] The scion of a family of royalist courtiers, he filled various diplomatic posts in Germany, Austria, and Holland.

[31] Preface of *Miscellanies or Amusements, in Prose and Verse* (1712). Morrice is not in *D.N.B.*, and I know nothing about his life.

In *The Muse,* he reminds the ambitious young Alexis of the lofty functions—and the material prosperity—of the poets of olden times:

> Wing'd by the Muse, Man's Soul to Heav'n did rise,
> She taught her first to know her native Skies;
> Fill'd her unactive Frame with quickning Fire,
> Did with Morality and Zeal inspire.
> Religion's Nurse, and then her Guide became,
> And thro' the World led the mysterious Dame;
> With earthly Blessings then supremely stor'd,
> By Princes cherisht, by Mankind ador'd.
> If such vast Trophies once adorn'd her Brow,
> Why meets she this despiteful Treatment now?

At present there is no money in poetry, and Alexis had better drop it.
Fostered by a generous patron, Morrice's muse might soar to heaven, but
as matters stand she sticks pretty closely to the earth.

A good deal of information is to be gleaned from the almost unknown
poems of John Glanvill (1664?-1735).[32] Though anything but a genius,
he rises a little above mediocrity in political panegyric, light amatory
verse, and translation. Practically all of his poems fall under one of these
heads.

His "state" poems reveal him as a passionately Whiggish admirer of
William III. Disapproval of the High Church party is seen in his description of conditions after William's death:

> Slaves of old Reigns now wanted to be free,
> Not from Oppression but from Liberty.
> Heady Republicans prepar'd the Way
> For the Return of arbitrary Sway.
> And English Churchmen (what was no new **Doom**)
> In Rage against *Geneva,* work'd for *Rome.*[33]

In his *Poems* the political pieces are followed by a sizable body of
amatory verse, much of which calls for the apology offered in his Preface,
where he says he is sorry "if the aims are levelled too directly at the
last End of Lovers, and the Persuasives are built too much upon the

---

[32] Glanvill came of gentle stock, and was educated at Oxford. His *Poems* appeared in
1725, and several of them bear dates or provide other evidence to justify placing him
in the 1700-1720 period.

[33] *Of the Times after the Peace, and His Majesty's Death.*

Foundations of Flesh and Blood, for the very politest and tenderest Sort of Readers; in short, if there is frequently more of the Libertine than the Lover."

Glanvill's compliments are sometimes blasphemous, as when he compares an eleven-year-old girl, on the score of her piety and precocity, to Jesus in the Temple.[34] Some three pages of the Preface are devoted to insisting that here he was thinking of Jesus only in His human aspect, and to denying the charge that this restriction implies Socinianism. But another poem he acknowledges to be beyond all defense: "As to the Stanzas upon the Friendship between three Ladies, the use of the Word Trinity in the first, and the Similitude from the Trinity itself in the last, are confessed to be much too free.... If they are shocking to the most serious and religious, I shall not wonder. I can only entreat their Pardon for having occasioned their being shocked." He pleads, however, that the poem was written in youth.

Glanvill's translations could be passed over were it not for the fact that his selection of material is almost always motivated by dislike of Christian beliefs and practises. These translations, furthermore, are very free and modernized. From *Seneca's Troas. Act II. Chorus* he draws a sweeping denial of immortality, but insists in his Preface that "the Subject Matter of what one translates is no good Indication that the Translator agrees to the Sentiments and Doctrine that are represented in the Translation." This to a certain extent is true, but surely persistent and almost exclusive devotion to a certain kind of subject matter *is* indicative of the translator's personal views.

Both *The latter Part of the second Satyr of Persius, Imitated* and *The latter Part of the tenth Satyr of Juvenal* cast doubt upon the value of petitionary prayer. The former is boldly defended in his *Preface:* "I make no scruple to declare that I esteem the carrying about in our Minds an awful Sense of the supreme Being, as a Principle to influence our Actions, to be the chief Work and Business of Religion, and out of all Proportion preferable to any costly Instances of Devotion, Ceremoniousness of Worship, or even much direct Application to God himself. And 'tis a wonder that any disinterested Person should think otherwise, who really believes that the Deity wants nothing of us, and knows beforehand what we

---

[34] *On a Paraphrase of the eighth Psalm in Verse, by the Honourable Mrs. Verney, at eleven Years of Age.*

want of him, and is no more to be moved by our much Speaking, than he is to be informed by our Speaking at all. Such Addresses indeed are approved, and commanded, and are therefore not to be neglected, and doubtless there was a Reason for the Command. But otherwise the Reason of the Thing itself, abstracted from the Command, is hard to be discerned." These are the thoughts, the tone, the argumentative technique of a cautious deist.

Other translations are allowed to stand without defense. Pythagoras' doctrine of metempsychosis as rendered by Ovid [35] is valued for its thrust at the Christian's "fantastic Dread of Death." Another weapon against the "vain fears" of the orthodox is provided by *The Beginning of the Second Book of Lucretius:*

> These Terrors then, this Darkness, and these Dreams,
> Not the gay Morning, not the mid-day Beams
> Of a bright Sun can vanquish and dispel,
> But Reason's Light, and Nature studied well;
> And these, and only these, the Mind will clear
> From gloomy Care, and from fantastick Fear.

Since Hobbes was regarded by his admirers as a great enemy of "fantastick Fear," it is not surprising to find Glanvill translating a seventeenth-century Latin poem, *Dr. Bathurst's Verses on Mr. Hobbs's Book of Human Nature.*[36] Hobbes, sweeping away "the Trash and Jargon of the Schools," has taught us to know ourselves:

> In Pieces took here we are shown the whole
> Clock-work and Mechanism of the Soul;
> May see the Movements, Labyrinths and Strings,
> Its Wires and Wheels, and Balances, and Springs;
> How 'tis wound up to its full Height, and then
> What checks, and stops, and settles it again.

The clockwork of Glanvill's soul began to tick about 1664, and he was a mature man by the end of the century. His mind is that of a seventeenth-century libertine who finds in Christianity an enemy of the sort of life he wishes to live. He rationalizes his sensuality by means of a philosophy compounded of Epicureanism, stoicism, Hobbism, and deism.

[35] *The Transmigration of the Soul. From Pythagoras's Speech in the fifteenth Book of Ovid's Metamorphoses.*

[36] This is Theodore Bathurst (died 1651), who translated Spenser's *Shepherd's Calendar* into Latin verse.

There is nothing to indicate that a sceptical interpretation of the new science influences his views,[37] but we know that he translated Fontenelle's *Plurality of Worlds* in 1688. He would be more interesting and worthier of respect if he spoke for himself. But he hides behind Seneca, Lucretius, and the rest, further protecting himself with a preface which, except for one of two deviations into honesty, is elaborately disingenuous.

Do the poets thus far considered furnish a basis for generalization? One simple but not unimportant fact suggests itself at once. Out of fifteen writers whose years of birth are known with certainty or probability, only three were born later than 1670—Farquhar, Oldmixon, and Lady Mary; and the last named is the only poet born later than 1680. Eight of the fifteen were born between 1660 and 1670, inclusive, and four even earlier. With few exceptions, then, the poets of this chapter were mature and in most cases middle-aged at the opening of the eighteenth century.

As regards political affiliations, nothing of significance emerges. If Halifax is a Whig, Lansdowne is a Tory, and so on through the list. But it appears that loyalty to the Church of England as a political institution is no evidence of warm religious feeling in such laymen as Buckingham or in such clerics as Sprat, Duke, and King. If Granville's High Churchmanship is of a somewhat more spiritual quality the fact is not to be inferred from his poems.

It is especially noteworthy that all the poets of this chapter are either persons of quality or aspire to write as if they *were* persons of quality. The cultivated gentleman devoting a few leisure hours to the composition of urbanely serious or elegantly witty verses—that is the impression they seek to give.[38] In subject matter, style, and feeling, this poetry is aristocratic or at worst genteel.

What now are its literary qualities? Mary Monck writes like an unlaid ghost of the court of Charles I; Granville derives from Waller a tinge of Cavalier idealism; Wycherley is more or less in the tradition of Oldham; Sprat is a petrified Cowley, King a Rabelaisian jester. These to a

---

[37] The lines on Hobbes might be taken as providing such evidence, but the materialism of Hobbes was inspired more by ancient atomism than by the new science.

[38] Two partial exceptions may be noted. There is a slightly bourgeois stuffiness about the work of Morrice, though he generally tries to sound like a gentleman. Lady Mary, thoroughly a part of the aristocratic tradition, nevertheless sometimes wearies of it.

large extent, and the others with absolute completeness, illustrate the meaning of the term, "neoclassicism." Their poems are essentially rhetorical—not life, but ideas *about* life versified and decorated with figures of speech. Instead of attempting the imaginative expression of emotion, they aim at the neat and clever restatement of familiar notions in correct, polished lines which will remind their readers of the poetry of Augustan Rome.

The scholar who explores this frigid zone for traces of "pre-romantic tendencies" will be disappointed. He will, to be sure, seize upon Sprat's fleeting sense of the divinity of creative imagination. Bezaleel Morrice twice sings the praises of rural retirement [39] in a spirit mainly classical but with a trace of sentimentalism. William King knows Shakespeare, Herrick, and Drayton better than most men of his time, and parts of his *Orpheus and Eurydice* are charmingly fanciful; yet his attitude toward earlier English literature and toward fairy lore is hearty, humorous, and realistic. At times Lady Mary's distaste for her environment approaches a kind of *Weltschmerz*. Her *Verses Written in Constantinople* display not only this trait but also an apparently sincere affection for external nature. Her lines on the billing doves, too, are pre-romantic in feeling. It must be remembered, however, that Lady Mary was born several years later than any other member of this group and lived on until 1762. With these scanty exceptions, the poets of this chapter will baffle the prospector for romanticism.

It is fairer, of course, to judge them as poets of their own thoroughly unromantic kind. Competent mastery of form, clear statement of the obvious, a little wit, a good deal of common sense, an air of cool elegance—these are more or less common characteristics. Four or five rise somewhat above this level. Garth is a satirist of some power and a clever technician in the heroic couplet. A few of Lady Mary's shorter pieces give an interesting illusion of direct, natural speech. King and Walsh can be amusing, and Granville mellifluously "polite." But they shrink into complete insignificance when compared with Dryden or Pope, and on this scale of values the other members of the group are less than nothing. These poets are not really distinguished practitioners even of their own neoclassical and rhetorical kind of poetry.

There is no single explanation which will account for the almost com-

[39] *The Request* and *The Ladies' Adiews.*

plete absence of religious thought and feeling in the verse of these writers. In the first place the type of poetry which they practised did not encourage the expression of deep, serious, personal emotions. Then too we do not always remember how persistently the true neoclassicist, even when not translating or directly imitating, tried to feel himself back among the ancients. The introduction of Christian elements into a poem meant to embody the atmosphere of Augustan Rome would be a breach of critical decorum.

A more important factor is the nature of the poets themselves and of the social class which they represent. Failure to write religious poetry is of course no proof that the poet is irreligious. Lord Lansdowne was a pillar of the Church, and Mary Monck and Bezaleel Morrice were probably good sober Christians. On the whole, however, these gentlemanly poets are simply not a devout lot. To expect men like Halifax, Buckingham, Congreve, Wycherley, Garth, Stepney, and Walsh to write ardently devout poetry would be absurd. There is little spirituality in them, little in the social class to which they belong or which they seek to imitate.[40]

Even those poets who seem hostile rather than merely indifferent to religion are intellectually unsatisfying. They do not, in any serious or systematic way, attack the faith which they dislike. Perhaps they were sometimes restrained by caution, or by the cynical feeling that one may as well keep up appearances, or by the extreme difficulty of deriving even a very unpoetical kind of poetry from an irreligious viewpoint. Even without these curbs, however, they would probably not have written much more boldly or searchingly. They shun "enthusiasm" too consistently to be enthusiastic even in their scorn of zeal. Their verses, as we have seen, sporadically display ideas which might be assigned to such pigeonholes as Cynicism, Epicureanism, Stoicism, Scepticism, Positivism, Hobbistic Materialism, Libertinism, and Deism. But these relics of the daring speculations of the seventeenth century [41] do not here, either singly or in combination, attain the dignity of a philosophy. They are merely devices seized upon from time to time to facilitate the expression of a

[40] One remembers such pious aristocratic families as the Thynnes of Longleat without feeling that they represented the dominant spirit of their class.

[41] Perhaps the phrase hardly applies to deism, considering its later development. Deism was, however, originally a Renaissance revival of such ideas on natural religion as may be found in Cicero.

mood. The chronological position of these aristocratic and would-be aristocratic poets brings them close to the turbulent waves of the Age of Hobbes, but also close to the more placid currents of the Age of Locke. They inherit from the past interesting and vital traditions of disbelief, but in their hands the heritage becomes sluggish, feeble, dull. They move toward a compromise in which irreligion will be almost as dead as religion.

Before concluding this chapter, however, we should consider the poems of three famous writers who are related in several ways to the group already discussed, but to whose complex and active minds the foregoing generalizations do not fully apply. Mandeville, Swift, and Prior are neither religious men nor great poets; but Swift is more religious and more poetic than Mandeville, and Prior more religious and more poetic than Swift. Achievement in poetry demands the acceptance of no particular creed, but it demands some capacity for belief in realities which lie beyond the work of the senses.

In this belief Bernard Mandeville (1670-1733), who of course was not a poet at all, was singularly deficient. Whatever else may be said of him, he cannot be called a man of compromise, for his savage paradoxes made him cordially detested by optimists of every stripe, both orthodox [42] and heretical. A detailed analysis of Mandeville's thought would be out of place in this study, since his scanty poems have only slight pertinence to our theme and since in any case Mr. F. B. Kaye has dealt with the subject exhaustively in the introduction to his edition of *The Fable of the Bees.*

Mandeville is willing to grant that reason must deduce from the orderly universe the idea of a First Cause, but he insists that man cannot discover the nature of this Supreme Being, and should not attempt to do so. There is no justification for ascribing human attributes to Him— or rather, It—nor for supposing that It is particularly concerned with the welfare of mankind. Mandeville is too wholeheartedly devoted to specific facts to be a deist of the geometrically rationalistic sort, and his Hobbesian ethics is diametrically opposed to the sentimental deism of Shaftesbury.

---

[42] For the purposes of this study, an "orthodox" person is one who considers it important to be what he regards as an orthodox Christian. From my use of the term the reader need not infer that I regard the theology of such persons as orthodox.

On the whole he must be regarded as a deist quite exceptional for the harshly cynical and negative empiricism of his outlook. After carefully weighing all the facts, Kaye reaches the conclusion that Mandeville "is lacking in any religious feeling or idealism. His rejection of all absolute laws and knowledge, his insistence on the animal facts of life—these are not the result of any rigoristic distrust of nature as it is, but of such complete faith in it that he feels no need for any beliefs by which to attempt to lift himself above it." [43]

The Grumbling Hive, the bitter little allegory which forms the kernel of *The Fable of the Bees,* includes, along with other social groups,

> ... the many priests of Jove,
> Hir'd to draw blessings from above.
> Some few were learn'd and eloquent,
> But thousands hot and ignorant;
> But all past muster that could hide
> Their sloth, lust, avarice, and pride;
> For which they were as fam'd as taylors
> For cabbage, or for brandy sailors.

The following lines speak of curates who toil half-starved while wealthy vicars loll at their ease.

When Jove grants the bees' prayer for honesty, *all* the clergy become industrious. Hence there is not enough work for them, and most of them abandon the profession.

> Few only with the high-priest staid,
> To whom the rest obedience paid:
> Himself employ'd in holy cares,
> Resign'd to others state affairs.
> He chas'd no starv'ling from his door,
> Nor pinch'd the wages of the poor;
> But at his house the hungry's fed,
> The hireling finds unmeasur'd bread,
> The needy trav'ler board and bed.

The clergy, then, have their place in the general fabric of the fable. Considering the satirical possibilities of the theme, however, Mandeville's treatment of it is weak and fumbling. Perhaps the difficulty lies in the fact that the change in the character of the bees would not really have had the same effect on the clergy as on the other professions.

---

[43] *The Fable of the Bees,* Introduction, pp. liv-lv.

A glimpse of Mandeville in slippered ease is furnished by the little volume entitled *Wishes to a Godson, With other Miscellany Poems* (1712). Nothing is said on the subject of religion apart from a fling at poor cracked Asgill,[44] but inferences may be drawn from the coarseness, brutality, and cynicism which pervade the whole collection. When little Theodore reaches his first birthday, his sponsor in baptism sends his best wishes for success in later life:

> May you've Credit in the City,
> And a hundred Pounds to spare;
> May y'at Noon in Hacknies dare
> By the Counter Gates to pass,
> Without drawing up the Glass.
> Of the handsome Female fry
> May you've still variety;
>
> .   .   .   .   .
>
> May your Whores be prudent, true,
> And Coquets to all but you;
>
> .   .   .   .   .
>
> May you never stick to one,
> Or by fondness be undone,
> But have Forty at a call,
> And be fit to serve them all.
>
> .   .   .   .   .
>
> May you never when y'are Drunk
> Stumble on a rotten Punk;
> Give offence to Fighting Blockheads,
> Or meet Jades that pick your Pockets,
> But go without more ado,
> Quietly to Bed, and Sp[u]e."

Making all due allowances for the manners of the age and for the author's detestation of cant, these lines suggest the inference that, if private vices really *are* public benefits, Mandeville was a public benefactor of the first order. Mr. Kaye, however, is very sceptical of the eighteenth-century gossip as to Mandeville's personal disreputableness.[45] Pious folk, as he reminds us, are notoriously fond of telling edifying lies about unbelievers.

[44] *A Letter to Mr. Asgil, writ at Colchester.* Asgill believed that man may be translated bodily into eternal life without passing through death.
[45] *Op. cit.,* pp. xxi-xxix.

Let us therefore be content with the obvious fact that Mandeville's verse is not very rich in spirituality.

Wishes to a Godson is just such a poem as Jonathan Swift (1667-1745) would have written with sardonic zest. Between him and Mandeville there are obvious resemblances. Both are harsh, bitter, cynically realistic— relentless haters of every sort of illusion, whether sincere or affected. Both are strongly tinged with materialism and scepticism. But life was more mysterious to Swift than to Mandeville, and he brooded over questions not to be answered by the human reason whose pretensions he so bitterly scorned. In certain moods he accepted, for want of anything better, the answers provided by the Christian faith. For himself and other men to do so was at least a means of holding society together and of curbing individual fools and rogues. In the Church of England as a state institution lay peace, dignity, authority, order. He was a loyal official of that institution and a propagandist for her political and ecclesiastical program.[46]

It may therefore be urged that Swift does not belong in this chapter at all. But where else should he be placed? Imagine the author of *A Tale of a Tub* on his knees in prayer; the author of *A Modest Proposal* baptizing an infant; the author of *Gulliver* celebrating the Eucharist. Like all men, Swift had his spiritual impulses, but he was not genuinely religious. He can appeal to Christian standards for satirical purposes, but his own faith was submerged in doubt, irony, and pessimism. He could more easily believe in sin than in salvation. Truthfully he tells us that he is

> Sunk over head and ears in matter,
> Nor can of metaphysics smatter;
> Am more diverted with a quibble,
> Than dream of worlds intelligible;
> And think all notions too abstracted
> Are like the ravings of a crackt head.[47]

But warmly emotional religion, on the other hand, he detested as "enthusiastic." Since reflection led to bewilderment, and irreflective feeling

[46] G. M. Trevelyan makes the important qualification: "As an Irish Protestant, he [Swift] was not wholly typical of the English High Churchman. He was more of a Williamite, and continued to the end more whole-heartedly hostile to the Pretender than his English Tory allies." (*Blenheim*, p. 62.)

[47] *The Dean's Reasons For Not Building at Drapier's-Hill.*

to superstition, where was he to turn? To the Establishment? Swift had
no real sense of the spiritual significance of the Church. He could be one
of her dignitaries, but never one of her children. No one was ever less
church-minded than this High Churchman.

Though not religious, Swift had interestingly elusive ideas *about*
religion; but since those ideas must be studied chiefly in his prose, we
may leave to others [48] the difficult task of interpreting them. Our sole
concern is with the poems. Many of them pertain to ecclesiastical politics,
and consideration of these must be postponed to the next chapter. Many
others, such as *The Curate's Complaint of Hard Duty,* amusingly
illumine the clerical life of the age,[49] but are of no real importance for
us. We may, however, pause to enjoy the whimsical musings of *Dr.
Swift to Himself, on St. Cecilia's Day,* where he pretends to wonder
whether he is right in opening the cathedral to "players and scrapers":

> To act such an opera once in a year,
> So offensive to every true protestant ear,
> With trumpets, and fiddles, and organs, and singing,
> Will sure the pretender and popery bring in.
> No protestant prelate, his lordship or grace,
> Durst there show his right or most reverend face:
> How would it pollute their crosiers and rotchets
> To listen to minims, and quavers, and crotchets!

But these pleasant trifles must be neglected in favor of poems indicative
of Swift's more serious thoughts. Serious enough, in all conscience, are
those early odes which convinced Dryden that Cousin Swift would never
be a poet. In three of them we see his sceptical distrust of reason. Perhaps
in the *Ode to the Honourable Sir William Temple* he scorns learning
partly because he wishes to treat Temple's retirement as a sort of "return
to nature"; but no such motive affects the *Ode to the Athenian Society,*
where he describes philosophy as hopelessly corrupted by "doubts, impertinence, and niceties."

The *Ode to Doctor William Sancroft* opens on a note of even deeper
scepticism. Truth abides eternally in heaven as the "First of God's darling
attributes." But how can it be found in a world where men talk only for
victory?

---

[48] Cf. C. Looten, *La Pensée religieuse de Swift et ses antinomies.*
[49] See also *Baucis and Philemon,* with its description of how Philemon lives after being
transformed into a parson.

> How shall we find Thee then in dark disputes?
> How shall we search Thee in a battle gain'd,
> Or a weak argument by force maintain'd,
> In dagger contests, and th'artillery of words?
> (For swords are madmen's tongues, and tongues are madmen's swords)
> Contriv'd to tire all patience out,
> And not to satisfy the doubt?

This world, he continues with an unexpected touch of Platonism, is merely the distorted reflection of the perfect world above. On this plane we see only

> Disjointing shapes as in the fairy land of dreams,
> Or images that sink in streams;
> No wonder, then, we talk amiss
> Of truth, and what, or where it is.[50]

But Swift soon abandoned the ode form for those versified bits of humor, satire, and bitter insight which we associate with his name. Most of these have nothing to do with religion, and a great many of them are such as could not be written by even the least spiritual dean of a modern cathedral.

Sometimes, however, he stands forth as the champion of orthodoxy, or at least as the enemy of the unorthodox. When urged to advise the youth of England to read Woolston,

> That noble genius, who unbinds
> The chains which fetter free-born minds,

he indignantly refuses to recommend "Such stupid blasphemy and nonsense." [51] *On the Death of Dr. Swift* lists this theological eccentric among those writers who have supplanted Swift in public esteem:

> He doth an honour to his gown,
> By bravely running *priest-craft* down:
> He shows, as sure as God's in Gloucester,
> That Moses was a grand impostor,
> That all his miracles were cheats,
> Perform'd as jugglers do their feats:
> The church had never such a writer;
> A shame he hath not got a mitre.

One of Swift's grudges against life was that *he* had no mitre.

---

[50] The remainder of this ode is chiefly of political interest, and will receive treatment in the next chapter.

[51] *A Dialogue Between an Eminent Lawyer and Dr. Jonathan Swift.*

Directions for Making a Birth-Day Song thrusts not only at the infidelity of the court [52] and its scribbling flatterers but at the popularity of Samuel Clarke, the leader of the "Intellectual School" and a noted latitudinarian:

> Reject with scorn that stupid notion,
> To praise your hero for devotion;
> Nor entertain a thought so odd,
> That princes should believe in God;
> But follow the securest rule,
> And turn it all to ridicule:
> 'Tis grown the choicest wit at court,
> And gives the maids of honour sport.
> For, since they talked with doctor Clarke,
> They now can venture in the dark:
> That sound divine the truth hath spoke all,
> And pawn'd his word, Hell is not local.

But Swift himself, in *The Place of the Damned,* can adapt Clarke's doctrine to satirical uses. Hell is located "where-ever the damn'd do chiefly abound." There follows a list of damned people, ending:

> Damn'd time-serving priests all over the nation;
> And into the bargain I'll readily give ye
> Damn'd ignorant prelates and counsellors privy.
> Then let us no longer by parsons be flamm'd,
> For we know by these marks the place of the damn'd:
> And Hell to be sure is at Paris or Rome.
> How happy for *us* that it is not at *home!*

That last couplet exhibits the loathing of cant which makes Swift suspicious of other people's orthodoxy. Unbelievers are enemies of Church and State, but the holier-than-thou folk who attack them are smug hypocrites more deserving of satire than the heretics themselves. In his eagerness to lash the Pharisee, this High Churchman can throw the creeds out of the window. When Thomas Rundle, the newly consecrated Bishop of Derry, is, like Clarke, accused of Arianism, Swift asks:

> Yet, were he Heathen, Turk, or Jew,
> What is there in it strange or new?
> For, let us hear the weak pretence,
> His brethren find to take offence,
> Of whom there are but four at most,
> Who know there is a Holy Ghost;

[52] The court is that of George II, the poem being dated 1729.

> The rest who boast they have conferr'd it,
> Like Paul's Ephesians, never heard it;
> And, when they gave it, well 'tis known,
> They gave what never was their own.
> Rundle a bishop! well he may;
> He's still a christian more than they.
> We know the subject of their quarrels:
> The man has learning, sense, and morals.

What more need be demanded of a bishop of the Holy Catholic Church? "Fools may doubt his faith in Jesus," but this objection comes strangely "from rogues who ne'er believed in God." On the other hand this defense of an Arian prelate [53] comes strangely from a believer in the Trinity. Perhaps a special reason for this inconsistency is the fact that Rundle is

> For liberty a champion stout,
> Though not so Gospel-ward devout.
> While others, hither sent to save us
> Come but to plunder and enslave us.[54]

A friend of the Irish people might think as he pleased about the Gospel.

Swift's own advancement in the Church, as everyone knows, was hindered by suspicions of his orthodoxy. His disappointment at receiving nothing better than the Irish deanery snarls out in *The Author Upon Himself. 1713:*

> By an old ———— pursued,
> A crazy prelate, and a royal prude; [55]
> By dull divines, who look with envious eyes
> On every genius that attempts to rise;
> And, pausing o'er a pipe with doubtful nod,
> Give hints that poets ne'er believe in God:

. . . . .

[53] The charge against Rundle appears to have been well founded. He was a member of William Whiston's definitely Arian "Society for Promoting Primitive Christianity." Rundle was one of the earliest admirers of Thomson's *Seasons,* praising it as an expression of the religion of Newton. Pope declared that "Rundle has a heart." (Léon Morel, *James Thomson: sa vie et ses œuvres,* p. 50 and *n.*) On learning to know Rundle personally, Swift also came to value him highly. (*Poems,* ed. Harold Williams, II, 819.)

[54] *On Dr. Rundle, Bishop of Derry.*

[55] The "old ————" is the Duchess of Somerset, who supported "the crazy prelate," Archbishop Sharp of York, in protesting to "the royal prude" that the author of *A Tale of a Tub* was an unseemly candidate for a bishopric.

> Swift had the gift of wit, no venial crime;
> Nay, 'tis affirm'd, he sometimes dealt in rhyme:
> Humour and mirth had place in all he writ;
> He reconcil'd divinity and wit;
> He mov'd, and bow'd, and talk'd, with too much grace;
> Nor show'd the *parson* in his gait or face.

This pose of being a swan among geese, too much the genius and fine gentleman to rise high in his calling, does not arouse much sympathy in us. Nor, unless we impute to Swift remarkable powers of self-deception, can we take very seriously the claim that "he reconciled divinity and wit." There is more wit than divinity in his little *Epigram. From the French:*

> Who can believe with common sense
> A bacon-slice gives God offence;
> Or, how a herring hath a charm
> Almighty vengeance to disarm;
> Wrapt up in Majesty divine,
> Does he regard on what we dine?

These lines are perfectly consistent with a kind of religion, but not with the kind of religion supposedly championed by the Dean of St. Patrick's.

No matter what one eats on Fridays, one can see no reconciliation of divinity and wit in *The Logicians Confuted,* where Swift, in his most misanthropic mood, sets animal instinct above human reason. *The Parson's Case,* a modernized version of an epigram by Martial,[56] takes a cynical view of the Christian's readiness to die. It is not surprising that the poor, overworked, hungry curate should speak cheerfully and even longingly of the grave;

> But now, should Fortune shift the scene,
> And make thy curateship a dean:
> Or some rich benefice provide,
> To pamper luxury and pride;
>
> .   .   .   .
>
> With underlings thy flock to teach,
> With no desire to pray or preach;
> With haughty spouse in vesture fine,
> With plenteous meals and generous wine;
> Wouldst thou not wish in so much ease,
> Thy years as numerous as thy days?

[56] Book XI, Epigram LVI. It was also translated by the sceptical Glanvill.

Of all the poems of Swift which touch upon matters of religion, *The Day of Judgment* is deservedly the most familiar. Everyone remembers how the sinners stand before Jove, trembling with fear but hoping "to see each other damn'd," and how Jove scornfully sends them packing with the words:

> The world's mad business now is o'er,
> And I resent these pranks no more.
> I to such blockheads set my wit!
> I damn such fools!—Go, go, you're bit.

It is appropriate that Lord Chesterfield, who possessed a manuscript of this poem, should have enclosed a copy in a letter to Voltaire.[57] Orthodox readers must not, however, be too quick to brand it as essentially irreligious. Swift hates the canting solemnity, the craven fear, the morbid glee at the eternal torture of unbelievers, which pervade so many "Judgment Day" poems of his time.[58] Occasionally it may be good for conceited sinners to be told that they are hardly worth damning, and for those "who never fell, from pride" that they are hardly worth saving.

Here as frequently elsewhere, then, Swift shows his remarkable gift for exposing the irreligion of supposedly religious people. Some may insist that his ability to criticize sham spirituality implies that he himself possessed genuine spirituality. But the logic of this argument is dubious, and in any case we must confine ourselves to the evidence actually before us. Scores of Swift's poems could hardly have been written by a man of religious nature, while none of them reveals the slightest trace of a reverent and loving personal faith in any sort of Divine Power.

No one who is likely to read this book need be informed that Matthew Prior (1664-1721) was neither a pious man nor a pious poet. The abundant and familiar evidence will not be brought into court. It was not his fault that in his Cambridge days he was forced to write a "divine ode" as a penalty for missing chapel. *Considerations on Part of the Eighty-Eighth Psalm* was also a college exercise, and the same is probably true

---

[57] For details about the publication of this poem and for proof of its authenticity, see Sidney L. Gulick, Jr., "Jonathan Swift's 'The Day of Judgement,'" *PMLA*. XLVIII, 850-855; and the Harold Williams edition of Swift's *Poems,* II, 577-578.

[58] Some of the most offensive of these are by Anglicans. I do not believe with Mr. Gulick that the line, "You who in different sects were shamm'd" indicates that the poem is directed merely against dissenting fanatics.

of *Charity. A Paraphrase on the Thirteenth Chapter of the First Epistle to the Corinthians*. The ode entitled *On Exod. III. 14. I Am That I Am* was written in 1688 as the annual poetic tribute of St. John's College to its benefactor, the Earl of Exeter. Here Prior first expressed what may be regarded as his favorite religious idea—that faith is necessitated by the weakness of human reason. At this time he considered the possibility of taking holy orders, but not from spiritual motives.

We cannot, however, dismiss so lightly the poem which Prior regarded as his most important work. Set amidst all the *vers de société* and bawdy tales, *Solomon* looks like a parson in a night club. How account for it? In the first place, Prior was a complete sceptic, who, like many other sceptics, wavered between frivolous negation and despairing affirmation. The former mood is dominant, but the latter is discernible in *Solomon* and in several other poems.

Furthermore, although in most respects thoroughly representative of the aristocratic tradition, Matt rose from a social level which, in the seventeenth century, was characterized by a stoutly Calvinistic Protestantism. One of his grandfathers was a farm-laborer; his father was apprenticed to a joiner; an uncle kept a tavern. The poet was baptized in the Church of England, but the theological atmosphere which surrounded his youth was probably free from High Church Arminianism. He began his literary and political career as a Whig, and turned Tory merely for reasons of expediency. One pair of grandparents were Presbyterians, and the *Epistle to Fleetwood Shepherd* draws a simile from childhood memories of the conventicle:

> So at pure barn of loud Non-con,
> Where with my grannam I have gone,
> When Lobb had sifted all his text,
> And I well hop'd the pudding next;
> NOW TO APPLY has plagued me more,
> Than all his villain cant before.

Despite the conventional Tory sneer, the preacher's "cant" may have impressed him more deeply than he realized. Modern psychology knows even better than Wordsworth that the child is father of the man. Prior's mother, who came of a "better" family than his father, appears to have been a pious woman. He remembered her "fervent anxious prayers" for him, and addressed her reverently:

> Ungrateful howsoe'er, mayn't I forget,
> To pay this small, yet tributary debt.
> And when we meet at God's tribunal throne,
> Own me, I pray thee, for a pious son.[59]

Some tincture of Calvinism remained with him to the end, for in the month before his death he planned and partly executed a long poem on predestination. If we may suppose that a doctrine impressed upon him in childhood became, in an altered guise, a main element in the unbelief which dominated his maturity, *Solomon* will seem more coherently related to the main body of Prior's verse.

The cynicism of Prior, though often frivolously expressed, arose from a more than superficial disillusionment. When Lord Portland expressed to him the fear that poets were atheists, Matt replied: "My Lord, you do us poets the greatest injustice: of all people we are the farthest from atheism. For the atheists do not even worship the true God, whom the rest of mankind acknowledge; and we are always invoking false gods whom every one else has renounced." [60] Poetry, he thinks, is devoted not only to false gods but also to false visions of happiness, yet after all we must deceive ourselves if life is to be tolerable. That man is fortunate who, like the poet,

> . . . can imagin'd pleasures find,
> To combat against real cares.
>
> .   .   .   .
>
> If we see right, we see our woes:
> Then what avails it to have eyes?
> From ignorance our comfort flows;
> The only wretched are the wise.
>
> We wearied should lie down in death:
> This cheat of life would take no more;
> If you thought fame but empty breath;
> I, Phillis, but a perjur'd whore.[61]

Very pervasive in Prior is this realization that Phillis is a whore and life a cheat. If he were a melancholy romantic instead of an Augustan

---

[59] *The Mice. A Tale.*

[60] R. B. Johnson, "Life of Prior" prefixed to his edition of *The Poetical Works of Matthew Prior* (1892), I, li.

[61] *To the Honourable Charles Montague.*

wit, one would say that he suffered from *Weltschmerz.* Weariness mingles with the fun of *Alma,* where the soul,

> Stunn'd and worn out with endless chat
> Of Will did this, and Nan said that,

longs for "some little crack" through which to escape from life into
death. Prior can forgive the soul her crimes, but not her immersion in
triviality:

> I view with anger and disdain
> How little gives thee joy or pain;
> A print, a bronze, a flower, a root,
> A shell, a butterfly can do't;
> Ev'n a romance, a tune, a rhyme,
> Help thee to pass the tedious time,
>
> .   .   .   .
>
> And cards are dealt, and chess-boards brought,
> To ease the pain of coward thought:
> Happy result of human wit!
> That Alma may herself forget.

This mood is not without some philosophical basis. "Your crabbed
rogues, that read Lucretius," he reminds Shepherd, deny the religious
view of poetic inspiration, holding rather

> That writing is but just like dice,
> And lucky mains make people wise;
> That jumbled words, if fortune throw 'em,
> Shall, well as Dryden, form a poem;
>
> .   .   .   .
>
> So atoms dancing round the centre,
> They urge, made all things at a venture.[62]

Prior does not attempt to refute the "crabbed rogues," and one suspects
that he had a goou deal of sympathy for their position. He was born
early enough to retain something of the Epicureanism which was more
popular in the seventeenth century than in the eighteenth.[63] The same

---

[62] *Epistle to Fleetwood Shepherd.*

[63] Cf. T. F. Mayo, *Epicurus in England (1650-1725).* On p. 213 of this dissertation the
author quotes from Prior's *Satire on the Modern Translators* a passage assailing Dryden
as fitted to "more debauch what loose Lucretius writ." But this early work, like *The
Hind and the Panther Transvers'd,* is motivated chiefly by the wish to damage Dryden;
and it is dangerous to infer from it, with Dr. Mayo, that Prior was hostile to Lucretius.
There is evidence that Prior, while by no means a convinced disciple, was much impressed by the Epicurean philosophy.

association of Lucretius' atomism with a doctrine of blind chance appears in *The Ladle:*

> The sceptics think, 'twas long ago,
> Since gods came down *incognito:*
> To see who were their friends or foes,
> And how our actions fell or rose:
> That since they gave things their beginning,
> And set this whirligig a-spinning,
> Supine they in their heaven remain,
> Exempt from passion, and from pain;
> And frankly leave us human elves
> To cut and shuffle for ourselves:
> To stand or walk, or rise or tumble,
> As matter and as motion jumble.

Not chance, however, but the close regulation of life by some inexorable fate, is the thought expressed in these lines from another poem:

> In vain we think that free-willed man has power
> To hasten or protract th'appointed hour.
> Our term of life depends not on our deed:
> Before our birth our funeral was decreed.

Is this mechanical determinism, or Calvinism? Fate again, licensed to operate by indifferent Lucretian gods, is the theme of a bitter little *Song:*

> You sigh and weep: the gods neglect
>   That precious dew your eyes let fall:
> Our joy and grief with like respect
>   They mind; and that is, not at all.
>
> We pray, in hopes they will be kind,
>   As if they did regard our state:
> They hear; and the return we find
>   Is, that no prayers can alter fate.

Prior is obviously impressed by both the gods and the atoms of Epicureanism, but he seems unable to decide whether this philosophy implies chance or fate. The inconsistency is less glaring than it may appear. Under a mechanistic system, the loss of divine guidance may give one the sense of living in a world of chance, or the loss of human freedom may give one the sense of living in a world of fixed unfriendly law. Prior seems to be unaware that Epicurus himself believed in free will.

In this matter he probably inherits the aristocratic Epicureanism of the court of Charles II, which was influenced by Hobbes's determinism. His own Calvinistic upbringing, perhaps slightly reinforced by seventeenth-century stoicism, would make Prior receptive to this prevalent distortion of the Epicurean philosophy.

But a maturer, more formidable, and historically more important kind of determinism underlies the following passage from *Alma:*

> Have you not seen a baker's maid
> Between two equal panniers sway'd?
> Her tallies useless lie, and idle,
> If plac'd exactly in the middle:
> But, forc'd from this unactive state
> By virtue of some casual weight,
> On either side you hear them clatter,
> And judge of right and left hand matter.
> Now, Richard, this coercive force,
> Without your choice, must take its course;
> Great kings to wars are pointed forth,
> Like loaded needles to the north.
> And thou and I, by power unseen,
> Are barely passive, and suck'd-in
> To Henault's vault, or Celia's chamber,
> As straw and paper are by amber.
> If we sit down to play or set
> (Suppose at ombre or basset)
> Let people call us cheats or fools,
> Our cards and we are equal tools.

> Poor men! poor papers! we and they
> Do some impulsive force obey:
> And are but play'd with—do not play.
> But space and matter we should blame;
> They palm'd the trick that lost the game.
> Thus to save further contradiction,
> Against what you may think but fiction,
> I for attraction, Dick, declare:
> Deny it those bold men that dare.
> As well your motion, as your thought,
> Is all by hidden impulse wrought:
> Ev'n saying that you think or walk,
> How like a country squire you talk!

"Attraction" of course means gravitation. These lines interpret Newton in an unusual way—unusual, because in Prior's day Newtonian science and what then passed for orthodox Christianity were generally on the friendliest terms. The compromise was temporary, but surprisingly solid while it lasted. The new science of the seventeenth century had aroused some anxiety among the Cambridge Platonists and other pious men. On the whole, however, the Church gave its blessing to the activities of the Royal Society. Boyle had demonstrated to the satisfaction of most people the harmony of science and religion. As for Newton, he was himself a devout Christian and an influential theologian. His discoveries strengthened that favorite apologetic weapon, the argument from design. They greatly encouraged belief in that natural religion which was, as many theologians thought, the firmest basis of Christianity. The Newtonian heavens declared the glory of God, and the Newtonian firmament showed His handiwork. Gravitation was simply God's will at work in the universe. Conflict between the hypothesis of unvarying natural laws and faith in a watchful Providence was evaded by various expedients. Respectable moralists and divines rather strangely regarded Newtonianism as a precious means of refuting the relics of ancient materialism which had survived the age of Hobbes. Thus when Richard Bentley delivered the first series of Boyle Lectures in 1692, he made great use of Newton in attacking Epicurus. In the Queen Anne period Berkeley stood almost alone in distrusting the mechanistic implications of the new science as well as those of ancient materialism. It is therefore surprising to find that, in Prior's opinion, Newton merely carries the older determinism still further.

Whence does Prior derive the feeling that the philosophy of "space and matter" is inimical to human freedom? It seems at least possible that his early training conditioned him toward disbelief in free will. He moved a long way from the Calvinism of his "grannam's" conventicle. But he moved—he did not jump. When, as he grew up, he associated with Montagu and other free-livers and freethinkers, it was natural for him to extract determinism from the still fashionable Epicureanism of the seventeenth century; and when Newtonianism came to his attention, it was natural for him to see in it another kind of predestination.

We are now better prepared to understand *Solomon*. From beginning to end the poem is an expression of Prior's scepticism, which for once is sufficiently thoroughgoing to lead him to an apparently religious conclusion. The final "Thy will be done," however, is little more than an admission of bewildered despair. Prior is no hypocrite, but it must be granted that his hero expresses doubt much more tellingly than he expresses faith.

Again one sees what I have been tempted to call Prior's *Weltschmerz* when Solomon describes "life, that fundamental ill," as a

> ...fatal search! in which the labouring mind,
> Still press'd with weight of woe, still hopes to find
> A shadow of delight, a dream of peace,
> From years of pain, one moment of release:
> Hoping at last she may herself deceive,
> Against experience willing to believe,
> Desirous to rejoice, condemn'd to grieve.

Is not this almost Byronic?

And again we find the poet unable to choose between chance and fate. Solomon asks:

> Esteem we these, my friends, event and chance,
> Produc'd as atoms from their fluttering dance?
> Or higher yet their essence may we draw
> From destin'd order, and eternal law?
> Again, my muse, the cruel doubt repeat:
> Spring they, I say, from accident, or fate?
> Yet such, we find they are, as can control
> The servile actions of our wavering soul.

Such views imply the futility of reason:

> Alas! we grasp at clouds, and beat the air,
> Vexing that spirit we intend to clear.
> Can thought beyond the bounds of matter climb?
> Or who shall tell me what is space or time?
> In vain we lift up our presumptuous eyes
> To what our Maker to their ken denies:
> The searcher follows fast: the object faster flies.
> The little which imperfectly we find,
> Seduces only the bewilder'd mind
> To fruitless search of something yet behind.

In Book I the gloomy monarch contemplates the physical universe, but finds only mystery where good Newtonians were finding evidence of a wise and benignant Deity:

> We seek great Nature's power, but seek in vain;
> Safe sits the goddess in her dark retreat;
> Around her, myriads of ideas wait,
> And endless shapes which the mysterious queen
> Can take or quit, can alter or retain:
> As from our lost pursuit she wills to hide
> Her close decrees, and chasten human pride.

Faced by these and many other perplexities expressed in his interminable soliloquy, Solomon is compelled to fall back upon a baffled and fundamentally cynical submission to God. The poem is what might be expected of a man whom determinism has completely disillusioned, but who has never quite been able to forget the religious teachings of his youth.

Near the close of his life Prior began a rough draft of a long poem on *Predestination,* completing about two hundred heroic couplets. Apparently the poem was to be a sort of sequel to *Solomon.* It is pious in tone, and gives an impression of sincerity. Satisfied with neither determinism nor free will, the poet desired a means of reconciling the two viewpoints; but death came before the problem could be solved.

For us, of course, the negative side of Prior's scepticism is more significant than the positive. Of all the poets studied in these pages, he is the first to realize that he is "eyeless in Gaza, at the mill, with slaves," the first in whom modern science has plainly helped to produce the view of life expressed in his epigram:

> What trifling coil do we poor mortals keep;
> Wake, eat, and drink, evacuate, and sleep.

Chapter II

POETS OF CONTROVERSY

"THE MAIN MOTIVE BEHIND THE PARTY PASSIONS AND POLITICAL MANOEUVRES of the age of Anne," says Trevelyan, "was religious, or if not religious in the higher sense, at least denominational. The world of Marlborough and St. John, of Defoe, Swift and Sacheverell does not appear religious in the same sense as the world of Laud and Baxter, of Cromwell and George Fox. The chief actors in Anne's reign, even when they are beating the drum ecclesiastic, do not seem to have essentially religious minds. Doctrine and ritual are no longer undergoing transmutation in the crucible of war and parliamentary debate.... The doctrine and ritual of the Church of England has become a fixed quantity that no one proposes to alter. The Dissenting Sects hold with easy minds the doctrines that their grandfathers sought sorrowing, and reached with doubts and divisions, groans and tears. And the Puritans no longer aspire to capture the Church of England. Controversy, therefore, has limits set within which it must move. Yet within these limits the rivalry of Church, Dissent, and that vague *tertium quid*—Free Thought—is the very pulse of the machine of politics." [1]

Another historian informs us that in 1713, during the turmoil which preceded the Queen's death, "a metrical edition or adaptation of some of the Psalms, written in the highest strain of Tory loyalty, and entitled 'The Loyal Man's Psalter,' was widely circulated throughout England." [2] The fact will serve to remind us that the politico-ecclesiastical controversies of the period were often reflected in its poetry. It was an age of polemic songs, ballads, and squibs. The Sacheverell case alone proved so rich in poetical possibilities that in 1710 a canny bookseller rushed into print with *A Collection of Poems, For and Against Dr. Sacheverell.*

[1] G. M. Trevelyan, *England under Queen Anne*, I, 283.
[2] W. E. H. Lecky, *A History of England in the Eighteenth Century*, I, 146. I have not seen the book to which Lecky refers.

At an earlier date the High Churchmen expressed their disapproval of Tillotson and his latitudinarian theology in such lines as:

> For holy cause, sir,
> You may break laws, sir,
> Nor treason then nor perjury will signify two straws, sir:
> So sad our fate is,
> Worser far than Papists,
> For Socinus rules the Church, and is ruled by an Atheist.
> The nation's damnation
> Was this last reformation,
> For you must either take the swear, or starve, or lose your station.[3]

Their subsequent disappointment in Queen Anne was voiced in the ruefully humorous quatrain:

> When she was the church's daughter,
> She acted as her mother taught her;
> But now she's mother of the church,
> She's left her daughter in the lurch.[4]

When the Bangorian Controversy broke out, they sneered:

> And how does Ben Hoadley?
> Oh, he's very well,
> A truer blue Whig
> You have not in hell.[5]

The Low Church Whigs retorted with:

> The pulpit thunders death and war
> To heal the bleeding nation,
> And sends Dissenters to the Devil
> To keep the Toleration.
> The High Church Clergy, mounted high,
> Like sons of Jehu drive,
> And o'er the true religion ride
> To keep the Church alive.[6]

And as the Queen's health began to fail they anxiously sang:

> Whoe'er is in place, I care not a fig,
> Nor will I decide betwixt High Church and Low.
> 'Tis now no dispute between Tory and Whig,
> But whether a Popish successor or no.

[3] Quoted by W. Sichel, *Bolingbroke and His Times*, I, 171.
[4] Quoted by Abbey and Overton, *The English Church in the Eighteenth Century*, I, 65.
[5] Quoted by Sichel, *op. cit.*, I, 13.   [6] *Ibid.*, p. 122.

> Over, over, Hanover, over,
>> Haste and assist our Queen and our State;
>> Haste over, Hanover, fast as you can over,
>> Put in your claims before 'tis too late.[7]

Such topics also received treatment in numberless longer and more formal poems. Although detailed examination of this material would lead us too far into contemporary politics and too far away from anything that merits the name of religion, we must not entirely disregard it. Since no fixed line of demarcation can be drawn between the political and religious passions of the age, many of these controversial poems shed light upon our subject. In this chapter, therefore, will be grouped certain poets who devote themselves mainly or exclusively to questions of Church and State.

The Tories may be permitted to speak first, and the verses of Thomas Brown (1663-1704) provide a convenient starting point. This scurrilous but sometimes amusing rascal, whose life the *D.N.B.* declares with prim accuracy to have been "as licentious as his writings," emerges as a pamphleteer and satirist in the closing years of Charles II's reign.

Tom Brown adheres to the thoroughly English belief that "Tobacco, Ale, and the Protestant Religion" are "the three great blessings of life."[8] He prizes the Church of England for its ability to preserve a just balance between sound reason and the nonsense required to capture the popular imagination. "A speculative religion," he declares, "is only calculated for a few philosophers, and not the gross vulgar....For this reason the popish priests amuse them with pictures, shows, and images; the presbyterian parsons with apish gestures, fantastic expressions, and sordid similies, that are full as gross as images: The church of England goes the middle way to work, and gives them half in surplices and organs, and t'other half in good sense and reason."[9] Evidently the churchmanship of this champion of the *via media* is "high" only in the political sense. He has not a grain of reverence for the spiritual aspect of the Church.

In fact Brown would like nothing better than to be free from the necessity of thinking about religion at all. With James II on the throne, he refuses to let fears of popery drag him from his bottle:

[7] *Ibid.*, p. 64.
[8] *The Works of Mr. Thomas Brown* (1744), III, 278.
[9] *Ibid.*, IV, 107.

What a pox d'ye tell me of the papists' design?
Would to God you'd leave talking, and drink off your wine.
Away with your glass, sir, and drown all debate;
Let's be loyally merry; ne'er think of the state.
The king (heavens bless him) knows best how to rule;
And who troubles his head I think is but a fool.

. . . .

Let chapels, in Lime street, be built or destroy'd,
And the test, and the oath of supremacy, void;
It shall ne'er trouble me; I'm none of those maggots,
That have whimsical fancies of Smithfield and faggots.[10]

Not of course that he has the slightest sympathy with Rome. "If the Eucharist be the true and real body of our Saviour," he asks with a triumphant libertine swagger, "why do you administer it on Fridays, when you prohibit eating flesh?" [11] Dryden's conversion is the theme of a mordant epigram:

Traytor to God, and rebel to the pen,
Priest-ridden poet, perjur'd son of Ben,
If ever thou prove honest, then the nation
May modestly believe Transubstantiation.[12]

Rather surprisingly, despite his loyalty to King James his Protestantism is strong enough to make him warn the dissenters against accepting the Declaration of Indulgence:

Trust me, this kindness either was design'd
T''inflame our quarrels, and our weakness find:
Or else the breach was open'd at a venture,
That at one hole both cowl and cloak might enter.
Pray heav'n there be no farther mischief meant,
But I'm afraid there's Roman opium in't.[13]

Yet when William Sherlock, after long hesitation, agreed to take the oaths, Brown gibes at both his politics and his theology in the lines:

The same allegiance to two Kings he pays,
Swears the same faith to both, and both betrays.
No wonder if to swear he's always free,
That hath two gods, to swear by, more than we.[14]

---

[10] *In Praise of the Bottle.*   [12] *Ibid.*, I, 127.
[11] *Works*, III, 278.   [13] *Ibid.*, IV, 94.
[14] Cf. also *To Dr. Sherlock, On Occasion of his Taking the Oaths, 1690.* The last line of Brown's epigram is explained by the fact that Sherlock's *Vindication of the Doctrine of the Trinity* (1690) aroused some suspicion of his own orthodoxy on this point.

Brown's loyalty to the Tory cause, however, is not to be ascribed to any fine flame of devotion. He simply defends the system which, if left undisturbed, would be most favorable to his own lazy, sensual, witty way of life, and he attacks anything that threatens the stability of that norm.

Thus though himself without a grain of spiritual feeling, he can praise Creech's introduction to his translation of Lucretius as a counterblast against atheism.[15] To *be* an unbeliever is harmless, but to *preach* unbelief destroys the comfortable balance of things. On the other hand he pursues Blackmore with relentless enmity [16] because the earnest Whig morality of the pious old physician goes too far in the opposite direction from Lucretius. Of course the dissenters, as menacing Brown's ideal of being "loyally merry," come in for a large share of his abuse. But Brown's views are expressed so much less fully and interestingly in his verse than in his prose that we had better turn to a richer source of the same kind of material.

Edward Ward (1667-1731) is generally regarded as Brown's lineal successor, for the two have much in common. Both qualitatively and quantitatively, however, Ward is by far the more important as a writer of verse. His ambition to emulate Samuel Butler is revealed in the title of *Hudibras Redivivus* (1705-1707). The main purpose of this satire, as he says in an "Apology" added to the second edition (1708), is to attack the "Fanaticks, Dissenters, Moderators, Whigs, Low-Church-men, Saints, Reformers, or whatsoever new Denomination they are pleas'd to rank themselves under, the better to disguise their old base Principles, as well as Practices." But the poem as a whole is more casual than this declaration would suggest. Somewhat in the manner of his prose *London Spy,* the author rambles about the city, commenting digressively on what he sees:

> Young Drunkards reeling, Bayliffs dogging,
> Old Strumpets plying, Mumpers progging,
> Fat Dray-men squabling, Chair-men ambling,
> Oyster-whores fighting, School-Boys scrambling,

---

[15] *Works,* IV, 225-226.

[16] In 1700 Brown edited a little anti-Blackmore miscellany, *Commendatory Verses on the Author of the Two Arthurs and the Satire against Wit by some of his particular Friends.*

> Street Porters running, Rascals battling,
> Pick-pockets crowding, Coaches rattling,
> News bawling, Ballad-wenches singing,
> Guns roaring, and the Church-Bells ringing.

But the bells ring to small purpose, for greed has taken the place of faith:

> Religion, once the nation's darling,
> Now bows its head to pow'rful Sterling.

Witness the debtors' prisons, which contradict the most essential of Christian precepts:

> The King of Christians gave his Bosome
> To Lazarus, when poor and lo'hsome,
> But modern Christians now, instead,
> Would heap more Mis'ries on his Head,
> And give him Stones, instead of Bread.

Christian charity is not, however, a powerful factor in *Hudibras Redivivus*. Ward is fully aware that

> ... he that writes in such an Age,
> When Parties do for Pow'r engage,
> Ought to chuse one Side for the Right,
> And then, with all his Wit and Spite
> Blacken and vex the Opposite.
>
> .   .   .   .
>
> Scurrility's a useful Trick,
> Approv'd by the most Politick.
> Fling Dirt enough, and some will stick.

Ward is being ironic here, but one cannot deny that he follows his own advice.

His political theory is simplicity itself:

> How shall a King bear Sov'reign Sway,
> Unless the Subjects do obey?
> And what can bind 'em, if they won't,
> But Pow'r to force 'em, when they don't?

The dissenters have a quite different standard, "The Lords the Rabble" are really much greater than the nobility,

> For surely those that can at Pleasure
> Make Kings, and give them Pow'r and Treasure,
> By Nature's Law much higher stand,
> Than those made Great at second Hand.

This sarcastic reference to "nature" as a basis for the puritan position is of some historical interest.

The Low Churchmen, who are so proud of their moderation, are merely the tools of the crafty dissenters,

> Design'd in some more wicked Times
> To bear the Slander of their Crimes,
> That when they find a proper Season
> T'attempt some Massacre or Treason,
> The cunning Saints may shift the Shame,
> And cast upon the Church the Blame.

Very much in Butler's manner is the description of a congregation of "fanatics,"

> Shelter'd beneath Umbrella Hats,
> And Canoniz'd with Rose Cravats,
> That by their Querpo's and their Quaints,
> The World might read them to be Saints;
> Their sweaty Rats-tail Hair hung down
> To th'Shoulders from each addled Crown,
> Kept thin, to cool their frantick Brains,
> And comb'd as strait as Horses Manes;
> Their Bodies almost Skelitons,
> Reduc'd by Zeal to Skin and Bones.

In what obscure alley, one wonders, could Ward have found such a collection of canting scarecrows? Probably he is satirizing the non-conformists of his own day for the eccentricities of their seventeenth-century forefathers.

The sermon delivered to this congregation is a fine piece of hypocritical cant:

> O sanctify this Congregation;
> Scatter their Seed throughout the Nation,
> And cleanse their wicked Souls within,
> From all the filthy Dregs of Sin;
> Wash from them all their Blots and Stains,
> As Housewives do their Pots and Pans:

> O stretch their Consciences I pray;
> O stretch 'em largely every way,
> That by that means they may embrace
> A greater Portion of thy Grace;
> Which well improv'd by Pray'r and Fasting,
> May make them Saints for Everlasting!
>   This he repeated o'er again,
>   And all the People cry'd, *Amen*.

Has any source-hunter suggested a relationship between this sermon and Burns's *Holy Willie's Prayer?* I suppose so.

In 1707 the time was hardly ripe for such violently intolerant Toryism. Ward was placed in the pillory, where, it is said, the mob pelted him with particular zest. Later, in 1710, the rising of the mob in favor of Sacheverell gave him the opportunity, by writing *Vulgus Britannicus,* to hurl back some of the rotten eggs which had been thrown at him.

The support of the mob was valuable to the Tories, but it was also embarrassing to them. Strange spectacle—an alliance between the despised rabble and the party of loyal Cavaliers, of High Church parsons, of landed gentry! Ward, who had his own reasons for detesting the *mobile vulgus,* wishes to show that "our Good Lords the People," as being full of the spirit of rebellion, are really at one with the Whigs, Low Churchmen, and Dissenters. The mob, he insists, supported Sacheverell merely because in so doing it could make trouble for the governing party. Had the Tories been in power, the mob would have risen against them in the same way. Sacheverell himself disliked the rabble. Ward refers to him with respect, but grants that he was headstrong and overzealous. *Vulgus Britannicus,* then, is directed against

> ...their S[overeign] L[ords] the Mob;
> Who now grown mad twixt Nob and Tipple,
> Declar'd themselves to be the *People,*
> Who had by Nature's Law a Right,
> To do whate'er themselves thought fit.

Again one observes that Ward regards belief in "natural law" as a favorite doctrine of his enemies.

From the viewpoint of the present study, this poem adds little to what has been gleaned from *Hudibras Redivivus*. Ward's loyalty to the Church is absolute:

> The stubborn Turk or faithless Jew,
> May say their own Opinion's true,
> And scribble, wrangle, lie, and bluster,
> To make the Alcoran pass muster;
> Or use a crafty strenuous Plea,
> In Right of Infidelity:
> But shall we to our wicked Shame,
> Forsake our Faith to Humour them?
>
> .   .   .   .
>
> No, to the Church let's stick the closer,
> When such bold Enemies oppose her:
> And never heed what 'tis they Write,
> Or say against her in their Spite.

The same principle applies to the dissenters. Enemies of Church and State, they deserve no toleration. But the Low Churchmen are almost as bad, for they are closer friends to Nonconformity than to the Establishment:

> These are the Janus-looking Fools
> The Faction work with as their Tools,
> Who with Church Discipline concede,
> Yet strongly for Dissenters plead;
> And for the sake of Peace and Union,
> Altho' they're of the Church Communion,
> Comply with e'erything that shows
> They're Friends to them that are her Foes.

All gentleness toward the sectarians, they are all bitterness toward the true Church. Such as these

> Would frequently at Church commune,
> And rail against her when they'd done,
> As if they only kiss'd the Chalice,
> To whet and sanctifie their Malice.

Yet we wonder how often Ned Ward himself was able to go to the altar rails, as the liturgy prescribes, in love and charity with all his neighbors. Malice is the very lifeblood of his work. It would be hard to imagine a man more stoutly loyal to the Church as a political institution, or one more devoid of any genuine religious feeling.[17]

[17] For other poems by Ward which pertain to our subject, see R. P. Bond, *English Burlesque Poetry*, pp. 246-247 and 287.

On the other side of the Scottish border, the Hudibrastic tradition of Tory satire was carried on by William Meston [18] (1688?-1745). *The Knight of the Kirk: or, the Ecclesiastical Adventures of Sir John Presbyter* is a long, though uncompleted, anti-Presbyterian and pro-Stuart imitation of Butler. Meston is a clumsy, coarse, wordy fellow, but occasionally strikes home. His eccentric hero, some people alleged,

> Was come of chaos and old night;
> Proving that he came from that border,
> Because he hates all form and order.

> . . . . .

> Cou'd we believe himself, he'll tell us,
> He is one of th'Apostles' fellows,
> With whom he did sit cheek for jowl,
> And voted when they made their Poll,
> As member of their first Assembly,
> Which makes him be with them so homely.

Needless to say, Sir John Presbyter is opposed to popish ritual in the Church. Observing that bishops pray on their knees, he

> . . . thought fit to teach
> His followers to sit on breech,
> Or, if they please, to lean their heads
> Upon their neighbour's shoulder-blades,
> Or lolling lye upon their haunches,
> With head on hand in the kirk-benches,
> Which postures are less superstitious
> He says, than kneeling, which is vitious.

Sir John is anxious that the Independents should not rob the Presbyterians of the •credit for the death of Charles I. The former merely completed the process initiated by the latter:

> . . . 'Tis sure we did unking him;
> They only to a block did bring him.
> Let any man say what he can,
> We kill'd the *King,* they kill'd the *man.*

[18] The son of an Aberdeenshire blacksmith. In 1715 he relinquished his post as Regent of Marischal College to fight for the Old Pretender. After the collapse of the rebellion he combined sponging on the Jacobite nobility with unsuccessful attempts to conduct schools. An example of the "learned witty drunkard" type of Scotsman. His poems did not begin to appear until 1720, but several of them had been written before that time. In any case, since he is interesting only in relation to the Rebellion of 1715, it would be absurd not to place him in this chapter.

Like the dissenters satirized by Ned Ward, the hero of this poem bases his treasonous views on belief in the rights of nature; but the nature which Meston makes him preach is a wild and lawless state like that imagined by Hobbes, who is referred to in a footnote. The Knight's views are severely tested when he is held up and robbed by the chief of the clan McGregor. The robber reminds him:

> You are a champion, most zealous
> For nature's rights; so are my fellows
> And I; We use the Self-same reason:
> Produce your purse; it is no treason
> To take it from you.

At this Sir John appeals to the laws of orderly civilization, but he is urged to be more consistent:

> Tush! quoth McGregor, Never flinch
> From principles, nor spurn, nor winch:
> Ne'er talk of laws 'gainst nature's right;
> You know far better things, good Knight:
> These cobwebs you have all swept down,
> By sweeping off your Sov'reign's crown.

And so the apostle of nature gets a taste of his own lawlessness.

A section of Meston's *Poetical Works* headed "Old Mother Grim's Tales" consists of fables and tales which curiously mingle extremely broad humor with indignant Jacobitism. Their point of view is illustrated by *Tale VII. A Vision:*

> At dead of night, after an evening ball,
> In her own father's [19] lodging at Whitehall,
> As youthful Tullia [20] unregarded lay
> By a dull lump of Netherlandish clay—[21]

her mother's shade appears and reproaches her, saying,

> Can any thing that's good from Frog-land [22] come,
> The very jakes and sink of Christendom?
> A Dutchman is a rogue, whate'er he seems;
> (No muddy fountain can yield chrystal streams.)

[19] James II.
[20] Queen Mary.
[21] William III.
[22] Not France, but Holland!

> Awake, Britannia, guard thy tott'ring crown,
> Which by republicans is pulling down;
> Ambitious Orange serves but for a tool,
> They set him up that they themselves may rule.

When Addison's *Cato* was produced, the Tories tried to claim its noble sentiments as their own. But Meston scorns any such compromise with the powers of darkness. In *Cato's Ghost* he says that the old Roman would be astounded to see himself in a play "where treason mounts on each brocaded line." Let us replace this false symbol of virtue with a living one—the rightful heir to the throne of England:

> Britons, for shame! behold the wondrous youth,
> With how much care he forms himself to truth!
> How just, how brave, how generous, and how wise,
> How good he is, without the least disguise!
>
> .   .   .   .
>
> Such is your Prince; how can you then be slaves
> To madmen, fools, whores, foreigners, and knaves?

More even than Ned Ward, Meston impresses one as living completely in the past. He broods over old, unhappy, far-off things like an "unreconstructed" Confederate. For him the Presbyterians of his own day are the very men who betrayed the Royal Martyr, and he will never forgive them. Exerting our utmost charity, let us grant the possibility that a little religion may have mingled with his Jacobite loyalty and hatred. In *A holy Ode, from Mount Alexander,* he says that since the ways of Providence are hidden from man, we should not let our sufferings make us lose faith. Then he applies this thought to the Pretender:

> O! sacred J[ames], let not thy lot,
>   Tho' seemingly severe,
> Make thee suspect thy cause forgot;
>   Thy crosses nobly bear.
> He, who thy heart has in his hand,
>   (Trust thou his sacred skill)
> Has too the people's at command,
>   And turns them at his will.

A believer in the divine right of kings must have some shadowy sense of divinity. In Meston's case, however, the evidence for this proposition is very slight, since this "holy ode" is the sole clue.

Hudibras is still the model for an anonymous satire of 1718 entitled *The Tower of Babel. An Anti-Heroic Poem. Humbly Dedicated to the B[ishop] of B[ango]r.* It represents a late phase in the controversial writing of the 1700-1720 period—the half-theological, half-political turmoil centering around Bishop Benjamin Hoadly. His *Preservative against the Principles and Practices of the Nonjurors* (1716) and his more famous sermon on *The Nature of the Kingdom or Church of Christ* (1717) gave rise to the acrimonious Bangorian Controversy. In these and other writings the bishop implicitly denied that he was a bishop at all. He interpreted the text, "My kingdom is not of this world" as a divine rebuke to the doctrine of one Holy, Catholic, and Apostolic Church. The Church of England was simply the Protestant denomination which had been selected as the national form of worship. Its clergy were priests only in a manner of speaking, and its sacraments were only more or less edifying traditional customs. Religion was essentially a matter of virtuous behavior, the relations between God and man were purely direct and personal, and any sincere belief was as good as any other sincere belief. Such views were common in the eighteenth century, but to see them advocated by a powerful prelate created a furor of mingled joy and execration.

In *The Tower of Babel,* the author's plan is to expose Hoadly chiefly by making him set forth his own views so absurdly that they will be easy to refute. Unfortunately he makes Hoadly speak a little too well for this purpose: the Whig prelate's ideas are less obviously nonsensical to the reader than to the satirist, who on the other hand, sublimely confident of his position, does not give himself enough telling points.

Hoadly, for example, is permitted to say:

> Religion in St. James's Days
> Had not a Grain of Pray'r or Praise,
> But like good Boaz courting Ruth,
> Pure Virtue was, and naked Truth;
> But since the Time and Place 'twas married,
> How has the holy Thing miscarried!

.   .   .   .

> For when Externals we profess,
> We wear it merely as a Dress,
> And fix a Badge on our Belief,
> Like that upon a Beggar's Sleeve;

.   .   .   .

In sacred Offices 'tis clear
The Outer-Man should disappear.
Worship's the Homage of the Spirit,
And can't endure the Body near it.

The burlesque, though not indiscernible, is not broad enough for satirical purposes. It is quite possible to read these lines as a straightforward expression of left-wing liberal Protestantism.

The author's answer to Hoadly on this particular point is not without merit. He says that he too is an enemy of empty formalism, but regards man as so complex a being that his spirit can never, in this life, be separated from his flesh. Hence instead of vainly attempting to sunder flesh and spirit, we should combine them in our worship.

But on the whole the satirist gives himself rather the worst of it, so that at the close he uneasily drops his good-natured mask and launches a direct attack:

Since then by Maxims vile and scurvy,
You've turn'd Religion topsy-turvy,
Unsettled States, and sapp'd your Bases,
By Dint of Queries, Hints and Cases,
Have left all Christendom i'the'Lurch,
And made each single Man, a Church;
Since common Sense, your Rev'rence saith,
Is the most certain Rule of Faith,
And Hereticks, sincerely giv'n,
Are in the ready Road to Heav'n;

. . . .

Since Truth you equally can fix on
The two Parts of a Contradiction;
Notions of Wrong and Right confound,
And Virtue prove an empty Sound;
Perversely paint the Devil White,
Call Truth a Lie, and Darkness Light:
Go on!—and with the Rebel Giants
To Heav'n and Nature bid Defiance;
Call for your Implements and Rabble,
And try to build a second Babel.

This passage contains some legitimately hostile criticism: it is quite true, for instance, that Hoadly's theories "made each single man, a church." But the author soon collapses into vague and silly abuse, and leaves a final impression of weakness. It may at least be said for him, however, that he sticks rather closely to the theological side of the controversy, and does not seem to be actuated merely by political malevolence.

Abel Evans (1679-1737), clergyman and wit, is a more gifted and more serious Tory [23] satirist than those previously considered. He directs *The Apparition* (1710) against the deist Matthew Tindal [24] as the foe of morals, religion, and orderly government. The device is that Satan visits Tindal in his Oxford rooms to congratulate him on his fiendish exploits. The "hot-brain'd Atheist crew" down in hell are delighted with him:

> Spinoza smiles, and cries, "The work is done;
> Tindal shall finish (Satan's darling son),
> Tindal shall finish what Spinoza first begun."
> Hobbes, Milton, Blount, Vanini with him join;
> All equally admire the vast design.

Epicurus and Lucretius add their voices to this chorus of praise. As for Judas, he positively envies Tindal.

Milton probably owes his place in the above list more to his political than to his theological heterodoxy. To an extreme "Highflyer," a man who wrote against kings might as well be called an atheist. Evans's High Churchism has a large political element: he finds Tindal's republican views quite as disturbing as his deism.

Inflamed by Satan's praise, Tindal longs to do even greater harm. He exclaims:

> Oh, were my will but once Britannia's law!
> Rome should again the servile nation awe;
> The Druids else regain their lost abodes,
> And Thor and Woden be Britannia's gods:
> Idols in every temple should be found,
> The poor in chains of superstition bound;
> The rich in luxury and atheism drown'd;
> All decency and order should be damn'd;
> And wild Enthusiasm run bellowing through the land.

[23] He was originally a Whig and a protégé of the Duchess of Marlborough, but had become a strong Tory by the time *The Apparition* was written.

[24] In the first edition Tindal's name is concealed as "L——t," but there is no doubt that he is aimed at. The subtitle of the poem as it appears in Nichols' *Collection*, III, 118, reads: "Occasioned by the Publication of Tindal's Rights of the Christian Church."

> All, in their turns, be prophets, priests, and kings;
> Distinctions are but meer fantastick things:
> All government does from the people flow;
> Whom they make priests or kings, are truly so.

Satan applauds these aims, but is doubtful of their speedy fulfilment. There are two obstacles, of which the second is by far the more formidable:

> False are our hopes, and profitless our pains,
> While bishops mitres wear, and ANNA reigns.
>
> .   .   .   .   .
>
> Oh Anna! When will thy devotion cease?
> When will thy streams of charity decrease?
>
> .   .   .   .   .
>
> Why art thou thus too generously great,
> To sink thy own, to raise the clergy's state? [25]
> What blessings still attend thy glorious reign!
> Oh Anna! most perversely pious queen.

The Prince of Darkness not only fears that it will be necessary to make haste slowly, but he also wishes that Tindal would be a little more subtle and insidious in his assaults on Church and State, lest their plots be exposed and crushed before they are ripe. The stage provides an example of his meaning. It was a most laudable agency of corruption, but it went so far that "fierce Jerry Collier rose" and checked the progress of evil in that direction.

Satan bids his favorite disciple farewell with the words:

> 'Tis well remember'd—take one parting kiss;
> Thine elder brother Judas sent thee this.

In short *The Apparition* is a good hot satire, especially instructive in showing the close interweaving in the author's mind of moral reform interests,[26] High Church religion and Tory politics.[27]

---

[25] An allusion to "Queen Anne's Bounty," which provided the Church with about £17,000 a year for the augmentation of small livings.

[26] High Churchmen played their part in the moral-reform movement of Queen Anne's reign—witness Jeremy Collier. I suspect, however, that this element in Evans's work may be a survival of his earlier Whiggery. It does not seem to be a common element in Tory satire.

[27] I have not read *The Second Part of the Apparition* (1710). There is nothing to the purpose in *Vertumnus*, nor in the epigrams for which Evans is chiefly known. *Præ-Existence. A Poem, in imitation of Milton* will be dealt with in Chapter IV.

Of all Swift's politico-ecclesiastical poems, only the *Ode to Doctor William Sancroft* [28] has a modicum of religious feeling. In the previous chapter we noted the scepticism of the opening stanzas. But Swift goes on to say that while the pure truth of heaven is unknowable on earth,

> Ill may I live, if the good Sancroft, in his holy rest,
>   In the divinity of retreat,
> Be not the brightest pattern earth can show
> Of heaven-born Truth below.

Few men, however, are capable of following so nearly perfect a model. They prefer to let their minds be swayed by popular opinion, "Till honesty and conscience are clear out of sight." To such men,

> ...holy Sancroft's motion quite irregular appears,
>   Because 'tis opposite to theirs.

In characteristic rage at the stupidity of the multitude, Swift despairs of enlightening them. England is thoroughly rotten, and William III, a rose "too much without a thorn," is too gentle to punish the evil-doers. Above this turmoil of sin, faction, rebellion, and misguided zeal, "primitive Sancroft" shines like a star showing "the way which leads to Christ" —the way neglected alike by the foolish rabble and the

> ...ignorantly wise,
> Among proud doctors and disputing Pharisees:
> What could the sages gain but unbelieving scorn;
>   Their faith was so uncourtly, when they said
> That Heaven's high Son was in a village born;
>   That the world's Saviour had been
>   In a vile manger laid,
>   And foster'd in a wretched inn.

This strikes a note almost unique in Swift's verse.

The political element, however, at once reasserts itself. Swift asks "why the church is still led blindfold by the state," apparently not perceiving, or refusing to perceive, the inevitable consequence of the High Church

[28] William Sancroft, who became Archbishop of Canterbury in 1678, was a High Churchman of the earlier-seventeenth-century type, desirous of reviving the Anglo-Catholicism of Laud. Because he held that William III should be declared *custos regni* rather than king, he was suspended August 1, 1689, deprived of his mitre February 1, 1690, and ejected from his see June 23, 1691. "We may surmise," says Harold Williams, "that the poem was begun in 1689, at the request of Francis Turner, Bishop of Ely, also a non-juror, and abandoned incomplete in 1692." (Swift's *Poems*, I, 34.)

views of regal power. Rather grimly, he expresses the hope that "the present mitre," unlike Sancroft's, may be disturbed by

> ... no unkind earthquake of the state,
> Nor hurricano from the crown.

But though deprived of his honors on earth, Sancroft is a prelate in the realms above:

> For, whate'er theologic levellers dream,
> There are degrees above, I know,
> As well as here below,
> (The goddess Muse herself has told me so),
> Where high patrician souls, dress'd heavenly gay,
> Sit clad in lawn of purer woven day.
> There some high-spirited throne to Sancroft shall be given,
> In the metropolis of Heaven;
> Chief of the mitred saints, and from archprelate here,
> Translated to archangel there.

The "happy saint's" prayers for the "miserable church" are needed in these days when her enemies are so bold:

> Some angel, say, what were the nation's crimes,
> That sent these wild reformers to our times:
> Say what their senseless malice meant,
> To tear religion's lovely face:
> Strip her of every ornament and grace;
> In striving to wash off th'imaginary paint?
> Religion now does on her death-bed lie,
> Heart-sick of a high fever and consuming atrophy.

This poem serves to remind us that Swift was a High Churchman long before he became a member of the Tory party. Once his political and ecclesiastical views were completely harmonized, he wrote only to hurt. A few examples will suffice. *Toland's Invitation to Dismal, to Dine with the Calf's Head Club* bitterly satirizes the political apostasy of Nottingham.[29] Toland appears merely as a wicked republican, not as a deist. Elsewhere the indifference of two notoriously irreligious Whigs to the High Churchmen's favorite slogan occasions a striking epigram *On the Church's Danger:*

---

[29] The Earl, a very strong High Churchman, was induced to support the Whigs' war policy by their agreeing to the Occasional Conformity Bill.

Good Halifax and pious Wharton cry,
The Church has vapours; there's no danger nigh.
In those we love not, we no danger see,
And were they hang'd, there would no danger be.
But we must silent be amidst our fears,
And not believe our senses, but the Peers.
So ravishers, that know no sense of shame,
First stop her mouth, and then debauch the dame.

The *Ballad* beginning "A wonderful age" expresses with a kind of bitter gaiety many of Swift's favorite grudges, but its most interesting feature is the author's linking of religious toleration with a widespread cult of relativism. People think, he snarls, that in Scotland Presbyterianism may well be the best form of religion; for just as different fruits thrive best in different soils,

The best church by far
Is what grows where you are,
Were it Mahomet's ass or his pigeon.

Hence it is not surprising that pensions and places are granted to rascally occasional conformists:

For if it be not strange
That religion should change,
As often as climates and fashions;
Then sure there's no harm,
That one should conform,
To serve their own private occasions.

In this topsy-turvy world of heresy, hypocrisy, and rebellion, Swift sees just one ray of light:

But now, sir, they tell,
How Sacheverell,
By bringing old doctrines in fashion,
Hath, like a damn'd rogue,
Brought religion in vogue,
And so open'd the eyes of the nation.

The author of the *Voyage to the Land of the Houyhnhnms* speaks out plainly in *On the Words Brother Protestants and Fellow Christians, So Familiarly Used by the Advocates for the Repeal of the Test-Act in Ireland. 1733:*

> But be they English, Irish, Scottish,
> What Protestant can be so sottish,
> While o'er the church these clouds are gathering,
> To call a swarm of lice his brethren?
>
> . . . . .
>
> Let folks in high or holy stations
> Be proud of owning such relations;
> Let courtiers hug them to their bosom,
> As if they were afraid to lose 'em;
> While I, with humble Job, had rather
> Say to corruption—"Thou'rt my Father."
> For he that has so little wit
> To nourish vermin, may be bit.

In a sense all men are Yahoos, but the purest specimens of the breed are the dissenters and their Low Church friends. Nevertheless his partisanship is thoroughly disillusioned; his *Advice to a Parson,* one feels, is meant to apply to clerics of every shade of opinion:

> Would you rise in the Church, be stupid and dull,
> Be empty of learning, of insolence full:
> Though lewd and immoral, be formal and grave,
> In flatt'ry an artist, in fawning a slave.
> No merit, no science, no virtue is wanting,
> In him, that's accomplished in cringing and canting.

Although savagely intolerant, Swift is usually keen and witty. The satires which ushered in the career of William Shippen, (1673-1743),[30] on the other hand, are as dull as they are bigoted. They teem with recondite personal allusions which we must not pause to unravel, but their general position is clear. *Faction Display'd* (1705) contrasts the evil present with the happy times "When Laud or Sancroft fill'd the Sacred Chair." The latitudinarian Whig prelates of today pretend great affection for Christian charity,

> But with a blind Enthusiastick Rage,
> For Schism and Toleration they engage;
> With strange Delight and Vehemence espouse
> Occasional Conformists' shameful Cause.

[30] Pope's "honest Shippen," a consistent Jacobite throughout a parliamentary career which extended from 1707 to his death. After the accession of George I, he led, with much courage and probity, the small group of Jacobite squires in the House of Commons.

These Low Churchmen, of course, are political radicals carrying on a plot against the throne. Clodio, a speaker in the more or less Miltonic council summoned by Faction, declares:

> The glorious Revolution was in vain,
> If Monarchy once more its Rights regain.
> Let all be Chaos, and Confusion all,
> Ere that damn'd Form of Government prevail.

Let us, he continues,

> Argue how th' Roman and Athenian State
> Were only when Republicks truly Great;
> Assert in Passive Jacobites despight,
> Rebellion is a Freeborn Peoples right;
> Disperse a thousand well invented Tales
> Of Foreign Gold, the Pope, and Prince of Wales.
>
> .   .   .   .
>
> Toland alone for such a work is fit,
> In all the Arts of Villany compleat.

Moderation Display'd (1709) differs in no important respect from the earlier diatribe. Both poems ascribe irreligion and treason to the opponents of the bill to prevent Occasional Conformity.

Now that the Tories have been allowed to voice their loyalties and hatreds, it is time to hear from the opposite side. In his prosperous early days, when the success of his bombastic tragedies aroused even Dryden's jealousy, Elkanah Settle (1648-1724) was a violently Protestant Whig. On the anniversary of Queen Elizabeth's birthday, November 17, 1680, he was unanimously chosen to organize the pope-burning ceremony. But the accession of James II found Dryden's Doeg in a very different frame of mind, and nothing could be more loyally Tory than *An Heroick Poem on the Coronation of the High and Mighty Monarch, James II* (1685). The poem, full of Biblical parallels, celebrates the occasion as an event in the history of Christianity no less than of England. The former pope-burner makes no direct reference to James's Catholicism, but carefully attributes the "Whore of Babylon" conception of Rome to the miscreants who slew the Royal Martyr. After declaring that all the woes of England's recent past will now cease, Settle adds the staggeringly blasphemous simile:

> So when th' Almighty Hebrew Child was Born,
> Immaculate Truth began her glorious Morn:
> Whilst the old Fiend, the Pagan Oracle,
> Was silenced down to his own Native Hell.
> Our World, Great Reconciling James, in Thee
> And thy blest Reign, shall equal Glories see.

Unfortunately Settle had so good a memory for his own inspirations that in 1702 he applied almost the same simile to the frustration of the designs of Rome by the House of Hanover:

> So the World's once famed Oracles of old,
> All by Infernal Inspirations told,
> Doom'd t' endless Silence, hid their Heads in Earth
> At the bright Dawn of the Great Hebrew Birth.

These lines occur in the English version of his *Eusebia Triumphans. Carmen Hannonianis Imperiali Coronae Angliae Successionibus Dicatum* (1702).[31] Settle, reconverted to Whiggery in 1688, desires to elevate his party's theory of government to lofty spiritual heights. Orderly government both in heaven and on earth, says he, is God's will. A king is the earthly representative of this divine principle. England is especially blest in that her government is based upon

> The Second to the great First Mover, Law.
> This beauteous Tutelar, with all her Charms
> Lodg'd in thy Walls, Britannia, in thy Arms,
> No wild Luxuriant Offspring of the Throne,
> Her whole Divine Creation's all thy own.
> Thy Popular Hands found thy Imperial Sway,
> Lords to make Laws, and Subjects to obey.

When "this Compact of Obedience and Command" was threatened, England called in William to preserve it. It is now, to the impotent chagrin of Rome, guaranteed by the Hanoverian Succession.

By this time Settle's emulation of the Vicar of Bray's tactics has discredited him. A shabby, half-absurd, half-pathetic figure as city laureate, he is descending toward the final humiliations of Bartholomew Fair and the Charterhouse. Except for characteristic wavering during the Tory years of 1710-1714, he remains a Whig to the end of his life. Indignant at the rebellion of 1715, he rushes into print the same year with *Rebellion*

---

[31] Latin and English versions on opposite pages. On the title-page of the British Museum copy the date is altered in ink from 1702 to 1703.

Display'd: Or, Our Present Distractions Set forth in their True Light.
Without confining himself to the religious aspect of the situation, he
nevertheless places the popish peril in the foreground. This paragon of
consistency reproaches the English for their fickleness—once so eager to
be rescued from Rome by William, now so willing to welcome the
Catholic Pretender. It is nonsense to suppose that the exiled Stuart would
uphold the Church of England:

> ...Would Rome such Sums disburse,
> Sums has she own'd so spent, if spent alone
> To mount *Our* Faith's Defender, not her Own?
>
> ·   ·   ·
>
> O Albion! what malignant Planet rules;
> Thy Sons debas'd below the Class of Fools,
> Such Zealots for their Church, and yet such Popish Tools?

Anything like a thorough examination of Settle's too copious verse
would be unprofitable. A fact at least worthy of mention, however, is
that he enjoyed writing lugubriously pious funeral elegies. These are a
trifle more "literary" than the puritan elegies studied by Professor
Draper,[32] but are plainly related to that type.

The missionary activities of Queen Anne's reign are so rarely celebrated
in poetry that we may dwell for a moment on *A Pindaric Poem, On the
Propagation of the Gospel in Foreign Parts* (1711).[33] Here Settle leaves
the Church-and-State sphere, but in his dedication flatters Anne's
"Radiant Piety" so grossly as to suggest hope of royal favor. He contrasts
her missionaries with those of the popish Spaniards: "Your Majesty's truly
Christian Hosts, march forth neither for Hostility, Rapine, nor Invasion;
not sent amongst them [the natives], to rob them of their World, but to
give 'em Your Heaven."

In Settle's eyes the East Indian is anything but a Noble Savage. He is
"Dark in Body, but more Dark in Soul...In Ignorance, not Innocence,
a Child." But "Evangelic Day" will soon shed its beams upon him:

> The Phosphor hastens thro' the Sky;
> To you, Ye Indians, it draws Nigh;
> 'Twill guide your following Eyes to Him above,
> The Source, the Author, and the Sum of Love.

[32] J. W. Draper, *The Funeral Elegy and the Rise of English Romanticism.*
[33] In the British Museum Catalogue this anonymous poem is assigned to Settle with
a query. The attribution seems thoroughly probable, though I cannot substantiate it.

Her [England's] Apostolick Sons with swelling Sails,
(Extensive as their Zeal) and Heavenly Gales
Approach your Coasts, while in their Hands they bear
Th' expanded Gospel, unconfin'd as Air,
And free, as Light, to All; where you'll behold,
An humble Shepherd, with an humble Fold;
His Sheep and Lambs wash'd in their Owner's Blood,
Whiter than Snow, tho' in a Crimson Flood,
As Virgin dreams are, Innocent and Good.

This is perhaps Settle's closest approach to religious poetry. Soon, however, he relapses into bumptious eulogy of England as a Christian land
blest with a pious Queen and a sublime bench of bishops.

Settle was false to himself only when writing as a Tory, though even
then he seems to be fully convinced of his own sincerity. He was by
nature an ultra-Protestant Low Church Whig whose apparently genuine
piety and indubitably genuine self-interest hung in ambiguous equilibrium.

John Tutchin (1661?-1707) once dreamed of being a poet. In 1685 he
published *Poems on Several Occasions,* an example of that shaggy type of
Restoration verse which, though hardly romantic, has not yet become
smoothly classicized. "I must confess," he remarks in his Preface, "I never
took that for Wit which was (to use a New-born word) *Un-by-any-Fancy-
fathomable.*" Nevertheless, he justifies poetry by urging that "Part of the
Sacred Writings were delivered in Verse: And It's well known, what
Use Divines have made of the Heathen Poets, in their Writings. . . . They
[the heathen poets] all seem'd to be Inspir'd by a Divine Spirit, and to
have some faint Glimmerings of the Eternal Mind diffused on their
Souls. . . . I must confess, the Abuse of Poetry has been very great in these
latter Ages; and since Mr. Cowley, there has been none that has endeavoured to Rectifie it. But if ever I exercise my Hand again this way,
it shall be on some Graver Subject. I hope, here are no Expressions can
offend the Tenderest Reader." Tutchin, we recall, came of a line of dissenting ministers.

As a matter of fact the volume, though it falls a little below the piety
of the passage just quoted, is not at all offensive. If he is coarse in two
or three satires, he can plead good intentions. In such pieces he imitates

Oldham, whom he greatly admires.[34] *A Satyr Against Vice* lashes out at Hobbes, "the Malmesbury Devil":

> As if thou Sin's Columbus meant'st to be,
> Thou view'dst the Orb of large Iniquity.
> And having view'd each Creek, thy fatal Breath
> Thou didst resign to Chance, that made thy Earth.
> And thus our mighty *Atheist* liv'd, thus fell
> The goodliest Brand that ever burnt in Hell.

A Satire Against Whoring is also very outspoken on the side of the angels. Elsewhere, praise of Rochester's genius is mingled with regret for "the bawdy flashes" of his poetry.[35]

Although the volume as a whole is more worldly than these selections would indicate, Tutchin at the outset of his career is plainly a friend of religion and good morals. He is also very much of a Whig, and as the years pass his Whiggery becomes more prominent than his religion. Witness his *Heroick Poem upon the late Expedition of His Majesty, to Rescue England from Popery, Tyranny and Arbitrary Government* (1689). Here Tyranny receives more stress than Popery, but William's English enemies are declared to be in league with Rome. There is much talk about the rights of the people. William is compared to Moses as an agent of the divine will.

In 1691 Tutchin addressed a *Congratulatory Poem to the Reverend Dr. John Tillotson, Upon His Promotion to the Arch-Episcopal-See of Canterbury*. To emphasize his pleasure, he refers to himself as

> I, who the Levite seldome did adore,
> And scarce e're knew a Priest I lov'd before.

Whether this refers to his own nonconformist background or to a more general anti-clericalism is uncertain. Perhaps something of both ideas is in his mind.

Now, the author continues, King William will be more than ever victorious in war, "For Heav'n will grant a Righteous Prelate's Pray'r." He sneers triumphantly at those "stubborn Levites"—the High Churchmen— who will resent Tillotson's elevation, and assures the new primate that

[34] Cf. *To the Memory of Mr. John Oldham.*
[35] *To the Memory of the Right Honourable the Earl of Rochester.*

> Thus by your Sway we hope for better Times,
> Men shall hate Vice, and shall abandon Crimes;
>
> .   .   .   .
>
> The Priests no longer shall be steep'd in Sloth,
> And 't shall be Scandal to refuse the Oath.

He is probably sincere in his hopes for moral betterment, but he is chiefly delighted to have a latitudinarian Whig at Canterbury.

By 1700, however, Tutchin shared the rather prevalent indignation at the favor shown by William to Bentinck and other Dutch followers. The result was the well-known verse-pamphlet, *The Foreigners*. In deference to *Absalom and Achitophel*, it has a vaguely "Israelitish" background. Tutchin carefully refrains from attacking William directly, saying that he has been misled by

> ... crafty Knaves at home,
> In combination with a Foreign Brood,
> Sworn Foes to Israel's Rights and Israel's Good.

But the implications of the poem are hostile to his former idol, and the emphasis on "Israel's Rights" has a radical tone which goes beyond the conventional Whiggish glorification of liberty. Tutchin had played an active part in Monmouth's Rebellion. The following lines suggest that Judge Jeffreys was not speaking aimlessly when he called him a rebel and the descendent of rebels:

> If Kings are made the People to enthral,
> We had much better have no King at all:
> But Kings, appointed for the Common Good,
> Always as Guardians to their People stood.
> And Heaven allows the People sure a Power
> To chuse such Kings as shall not them devour.

Quite without irony, he refers to the execution of Charles I as a "Glorious Feat." The Divine Right of Kings has become the Divine Right of the People.

But Tutchin had gone too far. Defoe, seizing the heaven-sent opportunity to prove his own loyalty at the expense of a rival, crushed him with *The True-Born Englishman*. Tutchin staggered to his feet and scribbled on until his death in 1707, but without adding anything to our understanding of him or of our subject. His career provides one more illustration of the absorption of religion by politics.

The poems of Daniel Defoe (1661?-1731) give a very imperfect notion of his literary genius, but they represent his characteristic views more satisfactorily than the verse of most of the great eighteenth-century prosemen. A systematic analysis of each poem would require a disproportionate amount of space, for some of them are very long [36] and most of them are crammed with matter. It will therefore be best to draw from a few of the most interesting pieces the materials for a brief sketch of Defoe's ideas on religion and the Church as seen in his verse.

For Defoe, the test of true religion is virtuous conduct:

> Blush England, hide thy Hypocritick Face,
> *Who has no Honesty, can have no Grace.*

. . . .

> Virtue's the Light by which Religion's known,
> If this be wanting, Heaven will that disown.[37]

Religion is not a complicated body of dogma, nor is it shrouded in mystery. Its principles can be understood by everyone:

> Naked and plain her Sacred Truths appear,
> From pious Frauds and dark Ænigma's clear:
> The meanest Sence may all the Parts discern,
> What Nature teaches all Mankind may learn:
> Even what's reveal'd is no untrodden Path,
> Tis known by Rule, and understood by Faith,
> The Negatives and Positives agree,
> Illustrated by Truth and Honesty.[38]

In other words, even Revelation is to be judged from the viewpoint of an ethical pragmatism. The best reasons for believing it are the "truth and honesty" of those who *do* believe.

In the passage just quoted, "nature" apparently signifies "the universe as it lies displayed to human reason." But in Defoe's thought the relation between nature and reason is very close. Since nature teaches all men through reason, nature herself is reasonable and reason is a natural faculty. Thus, if the two terms are not quite synonymous, reason may be regarded as nature within the human breast. *Jure Divino* is dedicated "To the Most Serene, Most Invincible, and Most Illustrious Lady REASON: ... Image of, and Ambassador Extraordinary from, the Maker

---

[36] *Reformation of Manners,* for example, runs to 64 pages, and *Jure Divino* to 278.
[37] *Reformation of Manners.*   [38] *Ibid.*

of all Things: The Almighty's Representative, and Resident in the Souls of Men; and one of Queen Nature's most Honourable Privy Council." And in the text of this poem reason is described as

> The light of heaven which shining in the soul,
> Instructs the Parts and Luminates the whole.

God, nature, and reason, then, are intertwined. God Himself lives according to the rules which he has imposed upon the Creation:

> The Laws of God, as I can understand,
> Do never Laws of Nature countermand.[39]

Indeed they cannot possibly do so, since the laws of God *are* the laws of nature.

Another term for the light of heaven within the soul is "conscience." Its power, we read in *More Reformation,* is felt even by the atheist who mocks it.

> Men never could commit Mistakes, would they
> This Constant wakeing Centinel obey;
> Would they within this Cabinet retire,
> And of this Faithful Councellor enquire
> Of every action, they might quickly know
> Whether it was an honest one or no.

We shall fail to understand Defoe if we saddle him with a stricter logic than he himself ever dreamed of. The essence of his ethico-religious theory is that every man possesses within himself a guide, a light, a voice which shows him the truth and directs him toward virtue. That faculty cannot be expressed in words, and yet Defoe must try to express it. Hence in various contexts he uses God, nature, reason, and conscience as more or less equivalent terms for the Inner Light. In all this, by the way, the similarity between him and Rousseau is striking.

These views underlie the arguments of *Jure Divino* (1706). He says in his Preface that the poem would not have been published "had not the World seem'd to be going mad a second Time with the Error of Passive-Obedience and Non-Resistance." Against the rising clamor of the High Churchmen he insists "that Kings are not Kings *Jure Divino,* that when they break the Laws, trample on Property, affront Religion, invade the

[39] *Jure Divino.*

Liberties of Nations, and the like, they may be opposed and resisted by Force."

For Defoe as for John Locke,

> Compact's the Womb of real Majesty,
> The rest is all Excentrick Tyranny.

The doctrine of Divine Right is not only absurd but positively irreligious, for it conflicts with the sacred standard of God-nature-reason:

> 'Tis horrid incoherent Blasphemy,
> Gives Nature, Sense, and Sovereign Truth the Lye:
> It Contradicts the Notion of a God,
> And all the Rules by which he's understood.

Human liberty, on the other hand, fully accords with the dictates of the voice within:

> ...Man, by Heav'n it self made free,
> Has an undoubted Claim to Liberty:
> The Bondage which his Nature feels within,
> Is not his Nature's Happiness, but *Sin*.

Thus man, for reasons left unexplained by Defoe, has departed from the God-given freedom and happiness of nature. He must now return to nature, as it were, by reasserting his right to liberty:

> The Freedom Heaven bestow'd, was giv'n in Vain,
> Unless he does the Mighty Gift maintain.

The promptings of nature within Defoe's own breast are capricious. When he is confronted by the Tory doctrine of Divine Right, she tells him to be a rather extreme latitudinarian; but when he is confronted by the vice and impiety of Englishmen in general, she tells him to be a rather old-fashioned puritan. One thinks of the contrast between the smug devoutness of *Mrs. Veal* and the vague charitable breadth of the religion arrived at by Crusoe and Man Friday as a result of their colloquies. Defoe is incurably a journalist, with all the journalist's readiness to adapt his ideas to the requirements of the subject and the demands of the reader. But this fact does not tell the whole story. Defoe very interestingly represents the nonconformist in transition from seventeenth-century Protestant orthodoxy to eighteenth-century latitudinarianism. The ideals of individual freedom of conscience, the rights of nature, and the Inner Light which the puritan had often used in defense of his Christianity are now in a fair way to become a religion in themselves, a religion only very tenuously related to the Protestantism which gave them birth.

In Defoe, however, this process has by no means completed itself. He is aware of no conflict between puritanism and the religion of reason and nature; in fact he appears to think that they are one and the same. Hence the ideas which have been outlined above are strangely mingled with the grim severity of one whose parents had intended him for the Presbyterian pulpit. The great storm of 1703 merely reminds Addison of the Duke of Marlborough,[40] but for Defoe the echo of each blast calls out "REFORM," and each falling timber cries "REPENT." [41]

Contemplating London's vices as a puritan satirist, Defoe asserts that

> No city in the spacious Universe,
> Boasts of Religion more, or minds it less.[42]

To a large extent the same condemnation applies to Englishmen in general. This defender of individual liberty is troubled by the individualism of his countrymen, for it appears that the voice of nature explains the grand and simple truths of religion in different ways to different persons:

> In their Religion they are so unev'n,
> That each man goes his own By-way to Heav'n.
> Tenacious of Mistakes to that degree,
> That ev'ry Man pursues it sep'rately,
> And fancies none can find the Way but he:
> So shy of one another they are grown,
> As if they strove to get to Heav'n alone.[43]

This comment on Protestantism comes unexpectedly from so stout a Protestant as Defoe.

Individual freedom of conscience must operate within carefully prescribed limits. Defoe is horrified to relate that London is full of Socinians,

> Worse Jews than those which crucified their God:
> They kill'd a Man, for they suppos'd him so;
> These boldly sacrifice the God they know,
> His Incarnation Miracles deny,
> And vilely Banter his Divinity;
> Their old Impostor, Socinus, prefer,
> And the long Voyage of Heaven without a Pilot steer;

*   *   *

[40] Cf. the famous simile in *The Campaign.*   [42] *Reformation of Manners.*
[41] *The Storm. An Essay.*   [43] *The True-Born English-Man.*

> But see the Badge of our Reforming Town,
> Some cry Religion up, some cry it down:
> Some worship God, and some a God defie,
> With equal boldness, equal liberty." [44]

Despite the fact that his views point directly through latitudinarianism toward deism, Defoe holds deists in abhorrence. Of a leader of the group he writes:

> Toland, if such a Wretch is worth our Scorn,
> Shall Vice's blackest Catalogue adorn.
> His hated Character let this supply—
> Too vile even for our University. [45]

A clumsy but forceful double compliment!

The puritanism of Defoe is especially strong in *Reformation of Manners* (1702). The reader is aware that the protests of Collier, Blackmore, and Law against the licentiousness of the stage were merely one aspect of a widespread reform movement which arose in the latter part of William's reign and continued into Anne's. Addison and Steele were by no means struggling against a rising tide of evil: they were riding the crest of a wave of bourgeois respectability. The utilitarian morality of the increasingly influential middle class was reflected in various organizations. The chief of these was the Society for the Reformation of Manners, whose membership included both Churchmen and Nonconformists. It not only distributed innumerable tracts against drunkenness, swearing, public indecency, and Sabbath-breaking, but instituted thousands of successful prosecutions against such offenses. Though these activities were excessively priggish and "snooping," it is generally admitted that they accomplished some desirable reforms, and that the standard of public and perhaps even of private morality improved considerably during the reign of Queen Anne.

Reformation of Manners, however, takes a thoroughly sceptical view of this movement. Defoe regards it as a pretentious sham which has done no real good. London, he says,

> ... boasts of her Regeneration,
> And tells us wondrous Tales of Reformation:
> How against Vice she has been so severe,

---

[44] *Reformation of Manners.*   [45] *Ibid.*

That none *but Men of Quality* may swear:
How Publick Lewdness is expell'd the Nation,
That Private Whoring may be more in fashion,
How Parish Magistrates, like pious Elves,
Let none be Drunk a Sundays, but themselves.
These, Ostia [London], are the Shams of Reformation,
With which thou mock'st thy Maker, and the Nation;
While in thy Streets unpunish'd there remain
Crimes which have yet insulted Heaven in vain;

    .   .   .   .

Superior Lewdness Crowns thy Magistrates,
And Vice grown grey usurps the Reverend Seats;
Eternal Blasphemies and Oaths abound,
And Bribes among thy Senators are found.

This theme is illustrated from various professions and social classes, with occasional mention of individuals. Here as elsewhere the author is very severe against the English vice of intemperance. Even the clergy are sodden with liquor. Defoe bids his satiric muse challenge the Bishop of London

...but to name the Priest,
Went sober from his Visitation Feast.
Tell him of sixteen Ecclesiastick Guides,
On whom no Spirit but that of Wine abides;
Who in contiguous Parishes remain,
And preach the Gospel once a Week in vain:
But in their Practices unpreach it all,
And sacrifice to Bacchus and to Baal.

Not all clergymen are content with mere drunkenness. One priest disguised as "Solid" is admittedly learned, eloquent, and strictly orthodox. But, alas, he

Dotes on a Bottle, and what's worse, a W[hore].

    .   .   .   .

Two Bastard Sons he educates abroad,
And breeds them to the Function of the Word.
In this the zealous Church-man he puts on,
And Dedicates his Labours to the Gown.

Literature is wholly given over to the service of vice. The nation's corruption is summed up in the fact that "One Man reads Milton, forty Rochester." "That Bawdy, Saucy Poet P[rior]" receives a special share of abuse, but as a vicious public servant rather than as a writer. He "was for his Wit and Wickedness advanc'd."

Defoe's ideas on many social problems are so "modern" that it is no surprise to find in *Reformation of Manners* an attack on those unchristian merchants who deal in slaves:

> The harmless Natives basely they trepan,
> And barter Baubles for the Souls of Men:
> The Wretches they to Christian Climes bring o'er,
> To serve worse Heathens than they did before.
>
> .   .   .   .
>
> To more than Spanish Cruelty inclin'd,
> Torment the Body and debauch the Mind:
> The lingering Life of Slavery preserve,
> And vilely teach them both to sin and serve.
> In vain they talk to them of Shades below,
> They fear no Hell, *but where such Christians go.*

Genuine reform, according to Defoe, must begin at the top of society, among magistrates, clergymen, and courtiers. Let them reform, and the lower classes will imitate their virtues just as they now imitate their vices. In conclusion the great ones of the earth are admonished:

> In vain you strive ill Manners to suppress,
> By the Superlatives of Wickedness:
> Ask but how well the drunken Plow-man looks,
> Set by the swearing Justice in the Stocks;
>
> .   .   .   .
>
> The Mercenary Scouts in every Street,
> Bring *all that have no Money* to your Feet,
> And if you lash a Strumpet of the Town,
> She only smarts *for want of Half a Crown.*

So much for Defoe as puritan moralist. His liberal ideals of nature, reason, conscience, and liberty return in full force when he wishes to attack the High Churchmen, whom he regards as the sworn foes of those ideals. Some people, he says, thought of the great tempest of 1703 as

> ...a High-Church Storm,
>   Sent out the Nation to reform;
> But th'Emblem left the Moral in the Lurch,
> For't blew the Steeple down upon the Church.
>   From whence we now inform the People,
> The Danger of the Church is from the Steeple.

> And we've had many a bitter stroke,
> From Pinnacle and Weather-Cock;
> From whence the Learned do relate,
> That to secure the Church and State,
> The Time will come when all the Town
> To save the Church, will pull the Steeple down.[46]

Defoe's assaults on the steeple are numerous and bitter. In *A Hymn to Peace* (1706), after observing that warring kings often plead that they are fighting for peace, he adds:

> In Ecclesiastick Quarrels 'tis the same,
> Where Hierarchy's the thing, and Peace the Name;
> Th' Enthusiastick Errors Mad Men broach,
> All cry the Peace and Union of the Church.
> The mighty Cheat's in strong Delusions drest,
>   And Peace becomes the Church's Jest;
> The Holy Varnish colours the Deceit,
> And *High-Church Projects* work beneath the sacred Cheat.
> Covered with Clouds, and Ecclesiastick Mists,
> In zealous Masks for Conscience' sake oppress,
> And damn Men's Souls to purchase Peace.

The Double Welcome (1705) hails Marlborough on his return from the wars, but warns him that having conquered armies abroad, he must now prepare to fight "devils" at home. These fiends—"Jesus, are these thy Sons!"—are the High Churchmen who are pushing the Occasional Conformity bill: [47]

> These are the strong Bandity of the Gown,
> Who preach for God's Sake, plunder for their own.
> Our State Divines that push the Party Cause,
> And swear and pray for Persecution Laws;

---

[46] *The Storm.*

[47] The Test and Corporation Acts barred from membership in civic corporations all persons who did not receive Holy Communion in an Anglican church at least once a year. But many Dissenters, either from latitudinarian indifference or self-interested hypocrisy, obeyed the letter of the law by practising what was called "occasional conformity." Largely from political motives, the Tories in 1702 introduced into the House of Commons a bill to prevent this practise. It imposed severe financial penalties on officeholders who, during their tenure of office, attended any conventicle of five or more (later, ten or more) persons. This bill, beloved by High Churchmen and loathed by Low Churchmen and Dissenters, was finally passed in 1711 after the Tories had come into power. In 1718, the Whigs being once more in the saddle, it was repealed along with the still more offensive Schism Act. The use of the Sacrament as a test for officeholders and as a political football had a most deleterious effect on the religious experience of Anglicans.

Own 'tis against their Doctrine and their Sence,
But freely grant they'd be at that Expence;
Would sell the Church, the Nation, and the Queen,
While all our mod'rate Clergy strive with them in vain.

Sacheverell, who fights in the front line of this army of bloody-minded priests, is characterized as

High Church Buffoon, the Oxford's stated Jest,
A Noisy, Sawcy, Swearing, Drunken Priest.

This Tory agitator also appears in *A Hymn to the Pillory* (1703) among those who really deserve the punishment which Defoe has unjustly suffered:

He from a Church of England Pulpit first
All his Dissenting Brethren curst;
Doom'd them to Satan for a Prey,
And first found out *the shortest way*.[48]

In its mad craving for slavery, the mob which rose in support of Sacheverell is said to have had only two precedents: Satan and his supporters in their rebellion against God, and the rabble that claimed Jesus from Pilate:

The First mob'd God Himself, to bring
Themselves in Slavery to a King;
And were the first in Spight of Prophecy,
That beg'd for Bondage, when they might be free:

. . . . .

The Second cry'd aloud to Crucifie,
And mob'd the Lord of Life and Liberty." [49]

A devoted admirer of William III, Defoe is indignant at the inconsistent and dishonest attitude of the "high" clergy toward that monarch. Having once begged William to save them from James, they now talk treason against the former and use the doctrine of non-resistance in support of the latter. *The True-Born English-Man* makes much of this point. In *Jure Divino* he reproaches those who in the reign of Anne would cast away the liberty that William gave them. And in *A Hymn to the Mob,* occasioned by the Sacheverell case, he expresses his astonishment

[48] Of course the allusion is to Defoe's own ill-fated pamphlet, *The Shortest Way with the Dissenters,* where he parodied Sacheverell's violence only too realistically.
[49] *A Hymn to the Mob.*

> To see a Free-born People rise,
> And what before they fought for, now despise;
> To see their Ancient Madness so restor'd,
>   Longing for what they once abhorr'd;
> Gorg'd with the Luscious Gust of being made Free,
> Grieving for Chains, and Sick for Slavery.

This enemy of High Church intolerance does not wish to stand forth in defense of all nonconformists. They are, he says in *Reformation of Manners,* either "the best of Christians, or the worst," according to whether their dissent arises from piety or merely from pride. Some of them are certainly worthy of the highest praise:

> With steady Faith they serve the Government,
> In Judgment, not in Charity, dissent:
>
> .   .   .   .
>
> The English Crown they cheerfully maintain,
> And wish that where it is it may remain.
> The Church they can't Conform to they defend,
> It's Civil Power uphold, its Sacred Power befriend;
> With Tolleration they are well content,
> And these are they the Tolleration meant:
> No Government would such as these oppress,
> Or wish to make their little numbers less.
> What tho' we think their Consciences mis-led,
> Conscience is positive, and must b'obeyed;
> And he that's faithful to its Dictates, goes
> Direct and steady to the Truth he knows;
> And they that find a nearer way than he,
> May blame his Knowledge, not his Honesty.[50]

Though Defoe regards the Occasional Conformity Bill as a tool of Tory oppression, the practise of occasional conformity by dissenters is distasteful to him. Nothing can be said for those hypocrites who

> Alternate Oaths and Sacraments can take,
> Alternate Oaths and Sacraments can break;
> On one hand can the Establish'd Church defie,
> And when occasion offers can comply:
> No Tollerating Laws can these defend,
> To these no Royal Promises extend.[51]

[50] *More Reformation.*

[51] *Ibid. Reformation of Manners* also reproaches "Those Ambo-Dexters in Religion" who practise occasional conformity.

It is unnecessary to trace the sinuous course of Defoe's later career. In these poems one sees the real man—a nonconformist Whig in whom the religious and moral standards of puritanism are permeated by a latitudinarian philosophy. The relation between these two elements will become more apparent as we proceed. It is noteworthy, however, that Defoe the moralist is more orthodox than Defoe the politician: his doctrine of the Inner Light is especially prominent when he is attacking the highflying Tories. The latitudinarianism of the Queen Anne period was greatly stimulated by the political policies of the Whigs, for whom it was important to emphasize as little as possible the doctrinal differences between nonconformists and Low Churchmen.

Fortunately for the reader's patience, most of the worthless poems of Edmund Arwaker the younger [52] appeared too early to warrant our examination. A word, however, may be devoted to his emblem book, *Pia Desideria* (1686); for although it is merely a translation from the Latin of the German Jesuit, Hermann Hugo,[53] it displays the rather hectic piety which Arwaker cultivated early in his career. The little poems accompanying the cuts abound in pseudo-erotic groans, sighs, and yearnings. But by 1704, when he published *An Embassy from Heav'n: Or, The Ghost of Queen Mary,* Arwaker has developed. He now writes smooth couplets in the best genteel tradition; he has learned the ways of the world and purged himself of the old enthusiastic taint; he can enlist divine poetry in the service of flattery and party politics. We must inspect this monstrous piece of baroque blasphemy.

While the shepherds Damon and Thyrsis, typifying the English people, are watching their flocks, the "Ghost" of Queen Mary descends from heaven, "Where Her Nassau presides among the Blest," to converse with them. She describes the anxiety of the blessed spirits, all of whom are Whigs, as they watched the Battle of Blenheim:

> Our Eyes on Vict'ry's dubious Motions wait;
> She, in suspense, expects the Nod of Fate.
> Jove gave the *Fiat,* from the Sky she fled,
> And crown'd with Palm the Conq'ring Marl'brough's Head;

[52] Not in *D.N.B.* He was an Anglican clergyman and had obtained an M.A. from one of the universities.

[53] Quarles was inspired to write his *Emblems* by Hugo's *Pia Desideria,* and copied most of his prints from that source.

> It thunder'd, and Nassau the Lightning threw,
> Your Foes, who dy'd not, or surrender'd, flew;
> Confusion rages through the scatter'd Rout,
> The Angels sing, the Danes and English shout.

The talk soon shifts to Queen Anne's coronation procession, which caused equal delight in paradise:

> Almighty Jove, pleas'd with the humble Show,
> Decree'd on High a Triumph for Nassau.

At Thyrsis' request, the Ghost of Queen Mary describes this celestial pageant. First comes an excellent band led by Purcell. Then poets— "Cowley sung David's Fame, and Waller William's Praise." After a group of painters,

> ...Noble Boyle a Troop of Sages led,
> By whose Attempts the World has profited.

Following these philosophers trips a bevy of Virtues which the Ghost says she need not particularize, since on earth "They meet and shine in your Illustrious Queen." After them march the noble "chiefs" who died at Blenheim, Liége, and Bonn.

> Next, Pious Souls, of all Religions, came;
> Their Worship Various, but their God the same.

They include Bates, Hammond, Baxter, Stillingfleet,

> Horneck, and Annesley, and Millions more,
> Alike are Happy, and alike Adore:
> All, all in Peace, all Prejudice forgot;
> From sev'ral Stations, at one Mark they shot:
> The Just reach Heav'n, altho' by different Ways;
> God is the Sun, and they his spreading Rays:
> Tho' at the Circle some are opposite,
> They meet, and center in Eternal Light.

From this we see that our seventeenth-century pietist has become an eighteenth-century latitudinarian.

Next in the procession, appropriately, comes Truth herself, with a bodyguard composed of the heroes of the Protestant Reformation. At their heels march some of the martyrs of English liberty—Gaunt, Essex, Cornish, Sidney, Russell.

> Next your ECCLESIA was by Angels drawn,
> Herself all Light, and all her Vestments Lawn;
> Cherubs above her, Saints around her fly,
> Her Locks are Constellations in the Sky.

On her right hand is Edward VI; on her left, Elizabeth.

Then appears Justice, attended by Hales, Coke, and Littleton. Then Archbishop Tillotson—

> Wisdom and Piety the Patriarch led,
> And MODERATION crown'd his Peaceful Head.

At the end of the procession walks great Nassau, with the Archangel Michael as his personal escort.

> Jove at the Triumph wou'd himself appear,
> But that he had decreed none shou'd be there
> Of greater Glory than the Triumpher.

But the Ghost is unable to describe Nassau's appearance, because "We could not see him for excess of Light."

We may omit the concluding flattery of Queen Anne, for the poem has already received more than its share of attention. Nevertheless this glimpse into the heaven of latitudinarian Whiggery is instructive, especially when we remember that Arwaker was a priest of the Church of England.

Arthur Maynwaring (1668-1712), political writer and politician, came of a noble Shropshire family.[54] During the Revolution of 1688 he was an ardent Tory who hailed the Nonjurors as

> . . . some who bravely stood in the Defence
> Of baffled Justice, and their Injur'd Prince;
> These shine to After-Times, each Sacred Name,
> Stands still recorded in the Books of Fame.

But soon after the accession of William he became an ardent Whig, and a Whig he remained to the end of his days—a leading member of the Kit-Kat Club, an advocate for the prosecution of Sacheverell.[55]

---

[54] My source for both biographical information and illustrative material is *The Life and Posthumous Works of Arthur Maynwaring, Esq.* (1715). The poems are woven into the biography, which is the work of John Oldmixon.

[55] Oldmixon tells us that in his last illness—he had consumption—Maynwaring was attended by the Whig physicians Garth and Blackmore. But some Tory relations insisted on his calling in the chief medico of their own party, Dr. Radcliffe. After that, of course, the patient took a turn for the worse and soon died.

Maynwaring's non-political verse consists mainly of translations which were well regarded in their day. Most of his original pieces are rough-and-tumble partisan ballads. Several of these, as we should expect, are directed against High Church policies. Oldmixon quotes from a ballad ridiculing the Occasional Conformity Bill:

> Dissenters they were to be prest
>   To go to Common Pray'r,
> And turn their Faces to the East,
>   As God were only there.

. . . . .

> Now some, I say, did think this Hard,
>   And strove with all their Might,
> That Subjects might not be debarr'd
>   Of Freedom, nor of Right.

> For who can think our Lord can care
>   From whence the Voice does sound?
> Tho' we should pray as Seamen swear,
>   The Compass Points around:

> Sure he, I say, our Pray'rs can hear,
>   Where-ever we do call;
> For if so be the Heart's sincere,
>   Oh that is all in all.

The passage unites the Whig ideal of political liberty with the Low Church ideal of "sincerity" as the all-important religious requirement. But another stanza shows a more realistic awareness of the political background of the dispute:

> For to tell Truth, some Peers did smoke,
>   That this same Bill's Progression
> Might by Degrees at length have broke
>   The Protestant Succession.

Maynwaring was distinctly a man of the world. Everyone knew of his *liaison* with Mrs. Oldfield, the noted actress. "Such liberties are too common," says Oldmixon, "for any Body to be surpriz'd at his taking them, and he was not so abandon'd to Pleasure, as to neglect the Affairs which fell to his Cognisance." It must also be granted that "he drank freely" of champagne and burgundy. But Oldmixon places an item on the credit side when he says, "I have omitted one thing which is very Exemplary, and that is an Abhorrence he had for those that Curs'd and Swore, talk'd Profanely and Irreligiously, or abus'd the Clergy.... If he wou'd Swear sometimes in Passion, he never offended in the other Articles, and a Gentleman who from a Child had been us'd to the gayest and freest Company may well be excus'd for falling into Temptation, in an Age when it is become so fashionable." With which charitable reflection we may take leave of this champion of the heart's sincerity.

Although very little of the controversial poetry of the age is written by women, an exception is provided by Martha Keinton's [56] *A Poem. Gen. XLIX. V. 23, 24, 25. The Archers have sorely grieved Him, and Shot at Him, and hated Him; But his Bow abode in strength, and the Arms of his Hands were made strong, by the Hands of the mighty God of Jacob: Even by the God of thy Father who shall Help thee; And by the Almighty who shall bless thee* (1716). George I, the hero of this effusion, is to England what David was to Judah.

Despite her technical clumsiness, the author delivers one or two good thrusts at George's foes. Thus she says of the still-vext question of Divine Right:

> God only has unalienable Right,
> Apply'd to Kings, 'tis against scripture Light:
> He sets up one, and puts another down,
> It is his right to give, or take a Crown.

Now since George can be occupying the throne only by God's will,

> For Non-Resisters then, 'tis something odd,
> Thus to resist the Ordinance of God.
> When Non-Resistance and Rebellion meet,
> It is a Solecism, amazing Great!

Regarding George I as "the Darling of Mankind," she is appalled at the ingratitude of those Jacobite "non-resisters" who have recently resisted him:

> Oh! Tell it not in Gath, nor Askelon,
> What English Protestants wou'd now have done:
> Dethron'd their King, and try'd the fatal Chance,
> O' th' Popish Idol, disciplin'd in France.

[56] Not in *D.N.B.* No other work of hers is listed in the British Museum Catalogue.

Martha Keinton, in short, is rather pious, very Whiggish, very Low Church. At least she provides a footnote to Addison's essay on "Party Patches."

A fairly well-written Whig and Low Church satire is the anonymous *Epistle from an English Jesuit to the Pope, Concerning the Present Affairs of Europe* (1718). The priest assures His Holiness that although of course England is heretical,

> Amidst this stiff-neck'd Crew, there still are some
> Firmly devoted to the Cause of Rome,
> Great Souls resolv'd, who Snarl at Pow'r, and dare
> Foment new Factions, and revive a War:
> With Loyal Tears that from true Sorrow spring,
> Behold the Fortune of their Exil'd King.

As a means of crushing Protestant Germany, the base Jesuit recommends an alliance between Spain, where Cardinal Alberoni is Prime Minister, and Turkey. Why not? "What's our Religion but to serve our ends?" Then when Germany is beaten, Alberoni can invade England and set Catholic James on the throne:

> Oh Glorious Deed! nor shall the pious Aid
> Of half the British Clergy be deny'd;
> They to the Cause have ever firmest been,
> Tho' Protestant without, all Rome within.

Thus, to the joy of all Jacobites, Papists, and "highflying" crypto-Papists, the good old days of Bloody Mary will return to England.

John Durant de Breval (1680?-1738), who usually wrote under the pseudonym of "Joseph Gay,"[57] came from a family of Huguenot refugees, and was the son of a prebendary of Westminster. Despite this promising background, he became one of Curll's henchmen, an unprincipled, scurrilous, obscene, rather nimble-witted Grub Street scribbler and satirical pamphleteer in prose and verse.

Breval's Whig politics and his personal libertinism combine in opposition to High Church theories of ecclesiastical authority. *The Church-*

---

[57] The same pseudonym was also used by Francis Chute, with resultant bibliographical confusion. *The Church-Scuffle* is assigned to Breval in the British Museum Catalogue, but I shall not quarrel with any specialist who considers it the work of Chute.

Scuffle (1719), dealing with a squabble between Sacheverell and Whiston,[58] amusingly confronts two types of Anglican cleric. The Arian defies the High Churchman:

> I am no Infidel, He said;
> What Sacred Writings teach
> I do most stedfastly believe,
> But not all that you preach.
>
> The lawless Pow'r usurp'd by Priests,
> I neither own nor fear;
> God's Word's my Guide, he is my Judge,
> And him I worship here.

Against this "broad" Protestant view Sacheverell opposes the authority of the Church:

> The Church, the Church, you shou'd obey,
> Nor once her Pow'r dispute;
> Sh' interprets Right, she never errs,
> And she is Absolute.
>
> But oh! what boots this learn'd Advice,
> Where Ignorance prevails:
> This Reas'ning Wretch, from Holy Church
> To's Bible still Appeals.
>
> Alack! Alack! that Book will prove
> Too strong, I plainly see,
> For Athanasius and the Church,
> With all their Mystery.

Fortunately the good old principle of "The Bible, the Religion of Protestants," has had many more creditable defenders than "Joseph Gay."

The Whigs admired Bishop Hoadly no less than the Tories detested him. This anti-prelatical prelate is not, on the whole, a helpful source of poetic inspiration. A very feeble anonymous panegyric, *A Familiar Epistle to the ... Lord Bishop of Bangor,* wallows in platitudes about truth and liberty, and congratulates Hoadly on being victorious over his foes. But

---

[58] William Whiston was the first important Arian clergyman of the period. He believed himself to be completely orthodox, for he thought that Arianism was the view of the earliest Christians. In his quest for the most primitive form of Christianity he finally left the Church of England and joined the General Baptists.

the nadir of controversial poetry is represented by *The Protestant Garland in Praise of the most Noble Bishop of Bangor*. Lovers of bad poetry will enjoy the following excerpt:

> He wrote against the Church of Rome,
> And was for Liberty at Home,
> He conquer'd the Whore of Babylon,
> And struck at the Pope with his Tripple Crown,
> And what Good Christian can be in anger
> With the most noble Bishop of Bangor?
>
> .   .   .   .   .
>
> All True Protestants open your Arms;
> Embrace the great Hoadly, and view his Charms,
> Sherlock looks pale and shivers and shakes,
> And Law the Nonjuror sadly quakes;
> And what good Christian, etc.
>
> He is lov'd by the King and fear'd by his Foes,
> King George protects him by whom he rose;
> The Church is afraid, the Dissenters rejoice,
> And hug the great Champion of their Cause;
> And what good Christian, etc.

On a much higher, though by no means on a towering, intellectual plane moves the unknown author of *Austin, and the Monks of Bangor* (1718). In Book IV of Milton's *History of Britain*—the work of another man who had no love for bishops—he has read the story of how the primitively Christian Abbot of Bangor resisted the popish arrogance of Augustine.[59] There had, then, been an earlier Bangorian Controversy. The British abbot will be Hoadly, and "Austin" will be a blend of Atterbury and Sacheverell.

Milton's story, as freely adapted by our satirist, relates how the monks of Bangor followed "The *Christian* Laws, as taught by *Christ*":

> They liv'd not, like a Popish cloister'd Drone,
> Lazy, and fed by Labours not his own.
>
> .   .   .   .   .
>
> And, thinking vain all Office for the Dead,
> The Souls and Bodies of the Living fed.

[59] *The Works of John Milton* (Columbia Edition), X, 147-150.

As for their abbot,

> Meekness and Love did ev'ry Action grace,
> And Heav'n it self was open'd in his Face.

The Roman persecutors descend upon the Bangorians

> With Crosses, Crucifixes, Bells and Beads,
> And all the Pageantry of Popish Creeds,

and Austin demands that the Abbot swear unconditional obedience to the Pope. Hoadly's prototype answers:

> ...We to None
> But Christ our Master such Obedience own:
> A Perfect Charity tow'rd all, nor less
> To you your selves, tho' Strangers, we profess;
> Him you call Pope, we, like a Brother, love,
> And, as a Christian, would our Love improve:
> We this allow, but more we cannot give,
> And keep that Sacred Rule by which we live.

Deaf to the appeal of Christian love, Austin's party massacres the Bangorians.

> The Monks of Bangor thus remov'd to Rest,
> The Church with Uniformity was Bless'd.

"Perhaps I now and then take my Glass too freely, or kiss a pretty Woman in a Corner; but I pay my Debts honestly and defraud no body." [60] This is the combined confession and apologia of Nicholas Amhurst (1697-1742), lively young scholar of St. John's, Oxford. Restive under every sort of authority, whether political, moral, or ecclesiastical, he found himself a Whig and a Low Churchman. At Oxford he belonged to the Constitution Club, that little island of Whiggery in an ocean of academic Toryism.

Amhurst was greatly stirred by the publication of Hoadly's sermon, Convocation's attempt to brand it as heretical, the proroguing of Convocation by the King, and the beginning of the long pamphlet war. He rushed into the lists with *Protestant Popery: or, The Convocation* (1718). Here and elsewhere the young satirist uses a limited intellectual

[60] Preface of Nicholas Amhurst's *Poems on Several Occasions* (1720). See also, in the same volume, *Advice to my self on being threatned to be expell'd*.

equipment with much cleverness, and shows a real knack for sharpening the point of a couplet.

The author's thesis is that the conception of ecclesiastical authority maintained by Hoadly's enemies is essentially Popish rather than Protestant:

> Fain would I tell how Gospel-Candour fails,
> And the old LAUDEAN Leven still prevails.

The High Churchmen would restore the evils of the Dark Ages:

> Abroad we conquer'd our Apostate Foes:
> But see! at Home a Race more fierce than those,
> Who plead to Tyranny a Right Divine,
> And trace it back in one unbroken Line:
> A Race, that loath th' old-fashion'd Gospel-light,
> New Doctrines coin, and foreign Gods invite.

The Bishop of Bangor is saluted as the great defender of true Protestantism against "Protestant Popery":

> From human Creeds you free the Christian Mind,
> And gain the publick Thanks of Lay-Mankind.

Other anti-prelatical prelates, however, receive their meed of praise:

> Fleetwood, untouch'd with Pontifical Pride,
> Refers each Christian to his Conscience-Guide:
> Not studious the Believer to enslave,
> Rejects all Pow'r, but what his Master gave.

These lines convey the essence of the latitudinarian position.

Such direct statements are more valuable to us than the main body of the poem, which consists of a little epic equipped with furies and guardian angels in the manner of Tasso. We are shown the realm of "The Goddess Priestcraft," who is attended by fiends labelled Inquisition, Bigotry, Superstition, Implicit Faith, Ignorance, and Hypocrisy. In Convocation their High Church tools raise the cry of "the Church in danger." But "the Genius of our Isle" warns the slumbering King. He awakes and saves Protestantism by proroguing Convocation.

The Protestant Session [61] (1719) represents Amhurst's joy at the recent repeal by Parliament of the Occasional Conformity Act. "Such," he cries,

---

[61] This anonymous poem, "By a Member of the Constitution-Club at Oxford," is credited to Amhurst in the British Museum Catalogue. *D.N.B.* considers the ascription "probable." There is plenty of internal evidence for Amhurst's authorship.

"are the fruits of Hoadly's learned Pain." He is friendly toward the hitherto oppressed dissenters. Though he does not approve of the execution of Charles, he asks:

> But must I therefore with unhallow'd Rage
> Accuse of ancient Crimes the present Age?
> Must I charge Men with a rebellious Cause,
> Who love their Country, and espouse her Laws?

We must remember, too, that the ancestors of present-day dissenters were revolting against intolerable oppression. The responsibility for Charles's death lies with both parties. They should

> Conjunctly mourn, what was conjunctly done,
> What Cromwell finish'd, and what Laud begun.

In Tory Oxford such ideas were distasteful; but Dr. Delaune, President of St. John's, hesitated to make a martyr of Amhurst while the Whigs were in the saddle. Fortunately the young satirist, despite his zeal for pure religion, was known to be a little too fond of wine and women. It was ostensibly on these grounds that Amhurst was banished from Oxford, but he insisted that he had been expelled "Imprimis, for loving foreign turnips and presbyterian bishops. Item, for ingratitude to his benefactor, that spotless martyr William Laud. Item, for believing that steeples and organs are not necessary to salvation. Item, for lampooning priestcraft and petticoat-craft. Item, for not lampooning the government and the revolution. Item, for prying into secret history."

This lively sarcasm is drawn from the Preface of *Poems on Several Occasions,* published in 1720, the year after his expulsion. The volume includes two Scripture-paraphrases (probably school or college exercises), a naïve account of how a freethinker was scared into saying his prayers, and a more mature elegy *Upon the Death of Mr. Addison.* On the whole, however, the collection is the work of a smart young worldling who aspires to emulate Prior. It consists mainly of frivolous little "occasionals," bits of gallantry, epigrams, droll and sometimes nasty tales, and imitations of Catullus.

In later years Amhurst was an active, though never a prosperous, anti-Administration Whig journalist who confined himself almost wholly to prose. These early poems of his have provided a clear statement of the extreme Low Church viewpoint and one more illustration of the fact that zeal for an ecclesiastical party is not inconsistent with an almost total lack of spirituality.

An anonymous satire entitled *The Pulpit-Fool* (two parts, both 1707) is credited in the British Museum Catalogue[62] to John Dunton (1659-1733). This popular journalist and pamphleteer has been characterized as "pietist and impostor"[63] in an article so damaging to his reputation that henceforth it will require a brave man to assert that Dunton wrote anything at all. But whoever wrote this clumsy, mean, extravagantly railing satire, it is an interesting document.

According to the Preface of Part I, a pulpit-fool is "a Levite, that Rails in the Pulpit, and Plots out of it." Specifically, the poem is occasioned by a sermon delivered by one Mr. Higgins, who said that "Those that brought the Royal Martyr to the Scaffold and to the Block, such as those are now prefer'd to the greatest Places of Trust in the Kingdom." In other words, pulpit-fools are extremists whose words and actions are disloyal or threatening to the peace and quiet of the realm.

The origin of the type is given in a passage adapted from Dryden:

> Natural Religion, easie first, and plain;
> Tales made it Mystery, Offerings made it Gain;
> Sacrifices and Feasts were at length prepar'd;
> The PRIESTS ate Roast-Meat, and the People star'd;
> And from that time the Pulpit Fool appear'd.[64]

Those who have done most violence to Natural Religion are of course those "Pimps to the Church of Rome," the Highflyers. Of their ancestors, the Anglo-Catholic prelates of the seventeenth century, it is said that

> Their Popish Whimsies did the Truth invade,
> And Laud's Inventions, Grounds of Faith were made.

In a long footnote Dunton—we may as well use his name—argues that Laud was "a Papist in his Heart." Of present-day pulpit-fools, that

---

[62] *Halkett and Laing* accepts the ascription, but provides no further evidence.

[63] C. A. Moore, "John Dunton: Pietist and Impostor," *Studies in Philology*, XXII, 467-499.

[64] E. C. Mossner observes that the first four lines of this passage appear, with insignificant variations, in Toland's *Letters to Serena* (1704), p. 130. (*Bishop Butler and the Age of Reason*, p. 65.) Since, as we shall see, Dunton is indebted to Toland for another passage of this satire, he may have drawn these lines from the deist rather than directly from Dryden.

"Fiery Madcap" Sacheverell is the perfect example, though Jeremy Collier and other High Churchmen are also satirized.

To give an impression of impartiality, Part I closes with a short section on nonconforming pulpit-fools, but Dunton finds very few of them. Though an Anglican, he greatly prefers Dissenters to High Churchmen. He can see no essential difference between Anglicanism and Presbyterianism, for he says of the latter:

> I am not such a Foolish Rhiming Sot,
> To mark my own Religion with a blot,
> My own: For CHURCH and *Presbyterians* are the same;
> Or if we differ 'tis but just in Name.
> Our Church and Presbyterians sure might close,
> For meer indiff'rent Things have made them Foes.

Though the differences between Anglicans and Baptists are more considerable, he is unable to discover a single pulpit-fool in the ranks of the latter sect. "In Life and Pulpit too, their Preachers shine." After all, they believe in baptism, being merely a little eccentric as to the proper time. Of Quakers it must be granted that "Their Light within does keep them in the Dark"; but there is much to be said for them,

> For they unite against the Roman Whore,
> Renounce the Pope, and Tackers do abhor;
> Are Friends at Heart, as well as in their Speech,
> (And tho' Bugg writes, and Keith against them Preach)
> Are very Just, as well as very Rich:
> Then wou'd they Christen, and Christ's Death revive
> I'th' Sacrament (where Souls do Feast and Live)
> They'd pass for Christians, and the best of Men,
> And to their Creed, we all would say Amen.

Part II opens with a renewed quest for pulpit-fools among the Dissenters. Abuse is hurled at Jacobs, the leader of the Philadelphians, full of "all corrupt and idle Whimsies," and Emlyn, "that bold Socinian." But it is significant that really prime specimens of nonconforming pulpit-foolery are to be found only in seventeenth-century fanatics like Muggleton and Nayler. After a brief exhumation of such figures, Dunton launches a diatribe against the Papists, all of whom are pulpit-fools by definition. Curiously he borrows several bitter lines on Romish priest-craft from Toland's *Clito,* a deistic poem to be considered later.

Most of Part II, however, is devoted to praising the antithesis of the pulpit-fool—the truly learned, pious, and moderate Christian minister. John Norris is lauded for his sacred poetry as well as for his broad theology. But most of those singled out for praise are less exciting people than Norris. In general they resemble Denham's river—"strong without rage, without o'erflowing full." Tenison, the Primate, is pre-eminently a man of "moderation." Of Hoadly we learn that "Moderation has inform'd his Breast," and of Burnet that "He loves Religion, but he hates Extreams."

But Dunton finds more of the true Laodicean spirit among the Dissenters than among the Anglicans. A long line of chapel preachers steps up to receive compliments.

> Sam Palmer is on purpose made by Fate,
> That Priests might have a Guide to imitate;

while Calamy illustrates the essential truth that

> For Moderation all good Men are bent,
> Such Men are Wise, and love through all Dissent.

Roswell, on the other hand, wins praise for the more old-fashioned reason that in a recent series of sermons

> The Pains of Hell he did so well explore,
> You'd (almost) think you heard the Damned roar;
> Who heard those Sermons, sure, will sin no more.

In this poem the passage on the corruption of natural religion and the anti-priestcraft lines borrowed from Toland suggest a deistic outlook. At such times, however, the author's enmity toward High Church principles has led him to say a little more than he means. For all his latitudinarian views, he preserves vestiges of a stricter Protestantism in his respect for baptism and his appreciation of hell-fire sermons.[65] But on the whole his position is that of an extremely "low" Anglican Whig with great sympathy for Nonconformity and a most immoderate passion for moderation.[66]

[65] C. A. Moore, op. cit., shows that Dunton's numerous religious publications gradually pass from a lugubriously graveyard sort of puritanism to a much "broader" position.

[66] At the end of Part II appears the following announcement: "There is preparing for the Press—HEAVEN, Or, The Celestial Court. An Heroic Poem. Attempted by the Author of The Pulpit Fool." I find no record of its having been published. No doubt this heaven would have been as full of Whigs as Arwaker's. As Moore's article shows, Dunton published a good deal of religious verse, chiefly of the "funeral elegy" sort; but the originality of much of his work is so dubious that I have ignored it to avoid grappling with bibliographical puzzles the solution of which would contribute little to my study.

For obvious reasons, the deists of this period were almost invariably Whigs. In theological controversy they could, albeit with caution, express something approaching their real views, but in the discussion of specific politico-ecclesiastical issues such frankness was generally regarded as bad tactics. In fighting the Occasional Conformity Bill, for example, there was no need to invite attack by preaching outright deism when the usual arguments of Low Churchmen would better serve to keep the Whig lines unbroken against the enemy.

John Toland (1670-1722), however, makes no effort to conceal his deistical opinions.[67] He qualifies for admission to these pages by a single long piece entitled *Clito: A Poem on the Force of Eloquence* (1700). The Preface, signed "W. H.," is friendly in tone. This "onlie begetter" declares that he is publishing the poem without Toland's permission or knowledge. After circulating "a good while" in manuscript, it got out of the hands of friends into the hands of enemies, and "strange representations were made of it. ... I am wholly ignorant what induc'd him first to write it, or why he did it in Verse, which is a Talent on which he was never heard to value himself beyond a Song or such slight performances. ... I cannot see how it should be displeasing to any, but such as are angry at bottom that Liberty and Religion are prefer'd to Slavery and Superstition."

This work of Toland's youth is written in crude but vigorous heroic couplets. Clito, darkly referred to in W. H.'s preface as "a certain eminent Man," asks Adeisidæmon (Toland)—meaning "Unsuperstitious," says W. H.—

> How far the Force of Eloquence cou'd go
> To teach Mankind those Truths which they mistake,
> And who the noble Task durst undertake.

Adeisidæmon replies that eloquence has limitless possibilities, and that he will undertake the noble task in person. The rest of the poem is his account of what he will accomplish through the spoken and written word.[68]

Toland will, first of all, "Dispel those clouds that darken human sight"

[67] At the time he wrote *Clito* he would have called himself a Christian, but only because he thought deism was true Christianity.

[68] Needless to say, the "force of eloquence" idea is mainly a protective device. If the authorities try to make trouble for Toland, he can plead that he has written a poem on rhetoric.

by answering every conceivable question about God, Nature, and Man, such as

> Who form'd the Universe, and when and why,
> Or if all things were from Eternity;
> What Laws to Nature were prescrib'd by Jove;
> Where lys his chiefest residence above;
> Or if he's only but the World's great Soul;
> Or parts the Creatures are, and God the whole.

Did Pope come upon this poem?

He will also overturn all political tyranny, "and form a Commonwealth." With the ardor of one who was reared a Catholic, he declares that he will drive the Pope from his seat, and expose the pretended mysteries and "holy cheats" of priests and "Female Orders of Religious Punks." But of course he makes the deistic distinction between priestcraft and true religion:

> Religion's safe, with Priestcraft is the War;
> All Friends to Priestcraft, Foes to Mankind are.[69]

This assault on bigotry and superstition will merely be preliminary to his convincing all mankind that

> There's but one, true, all-perfect Deity.
> Sound Reason is the law that likes him best,
> Of Good and Ill the never-erring Test.
> His sacred Temple's every good Man's Heart,
> Where his choice Gifts he freely does impart.

Evidently Toland the deist shares with Defoe the nonconformist the conception of God and reason as abiding within the heart. Belief in this God of sound reason, he continues, will banish threats of hell and promises of heaven as ethical agencies, substituting the purer idea that "Virtue's its own reward."

In later years Toland, who was not without sophistication and humor, may have smiled to remember this youthful rhapsody. Nevertheless *Clito,* despite its extravagance, predicts what he seriously attempted to do throughout his career. The poem might have been written by a very unpoetical young Shelley. It is the *Queen Mab* of 1700.

---

[69] The passage on which this paragraph is based is the one used by Dunton in *The Pulpit-Fool.*

As regards their dates, these poets of controversy closely correspond to the writers considered in the first chapter. Out of thirteen authors for whom the facts are available, six were born between 1660 and 1670, inclusive. Only four were born later than 1670: Evans in 1679, Breval (probably) in 1680, Meston (probably) in 1688, and the exceptionally youthful Amhurst in 1697. These figures are too meagre for statistical value, but as far as they go they suggest that the Church-and-State poetry of this period was produced mainly by middle-aged men whose ideas had taken form before the end of the seventeenth century.

What might be called the social distribution of these writers is wide and varied. There are three Anglican clergymen—the High Churchmen Swift and Evans, and the Low Churchman Arwaker. No dissenting minister figures in the list. Defoe and Tutchin are lay nonconformists, while Toland is a deist. Gentlefolk such as Swift, Maynwaring, and Evans are balanced by men of humble birth such as Brown, Ward, Defoe, and Meston. Even the gentry, however, make little attempt to maintain the aristocratic and classical literary tradition. Whatever its shortcomings in other respects, the verse studied in this chapter has a heartiness and vitality very different from the vapid elegance of "Granville the polite." At least these men are writing on subjects of real interest to them instead of toying affectedly with pen and ink.

As they come to the end of this chapter, however, religious-minded readers will be depressed at having found so much blind prejudice and will-to-hurt, so little charity even in those writers who prate of it, so little evidence that those engaged in these controversies have any spiritual motive. In these respects the Whigs may seem less culpable than the Tories. They often speak in a more earnest and pious tone, and to a modern liberal the emphasis which they place on breadth and toleration is likely to give an impression of spirituality. One might risk the generalization that the Tories have a religion which they do not use, while the Whigs are a little more religious without possessing any religion in particular.

The comparatively greater religiosity of the Whigs, however, is not without a large element of cant. The turncoat Settle, the bootlicking Arwaker, the young libertine Amhurst, the "impostor" Dunton—is there much to choose between their ardor for undefiled religion and the open rascality of Tom Brown and Ned Ward? As for their moderation, it is the result of indifference to, rather than concern for, the things of the spirit. The only strong and positive force behind it is a political one. If the solidarity of the Whigs is to be preserved, it is very important that doctrinal differences between the Establishment and Nonconformity should be minimized. The Low Churchmen are beautifully tolerant of their political allies the Dissenters, but fiercely intolerant of the Tory High Churchmen.

In this chapter the numerical predominance of Whigs over Tories is partly the misleading result of my casual method of sampling materials which I had no intention of treating exhaustively. Nevertheless, although I cannot present statistics, I am sure that in glancing through volumes of pamphlets in the British Museum I noticed more Whig poems than Tory poems. This applies chiefly to longer and more ambitious pieces. In ballads and short squibs the balance is probably about even.

Much more important for us is the fact that the Tories make a poor showing not only quantitatively but qualitatively. The reasons are not hard to understand. For the Tories it is essential that Low Churchmen and Dissenters be branded as traitors, but this can only be done retrospectively. During the Civil Wars, or even in the days of *Hudibras,* Low Churchmen and Dissenters frequently *were* traitors from the Tory viewpoint. In the reigns of William, Anne, and George I, however, these groups were more loyal subjects than the Tories themselves, and for a party stained with Jacobitism to accuse them of treason was no less absurd than perilous.

The Tories made much of loyalty to the monarch. But to *what* monarch? To the exiled Stuart of the past, to the ambiguous Anne of the present, or to the Hanoverians of the future? Later in the century their predicament was summed up in John Byrom's epigram:

> God save the King—I mean our realm's defender;
> God bless—no harm in blessing—the Pretender.
> But who Pretender is, and who is King—
> God bless us all—that's quite another thing!

Loyalty to the Church was another main plank of the Tory platform. The Holy Catholic Church is necessarily independent of, and within its own spiritual realm superior to, any worldly power. The Church of England, however, was a *national* church—an integral part of the government, with the monarch as its official head. Hence the only way in which the Establishment could avoid rendering unto Caesar the things which are God's was to make a god of Caesar. In the first half of the seventeenth century, Anglo-Catholicism identified itself with the interests of the friendly House of Stuart, and at the Restoration this dynastic loyalty was revived in contrite remembrance of the Royal Martyr. The doctrines of Divine Right and of absolute non-resistance were preached in their extremest form, and indeed were often regarded as essential articles of the Christian faith. This Tory zeal outwardly strengthened Restoration Anglo-Catholicism, but inwardly weakened it. The prominence of the dynastic question in ecclesiastical affairs diverted the Church from her spiritual tasks and immersed her in the ugly maelstrom of politics.

At the Revolution of 1688 the great majority of High Churchmen proved false to their own most cherished doctrines, with a resultant loss of morale. The withdrawal of the Nonjurors, wrong-headedly fanatical though they were in some respects, was a blow to the Catholicism of the Church of England, for it deprived the High Church wing of many of its ablest and most genuinely spiritual members. It is true that many High Church clerics who remained within the Establishment, and many laymen as well, maintained something like the older Anglo-Catholic spirit; but most of these were, chronologically or psychologically, survivors of the seventeenth century. Even Wakeman, whose view of Queen Anne High Churchmanship is more sanguine than that of most historians, grants that "descending into the arena of party strife, the Church quickly lost her spiritual ascendancy.... Victories at the polls were more sought after than triumphs of the Cross, and Atterbury takes the place of Ken as the typical Churchman of his time." [70] Those were the days when simple laymen complained that they heard more from High Church pulpits of Charles the Martyr than of Jesus Christ.[71]

It was impossible for Tory controversialists to argue for Anglicanism as an authentic expression of the ideal of the Holy Catholic Church without using language suggestive of Romanism. Yet with James II a vivid memory and with the Pretender just across the Channel, any lapse from Protestantism on the part of the Tories would furnish deadly ammunition to the Whigs. As a matter of fact, however, most High

[70] *An Introduction to the History of the Church of England*, p. 400.
[71] *Ibid.*, p. 404.

Churchmen were quite as anti-Roman as anyone else, though their enemies constantly accused them of "Protestant Popery."

A majority of those who, as Tories, regarded themselves as the defenders of the Church were strongly tinged with the individualism, the anti-clericalism, the hatred of enthusiasm and mystery, and the worldly common-sense of the *Zeitgeist*. They were loyal to the Church as England's official form of Christian worship and hence as a part of the government, but not as the Bride of Christ, not as the mother of all faithful people in this world and the next. When they asserted the spiritual authority of the Church they really meant the political authority of the Crown. It is not surprising, then, that the Tory controversialists are so prone to impotent sneering and snarling, for there is not much that they can say for themselves. Of course they can plead for peace with France and expose the political corruption of the Whigs, but even in this they are merely sniping at the enemy without solidifying their own position.

The Whigs, on the other hand, are deeply intrenched in the very soil of their age. Their commander-in-chief, not far behind the lines, is the empirical John Locke. Their best troops are recruited from the rising middle class, which knows that tolerant indifference in matters of belief is good for business. They have all the best pieces of artillery—liberty and individualism within limits fixed by the spirit of compromise, moderation, ethical pragmatism, broad and vague Protestantism as a breastwork against the popish peril. These facts hardly require detailed exposition. It is impossible to compare the Whigs and the Tories of this chapter without recognizing that the Whigs represent the forces which are to dominate modern civilization.

All this is said without forgetting the intense activity of the Tories during the reign of Anne, the marked acceleration of their progress which began about 1708, and the brief triumph which they enjoyed between 1710 and 1714. A river flowing toward the sea may be so ruffled by winds that it seems to be moving in the opposite direction. So it is with the reign of Queen Anne. Looking at the surface of the water, we feel that the river has a Toryish appearance. But seen from a longer historical perspective the cries of "the Church in danger," the Occasional Conformity and Schism Acts, the Sacheverell turmoil and so on are merely squalls blowing up the channel. When the squalls subside a few years after Anne's death it becomes plain that the river has all along been moving in the direction of latitudinarian Whiggery.

Hence for the historian of ideas the Whigs of this chapter are much more significant than the Tories. Their work shows how puritan Protestantism gradually becomes permeated by latitudinarian views which are sometimes so "broad" as to be indistinguishable from those of deism. Furthermore, their tendency to reject outward authority and to regard God, or nature, or reason, or conscience, as a universal instinctive faculty of the human heart contains the seeds of a new literature and a new religion.

Chapter III

DIVINE POETS

THUS FAR THE STORY HAS BEEN ONE OF INDIFFERENCE, HOSTILITY, SCEPTICISM, and the subordination of religion to the spirit of faction. But despite these adverse influences a large amount of religious verse was produced during the 1700-1720 period, and some of it may now be considered. The present chapter is concerned with writers who devote themselves exclusively, or almost exclusively, to what the age called "divine" poetry. The next chapter will deal with less specialized writers whose work mingles divine and secular poetry in various proportions.[1]

As we begin with a group of Anglican poets, we are plunged into an atmosphere startlingly different from that of the first two chapters.

> Praise God, from whom all Blessings flow;
> Praise him, all Creatures here below;
> Praise him above, ye Heavenly Host;
> Praise Father, Son, and Holy Ghost.

Not many of the innumerable Christians who have sung this doxology are aware that it was written by the courageous and saintly nonjuring bishop, Thomas Ken (1637-1711).[2] The famous stanza concludes each of the *Three Hymns for Morning, Evening, and Midnight*. Besides these and other pieces published in one or another of his numerous devotional works, he left behind him at his death four stout volumes of divine poetry.[3] So large a body of verse cannot be described in detail without

---

[1] The reader is reminded that this book is not intended to cover psalmody or hymnody, though it considers the hymns of several writers who also wrote divine poetry in the more general sense.

[2] It may be felt that Ken is too early a figure for inclusion in this book. But he composed many of his poems after his withdrawal from the Establishment in 1689, and continued writing until close to his death. His poetical *Works* were not published until 1721. In any case, he provides a useful basis for comparison and contrast with other poets.

[3] These comprise *The Works of the Right Reverend, Learned, and Pious, Thomas Ken, D.D.... Published from Original Manuscripts, by William Hawkins, Esq.*, London, 1721.

injury to the proportions of this book, but it well deserves close attention.

For Ken poetry is not, as it is for the aristocratic poets of our first chapter, a politely frivolous pastime. In *An Essay on Hymn* [4] he writes:

> Bless'd Poetry! Immortal Soul refin'd,
> Pure Love with bright Illumination joyn'd,
> The Spirit lost in an Ecstatick Height,
> Imagination soaring out of Sight,
> Seraphic Ardour circling in each Vein,
> The Majestatick Presence in the Brain,
> Inspir'd to make Mankind with Angels vie,
> To emulate the Anthems sung on high.

Evidently Ken closely associates religious and poetical inspiration, and does not share the prevalent dread of warmth and rapture either in faith or in art.

To sing God's praises is to exemplify Ken's personal definition of the term "man":

> Something like Reason is in Brutes; Mankind,
> A Creature hymning God is best defin'd.

He sadly admits that this definition may now hardly seem applicable, but feels that a revival of sacred poetry would do much to reform the irreligion of the times. It is his great hope that his own writings may further such a revival.

Like so many divine poets before and after him, Ken cites scriptural precedents for his art. Adam, Moses and the patriarchs, and David praised God in song. Solomon "couch'd celestial Love in Past'ral sweet":

> But none cou'd ever reach the Hymn composed
> By Mary, when her womb God-Man enclosed.

Incarnate God Himself "his Devotion in a Hymn express'd"; and after the Ascension

> He in the Church first Hymn'd his Father's Name,
> And from God-Man Church-Hymn derives its Flame.
> The Gracious Dove in cloven Tongues of Fire,
> When hovering o'er the Apostolic Quire,

[4] The poem serves as the introduction to that section of his *Works* entitled *Hymns for all the Festivals in the Year.* Ken often uses "Hymn" as a generic term for all divine poetry.

That Flame fomented, Saints God's Wonders sung,
And spread them with a multifarious Tongue;
Taught by the Spirit Anthems to indite,
They made God's awful worship a delight;
In Psalm, and Hymn, and in Spiritual Song,
They preach'd Salvation to the list'ning Throng,

. . . . .

And ever since those sweet harmonious Days,
The Church in sacred Numbers sang God's Praise.

This view of "hymn" as an art practised by God-Man, imparted by
Him with the Holy Spirit to the Apostles at Pentecost as one aspect of
the Gift of Tongues, and from them uninterruptedly handed down in the
Church, is thoroughly characteristic of Bishop Ken. He is a poet not only
of Christianity but of Holy Church. He summarizes almost the complete
program of seventeenth-century Anglo-Catholicism when he describes his
tiny flock of nonjuring communicants as

A Remnant who the gaps of Schism shall close,
Whom no minacious Cross shall discompose,
Who Sin shall by due Penance over-awe,
By sacred Censures curb Erastian Law,
Blasphemers Atheistical expell,
Who ne'er will turn Believers till in Hell;
Hereticasters anathematize,
No Papal Innovations idolize,
Subject their Faith to no one modern Name,
All Latitudinarian Fraud disclaim,
With Meekness to the Fold recal the Stray,
And guide, not drive him to the narrow Way;
No bold Encroachments make on Regal right,
The Church and State in mutual Band unite,
The ancient holy Discipline revive,
Truth Catholick from God's own word derive,
Primæval Fathers reverently peruse,
Primæval Sanctity from them transfuse,
Primæval Faith and Charity restore,
And the Church water'd by the Martyr's gore.[5]

How different is this viewpoint, in its deeply religious feeling for the
Church and in its intermingling of orthodoxy and charity, from the
merely political High Churchmanship of the Tories and the merely

[5] *The Introduction*—the poem which acts as the preface to the *Works* of 1721.

political "moderation" of the Whigs considered in the preceding chapter! The same note is even more emphatically struck in the lines *On King Charles the Martyr:*

> May I in Bliss obtain a Seat
> At our bless'd, martyr'd Sov'reign's Feet;
> His Foes will have the same Desire,
> If Penitent, when they expire:
> My God, indulge them when they die,
> To be as near bless'd Charles as I.

This poem includes a comparison between Charles and that other royal saint and martyr, King Edmund:

> Both after Jesus Copies drew,
> Charles seem'd the likest of the Two.

The same analogy between the Stuart and the Saxon martyr is implicit in *Edmund, an Epic Poem.* The "fable" of this interminable work must be passed over so that we may attend the synod which occupies Book VIII. Lucio, Edmund's favorite bishop, sets forth the primitive doctrine of the one Holy, Catholic, and Apostolic Church. The high priest of this Church is Christ:

> He on the Twelve his Church was pleas'd to rear,
> Peter himself the Church was bound to hear.[6]

After the Resurrection,

> Full forty Days he with the Flock convers'd;
> His holy Life all saving Truths dispers'd;
> Set all things in a clear, unerring Light;
> Instructed them in ev'ry sacred Rite.

To them, also, He gave the power to bind and loose and the guidance of the Comforter.

But Lucio has opponents in the synod. One is Romano,

> Zealous all Reformation to oppose;
> To him all Changes, Innovations seem'd;
> He old Corruptions, aged Truths esteem'd;
> He primitive Simplicity contemn'd,
> And fond of new Mistakes, old Truths condemn'd.

[6] Peter is the subject, not the object, of this thoroughly Anglican sentence.

His papistical oration is rebutted by Bishop Lucio:

> It is no Schism from Errors to abstain,
> No Schism to be what Jesus' Laws ordain;
> It is no Innovation to restore,
> And make God's Spouse as beauteous as before.

Lucio adds a protest against papal supremacy, emphasizing the Anglo-Catholic view that the Church of England is more uncorruptedly Catholic than the Church of Rome.

Now appears an enemy even more dangerous than Romano:

> Sly Proteo then rose next, the Head of them
> Who, Scepticks, all Religious Truth contemn;
> Who, or to none, or any Faith adhere,
> Determin'd by Self-Interest or Fear.

He delivers a speech embodying several of the ideas which were voiced by the latitudinarian Whigs of the preceding chapter. "Religion should be free and unconstrain'd." God damns nobody for his sincere opinions. Charity is more important than faith. One of Proteo's arguments will assume special significance in the intellectual history of the eighteenth century. "God," he avers, "in Variety takes most Delight." Hence His "goodness opens numerous ways to Bliss," and He approves of diversities of belief.[7] Proteo is rebuked by the indomitable Lucio, who gives an excellent description, too lengthy to be quoted, of the Anglican Church as envisaged by Ken.[8]

Ken not only believes in the doctrines and practises of Holy Church, but finds them ever-flowing springs of poetic stimulation. He glories in the divinity of Jesus and in His miraculous birth:

> Down to the Virgin Filial God
> With Chariots of Salvation rode;
> Of her Heart Blood by Love inflam'd,
> He for himself a Temple fram'd;
> Debasement was his sole intent,
> To Heav'n his Chariot empty went.[9]

Ken's reverence for the Mother of God is that of a devout and well-instructed Catholic. She alone of all the saints does not attend the great gathering on Mount Tabor, for with perfect humility she shrinks from

---

[7] Cf. A. O. Lovejoy, "Optimism and Romanticism," PMLA, XLII, 921-945.
[8] Works, II, 222 ff.   [9] On the Annuntiation. See also On the Incarnation.

hearing "her own Encomiums." [10] Elsewhere lines imbued with a tender and not unattractive concettism depict the mingled emotions with which she regards the Holy Babe:

> God-Man then seem'd her passions to divide,
> She to act Votry, and the Mother try'd,
> She both familiar was, and would adore,
> Would help her Child, and yet his Help implore,
> Would love her Babe, and her Creator dread,
> Beg Food from him, whom with her Milk she fed,
> Wou'd for, and to, her little Infant pray,
> Contemplate on him, and yet with him play,
> Wou'd kiss her Son, and then her God wou'd praise,
> Swadling him by the Light of his own Rays. [11]

That last line embodies a whole lost world of poetically imaginative faith.

All the great saints are living realities in Ken's mind. In heaven they do not forget the struggles of humanity:

> You know the Conflicts well,
> We have with Flesh, the World and Hell,
> You safe the Gulf have shot,
> Eternal Glory is your Lot,
> You on the Dangers think yourselves have felt,
> And for our State with dear Compassion melt.

This poem, *On all Saints*, does not say outright that the saints pray for us, but the implication is clear.

Angels too arouse poetic feeling in Ken precisely because he thinks of them as more than mere figments of poetry. His guardian angel repeatedly appears. Once the angel banishes the pains of Ken's illness by singing him the joyful hymn sung by his fellow-angels in heaven when a sinner repents. [12] In the long allegorical narrative *Sion*, Psyche, the soul personified, addresses her guardian angel in the rather beautiful words:

> O dear Embraces of sweet Plumes,
> Which breath restorative Perfumes,
> O kind Angelick Breast,
> Safe Shelter, and soft Rest,
> O Heav'n below within these Wings,
> Where my Soul loves, and joys, and God-ward springs.

[10] *Mount Tabor.*   [11] *On the Incarnation.*

[12] *Anodynes.* On another occasion the guardian persuades one of the seven angels who wait with their trumpets by God's throne to give a private, pre-Judgment Day blast for Ken's special benefit.

The whole drama of the Christian Year provides Ken with poetic material. He writes on the Annunciation, Nativity, Circumcision, Epiphany, Presentation, and so on to Pentecost. A two-hundred-page section of his *Works* is entitled *Hymns for all the Festivals in the Year*.

Like almost all Anglo-Catholics, Bishop Ken is an Arminian. Twice he makes Satan advocate predestination—once to lure a good Christian into Antinomianism, once to corrupt a good Christian through fear of *not* being one of the elect.

Ken's private devotions are such as would be familiar to any modern Catholic. For him, words like "retreat," "ejaculation," "meditation," and "contemplation" have precise and even technical meanings:

> Ejaculations are Pearls loose;
> Strung, Meditation they produce.
> 'Tis by Continuation, Thought
> Is up to Contemplation wrought.
> Love, when Faith sees my Jesus near,
> Will say, 'Tis good to mansion here.[13]

Ken is also thoroughly Catholic in his belief that the supreme vehicle of grace is the Holy Eucharist:

> The greatest Love unbounded God cou'd show,
> Was to resign his Son to bear our Woe.
> The greatest Love cou'd from the Son proceed,
> Was to assume our Flesh, and for us bleed.
> The Eucharist to Souls both Loves displays,
> Love emulous of infinite to raise;
> As if to dye had been a Love too low,
> He on his Lovers wou'd himself bestow.[14]

It might be argued, however, that in regard to the Lord's Supper his theological views are less genuinely Catholic than his feelings. According to Paul Elmer More, "The Anglicans widely admitted the 'real presence,' not corporal but spiritual, of the body and blood of Christ in the Eucharist. In so far, they tended away from Reformation Eucharistic theology toward the Objectivism of Rome. But in a different respect, namely in their emphasis on the need for the coöperation of faith in the communicant, they leaned towards the Protestant position." [15] Like most Anglo-Catholics of his day, Ken avoids any specific account of exactly what

---

[13] *Meditation on Jesus.* See also *Jesus in our Retreat.*
[14] *On the Eucharist.*   [15] *Anglicanism,* p. xxxvi.

happens in the Eucharist. When he grapples with the mystery, as in the following lines, his desire to avoid the taint of Romanism gives somewhat negative results:

> That Bread and Wine Christ's Flesh and Blood shou'd be,
> No Saint can think, who shall his glory see:
> For Flesh and Blood which corruptible are,
> In heav'nly Incorruption cannot share.
> His Sacred Body and Blood by frail Mankind
> Cannot be broke, eat, spilt, when 'tis refin'd,
> Yet its Memorial may, Saints, who frequent
> The Symbols, gain the Grace they represent;
> That 'tis true Bread which Shall on Altars lye,
> They'll know by Touch, by Taste, their Smell, and Eye.
>
>   .   .   .
>
> Christ when in Heaven, in Heaven he must remain,
> Till the great Day he'll ne'er return again;
> Yet he'll below on Elements when blest,
> By Union, not Conversion deign to rest.[16]

In our attempt to understand Ken's position in the history of religious thought we have been forced to neglect a host of short poems of inward religious experience—poems of Christian penitence, hope, gratitude, and yearning for union with Jesus. This defender of creeds and forms is no mere bigot or formalist: his Christianity is a living thing—rich, fervent, deeply sorrowful and deeply joyful.

Ken thinks poetically of religion and religiously of poetry. Faith and song are inextricably entwined in his heart. He is not, however, a great religious poet. The age gave him too little of the peace which his gentle nature needed, and often forced him to preach and argue in verse. At such times he tends to be flat and verbose. Without possessing a truly "metaphysical" genius, he sometimes indulges in conceits which are quaintly rather than movingly outlandish. He is too fond of fussy allegorical devices and of strange adjectives like "cotrine," "antesolar," "salvifick," and "chaolick." His sins of omission are even easier to feel, though harder to define. In general he writes like a contemporary of Phineas Fletcher who has lived on into times which nourish neither his thought nor his art.

Yet it cannot be denied that Ken had a truly poetic spirit. Though he

---

[16] *On the Eucharist.*

was seldom sufficiently the artist to get his feelings on paper, he occasionally reveals a glimpse of the poem which filled his devout and imaginative heart. This applies, I think, to *Jesus in our Retreat*:

> My Lord, O in my Closet stay,
> Let me not lose thy gracious Ray;
> Thou me, shou'dst Thou my Cell forsake,
>   Must with Thee take.
>
>   .   .   .   .
>
> Shou'dst Thou, Thy Face a while to hide,
> Retire to thy celestial Bride,
> And while Thou dost from me recede,
>   On Lillies feed,
>
> Thither I after Thee will fly,
> And hymning Thee, will prostrate lye,
> In hope to pluck a Lilly sweet,
>   Kiss'd by thy Feet.
>
> Odour and Beauty never fade,
> In Lillies sweeten'd by thy Shade,
> 'Twill Virtue from thy Touch derive,
>   Love to revive.
>
> T'wards Heav'n it will aspiring tend,
> Grow fairer as it shall ascend;
> T'wards Heav'n, to teach me ev'ry Hour
>   To rise and flow'r.

It is related that on rising in the morning Bishop Ken would take his lute and sing his own *Morning Hymn* to the accompaniment of music which he himself had composed.[17] How thoroughly antiquated—almost more Elizabethan than of the seventeenth century—is this picture! No such eccentric conduct is reported of eighteenth-century bishops, whether they be high as Atterbury or low as Hoadly. When Ken and his associates became Nonjurors, there passed from the Church of England certain values which were not to be regained for well over a century.

In some respects, however, Ken had a kindred spirit in his contemporary John Norris (1657-1711).[18] Both men possessed that fragrance and

---

[17] Abbey and Overton, *The English Church in the Eighteenth Century*, II, 230.

[18] His poems were first published in 1684, and he wrote little or no verse after 1700. But he was an active intellectual force up to the year of his death, and his poems were several times republished in the eighteenth century. They reached a tenth edition in 1730.

radiance which illustrate the meaning of "newness of life," and in their minds religion, poetry, and music were inseparable. Ken, who loved his lute, would have understood Norris's defense of *A Musician Supposed to be Mad with Musick*:

> His soul is only set t'an higher strain.
>
> .   .   .   .   .
>
> Musick, thou generous ferment of the soul,
> Thou universal cement of the whole;
> Thou spring of passion, that dost inspire
> Religious ardours, and poetick fire,
> Who'd think that madness should b'ascribed to thee,
> That mighty discord to thy harmony?

Neither poet was afraid of a little spiritual inebriety.

Despite peculiar ideas which must be noted later, Norris, like Ken, is often inspired by the basic Christian doctrines as externalized in the events of sacred history. In *The Passion of Our Blessed Saviour* the spirit of Catholic devotion is strong, and it is even stronger in *The Passion of the Virgin Mother, Beholding the Crucifixion of Her Divine Son*:

> She sees now by the rude inhuman stroke,
> The mystic river flow, and in her breast
> Wonders, by what strange figure th' angel spoke,
> When amongst all the daughters he pronounced her blest.

Elsewhere he hopes that "the preciser sort" will not think him popish if he prays to a dead child as his "little saint."

Norris, however, is a better poet than Ken. The Nonjuror could never have written this paraphrase of the *Second Chapter of the Canticles, from Verse 10 to 13*, which is here given entire:

> It was my Beloved spake,
>   I know his charming voice, I heard Him say,
> Rise up, my love, My fairest one awake,
>   Awake, and come away.
>
> The Winter all is past,
>   And stormy winds that with such rudeness blew;
> The heavens are no longer overcast,
>   But try to look like you.

> The flowers their sweets display,
>   The birds in short preludiums tune their throat,
> The turtle in low murmurs does essay
>   His melancholy note.
>
> The fruitful vineyards make
>   An odorous smell, the fig looks fresh and gay;
> Arise, my love, my fairest one awake,
>   Awake and come away.

He is by no means always so successful. Pindarics exert a fatal fascination upon him, and too often the abstract ideas which he loves are not converted into images before they are expressed. On the whole, however, he was not unworthy of becoming the rector of George Herbert's old parish of Bemerton. In him the noble tradition of seventeenth-century religious poetry, though decadent, retains some of its old beauty. He writes well enough to remind us that Henry Vaughan did not die until 1695.

But Norris differs from Ken chiefly in being much more deeply saturated in secular philosophy. He was an enthusiastic disciple of Malebranche, and his *Essay toward the Theory of an Ideal and Intelligible World* uses the Frenchman's theory of the vision of all things in God in an endeavor to refute Locke. Norris values Malebranche as a fellow-Platonist, for he inherits the more mystical and less rationalistic features of the thought of Cudworth, Whichcote, and More. He corresponded with More on metaphysical subjects, and had the deepest admiration for him.[19] In fact Norris is a link between the Neo-Platonism of the Cambridge school and that of Shaftesbury. The very different Platonism of Berkeley's later writings may also, in some measure, reflect his influence.

The salient feature of Norris's poetry is his longing for those perfect ideas of truth, beauty, and love which exist in the mind of God:

> How long great God, how long must I
> Immur'd in this dark prison lye!
> Where at the gates and avenues of sense
> My soul must watch to have intelligence;
> Where but faint gleams of thee salute my sight,
> Like doubtful moon-shine in a cloudy night.[20]

Those "faint gleams," those dim reflections on the walls of the cave,

[19] See *To Dr. More. An Ode.*   [20] *The Aspiration.*

both inspire and thwart his strivings toward the ideal reality. Much as he loves learning, he knows that books can never lift him to the heights. His friends are wrong, he says in *The Discouragement,* if they think that he despises knowledge,

> Or that t'enthusiasm I incline,
> And hope by inspiration to be wise.

But the thought has struck him that perhaps earthly knowledge is not deemed knowledge at all in heaven: "Perhaps they've other rules to reason by." Then why should he not put away his books and wait a few years until death gives him the real truth at a single stroke? *The Curiosity,* where he longs for some kind angel to enlighten him all at once, is written in the same mood.

The only way of obtaining a foretaste of the perfect heavenly truth is not through the senses, not through books, but through contemplation— the exercise on earth of something akin to *Seraphick Love:*

> Through Contemplation's optics I have seen,
> Him who is "fairer than the sons of men":
> The source of good, the light archetypall,
>   Beauty in the original.

> To thee, Thou only fair, my soul aspires
> With holy breathings, languishing desires,
> To thee m' inamoured, panting heart does move,
>   By efforts of ecstatic love.

> How do thy glorious streams of light
> Refresh my intellectual sight!
> Tho' broken, and strain'd through a skreen
> Of envious flesh that stands between!
> When shall m' imprisoned soul be free,
> That she thy native uncorrected light may see,
> And gaze upon thy beatifick face to all eternity?

Sometimes, however, the force of contemplative love sweeps aside what Blake calls the "little curtain of flesh on the bed of our desire." Such a joyful moment is described in *The Elevation.* The poem, says Norris in his notes, is intended to "represent the gradual ascent of the soul by contemplation to the supreme good, together with its firm adherency to it, and its full acquiescence in it. All which is done figuratively, under the allegory of a local elevation from the feculent regions of this lower world."

The doctrine of pre-existence appears when the soul, rising above the earth, finds heaven strangely familiar:

> But see, to what new region am I come?
> I know it well, it is my native home.
> Here led I once a life divine
> Which did all good, no evil know.

Then comes the ineffable moment:

> With piercing rays, th' eternal day doth break,
> The beauties of the face divine
> Strike strongly on my feeble sight:
> With what bright glories does it shine!
> 'Tis one immense and ever-flowing light.[21]

Some Neoplatonists are inclined to view the creation as the result of a sort of struggle between God's shaping spirit of imagination and the stubborn shapelessness of matter. No such conflict appears, however, in Norris's *Divine Hymn on the Creation,* where God simply responds to the promptings of Love, and smiles His own beautiful ideas into being:

> Love, gentle Love, unlockt His fruitful breast,
> And woke the Ideas where they dormant lay.
>   Awak'd their beauties they display;
>   Th' Almighty smil'd to see
>   The comely form of harmony
>   Of his eternal imag'ry;
> He saw 'twas good and fair, and th' infant platform blest;
> Ye seeds of being, in whose fair bosoms dwell
>   The forms of all things possible,
> Arise and your prolific force display.

From contemplation of this fecund and harmonious universe, so interestingly prophetic of Shaftesbury's, the mind rises to contemplation of the divine reality. The twin poems entitled *Love* and *Beauty* are attempts to describe the goal of the mystic quest. The former declares that

> The Universe is kept in tune by love.

>   .   .   .

[21] Somewhat regrettably, Norris does not mention the fact that *The Elevation* is considerably indebted to Casimir's *E rebus humanis excessus* (Book II, Ode V).

> The happiest order of the blest
> Are those whose tide of love's most high,
> The bright seraphick host, who're more possest
> Of good, because more like the Deity.
> T'him they advance as they improve
> That noble heat, for God is love.

God is not only love, but that beauty toward which love aspires. Norris declares in one of his prose essays that Plato shows how, through love, "we may gradually ascend from the many Fairs to the chief Fair, that is to God, in whom is true Felicity." [22] This is precisely the theme of *Beauty*. God is

> ... Beautie's vast abyss and boundless sea,
> The primitive and greatest Fair;
> All His perfections beauties are,
> Beauty is all the Deity.
> Some streams from this vast ocean flow,
> And that is all that pleases, all that's fair below.

>   .   .   .   .   .

> But do not thou my soul, fixt here remain;
> All streams of beauty here below
> Do from that immense ocean flow,
> And thither they should lead again.
> Trace then these streams, till thou shalt be
> At length o'erwhelmed in Beauty's boundless sea.

Norris is a latitudinarian of an earlier, more adventurous, more genuinely spiritual type than the "moderation men" of the foregoing chapter. His aim is not to achieve a safe-and-sane compromise, but to find God. Imbued with real love for the Christian faith and with real love for reason of an intuitive and transcendental kind, he seeks to reconcile his two loves by means of Neo-Platonism. In some minds, a sort of Platonism may remain standing long after the collapse of the Christianity which it was originally intended to buttress, but this is hardly true of Norris. He does, to be sure, speak *either* in technically Platonic *or* technically Christian terms, a fact which hints that the two aspects of his religion are in some danger of drifting apart. The separation, however, has not

[22] *An Account of Plato's Ideas, and of Platonic Love. A Collection of Miscellanies...* By John Norris (1706), p. 363.

taken place. Nothing in his poetry is inconsistent with Christian orthodoxy: the God of beauty and love is still, for him, the God who so loved
the world that He gave His only begotten Son. But as we continue our
investigation we shall find poets who have something like Norris's Platonism without his Christianity—men who worship truth, love, and
beauty without worshipping Father, Son, and Holy Spirit.

From Ken and Norris to the next poet on our list the descent is steep.
Samuel Wesley the elder (1662-1735) shows all too plainly that he belongs
to a later generation. His *Maggots* (1685) we may pass by as a volume
of youthfully facetious verse belonging to the period when he was still a
dissenter.[23] But in 1693 we find Wesley a priest of the Church of England
and the author of *The Life of our Blessed Lord and Saviour Jesus Christ.
An Heroic Poem.* This sacred epic in ten books, dedicated to Queen
Mary, was issued as a handsome folio with sixty copper-plates by
Faithorne.

The Preface is a well-informed *Essay on Heroic-Poetry* with special
emphasis on moral instruction as the final purpose of the type and with
arguments in defense of the Christian epic. His strongest point is that to
use poetic imagination in treating a sacred theme is not necessarily to
impose falsehood upon it. As compared to Ariosto, Spenser is "almost
as Irregular, but much more Natural and Lovely." The style of *Gondibert*
is "rather stiff than Heroic." His high praise of Cowley in general and
of *Davideis* in particular is disappointing, but one likes his comment, "As
for Milton's *Paradice* [sic] *Lost* it's an Original, and indeed he seems
rather above the common Rules of Epic than ignorant of them. It's I'm
sure a very lovely Poem, by whatever Name it's call'd." It is evident
that Wesley can throw pedantry overboard when he stands in the presence
of greatness.

Plunging *in medias res,* the author begins his poem with the Transfiguration and the entry into Jerusalem. After the conversation of Peter,
James, and John has related the earlier events of Christ's life, the story
moves through the Crucifixion to the Ascension. Unfortunately, though

---

[23] His father, an ejected clergyman of 1662, became an Independent minister. His
wife, John Wesley's mother, had exactly the same background, but it is interesting to
observe that before her marriage she "had been a benevolentist with leanings toward the
fashionable Unitarianism." (Norman Sykes, *Church and State in England in the Eighteenth Century,* p. 391.)

Wesley has a sound critical understanding of the requirements of epic, he is not equipped by nature to rise to the height of his great argument. Furthermore he is so eager to prove the suitability of the subject for heroic treatment that he smothers both its literary and spiritual values in stock devices and decorations. The loss of Malchus' ear at the betrayal, for instance, is absurdly rendered as an epic combat.

Worse than absurd is the simile arising from the following incident. At the words, "My God, my God, why hast thou forsaken me?" the angels are moved to descend and rescue their Lord.[24] While Jesus suffers on the cross, heaven is full of military bustle. Michael arms himself to lead his cohorts:

> . . . On a Cloud, with Thunder charg'd, he rode
> Above 'em all, and only not a God.
> Thus, might we Mortal match with things Divine,
> Thus look'd our Godlike Heroe at the Boyne:
> The same fair Ardor for the glorious Prize,
> The same just Anger lightning in his Eyes:
> Thus he appear'd, thus those who round him rode,
> They all like Heroes fought, he like a God.

Only a true-blue Whig would bring William III and the Boyne into an account of the Crucifixion. Two years later (1695), when he publishes his *Elegies on the Queen and Archbishop,* Wesley is still a Whig. In the first[25] of the two pieces composing this slender volume, Mary is praised for her benign religious influence on her court and her lowlier subjects. "A Pattern of the Active Life," she steered along the channel of practical beneficence, avoiding the extremes of immorality and sterile, superstitious asceticism.

To honor her arrival in heaven, the angels have prepared a special hymn which should be quoted as one of Wesley's rare attempts in elevated religious lyric:

> O Holy Father! Spirit! and Son!
> Dread Holy Three! Dread Holy One!
> Thy eyes, how perfect and how pure!
>   All those approve
>   Who Virtue love

[24] God eventually calms them by revealing to them His plan of redemption.
[25] *On the Death of Her Late Sacred Majesty, Mary Queen of England, etc. A Pindarique Poem.*

> Nor can the smallest Stain of Guilt endure.
> Though long the stupid World has been
> Enslav'd to Error, lost in Sin,
> Did long thy saving Health despise,
> Now the fair years in comly Order rise!
> The stupid World shall worship Fiends no more
> (Their Temples by th'Almighty's Frown,
> Their smoaking Altars thunder'd down)
> But thee and thy dread Son, O King of Kings! adore.

These lines are not very moving, but they suggest that the author was moved when he wrote them.

Queen Mary's active and practical religion found a worthy agent in her primate, Tillotson. Wesley's elegy on the dead archbishop [26] is valuable as describing one who embodied the ideals which were long to dominate the Church of England. Tillotson's serene and cheerful spirit, he says, was untouched by the gloomy, fearsome views born of superstitious ignorance. Eminently a man of reason, he showed God's "footsteps" in nature:

> Yet his strong Reason to his Faith he bent,
> By new Elastic Pow'rs still stronger made;
> Yet more-than-nat'ral Truths had his Assent,
> Who where he could not comprehend obey'd.

The Archbishop exposed the frauds of Rome and in general had a great genius for controversy,

> Yet no wild Motions e'er disturb'd his Breast,
> His Reason, not his Passion kept him warm;
> No warring winds his peaceful Soul opprest,
> Where blew a gentle Breeze, but not a Storm.

Above everything he was a man of balance, mildness, moderation. As a preacher, "the Standard he of English Eloquence":

> 'Twas Music, Poetry, and Rapture all,
> The Sweets of his orac'lous words to share;
> As soft they fell as balmy Dew-drops fall,
> As smooth as undisturb'd etherial Air.

An Epistle to a Friend Concerning Poetry (1700) is a rather mediocre "art of poetry" with remarks on contemporary writers. The religious and

[26] *A Poem on the Death of his Grace John Late Lord Arch-Bishop of Canterbury.*

moral element, however, is so large as to make the poem in part a contribution to the "reformation of manners" movement. In the Preface, which is more exclusively pious than the poem itself, Wesley shows alarm at the prevalence of atheism: "There's too great reason to apprehend, that this Infection is spread among Persons of almost all Ranks and Qualities; and that though some may think it decent to keep on the Masque, yet if they were searched to the bottom, all their Religion wou'd be found that which they most blasphemously assert of Religion in general, only a state Engin to keep the World in Order." Freethinkers are merely rationalizing their desire to live sinfully: "How came Men to fall into these damnable Errors in Faith, but by Lewdness of Life? The Cowards wou'd not believe a God because they dare not do it, for Woe be to 'em if there be one, and consequently any Future Punishments."

In the text of this poem he expresses admiration for Dryden, but laments the looseness of his comedies. On the Day of Judgment,

> How will he wish each lewd applauded line
> Will make Vice pleasing, and Damnation shine,
> Had been as dull as honest Quarles' or mine!

The stage in general is castigated:

> Why thrive the Lewd, their Wishes seldom crost,
> And why Poetic Justice often lost?
> They plead they copy Nature.—Don't abuse
> Her sacred Name with such a vile Excuse!
> She wisely hides what these, like Beasts, display."

In Tennyson's words, then, the comic dramatists "Paint the mortal shame of nature with the living hues of art."

In 1704 we find Wesley returning to divine poetry in the more restricted sense in *The History of the Old and New Testaments Attempted in Verse*.[27] The dedication to Queen Anne strikes a new note of Toryism:

> O! Of the Royal Martyr's Sacred Race!
> (Long may the Royal Martyr's Race remain!)

Wesley underwent a political conversion at the beginning of the new reign. He remained a Tory and consequently a High Churchman from that time to his death.

[27] The third and last volume, devoted to the New Testament, did not appear until 1715.

The core of this work is John Sturt's three hundred and thirty en-
gravings, so chosen and arranged as to form a pictorial history of the
Bible. Each cut is accompanied by the Biblical account of the scene
represented and by a poem in which Wesley gives an interpretive paraphrase of the Scripture passage. The verses, all in heroic couplets, are
less burdensomely elaborate than in *The Life of Christ*. Wesley is now
writing for the edification of the plain man, and does not try to be literary. On the other hand his little poems are rather crude and flat, giving
an impression of perfunctory haste.

What Wesley declares to be "the last effort of a retiring Muse" is *A
Poem in Memory of Robert Nelson Esquire* (1715). Nelson, the much-
loved nonjuring layman, was his close friend; but this sober elegy is not
rich in emotional quality. One point, however, is worth noting. Wesley
tells us that as a youth Nelson was pious and virtuous from natural
impulse, and needed only to obey his own heart in order to do right:

> Happy the Man, whom Heaven did so compose,
> That ev'ry Vertue from his Temper flows;
> So just the Frame, he wants not Reason's Art
> To win the Passions, nor to warm the Heart;
> Thro' heedless Youth by happy Impulse goes
> And loves the Vertue that not yet he knows:
> When riper Age doth make the vertuous Choice,
> With Joy he finds the same was Nature's Voice.

Had Nelson lived later in the century, he would have been classified as
a *belle âme* in whom the instinctively good child was father of the consciously good man.

Wesley was certainly a man of solid piety and a competent practitioner
in what his age regarded as divine poetry, but how drab and arid he
seems after Ken and Norris! He was impelled to write by no deep
spiritual passion, and almost never reveals a personal religious experience.
He never fully came alive as man, priest, or poet. After reading his poems
one realizes more keenly than ever how triumphantly John Wesley
was his mother's son, and how tragically the younger Samuel was his
father's.

The other Anglican divine poets who have been swept into my net
are small fry. Basil Kennett (1674-1715), although a clergyman, distin-

guished himself chiefly as an antiquarian.[28] His only published verse is found in *An Essay towards a Paraphrase on the Psalms, In English Verse. To which is added A Paraphrase on the Third Chapter of the Revelations* (1706). Rather less than half of the psalms are dealt with—occasionally in hymn-stanzas, more often in heroic couplets, but generally in iambic pentameter lines arranged in variously interwoven rhyme-schemes. His aim is not to provide material for congregational worship, but to turn the psalms into English poetry.

Granting the validity of this aim Kennett must be credited with some measure of success. At his worst he is very pedestrian, but at his best he writes as he does in *The Third Chapter of the Revelations Paraphras'd*:

> Let the bright Watchman, that defends
> The Sardian Gate, hear what his Lord declares,
> Whose Throne the Sev'n-fold Pow'r attends,
> And whose Right-hand sustains the Mystick Stars:
> I love thy Vows, but hate thy Sin:
> Without thou feignest Life, I see thee dead within.
>
> If yet around thine Heart there move
> Some warm Remains of Life not given o'er,
> With Care the Heav'nly Spark improve,
> And guard expiring Faith with all thy Pow'r.
> Too long uncertain Thou hast stood,
> Novice in Arts Divine, and incomplete in Good.

In such passages the verse is interestingly managed, and the diction has a restrained dignity. If this praise is excessive, one may at least be thankful for the absence of that periphrastic decorativeness which ruins most Scripture-paraphrases of the century. This scholar has classicized the original, but his classicism is more nearly genuine than "pseudo." We vainly wonder how his religion and his scholarship would have combined in original poetry.

The author of *Sacred and Moral Poems* (1716) disguises himself as "A Cambridge Gentleman"; but if, as seems likely enough, he is the same

---

[28] His *Romae Antiquae Notitiae* attained its eighteenth edition as late as 1820. In the field of theology he published sermons and a short treatise on the Apostle's Creed, besides translating Pascal's *Pensées* and La Placette's *The Christian Casuist*. He came of a good family, and was the younger brother of White Kennett, Bishop of Peterborough. Probably he followed his brother in being a Whig and Low Churchman.

"Cambridge Gentleman" who published *A Letter to the Reverend Dr. Henry Sacheverell* in 1710, he is an otherwise unknown Mr. Rawson.[29] He dedicates the volume to God the Father, and in a prefatory poem welcomes only those readers

> Who do not love their Errors or Disease;
> Whom Truth, tho' plain, and wise Instructions please.
> Such I invite with me to taste those Joys
> Which Death survive.

To accept this invitation is to be disappointed. Mr. Rawson—if he *is* the author—is pious in a simple, straightforward, unsentimental way, but he lacks both the form and the spirit of poetry.

The sacred pieces marshal sober truisms under such titles as *For the Lord's-Day, For Good-Friday, On Man's Unwillingness to Die,* and *No Condition without its Comfort.* Even the poems which the author would probably classify as "moral" are given a religious turn: *On Friendship,* for instance, rises to the conclusion that the one necessary and perfect friend is God.

Without being morbidly gloomy, the writer has a rather strong sense of sin,[30] accompanied by a lively distrust of nature as a moral guide:

> By Nature Man discerns not the great Price
> Of a meek, quiet Spirit, nor of Vice
> In his own Life can see the Turpitude,
> Till by Assistance from Above subdu'd. [31]

To follow nature is to live like an animal:

> The most, proceeding as the Stream does drive,
> Let Nature steer, and only would arrive
> At the Beast's Paradise.[32]

Is he perhaps reacting against a growing tendency of naturalism?

Our Cambridge poet seems too artless and unlearned to be of the university, and even his label of "gentleman," though not unbelievable, is somewhat surprising. One pictures him as an elderly, old-fashioned Whig with some claim to inclusion among Cambridgeshire gentry, of puritan ancestry, and a more than usually earnest and precise Low

---

[29] Cushing, *Initials and Pseudonyms,* p. 49.
[30] See *For Good-Friday.*
[31] *On our Natural Inability in Holy Things.*
[32] *No Condition without its Comfort.*

Churchman. Such men are links between seventeenth-century puritanism and the Evangelicalism of the later eighteenth century.

Of the Reverend Samuel Catherall I know next to nothing. In 1720 he was a fellow of Oriel College, Oxford, and presumably rather more than middle-aged, for he had published a funeral sermon as early as 1692. *An Essay on the Conflagration* (1720) is, in the first place, a Judgment-Day piece written with the usual minatory intentions. Considering the prevalent "infidelity, heresie, and profane scoffing at religion," says Catherall in his Preface, the day of wrath may well be close at hand.

But besides being gloomily pious, the poem is self-consciously literary. It is a labored imitation of Milton's blank verse,[33] and indeed one suspects that Catherall selected the subject at least partly because it provided an opportunity to handle with Miltonic grandeur

> No vile, or abject theme; but earth's whole frame
> Dissolv'd, and Christ to judge mankind return'd.

The imitation is particularly close in the first book, a dialogue between the Adam-like poet and an angel whose instructions prepare him for the vision of Judgment comprising the second and concluding book. The invocation, too, pays Milton sincerest flattery:

> O thou Eternal Spirit, who first didst move
> Upon the vast Abyss with wings outspread,
> Creating light from darkness, and this earth
> From a rude chaos; aid my aspiring song.
>
> . . . . .
>
> . . . Send a bright seraph down,
> And from thy burning altar let him take
> A living coal, and lay the sacred fire
> On my unhallow'd mouth. Then purg'd from sin
> I'll soar the height of this great argument,
> Describe the flaming globe, and like a trump,
> My verse shall sound, shall make the atheist shrink,
> And deist tremble.

Another feature of this poem is its enlistment of natural science in the attack on atheism and deism. An engraving of Thomas Burnet forms the frontispiece,[34] and the instructive angel in Book I has read that divine's

[33] The debt is acknowledged in preface and text.
[34] Catherall, therefore, is probably a Whig and a Low Churchman.

Telluris Theoria Sacra. Hence he is able to tell the poet that the earth is full of "fiery vapours"—witness the volcanoes all over the world. The final conflagration will be a general eruption of these vapours, reinforced by lightning flashed down from heaven. But whenever the poet's curiosity on these matters goes too far, the angel checks him with speeches of the "impious worm, inquire no further" sort. Judgment Day can be supported by science, but does not require such support. The essential point is that all this will happen because God has said so. In Book II, in order to rationalize the traditional conception of Hell, Catherall has borrowed "some useful suggestions of the pious and learned Dr. Sherlock," who believes "that, after the saints are received into bliss, and the sentence is passed upon wicked men, the world shall kindle into flames, and make a Hell for them."

To this compound of Milton, threatening piety, and physico-theological science, is added a spice of flattery. Among those especially singled out for divine favor on Judgment Day, this ambitious clergyman beholds in his vision the Bishop of Durham, the Bishop of London, "unblemish'd Hooper," [35] and the Duke of Chandos, "gen'rous beyond compare." [36]

The foregoing pages by no means constitute an exhaustive treatment of Anglican specialists in divine poetry during this period, but they include all the important figures and several unimportant ones. Using roughly the same scale of selection, we now consider the work of a few Nonconformists. At once, of course, there comes to mind the name of Isaac Watts (1674-1748).

No fixed dividing line can be drawn between the dissenters of the seventeenth and of the eighteenth century. Queen Anne's London had plenty of hale old men who could remember the days when puritan zeal burned most hotly. As an infant, Watts had been suckled on the steps of the jail where his nonconforming father was imprisoned; and as a student at Rowe's academy he often went to hear the preaching of Oliver

[35] George Hooper (1640-1727), Bishop of Bath and Wells. He at least was responsive to this praise, for by 1725 Catherall had become a prebendary of Wells Cathedral.

[36] In 1725 Catherall published *Cato Major. A Poem. Upon the Model of Tully's Essay of Old Age.* This much-inflated paraphrase in blank verse is of no interest to us except for a remark in the preface that the moral ideals of the heathen philosopher put to shame those of many professed Christians. I have not seen Catherall's Εικων Σωκρατικη : *or a portraiture of Socrates, extracted out of Plato : in blank verse,* 1717. Probably it deals with Plato as *Cato Major* does with Cicero.

Cromwell's former chaplain, John Howe. Under the alias of Clarke, Richard Cromwell himself survived as a member of Howe's congregation.

High Churchmen, vividly remembering the rebels of earlier days, continued to revile their dissenting contemporaries as fanatics. In the reign of Anne, however, this term was rather a party catchword and a survival of the satirical tradition established by *Hudibras* than an accurate description of the dissenter as he really existed. The zealot was now the business man, either prosperous or doing his best to become so. He kept on good terms with the Establishment, and the Low Church wing of the Establishment kept on good terms with him, because sensible merchants do not quarrel with their clients. In the words of the modern slogan, "The customer is always right."

Hence we must not picture Isaac Watts as a seedy enthusiast thumping his tub in a back alley. He was the close friend as well as the chaplain of Sir Thomas Abney, Lord Mayor of London, and a majority of his congregation were men of substance. Until ill health forced him to retire from regular preaching in 1712, he devoted his efforts to pushing camels through the needle's eye. He was on familiar terms not only with the merchant princes of London and their families, but with landed aristocrats like the Weymouths and Hertfords. A man of learning and culture, his literary orbit intersected that of the Addison-Steele group. His paraphrase of Psalm CXIV appeared in *Spectator*.[37] The dramatist John Hughes had been his schoolmate, and remained his friend.

Queen Anne Nonconformity was not rich in religious ardor. By 1702 membership was at a standstill and had probably already begun to decline. The children of the wealthier dissenters were showing a tendency to drift back to the Establishment; for Episcopalianism, then as now, was cursed with being the church of the really nice people. Up to the Revolution of 1688, the mainspring of Nonconformity had been the fight for liberty. Now the fight was over, and zeal cooled as the polemic tension slackened. The Revolution, to be sure, had given only toleration, not complete freedom. But the dissenter had grown less uncompromising as he grew more prosperous and respectable. Why should he be dissatisfied with his bargain? He had much more freedom than his persecuted forebears—quite enough to enable him to do business in peace and quiet. If

---

[37] No. 461, August 19, 1712. The paper includes also a letter by Watts, and a little introduction by Steele.

his ambitions soared to membership in a corporation, it was easy enough to kneel at an Anglican altar rail once a year. London was worth a Mass. He was rather anxious to live down his old reputation as an enthusiast, to show that he could be as sound and sober as the most respectable Anglican. Indeed, if he rose high enough in the social scale to acquire a little sophistication, a discreet latitudinarianism was more attractive to him than the grim theology of his parents. As the intolerance of the High Church party increased during the reign of Anne, Nonconformity regained something of its old fighting spirit. But with few exceptions the partisan bitterness thus aroused was no longer accompanied by deep religious feeling, and in any case it was merely a fitful awakening. When the Queen died the dissenters gave thanks to God and prepared to enjoy in torpid contentment the renewed tolerance granted by the Hanoverians.

Although the stigma of "enthusiasm" was imputed to all dissenters by high Anglicans, the historian must be more discriminating. The Presbyterians, even in the seventeenth century, had been staunch opponents of enthusiasm and had regarded themselves as better Anglicans than the Episcopalians. They had never sought Nonconformity: that status had been thrust upon them by the monarch whose restoration they had helped to effect. The case of the Independents or Congregationalists, the sect of Watts, is more complex. In the seventeenth century they had not consciously attacked what they conceived to be the true conception of the historic Church. They wanted freedom for each congregation, not absolute individual liberty. In 1643, to be sure, the predominance of the conservative Presbyterian element in the Assembly of Divines caused many Independents to identify their interests with those genuine enthusiasts, the members of the mystical, antinomian, and politically radical Separatist sects like the Ranters and Levellers. Obviously, too, the congregational system would permit a latitude in the expression of religious belief running all the way from stodgy sobriety to violent eccentricity. On the whole, however, the seventeenth-century Independents cannot be summed up as enthusiasts or political extremists. "The logic of events," says Professor Haller, "drove them in the direction of a larger freedom than they could approve, and, when the time came, they retreated willingly to the Cromwellian compromise, which tolerated only such quiet, respectable, law-abiding groups as would support the existing government." [38] It is not

---

[38] William Haller, *Tracts on Liberty in the Puritan Revolution*, I, 34.

surprising, then, that in the more relaxed days of Queen Anne the Independents were far from being wild-eyed fanatics in religion or politics.

This seeming digression is intended to suggest the importance of Isaac
Watts. Although he was in several respects a typical Independent minister
of his age, he was one of a very few men who, under the conditions
which have just been described, preserved the old spiritual ardor of Dissent; and he was literally the only man who gave that ardor anything
like a significant poetic expression. His ministry and his writings form
a link between the zeal of the seventeenth and the revived zeal of the
later eighteenth century. He who had listened to the sermons of John
Howe lived long enough to clasp the hands of Zinzendorf and Whitefield.
Nor is this connection merely an accident of chronology: it implies a
tenuous but unbroken continuity of doctrine and temperament.

After about 1718, when he turned from poetry to theology and metaphysics, Watts began to indulge in speculations of not impeccable orthodoxy.[39] As we see him in his poems, however, he is a Calvinistic Protestant
of the strictest kind. The emphasis which he lays on sin and its
eternal punishment in hell fills many of his hymns and divine poems
with a repulsive gloom. Though he obviously accepts the doctrine of
predestination, however, he seldom explicitly refers to it. The book of the
fates of men is chained to God's throne:

> Not Gabriel asks the reason why,
>   Nor God the reason gives;
> Nor dares the favourite-angel pry
>   Between the folded leaves.

It is best not to be too curious about matters so far beyond the scope of
the human mind. We can only breathe an humble prayer for mercy and
keep ourselves as spotless as we can until death reveals what has been
ordained for us:

> My God, I never long'd to see
> My fate with curious eyes,
> What gloomy lines are writ for me,
> Or what bright scenes shall rise.

---

[39] He believed that the only *established* church should be based on the principles of
natural religion, to which he attached much importance. Bradbury, his fellow-Independent,
accused him of Socinianism. The charge was probably unjust, but it appears that Watts
found it difficult to believe in the full personality of the Holy Spirit, and that this
in turn gave him a somewhat uncertain conception of the Trinity which led some of his
contemporaries to regard him as an Arian.

> In thy fair book of Life and Grace
> May I but find my name
> Recorded in some humble place
> Beneath my Lord the Lamb.[40]

The absolute inscrutability of God, indeed, is one of Watts's favorite themes. Far more than most men of his time he is imbued with the sense of mystery. "Thine essence is a vast abyss," he cries to God;

> In vain our haughty reason swells,
> For nothing's found in thee
> But boundless inconceivables,
> And vast eternity.[41]

To judge from the images which abound in his poems, Watts must have been a keen and loving observer of nature. He thinks of nature as offering constant homage to God:

> The lark mounts up the sky,
> With unambitious song,
> And bears her Maker's praise on high
> Upon her artless tongue.[42]

Nevertheless he is not one of those who confidently use the creation as a means of explaining the Creator. God and nature have nothing in common except in the sense that nature bears witness to the divine power:

> Thy voice produc'd the seas and spheres,
> Bid the waves roar, and planets shine;
> But nothing like thy Self appears,
> Through all these spacious works of thine.
>
> .   .   .   .   .
>
> None but thy wisdom knows thy might,
> None but thy word can speak thy name.[43]

Far from agreeing with the Newtonian conception of God as a celestial mechanic hired by the universe to keep it in running order, Watts insists upon *God's Absolute Dominion*:

> Nature, compell'd by a superior cause,
> Now breaks her own eternal laws,
> Now seems to break them, and obeys
> Her sovereign King in different ways.

[40] *God's Dominion and Decrees.*
[41] *The Infinite.* Emily Dickinson might have written the last two lines of this stanza.
[42] *Sincere Praise.*   [43] *The Creator and Creatures.*

Father, how bright thy glories shine!
How broad thy kingdom, how divine!
Nature, and Miracle, and Fate, and Chance, are thine.

Since the Christian revelation declares that this inscrutable and almighty power hates and punishes human sin, and that a large proportion of the human race is foredoomed to damnation no matter how virtuous their conduct may appear in the eyes of men, fear is an important element in Watts's religion. He cannot turn his eyes away from the dreadful pit:

Hark, the shrill outcries of the guilty wretches!
Lively bright horrour, and amazing anguish,
Stare through their eye-lids, while the living worm lies
    Gnawing within them.

.   .   .   .

Hopeless immortals! how they scream and shiver,
While devils push them to the pit wide yawning
Hideous and gloomy to receive them headlong
    Down to the centre! [44]

This is a note which we must expect to hear frequently struck in the work of a Calvinist. It is hard to forgive Watts, however, for scaring little children with poems like *Heaven and Hell*:

There is beyond the sky
    A Heaven of joy and love;
And holy children when they die
    Go to that world above.

There is a dreadful Hell,
    And everlasting pains;
There sinners must with devils dwell
    In darkness, fire, and chains.

.   .   .   .

Then will I read and pray,
    While I have life and breath;
Lest I should be cut off to-day,
    And sent t'eternal death.

And the child who has been forced to memorize such lines is expected to rise on Sunday morning happily exclaiming,

[44] *The Day of Judgment.*

> I'll leave my sport, to read and pray,
> And so prepare for Heaven:
> O may I love this blessed day
> The best of all the seven! [45]

But Watts scared children only because he longed to snatch them from hell before it was too late. He loved them—loved them even too much, he sometimes thought, for his soul's good:

> Nature has soft but powerful bands,
> And Reason she controls;
> While children with their little hands
> Hang closest to our souls.
>
> Thoughtless they act th' old Serpent's part;
> What tempting things they be!
> Lord, how they twine about our heart,
> And draw it off from thee! [46]

Perhaps his child psychology was not so absurd as it may appear. Children loved to be scared a little: it appeals to their sense of drama. Lady Hertford wrote to Watts: "I assure you my little boy is grown a great proficient in your songs for children, and sings them with pleasure." [47] Of course it is possible that the young Viscount Beauchamp's pleasure was derived mainly from the milder and more whimsical pieces in *Divine Songs for Children*. Some of these, like "How doth the little busy bee," " 'Twas the voice of the sluggard," and "Let dogs delight to bark and bite," are pleasant enough. And *A Summer Evening* has often been praised for its comparison of the Christian's life to the sun which rises in mist but sets in a glory of purple and gold.

In fact the hell-fire side of Watts, although certainly prominent, has been somewhat exaggerated by modern students who are astounded at the notion that our conduct in this life has any relation to our state in the next. There was much love in the man, and much love in the God whom he worshipped. Poems of mingled fear and joy are more common in his work than poems of unrelieved gloom. Despite the grimness of its opening stanzas, *The Day of Judgment* ends with a glad hope. When the sense of guilt oppresses him, he remembers that

[45] *For the Lord's-Day Morning.*
[46] *The Hazard of Loving the Creatures.*
[47] Quoted by Thomas Wright, *Isaac Watts and Contemporary Hymn-Writers*, p. 148.

> Jesus the Saviour stands
> To court me from above,
> And looks and spreads his wounded hands,
> And shows the prints of love.[48]

Nor can the Father who gave his Son be only a God of fear:

> Destruction waits t' obey his frown,
> And Heaven attends his smile;
> A wreath of lightning arms his crown,
> But love adorns it still.[49]

And not a few of the poems are wholly sanguine in spirit. Watts often thinks of the joys of heaven, where the Saviour

> ... scatters infinite delights
> On all the happy minds.[50]

In *The Law and the Gospel*, he contrasts the thunders of Sinai with Christ's merciful love:

> Go you that rest upon the law,
> And toil, and seek salvation there;
> Look to the flames that Moses saw,
> And shrink, and tremble, and despair.
>
> But I'll retire beneath the cross:
> Saviour, at thy dear feet I'll lie;
> And the keen sword that justice draws,
> Flaming and red, shall pass me by.

For one who believes that strict justice would damn us all, the implications of Calvinism are not altogether sombre, for predestination at least holds out the hope of a mercy absolutely unrelated to legal principles. There is a frightful peril, but there is a gloriously irrational chance of escaping it.

Watts's view of man as a weak, sinful worm is strangely mingled with a more or less transcendental belief in the greatness of the human soul and the powers of the human mind. This is by no means a prominent feature of his thought, but its historical interest justifies some attention. Exactly the same inconsistency appears in Edward Young.

True Wisdom, according to Watts, teaches that

[48] *Confession and Pardon.*   [49] *Worshipping with Fear.*
[50] *The Song of Angels Above.*

Heaven is my home, and I must use my wings;
Sublime above the globe my flight aspires:
I have a soul was made to pity kings,
    And all their little glittering things;
I have a soul was made for infinite desires.

The triumphant drive of the spirit toward the freedom and power of
eternal life constitutes *The Life of Souls:*

Sure there's a mind within, that reigns
O'er the dull current of my veins;
I feel the inward pulse beat high
With vigorous immortality:
Let earth resume the flesh it gave,
And breath dissolve amongst the winds;
Gibson, the things that fear a grave,
That I can lose, or you can save,
    Are not akin to minds.[51]

"Mind" and "soul" are apparently synonymous terms for a spiritual element which "reigns" over the physical.

Still more revealing is the poem entitled *Free Philosophy,* dedicated
"To the Much Honoured Mr. Thomas Rowe,[52] the Director of My
Youthful Studies." Here he cries out against the tyranny of custom in
the intellectual realm, asserting that "Souls were not born to be confin'd."
Rowe, who evidently encouraged his pupils to think for themselves, is
told that

Thy gentle influence, like the Sun,
Only dissolves the frozen snow,
Then bids our thoughts like rivers flow,
And choose the channels where they run.

Thoughts should be free as fire or wind;
The pinions of a single mind
    Will through all nature fly:
But who can drag up to the poles
Long fetter'd ranks of leaden souls?
A genius which no chain controls

[51] Thomas Gibson was a well-known physician to whom this poem is addressed.
[52] An uncle of the Thomas Rowe who married Elizabeth Singer. He was principal of a
nonconformist academy attended by Watts, John Hughes, and other students who later
became famous.

> Roves with delight, or deep, or high:
> Swift I survey the globe around,
> Dive to the centre through the solid ground,
> Or travel o'er the sky.

This doctrine of the free, unique, and creative mind seems to be related to Watts's idea of poetic inspiration. The poem just cited is an early plea in behalf of "original genius." The same feeling appears in *Two Happy Rivals, Devotion and the Muse,* where his "Pindaric song" is associated with the untrammelled liberty of the inspired religious bard:

> Loud as the noisy thunder, as a deluge strong,
> Are my thoughts and wishes free,
> And know no number nor degree?
> Such is the Muse: Lo, she disdains
> The links and chains,
> Measures and rules, of vulgar strains,
> And o'er the laws of harmony a sovereign queen she reigns.

Again, *The Adventurous Muse* declares that Urania cares nothing about rules, and scorns poetry which aspires only to be "correctly dull." "Give me," cries Watts,

> ...the Muse whose generous force,
> Impatient of the reins,
> Pursues an unattempted course,
> Breaks all the critic's iron chains,
> And bears to Paradise the raptur'd mind.

Evidently, then, this exuberant, quasi-transcendental element in Watts is related to his belief in the rights and powers of genius. Poetic and religious inspiration—divine madness and divine truth—are for him closely akin. He was a learned man, well able to draw from the past ideas congenial to his temperament. Apparently he inherited from the seventeenth century certain Renaissance critical theories concerning the poet as a priest and seer who expresses sublime truths under the influence of poetic fury. Here again Watts appears as an historical link, for in this respect he looks not only backward but forward to the romantic identification of the transcendental faculty with poetic genius. Such views are less inconsistent with Watts's theology than might at first appear. As a child of Adam he is a weak and helpless worm, but as one of the elect he is a being of goodness, freedom, and power, full of "the glorious liberty of the children of God." A kind of intellectual antinomianism combines with his Platonic doctrine of the inspired rhapsode.

Thus we are led to a consideration of Watts as a poet. He had more than one motive for writing. In the first place, poetry provided a means of externalizing his own strongly imaginative and religious nature. Even the hymns reflect the inward feelings of his heart. Secondly, he aspired to restore poetry to her original status as the favorite handmaid of religion. Thirdly, as a hymn-writer he hoped to increase the beauty and ardor of Christian worship. In 1700 his brother Enoch urged him to publish his hymns, complaining that in other hymn-writers he found " 'a mighty deficiency of that life and soul which is necessary to raise our fancies and fire our passions.' " [53] Finally, it was Watts's ambition to prove that the dissenters, far from being averse to the arts, could produce and enjoy good poetry and make religious use of it.

That he had a well-reasoned critical basis for his work is shown by the Preface to *Horae Lyricae*. Though he is thoroughly steeped in Renaissance and seventeenth-century discussions of divine poetry, he has plainly digested his material and made it his own. The Preface, in fact, is one of the most significant documents in eighteenth-century literary criticism.

He begins by lamenting "that an art, inspired from Heaven, should have so far lost the memory of its birth-place, as to be engaged in the interests of Hell." The religious origin of poetry is clearly shown in the Scriptures. Pagan poetry, too, arose in connection with worship. "But some of the latter poets of the Pagan world have debased this divine gift; and many of the writers of the first rank, in this our age of rational Christians, have, to their eternal shame, surpassed the vilest of the Gentiles." So utterly corrupt has poetry now become that "some weaker Christians" suppose that all poetry is at worst vicious and at best trifling and frivolous. "They will venture to sing a dull hymn or two at church, in tunes of equal dulness; but still they persuade themselves and their children, that the beauties of poesy are vain and dangerous.... It is strange, that persons that have the Bible in their hands should be led away by thoughtless prejudices to so wild and rash an opinion."

Then Watts opens his Bible, and through comment and illustration proceeds to show that to scorn poetry is to scorn God's holy word. For the Bible is full of poetry, "and the figures are stronger, and the meta-

[53] Thomas Wright, *Isaac Watts and Contemporary Hymn-Writers*, p. 46.

phors bolder, and the images more surprising and strange, than ever I read in any profane writer." His examples are all chosen with a view to substantiating this statement. He is pleading explicitly for a reunion of poetry and religion, but implicitly for a bolder, more concrete, and more exciting sort of poetry than neo-classicism provides.

Boileau's objections to the use of Christian material in poetry are refuted not only by the writings of his own countrymen, Corneille and Racine, but by Cowley's *Davideis* and Blackmore's Arthurian epics. Norris's shorter pieces are favorably mentioned. John Dennis, whom we must consider later in this connection, is praised as a critic who has "made a noble essay to discover how much superior is inspired poesy to the brightest and best descriptions of a mortal pen."

The literary possibilities inherent in "the wonders of creating power, of redeeming love, and renewing grace" are recommended to modern writers. Treatments of such themes need not always be set in the days of the patriarchs or the martyrs: "Modern scenes would be better understood by most readers, and the application would be much more easy." Hence while Watts approves of Christian epic and tragedy of the seventeenth-century type he more warmly advocates a definitely modern religious poetry which will deal in a serious, lofty, and impassioned way with "the anguish of inward guilt; the secret stings and racks and scourges of conscience; the sweet retiring hours and seraphical joys of devotion; the victory of a resolved soul over a thousand temptations; the inimitable love and passion of a dying God; the awful glories of the last tribunal; the grand decisive sentence, from which there is no appeal; and the consequent transports or horrours of the two eternal worlds.... How might such performances, under a divine blessing, call back the dying piety of a nation to life and beauty!"

Such is the poetry that Watts himself undertakes to write. To what extent did he succeed? A good hymn should be singable. It should be not only religious but thoroughly Christian in doctrine and tone. Without being mere *pastiches* of Bible texts, the most successful hymns have been richly reminiscent of the Scriptures. But above all, a good hymn should achieve a balance between two opposing factors: without going beyond the intellectual and emotional range of the congregation, it should possess something of that individuality of thought and style which is essential to poetry.

Watts is by no means uniformly successful in meeting these requirements. He writes too much and too hastily. He is often dull, flat, and
prolix. He must have lacked the faculty of self-criticism, for he is sadly
uneven and fitful. One could draw from his work an excellent little
anthology of lines and stanzas without finding many entire hymns that
would be worthy of inclusion. But hymns are written for the people, and
the people must be allowed to judge of their value. Several of Watts's
hymns have held their place in various collections for well over two
centuries, and some of them are among the most famous examples of
the type—"When I survey the wondrous Cross," "Come Holy Spirit,
heavenly Dove," "I give immortal praise," "There is a land of pure
delight," "O God, our help in ages past," "From all that dwell below
the skies." He unquestionably raised the standard of English hymnody
and exerted a strong influence on the hymn-writers of his century.

In divine poems other than hymns, he tends to be either too pedestrian
or too flamboyant. He is at his best in simple devotional lyrics which
might be classified as hymns except for the predominance of personal
over communal feeling. His frequent attempts to write *geistliche Minnelieder,* however, are clumsy and sometimes offensive. Here for once his
sincerity seems to desert him: mystical love is not congenial to his nature,
but he feels that the theme is poetic and must be essayed. He is obsessed
with the notion that the pseudo-pindaric ode is the ideal form for the
exercise of original genius; but his *furor poeticus* is at best unconvincing
and at worst absurd. The *Elegy on Mr. Thomas Gouge* [54] begins:

> Ye virgin souls, whose sweet complaint
> Could teach Euphrates not to flow,
> Could Sion's ruin so divinely paint,
> Array'd in beauty and in woe:
> Awake, ye virgin souls, to mourn,
> And with your tuneful sorrows dress a prophet's urn.
> O could my lips or flowing eyes
> But imitate such charming grief,
> I'd teach the seas, and teach the skies,
> Wailings, and sobs, and sympathies:
> Nor should the stones or rocks be deaf;
> Rocks shall have eyes, and stones have ears,
> While Gouge's death is mourn'd in melody and tears.

[54] Thomas Gouge (1665?-1700) was a well-known Independent minister. He was the
son of the Independent divine Robert Gouge (1630-1705).

Heaven was impatient of our crimes,
    And sent his minister of Death
To scourge the bold rebellion of the times,
    And to demand our prophet's breath;
He came commission'd for the Fates
Of awful Mead, and charming Bates;
There he essay'd the vengeance first,
Then took a dismal aim, and brought great Gouge to dust.

When we have smiled at these lines, let us pause to remember that in this period a poet who "lets go" and is not afraid to make a fool of himself is rare enough to command a certain respect. And after all Watts does not often commit such atrocities. With all his faults, he has religious and poetic earnestness, he has a desire to sing, and he has an abundance of vivid, concrete images. While most of his contemporaries are versifying ideas, he is primarily engaged in the imaginative expression of strong feelings. In the works of what other writer who flourished between 1700 and 1720 shall we find stanzas like these:

Go, shepherds, where the infant lies,
    And see his humble throne;
With tears of joy in all your eyes,
    Go, shepherds, kiss the Son.[55]

There, like a trumpet, loud and strong,
    Thy thunder shakes our coast;
While the red lightnings wave along
    The banners of thine host.[56]

What Heavenly Man, or lovely God,
Comes marching downward from the skies,
Array'd in garments roll'd in blood,
With joy and pity in his eyes? [57]

Ye slumbering saints, a heavenly host
Stands waiting at your gaping tombs;
Let every sacred sleeping dust
Leap into life, for Jesus comes.

·   ·   ·   ·

[55] *The Nativity of Christ.*
[56] *A Song to Creating Wisdom.*
[57] *A Preparatory Thought for the Lord's Supper.*

> Our airy feet with unknown flight,
> Swift as the motions of desire,
> Run up the hills of heavenly light,
> And leave the weltering world in fire.[58]

The Day of Judgment, a particularly striking example of the vividness and intensity of Watts's best work, has already been quoted in another connection. When such writing is placed beside Garth's *Dispensary,* Addison's *Campaign,* or Pope's *Pastorals,* the intrinsic worth of Watts must be recognized as considerable, and his historical significance as very great indeed.

Like her close friend, Watts, Elizabeth Singer (1674-1737), who became the famous Mrs. Rowe, is firmly linked with seventeenth-century puritanism. In the reign of Charles II, her father, a pious dissenter of good Somersetshire stock, was imprisoned for his religious convictions. The girl's early environment was by no means one of ignorant and ill-bred fanaticism. Her father was a prosperous and cultivated man who enjoyed the friendship of Lord Weymouth and Bishop Ken. Reared on the family's comfortable estate near Frome, Elizabeth was well grounded in such ladylike accomplishments as drawing and music. French and Italian, too, she learned from Henry Thynne, the son of Viscount Weymouth.

A precocious child, she began to lisp in numbers at the age of twelve. In 1694 and 1695 she was the chief contributor of verse to Dunton's *Athenian Mercury,* and in 1696 she published her first volume under the pseudonym of "Philomela." Some of these early pieces were sentimental pastorals of the sort so popular among seventeeth-century ladies, and in graver years she regretted their worldliness; but even at the outset of her career she was primarily a religious poet.

According to her biographer,[59] Elizabeth Singer was not a "regular beauty," but she was decidedly attractive and had a fine head of auburn hair. Among her many admirers were such incongruous figures as Matthew Prior and Isaac Watts. In 1710, however, she gave her hand to Thomas Rowe, the learned young scion of another well-known nonconformist family. She was then thirty-six, and he twenty-three. When he

---

[58] *Come, Lord Jesus.* The second stanza is pure Blake.
[59] The memoir prefixed to the *Miscellaneous Works* of 1739 appears to be partly by Henry Grove and partly by her brother-in-law Theophilus Rowe.

died after five happy years, his widow retired for the rest of her days
to her Frome estate. There she gave her life to prayer and meditation,
church-going, practical charity, and the writing of devotional prose and
verse.

Such an existence is so repugnant to most moderns that they will
imagine Mrs. Rowe as a sour, gloomy prig. On the contrary, her spirit
was serene and she was probably very happy when she could forget her
lost husband. Despite her other-worldliness she remained a well-bred
elegant woman, and numbered among her multitudinous correspondents
many people of rank and fashion. Her letters show plenty of broad-
mindedness, humor, and frank humanity. Exacting in her demands on
herself, she was tolerant of others. Though she remained a nonconformist, she was well disposed toward all good Christians both within and
without the Establishment.

Mrs. Rowe's amiable and tolerant spirit does not prevent her from
thinking earnestly of "the four last things"—death, judgment, heaven, and
hell. In *The Conflagration* she essays, without much success, a sublimely
pindaric treatment of the familiar theme. The darker side of her faith
also finds expression in *A Description of Hell. In Imitation of Milton.*
Hell is a fearsome place

> Whence issue long, remediless complaints,
> With endless groans, and everlasting yells.
> Legions of ghastly fiends (prodigious sight!)
> Fly all confus'd across the sickly air,
> And roaring horrid, shake the vast extent.

Here, as in Catherall, a definite literary tradition combines with Mrs.
Rowe's religious feeling. Divine poetry is carrying Milton from the seventeenth century into the eighteenth.

But hell-fire plays only a small part in Mrs. Rowe's work. She is much
more herself in the numerous little meditative pieces which express some
aspect of her personal religious experience. Particularly striking in this
respect are the two series of short meditations entitled *Devout Soliloquies,*[60] which give the effect of a sonnet-sequence. The same tendency
to share her inward feeling with the reader, however, is strong throughout her writings.

[60] The first series consists of twenty-two poems in heroic couplets; the second, of forty-
two poems in blank verse.

Philomela is not philosophical nor even theological. Religious ideas, as such, are of small concern to her. She simply loves Jesus, and longs for union with Him. That of course is not her only theme, but it is the one which remains uppermost in one's mind after a reading of her poems. *Seraphic Love* is characteristic:

> How strongly thou, my panting heart, dost move,
> With all the holy ecstasies of love!
> In these sweet flames let me expire, and see
> Unveil'd the brightness of thy deity.
>
> Oh! let me die, for there's no earthly bliss
> My thoughts can ever relish after this;
> No, dearest Lord, there's nothing here below,
> Without thy smiles, to please, or satisfy me now.

In order to enjoy this spiritual love, it is necessary to withdraw from the crowd. Accordingly Mrs. Rowe is a great believer in meditative retirement. In the solitary grove she thinks much of the sins of the world, much of her own widowed loneliness, but mainly of the infinite spaces separating her from her Lord. But the Christian melancholy which mingles with her Christian joy is neither morbid nor, with rare exceptions, cultivated for mere literary effect. The serenely pensive twilight in which she moves is but the earthly shadow cast by the wings of an unattainable bliss.

The woodland scenes which surround Mrs. Rowe in her retreat are regarded as instruments rather than as ends. "Madam," she writes to a friend who has just gone to the country, "the woods and streams, and country scenes, to which you are now retiring, will yield, to a temper like yours, more real delights than all the noisy pleasures of the town; and yet, if there was no superior happiness to be secur'd, I should think plays and operas the height of human enjoyments. I can't be guilty of dissimulation, and pretend to an indifference for those entertainments, on any other view, but the hopes of something more noble and lasting, in exchange for present pleasures; otherwise the birds might sing, and the rivulets murmur at their leisure for me." [61]

But she liked the country better than this momentary hankering for the opera permitted her to realize. It not only shielded innocence, but bore witness to God's power and goodness:

[61] *Miscellaneous Works,* Letter XLI.

> Beauty complete, and majesty divine,
> In all thy works, ador'd Creator, shine.
> Where'er I cast my wond'ring eyes around,
> The God I seek in ev'ry part is found.
> Pursuing thee, the flow'ry fields I trace,
> And read thy name on ev'ry spire of grass.
> I follow thee thro' many a lonely shade,
> And find thee in the solitary glade.
> I meet thee in the kind, refreshing gale,
> That gently passes thro' the dewy vale.
> The pink, the jess'min, and the purple rose,
> Perfum'd by thee, their fragrant leaves disclose.[62]

Such moods never approach a pantheistic confusion of God and nature. It cannot even be said that Mrs. Rowe uses natural objects as a means of ascending toward the mystical experience. She regards the Creator of the universe with due reverence, but the true goal of her yearning is an

> . . . infinite abyss
> Of ecstasy and life.[63]

When she thinks of *that,* she sweeps physical things aside with an ardent scorn:

> What is the day? what is its useless light,
> Unless it shews me that transporting sight?
> No beauteous object smiles below the skies,
> To charm my thought, and fix my longing eyes;
> Celestial excellence my eyes inspires,
> And kindles in my breast immortal fires.
> Thou bright, unrivall'd object of my love,
> To thee alone my soft affections move;
> Thine are my rising hopes, my purest fires,
> My noblest wishes, and sublime desires.[64]

If Mrs. Rowe possessed a larger share of poetic power and of intellectual and spiritual austerity, such utterances might not arouse the suspicion that she tends to mistake earthly for heavenly love. Unfortunately there is something sentimental, hectic, and even a little sensational about her writings. This element contributed not a little to her great popularity. Her lines *On Heaven* describe the happy realms where

---

[62] *On the works of Creation.*   [63] *Devout Soliloquies.*   [64] *Ibid.*

> Fair spirits in melodious concert join,
> And sweetly warble their heroic loves.
> For love makes half their heaven, and kindles here
> New flames, and ardent life in ev'ry breast;
> While active pleasure lightens in their eyes,
> And sparkling beauty shines on every face:
> Their spotless minds, all pure and exquisite,
> The noblest heights of love prepar'd to act,
> In everlasting sympathies unite,
> And melt, in flowing joys, eternity away.[65]

Doubtless these spirits love God, but apparently they spend a great deal of their time in loving each other.

The *History of Joseph,* a long narrative poem in heroic couplets, tells the familiar story from the hero's birth to his rise to prosperity and power in Egypt. The author is not attempting to write a Christian epic, but provides a few heroic trimmings—a formal invocation of the Divine Spirit, a "Congress of infernal Powers" who plot and speechify, and so on. To Mrs. Rowe, however, Joseph's career is not so much an epic as a romance. The story of Potiphar's wife is so warmly elaborated as to suggest that Philomela is using Scripture as an outlet for emotions other than strictly religious. Though not published until 1736, the poem was written soon after her husband's death in 1715. Mr. Wright believes that in the character of Joseph, Thomas Rowe's "person is reflected as in a mirror." [66]

But it was the *Song of Solomon* which perfectly expressed the joys toward which Mrs. Rowe aspired, and paraphrases drawn from it repeatedly appear in her work. Sometimes they are lyrical:

> Ye pure inhabitants of light,
>   Ye virgin minds above,
> That feel the sacred violence
>   And mighty force of love;
>
> By all your boundless joys, by all
>   Your love to human kind,
> I charge you to instruct me where
>   My absent Lord to find.[67]

---

[65] The same conception of heaven is even more cloyingly set forth in her prose work, *Friendship in Death.*

[66] Thomas Wright, *Isaac Watts and Contemporary Hymn-Writers,* p. 103.

[67] *A Hymn. In imitation of Cant. V, vi, vii.*

Once the original is arranged as a pastoral dialogue between "He" and "She." The woman is made to say:

> But oh! what sweetness like his rosy breath?
> Not myrrh new bleeding from the wounded tree,
> Nor blest Arabia thro' her spicy groves
> Such fragrance blows. He all the silent night
> Shall lean his head upon my peaceful breast.[68]

Sometimes these paraphrases sound like unsuccessful imitations of *Eloisa to Abelard*:

> O! if you meet the object of my love,
> Tell him what torments for his sake I prove;
> Tell him how tenderly his loss I moan,
> Tell him that all my joys with him are gone,
> Tell him his presence makes my heaven; and tell,
> O tell him, that his absence is my hell![69]

Is this the Heavenly Bridegroom, or the dead Thomas Rowe? Elizabeth Singer was an attractive girl, vivid and strongly sexed, whose impulses were stifled by the puritanism of her environment. In early adolescence she sought an outlet in the writing of religious verse—an unforbidden form of emotional expression. When in danger of becoming an old maid she married and passionately loved a man, thirteen years younger than herself, who was snatched from her arms much too soon and a little too late. What more natural than that she should specialize in poems of mystical union and paraphrases of *Canticles*?

This interpretation possesses just enough truth to be misleading. Regarded from a long historical perspective, Philomela may seem to predict a stage in which religious faith will become merely one aspect of sentimentalism. She herself, however, has not yet arrived at this stage. Her shortcomings as a poet do not in themselves justify our questioning the validity of her faith. The trouble with her is not that she is a normal woman, but that she is seldom enough of an artist to convey her feelings through images instead of through languishing remarks *about* the inexpressible.

Granting that she had a good deal to sublimate, the fact remains that she met her difficulties with some success. And the main factor in the

[68] *A Paraphrase on Canticles. In blank verse: a Divine Pastoral.*
[69] *Cant. chap. V.*

sublimation is no subconsciously hypocritical desire to conceal her real feelings, but a genuine willingness to merge her love of Thomas Rowe in her love of God. Hence, although she is not a great religious poet, she is anything but a despicable one. She is a little too sentimental and too earth-bound to be a true mystic, but I am ready to credit her with a genuine aspiration toward what she calls the

> Immortal fountain of my life,
>   My last, my noblest end:
> Eternal centre of my soul,
>   Where all its motions tend!
>
> Thou object of my dearest love,
>   My heav'nly paradise,
> The spring of all my flowing joys,
>   My everlasting bliss!

Unless God is merely another term for the *libido,* the Being worshipped in this *Hymn* is not quite identical with Thomas Rowe.

The powerful influence of Isaac Watts may be illustrated by brief treatment of three minor nonconformist writers. Despite its rather misleading title, the *Hymns and Spiritual Songs* (1720) of Simon Browne (1680-1732)[70] consist entirely of hymns—chiefly of the sort which force the congregation to summarize points of doctrine crisply and systematically. The Preface, however, is of some critical interest, for it uses Watts's ideas on divine poetry in a defense of hymnody. Though anything but a poet, Browne has sensed the importance of the poetic element in worship. "The noblest part of divine worship," he declares, "is praise.... Poetry enlivens praise. What is written under a kind of inspiration may be recited in rapture. Lively thoughts, gay images, proper and florid diction, and easy flowing numbers, naturally strike and enliven the mind: And then is the mind most in tune for the work of praise, when its powers are in most vigorous exercise: When the thoughts are bright and intense, the passions warm, and the whole soul awake."

Browne is not one of those who regard psalmody as more justifiable than hymnody. If anything he inclines to the opposite opinion, doubting

---

[70] An Independent minister who became pastor of the Old Jewry Chapel in 1716. He published sermons and wrote against deism. In the Salters' Hall controversy of 1719, he was one of those who voted against imposing a Trinitarian test. He went mad in 1723.

whether all of the psalms "are still fit to be sung in Christian-worship."
At a time when an historical view of the Scriptures was still very rare,
he is something of a radical when he adds: "I see no reason, why Christians should be ty'd down to the use of forms of praise, that were
peculiarly fitted to a very different state of religion from their own, and
to many peculiar circumstances of a single nation."

As regards the accompaniment of either psalms or hymns by instrumental music Browne is more hesitant. Though he "will not censure"
the practise, he reminds his readers "that it is but too common and easy
for the sensual delight to drown the seriousness of the Spirit, and the
entertainment of the musick to extinguish devotion; and yet persons all
the while imagine they are in a temper of mind highly pleasing to God,
because they feel an uncommon satisfaction, and a sort of transport in
themselves." Even those most inclined to smile at Browne's puritan
scruples will grant that he knows something about the psychology of
worship.

Browne assures us that he wishes merely to supplement, not to rival, the
work of Isaac Watts, which unites "the lively imagination, and the devout
heart." His admirer is also trying, less successfully and not without some
qualms, to restore poetry to Protestant worship.

For fourteen years Thomas Harrison (1693-1745), like his father before
him, served as a Baptist minister in London; but in 1729 he conformed
and ended his days as vicar of Radcliffe-on-the-Wreke in Leicestershire.
All his published poems, however, were written before he joined the
Establishment. *Belteshazzar; or the Heroic Jew* (1727) I have not seen,
but his *Poems on Divine Subjects* (1719) will tell us all that we need
to know.

Since Harrison was born in 1693, these are the poems of a young man.
They are dedicated to his flock, "the Church of Christ meeting in Little-
Wild-Street," in the hope that they "might be useful to solid Christians,
and at once divert their Minds, and bring them under the strong Impressions of heav'nly Objects, and be instrumental, thro' the Agency of the
divine Spirit, for preparing them to sing the Song of Moses, and the Song
of the Lamb in the Kingdom of Glory."

He goes on to justify divine poetry along the lines laid down by Watts,
and refers his readers to the preface of *Horae Lyricae*. On the whole vol-

ume, indeed, the influence of Watts is strong. Like *Horae Lyricae,* it combines congregational hymns with sacred poems—chiefly pindaric odes —of a more personal and ambitious kind.

The hymns of Part I hammer away doggedly at fundamentals:

> Under the dreadful, fiery Sea,
> Held down in Adamantine Chains;
> The Criminals by Christ condemn'd
> Shall suffer everlasting Pains.[71]

But the title of *Repentance and Faith* points the way to a better hope:

> My Soul looks back, and views the Weight
> Thou, spotless Lamb, didst bear,
> Nail'd to the painful, shameful Tree,
> Naked in open Air.
>
> .   .   .   .
>
> To him I now all Praise ascribe,
> Who my Deliv'rance wrought;
> Glory to thee, O Lamb of God,
> Who hast my Ransome bought.

In Part II Harrison treats a variety of themes. Of course he sings *The Day of Judgment.* Richer in personal feeling are two poems of self-dedication and gratitude, *An Ode for the Morning* and *An Ode for the Evening.* The allegory of *The Spiritual Traveller* is faintly Bunyanesque. A wayfarer is hastening from Egypt to Canaan along a rough, narrow path hemmed in by thorny bushes. He prays that Jesus may guide him and protect him against the wild beasts.

The impulse to escape from a sinful world motivates several of Harrison's poems. Once he refreshes himself with *A View of Heaven:*

> M'aspiring Thoughts now on swift Wings
> Of stedfast Faith, and flaming Love,
> Mount to the King of Kings,
> Who dwells in pure, unmixed Light above.

He would gladly die in order to "enter that bright Place."

Rural retirement provides another form of release. *The Wish; or a Desire after Retirement from the Hurries of the World* is Pomfret's

[71] *Death's Approach to the Sinner.*

Choice rewritten in blank verse by a Baptist minister. His desires are a mixture of worldliness and other-worldliness. There must be enough money to spare him the necessity of working for a living and to enable him to be charitable to the less fortunate. His "little Seat" should be placed

> Amidst the fragrant Bowers, and purling Streams,
> Where the wing'd Choristers resort, and where
> In tuneful Notes they warble forth to him
> The Tribute of their Praise, who gave them Breath.

But his "unfrequented Grove" must be "Near some fair Town furnish'd with all Supplies." There he will go to chapel every Sunday, but on weekdays also he will think much of heaven and how to attain it. Not that worldly learning is to be despised: he will read deeply in classical philosophy and poetry,

> And when my weary Mind demands a loose,
> I'd have one fair, one kind, ingenious She,
> With whom to hold sweet Converse, till my Strength,
> By Contemplation long and fixed spent,
> Needful Recruits obtains.

The Dream indulges in similar longings, but ends with a sharp recall to actualities:

> But suddenly the pleasing Vision fled;
> Awak'd I lay lamenting on my Bed
>   That still I must remain
> Without Relief amidst perplexing Cares,
> Encompassed by num'rous hidden Snares,
>   And drag a heavy Chain.

He can only try to be patient and faithful until the end.

Though Harrison's verses have almost no intrinsic merit, one may at least say that he feels what religious poetry is, and strives hard to write it. His work deserves gentle treatment because of the extreme rarity of Baptist poetry during the 1700-1720 period. He expresses, however, none of the special doctrines of his sect.[72] Ten years after the publication of his volume he became an Anglican—and ceased to write poetry.

---

[72] To be sure he belonged not to the Particular but to the General Baptists, a denomination only slightly less "respectable" than the Presbyterians and Independents.

As an Independent minister, Samuel Say (1676-1743)[73] followed in his father's footsteps. At the Reverend Thomas Rowe's academy he was the school-fellow of Isaac Watts, whose friend he remained in later years. Another boyhood companion, William Duncombe, edited Say's poems in 1745. He is anxious to clear the author of any imputation of narrowness or fanatical gloom, insisting in his Preface that "Mr. Say had a Heart susceptible of every tender, social, and humane Passion." Theological and political controversies were distasteful to him. "He had great Candor and Good-breeding, without Stiffness and Formality, an Open Countenance, and a Temper always Communicative." Far from being an enemy of worldly learning, "he was well versed in Astronomy and Natural Philosophy, had a Taste for Music and Poetry, was a good Critic, and a Master of the Classics."[74]

This is an idealized but probably not a seriously falsified sketch of the best type of nonconformist minister in the first half of the eighteenth century—broad, amiable, well-educated, soberly and sensibly pious if not exactly aflame with zeal. The full self-expression of such a man in verse would be of some historical value. Unfortunately, as Duncombe says, most of Say's poems "were written in the Author's younger Years, chiefly as an Amusement from graver Studies, and never intended for the Press."

One "Cecilia" is the subject of a group of youthful "Love-Verses: Chiefly written in the Year 1701." "They contain," Duncombe hastens to assure us, "nothing but what is Chaste and Innocent." But on his twenty-sixth birthday, Say takes stock of himself and finds that he has been too much the slave of worldly desires. Henceforward, he declares in *Die Natali, 23° Mar. 1702,* he will dedicate himself and his poetry to God alone:

> Louder, already, sounds my tuneful Voice,
> Swells bolder Notes, and with more spritely Noise:
> High in the Air, disdainful of the Ground,
> I soar aloft, midst towĕring Eagles' sound,

---

[73] His *Poems on Several Occasions* appeared in 1745, two years after his death. Enough of them are dated to justify placing him in the 1700-1720 period. His editor, too, says that most of his poems were written early in his career.

[74] He really was "a good critic." The two essays printed with his poems, *On the Harmony, Variety, and Power of Numbers, whether in Prose or Verse* and *On the Numbers of Paradise Lost* are far ahead of their time in gra_p of prosodic theory and appreciation of Milton's technique. His classical interests are shown in a section of his poems, *Epistles of Horace in Blank Verse.* Observe the unusual choice of form.

There strike my Harp, and shake the trembling Strings;
Music, divinely sweet, Harmonious rings
Thro' all the Vault of Heaven, and thence rebounds,
Repeated from the Hills in glad redoubled Sounds.
O may I never, never hence descend!
But, like the Early Bird of Morn, still bend
Upwards my aëry Flight from Earth, and raise
In worthy Songs my great Creator's Praise;
His Praise, the only Subject of my Muse
Henceforth, that now shall genĕrously refuse
All lower Themes. No more in artful Strains
Cecilia's Name shall charm the listĕning Swains:
Ev'n She, whom impious once I did adore,
Of Heaven itself Neglectful, Now no more
Shall fill my Numbers, which in juster Verse
The Great Eternal Beauty shall rehearse.[75]

From these lines it is plain that Say associates divine poetry with rapt and passionate sublimity. The "Eagles" in the fourth line hint that he is thinking of Pindar. In his own sober verses, however, he is quite unable to rise to bardic heights. Rather more than half of his poems are conventional paraphrases of Scripture in hymn-stanzas. The original pieces, though competently put together, lack color, warmth, and energy of thought and expression.

According to Duncombe, Say was "a tender Husband," but tenderness is not quite the word for the lines addressed *To Mrs. Say, on her being Uneasy at the Author's going a Journey alone on important Affairs.* He informs Mrs. Say—did he marry Cecilia?—that God expects better conduct of a "Christian Wife":

> Cease, then, with vain foreboding Fears,
> With Parting Kisses, Flowing Tears,
> And Every Female Charm,
> The firmness of the MAN to try,
> And ev'n of all his Constancy
> The CHRISTIAN to disarm.

For all his breadth and moderation, indeed, Say is no vaguely beaming latitudinarian. He knows that Christ came into the world to save sinners:

---

[75] The diacritical marks over words like "towering" and "listening" reflect Say's disapproval of mangling words for the sake of metrical regularity. He believes in the principle of syllabic equivalence.

> We tremble when we view our Crimes;
> How Great the Guilt! how Vast the Sum!
> Oh! change our Hearts; forgive our Sins:
> Come, Jesus, Mighty Saviour, Come! [76]

But *Written in a Storm* shows that Christian experience is more than mere trembling:

> Sinners feel *only* Fear: Their Father's Voice
> The Righteous own; and *tremble* and *rejoice*.

These lines are rather above than below Say's average level of accomplishment. Like many people whose temperaments are primarily critical and scholarly, he conceived of a much loftier kind of poetry than he was able to write.

For a brief sketch of Quaker verse between 1650 and 1725 the reader should consult Luella M. Wright's *The Literary Life of the Early Friends*.[77] Here I shall bring forward only two poets of this denomination.

> Of Worship I presume to sing,
> Yet from the Nine no Aid implore,
> Shiloh's outvies Castalia's Spring,
> Assist blest Pow'r whom I adore;

> . . . . .

> Momus, be gone, fly all ye Vain
> Who the Wit of Poems place
> In florid Strains; my Muse is plain;
> Fine Cloth exceeds fantastick Lace
> On Kersey set; I leave those Flights,
> To such as Fiction most delights.[78]

This is fair warning from Thomas Ellwood (1639-1713),[79] Milton's Quaker friend. His sect was as scornful of poetic as of sartorial ornament. Ellwood says what he wants to say plainly and clearly, despite an occasional tangle caused by the difficulty of fitting words to rhyme and metre. He is so utterly sincere that he sometimes imparts an emotional experi-

[76] *The Conversion of St. Paul. A Hymn on Acts ix. 6.*
[77] Pages 131-135.   [78] *Divine Worship.*
[79] Perhaps too early a figure for inclusion in this study. But his poems were first collected and published in the eighteenth century, and he wrote a large part of his longest poem after 1700.

ence,[80] but generally poetic form is for him an obstacle rather than a congenial medium of expression.

Hence the posthumous *Collection of Poems on Various Subjects* [81] is interesting chiefly because every poem embodies some aspect of Quakerism. Ellwood traces maypoles back to the pagan cult of Flora, "a most lascivious Dame," [82] and arraigns the clergy as proud, rich, selfish, and lazy.[83]

Divine Worship shows his dislike of external forms. The acts of "legal Worship" exacted of Abraham and his seed

> Were Types of that eternal Good,
> To which the Gospel all invites;

but under the new, non-legal dispensation such observances are needless:

> 'Tis not the fatted Calf that skips
> Is offer'd now, but *Calves of Lips*.

The true Quaker ideal is set forth:

> This then of Worship is the Sum,
> To wait in Spirit on the Lord,
> That at what Time He deigns to come,
> The soul may hear His living Word,
> And with Alacrity fulfill,
> What He makes known to be His Will.

But in life's hubbub the still small voice of calm cannot always be heard. The blessed quiet of the Pennsylvanian forest is therefore alluring. Ellwood writes *To a Friend in America* that he dares not hope

> That to America I may be brought;
> Where I that peaceful Solitude may find,
> Which more than Riches would delight my Mind.

This Quaker would enjoy the American scenery without making it an important part of his religion. In *A Prospect* we see him walking at eventide by the margin of a brook,

---

80 To some extent at least he does so in *Divine Worship, Inward Peace,* and *A Prospect.*
81 London, n.d. British Museum Catalogue queries 1730.
82 *Floralia: Or, an Account of the Rise of May-Games, and May-Poles.*
83 *The bleating Sheep; or the Flock's Complaint of their Shepherds.*

> Whose crystal Streams so small did slide,
> As if they fear'd to be descry'd,
> Save that a Pebble, here and there,
> Whisper'd their Flight into mine Ear.

He takes "sweetest innocent Delight" in the birds, bees, and flowers;

> But stay'd I there? Oh no, my Heart
> Cry'd still, Give me the better Part;
> Let me with Him for ever live,
> That to these Things doth Being give;
> Exterior Things may please each Sense,
> And be enjoy'd without Offense,
> But nothing but a Power divine,
> Can make their Virtues truly mine.

These pleasant objects are meaningless unless seen, as Blake would say, "through, not with, the eye" of a man who has found God in his heart. And so the core of religion is *Inward Peace*. The title is self-explanatory, but the final stanza may be quoted to show Ellwood at his best:

> No Tongue is able to declare
> How dear to God His Children are;
> Only the Sense of it is felt,
> Which breaks the Heart and makes it melt.

Here Ellwood and the reader could part friends were it not for the fact that in 1712, the year before his death, he published *Davideis. The Life of David King of Israel: A Sacred Poem. In Five Books.* According to the Preface the first three books were written in 1688 and the last two in 1711. He had taken no more than a glance at Cowley's *Davideis* before completing his own work. He has now (1712) read Cowley's poem, and is glad that he has not done so earlier, "lest his great Name, high Stile, and lofty Fancy should have led me, unawares, into an apish Imitation of them. . . . I am not so wholly a Stranger to the Writings of the most Celebrated Poets, as well Antient as Modern, as not to know, that the great Embellishments of their Poems consist mostly in their extravagant, and almost boundless Fancies; Amazing, and even Dazeling Flights; Luxurious Inventions; Wild Hyperbles [*sic*]; Lofty Language: with an Introduction of Angels, Spirits, Daemons, and their respective Deities, etc. Which, as not suitable to my Purpose, I industriously abstain from."

The long-winded narrative is certainly as unbedizened as the severest Friend could desire. Here is Doeg slaughtering the priests:

> He, in their Blood, did bathe his reeking Blade;
> And, on the soiled Earth, them senseless laid.
> The bloody Wretch did them of Life bereave,
> And, in their warm Gore, did them weltring leave,
> All Man by Man: Nor did he leave alive
> One Ephod-wearer, out of Eighty-Five.

In the year following the publication of *Davideis* Ellwood was laid to rest beneath the turf at Jordan's. Old age, however, cannot be pleaded in extenuation of the lines just quoted; for they are found in Book II, written when he was only forty-nine. One concludes that Ellwood, a true Quaker, most closely approaches poetry when he looks within his own heart rather than outward upon sacred history.

A later generation of Quakerism is feebly represented by Richard Bockett the younger (1693-1721). According to the "Testimony" of his parents, he very early had religious experiences "wherein he met with that Peace and Satisfaction, as we conclude engaged him, in his very young Age, to write these Exhortations and wholesome Advice laid down in the following Lines, which came to Hand since his Decease, which we freely made publick, in Hopes it may be of some Service, especially to the Youth." Richard died edifyingly in 1721, but his poems were all written between 1710 and 1714—that is, between the ages of seventeen and twenty-one. Hence we are not dealing with the work of a mere child. His parents published the verses in a little volume called *Fruits of Early Piety*.[84]

Bockett is barely literate and quite without even such stirrings of imagination as might be expected of a pious youth of his age. At any rate humility is one of his virtues, as we may learn from a passage which somehow recalls Shakespeare's Athenian mechanics:

> I know my Matter's in a mean Stile pen'd,
> Neither did I in writing it design,
> To please the Critick, for I don't pretend
> To Wit or Learning, neither of 'em's mine.

[84] The British Museum has only the third edition, n.d., but conjecturally assigned to 1722 in the catalogue. Since Bockett died in 1721, the first edition presumably appeared either in that year or the next.

> The chief Design of these my Verses are,
>> That such as read them happily may End,
> And by the Deaths of wicked Men beware,
>> Whose Souls at last great Terror doth attend;
> But, that all may escape that dismal State,
>> 'Tis needful that we often think upon
> Our latter End before it be too late;
>> Time cannot be recall'd, when once 'tis gone.[85]

These lines express all that he has to say, though there are some special variations of the theme in his friendly admonition to a schoolmate who has been making faces at him in meeting [86] and in *A Word of Advice to the Batchelor:*

> In my Mind, a religious sober Wife,
> Should add much Comfort to a married Life:
> Which if young Men in marrying would obtain,
> Let them all high fantastick ones refrain.

Only once does this officious youth cease nagging at others and gets down on his own knees. *A Meditation* is a bad poem, but we shall not laugh at the lines,

> Oh! that sweet Solace, that unmixed Wine,
> Which thou the Lord art pleas'd to give to thine,
> Give me to drink thereof abundantly,
> That so my soul may be refresh'd thereby.

Fruits of Early Piety is almost completely lacking in distinctively Quakerish doctrine and feeling. Except for one brief passage about the Inner Light in *Some serious Observations* these poems might have been written by any ignorant and untalented young nonconformist. In the author's days the Quakers, grown prosperous and a little smug, were trying to live down their old reputation for fanatical enthusiasm. Richard Bockett was plainly brought up, not on introspective mysticism, but on the "Be good or be damned" principle.

Perhaps the most noteworthy fact about this volume is that it speedily ran through three editions. The phenomenon at once broadens and perplexes one's conception of the eighteenth century.

---

[85] *Some serious Observations of several Visitations of God unto Mankind; and the States and Conditions of some on a Bed of Sickness, with Instructions to the Ignorant.*
[86] *To I. B.*

I have reserved for the end of this chapter a man whose work points forward to later phases of eighteenth-century thought. John Reynolds (1666-1727) was an intelligent and learned Presbyterian minister, an intimate friend of Isaac Watts, and a Christian of warmly emotional piety. He wins at once our favorable attention by his admiration for George Herbert.[87] He greatly prefers him as a religious poet to Cowley, whose *Mistress* and *Anacreontics* have done more harm than his *Davideis* has done good. Herbert is imagined as warring against the pagan spirit in literature and restoring the original kinship between poetry and religion.

Though not prolific in verse, Reynolds himself acts upon the belief that poetry should be redeemed to spiritual uses. A handful of shorter divine pieces must be neglected to gain space for examination of *A View of Death: or, The Soul's Departure from the World. A Philosophical Sacred Poem, With a Copious Body of Explanatory Notes.*[88] This poem was several times reprinted and found a place in the third edition, 1719, of *A Collection of Divine Hymns and Poems.* The title-page of that miscellany describes it as "writ at the request of the late Mr. Locke"—a significant statement which I cannot corroborate.

Reynolds is both an earnest Christian and an earnest student of "natural philosophy." Hence, as he explains in his Preface, he has undertaken to write a poem at once philosophical and religious. He hopes that scientific knowledge is spreading rapidly, especially among young people. "It would enlarge the mind, lead us to the admiration of the Maker, and to religion, and employ the thought and time in pleasant speculations, that would mightily preclude the follies and vagaries of unthinking and unstudied youth."

The poet projects his imagination beyond the grave, never doubting that death will reveal the complete harmony of scientific and religious truth:

> Welcome, ah welcome rare informing light!
> That cures my old mistakes, and scouts
> My num'rous philosophic doubts,
> And chases all my scepticism quite!

[87] *To the Memory of the divine Mr. George Herbert, Author of the Temple.*

[88] J. W. Draper, in *The Funeral Elegy and the Rise of English Romanticism*, p. 184n, says that the poem was published in 1725 but that Reynolds died in 1703. Considering the ideas expressed, this would imply a startlingly early date of composition. But as a matter of fact—see *D.N.B.*—Reynolds died in 1727, and *A View of Death*—see British Museum Catalogue—was first published as *Death's Vision* in 1719. The 1725 edition is the second.

His disembodied soul will learn that since "attraction" is love at work in matter, the Christian God of love is the God of Newton's universe:

> Now the mysterious love I duly trace,
> That binds and acts the vast corporeal whole,
>   That plays the universal soul,
> Assigning all their order and their place.
>
>   .   .   .   .
>
> Yea his great signature the God of love
> Imprints on what is most unapt to move;
> Ev'n matter's self is urg'd with am'rous suit,
> Inclin'd, in all its parts, to mutual salute.

Throughout most of the poem Reynolds' practise is to suggest questions in his stanzas and answer them in his elaborate notes. These, as we should expect, refer to such authorities as Descartes, Newton, Locke, Ray, Burnet, Boyle, Derham, Dampier, Halley, Huygens, Liewenhoek, and Hook. Names less frequently found in physico-theological poems are those of Aristotle, Bacon, Ficino, Henry More, Glanvil, Agricola, St. Augustine, Richard Baxter, and his favorite George Herbert. There are numerous references to Scripture, but very few references to strictly theological works.

A question as to the nature of the soul will illustrate the author's curious method. The passage runs:

> What start will shake me, at the dread surprize,
>   To see an uncompounded-self arise!
> To see, what 'tis will then leap out alive,
> A novel self that must my self survive!
>   This indivisible, extended point,
>   That scatters life through every joint!

The note reads: " 'Tis plain, that here (in so abstruse a subject) several philosophies are conjoined and complicated. Some (as the Cartesians) suppose that the soul is an indivisible (almost mathematical) point. Others (as Dr. H. More) that it is (physically) indivisible, (or in their language, indiscerptible) though it have (as they call it) metaphysical amplitude. Some, (as the Cartesians, who call it res cogitans, or even cogitatio ipsa) suppose, it always thinks. Others (as Mr. Locke) suppose it may exist without thought. But its ability to think or not to think (sometimes, for no person can always stay his thought) may be as good a note of its incorporeity, as if it did always think." I trust the reader has followed this.

In his Preface, Reynolds urges that "natural phænomena are the subject of many scriptural songs; and what else but the basis of such phænomena must be the theme of the evangelical anthems, sung at laying the foundation of this system?" One such anthem appears in the poem itself, for we learn that at the Creation the angels sang:

> O, O, the treasures of eternal might!
> The magazines of boundless love and light!
> Though in our realm new admirations grow,
> Where immaterial wonders always flow,
>   Turn we aside, and stoop to see
> Now matter's maze, and multiform variety!
> Matter! whose dusky nature can surprize
>   Our shining intellective faculties!
> That gravels them with undissolved knot;
> 'Tis still divisible, and yet 'tis not;
> Bless us! how matter and its motion can
> In all the pomp of intricacy reign!

When pure spirit, a little bored with "immaterial wonders," bends down in admiration and almost in worship of matter, something like a revolution in religious thought is near at hand. But Reynolds' physico-theological enthusiasm is undisturbed by any glimpse of the future. Never doubting his orthodoxy, he wrote *A Confirming Catechism* (1708) and *Three Letters to the Deist* (1725). He was, indeed, an authority on angels, for he answered, also in prose, certain *Inquiries concerning the State and Economy of the Angelical Worlds* (1723). No one could be better qualified to tell what happened when the Newtonian stars threw down their spears.

Since a large amount of divine poetry remains to be considered in the following chapter, we are not yet prepared for anything like a complete summary, but a few facts may be drawn together at this point. Dates of birth and death available for twelve of the writers indicate that the group is somewhat later than those of the first two chapters. Only three were born before 1660; seven were born later than 1670, and three of these later than 1680. Thus more than half of these poets had not yet reached middle age by the beginning of the eighteenth century.

All the Anglican poets except "A Cambridge Gentleman," and all the Nonconformist poets except of course Mrs. Rowe and the two Quakers, Ellwood and Bockett, are clerics. Several of the Nonconformists we know to be Whigs, and that the others adhere to that party is a safe assumption. The Anglicans naturally show more variety in this respect. Ken and Norris are Tories. Wesley shifts from Whiggery to Toryism about 1702. Kennett, Catherall, and "A Cambridge Gentleman" appear to be Whigs. The Anglicans may be grouped as "high" or "low" according to their politics. Ken, however, is an Anglo-Catholic of the old school; and Norris, though his imaginative sympathies are "high," is theologically a Neo-Platonic latitudinarian. The Nonconformists include four Independents, one Presbyterian, one General Baptist, and two Quakers.

If Ken and Norris are set aside as seventeenth-century poets who serve to illustrate what the Queen Anne period had lost rather than what it possessed, the religious and poetic value of the Nonconformists appears considerably greater than that of the Anglicans. Deprived of Ken and Norris, the latter can produce no writer of real importance. Samuel Wesley the elder cannot be compared with Isaac Watts, or even with Elizabeth Rowe. In his special field of paraphrase Basil Kennett is praiseworthy, but not remarkable. In competition with "A Cambridge Gentleman" and Catherall, minor Nonconformists like Harrison, Say and Reynolds seem richly gifted. Though allowance must be made for the strong personal influence of Watts, one feels drawn toward the tentative conclusion that Queen Anne Nonconformity, smug and sleepy as it was, possessed somewhat more imaginative vitality than the Anglicanism of the period.

Without further comment, the reader is asked to remember the religious conception of poetry set forth in different ways but with fundamental harmony of motive by Ken and Watts, the Platonism of Norris, the sentimental strain in Mrs. Rowe, and the medley of science and theology in Reynolds' *View of Death*. These are clues which will prove useful when the plot thickens, as it is now about to do.

Chapter IV

MIDDLE-CLASSICISTS

THE PRESENT CHAPTER IS DEVOTED TO POETS WHO, THOUGH NOT SPECIALISTS IN divine poetry, practise that type to some extent and show a more friendly interest in religion than the poets of the first chapter. This loose classification comprises a few men who are anything but distinguished for the spirituality of their work and a few definitely pious writers who might almost as well have been placed among the divine poets. The others occupy various positions between these extremes.

We begin with a quartette of poets whose contribution to our subject is very slight. Thomas Rowe (1687-1715), the obscure and short-lived husband of Elizabeth Rowe, wrote a few mediocre poems which his wife's biographer characterizes as "the elegant amusements of some hours of relaxation from severer studies." [1]

The son of a dissenting preacher and schoolmaster, Rowe was himself a pious young man, but his piety did not get into his verses. *David's Lamentation over Saul and Jonathan* is a paraphrase. The very flat *Ode on Virtue* and *Ode on Liberty* reflect the tendency, later more common, to wallow in muddled sublimities about ethical abstractions. The former pays frigid compliments to a long list of virtuous personages; the latter, very Whiggish, praises ancient heroes who dared to oppose tyrants. His other poems have, if possible, even less relation to our theme.

William Tunstall,[2] while imprisoned in the Marshalsea for taking part in the Preston Rebellion, published *A Collection of Ballads, And some other Occasional Poems* (1716). These consist of trivial songs and jocular or complimentary occasional pieces. But in 1725, still a prisoner at the age

---

[1] *The Miscellaneous Works...of Mrs. Elizabeth Rowe* (1739), I, lii.
[2] Not in *D.N.B.* He called himself "Gent.," came from Yorkshire, and was born in or about 1665.

of sixty, he produced *St. Cyprian's Discourse to Donatus. Done into English Metre.* Cyprian's purpose, apart from that of displaying his excessively aureate style, was to emphasize the advantages of Christianity by describing the vices of pagan Rome, and Tunstall may have felt that much of the discourse applied to his own times. In his Preface he represents the Muse as appearing to him in prison, and bidding him turn from trifles to serious themes. A moment later, however, he admits, "I did it purely to divert myself in my Confinement, and for Subsistence to support me against the vast Expences of a Jayl. It prov'd indeed, a very hard Tugg."

This translation deserves mention only because of the paucity, during our period, of interest in the Fathers. At this time patristic lore is cultivated almost wholly by Nonjurors and by a few other High Churchmen who have retained something of the older Anglo-Catholic spirit. One might assume that since Tunstall was a Jacobite he was "high" in his ecclesiastical views. It is equally probable, however, that he was a Roman Catholic, for several Yorkshire Tunstalls were of that faith.[3]

For all I know, Samuel Cobb (1675-1713) may have been a man of exemplary piety, but his poems do not suggest that religion had much meaning for him. In 1695, while still a student at Trinity College, Cambridge, he published *Bersaba: Or, The Love of David,* a fifteen-page poem in heroic style. He confesses that he "took the hint" of the work from Beza, but asserts his essential originality.[4] Cobb's classical affectations deprive the story of all literary or religious value. David is called "Jessides," and the God of Love, described as the mightiest of deities, shoots arrows at him. Later, "the Father of the Gods" is angry at Uriah's death.

This writer's *Poems on Several Occasions* (1710) consist mainly of military pindarics and imitations of the ancients. He transforms three psalms into "irregular odes," however, and in *Of Poetry* emphasizes the religious origin of the art and the poetic qualities of the Old Testament. Elsewhere, too, religious themes, allusions, and metaphors are fairly frequent, but always to achieve a clever "turn" or an ingenious compliment. Thus he says of *A Lady, of a Voice incomparably sweet, who died Young* that her singing will "enhance the Blessings" of heaven; and Dr. Blow,

---

[3] This writer is not worth much genealogical research, but see, in *D.N.B.,* the articles on Cuthbert Tunstall (1474-1559), Thomas Tunstall (d. 1616), and Marmaduke Tunstall (1743-1790), all Yorkshiremen and Romanists.

[4] I have not investigated the extent of Cobb's indebtedness.

deceased organist and choirmaster, is a perfect subject for a similar conceit.[5] In political eulogy his piety sometimes becomes even more impious, as in these Whiggish lines from *On the Electoral House of Hanover:*

> If to a Conclave Modern Rome assign
> The certain Help of Influence Divine,
> God sure to this Succession gave Consent,
> And breath'd upon th' adopting Parliament.

Even his scanty divine poems seem written to parade what he considers a pretty gift for epigram. *On the Ceasing of the Oracles upon the Birth of our Blessed Saviour* concludes:

> The Delphick Priestess was no more inspir'd,
> Phoebus stood silent, and in Mists retir'd.
> More strong than Thunder were this Infant's Nods,
> That strikes the Lofty Temples, These the Gods.[6]

As for the deeper mysteries of religion, the vain attempt to solve them by the use of reason only makes one uncomfortable. Let them alone, and be cheerful in ignorance:

> Let trifling To[lan]d and his empty Tribe
> Presumptuously attempt to find
> The Counsels of th' Eternal Mind,
> And shallow Reason for a Rule prescribe.
>
> .   .   .   .
>
> To Wisdom Infinite we wisely leave
> What our short Opticks never can conceive.
> We justle in the Dark to know
> The secret Cause of Things below.
> And if We some small Knowledge get,
> 'Tis hammer'd out with Pains and Sweat.
> Then let old Nature's Mysteries alone
> To Ray, to Lister, or to Sloane;
> While thus more chearfully we sit,
> And taste the Season of the Year
> Beneath this spreading Oak, and hear
> The sportive Innocence of Wit.[7]

---

[5] *Amphion. An Ode on the Death of Dr. Blow.* Blow, choirmaster and organist at Westminster Abbey, was the teacher of Purcell.

[6] The same smart antithetical crackle is heard in *Descensio Sancti Spiritus.* I suspect that these religious epigrams are translations from some Latin poet of the seventeenth century. Nevertheless they reveal Cobb's taste in these matters.

[7] *To William Jordan of Gatwick, Esq. Horace's 9th Ode, B. 2d. imitated.*

Here he is freely paraphrasing Horace, but seems to have made the mood of the original his own. This lazily aristocratic scepticism falls strangely from the lips of a man whose father was a London cooper; but we may suppose that at Cambridge this young cockney, eager to resemble his social superiors, achieved a working compromise between religiosity and gentility.[8]

George Waldron (1690-1730?)[9] delights in saying "the right thing" about the birthdays, marriages, and funerals—especially funerals—of important persons. In such poems the triumphal reception in heaven is one of his favorite devices.[10] He might have been included in the second chapter, for his political interests are strong. An enthusiastic Whig, he smites the lyre in honor of George I:

> All hail, ye sacred Powers above,
> Exceeding full of Care and Love,
> Who have sent One to save us,
> From those who would enslave us.
>
> .   .   .   .
>
> Designing Papists smil'd to see
> Our near approaching Misery,
> While Protestants groaning
> Our Fate were bemoaning,
> Expecting all a Fatal Share,
> Till welcome News remov'd their Fear,
> That the base Act was ended,
> And the Scene would be mended:
> Thus George Great and Glorious
> Reviv'd the sweet Chorus.[11]

[8] Strangely, the *Discourse on Criticism and the Liberty of Writing* published with Cobb's *Poems* is an early defense of the rights of original genius. He transfers his Whig ideal of liberty from politics to critical theory. This independent spirit, however, is quite absent from his poems.

[9] A gentleman. He matriculated at Queen's College, Oxford, in 1706. Most of his life was spent on the Isle of Man as excise commissioner. His chief work was the prose *Description of the Isle of Man*. The *Compleat Works, in Verse and Prose* were not published until 1731, but most of his versifying belongs to the end of the 1700-1720 period.

[10] For example, in *A Funeral Poem on the ... Duke of Marlborough* and *A Poem on the Death of the Earl Stanhope*.

[11] *An Ode, Humbly devoted to His Most Sacred Majesty King George the First, On His Birthday*. Observe the curious mixture of pindaric ode and political ballad.

The "Base Act" is either the Occasional Conformity Act or the Schism Act,[12] both of which were repealed by Parliament in 1718. This event also furnished the occasion for one of Waldron's more ambitious poems, *Christianity without Persecution*. Religion, personified, declares:

> My Sons are born by Nature to be Free,
> Freedom of Conscience is True Liberty;
> 'Tis Romish Persecution to controul
> The glorious Operations of the Soul.

Rome, continues Religion, is her only real enemy, against whom all English Protestants should unite. The Trinitarian Controversy is an obstacle to this union and should be abandoned. Of course all Christians *should* believe in the Trinity, but this is no time to argue about it. Lesser mysteries—by implication the Eucharist is included—are not worth arguing about at any time:

> But Ceremonials no such Weight afford,
> They are but Customs, not th' eternal Word;
> Customs improv'd beyond their first Design,
> Beyond the Rule of decently Divine;
> Customs which have been made compelling Laws,
> For Persecution not a sacred Cause.

Rejoicing that bigotry has now been swept away, Religion congratulates Parliament on having the guidance of a monarch

> Who never cramps his Subjects' fervent Prayers,
> Nor from true Christian Zeal their Faith debars.
>
> . . . . .
>
> Methinks I hear the blest harmonious Choir
> Applaud his Wisdom, and your Zeal admire,
> Praise steady Protestants, of ev'ry Name,
> Because their real Faith is all the same,
> And Heav'n, and God, their Great, their Glorious Aim.

---

[12] For the former, *vide supra*, p. 74*n*. The Schism Act forbade anyone to conduct a school unless he had presented to a bishop a certificate showing that he had communicated according to the Anglican rite within the preceding year. The applicant was also compelled to sign a general declaration of conformity to the Anglican liturgy. The act was passed in the spring of 1714, but Queen Anne died on the day (August 1) when it was to go into effect, and almost no attempt was made to enforce it under George I. Waldron's poem should be compared with Nicholas Amhurst's *The Protestant Session*.

[16] *Vide infra*, pp. 179 and 367.

Religion is evidently a strong latitudinarian, and keeps her eye on the political situation.

In his only witty lines, Waldron refuses to range himself with those who might take as their motto:

> I do not love the Thing call'd High-Church,
> The Reason is, it is not my Church;
> Nor am I hearty for the Low-Church,
> Because I really am for no Church.[13]

But although his allegiance to Low Church principles is unshakable, he asks pardon

> ... if I prefer
> A High-Church Peace to Low-Church War.[14]

The great desiderata are not reprisals against the highflying Jacobites, but peace and Protestant unity.

A Poem, on the Parliament, evidently written somewhat earlier than *Christianity without Persecution,* casts additional light on the author's motives. Parliament, he says, has two great questions to consider: religious toleration, and the improvement of commerce. As excise commissioner for the Isle of Man, Waldron has a special interest in the latter. The relation between the two issues, though not explicitly shown, is obvious: persecution and sectarian strife are bad for business.

Rather surprisingly, Waldron's poems are not without traces of religious feeling. The paraphrase of *Psalm XCIII* is unimportant as evidence, but the paraphrase of *Some Versicles out of the Litany* is more striking in an age when efforts to distill poetry from the Book of Common Prayer are almost non-existent. The little poem ends:

> Save me, Coequal and Coeval Three,
> Great, Glorious, Wondrous, in thy Unity.
> Save me by that Effusion of thy Blood;
> Virtue immaculate, Thou Son of God,
> Blest Lamb, may thy dire Sacrifice appease
> Thy Father's Wrath, and I enjoy the purchas'd Peace.

That sacrifice and its benefits form the theme of *A Poem on Good Friday.* The day means sorrow, but it also means unspeakable joy:

---

[13] *An Answer to Mr. Burnett's Letter.* Of course Waldron may be quoting some contemporary squib. The lines are not very characteristic of him.
[14] *Ibid.*

> Now could I ever weep, but that those Eyes,
> Which saw their Saviour die, saw him arise.

I may be wrong in feeling that this poem and *A Poem, on the Parliament* represent radically different kinds of religion. In any case the inconsistency, if such it be, would probably not have been apparent to Waldron. It seems likely, however, that *A Poem on Good Friday* and the two paraphrases were composed some years earlier than the Church-and-State pieces. They may well date from his Oxford days, when he did not yet grasp the political and commercial importance of repealing the Occasional Conformity and Schism Acts.

Let us turn from these nonentities to a group of poets who for one reason or another are a little more rewarding to a student of our subject. John Philips (1676-1709), specialist in both comic and serious imitation of Milton's blank verse and a pioneer in the eighteenth-century *Georgics* tradition, was the son of an archdeacon and was himself regarded as a good though very convivial Christian. "We are assured by his friends," writes George Sewell, "that he intended to write a Poem upon the Resurrection, and the Day of Judgment.... Milton has given us a few fine touches upon the same; but there still remains an inexhaustible Store of Materials to be drawn from the Prophets, the Psalmists, and the other inspired Writers.... The meanest Soul, and the lowest Imagination cannot think of that Time, and the Descriptions we meet with of it in Holy Writ, without the greatest Emotion, and the deepest Impression. What then might we not expect from the believing Heart of a good Man, and the regulated Flights and Raptures of an excellent Christian Poet?" [15]

There is no reason to doubt the truth of Sewell's statement, which is corroborated by "Rag" Smith's elegy on his college chum and by Leonard Welsted's *Poem to the Memory of the incomparable Mr. J. Philips.*[16] Philips was only thirty-two when he died in 1708. He was a scholarly, self-conscious, fastidious writer, who might well have meditated a divine poem in his favorite Miltonic verse without quite daring to write it.

Cheated of this unwritten work, we are left with very little. *Cyder,* which might at least say something about "Nature and Nature's God,"

[15] *The Life and Character of Mr. John Philips,* in the third edition, 1720, of Philips' *Poems on Several Occasions.*
[16] *Vide infra,* pp. 179 and 367.

says nothing of the kind, but goes about its business of imitating the *Georgics*. In Book I the remarks on love and hate as elements pervading all creation and the praise of the simple life are thoroughly classical. His momentary enthusiasm for the marvels revealed by the microscope strikes a modern note, but science suggests to him no philosophical or religious generalizations.

Cyder does, however, provide evidence of Philips's Toryism. He regards Charles I as the "best of kings," a martyr slain by "apostate atheist rebels" who were inspired by the devil. He reminds the apple-grower that God will reward him if he pays his tithes and punish him if he does not. He regrets the disloyalty of the poet whom he apes so sedulously:

> Oh, had but he that first ennobled Song
> With holy Raptures, like his Abdiel been,
> 'Mong many faithless, strictly faithful found;
> Unpity'd, he shou'd not have wail'd his Orbs,
> That roll'd in vain to find the piercing Ray,
> And found no Dawn, by dim Suffusion veil'd.

The staunch Tory Churchman would be puzzled by this scrutiny of his work. Why, he might ask, should we expect to find any religion in Miltonic parodies and imitations of Virgil? Each type of poetry has its own requirements, and the place for religion is divine poetry. He was about to undertake that "kind" when consumption forestalled his "regulated Flights and Raptures."

The poems of Richard Lely [17] are chiefly translations, imitations, anacreontics, and occasional pieces. Two of the trifles are mildly obscene, but on the whole the author is a sober fellow. He abounds in ethical commonplaces and sometimes, without expressing anything that could quite be called religious emotion, displays a Christian point of view. He translates Rapin's eclogue, *Jesus in agro ludens cum Matre*. One of his occasional pieces is addressed *To a Contemplative Lady, With a Present of a small Amber Hour-Glass:* for the recipient, every grain of sand will be a prayer. Perhaps he is reciprocating the gift acknowledged in *To a Religious Lady, occasion'd by her Present of a Standish*. *A Thought on*

---

[17] Not in *D.N.B.* His *Poems and Translations* were published in 1723 and achieved a second edition in 1727. They give the impression that he was a "person of quality." To judge from his epistle *To Ambrose Philips*, he was a Whig.

Self-Resignation goes a little deeper, though with unfortunate results. He reminds us:

> Short the Duration of our human State,
> And scarce we breathe, e'er yield we must to Fate:
> Then, grant Affliction be our painful Lot,
> The Cup (tho' bitter) will be soon forgot.
> But Oh, How ravishing the bliss divine
> Which waits that Soul, who could with Joy resign!
> Whose zealous Mind, of future Ease assur'd,
> Content th' Award of Providence endur'd.

Such patient souls are received in heaven with special rejoicing.

Lely's work is too flat, faint, and clumsy to present a real picture of a mind. One imagines him, however, as a respectable Whig, far from other-worldly or enthusiastic, but quietly attached to a common-sense Protestant religion of good morals. His imagination is not kindled by his faith, but one must add that it is not kindled by anything.

It was largely because of his tragedies that Nicholas Rowe (1674-1718) succeeded Tate as poet laureate. Except for two or three pleasingly simple lyrics, his non-dramatic verse is negligible. He is one of those slightly sentimental writers who, although they have no real gift for the regulation neoclassical forms, lack the imaginative force to break out of the groove.

In his life of Rowe, Johnson says that he was "so keen a Whig that he did not willingly converse with men of the opposite party." It follows that he was a Low Churchman. Dr. James Welwood, in his *Character of Mr. Rowe,* reports that much as he loved the Church of England, he "never condemned those who dissented from it."[18] His private conduct was as highly moral as his writings, and he was a devoted reader of the Bible. Welwood is quite correct in saying that "there runs through all his Tragedies a strong vein of Religion and Virtue."[19] In his poems, however, he does not genuinely express himself. From the Latin of Johann Gerhard[20] he translates *On the Last Judgment, and the Happi-*

---

[18] *Miscellaneous Works of Nicholas Rowe* (1733), pp. xiv-xv.

[19] G. W. Whiting has suggested that herein Rowe is partly inspired by *Paradise Lost,* which had a marked influence upon his dramatic work. "Rowe's Debt to 'Paradise Lost,'" *Modern Philology,* XXXII, 278-279.

[20] A well-known Lutheran theologian, 1582-1637, who wrote some religious poetry in Latin. Cobb also translates from Gerhard a short ethical piece *On Contentment.*

ness of the Saints in Heaven. The poem is somewhat unusual in its avoidance of gloomy terrors.

On the whole Rowe's Whiggery is more obvious than his piety. *Ode for the New Year, 1716* is a laureate effusion presenting a sort of tableau in which the Church of England appears beside King George:

> On the monarch, standing by,
> Still she bends her gracious eye,
> Nor fears her foes' approach, while Heaven and he are nigh.

It is not surprising that he wrote a harsh prologue for Cibber's *Nonjuror,* stigmatizing these extremists as traitors:

> Why since a land of liberty they hate,
> Still will they linger in this free-born state?

Let them be off to Italy, the land of bigots and slaves.[21]

But mulling over these trivialities is unjust to Rowe. Those who wish to know him as he really was must seek him in his plays.

The accession of George I found George Sewell (d. 1726)[22] hastily scrambling from Toryism to Whiggery. In 1712 he had eulogized Harley in *The Patriot,* but in 1714 he wrote with equal rapture *Upon His Majesty's Succession.* The latter poem hails George as the true descendant of those original German champions of Protestantism, who

> ... soonest pierc'd the Church's darksome Gloom,
> And snatch'd Religion from the Chains of Rome;
> Taught Bright-ey'd Faith to soar above the Skies,
> And leave her Legends, Venerable Lies;
> Then Superstition, of a motley Hue,
> With all her Idol-Saints and Gods withdrew;
> While Hood-wink'd Ignorance her Reign resign'd,
> Reason resum'd her Empire o'er the Mind.

Sewell's two volumes of verse are stodgy and sober, much richer in "Reason" than in "Bright-ey'd Faith." One of the almost inevitable psalm-paraphrases of course appears. In the poetry of the period references to the

---

[21] He takes another fling at the Nonjurors in his epilogue to Mrs. Centlivre's *The Cruel Gift.*

[22] Son of the treasurer and chapter-clerk to the dean and canons of Windsor. After attending Eton and Peterhouse he studied medicine at Leyden and Edinburgh, receiving his M.D. at the latter. Despite this sound preparation he was not successful in medical practise and became a bookseller's hack.

Eucharist are so rare that the following lines from *On the Death of Mr. Hawtrey* may be noted:

> Ye Sacred Doors, his frequent Visits tell,
> Thou Court where God himself delights to dwell:
> Thou Mystick Table, and thou Holy Feast,
> How often have you seen the Sacred Guest!
> How oft his Soul with Heavenly Manna fed,
> His Faith enliven'd, while his Sin lay dead!

Perhaps some allowance may be made for the fact that Sewell is here lamenting the death of a pious man. When he writes *To the Memory of my dear Friend, Sir Samuel Garth,* he says nothing about religion.[23]

Sewell's only poem of real value for us is a four-page essay *On Conscience.* The pricks of conscience, he says, are inescapable, and often inflict bitter shame and sorrow. But conscience can equally well be a source of joy, for there are blessed moments

> When Man reviews himself with thought sincere,
> And sees his Actions fair, his Bosom clear;
> No unrepented trace of Sin behind,
> To taint and rankle in the fester'd Mind,
> The Soul well-pleas'd, its own fair Picture loves,
> And Conscience ratifies, what Heaven approves.
> Then Peace is sown within, the pregnant Seed
> Quickens with active Life, and Blessings breed;
> The Face with social Humour shines, the Eye
> Darts Joy, the Hand is ready to supply,
> And Heav'n is half obtain'd—before we die.[24]

In this passage the association of a clear conscience with active humanitarianism is significant. This is not so much the conscience of traditional Christianity as that of eighteenth-century sentimentalism—the spotless soul, smirking with approval at its own picture; its owner, his face beam-

[23] Sewell may have been more interested in divine poetry than one would judge from *Poems on Several Occasions* (1719) and *A New Collection of Original Poems* (1720), for according to *D.N.B.* "he contributed to, and probably supervised, a volume of 'Sacred Miscellanies.'" I have not seen the *Sacred Miscellanies* published by Curll in 1713, but observe that A. E. Case's *Bibliography of English Poetical Miscellanies* indicates nothing as to its editorship. Even if Sewell's contributions could be identified, they would be of scant importance.

[24] This poem is interesting enough to be worth dating. It appears on pp. 1-4 of *A New Collection of Original Poems, Never Printed in any Miscellany* (1720). I find nothing to indicate that it was published separately. It can hardly have been written much earlier than 1720.

ing with "social Humour" and his hand in his change pocket. Why should the Man of Feeling go to heaven? It is such heavenly fun to do good right here on earth.

Although a Scot, Dr. John Arbuthnot (1667-1735) was the son of a High Church clergyman, and he always remained a Tory with slightly Jacobite leanings. Furthermore, he always remained a Christian. Samuel Johnson honors him as "a wit who, in the crowd of life, retained and discovered a noble ardour of religious zeal." He also quotes the unsneering report of Chesterfield, who with Pope visited Arbuthnot on the evening of his death: "He took leave of us with tenderness, without weakness, and told us that he died not only with the comfort, but even the devout assurance of a Christian." The first bequest in his will reads: "I recommend my Soul to its merciful Creator, hoping to be saved by the Merits of Jesus Christ."

Late in life Arbuthnot composed a religious poem entitled ΓΝΩΘΙ ΣΕ'ΑΥΤΟΝ, *Know Yourself*.[25] The "advertisement" declares that it "contains some thoughts of Monsieur Pascal, which cannot make it less acceptable to the public."

In a general way, Arbuthnot's sceptical analysis of the weakness and the duality of man recalls the earlier chapters of the *Pensées*. It has been shown, however, that the poet is more substantially indebted to the *Entretien de Pascal avec Saci*.[26] One important difference observed by Mr. Beattie is that for Pascal man is a corrupt being, while for Arbuthnot he is a perfect being who has become corrupted.

In the opening lines unanswerable questions are proposed:

> What am I, how produc'd? and for what end?
> Whence drew I being? To what period tend?
> Am I the abandoned orphan of blind chance,
> Dropt by wild atoms in disordered dance?
> Or from an endless chain of causes wrought?
> And of unthinking substance, born with thought?

[25] It was first printed in 1734 with the statement that it "was wrote several years ago." Since it draws upon Pascal's *Entretien de Pascal avec Saci*, which was first published in 1728, it cannot have been written in its present form earlier than that year. At the cost of some inconsistency, however, I include Arbuthnot in Part I along with his fellow-wits of the Queen Anne period.

[26] L. M. Beattie, *John Arbuthnot, Mathematician and Satirist*, pp. 377-382.

> By motion, which began without a cause,
> Supremely wise, without design or laws?
> Am I but what I seem, mere flesh and blood;
> A branching channel with a mazy flood?

But this physician denies that his body is "that thinking I....I call it mine, not me." His mother is earth, but his father is God, who added to his unthinking flesh-and-blood an immortal soul. The dualism of human nature has distressing consequences. When his mind is revelling in "godlike thoughts,"

> Some beastly want, craving, importunate,
> Vile as the grinning mastiffs at my gate,
> Calls off from heavenly truth this reasoning me,
> And tells me I'm a brute as much as he.

The dilemma is potentially romantic:

> To bliss unknown my lofty soul aspires,
> My lot unequal to my vast desires.

It is the cry of Childe Harold and of René. "Man's unhappiness comes of his greatness," says Carlyle. But Arbuthnot's solution of the difficulty is not romantic, for the way out is through humble faith in the truths set forth by Scripture. There he finds what Zeno and Epicurus have been unable to give him—a satisfying explanation of human duality. Man, possessed of free will, turned away from God. And yet,

> Thou still retain'st some sparks of heavenly fire,
> Too faint to mount, yet restless to aspire;
> Angel enough to seek thy bliss again,
> And brute enough to make thy search in vain.
>
> In vain thou hop'st for bliss on this poor clod,
> Return, and seek thy father, and thy God:
> Yet think not to regain thy native sky,
> Borne on the wings of vain philosophy;
> Mysterious passage! hid from human eyes;
> Soaring you'll sink, and sinking you will rise;
> Let humble thoughts thy wary footsteps guide,
> Regain by meekness what you lost by pride.

Thus, in a spirit like that of Prior's *Solomon,* the poem ends. It may represent a passing mood, or may even be an intellectual exercise in setting forth arguments not extremely vital for him; but the personal religion of this physician, mathematician, and satirical wit was not improbably tinged with fideism. In any case, Arbuthnot has given us, with Pascal's help, a workmanlike statement of the sceptical approach to faith.[27]

In Chapter II, Abel Evans's *The Apparition* mingled with its Toryism an apparently genuine concern for morals and religion. Hence it is with hopeful curiosity that we open *Præ-Existence. A Poem, in Imitation of Milton* (1714),[28] which may be the work of the same author. In Havens' opinion this piece "is couched in some of the best blank verse written during the period.... In style and diction the piece is quite as Miltonic as in subject-matter; yet it escapes the pitfalls of tumidity and dull prose into one or the other of which most contemporary blank verse fell, and at its best is not without dignity and nobility of utterance." [29]

This praise is deserved: *Præ-Existence* is one of the best of the forgotten "Miltonic" poems of the century. From the religious viewpoint, however, the poem is a strange one. As it opens we see the exultant return of the angels from their victory over Satan. A few of the rebellious angels who have repented of their crime beg for mercy. The Almighty pronounces upon them a special doom, half-merciful and half-cruel. Unlike their hardened brethren, they will not spend eternity in hell. Instead, they will become men, the unhappy inmates of the earth which is about to be created. After having expiated their sin by enduring the dreariness of mortal existence, they may hope to be restored to angelic status after undergoing death. Despite the religious background and machinery of the poem, it seems to have been written chiefly to set forth the author's sense of the utter worthlessness of human life. Nor is there any suggestion that these half-fallen angels, now to be called men, are to raise themselves through faith in a Redeemer. Life is to be for them a prison from which death provides the only escape:

[27] It will also be remembered that Arbuthnot collaborated with Pope in *Esther, An Oratorio.*

[28] Not listed in *Halkett and Laing* or credited to Evans in the British Museum Catalogue. Printed without indication of authorship in Dodsley's *Collection.* Herbert Schöffler, in *Protestantismus und Literatur,* p. 81, assigns the poem to Evans. P. J. Dobell, in his very scholarly *Catalogue of Eighteenth Century Verse* (Catalogue No. 99, London, 1933), lists a copy of the 1740 edition, which I have not seen, among other works by Evans.

[29] R. D. Havens, *The Influence of Milton on English Poetry,* p. 109. Professor Havens says nothing as to the authorship of the poem.

... The blended loads
Of punishment and crime deform the world,
And give no rest to man; with pangs and throes
He enters on the stage; prophetick tears
And infant cries prelude his future woes;
And all is one continu'd scene of grief,
'Till the sad sable curtain falls in death.

A third group of poets falling within the scope of this chapter is of considerable interest to a student of our subject. John Pomfret (1667-1702) seems to have written nothing after 1700, but the great popularity of *The Choice* and to a less extent of his other poems throughout the eighteenth century justifies his inclusion.

Young Pomfret, the son of a Bedfordshire rector, did not wholly confine himself to divine poetry, but the main trend of his work is pious. Obviously an admirer of Cowley, in his pseudo-pindaric muse he soars to the most sublime themes—*Upon the Divine Attributes, Dies Novissima, On the General Conflagration*. In such poems he affects complete submission to poetic rage:

How my breast heaves, and pulses beat!
I sink, I sink, beneath the furious heat:
The weighty bliss o'erwhelms my breast,
And overflowing joys profusely waste.[30]

But the poems deny this claim to inspiration. Pomfret occasionally throws out a striking line or phrase, but on the whole, in this genre, he represents the metaphysical tradition in its death agonies. His craving to be pindaric conflicts with his dread of being absurd, and he never quite knows whether he is singing or arguing. At bottom he is a man of good sense vainly lashing himself into ecstasies which he does not feel. The ode *Upon the Divine Attributes* can reach no loftier conclusion than that "the only fountains of sincere delight" are "competence, content, and peace"—essentially the thought of his secular epistle *To His Friend Inclined to Marry*:

For that which makes our lives delightful prove,
Is a genteel *sufficiency* and *love*.

Pomfret's smug common sense, however, has done little to soften the rigor of his severe and rather grim piety. His faith gives him little joy, for he broods much upon that

[30] *Dies Novissima.*

> ...inexpressible, stupendous punishment,
> Which cannot be endur'd, yet must be underwent.[31]

He spurns the idea that the everlastingness of heavenly bliss is to be understood literally, while the everlastingness of hell-torment is not,

> Though none can give a solid reason, why
>   The word eternity,
> To Heaven and Hell indifferent join'd,
> Should carry senses of a different kind;
> And 'tis a sad experiment to try.

For some people, however, death holds no terrors. *A Pastoral Essay on the Death of Queen Mary, Anno 1694* depicts the late Queen's triumphant entrance into heaven. The blessed spirits are dazzled by "the excessive splendour of her rays." In life she had been a being of "virtue unmix'd," and hence she

> ...knew what best great Pan [32] would please
> And still perform'd it with the greatest ease.

This flattery prompts the conjecture that he is deliberately transferring the virtues of Mary, Queen of Heaven, to Mary, Queen of England. By this time the young writer of pindarics is eager to rise in the clerical profession, and the world is closing in on him.

The pieces mentioned thus far were all included in the 1699 *Poems on Several Occasions,* and it is known that most of the poems in this volume had been written before Pomfret left Cambridge in 1688. In 1700, he separately published three poems: *A Prospect of Death, Reason,* and *The Choice.* The first of these, if written after 1699, must represent a revival of an earlier mood, since in theme, tone, and form it closely resembles *The General Conflagration.* Pomfret hopes to give sinners a good scare by painting death in the sombrest hues. The poem looks backward to the puritan funeral elegies and forward to *Night Thoughts.*

Reason was written in 1700. The author partially accepts the sensationalism of Locke, but draws from that philosopher interestingly sceptical and pessimistic implications. Since William III had recently forbidden the further publication of controversial views on the Trinity, it was expedient to show the futility of polemics by showing the futility of reason. Pomfret writes, however, as if he had other than merely politic motives for this

---

[31] *On the General Conflagration.*
[32] The poem has a vaguely pastoral background.

treatment of the theme. What he calls "Infant Reason" is a "natural light," a universal gift of God. But as we grow up, "the cheats of sense" and "false opinions" quench the flame of this faculty. Vain the endeavor to compensate for its loss by gaining knowledge "from outward objects, and from sense," because

> Our prepossessions and affections bind
> The soul in chains, and lord it o'er the mind,

and we avidly adopt any "unexamin'd principles" which agree with "self-interest."

Formal education is no remedy, for it merely enforces custom and thus perpetuates the errors of the past. Book-learning is but "the idle knowledge of laborious fools." The dusty tomes of Aquinas and Scotus, the learned bickerings of Sherlock and South, only obscure the truth, "When passion or conceit still hurries us away," controversial points cannot be decided rationally. In short,

> How do we know, that what we know, is true?
> How shall we falshood fly, and truth pursue?
> Let none then here, his sacred knowledge boast,
> 'Tis all but probability at most;
> This is the easy purchase of the mind,
> The vulgar treasure, which we soon may find:
> But Truth lies hid, and e'er we can explore
> The glitt'ring gem, our fleeting life is o'er.

Such scepticism has brought many a man to his knees. Pomfret, however, is not a Pascal, a Dryden, or even an Arbuthnot. As a matter of fact, when he wrote this poem his faith lay behind him rather than before. His desire for "a genteel sufficiency" has conquered his fear of God. This distrust of reason is merely a way of rationalizing a cozy bourgeois Epicureanism.

We know what Pomfret wants in *The Choice*, that completely unromantic retirement-poem which comprised the ideals of so many of his contemporaries: an unpretentious but comfortable seat "near some fair town"; a garden, with a study full of classical authors; money enough to live "genteely, but not great"; a good plain table; a well-stocked wine cellar for temperately convivial hospitality; two male friends, with pleasantly balanced traits; one female friend to converse with—not too often; no law suits; and as he grows old, "some kind relation (for I'd have no wife)" to manage his affairs. Except for perfunctory recognition of the fact that these blessings must flow from "bounteous heaven" there is not a word of religion in the poem. The gloomily pindaric young Cambridge puritan has now become quite worldly enough, one would suppose, to receive a really good living. But a malicious report reached the ears of Henry Compton, Bishop of London, that "for I'd have no wife" implied a preference for a mistress; and when Pomfret died of smallpox in 1702 he was still a little country parson.[33] The story of his career is not lacking in irony.

Thomas Yalden (1671?-1736)[34] is another of those writers who carry the pseudo-pindaric tradition from the seventeenth century into the eighteenth. Like Cowley, he has a *Hymn to Light;* and like John Norris, a *Hymn to Darkness.* Somewhat more than half of his poems—fables and trifles excluded—are "irregular odes," but he errs in thinking himself qualified for success in this type.

Yalden's divine poems, which are few in number, do not seem to express a personal religious emotion. His High Church predilections sometimes come to the surface. Thus, although he admires Milton's poetry, he detests his prose, comparing him to his own fallen angels:

> Apostate bard! may not thy guilty ghost,
> Discover to its own eternal cost,
> That as they Heaven, thou Paradise hath lost![35]

And in praising the piety of the dead Sir Willoughby Aston, he takes pains to relate that

> The Liturgy employ'd his daily care,
> His public worship, and his private prayer:
> To all its rites conformity he paid,
> The service lov'd, and discipline obey'd.[36]

---

[33] In the year of his death he was instituted to the rectory of Milbrook in Bedfordshire. I do not know whether the change implied any substantial advancement. In any case it came too late.

[34] After graduating from Magdalen, Oxford, he took orders and received a Warwickshire living; but he was also a fellow of his college and lecturer in moral philosophy. Though involved in "Atterbury's Plot," he was able to establish his innocence. He was too "high," however, to hope for much preferment after the downfall of the Tories in 1714.

[35] *On the Re-Printing of Milton's Prose Works With His Poems.*

[36] *An Essay on the Character of Sir Willoughby Aston.*

But Yalden derives no real spiritual or poetic stimulation from his High Churchmanship.

This poet's two major efforts, *Hymn to the Morning. In Praise of Light* and *Hymn to Darkness* are strange compounds of Christianity and mythology. Light and Darkness are apostrophized almost as independent powers, with only the vaguest recognition of the God behind them. Criticizing *Hymn to the Morning* in his life of Yalden, Johnson rightly objects to the first line of the couplet,

> Awhile th' Almighty wondering view'd,
> And then himself pronounc'd it good.

"Infinite knowledge," growls the Doctor, "can never wonder. All wonder is the effect of novelty upon ignorance."

In *Hymn to Darkness,* by far his best poem, Yalden expresses with a kind of gloomy majesty his sense of the eternity, the power, the inescapable reality of the blackness which enshrouds human life. Darkness is "the great monarch of the grave and womb." From it we have emerged; to it, "where-e'er our souls shall go," our bodies shall return. The author of the *Dunciad* remembered the final stanza:

> Yet fading Light its empire must resign,
> And Nature's power submit to thine;
> An universal ruin shall erect thy throne,
> And Fate confirm thy kingdom evermore thy own.

This poem is Yalden's completest externalization of the pessimism which is the most obvious feature of his thought. In this respect he has been likened to Young; but his melancholy is not, like Young's, balanced by religious hope. One suspects that Yalden's melancholy is more physiological than spiritual. There is something cold, sluggish, and heavily bitter in his nature—distrusting this life without clear happy vision of any other life. *Against Enjoyment* provides another example. Our passions urge us toward illusory joys, but "Fruition only cloys the appetite." We are all like King Midas—when we get what we want we lament our success.

Even Yalden's scripture-paraphrases manage to express his interestingly unpleasant character. In *The Curse of Babylon,* a version of *Isaiah xiii,* he seems to revel in the vengefulness of the original. The second chapter of *Ecclesiastes* is rendered as *Human Life. Supposed to be Spoken by an*

Epicure. The "epicure" is allowed to preach his unbelieving and sensual philosophy with a force which almost arouses our suspicions of the author. Not until the close does the speaker drop his mask. Let us drink deep, he says, so that when we are dead,

> Then our recorded vice shall flourish on,
> And our immortal riots be for ever known.
> This, this is what we ought to do,
> The great design, the grand affair below!
> Since bounteous Nature's plac'd us steward here,
> Then man his grandeur should maintain,
> And in excess of pleasure reign,
> Keep up his character, and lord of all appear.

Since the relations between science and religion are of special interest to us, we may glance at the epistle *To Mr. Watson, On His Ephemeris of the Celestial Motions:*

> While your celestial bodies thus I view,
> They give me bright ideas of the true;
> Inspir'd by them, my thoughts dare upward move,
> And visit regions of the blest above.

But probably Yalden is just paying a compliment. At any rate, so far as one can judge from his poetry, which is unusually self-revealing for its period, his thoughts did not often soar to heaven. He was a loyal Churchman without much love, hope, or joy.

Nahum Tate (1652-1715),[37] the son of a puritan clergyman, was of course an all-around secular scribbler, but he was also a persistent writer of divine and semi-divine verse. As poet laureate he found the composition of elegies on Queen Mary and Archbishop Tillotson a task no less congenial than obligatory. Of the late queen he exclaims,

> Let Heav'n (with Heav'n she correspondence held)
> Say how my Saint in Piety excell'd.
> Its sinking Empire how She did support,
> And to a Sanctu'ry reform'd a Court.[38]

---

[37] Although primarily a poet of the seventeenth century, he produced enough work in the eighteenth to warrant his inclusion. I have read by no means all of his verse, but have sampled it sufficiently. The second part of *Absalom and Achitophel* has intentionally been excluded from consideration.

[38] *A Funeral Poem on Her Late Majesty of blessed Memory.*

His view of Tillotson coincides, almost point for point, with Samuel Wesley's. He praises the Archbishop as an eloquent preacher, "Courtly Familiar, and Majestick Plain," and as the hero who slew the dragons of Atheism and Popery. Tillotson was a great ethical teacher who

> ... Vertue in her native Beauty drew:
> Of her bright Paths a Prospect did display,
> Where smiling Peace and harmless Pleasures lay;
> Did straying Souls to her Enclosure bring,
> With charming Accents, such as Halcyons sing,
> Or Evening Zephyrs when they woo the Spring.
> Heav'n He describ'd as 'twere His native Home,
> And He an Envoy from those Regions come.[39]

But above all, of course, the lamented prelate was a man of moderation—

> Of Temper calm, and Sanatively cool,
> As Jordan's Current, or Bethesda's Pool:
> By Grace Instructed, and by Nature Mild,
> Nor relisht Life but when he *Reconcil'd*.

Close on the heels of these elegies came *A New Version of the Psalms of David, Fitted to the Tunes Used in Churches* (1696), in which Tate's collaborator was Nicholas Brady (1659-1726). The purposes of our study happily relieve us from the obligation of discussing this work with any thoroughness. The Tate and Brady version is certainly smoother, clearer, and more shipshape than the quaint and clumsy old version of Sternhold and Hopkins. It is also flatter and duller, less imaginative and less religious in feeling.

The same year saw the publication of *Miscellanea Sacra: Or, Poems on Divine and Moral Subjects*. Tate not only edited this collection but contributed nine of his own pieces. His preface shows that his plan was to issue an annual miscellany of divine and moral poems.[40] He wishes to draw people, especially the young, to religion through the pleasures of verse. "That Religion and Morality are capable of all the Embellishments of Poetry, has been confirmed by the Suffrage and Performance of the best Poets in all Ages. 'Tis there the Muses breath their native Air. After

---

[39] *An Elegy on the Most Reverend Father in God, His Grace, John, Late Lord Archbishop of Canterbury.*

[40] This project was never carried out by Tate. "Vol. I" of the first edition appeared in 1696, but no more was published. In 1698, however, this volume was reissued with additions. The title-page of a third edition, 1707, reads "collected by Samuel Phillips."

all their Prodigal pursuits of Vanity; 'Tis thither they must come, to recover Strength and Beauty."

Though neither strength nor beauty characterizes Tate's own contributions to this miscellany, three of them deserve brief mention. *The Blessed Virgin's Expostulation, When our Saviour at Twelve Years of Age had withdrawn Himself. Luke c. 2. v. 42* makes Mary think and speak like a character in some affecting tragedy of the period. She exclaims to her absent Son:

> Was it a waking Dream that did foretel
> Thy wondrous Birth? No Vision from Above?
> Where's Gabriel now that visited my Cell?
> I call—He comes not—flatt'ring Hopes, Farewell.
>   Me Judah's Daughters once Caress'd,
>   Call'd me of Mothers the most Blest;
> Now (fatal Change!) of Mothers, most distress'd!
>   How shall my Soul its Motions guide,
>   How shall I stem the various Tide,
> Whilst Faith and Doubt my lab'ring Thoughts divide?
> For whilst of thy Dear Sight I am beguil'd,
> I trust the God— But oh! I fear the Child.

A short poem addressed to the children slaughtered by Herod's command ends with the lines:

> If then 'tis Glorious to pursue
> His [Christ's] great example, what must be your Due,
> Who Dy'd for him before he Dy'd for you.[41]

The conceit is not lacking in religious feeling. One fears, however, that Tate got more real pleasure from writing *Upon the Sight of an Anatomy*. With a touch of macabre humor, he urges us to "converse" with the skeleton,

> ...and you will say
> You cannot better spend the Day;
> You little think how you'll admire
> The Language of those Bones and Wire.
> The Tongue is gone, but yet each Joint
> Reads Lectures, and can speak to th' Point.

Then he "improves" the main parts of the body. In life, for example, the eyes may have been either quick-sighted or dim,

---

[41] *The Slaughter of the Innocents. Matth. ii. v. 16.*

Yet if they were from Envy free,
Nor lov'd to gaze on Vanity;
If none with scorn they did behold,
With no lascivious Glances rowl'd:
Those Eyes, more bright and piercing grown,
Shall view the Great Creator's Throne.

As late as 1713, two years before his death, Tate still regards divine
poetry as an agent of religious conversion and moral reformation. In that
year, with the help of Edmund Smith "and others," he edited and wrote
large portions of a broadside periodical of moral and religious verse called
The Monitor,[42] "Intended for the Promoting of Religion and Virtue, and
Suppressing of Vice and Immorality." Evidently an outgrowth of the
moral reform movement of Anne's reign, *The Monitor* was published
"In Pursuance of Her Majesty's Most Gracious Directions." A long list
of bishops and other clergy, "besides Many of the Nobility, and great
Numbers of the Gentry," supported it by their subscriptions. Certain
benevolent persons sent in special contributions enabling the editors to
supply two charity schools with the paper.

The Introduction ... Humbly Address'd to Her Most Sacred Majesty
informs Anne that her piety has awakened Urania, the muse of divine
poetry. After stock remarks about the religious origin of poetry and its
present corrupt condition, the author—pretty certainly Tate—concludes
by exhorting Urania:

Fair Mourner Rise, Britannia chides your Stay,
Her Anna calls, Fair Mourner come away;
Our Queen, for Peace, did War's Alarms pursue,
And Peace, her Realms worst En'mies to subdue;
Not Born alone to Rescue, but Reform,
And strongest Forts of Desp'rate Vice to Storm;
And since no Foes such Ravages commit
As Poison'd Poetry, and Painted Wit,
Your Province is, with Salutary Verse,
Th' Inchantments of those Syrens to disperse;
'Till British Youth their Virtue shall Regain,
And Worthy prove of Anna's Sacred Reign.

[42] It appeared Mondays, Wednesdays, and Fridays from March 2 to April 24, 1713—
twenty-one numbers in all, plus an unnumbered introductory sheet. Each issue is simply
a sheet, printed on both sides, containing one long poem or two or three shorter ones.
Forty-one poems were thus published. There is no prose matter save a few editorial
notices to the public.

Some of the poems, such as *An Exhortation to the Youths of Great-Britain, The Swearer,* and *The Gamester,* are directly and urgently moral rather than religious. Others—*The Charnel-House, The Day of Judgment* —use pious threats to scare the reader into virtue. A few, like *Upon the Annunciation of the Blessed Virgin* and *On our Saviour's Passion* are attempts at divine poetry of a less instrumental sort. There is nothing to indicate the authorship of any of the contributions. The worst are a trifle below, the best a trifle above, Tate's average level. Most of them, however, sound very much like him.

Robert Southey quotes Oldys as saying that Tate was "a free, good-natured, fuddling companion." [43] Toward the end of his life he was so heavily in debt that he lived in the Mint to protect himself from duns. It is tempting to suppose that, having failed on the more aristocratic levels of literature, he tried to keep alive by dispensing cheaply pious verses to the lower middle class. But with all his faults Tate was reputed to be an honest fellow, and he may be credited with a reasonably sincere devotion to the sort of religion which he exploits. Despite his laureate admiration for Tillotson, he is much more of a puritan than a latitudinarian. In fact, although his poems are destitute of intrinsic worth, they are of some historical value as showing that the Low Churchmanship of his age was sometimes genuinely "low" rather than "broad" in the nineteenth-century sense. If Whig policies encouraged theological vagueness, the vices of the age sometimes encouraged a severer and more old-fashioned Protestantism as a weapon of moral reform. There was no complete gap between the Anglican puritanism of the seventeenth century and the Evangelicalism which arose later, in the second half of the eighteenth.

A familiar type in all ages is the morally weak man who has a sincere respect for religion and carries a bit of unused piety in his heart. Learned, witty, lazy, slovenly, and dissipated, John Philips's college chum and elegist Edmund Smith (1672-1710) was expelled from Oxford in 1705 and cast in his lot with the Whig group during the five shady years which remained to him. His scanty poems, most of which are in Latin, have but little pertinence to our subject. This amiable Bohemian, however, is wistfully impressed by the piety of his friend Philips, who at the time

[43] *Specimens of the Later English Poets,* I, 173.

of his death was meditating a poem on Judgment Day.[44] Nor, we may believe, was it merely for money that "Captain Rag" joined Tate and "others" in writing the poems of *The Monitor*.

As has already been explained, none of the poems in that periodical bears the name of its author; but remembering that Smith, the author of *Phædra and Hippolitus*, was much better acquainted with Greek drama than anyone else who is likely to have written for *The Monitor*, we may tentatively ascribe to him at least two contributions. Joseph and Judah fill a sheet with stichomythia in *Joseph's Discovery of Himself to his Brethren. Written in Latin by H. Grotius, imitated in Blank Verse.* Another blank-verse poem, *Upon the Crucifiction of our Blessed Saviour. A Dialogue between a Disciple and several Messengers,* is a "messenger scene" in the manner of Greek tragedy. Its dignified simplicity demands respect. The use of blank verse in both poems adds some weight to the ascription, for Smith's elegy on Philips, though written in the heroic couplet, decries the bondage of rhyme and praises the favorite verse-form of his idolized friend.

There would be pathos in the scholarly rascal's attempt thus to enlist his learning in the cause of piety and virtue. All this, however, is the merest guesswork. He may have written other *Monitor* poems, and may not have written these. All one can definitely say of Rag Smith is that he was a weak man who sometimes wished to escape from his weakness, but that neither side of his character found a satisfactory outlet in his poems.

The religion of Joseph Addison (1672-1719) had much in common with the pragmatic, ethical Christianity of Locke and Tillotson. The important thing was good moral conduct, not creeds or mysteries. But it was demonstrable that Christianity embraced the purest and most beneficent system of morals, and on this empirical rock the faith of Addison was founded. The simple fundamentals of Christianity were attested by documentary evidence. Deeper mysteries eluded tangible proof, but a sensible man would accept them because of their salutary influence.

All this sounds rather cold-blooded, and indeed it must be granted that Addison's religion was far from ecstatic. He maintained his temperance and lucidity even on his knees—even on that edifying but rather smug

---

[44] *To the Memory of Mr. John Philips. Vide supra,* p. 161.

deathbed. Yet we do Addison scant justice if we suppose that his faith was purely utilitarian and prudential. By no means a mere latitudinarian or Christian Rationalist, he had, as a matter of sincere conviction, considerably more traditional and orthodox piety than Locke. He believed that Christ died to save him, and felt a measured joy in that thought. At times his imagination could respond with decorous but genuine warmth to the emotional appeal of Christianity.

Addison's secular poetry contains nothing of importance for us. The reader who is sensitive to blasphemy will wince to recall the famous "So when an angel" simile in *The Campaign,* which implicitly deifies Queen Anne. The early *Song for St. Cecilia's Day at Oxford,* on the borderline between secular and divine poetry, is at least more religious in tone than most of these imitations of Dryden. But of course any discussion of Addison's verse in relation to this subject must be focussed upon his five famous "hymns." All of them appeared in *Spectator,* and each illustrates the text of the essay to which it is attached. Hence these poems are a part of the author's educative program: he seeks to show his readers the possibility of combining poetry and religion, and of relating the combination to the *Spectator's* norm of temperate good sense and morality.

Spectator No. 453 urges that gratitude, the exercise of which gives pleasure to every generous mind, should lead to religious rapture. And what more just and natural than that this feeling should be expressed in poetry? In this respect Christians should follow the example of the Hebrews. As an illustration of his meaning he offers a song of thanksgiving for divine guidance, *When all thy mercies, O my God.* Some readers of this book may have sung it in church.

Not rapturous gratitude toward God, but quiet trust in Him, is the theme of *Spectator* No. 441. Such trust is particularly precious in the hour of death. This thought is expressed in "a kind of Pastoral Hymn," a free and not very successful paraphrase of the Twenty-third Psalm. "He maketh me to lie down in green pastures," etc., is transmogrified into:

> When in the sultry glebe I faint,
> Or on the thirsty mountain pant;
> To fertile vales and dewy meads,
> My weary wand'ring steps he leads;
> Where peaceful rivers soft and slow,
> Amid the verdant landskip grow.

In his anxiety to show the suitability of Christianity for poetic uses, he
over-develops the pastoral side of the psalm at the expense of its spiritual
values.

Another *Spectator* paper, No. 489, includes a hymn originally written
to express his own gratitude on escaping from shipwreck in the course
of his early travels. In the essay he observes how often his religious imagination has been stirred by the majesty of the sea, especially during a
storm. He glances at his personal experience, but describes *How are thy
servants blest, O Lord* merely as "a divine Ode, made by a gentleman
upon the conclusion of his travels." The best stanza is probably

> For tho' in dreadful whirles we hung,
>   High on the broken wave,
> I knew thou wert not slow to hear,
>   Nor impotent to save.

In No. 513, Addison assumes the mask of the clerical member of the
Club. The good parson has been led to serious thoughts of death by an
illness from which he has only partly recovered. The hymn included in
his letter, *When rising from the bed of Death,* is the most definitely
Christian of Addison's divine poems. Earnestly and reverently it expresses fear of divine judgment, repentance, and finally hope of pardon:

> For never shall my soul despair
>   Her pardon to procure,
> Who knows thine only Son has died
>   To make her pardon sure.

The spacious firmament on high, Addison's best-known divine "ode,"
occurs in No. 465. The essay arrives at the point that habitual adoration
of God is the best means of strengthening one's faith. "The devout man
does not only believe, but feels there is a Deity. He has actual sensations
of him." And these sensations are likely to be stimulated by retired contemplation of God in his wonderful works. "The Supreme Being has
made the best arguments for his own existence in the formation of the
heavens and earth; and these are arguments which a man of sense cannot
forbear attending to, who is out of the noise and hurry of human affairs.
... The psalmist has very beautiful strokes of poetry to this purpose in
that exalted strain, 'The heavens declare the glory of God: and the
firmament sheweth his handy-work. One day telleth another: and one
night certifieth another. There is neither speech nor language, but their

voices are heard among them. Their sound is gone out into all the lands: and their words unto the ends of the world.' As such a bold and sublime manner of thinking furnished very noble matter for an ode, the reader may see it wrought into the following one." Then follow the well-known lines, for which Addison has prepared his public by a compound of rationalistic Newtonian Christianity, the contemplative-retirement tradition, a dash of orthodox piety, and the contemporary theory of divine poetry.

The still frequent use of this poem as a hymn is not altogether easy to understand. The words, to be sure, are dignified and eloquent; and the music to which they are usually sung fits them admirably. But the poem has a formal, cornerstone-laying quality which might be expected to militate against its success. Addison never intended it—or any of the other hymns, for that matter—to be sung in church. He thought of these poems as odes. Remembering that *The spacious firmament* has found its widest currency among the "broader" Protestant churches, we may ascribe its popularity at least partly to the fact that it is earnestly religious without being very specifically Christian. A man of the eighteenth century might say that it represents that religion of reason and nature upon which Christianity is based.

Though the poem is perhaps too familiar for quotation, the last stanza embodies a thought which may not have been noticed. Speaking of the planets, Addison says:

> What though, in solemn silence, all
> Move round the dark terrestrial ball?
> What though no real voice nor sound
> Amid their radiant orbs be found?
> In Reason's ear they all rejoice,
> And utter forth a glorious voice,
> For ever singing, as they shine,
> "The hand that made us is divine."

This reason which perceives a truth beyond what men call reality is not the reason to which Addison is usually loyal. In order to hear the divine poetry of the spheres, he must rise above the Newtonianism which inspired him to begin the poem.

But this passage, though not insignificant as an historical symptom, is too exceptional to be of value in the interpretation of Addison. On the

whole his divine poems bear witness to "the reasonableness of Christianity" in a sense very far from transcendental. Breadth without heresy,
strength without violence, beauty without mystery, faith without superstition, warmth without enthusiasm—such is the Addisonian norm. And
hence it is that these poems win our respect without deeply stirring our
feelings. The experience of reading them is like the experience of trying
to pray in a formal Palladian church of the period. Everything is decorously and rationally devout, full of good form and right feeling, but it
is not easy to find God there. Yet it must be granted that these poems
rather more than adequately express whatever is poetical in the Christianity of Locke, Newton, and Tillotson. Were they stranger, more self-
revealing, more passionately spiritual, they would not be the divine
poems of Mr. Spectator.

Several of the prose works of John Dennis (1657-1734) betoken his
interest in politico-ecclesiastical questions, in the moral-reform movement,
and even in theology. In *The Danger of Priestcraft to Religion and Government* (1702) he opposed Sacheverell's early activities, and in *Priestcraft Distinguish'd from Christianity* (1715) he branded the Jacobite
clergy as disciples of Antichrist. The reformer appeared in *An Essay
upon Publick Spirit; being a Satire in Prose upon the Manners and
Luxury of the Times* (1711). *Vice and Luxury Public Mishaps* (1724)
was a shocked attempt to refute Mandeville's paradox. The puritan and
the dramatic critic united in a severe *Essay on the Operas after the
Italian Manner, which are about to be establish'd on the English stage*
(1706).[45] Among the works of his last years were translations of two
Latin theological treatises by Thomas Burnet. From all this the reader
will perceive that Dennis was a Whig and a Low Churchman of the
half-puritanical, half-latitudinarian sort. To complete the picture, he was
the son of a saddler who was prosperous enough to put him through
Harrow and Cambridge.

Contrary to the expectations raised by the foregoing paragraph, very
few of Dennis's cumbersome baroque poems are strictly "divine." Indeed
one finds nothing of that sort except three paraphrases: of the *Te Deum,*
of the Eighteenth Psalm, and of a passage from *Habbakuk.* Nevertheless

---

[45] Nevertheless he defended the stage against Jeremy Collier and William Law. He
opposed operas because he thought them effeminate, frivolous, and "luxurious."

all of his poems display a more or less religious earnestness and strive for both spiritual and poetic elevation.[46] Even without acquaintance with his literary criticism it is easy to see that he has a religious conception of poetry and considers himself a *vates*. Thus in his longer, more ambitious pieces [47] Dennis is not merely flattering his heroes or decorating his lines when he regards events in the history of England as events in the history of Protestant Christianity.

Dennis is an admirer of the Renaissance Christian epic, and especially of Tasso and Milton. *The Battel of Ramellies* drags its slow length along in supposedly Miltonic blank verse with the aid of councils in hell, meddlesome furies, and guardian genii. Even into the epic, however, Dennis imports the *furor poeticus* of the pindaric tradition. When preparing to celebrate Blenheim in *Britannia Triumphans*, he fairly foams at the mouth:

> Begin my soul, and strike the living lyre,
> O raise thy self! O rouze thy utmost pow'rs!
> Contemn the world, and ev'ry thing below,
> And soaring tow'r above mortality,
> To meet and welcome thy descending God.
> 'Tis done. O raptures never felt before!
> Tempestuous whirlwind of transporting flame!
> O whither am I caught! O whither rapt!
> To what immense unutterable heights?

These amusing lines will remind us that the contemporary opposition to "unnatural flights" was powerless to prevent writers like Dennis from admiring a poetry of "transporting flame." Though quite unable to write such poetry, they believed that it *should* be written.

Somewhat less afflatic but valuable for the complex of ideas which it presents is *A Poem upon the Death of ... Queen Anne, and the ... Accession of ... King George.... With an Exhortation to all True Britons to Unity* (1714). Woe for the Queen's death changes to joy at the coming of George. There is jubilation not only on earth but in heaven. The spirit of William III now sees the fulfilment of all his labors.

[46] *Poems in Burlesque* (1692), that strange outburst of pedantic jocosity, is an unimportant exception.

[47] *The Monument* (on the death of William III), *Britannia Triumphans: or, a Poem on the Battel of Blenheim, A Poem on the Battel of Ramellies, A Poem upon the Death of ... Queen Anne, and the ... Accession of ... King George.*

Under great George will begin an era of unity in politics and religion. We shall have

> A Church in its own Excellence secure,
> Abhorring Violence, abhorring Blood,
> And mean Mistrusts, and vain fantastick Fears,
> Relying firmly on establish'd Law,
> And Promises Divine...
>
> . . . .
>
> The true Britannick Tory, and Church Whig,
> Mean nought but this, and therefore should be Friends.
> And the Dissenter from establish'd Rites,
> The sober, scrupulous, conscientious Man,
> In Principles political's the same:
>
> Let them be three by barbarous Terms no more,
> But by Affection one, and one by Name.
> Let them all three be to each other true,
> As to the original Compact they are just,
> And to their Country's Constitution true.

Without emphasizing the spiritual benefits of the new Hanoverian unity, Dennis declares that it will be useful for military purposes. And it will be even better for business:

> But when this glorious long continu'd peace
> Shall advance commerce to its utmost height;
> Base poverty, and baser passions then
> For ever shall be banish'd from our Isle.
>
> . . . .
>
> The merchant shall in sparkling ruby drink,
> And under golden canopies shall sleep,
> And balmy shall his slumbers be and long:
>
> . . . .
>
> And Virtue under Liberty grow strong.
> For ever property shall be secure,
> The publick credit be for ever fix'd.
> The busy Britons, like industrious bees,
> Shall drive the idle drones from forth their hive,[48]
> And idleness be deemed the source of every vice.
> Pernicious luxury shall be restrain'd

[48] How Mandeville must have laughed if he read this poem!

By wholesome and by sumptuary laws.

. . . .

Devotion to the Heav'n of Heav'ns shall soar
Upon the flaming wings of Charity,
And fall again in blessings on mankind.

. . . .

No passion here but Love shall reign, and Joy,
The lawful and the charming child of Love.
Each noble art shall flourish, as in days
Of great Augustus, or great Alexander.

Toleration, unity, internal peace, successful foreign wars, commercial prosperity, merchants snoring under golden canopies, liberty and virtuous activity, sound morals, "lawful" love and joy, the religion of practical charity, Augustan culture—all this without a trace of any vitalizing spiritual impulse. One could hardly find a more complete description of the Whig ideal.

In his own day no less than at present, Dennis was more widely known as a literary critic than as a poet, and his criticism bears directly upon our subject. The thesis of *The Advancement and Reformation of Modern Poetry* (1701) is clearly set forth in its sub-title: "A Critical Discourse in Two Parts. The first shewing that the Principal Reason why the Ancients excell'd the Moderns in the greater Poetry, was because they mix'd Religion with Poetry. The Second, Proving that by joining Poetry with the Religion reveal'd to us in Sacred Writ, the Modern Poets may come to equal the Ancients." True religion, Dennis insists, is not the enemy of the human passions. Her aim is rather to restore that harmony between reason and passion which was shattered by the sin of Adam. And this is precisely the aim of "the greater poetry."

The same ideas are expressed more systematically and with closer adherence to the ideal of "the rules" in *The Grounds of Criticism in Poetry* (1704). According to Dennis the divine art of poetry "is sunk and profan'd, and miserably debas'd," not because modern poets lack ability, but because they do not know the rules. He proceeds to enlighten them. "Poetry has two Ends, a subordinate, and a final one; the subordinate one is Pleasure, and the final one is Instruction." Now not only the subordinate but the final end is attained "by exciting Passion," for poetry instructs through the feelings.

Philosophy corrects passion through reason; poetry corrects reason through passion. "And therefore," since men are swayed chiefly by their emotions, "Poetry instructs and reforms more powerfully than Philosophy can do." But religion also works upon men's reason through their passions: the method of poetry is the method of religion.

There are two kinds of passion—vulgar, and enthusiastic. The distinction is not easy to grasp, but apparently vulgar passion is the immediate response to sense-experience. It "is moved by the Objects themselves, or by the Ideas in the Ordinary Course of Life. . . . Enthusiastick Passion, or Enthusiasm, is a Passion which is moved by the Ideas in Contemplation, or the Meditation of things that belong not to common Life. Most of our Thoughts in Meditation are naturally attended with some sort and some degree of Passion; and this Passion, if it is strong, I call Enthusiasm." Dennis's assumption that enthusiasm is a supremely desirable quality in both poetry and religion shatters our over-simplified picture of the Age of Reason.

The principal enthusiastic passions are six: "Admiration, Terror, Horror, Joy, Sadness, Desire." He proceeds to show "that the strongest Enthusiastick Passions, that are justly and reasonably rais'd, must be rais'd by religious Ideas; that is, by Ideas which either shew the Attributes of the Divinity, or relate to his Worship." Aristotle, Hermogenes, and of course Longinus are cited as authorities. Examples of great poetry inspired by religious enthusiasm are drawn from Homer, Virgil, Tasso, and Milton. Milton is by far his favorite source of illustrations, with Tasso a fairly close second.

We are to conclude that "as great Passion only is the adequate Language of the greater Poetry, so the greater Poetry is only the adequate Language of Religion; and therefore the greatest Passion is the Language of that sort of Poetry, because that sort of Poetry is the worthiest Language of Religion." The present extravagance and triviality of poetry must therefore be ascribed to its divorce from religion. Dennis rather acutely observes that "the modern Poetry being for the most part profane, has either very little Spirit; or if it has a great one, that Spirit is out of Nature because it bears no manner of Proportion to the Ideas from which it is forcibly deriv'd." In other words, the modern poet, having no religious enthusiasm, either does not attempt to be sublime or, if he *does* attempt to be sublime, has no genuine basis for the effort.

If poetry needs religion, it is equally true that religion needs poetry for "the offering of Praise and Thanksgiving, and several sorts of Prayer to God, and celebrating the Wonders of his Might. Because if the Ideas which these Subjects afford, are express'd with Passion equal to their Greatness, that which expresses them is Poetry." Not only is the Bible full of great poetry, but Christ's method of teaching "was entirely Poetical: that is, by Fables or Parables, contriv'd, and plac'd, and adapted to work very strongly upon human Passions." The cause of religion would be furthered if all the poetical parts of Scripture were rendered in verse by good poets. With astonishing *naïveté* he supposes that this would particularly attract the gentry, "For they of extraordinary Parts for the most part being extremely delighted with Poetry, and finding the greatest and most exalted Poetry upon Religious Subjects, would by degrees become more us'd to be moved by Sacred Ideas, than they would by Profane; that is, would by degrees become reform'd."

The essence of this hair-splitting analysis of imponderables is summed up by Dennis as follows: "The fundamental Rule then that we pretend to lay down for the succeeding or excelling in the greater Poetry, is that the Constitution of the Poem should be religious, that it may be throughout pathetick." [49] He forgets a rule even more fundamental: that the constitution not only of the poem but of the poet should be religious, and religious in a deeper sense than his own poem on the accession of King George.

Both the specific and the general sources of Dennis's views have been ably discussed by Dr. Paul.[50] Dennis, like Watts, inherits the Renaissance view that poetic and religious enthusiasm are closely akin, that the poet is a divinely inspired *vates,* and that the function of poetry is to instruct through delight. He was thoroughly familiar with earlier discussions of the relationship between Christianity and poetry.[51] The influence of Milton, Tasso, and Cowley seems to have been especially strong. Milton's entire career, of course, is a demonstration of the interfusion of the Platonic view of poetry with puritan religious feeling. In Dennis the Renaissance tradition has combined with the moral-reform interests of a sober

[49] By "pathetick," of course, he means "calculated to stir the passions."
[50] H. G. Paul, *John Dennis, His Life and Criticism,* pp. 120-140.
[51] All the essentials of his theory may be found in such seventeenth-century critical documents as the prefaces to Cowley's *Davideis* and to Edward Phillips's *Theatrum Poetarum.*

bourgeois Whig whose puritanism has acquired a slight latitudinarian tinge, and who, without being a neoclassicist in the strict sense, has all of the neoclassical passion for "the rules."

In Dennis's later years his reputation suffered as a result of quarrels with Pope and other wits; but from Dryden's death until about 1710 he was recognized as a leading critic, and even up to 1725 he had more admirers than detractors. It is significant that Thomson, Mallet, and Aaron Hill were among the friends of his old age. Dennis's not inconsiderable influence on other poets and critics receives attention in Dr. Paul's dissertation.[52] To his list of those who owe something to Dennis the name of Isaac Watts should be added.[53] But the direct influence of Dennis is not easy to estimate, for his chief importance lies in the fact that he represented tendencies widely current in the thought of his time.

One of Dennis's kindred spirits was Sir Richard Blackmore (d. 1729). The literary physician was angered by Dennis's *Remarks* on his epic *Prince Arthur,* but the two later became great friends and mutual log-rollers. The hardiest explorer of letters must shrink in dismay from the mountains of print which constitute the works of Blackmore,[54] especially since he is notoriously heavy-footed and long-winded. Modern students, however, should not be content to draw their impression of him from the mockery of his enemies, the wits. Professor Cazamian finds in his poems "a certain noble ambition, which is too frequently given over to edifying nonsense, and loses itself in arid deserts, but which shows itself capable upon occasion of vigour, of subtle and compact argumentation, of enthusiasm and eloquence." [55] This is a little more than just, but it comes closer to the truth than the undiscriminating abuse which usually falls to Blackmore's lot. Certainly, however great his artistic deficiencies may have been, his poems are a perfect mine of historically significant ideas.

Blackmore is shocked at "the Universal Depravation of our Manners, and horrible Contempt of Sacred and Divine Things." He is glad that William III "has been pleas'd to recommend from the Throne the Suppressing of Vice and Irreligion," and that Parliament has expressed "a

[52] *Op. cit.,* pp. 202-211.
[53] Dennis is favorably mentioned in the preface of *Horae Lyricae. Vide supra,* p. 131.
[54] I have not read all of his verse, but my bibliography will show that I have suffered enough.
[55] Legouis and Cazamian, *A History of English Literature,* p. 733.

ready and becoming Zeal for the accomplishing this Great and Good Design." [56] The reformers should turn their attention to the stage and to literature in general, since poetry, which could be a potent force for good, "was never in the worst of Times, or among the worst of Men, employ'd to more detestable Purposes than it has been by the writers of this Age." [57]

Against these licentious dramatists and poets and their admirers Blackmore launches his *Satyr Against Wit* (1700). It has become so fashionable to sneer at religion and virtue, he declares, that London teems with "Hypocrites in Vice" who

> To Wickedness pretend, that's not their own.
> A Bantring Spirit has our men possest,
> And Wisdom is become a standing Jest.[58]

He is hardly more alarmed by the irreligion of the wits than irritated by the frivolity with which they express it. To his sober and literal mind, their gay "turns" are not merely impious but irrational:

> The Mob of Wits is up to storm the Town,
> To pull all Virtue and right Reason down;
> Quite to subvert Religion's sacred Fence,
> To set up Wit, and pull down common Sense.

The rascals may urge that they aim to chastise the follies of the times, but surely

> Those who by Satyr would reform the Town,
> Should have some little Merit of their own,
> And not be Rakes themselves below Lampoon.

Not only religious but political considerations enter into Blackmore's views. In *The Nature of Man* (1711) as well as in the *Satyr* he insists that wit is a form of treason, for those who defy the laws of God will end by defying the laws of the state.

The inseparable bond connecting wit, irreligion, and immorality is as old as "Athens, whose refin'd Wits were plung'd in the most senseless

---

[56] Preface of *A Paraphrase on the Book of Job* (1700).

[57] *Ibid.*

[58] Here Blackmore is probably not glancing at any particular writer, but he may have Shaftesbury's *Letter Concerning Enthusiasm* in mind when he says in the preface to *Creation* (1712): "I know the gentlemen of atheistical notions pretend to refin'd parts, and pass themselves off on the world as wits of the first rank: yet in debate they decline argument, and rather trust to the decision of raillery."

idolatry." [59] In England the sinister alliance was given full scope by the Restoration. But conditions are even worse than they were in the days of Charles II, for we have moved from thoughtless libertinism to a more conscious and deliberate unbelief. "The atheist in practice is become one in speculation, and looseness of manners improv'd to intellectual impiety." Irreligion is now active and articulate, with its own bigotry and fanaticism.[60]

Literature is decadent because the great majority of writers are sceptics. She must be redeemed not only through frontal attacks like the *Satyr Against Wit*, but through the good example of religious and moral poetry. "I was willing," says Blackmore in the preface to *Prince Arthur* (1697), "to make one effort towards the rescuing the Muses out of the hands of these ravishers, to restore them to their sweet and chaste mansions, and to engage them in an employment suitable to their dignity." As the following pages will show, he made far, far more than *one* effort of this kind.

Although Blackmore was preaching the religious importance of poetry before Dennis published his *Advancement and Reformation,* the preface of his late poem *Redemption* (1722) seems to reflect the direct influence of his friend's theories. Here Blackmore represents himself as a lover of reason, but not a foe of passion. "Reason does indeed refine and exalt the passions; and on the other hand, the passions exalt reason, while, as active ministers, they carry it up in a flame of fire, and convey it in a sacred tempest to the regions of bliss. Thus reason and the passions mutually assist and advance one another, as the Author of them intended they should do, whence an harmonious dependence is preserv'd between them." For this harmony the sin of Adam substituted division and strife. Ancient philosophy could only increase the discord: the Stoical emphasis on reason clashed with the Epicurean emphasis on the passions. But the Christian Revelation has ended the war for those who believe in it. Far from condemning the passions, Christianity has taught us how to use them rationally, "in a just degree upon the proper objects. Immortal Bliss, the transports of glorified Saints and Martyrs, and celestial, ineffable delights are something else than oscitant contemplation, or the dry exercise of reason. By reason we may know God, but it is by love that we must enjoy him; when by this passion, refin'd and exalted to the utmost per-

[59] Preface to *Creation* (1712).   [60] *Ibid.*

fection, we adhere to the Divine Being, the Fountain of all goodness, we have then the fruition of Him."

Is not this that horrid thing, enthusiasm? Blackmore answers that the exercise of religious "love, desire, hope, and delight" within the bounds prescribed by reason "is so far from being a wild and extravagant temper of mind, that it is a most rational and praise-worthy enthusiasm, and the nearest resemblance of the happiness of the blest in Heaven, that we can find in this life. It is true, vehement emotions of monkish and fanatical visionaries, that are not rais'd by the force of reason, nor are govern'd and directed by it, but spring from the power of an overheated fancy, and the violence of strain'd contemplation, have brought an ill fame upon enthusiasm; but that word, in its genuine and original sense, signifies no more than an extraordinary, but regular passion, occasion'd by strong and lofty ideas."

If Blackmore resembles Dennis in his defense of enthusiasm, he resembles Watts in associating divine poetry with creative originality.[61] Dr. T. F. Mayo observes that Wotton's *Reflections upon Ancient and Modern Learning* (1694) "is full of indications that 'Modernism' in general was part of a Christian reaction against classicism." [62] If for "was part of" we substitute "was related to" or "overlapped with," we shall have an important fact which is clearly illustrated by Blackmore. Of course he advocates the use of Christian machinery in the epic,[63] but the question is broader and more fundamental than that. Christians, he repeatedly insists, should write Christian poetry. In all branches of the art we too slavishly imitate the ancients. "We have no Originals, but all Copiers and Transcribers," he cries in the preface of his *Paraphrase on the Book of Job* (1700). " 'Tis therefore to be wish'd that some good Genius, qualify'd for such an Undertaking, would break the Ice, assert the Liberty of Poetry, and set up for an Original in Writing in a way accomodated to the Religion, Manners, and other Circumstances we are now under.... What have we to do with Jupiter and Juno, Mars and Venus, and the rest? ... Are our Poets then so dry and barren, ... that they are not able to furnish themselves with proper Allusions, surprizing Metaphors, and

---

[61] No influence of Watts upon Blackmore is to be inferred. Blackmore's *Paraphrase on Job,* in the preface of which this view is clearly stated, was published in 1700, six years earlier than *Horae Lyricae.* On the other hand, it is possible that Watts was influenced by Blackmore.

[62] *Epicurus in England,* p. 195.   [63] Cf. preface to *Prince Arthur.*

beautiful Similes, without reviving the old exploded Idolatry of the Heathens? As in this Book of Job, they will find a Poem that is indeed an Original, and not beholding to the Greek and Latin Springs; so they will find, if it be not depress'd by the Paraphrase, a sublime Stile, elevated Thoughts, magnificent Expressions where the Subject requires them, and great richness and abundance throughout the whole, without the Aids of the Pagan System of Divinity."

Thus from Blackmore's puritanical dread of wit arises the conception of a serious, lofty, and non-witty kind of poetry—a Christian poetry of enthusiasm and originality. But his attempts to write such poetry are rare and unsuccessful. Not very surprisingly, he found it difficult to be enthusiastic without being "over-heated," to express spiritual raptures without suggesting "the vehement emotions of monkish and fanatical visionaries." It is significant that his strongest plea for originality should be prefixed to a volume of paraphrases.[64] The preface has more vitality than the contents. His *New Version of the Psalms of David* (1721)[65] is more dignified than "Tate and Brady," but too pompous for congregational singing. In original religious lyric he is flat when he is simple and ungainly when he soars.

The best that can be expected of Blackmore as a divine poet is to be found in Book III of *Prince Arthur*, where he describes the joys of the angels:

> Down from his [God's] throne, as light does from the sun,
> Rivers of fresh delight for ever run.
> With ravish'd eyes they drink in heav'nly beams,
> Which from his face flow down in glorious streams.
> They gaze so on the beatifick sight,
> Till they become all intellectual light:
>
> So quick they feel the mighty influx come,
> The most capacious, thirsty souls want room:
> They widen and extend themselves, to hold
> Those floods of joys, which to their breasts are roll'd.

[64] *A Paraphrase on the Book of Job: As likewise on the Songs of Moses, Deborah, David: On Four Select Psalms: Some Chapters of Isaiah, and the Third Chapter of Habbakuk* (1700).

[65] This collection was "Fitted to the Tunes used in Churches." Its use in congregational worship in the Church of England was permitted by order of the Lords Justices of the realm.

This scene is balanced by a conventionally terrific description of hell, which, needless to say, is full of "scoffers."

Of some interest also is the *Hymn to Christ the Redeemer* appended to *Redemption*. It bursts forth in praises which freely paraphrase Psalm CXLVIII:

> Praise him each vapour, that to heav'n aspires,
> Praise him, ye shooting stars and lambent fires:
> Ye storms of thunder, with your awful sound
> Make his loud praises sing in peals around.
> Ye soaring eagles, who the earth despise,
>
> . . . .
>
> Ye princes of the feather'd nations, raise
> To heav'n, as you ascend, the Saviour's praise;
> And all ye num'rous flying brotherhoods,
> That roust [sic] in rocks and hills, or seek the floods,
> That with your musick from the dewy grove
> Salute the rising sun, and you that rove
> From clime to clime, that high uplifted sing,
> Or sweep the ouzy shore with easy wing,
> Joyn'd with your chiefs, that dwell sublime in air,
> Of praising *Christ,* the Lord, the honour share.

Perhaps Thomson remembered these lines when, in language more poetical and less Christian, he hymned the God of nature at the close of *The Seasons.*

Literature was to be reformed by writing not only divine poetry but secular poetry imbued with a religious spirit. Blackmore's three epics, *Prince Arthur* (1695), *King Arthur* (1697), and *Eliza* (1705) are closely related to his campaign for the redemption of poetry. The preface to *Prince Arthur* declares that the aim of poetry in general and of epic in particular is "to give men right and just conceptions of religion and virtue, to aid their reason in restraining their exorbitant appetites and impetuous passions, and to bring their lives under the rule and guidance of true wisdom, and thereby to promote the publick good of mankind." In elaborating this statement he considers the epic as a religious or moral treatise in the form of an allegorical narrative. To paraphrase Spenser's prefatory letter to Raleigh, *Prince Arthur* might be called an attempt "to fashion a Protestant Whig or true Englishman in virtuous and gentle discipline." It emphasizes the religious element in the conflict between

Arthur—constantly called "pious" in a sense different from Aeneas—and the pagan Saxons. God and Christ support the former; Satan and his henchman Thor, the latter.

I have not read the second of the two Arthurian epics, but can testify that *Eliza* is rich in morality and sturdy Protestantism. Blackmore's no-popery heroine is Queen Elizabeth,

> Who zealous pure religion to defend,
> Did to the Belgick Shore her Cohorts send,
> To save reform'd Batavia, and restrain
> The persecuting rage of superstitious Spain.

The Armada also figures importantly. The machinery is what one would expect. Christ, for example, bids Gabriel, England's guardian angel, warn Elizabeth not to trust the Spanish: "Those who have me betray'd, will her betray." At a feast held in Book VII, Spenser appears as an Homeric bard to summarize sacred history from the revolt of Satan down to Deborah, who rejoiced in the drowning of the Egyptians as Elizabeth now rejoices in the destruction of the Armada.

In Book VIII Elizabeth, like Milton's Adam, is vouchsafed a vision of the future. Without mentioning the Civil Wars or the execution of Charles I, Gabriel, who interprets the vision, tells her that

> The three great kings, who next shall fill the throne,
> Shall faith reform'd and pure religion own.
>
> . . .
>
> The fourth (unhappy prince!)who mounts the throne,
> Shall be, imperious Rome, thy zealous son.

But God will send "a mighty hero of Nassovian blood" to free England from Popery. And when William dies, his place will be worthily filled by "a new Eliza." Queen Anne's Marlborough will prove "a wiser Cecil, and a greater Vere." Anne will have a promising son in Prince William, but his life will be cut short as a judgment upon England's

> . . . fierce divisions, mutual hate and strife,
> Corrupted manners, and flagitious life.

From the viewpoint of this study, these ponderous epics are less important than Blackmore's versified apologetics. From any viewpoint, indeed, his most ambitious and most successful work is *Creation. A Philosophical*

Poem. Demonstrating the Existence and Providence of a God (1712).[66] His long preface asserts that "there are two sorts of men, who without injustice have been called atheists; those who frankly and in plain terms have deny'd the being of a God; and those, who tho' they asserted his being, deny'd those attributes and perfections, which the idea of a God includes." Deists are simply atheists of the latter type, for the God in whom they say they believe, "perfectly unconcern'd with the direction and government of the world," is the same as no God at all. Perhaps not all deists deserve the stigma of atheism, but can they expect better treatment? Never attacking irreligion, they laud the virtues of heathens and expose the faults of Christians; and they will make no public profession of their own religious beliefs.

Among philosophical atheists of ancient times the most formidable was Epicurus, who has been admired by "several great wits in this last age." [67] But even Aristotle's philosophy, which dominated the Middle Ages, was atheistic in its implications, for it taught the fatalistic doctrine of an eternal world. In the Renaissance "many wise men ... combin'd to pull down the Peripatetick Monarchy, and set up a free and independent State of Science." In getting rid of Aristotle, however, they "had recourse to the *Corpuscularian Hypothesis,* and reviv'd the obsolete and exploded system of Epicurus." Epicurus, he grants, professed a belief in God, but "by his description he entirely destroys the Divine Nature." Since this is equally true of the deists, Blackmore couples Epicureanism and deism as kindred manifestations of that accursed thing, "wit."

In so doing Blackmore appears to disagree with Addison's remark in *Spectator* No. 186 (October 3, 1711): "Infidelity has been attacked with such good success of late years, that it is driven out of all its out-works. The atheist has not found his post tenable, and is therefore retired into deism, and a disbelief of revealed religion only." Dr. Mayo, who quotes this passage, says that after 1700 "Epicureanism, though still present and occasionally audible, resigned its role of chief heresy to the less alarming

---

[66] I know of no evidence for Ambrose Philips's story, preserved by Dr. Johnson, that "a club of wits" helped Blackmore in the composition of this poem. He might of course have sought the advice of such religiously disposed Whiggish wits as Addison, John Hughes, Nicholas Rowe, Dennis, and Tate. But there is nothing in the poem that Blackmore himself was incapable of thinking and writing. It rises above his usual level because it is the only poem in which he does what he is best fitted to do.

[67] Blackmore is thinking chiefly of Hobbes, who, he insists, added nothing essential to the thought of Lucretius.

figure of Deism, an intellectual offspring, ironically enough, of that useful champion of seventeenth century orthodoxy, the 'New Science' of the Royal Society." [68] The materialism of the Restoration Epicureans, on the other hand, was only slightly indebted to the New Science. Mayo stresses the fact that deism was less radically irreligious than Epicureanism. He finds also that while Epicureanism had been fashionable and aristocratic, deism in the reign of Anne was unfashionable and bourgeois.[69]

In these matters Blackmore lacks the modern scholar's perspective, and in any case his mind is not of the sort that draws fine distinctions. Then, too, having been born about 1650,[70] he naturally tends to interpret the deism of 1712 in relation to the Epicureanism of Restoration times. On the other hand deism was sometimes more radical, less soberly bourgeois and less completely distinct from the Epicurean spirit than Mayo supposes. Aristocrats like Bolingbroke could use deism as a means of rationalizing a libertine viewpoint which in the seventeenth century would probably have been expressed in Epicurean or Cyrenaic terms. Blackmore is too undiscriminating and extravagant, but he is not utterly wide of his mark.

Creation is intended to be a Christian *De Natura Rerum*. A good disciple of Locke, Blackmore rejects all innate ideas of God and grounds his whole case upon the argument from design:

> I would th' Eternal from his Works assert,
> And sing the wonders of creating art.

"The First Book," to quote the Argument, "contains the proof of a Deity, from the instances of design and choice, which occur in the structure and qualities of the earth and sea." Here and elsewhere Blackmore's favorite device is to describe complex phenomena and then ask how they are to be explained without positing a God. He buttonholes Descartes to demand:

> If your magnetic atomes always flow
> From pole to pole, what form'd their double source,
> What spurr'd, what gave them their inflected course?
> Tell, what could drill and perforate the holes,
> And to th' attractive rays adapt their poles?

---

[68] *Epicurus in England*, p. 113.   [69] *Ibid.*, p. 200.
[70] The year of his birth is unknown, but he entered St. Edmund Hall, Oxford, in 1668.

The second book relentlessly "pursues the proof...from the celestial motions, and more fully from the appearances in the solar system and the air." The mysterious movement of the globe occasions this address to the sceptic:

> Since you the spring of motion cannot show,
> Be just, and faultless ignorance allow;
> Say 'tis obedience to th' Almighty Nod,
> That 'tis the will, the pow'r, the hand of God.

Book IV refutes "the hypothesis of the Atomists or Epicureans, and other irreligious Philosophers" chiefly by arguing that matter could not have arranged itself into the ingenious patterns and systems displayed by nature. Once again, God is the only answer to a riddle. "In the Fifth, the doctrine of the Fatalists or Aristotelians, who make the world to be eternal, is consider'd and subverted." The mechanical determinist, says Blackmore, speaks of "Nature" as the creative force of the universe. But what does he mean by this term?

> Sometimes by Nature your inlighten'd school
> Intends of things the universal whole.
> Sometimes it is the order, that connects,
> And holds the chain of causes and effects.
> Sometimes it is the manner, and the way,
> In which these causes do their force display.
>
> . . . . . .
>
> She's now the building, now the architect,
> And now the rule which does his hand direct.
> But let this Empress be whate'er you please;
> Let her be all, or any one of these;
> She is with reason, or she's not, endu'd:
> If you the first affirm, we thence conclude
> A God, whose being you oppose, you grant:
> But if this mighty Queen does reason want,
> How could this noble fabrick be design'd,
> And fashion'd by a Maker brute and blind?

If the unbeliever attempts to answer that

> Things what they are, are by Necessity,
> Which never else so aptly could conspire
> To serve the whole, and Nature's ends acquire;
>
> . . . . .

> Ready we this assertion will allow,
> For what can more exalted wisdom show?
> With zeal we this Necessity defend
> Of means directed to their useful end;
> But 'tis not that which Fatalists intend,
> Nor that, which we oppose in this debate,
> An uncontroul'd Necessity of Fate,
> Which all things blindly does, and must produce,
> Unconscious of their goodness and their use.

Nature and Necessity explain nothing unless they are regarded as agents of divine power.

In Book VI "the argument of the first two Books is resum'd, and the existence of a God demonstrated from the prudence and art discover'd in the several parts of the body of man." As a physician, Blackmore revels in the providential arrangements of the digestive system. "In the Seventh, the same demonstration is carry'd on from the contemplation of the instincts in brute animals, and the faculties and operations of the soul of man. The Book concludes with a recapitulation of what has been treated of, and a Hymn to the Creator of the World."

Blackmore would say that he uses science to prove the "existence and providence of a God." More often than not, however, he does not attempt to reason his way to God through science, but shows the impotence of science without religion. As he says in Book I,

> These paths in vain are by enquirers trod:
> There's no Philosophy without a God.

Despite his enthusiasm for science, he is more fideistic than later physico-theological writers.[71] He is also particularly anxious that God should not be thought of as controlled by the laws which He has imposed upon nature. A passage from Book VII of *Eliza* admits that

> Things chiefly here in the same order go,
> As rivers in their known frequented channels flow.
> Common effects from common causes spring,
> And nature runs her customary ring.

[71] In the preface to *King Arthur* he says that one reason for his writing that poem was "that I am so fallen out with all hypotheses in Philosophy, and all doctrines of Physic, that I am almost reduced to a sceptical despair." He would not say this of *Creation*, but the poem is not wholly free from the same feeling.

The strong subdue the weak by usual fate,
The wise and subtile triumph in debate.

· · · ·

But lest mankind to wrong conceptions prone,
Should heav'n's superior will and pow'r disown;
Should impious thoughts unworthy God imbibe,
Should providence dishonour, and ascribe
Private events, and publick turns of state
To a fixt chain of things, and necessary fate;
He sometimes bids his servant nature take
A path unknown, and her old course forsake:
Bring forth events by unexpected ways,
Awe to produce, astonishment to raise,
That God's controlling will mankind may fear,
Adore his wisdom, and his pow'r revere.

Blackmore does not perfectly trust the science from which he draws his ammunition.

Creation presents only a religion of natural reason. Except for his frequent assertion that the intricate wonders of nature prove not only the existence but the providential care of a Supreme Being, Blackmore does not advance far beyond the deism which he execrates. In 1722, however, he completed his defense of religion in *Redemption*. The interesting preface and the supplementary *Hymn to Christ the Redeemer* have already been cited. The body of the poem—an old man's work, of course—is extremely dull and feeble; *Creation* is a work of genius in comparison. The first three books "defend Christianity against the Deist" by arguing that man cannot live by the light of natural religion because he is a fallen creature who needs revelation and redemption. The last three books contain a demonstration of "our Saviour's strict Divinity, by clear and direct arguments contain'd in the inspir'd writings." Prophecy and miracle are the mainstays of his circular logic. He also makes much of the point that Arians are idolaters because they worship Christ without regarding him as divine.[72] There is a sad discrepancy between the genuine religious feeling of the preface and the bungling, pedestrian rhetoric of the text. Poetically and polemically worthless, *Redemption* merely serves to show the futility of a narrowly rationalistic defense of Christianity.

[72] Blackmore made two prose contributions to the Arian controversy: *Just Prejudices Against the Arian Hypothesis* and *Modern Arians Unmasked*.

This discussion of Blackmore may seem unduly lengthy, but it is conciseness itself compared to the poet with whom it deals. It may be concluded by a summary of the main elements of his work: the political, ecclesiastical and social views of a Whig whose Low Church Anglicanism has been but little affected by latitudinarian thought; puritanical concern for moral reform; opposition to "wit" as making for vice and irreligion; a campaign against atheism, Epicureanism, deism, and Arianism, with a tendency to lump them all together; belief in Christian, original, and *rationally* enthusiastic poetry as a means of reforming the age and its literature through a harmony of passion and reason; the use of scientific materials in the defense of religion, combined with distrust of scientific philosophy; the reliance upon a non-religious conception of reason in the attempt to argue for orthodox Christianity. Blackmore, in short, is a satisfyingly representative figure. Whatever the critic may say about his poetry, the student of the history of thought should be grateful to a man who gives him so much.

Both Alexander Pope and Edward Young began their long careers during the 1700-1720 period. *The Messiah* and *The Dying Christian to His Soul* would entitle the former, and *The Last Day* the latter, to a place in this chapter. Here, however, common sense enjoins inconsistency. For our purposes the author of the *Essay on Man* belongs in the 1720-1740 period, and the author of *Night Thoughts,* for reasons explained in my preface, to the next volume of this series. At present one need only observe the obvious kinship between Young and such pious Whigs as Dennis, Blackmore, and Addison. Pope, on the other hand, appears in this period as a follower of the aristocratic tradition who briefly reflects, in a few of his poems, the influence of the Addison circle.

We must not pretend to draw any hard-and-fast distinction between the poets of this chapter and those of Chapter I. Both groups, in the broad sense of the term, are neoclassical; and both, on the other hand, reflect the blurred standards of an age of compromise. The witty aristocrats are neither very gay nor very aristocratic; the sober moralists try to write as genteelly as they can. But the fact remains that between the more fully representative members of the two groups there are important differences. Generally speaking, the poetry considered in this chapter is Cavalier in form, but Puritan in content.[73] Even in accepting neoclassicism, these poets impose upon it something of the religiosity, the moral urgency, the sober utilitarianism, the suppressed emotionalism, of the rising middle class. Hence the punning title of this chapter.

About half of these writers are bourgeois. The rest are technically "gentlemen"; but none is a nobleman, and with the partial exception of Addison none, either in life or in art, moves in a genuinely aristocratic atmosphere. Their social origins are less significant than the fact that, whether gentlemen or not, they think and feel like members of a middle-class civilization. It is noteworthy that the list comprises twelve Whigs as against five Tories: a large majority is of the party chiefly dominant in the compromise between aristocratic and bourgeois standards.

Out of fifteen writers on whom sufficient information is available, three were born 1650-1659; three, 1660-1669; seven, 1670-1679; one, 1680-1689; one, 1690-1699. In Chapter I, only three poets out of fifteen were born later than 1670 as against nine out of fifteen in the present chapter. Despite the meagreness of the data, one is drawn toward the conclusion that aristocratic neoclassicism is receding before the advance of middle-classicism.

By no means all of the poets in this chapter, however, are of much importance as regards their religious interests. Let us then separately scrutinize the final group, which has provided the most abundant and interesting material. Addison and Smith were born in 1672, Yalden in 1671, Pomfret in 1667, Dennis in 1657, Tate in 1652, and Blackmore about 1650. The dates of the last three are especially significant. The average for this group of more definitely pious poets, then, is considerably earlier than the average for the whole chapter. Thus although middle-classicism is rising, its specifically Christian element seems to be diminishing.

All of these poets are Anglicans with the possible exception of Tunstall, who may be a Romanist. Hence the predominance of nonconformists over Anglicans which was noted in the preceding chapter is reversed. The dissenters have several specialists in sacred verse, but almost no piously disposed secular poets. With the Anglicans the opposite is true. Disregarding Ken and Norris, they have no exclusively divine poets who can rival

[73] I owe the turn of this phrase to J. W. Draper, *The Funeral Elegy and the Rise of English Romanticism*, p. 186.

Watts and Mrs. Rowe, but they have a large number of secular poets who practise divine poetry to a considerable extent.

Anglicanism, however, is a broad, loose term. The twelve Whigs in this chapter are all Low Churchmen whose religion is no important respect distinguishable from the Nonconformity of Presbyterians and Independents. Of the four Anglican Tories, none is "high" in any but a political sense. Hence from this and the foregoing chapter we may conclude that religion as it appears in the poetry of this period is predominantly the religion of the middle class, of Whigs, of Low Churchmen and nonconformists.

Between 1700 and 1720, the expression of religious thought and feeling in verse is more abundant and less confined to nonentities than is generally supposed. The Age of Anne certainly did not ignore Christianity as a poetic theme. Furthermore, the religious-minded poets of the time are of great value to the literary historian. Some of them transmit from the seventeenth century to the eighteenth a serious and lofty conception of poetry as impassioned wisdom. When, turning from theory to practise, we hunt for evidence that imaginative and emotional poetry survived even in this age of versified rhetoric, it is among them, and almost nowhere else, that we find such evidence. And, as will be shown in the following chapter, it is among them that the seeker of "pre-romantic tendencies" must begin to dig for his elusive ore. Not all of them, of course, are valuable in these respects, but the group as a whole is rich in suggestiveness for the future.

Yet from a critical viewpoint how unsatisfying, both as religion and as poetry, is the material which has been examined in these last two chapters! If even Ken, Norris, Watts, and Mrs. Rowe cannot unreservedly be admired, what is to be said of the rest? Simply that they lack ardor and depth of feeling, that they do not think about religion with much originality or penetration, and that the proportion of poetry to rhetoric in their work is after all very slight.

The historian must be recalled to explain the deficiencies which have pained the critic. Dennis and Blackmore are particularly clear examples of the difficulties besetting religious-minded poets of the age. Both are learned, intelligent, and eloquent; both are truly pious Protestant Christians. They regard Christianity as inherently poetic—a religion of wonder and rapture. Conversely, great poetry is for them the expression of strong emotions which at their height are religious. In all this they are admirably qualified to write divine poetry, but in other respects they are completely disqualified. Their religion of wonder and rapture must be warm, but not very hot. It must steer a middle course between the enthusiasm of sectarians and the superstition of papists. Doctrinally, it must be neither so broad nor so narrow as to threaten the peace of Whiggery. It must not conflict with that religion of reason and nature of which Christianity is the most reasonable and natural expression. It must rebuke Epicureans and deists and must contribute to the reformation of manners. The poetry which expresses this religion must be sublime and original without "unnatural flights," must swoon with inspiration without breaking any of the rules. We have seen the results of this compromise, and we are bored.

In the 1700-1720 period, orthodox Protestantism survives by swearing fealty to a thoroughly unpoetical conception of reason. It strengthens its appeal to common sense, but it weakens its grip on human feeling and imagination. Though politico-ecclesiastical controversy and, to a less extent, the moral reform movement foster a quasi-religious warmth, there can be no doubt that the period under discussion shows a progressive desiccation of the emotional and imaginative side of Christianity. The writers of this and of the preceding chapter resist this process more successfully than most of their contemporaries, but even they are strongly affected by it. They try to sing of a faith which is anxiously purging itself of its own poetry.

This situation cannot long continue. Indeed, our chronological findings suggest that even among the middle-classicists the responsiveness of poets to Christianity is waning. Meanwhile the undying spiritual emotions of men, though temporarily dulled and submerged, will not long be denied expression. If they cannot be expressed through Christianity, they will find some other outlet.

Chapter V

THE BEGINNINGS OF SENTIMENTALISM

THE ASSERTION THAT DURING THE 1700-1720 PERIOD THE RELIGIOUS-MINDED poets are almost the sole preservers and transmitters of the trends commonly labelled "pre-romantic" deserves to be amplified and illustrated. Discussion of this topic does not demand a hard-and-fast definition. Whatever romanticism may be, certain ways of feeling, thinking, and writing were markedly prevalent in the period which scholars seem determined to call the Romantic Period. The slow and irregular ascent of these tendencies from obscurity to prominence during the eighteenth century justifies our use of the term, "pre-romanticism."

It has already been noted that these tendencies are almost non-existent in the aristocratic and neoclassical poetry which furnished material for Chapter I. Nor, with a few exceptions to be recalled later, do they thrive amidst the politico-ecclesiastical bickering of the second chapter. They find a friendlier atmosphere among the divine poets of Chapter III and the more or less piously disposed middle-classical secular poets of Chapter IV.

The romanticist takes a serious and lofty view of poetry. For him, the true poet is a bard, a prophet, a priest, inspired by some power greater than himself, pouring out floods of wisdom in rapturous song. The poet's imagination, soaring above ordinary reason, gives him insight into the deep spiritual truth of things—gives him power even to create such truth. This conception of poetry was of course not invented by Wordsworth, Coleridge, Shelley, or Keats. It is at least as old as Plato's *Ion,* and it was popular in the literary criticism of the Renaissance. During the second half of the seventeenth and the first half of the eighteenth century, however, it fell upon evil days. Enthusiasm in poetry, like enthusiasm in religion, was under suspicion, and genius was curbed by judgment and the rules. The making of couplets was the amusement of gentlemen.

Versified rhetoric supplanted "truth carried alive into the heart by passion." In the face of these obstacles, the lofty old view of poetry was preserved and passed down to the next generation by a little group of pious writers who thought religiously of poetry and poetically of religion—Ken, Norris, Mrs. Rowe, Watts, Blackmore, Dennis, Samuel Say.

The favorite romantic idea that genius is superior to all rules is a venerable corollary of the view of poetry which has just been described. Although critics at no time deny the existence of "a grace beyond the reach of art," exaltation of original genius is alien to the neoclassical spirit. Hence in the 1700-1720 period, we again find an unfashionable viewpoint surviving chiefly among the religious-minded poets. In the preface to his paraphrase of Job, Blackmore decries the imitative classicism of the age, and calls for original geniuses who will write modern, Christian poetry.[1] Samuel Cobb holds that the rules are useful in restraining the vagaries of youth, but that a mature poet should lay them aside. "To judge well and candidly, we must wean ourselves from a slavish Bigotry to the Ancients.... Let a man follow the Talent that Nature has furnish'd him with, and his own Observation has improv'd, we may hope to see Inventions in all Arts, which may dispute Superiority with the best of the Athenian or Roman Excellencies." We call that irregular which is too lofty for our little minds. "Who knows the secret Springs of the Soul, and those sudden Emotions, which excite illustrious Men, to act and speak out of the Common Road? They seem irregular to Us by reason of the Fondness and Bigotry we pay to Custom, which is no Standard to the Brave and the Wise." [2] At least three of Watts's poems assert the prerogatives of a genius which "breaks all the critic's iron chains," [3] and Elizabeth Rowe's biographer informs us that "she read no critics, nor could her genius brook the discipline of rules." Such utterances are prophetic of Young's *Conjectures on Original Composition.*[4]

Even the most strenuous champion of originality, however, must provide examples and models. Englishmen must be shown that their native bards have composed original poetry of a religious and nobly emotional

---

[1] *Vide supra,* p. 192.

[2] *A Discourse on Criticism, and the Liberty of Writing,* prefixed to his *Poems on Several Occasions.*   [3] *Vide supra,* pp. 128, 129.

[4] Here I must observe that Mr. S. H. Monk's excellent study of *The Sublime* greatly underestimates the importance of religious thought in relation to his subject.

kind. Of this fact Milton would be the prime example. Professor Havens rightly states that the preservation and the first stages of the gradual enhancement of Milton's reputation were the work of men who thought highly of divine poetry.[5] Among early admirers, imitators, and critical champions of Milton are Samuel Wesley the elder, Dennis, Blackmore, Watts, Mrs. Rowe, John Philips, Addison, Say, Cobb, Catherall, Evans, and Edmund Smith—all divine poets or middle-classicists favorably disposed toward religion. Outside of such writers enthusiasm for Milton at the outset of the century is very slight. From them later and more obviously pre-romantic writers will inherit the Miltonic tradition.

A more remote, more "Gothic," and less sublimely religious figure than Milton, Spenser was genuinely appreciated by none of the poets who have thus far been considered. It may be noted, however, that he is mentioned more often and more admiringly by the poets of Chapters III and IV than by those of Chapter I. In the preface of his *Life of Christ,* Wesley objects to the irregularity of the *Faerie Queene,* but finds it "much more Natural and Lovely" than Ariosto, and full of "Sweetness and Variety." Spenser is briefly praised in Edmund Smith's elegy on John Philips and—coupled with Cowley—in Yalden's *Essay on the Character of Sir Willoughby Aston* and Lely's *Maevius Anglicanus.* Blackmore seems to recognize Spenser's significance as an epic poet of the Protestant Reformation.[6]

Of somewhat greater interest is George Sewell's *The Force of Musick, a Fragment after the Manner of Spenser.* The author describes the palace of personified Music in heroic couplets, for he aims merely to capture the luxuriance of Spenser's descriptive imagery. In a prefatory note Sewell "owns, that the Picturesque manner is extremely delightful to him, but they who never read Homer, Virgil, Tasso, Milton, and above all, Spenser, will never taste Beauties, or find Imperfections in this kind of Poetry. He might have mentioned Shakespeare too, if it were only to shew the Poet's Judgment, who uses them ['picturesque' descriptions] frequently, but seldom of any length, as more improper for the Drama. ... This Essay, however accepted, he [Sewell] confesses he writ with Pleasure enough to make amends for every opposing Cavil, or Cen-

---

[5] R. D. Havens, *The Influence of Milton on English Poetry,* pp. 33-34.
[6] *Vide supra,* p. 195.

sure." Though we can see nothing Spenserian in Sewell's lines, we may be glad that he so heartily enjoyed himself. These clues are very slight, but they suggest that these sober poets are related to the Spenserian as well as to the Miltonic revival.

The writers of Chapters III and IV display some interest in other poets who are to figure in the romantic renascence of the earlier national literature. In connection with Shakespeare, one thinks at once of Addison and Nicholas Rowe, and remembers that Sewell assisted Pope in his editorial labors. Cobb's modernization of Chaucer's *Miller's Tale* can hardly be called a contribution to the Romantic Movement; but for Sewell, Chaucer is more than a teller of broad stories. In a spirit of serious admiration he modernizes the apocryphal *Proclamation of Cupid* and an emotional passage from *Troylus and Criseyde*. Sewell's interest in earlier English literature might, in fact, be worthy of separate treatment, for he studied not only Chaucer, Spenser, and Shakespeare but the Earl of Surrey.[7] Elizabeth Rowe's poems include *A Pastoral. In imitation of Drayton's second Nymphal*, and we have seen that Reynolds admired George Herbert.

Interest in early popular poetry is slight in the writers of this group, but Addison's influence on the ballad-revival is known to have been considerable. Curiously enough, one of Mrs. Rowe's few secular poems is *A Laplander's song to his mistress*.[8]

Here we may digress to observe that Mrs. Rowe is also interesting as a strand in a network of personal relationships. In girlhood she was a protégée of the pious and cultivated Thynnes of Longleat, where Bishop Ken, her father's friend, was often an honored guest. The Countess of Hertford, daughter of Henry Thynne, Viscount Weymouth, was a lifelong friend of Mrs. Rowe and of Isaac Watts. Though she became lady-in-waiting to the deistic Queen Caroline, she was a deeply religious woman. Impressed by Whitefield's preaching, she allowed him to use her drawing-room as a chapel; and she encouraged the Countess of Huntingdon in her efforts on behalf of the early Evangelicals. But Lady Hertford also dabbled in verse, and was an enthusiastic patron of preromantic poetry. Thomson, Shenstone, and Savage had reason to bless

[7] He edited "Tottel's Miscellany" in 1717.

[8] The history of this song, generally known as *Orra Moor*, is treated by F. E. Farley in "Three 'Lapland Songs,'" *PMLA.*, XXXI, 1-39.

her name. It may be added that Bishop Percy dedicated his *Reliques* to her daughter, the Duchess of Northumberland. The importance of these facts may be variously estimated, but to me they hint that pre-romanticism is somehow related to these pious poets and gentlefolk whose lives run from the seventeenth century into the eighteenth. At least it is appropriate that Mrs. Rowe, in her later years, should have been a warm admirer of Thomson.[9] She is a devout Christian and he a vaguely deistic sentimentalist; but some common bond, as yet undefined, proves stronger than their religious differences.

The dominance of the heroic couplet even in relatively pure neoclassical verse is often exaggerated. Nevertheless the frequent use of other forms, when combined with more significant factors, is legitimate material for the seeker of pre-romanticism. Although I have gathered no detailed statistics on this topic I can convince any interested reader that blank verse, pseudo-pindaric odes, octosyllabic couplets and short lyrical stanzas with interwoven rhyme-schemes (the last two in *serious* poetry) are much more abundant in the writers of Chapters III and IV than in those of Chapter I.

It has already been granted that Dennis, Blackmore, and the rest were unable to write the sort of poetry which they advocated. But they sometimes tried to write such poetry, and they came nearer to writing it than any other group. Where among the elegant neoclassical versifiers will one find anything remotely comparable, in passion and power, to Watts's *Day of Judgment?* The historian of serious lyrical poetry must traverse a desert lying between the seventeenth-century singers and the eighteenth-century precursors of the great romantic lyricists. Yet there are a few relatively green oases amidst the sands—Ken, Norris, Mrs. Rowe, Watts, Addison, Nicholas Rowe, and a few other writers to be considered later in this chapter. In them the song of inward feeling, albeit precariously and fitfully, continues to exist.

The poets of Chapter I substantiate almost perfectly the common notion that the Age of Pope cared little about external nature and made no attempt to render in verse its real appearance. In the poets of Chapters III and IV, exceptions to this generalization are fairly frequent. Ellwood,

---

[9] See her poem *To Mr. Thomson;* also letters XIX, XXXVI, and XLVII in the *Miscellaneous Works* of 1739.

Norris, Watts, Harrison, and John Philips—to mention only indisputable examples—regard natural objects closely and with enjoyment.

These sober poets are Christians, not nature-worshippers. Not infrequently they guard themselves against any suspicion of pantheism by asserting the complete dependence of nature upon God. In Blackmore and Reynolds, natural science supports the Christian Rationalism of the age. Several other poets combine a more emotional Christianity with a less scientific response to nature. In his *Grounds of Criticism,* Dennis regards external nature as well adapted to the expression of those "enthusiastic passions" which appear at their height in religious poetry. "The Wonders of the Universe," says he, "afford the more admirable Ideas, and a more admirable Spirit, the more they shew the Attributes of the Creator, or relate to his Worship. . . . Natural Philosophy is absolutely necessary to a Poet, not only that he may adorn his Poem with the useful Knowledge it affords, but because the more he knows the immense Phænomena of the Universe, the more he will be sure to admire them. For the more we know of Things that are never to be comprehended by us, the more that Knowledge must make them appear wonderful." Here is a noteworthy attempt to draw from nature both the joy of understanding and the joy of *not* understanding.

In crossing the Alps, Dennis shuddered with "a delightful Horrour, a terrible Joy." [10] Addison's feelings in the same situation were very different, but we know that amidst more peaceful surroundings his heart was lifted up when he beheld the moon "walking in her brightness," and that he heard the stars singing, "The hand that made us is divine." [11] Watts, too, thinks of nature as praising God,[12] and Elizabeth Rowe in her pious retirement sees the impress of the divine hand on all the works of creation.[13]

The love of retirement, though a popular theme in the poetry of the seventeenth century, is often regarded as a pre-romantic tendency. We have seen that Mrs. Rowe values nature less for its own sake than as a means of shielding her soul from sin.[14] Watts is genuinely fond of nature, but he can find all the spiritual benefits of woodland solitude by closing the door of his study:

[10] Quoted by H. G. Paul, *John Dennis,* p. 5.
[11] *Vide supra,* p. 182.   [13] *Vide supra,* p. 137.
[12] *Vide supra,* p. 124.   [14] *Vide supra,* p. 136.

> Gunston, the lark dwells in her nest
> Till she ascend the skies;
> And in my closet I could rest
> Till to the Heavens I rise.
>
> .   .   .   .
>
> When I within myself retreat,
> I shut my doors against the great;
> My busy eye-balls inward roll,
> And there with large survey I see
> All the wide theatre of me,
> And view the various scenes of my retiring soul.[15]

This self-scrutiny will prepare him for the final examination before the Judgment Seat.

We have already observed that Ellwood, as a good Quaker, craves solitude in order to hear the still small voice.[16] *To a Friend in America* does not suggest that the appeal of scenic beauty is a factor in this desire, but *A Prospect* shows that natural objects could give him "sweetest innocent Delight." Thomas Harrison's *The Dream* combines the joys of pious meditation with those of observing "Nature's works" within a "blest Grove."

There is nothing romantic in wishing to withdraw from the noisy irrationality of the town to a snug little suburban retreat where one may cultivate the society of a few good friends, read the ancients, eat sensible food, and plan a formal garden. The prospector who discerns a glint of romanticism in Pomfret's *The Choice,* for example, must have a very sharp eye. John Norris's earlier poem of the same title is also predominantly classical though less cozily bourgeois. In *The Retirement* he says,

> Here in this shady lonely grove,
> I sweetly think my hours away;

but the main themes of the poem are the advantages of quiet study, scorn of worldly ambition, and detached Lucretian observation of the futile struggles of men. *Sitting in an Arbour,* though a trifle richer in *Naturgefühl,* is hardly prophetic of romanticism. Rather surprisingly, none of Norris's three retirement-pieces strikes a religious note.

The close relationship between retirement of the less classical sort and

---

[15] *Happy Solitude.* Avowedly imitated from an ode by Casimir.
[16] *Vide supra,* p. 147.

mildly pensive melancholy is familiar to all students of this period. Traditionally, retirement and contemplation were inseparable, and an *Il Penseroso* kind of melancholy was an essential trait of the contemplative man. Then, as now, however, the diverse shapes which melancholy may assume were puzzling to her devotees. In *To Melancholy*, Norris regards his subject as a fascinating mystery. "Thou mak'st us wise, yet ruin'st our philosophy.... No pain is like thy pain, no pleasure too like thine." This paradox results from confusing the melancholy which is banished in the opening lines of *L'Allegro* with the melancholy which is praised in *Il Penseroso*. A similar confusion between shades of melancholy appears in Mrs. Rowe's *Despair,* in which genuine sorrow at the death of her husband struggles for mastery against literary affectation:

> Oh! lead me to some solitary gloom,
> Where no enliv'ning beams, no chearful echoes come;
>
> . . . . .
>
> Far from the studious follies of the great,
> The tiresome farce of ceremonious state:
> There, in a melting, solemn, dying strain,
> Let me, all day, upon my lyre complain,
> And wind up all its soft, harmonious strings,
> To noble, serious, melancholy things.
>
> . . . . .
>
> Nor let a bird of chearful note come near,
> To whisper out his airy raptures here.
> Only the pensive songstress of the grove,
> Let her, by mine, her mournful notes improve;
> While drooping winds among the branches sigh,
> And sluggish waters heavily roll by.
> Here, to my fatal sorrows let me give
> The short remaining hours I have to live.
> Then, with a sullen, deep-fetch'd groan expire,
> And to the grave's dark solitude retire.

Prior's *Solomon* will remind us that melancholy is not monopolized by the poets of Chapters III and IV, and that the cynicism of other elegant versifiers may hover on the borderline between mockery and despair. Nevertheless, the most numerous and striking examples of this tendency are provided by the divine poets and the middle-classicists. Yalden is almost always disillusioned and sombre, while for Abel Evans human

existence is a dreary penance for rebellious angels. Arbuthnot and Pomfret, like Prior, are saddened by the impotence of reason and the disparity
between human desire and human power.

The gloom of Watts, though often exaggerated by modern students, is
an important element in his work. *The Mourning-Piece* opens with lines
which, both in form and mood, look forward to Young:

> Life's a long tragedy: this globe the stage,
> Well fix'd and well-adorn'd with strong machines,
> Gay fields, and skies, and seas: the actors many:
> The plot immense: a flight of demons sit
> On every sailing cloud with fatal purpose;
> And shoot across the scenes ten thousand arrows
> Perpetual and unseen, headed with pain,
> With sorrow, infamy, disease, and death.
> The pointed plagues fly silent through the air,
> Nor twangs the bow, yet sure and deep the wound.[17]

The crudely macabre melancholy of ghosts, skeletons and worms, as
Professor Draper has shown, develops from the funeral elegies of the
seventeenth-century puritans.[18] In our period this tendency is still chiefly
sub-literary, and examples of it in the poets thus far considered are rare.
But Tate's *The Charnel House* and *On an Anatomy*[19] belong to this
lugubrious tradition, as does Watts's *Death and Eternity:*

> These skulls, what ghastly figures now!
> How loathsome to the eyes!
> These are the heads we lately knew
> So beauteous and so wise.

But for further illustrations Draper's study may be consulted.

No one who has read Miss Whitney's *Primitivism and Progress*[20] will
regard primitivism as a purely romantic trend, but the fact remains that
the romantic impulse often expresses itself through a soft kind of primitivism. And since hard and soft primitivism are confused in literary
practise much more readily than in pure logic, this element of eighteenth-

---

[17] It is only fair to say that this poem is merely the first part of a nuptial trilogy so
arranged as to rise from a gloomy to a piously happy view of marriage.

[18] J. W. Draper, *The Funeral Elegy and the Rise of English Romanticism.*

[19] *Vide supra,* p. 176.

[20] Lois B. Whitney, *Primitivism and the Idea of Progress in English Popular Literature of
the Eighteenth Century.*

century thought will always interest the student of romanticism. In his *Satyr Against Wit* Blackmore laments the passing of those

> ...old unpolish'd Times,
> As free from Wit as other modern Crimes!
> As our Forefathers Vig'rous were and Brave,
> So they were Virtuous, Wise, Discreet, and Grave,
> Detesting both alike the Wit and Knave.

In *Creation,* he longs for the return of an apparently more remote Arcadia, where man, shunning the demoralizing knowledge which leads to scepticism, concerned himself only with that which was practically useful:

> Thro' metaphysic wilds he never flew,
> Nor the dark haunts of school Chimaeras knew,
> But had alone his happiness in view.
> He milk'd the lowing herd, he press'd the cheese,
> Folded the flock, and spun the woolly fleece.

Here is hard primitivism of a kind that can easily turn soft.

Nicholas Rowe's primitivism is more obviously pre-romantic in his *Epistle to Flavia, On the Sight of two Pindar Odes (on the Spleen and Vanity) Written by a Lady her Friend.* I give the full title because it is noteworthy that Lady Winchilsea's odes should have inspired him to write these lines in praise of free poetry and free love:

> Sure in the better Ages of old Time,
> Nor Poetry nor Love was thought a Crime;
> From Heav'n they *both,* the Gods' best Gifts, were sent,
> Divinely perfect both, and innocent.

> .   .   .   .

> Beneath cool Shades our happy Fathers lay,
> And spent in pure untainted Joys the Day:
> Artless their Loves, artless their Numbers were,
> While Nature simply did in both appear,
> Nor could the Censor or the Critic fear.

To the Noble Savages exhumed by Dr. Bissell and by the present writer [21] may be added the hero of George Waldron's *The Aged Creole.* When asked how he has managed to live so long, he replies that, unlike

---

[21] B. H. Bissell, *The American Indian in English Literature of the Eighteenth Century;* H. N. Fairchild, *The Noble Savage.*

more civilized men, he has not shortened his life by straining to rise above his fellows:

> In smallest Compass all I ask,
> And all I hope does move;
> Of rum I keep a moderate Cask,
> And eat the food I love.

He has never been plagued by "loss of land or gold," has never gone to law, has avoided harlots, and has stuck to one woman all his life. The old fellow has too much common sense to be richly satisfying to the romantic impulse, but at the close he forgets his "moderate Cask" and gravely counsels the inquirer:

> Revere the God that dwells on high,
> And rules the Day and Night;
> Lift up to him an holy Eye,
> He'll surely guide thee right.

Modern students of the eighteenth century attach great importance to "sentimentalism." To employ a term of critical opprobrium in historical scholarship may be confusing, but who can withstand the force of usage? The critic hurls the charge of sentimentalism when he regards the writer's emotional response to a stimulus as excessive in relation to the normal force of that stimulus. In the history of literature, on the other hand, "sentimentalism" properly pertains not to the sentimental, but to sentiment. Some ambiguity is inevitable, however, because the eighteenth-century literature of sentiment so often strikes the modern reader as being, in the pejorative sense, sentimental.

The tap-root of sentimentalism is belief in the natural goodness of the human emotions. If man's feelings are good, then the more he feels about the more things, and the more freely he externalizes feeling, the better. The pre-romantic tendencies already glanced at are today often described as different ways of satisfying, directly or indirectly, the fundamental impulse of sentimentalism. Thus in historical usage "sentimentalism" becomes practically synonymous with "pre-romanticism." It implies a romanticism which has not yet become fully self-conscious, free, and dominant—romantic hankering which has not achieved complete romantic expression. With these familiar views we need not quarrel, though in time we may hope to dig a little deeper.

In the earliest stages of any historical process, superficial symptoms are often more obvious than their underlying causes. Thus in the 1700-1720 period, direct literary reflections of the basic attitude of sentimentalism are much less frequent than they will become later in the century. Nevertheless, they are by no means wholly lacking in the years now under discussion. Were this study not confined to poetry, Richard Steele would provide abundant material. Defoe substantially equates nature, reason, and conscience;[22] Toland thinks of religion as a light which shines in "every good Man's Heart,"[23] and he would probably deny that any man is otherwise than good by nature. The latitudinarianism which is expressed by several other Whig controversialists in Chapter II has sentimental implications.

Lady Mary Wortley Montagu's lines on the billing doves imply "the holiness of the heart's affections."[24] Other writers seem to restrict this idea to a few specially favored persons. Wesley supposes that Robert Nelson, as a child, never had to learn to be good,[25] and Pomfret avers that Queen Mary, being made of "virtue unmix'd," needed only to follow the dictates of her heart.[26] We are not told that these *belles âmes* have preserved, amidst the corruptions of civilization, a universal privilege of the state of nature. For some time the eighteenth century will be unable to decide whether the moral sense is aristocratic or democratic, but on the whole the latter view will win the day.

The pious raptures of Mrs. Rowe, especially in depicting heavenly joys, should perhaps be called sentimental in the critical rather than in the historical sense: she is too orthodox to indulge in illusions about the natural goodness of the human impulses. But that she would very much *like* to entertain such illusions may legitimately be inferred from the tone of her work.

The warmth of one's virtuous feelings should of course be reflected in deeds. Hence arises the theme of the joys of practical benevolence. In the 1700-1720 period the best examples of this idea are found in the latitudinarian sermon, the sentimental comedy, and the periodical essay. But although it has not yet invaded poetry to any marked extent, it plainly appears in George Sewell's unctuous picture of the good man's conscience[27]

[22] *Vide supra,* p. 67.   [25] *Vide supra,* p. 116.
[23] *Vide supra,* p. 92.   [26] *Vide supra,* p. 170.
[24] *Vide supra,* p. 7.   [27] *Vide supra,* p. 165.

and in Dennis's Whiggish theory that charity is the inevitable fruit of commercial prosperity.[28]

In his valuable article "On the Discrimination of Romanticisms," [29] Professor Lovejoy makes an emphatic distinction between the sentimentally naturalistic romanticism of the eighteenth century and the transcendental romanticism of the nineteenth. But the gulf between the two is not impassable, for sentimentalism has transcendental implications. If the human feelings are naturally good, then much that Christian orthodoxy has assigned to God alone may reside within the human breast—divine goodness, divine wisdom, something even of divine creative power. Later sections of this study will reveal a considerable amount of transcendentalism in eighteenth-century poetry. In the 1700-1720 period, of course, transcendental views are extremely rare. They are preserved chiefly by the Renaissance-Platonic theory of poetic enthusiasm and inspiration. That this is true of Isaac Watts has already been shown.[30] The sub-title of Toland's *Clito: A poem on the Force of Eloquence* may imply some vague notion of the creative powers of imagination. At all events he writes:

> A Noble Fury does possess my Soul,
> Which all may forward, nothing can controul;
> The fate of Beings, and the hopes of Men,
> Shall be what pleases my creating Pen.

This looks backward to the *furor poeticus* of earlier critical theory and forward to that "shaping spirit of imagination" which for Coleridge is another name for the transcendental faculty. And who could more justly lay claim to poetry's creative fury than he whose heart is filled with the power of natural goodness?

The reader will not, I trust, accuse me of attempting to portray the 1700-1720 period as a hotbed of romanticism. My purpose has been to show that the tendencies which have been discussed in the foregoing paragraphs are, with only a few exceptions, confined to the divine poets of Chapter III, to the sober middle-classical poets of Chapter IV, and to a few middle-classical Whig controversialists of Chapter II.

These so-called pre-romantic tendencies were not invented by the eighteenth century: they are all of venerable lineage. But since they do not

[28] *Vide supra*, p. 186.   [29] *PMLA*, XXXIX, 229-253.   [30] *Vide supra*, p. 129.

readily harmonize with the rationalistic temper and the neoclassical literary standards of the Enlightenment, their survival throughout the 1700-1720 period is precarious. That they should owe their preservation chiefly to religiously-inclined poets is readily explained.

Earnest Christians whose culture is sufficient to raise them above a vulgarly pious prejudice against art will always regard poetry as fundamentally religious; and they will strongly oppose its cultivation as a merely frivolous secular amusement. Such persons are likely to draw a close connection between religious and poetic inspiration, and to make much of the original genius of the ardently Christian poet. Piously disposed poets and critics generally supported the moderns in the famous "quarrel." The ancients, after all, were pagans; the beauties of purely Christian, and therefore of native, literature must be emphasized. Hence the friendly attitude of the more devout literati toward the earlier English poetry.

Even in an age when religion is strongly dominated by rationalism, the emotional and imaginative side of Christianity cannot wholly disappear. It is only natural that the divine poets and the pious secular poets should have been somewhat more willing to sing and to "let themselves go" than writers for whom all enthusiasm, both religious and literary, was anathema.

Of all people, the devout Christian would be least likely to champion the man-made town against the God-made country. With memories of the psalmist in his mind, he would delight to trace the divine hand at work in the visible universe. The telescope and microscope at first only increased his reverential awe and provided him with teleological ammunition against the infidel.

It is quite to be expected that retirement, either to the leafy grove or to the quiet chamber, should particularly attract the Christian poet. The practise of "retreat" for the sake of religious meditation had not yet become a Catholic monopoly. Though Protestantism had already gone far toward making a cardinal virtue of commercial bustle, the process was far from complete. Retirement was still a living tradition in Protestant Christianity and one that exerted a strong influence upon sensitive puritans who recoiled from the worldliness or the contentiousness of their environment.

Modern liberal religion is so cheery that some readers may be surprised by the assertion that melancholy is an essential element of Christianity.

But of course the sorrowful mysteries are no less a part of Christian experience than the joyful and glorious ones. If Good Friday looks forward to Easter, Easter remembers Good Friday. The fall of our first parents, the sacrifice of the Cross, the continued sinfulness of even the most ardent believer, the dread of Judgment—such thoughts are woven into the fabric of the faith. Hence it is not very surprising that, in this period, melancholy moods can be found more easily in Christian than in non-Christian poets.

Certain kinds of primitivism, too, are especially congenial to Christian writers. The traditional conception of the Fall is essentially primitivistic: man has deteriorated from a primal state of goodness. In literary tradition if not in theology, the Garden of Eden and the Golden Age are almost interchangeable.

To assert that these tendencies are peculiarly Christian would be absurd. My contention is merely that they harmonize with Christianity and are well adapted to the expression of various aspects of Christian feeling. They owe to Christianity their survival during the 1700-1720 period. They survive obscurely and feebly because in this period Christianity itself has lost most of her emotional power and imaginative warmth.

But a difficulty arises when we consider the relationship between Christianity and the basic doctrine of sentimentalism. The Christian, ideally speaking, should have quick and ardent feelings. He should be tender-hearted, charitable, and forgiving. His faith opposes any attempt to deny the importance of emotion as a factor which may combine with reason in the search for truth. Thus far Christianity is, in the unpejorative sense, sentimental. There seems, however, to be a wide chasm between the orthodox Christian doctrine of the heart's essential sinfulness and the sentimental doctrine of the heart's essential goodness. In modern times the practise of applying the term "Christianity" to the religion of sentiment has become so common that not all readers will appreciate the radical difference between the two viewpoints. But whatever "Christianity" *ought* to mean, up to the close of the seventeenth century it meant that man is a weak and sinful being who requires redemption through the Cross, and that nature is devoid of goodness except when regarded as the work of the God who gave His only-begotten Son. It is obvious that this is a completely different religion from the religion which describes man as a naturally good part of the universal harmony.

Yet we have seen that it is chiefly the Christian poets of the period who preserve those tendencies which are to become vehicles for the expression of sentimentalism. Here we are faced by a problem with which we are not yet ready to grapple. We may prepare to do so, however, by examining a small group of 1700-1720 poets who have not yet appeared in these pages. They are singled out for separate consideration because they are relatively rich in those pre-romantic tendencies which the literary historian associates with the sentimentalism of the eighteenth century.

Thanks to Pope's *Odyssey*, the name of Elijah Fenton (1683-1730) has been preserved like the proverbial fly in amber. Though his poems are in no important respect pre-romantic, they lack the cool precision of genuine neoclassicism. He admires Milton [31] and Shakespeare, and likes to write pathetic love-epistles in imitation of the *Heroïdes* and of *Eloisa*. But on the other hand he can be decidedly racy. Several of his poems—*The Fair Nun* is a sufficiently malodorous example—are fabliaux in Prior's vein, and he is coarse also in his *Tale, Devised in the Plesaunt Manere of Gentil Maister Geoffrey Chaucer*. One is not surprised to find him poking fun at Blackmore in *A Letter to the Knight of the Sable Shield*.

Very decent men, of course, have written very indecent verses. The coarseness of eighteenth-century poetry is often quite as superficial as its piety. Pope, who wrote an epitaph on his old amanuensis, described him in prose as an "amiable, quiet, deserving Christian and philosophical character." [32] In Johnson's *Life* he appears as sincere, modest, amiable, and virtuous. Broome, his collaborator on the *Odyssey*, declares that he

> . . . deign'd but to high themes to tune the string,
> To such as heav'n might hear, and angels sing.[33]

A note on the word "high" explains: "Mr. Fenton intended to write upon moral subjects."

As in the case of John Philips, however, this ambition was denied by death, so that Broome's lines are an unfulfilled hope rather than a description of what Fenton actually wrote. His only poem of religious interest is *An Ode*, which declares that life is a mystery inscrutable to human reason, a puzzle to be solved only on Judgment Day:

[31] Besides revealing this fact in his poems, he published a life of Milton in 1725.
[32] Quoted by George Paston, *Mr. Pope*, I, 311n.
[33] *On the Death of my Dear Friend, Elijah Fenton.*

> Instructed then by intuition, we
> Shall the vain efforts of our wisdom see;
>   Shall then impartially confess
>   Our demonstration was but guess;
> That knowledge, which from human reason flows,
>   Unless Religion guide its course,
>   And Faith her steady mounds oppose,
> Is ignorance at best, and often worse.

Here is a clear instance of fideism—the grounding of faith upon distrust of the powers of reason.

Otherwise there is little to be gleaned from Fenton. He presents a short satirical sketch of one *Olivia,* who is "lewd, but looks devout," and he paraphrases in blank verse *Part of the Fourteenth Chapter of Isaiah.* On the whole Fenton, who came of a good Staffordshire family, has the intellectual outlook and the aesthetic ideals of the aristocratic tradition. Rather than swear fealty to William, he left Cambridge without his degree; and his literary career was that of a minor satellite of the Tory wits. His only distinguishing feature is the combination of a slight tenderness with a not very shocking but fairly persistent nastiness.

In the work of Richardson Pack (1682-1728) a temperament much like Fenton's receives fuller and more interesting expression. What this soldier-poet thought of his own character may be learned from *An Epitaph:*

> The Man, who lies beneath this Stone,
> Liv'd no One's Foe besides his own:
> The Faults he had were not a few,
> But most of a Good-natur'd Hue:
> When sudden Gusts his Anger mov'd,
> With Zeal he hated, as he lov'd;
> But gentler Pow'rs soon rul'd his Mind,
> The Peevish yielded to the Kind:
> Where he found Friend or Mistress true,
> He melted like descending Dew:
> Free from all mean Distrust, or Art,
> Sincere and open was his Heart:
> He honour'd Merit in Disgrace,
> And scorn'd a Villain in high Place:
> To God and Cæsar Tribute gave,
> Yet neither Bigot was, or Slave;
> And in three Words, to sum the whole,
> Was a warm, honest am'rous Soul.

These lines provide a satisfying early description of the Tom Jones type of sentimentalist—the man of feeling who prides himself on being neither very good nor very bad, but sincerely and warmly human. His ancestors, no doubt, did what they pleased in Rabelais' Epicurean abbey. Pack is quite sure that his heart is in the right place, but he would rather die than be taken for a solemnly virtuous prig. His background is antipuritanical. Though a Whig, he is a country gentleman's son, an Oxford man, a professional soldier, and something of a libertine in his life and in not a few of his writings. It is interesting to recall that he was a friend of the aged Wycherley.

Although no one would champion Major Pack as a neglected genius, he rises so far above mediocrity that it is hard to understand his failure to win a modest place in literary history.[34] Most of his work, to be sure, lacks that precursorial quality which we now demand of the minor poets of his age. It is regulation neoclassical stuff, marked by imitation of Prior in the more gamesome pieces. Even when he is serious, he does not "melt like descending dew." Nevertheless, he represents more clearly than Fenton a loosening and softening of the aristocratic tradition. His amoristic verses, though sometimes coarse, usually emulate "Waller's sweetness." In the translations which constitute almost half of his work he prefers the tenderer Romans—Tibullus most of all, with Propertius, Ovid, and Catullus as other favorites. This elegant wit has a heart.

That heart, however, does not beat in sympathy with Christian orthodoxy. Pack would appreciate Blake's "garden of love," where

> . . . priests in black gowns were walking their rounds,
> And binding with briars my joys and desires.

He likes to sneer at the hypocritical fleshliness of parsons.[35] A cynical tale called *Religion and Philosophy* rationalizes his dislike of control through its thesis:

> Dull are our Maxims! False our grave Pretence!
> Reason, at last, will prove the Dupe of Sense.
> Our Age is influenc'd as our Youth inclin'd,
> And the same Byass always rules the Mind.

[34] See, however, R. D. Crain, "Richardson Pack," *Notes and Queries*, CLXX, 344. The article adds some details to the poet's biography, but does not recognize the interest of his work.

[35] Cf. *To John Creed*, and *An Expostulation with an Acquaintance, Who was going to Marry an Old Rich Parson.*

Distrust of reason is double-edged. To Fenton, in one poem at least, it preaches the life of faith; to Pack, it preaches the life of impulse.

Pack is very much himself when he confutes a freethinker with the following argument for immortality:

> Ah Wretch profane! did you but know
> The Bliss in Cloe's Arms I prove,
> You'd own the Joys of Love below
> Were earnest of a Heav'n above.[36]

Without taking this blasphemous gallantry too seriously, we may remember that Rossetti will write in all earnestness,

> Thy soul I knew not from thy body, nor
> Thee from myself, neither our love from God.[37]

The anti-clericalism of Pack is explained in *A Fragment of a Letter to the Honourable Mr. James Brudenell*. It begins:

> Curse on the lazy, fawning, treach'rous Tribe!
> Who meanly wou'd our Freedom circumscribe;
> And bred themselves in Slav'ry and in Vice,
> Would prostitute our Reason to their Lies.

He adds what we should not otherwise have suspected—that he reveres

> ...those good Men, who zealous but sincere,
> Serve at the Altar with religious Fear,
> Practise th' Austerities they gravely teach,
> And in their Lives as well as Sermons preach.

Observe the implications of "zealous *but* sincere." He now approaches the root of the matter:

> But when some sawcy Pedant of the Schools
> Would bridle Senates by fantastick Rules,
> When Mother Church turns Bawd to regal Pow'r,
> That her black Locusts may the Land devour,
> Each honest Briton should assert his Right,
> And put those spiritual Dragoons to Flight.

He refers to the Sacheverell turmoil:

> Too fully did a late Example show
> What ill Effects from Superstition flow.
> Our Laws and Treaties were become a Jest,
> And blind Obedience was the only Test.

---

[36] *To a Free-Thinker.*   [37] *The House of Life*, Part I, No. 5.

> Some Prigg Divine was ready still at hand,
> With spread Phylactery, and well-starch'd Band,
> (The solemn Ensigns of the Fop's Command)
> To recommend the Folly to the Land.
> All Orders and Degrees of Men infected,
> Acted as the smooth Hypocrites directed.

Pack's Whiggery was not of the sober, sensible, bourgeois kind. Like that of his kindred spirit, Nicholas Amhurst,[38] it was the expression of a distaste for any sort of curb. It is obvious that as he reached maturity in the reign of Queen Anne, he acquired a strong animus against the High Church party. This feeling, despite a vague admiration for a more or less Chaucerian type of ideal parson, easily expanded into a general opposition to the whole Church idea. But although the negative side of latitudinarianism such as Hoadly's won his allegiance, its positive side did not attract him. Lacking any strong religious feelings, and not finding any form of Christianity which did not either restrict or bore him, he decided to live according to his own "warm, honest, am'rous" impulses. His philosophy, if such it may be called, is a sentimentalized Cyrenaicism:

> The Gay, the Witty, and the Fair,
> Are all the Parties worth our Care;
> The rest would but enslave us.
> Let us adore the God of Wine,
> Submit to Beauty's Right Divine,
> And trust to Chance to save us.[39]

Since a man like Pack must be allowed his little inconsistencies, one need not be startled on turning from these lines to those *Upon Religious Solitude. Occasioned by reading the Inscription of the Tomb of Casimir King of Poland, who abdicated his Crown, and spent the Remainder of his Days in the Abbey of St. Germain's at Paris*. The poet praises the king for spurning worldly vanities, and craves for himself the spiritual benefits of solitude:

> Hail, gentle Piety! (unmingled Joy!)
> Whose Fulness satisfies, but ne'er can cloy:
> Spread thy soft Wings o'er my devoted Breast,
> And settle there, an everlasting Guest.

From this we may conclude that our libertine sentimentalist has discovered the possibility of being sentimental about religion.

[38] *Vide supra,* p. 85.   [39] *Le Chevalier sans soucis.*

If Pack develops the implications of Fenton, Samuel Croxall (1689-1752) develops those of Pack. Seekers of the pre-romantic should read him with care. He is a poet of feelings rather than of ideas; he is decidedly sensuous and rich in images; he can at times be seriously, rather than wittily or coarsely, erotic; he delights in external nature; and he is an intelligent lover of the earlier English literature. Furthermore, Croxall's work has a good deal of intrinsic merit. His trail-blazing imitations of Spenser—known to students at least by title—are excellent of their kind, and elsewhere in his work there are glints of the true ore.

Croxall, who in the Romantic Period would have been a minor Keats, began his career as a party writer. His *Original Canto from Spencer* (1713) and *Another Original Canto from Spencer* (1714) are narrative allegorical satires against Tory policies in Church and State. Gloriana is Queen Anne; Arthegall, the Elector of Hanover; Talus, Marlborough; Archimago, Harley; Duessa, Mrs. Masham; and so on. In 1715 the glorious Hanoverian and Protestant Succession is hymned in *The Vision,* a poem written in heroic couplets but Spenserian in style. Queen Elizabeth, appearing in a Protestant and anti-French allegorical pageant, delivers a speech about the peril of Rome. George, she declares, will preserve England from popery and the French.

Once England has been saved by George, Croxall no longer felt impelled to express his natural sensuousness in "state" poetry. In 1720 he published *The Fair Circassian, a Dramatic Performance.* This free paraphrase of the *Song of Solomon* he dedicated in fervent terms to Anna Maria Mordaunt, pretending that the poem, and some minor pieces included with it, were the work of a young Oxford student who had recently died of love. *The Fair Circassian* is "dramatic" only in being arranged as a dialogue between "He" (Solomon) and "She" (Saphira) with a few eruptions from a "Chorus of Virgins." The poem reflects the influence of the popular "Abra" episode in Book II of Prior's *Solomon.*[40] Croxall's motives for handling the theme are by no means religious: he chiefly wishes to exploit the voluptuousness of the original.

---

[40] The fact is not observed by H. G. De Maar, who provides, however, some interesting facts as to seventeenth-century paraphrases of *Canticles* in Spenserian stanzas both pious and voluptuous. (*Elizabethan and Modern Romanticism in the Eighteenth Century,* pp. 62 ff.) "Croxall," says De Maar, "turned the inconsistent blend of morality, religion, and sensuous warmth favoured by his Spenserian predecessors into downright carnality, which gave its author an unpleasant notoriety." (*Ibid.,* p. 65.)

Of the slighter pieces appended to *The Fair Circassian, On Florinda, Seen while She was bathing* and two love-epistles *To Sylvia* are sensuous to the point of sensuality. Their tone may be indicated by the fact that the second of the two Sylvia poems contains an offensive misapplication of Jacob's wrestling with the angel. Croxall knows his Ovid, and perhaps some of Ovid's Elizabethan admirers. From the *Fasti* he draws, for the sake of their raciness and their sneeringly sceptical quality, two tales entitled *Heathen Priestcraft* and *The Naked Truth*.

It is important to remember that the author of these unedifying poems, after a gentlemanly education at Eton and Cambridge, had a prosperous career as a clergyman of the Church of England. He was successively a Prebendary of Hereford Cathedral, Archdeacon of Shropshire, and Chancellor of the Diocese of Hereford.

He who functions as a priest long enough may sometimes acquire a little religion in spite of himself. In 1750, two years before his death, he published *The Royal Manual*. This long poem is an apparently sincere devotional address to God, lauding Him for His wonderful works and praying for wisdom and goodness. In this poem Croxall's love of nature merges with religious feeling, for the "royal manual" is the visible universe:

> The beauteous Heav'ns thy lasting Truth declare,
> With constellations rang'd in meet array;
> The sea-bound Earth, with verdure fresh and fair,
> Proclaims the wisdom of thy mighty sway.
>
> •   •   •   •
>
> Nature, with all her workings, is thy book,
> The patent that contains thy sov'reign will:
> Let me therein, with close inspection look,
> And ev'ry precept faithfully fulfill.
>
> •   •   •   •
>
> That brook, that glides; this earth, that solid stands,
> Thy laws, with properties diverse, obey.
> Grant me, obsequious to thy great commands,
> To act my part as regular as they.

Croxall's God, to judge from this poem, is not the Father who gave His only-begotten Son, but a Supreme Being who reveals himself solely through a creation which is both beautiful and law-abiding. Yet He is not a mere pantheistic force, for He can be prayed to with hope of under-standing and forgiveness.

Croxall may be summed up as a very low, broad, and Whiggish Angli-can clergyman whose religion is much less prominent than his gift for writing pleasingly sensuous verses. First he expresses himself through partisan allegories and visions. Next he dabbles in rather mild eroticism. At last, with the reaper at his heels, he turns to a God who is not quite the God of the deist and not quite the God of the Christian.

Fenton, Pack, and Croxall were all born in the 1680's. All three are gentlemen. All three (Fenton less markedly than the others) live by their feelings rather than by their brains. In varying measure, they display leanings toward the soft, the sensuous, the erotic. Their imaginations have a strain of licentiousness. Fenton stands somewhat apart from the others because in him these tendencies are more obscure. Furthermore, he is a Tory and presumably a High Churchman, while Pack and Croxall are latitudinarian Whigs. Pack's latitudinarianism is merely the reflection of a rebellious nature; Croxall's, as befits his cloth, includes a vague nat-uralistic piety. Neither Fenton nor Pack is conspicuously pre-romantic, but Croxall's work shows how easily this temperament merges with a love of nature, of Spenser, and of emotional and imaginative expression. For want of a better term, let us call these writers "libertine senti-mentalists."

There is some justification for applying the same title to John Gay (1685-1732). Lazy, sybaritic, witty, cynical, moody, amiable, childlike, he gave himself up to the sway of his inconsistent impulses. Like all really important writers of any period, however, he cannot be pigeon-holed as easily as less gifted men.

Gay is too worldly and frivolous, too sceptical and realistic, too much the Tory wit, to be in harmony with the sober middle-classicists of the preceding chapter. Blackmore, whom he rather amusingly satirizes,[41] would be shocked at the celebrated "Life is a jest" couplet. The world of *The Beggar's Opera* is not a world in which religion greatly matters. Gay is one of those not very moral people who enjoy dwelling on the immorality of the "unco' guid." Two of his tales, *Work for a Cooper* and *The Equivocation,* sneer at the lustfulness of Roman Catholic priests.

[41] *Verses to be Placed under the Picture of Sir Richard Blackmore.*

They illustrate a habit very common among eighteenth-century wits—that of using apparent dislike of popery as a cloak for their real dislike of all ecclesiasticism. Similarly, a general prejudice against religious ardor may be expressed through attacks on the fanaticism of dissenters. Thus in *The Espousal, a Sober Eclogue,*[42] we hear a Quaker and Quakeress wooing each other in a sanctimonious jargon which exposes the foibles of the sect with special reference to the sexual aspect of enthusiasm. At the climax Tabitha cries:

> Espousals are but forms. O lead me hence,
> For secret love can never give offence;

and the poet imputes to the Quakers a view of love which might be championed by Shelley:

> Thus hand in hand the loving mates withdraw:
> True love is nature unrestrain'd by law.
> This tenet all the holy sect allows;
> So Tabitha took earnest of a spouse.

But Gay is not to be placed among the neoclassical writers of the aristocratic tradition without important reservations. His keen-eyed realism, his fondness—perfectly genuine though often whimsically expressed—for country scenes and country people, his interest in Spenser,[43] and his cultivation of the popular sentimental lyric have long been recognized as looking forward to certain aspects of the Romantic Movement. His boyhood did little or nothing to prepare him to be the associate of Pope, Swift, and Arbuthnot. Reared in Devonshire, he never forgot the rustic lore which he had absorbed in the neighborhood of Barnstaple. His old and respectable but shabby family had accepted the standards of the social class to which poverty had reduced it, and could do no better for the boy than apprentice him to a London mercer. On returning to Barnstaple discouraged and ill as a result of this experience, he spent some time with

---

[42] The poem develops a hint in Swift's letter to Pope of August 30, 1716—the same letter in which Swift, by recommending "a Newgate pastoral," provided the germ of *The Beggar's Opera.*

[43] I refer, of course, to the strong Spenserian element in *The Shepherd's Week.* See also the *Proeme* of that work, a remarkable burlesque which could have been written only by a man thoroughly saturated in the vocabulary and cadences of Elizabethan prose.

his uncle John Hanmer, a nonconformist minister who doubtless did not regard life as a jest. When he finally established himself in London, his first employment was as secretary to Aaron Hill, whose solemnly emotional and religious view of poetry was much like that of John Dennis.

These circumstances did not prevent Gay from casting in his lot with the Tory wits. He was drawn toward them by a kind of temperamental gravitation combined, no doubt, with political motives. A young man who began his career in 1708 could easily see that the tide of Toryism was rising, that Bolingbroke was a man to be cultivated and that Pope and Swift were his friends. Nevertheless Gay's boyhood environment was not without influence. His description of the *Present State of Wit* in 1711 displays a strong and rather Whiggish-sounding admiration for *Tatler* and *Spectator;* and his work about this time, like Pope's, is tinged by the earnest morality of the Addison-Steele group.

Thus the middle-classicists would certainly approve of *A Thought on Eternity,* which contrasts infinitude with the petty time-scale of this world and concludes:

> Who then would wish to stretch this narrow span,
> To suffer life beyond the date of man?
> The virtuous soul pursues a nobler aim,
> And life regards but as a fleeting dream;
> She longs to wake, and wishes to get free,
> To launch from Earth into Eternity.

Appropriately, *A Contemplation on Night* appeared in Steele's *Poetical Miscellanies* of 1713. Gay looks up at the starry Newtonian sky and muses:

> Whether amid the gloom of night I stray,
> Or my glad eyes enjoy revolving day,
> Still Nature's various face informs my sense,
> Of an all-wise, all-powerful Providence.

Yet it is not the face of nature that he worships. Even when the stars and the sun have been extinguished, their creator will "for ever shine the same."

A passage in Canto I of *Rural Sports* has often been quoted for its combination of vivid nature-description and religious feeling, but the lines are too valuable to be omitted:

Or when the ploughman leaves the tasks of day,
And, trudging homeward, whistles on the way;
When the big-udder'd cows, with patience stand,
Waiting the stroakings of the damsel's hand;
When no rude gale disturbs the sleeping trees,
Nor aspen leaves confess the gentlest breeze,
Engag'd in thought, to Neptune's bounds I stray,
To take my farewell of the parting day;
Far in the deep the Sun his glory hides,
A streak of gold the sea and sky divides:
The purple clouds their amber linings show,
And, edg'd with flame, rolls every wave below:
Here pensive I behold the fading light,
And o'er the distant billow lose my sight.
Now Night in silent state begins to rise,
And twinkling orbs bestrow th' uncloudy skies;
Her borrow'd lustre growing Cynthia lends,
And on the main a glitt'ring path extends;
Millions of worlds hang in the spacious air,
Which round their suns their annual circles steer;
Sweet contemplation elevates my sense,
While I survey the works of Providence.
O could the Muse in loftier strains rehearse
The glorious Author of the universe,
Who reins the winds, gives the vast ocean bounds,
And circumscribes the floating worlds their rounds;
My soul should overflow in songs of praise,
And my Creator's name inspire my lays!

There is a hint of Newtonianism in "millions of worlds," but on the whole he is less concerned with an abstract mathematical system than with the actual beauty of nature. Contemplation of the sunset merges into contemplation of a Deity who in this case is very closely related to the lovely scene.

Gay would have been well qualified to develop, in the direction of greater realism and immediacy of impression, this more or less Addisonian reverence for "the spacious firmament on high," but his life and his writings took a very different turn. He is always, however, ambiguous and elusive. In his fable, *The Ravens, The Sexton, and the Earth-Worm,* the ravens smell what they suppose to be a dead horse, but the sexton tells them that the squire has died and will be buried tonight. He is outraged by their failure to smell the difference, but the ravens assure him that a dead horse smells just as good as a dead man. Then a worm—a very remote ancestor of the worm in Blake's *Book of Thel*—appears to referee the debate. As an expert he reports that there is little to choose between different kinds of carrion, except that a glutton's corpse is "the rankest." But in more serious vein he continues:

> The only true and real good
> Of man was never vermin's food:
> 'Tis seated in th' immortal mind;
> Virtue distinguishes mankind,
> And that (as yet ne'er harbour'd here)
> Mounts with the soul we know not where.

Then without a break the worm ends on the note with which he began:

> So, Good-man Sexton, since the case
> Appears with such a dubious face,
> To neither I the cause determine,
> For different tastes please different vermin.

Perhaps this mixture of earnestness and cynicism, of Addison and Swift, is as good a clue as can be found for an understanding of Gay. The slight sentimentalism in his work may be ascribed to a temperamental tendency to soften the polished brittleness of the aristocratic tradition which on the whole he accepted. We have seen, however, that his sentimentalism, especially its religious aspect, includes a strong middle-classical element derived partly from his early environment and partly from the influence of the Addison group. He was, of course, not a religious person, but beneath all his witty chatter of vermin and thieves and whores there was a strangely innocent, childlike heart which sometimes leaped up when the setting sun cast its rays upon the sea.

Thomas Parnell (1679-1718), another member of the Tory circle, has been widely hailed as a pre-romanticist. The nature-feeling and Miltonism of *A Hymn to Contentment*, the blend of mild *Il Penseroso* melancholy with graveyardism in *A Night-Piece on Death*, the lyrical quality of *My days have been so wondrous free* and other songs, the jocular but affectionate medievalism of *The Fairy Feast*—these are classroom commonplaces. The fact that only a few of his poems can be regarded as precursorial does not lessen their importance, and one may find even in his neoclassical writings some evidence that his real abilities lay in another direction.

This poet abounds in inconsistencies. The *Essay on the Different Styles of Poetry* shows the jumble of classical and romantic views which underlies his work. His character, too, oscillates perplexingly: he is a melancholy wit and a pious sot. Those who associate sentimentalism with a lack of centrality and steady rational control will probably apply the term to Parnell. But this diagnosis must be qualified by recognizing that Parnell, although a feeler, does not preach the pure gospel of feeling. The preromantic traits of his poems are closely related to a Christian faith which, for his day, is unusually ardent.

Parnell is one of those who take a lofty view of divine poetry. In *The Gift of Poetry* he prays that the "bright gift of verse" may descend to him from the throne of grace so that he may inspire other men with religious fervor; and in *Piety: Or the Vision,* Piety urges him to consecrate his poetic powers to God:

> But urge thy powers, thine utmost voice advance,
> Make the loud strings against thy fingers dance;
> 'Tis love that angels praise and men adore,
> 'Tis love divine that asks it all and more.
> Fling back the gates of ever-blazing day,
> Pour floods of liquid light to gild the way;
> And all in glory wrapt, through paths untrod,
> Pursue the great unseen descent of God;
> Hail the meek virgin, bid the child appear,
> The child is God, and call him Jesus here.

Though not a great religious poet, Parnell outstripped most of the other writers who held this theory of loftily impassioned divine poetry. This praise must be withheld from the series of long and stodgy Biblical paraphrases written, one gladly believes, early in his career: *Moses, Deborah, Hannah, David, Solomon, Jonah, Hezekiah, Habbakuk.* But as a writer of original religious lyrics he deserves respect. His three "hymns" for *Morning, Noon,* and *Evening* are prayers arising from his personal meditations, attempts to

> Send devotion up on high,
> Wing'd with heat, to reach the sky.[44]

---

[44] *A Hymn for Morning.*

They are not remarkable in expression, but their unmistakable sincerity is moving. In *A Hymn for Noon* he prays that just as the sun illumines the earth, so may his love for God illumine his heart:

> Let its glory more than vie
> With the sun that lights the sky:
> Let it swiftly mount in air,
> Mount with that [the sun] and leave it there,
> And soar with more aspiring flight
> To realms of everlasting light.
> Thus, while here I'm forc'd to be,
> I daily wish to live with thee,
> And feel that union which thy love
> Will, after death, complete above.

While Parnell is hardly a genuine mystic, this desire for union with divinity is prominent in his religious poems. It is expressed in *The Convert's Love* through devoutly erotic imagery which recalls the *geistliche Minnelieder* of the Middle Ages:

> My tender heart within its seat
> Dissolves before the scorching heat,
> As softening wax is taught to run
> Before the warmness of the sun.
> O my flame, my pleasing pain,
> Burn and purify my stain!
> Warm me, burn me, day by day,
> Till you purge my earth away,
> Till at the last I throughly shine,
> And turn a torch of love divine!

"Pleasing pain" is a false note derived from the contemporary jargon of gallantry, but the passage otherwise rings true. A similar feeling pervades *On Divine Love. By Meditating on the Wounds of Christ*:

> Holy Jesus! God of Love!
> Look with pity from above,
> Shed the precious purple tide
> From thine hands, thy feet, thy side;
> Let thy streams of comfort roll,
> Let them please and fill my soul:
> Let me thus for ever be
> Full of gladness, full of thee;
> This for which my wishes pine,
> Is the cup of love divine.

Very few Queen Anne clergymen would dream of anything so popish as meditating on the wounds of Christ. Parnell descended from supporters of the parliamentary party during the Rebellion; and his father, a close friend of the regicide John Bradshaw, moved to Ireland as a place where his aggressive nonconformity would be sanctioned as a counterpoise to Romanism. Precisely when Parnell began to call himself an Anglican we do not know. His early background was Whiggish, and it has always been assumed that his shift to the High Church party at just the proper time was merely prudential. In all the verses which have been quoted, however, one feels a Catholic spirit. Did Parnell transfer his puritan emotionalism to the high Anglicanism which he espoused? Was his change of party a little more spiritual and a little less politic than our knowledge of the age would suggest? Was he perhaps impressed by the fervor of the Roman Catholicism which surrounded him in Ireland? Was he acquainted with medieval religious poetry? As to the last question a curious bit of evidence is provided by his *Translation of Part of the First Canto of the Rape of the Lock into Leonine Verse, After the Manner of the Ancient Monks.*

In the absence of more definite knowledge about Parnell, this problem should be approached with caution. There was always plenty of the Whig moralist in him. Even after becoming a Tory he remained friendly with Addison and his circle. His famous *Hermit* is a poem that would be expected neither from a Scriblerus Club wit nor from an ardent Anglo-Catholic. The work of Watts and Mrs. Rowe, too, shows that the puritans had their own tradition of mystical eroticism. Nevertheless there is a quality in Parnell's aspiration toward union with God which is not to be found in those writers. That quality is combined with a doctrinal peculiarity in *A Hymn for Evening:*

> When grace and love in one agree,
> Grace from God, and love from me,
> Grace that will from Heaven inspire,
> Love that seals it in desire,
> Grace and love that mingle beams,
> And fill me with increasing flames.

Here is a very "high" Arminian conception of grace, implying that man as well as God plays a part in establishing the union of humanity with divinity. These lines agree in spirit with the stress placed on the Incarnation in *Piety* and with the prayer to the Trinity which concludes *A Hymn for Morning*. To deny the existence of an Anglo-Catholic element in Parnell would be no less uncritical than to exaggerate its importance.

The pre-romantic qualities of the *Hymn to Contentment* and *Night-Piece on Death* should not blind us to the fact that both are divine poems. The *Hymn* looks forward to Wordsworth less certainly than it looks backward to Cardinal Bona, for it was suggested by an ode in his *Divina Psalmodia*.[45] It tells us that contentment is a prize reserved for those who curb their passions and lift their thoughts to God. Parnell values rural retirement as providing opportunity for religious retreat and meditation in the proper technical sense of those terms:

> Oh! by yonder mossy seat,
> In my hours of sweet retreat,
> Might I thus my soul employ,
> With sense of gratitude and joy!
> Rais'd, as ancient prophets were,
> In heavenly vision, praise, and prayer.

He sings of natural objects chiefly to help them in praising God:

> All of these, and all I see,
> Should be sung, and sung by me:
> They speak their maker as they can,
> But want and ask the tongue of man.

In the *Night-Piece*, graveyardism of the type which descends from the puritan funeral elegies is tempered by the milder, more contemplative melancholy of the *Il Penseroso* tradition. The poem is a lyrical counterpart of *The Hermit* to the extent that it embodies the strain of Whiggish didacticism which mingles with the more mystical element in Parnell. Nevertheless it is essentially religious, and its moralizing leads straight to the pious conclusion:

> Death's but a path that must be trod,
> If man would ever pass to God.

Though it may be argued that the nature-feeling of *Hymn to Contentment* and the melancholy of *Night-Piece on Death* are more important than the religiosity of these poems, I doubt whether the author intended to give this impression. In many writers of the century these tendencies

[45] *Poetical Works* (ed. G. A. Aitken, 1894), p. 224.

will break loose from Christianity and become the vehicles of a religion of sentiment. But in Parnell this fissure, if it exists at all, is no more than a faint crack. The strange inconsistencies which divide the man and his work suggest the type of character which we associate with sentimentalism. The religion of this sentimentalist, however, is still the Christian religion. His "pre-romantic" pieces are merely divine poems of an unusually warm, lyrical, and imaginative kind.

Wordsworth's authority has made the pre-romanticism of Lady Winchilsea (1661-1720) as familiar as that of Parnell. Much of her work, to be sure, is merely the occasional prattle of a versifying noblewoman; but at times she can regard natural objects closely, can sing a little, and can express herself with a telling simplicity and directness. Of course a woman who began to write verses in about 1685 can hardly be in revolt against the neoclassical tyranny of the eighteenth century. It is simply that she carries from the reign of James II into the reign of Queen Anne ways of thinking and writing which by the latter period were temporarily out of fashion.

Divine poems comprise a much larger proportion of her work than the more famous nature-pieces, and they are above the average of merit for their time. Before we sample their qualities, however, something should be said of the poet's background.

As maid of honor to Mary of Modena,[46] Anne Kingsmill breathed, with her friend Anne Killigrew, a congenial atmosphere of mingled loyalty and piety. In 1684 she married, to her lasting happiness, that gentle, studious, dreamy-headed soldier and courtier, Heneage Finch. Him she warmly seconded in refusing to take the oath of loyalty to William III, and found that retirement and "the spleen" were not mere figments of the pen.

It was not long, however, before the couple found a permanent home at Eastwell, the estate of young Charles, third Earl of Winchilsea, whom his uncle Heneage was later to succeed. Gradually the very real emotional shock caused by the fall of James II passed away. The life of the large family circle, cut off from participation in court and political affairs, was serene, cultivated, virtuous, and quietly devout. Their most intimate friends in the country were also of the sort that one too easily forgets in thinking of the aristocracy of the period. Besides Lord Thanet of Hoth-

---

[46] Then Duchess of York. Our poet left her service to marry before her accession in 1685.

field and his wife, formerly Catherine Cavendish, there were the Thynnes of Longleat, generous and congenial hosts to Elizabeth Singer and Bishop Ken. Anne Finch and Lady Hertford [47] were warmly attached to each other. Miss Reynolds finds no evidence of intimacy between Ardelia[48] and the future Mrs. Rowe, but shows that she greatly admired the nonjuring prelate.[49]

Lady Winchilsea was a staunch Churchwoman. *Ardelia's Answer to Ephelia* shows that it was natural for her to slip into a church to pray even when no service was in progress, and that she resented the fashionable town habit of sneering at the clergy. Her "high" sympathies are amusingly revealed in *A Pindarick Poem Upon the Hurricane,* where she supposes that the great storm of 1703, which damaged the episcopal palace at Wells and killed Bishop Kidder and his wife, would have spared "strictly pious Ken" had he remained as the incumbent. She set her face against all heterodoxy. She *may* have written *Free Thinkers* (1711), a poem which attacks Hobbes and Toland and answers Shaftesbury's *Letter concerning Enthusiasm* by associating freethinking with immorality.[50]

Ardelia believes that although poetry is now the slave of Mammon, its true function is

> To elevate the hearts of Men
> And lead them to those Blissful seats agen
> Whence all harmonious Sounds and lofty Numbers flow.[51]

She relates the contemporary theory of divine poetry to her scorn of the frivolities to which men have confined her sex. There are plenty of female singers in the Bible—why should not a modern woman hymn God's praises?[52] Most of her numerous Scripture-paraphrases read like exercises in versification, but a few of the freer ones convert the original passages into religious lyrics of some merit. Her funeral-poems eschew graveyardism in favor of quietly orthodox inducements to consolation.

Several poems concern the mysterious ways of Providence. In *Some Reflections,* Ardelia murmurs at the prosperity of the wicked and the

[47] *Vide supra,* p. 208.   [48] Lady Winchilsea's pen name.
[49] *The Poems of Anne Countess of Winchilsea* (ed. Myra Reynolds), pp. xxxix, xl.
[50] See R. P. Bond, *English Burlesque Poetry,* pp. 266-267. Bond questions the attribution, which he derives from *Halkett and Laing.* The poem does not appear in Myra Reynolds' edition.
[51] *Upon the Death of King James the Second.*   [52] *The Introduction.*

miseries of the virtuous but is brought to a better way of thinking by her friend Teresa, who urges:

> Who leads thee throo' this Vale of tears below,
>   To bring thee to thy Country, safe att last?
> Who in the way, does all thou want'st bestow,
>   For more than this, his sacred word n'ere passt,
> And all thou truly want'st, assuredly thou hast?
>
> What if to prove thee, when the billows rise,
>   He from thy danger turns, and seems to sleep,
> Wilt thou to murmures, strait convert thy crys,
>   The crowd we see, the shoar may safely keep,
> Whilst the distinguish'd twelve are threatn'd by the deep?

The same view of the disciplinary value of adversity is set forth in *On Affliction*. With a pleasantly dry humor, *Man's Injustice Toward Providence* describes a merchant who credits himself with his successes but blames God for his failures. Her best-known fable, *The Atheist and the Acorn*, a version of La Fontaine's *La gland et la citrouille*, tells the story of the atheist who thinks that in a properly ordered universe acorns should grow on low vines and pumpkins hang from great trees. But when a falling acorn hits him in the eye he is glad that it is not a pumpkin.

Lady Winchilsea's views on Providence, though perhaps edifying, are conventional. Naturally she is more distinctive when she reveals the quality of her personal religious feeling. *A Preparation to Prayer* might have as its motto the speech of Shakespeare's Claudius, "Words without thoughts never to heaven go." She reproaches herself for the sluggishness of her spirit:

> Think, with what reverence, and state,
>   Thy Maker is ador'd above,
> What mighty Beings, round him waite,
>   And pay their Worship, and their Love:
> That Cherubims, are in his sight afraid,
> And with enfolded wings their glorious faces shade.
>
> How must that Guardian Angel grieve,
>   That to attend thy soul is sent,
> Such cold petitions to receive,
>   As his warm zeal can n'ere present?
> How must he grieve, thy empty forms to see?
> In spirit and in truth, his God must worship'd bee.

THE BEGINNINGS OF SENTIMENTALISM

For the Countess there is ceremonial even in heaven, but like many people whose religion is rich in external forms she is on her guard against the snare of formalism.

Both in stanza-pattern and emotional quality, *On Easter Day* is at least remotely akin to Smart's *Song to David:*

> In vain the silly Rabbins strove,
>   A Strattagem of force to find,
>   The Lord Omnipotent to bind.
> Too weak,. to stop Almighty love,
> Their guard, their stone, their seal must prove,
> The trembling Earth, does all remove
>   Like dust before the wind.
>
>   ·   ·   ·   ·
>
> Unfold, ye Everlasting Gates,
>   That guard the great Jehova's Towers,
>   Those sacred, mystick leaves of yours,
> The King of Glory for you waits.
>   Receive him, oh! ye blissfull Bowers,
>   Ye Thrones, Dominions, Scepter'd Powers,
>   He comes! accomplish'd are the hours,
> Appointed by the Fates.[53]

Hallelujah sings with fervor her own hope of triumphing over death and the grave through faith in the risen Jesus. Several other examples might be adduced to show that Lady Winchilsea's imagination responds warmly to the poetic appeal of orthodox Christianity.

But what of the poems which are most frequently used in emphasizing Ardelia's pre-romanticism? *The Tree, The Bird,* and *To the Nightingale* are wholly without religious feeling, but on the other hand they disclose no very warm or thoughtful response to natural objects. They are slight, half-whimsical pieces in which piety would hardly be expected. There is no reason why a pious woman cannot enjoy trees and birds without constantly raising her eyes to heaven. In general her attitude toward nature shows a realism of the mind as well as of the eye. She genuinely likes natural objects and enjoys getting them down on paper, but she is not one to talk nonsense about them. The rivers and flowers and caves *should* lament the death of Sir William Twisden, but they do nothing of the sort:

[53] Dr. Johnson would quite properly complain that "the Fates" have no business in such a poem.

But oh! in vain, things void of sense, we call,
In vain, implore the murmuring sound
Of hollow groans, from underneath the ground;
Or court the loud laments, of some steep water's fall;
On things inanimate, would force
Some share of our divided greif,
Whilst Nature (unconcern'd for our relief)
Persues her settl'd path, her fixt, and steady course,
Leaving those ills, which Providence allows
To check our Pleasures, and contract our Brows,
Freely to act their uncontrouled part,
Within the center of the human breast.[54]

That charming retirement-piece, *The Petition for an Absolute Retreat,*
bespeaks a genuine fondness for country scenes. Despite the serene gaiety
of the poem, however, the pietistic element is strong. She moralizes natural objects, introduces several Biblical allusions, and concludes by saying
that the chief pleasure of her retreat will be the contemplation of heaven.
And this joy, we learn from a *Fragment,* is but the shadow of an ecstasy
which can fully be attained only beyond the grave:

Th' Expanse, the Light, the Harmony, the Throng,
The Bride's Attendance, and the Bridal Song,
The numerous Mansions, and th' immortal Tree,
No eye, unpurg'd by Death, must ever see,
Or Waves which through that wond'rous City roll.
Rest then content, my too impatient Soul:
Observe but here the easie Precepts given,
Then wait with chearful hope, till Heaven be known in Heaven.

Lady Winchilsea has a keen eye for external nature, but she seldom
feels very strongly about it. When she does, her feelings are those of a
Christian, not those of a sentimental naturalist.

In her rural retreat Ardelia does not cultivate the pleasures of melancholy. Perhaps, as an actual victim of the fashionable ailment,
she has no wish to praise its charms. In *The Spleen*—her most
popular poem throughout the eighteenth century—she describes this
malady in a more or less Burtonian manner as an elusive spirit of many
guises which may pervade and mar every aspect of life. Its evil effect on
religion is thus described:

[54] *Upon the Death of Sir William Twisden.*

> By Thee Religion, all we know,
> That shou'd enlighten here below,
> Is veil'd in Darkness, and perplext
> With anxious Doubts, with endless Scruples vext,
> And some Restraint imply'd from each perverted Text.
> Whilst Touch not, Taste not, what is freely giv'n,
> Is but thy niggard Voice, disgracing bounteous Heav'n.

The Countess, then, has no sentimental enthusiasm for melancholy, and does not regard it as the friend of religion.

Wordsworth was right in singling out *The Nocturnal Reverie* for special praise. Nowhere else does Ardelia look at things so sharply or feel about them so deeply. The closely-observed details of sight and sound give her spirit a "sedate Content," and

> ... silent Musings urge the Mind to seek
> Something, too high for Syllables to speak;
> Till the free Soul to a compos'dness charm'd,
> Finding the Elements of Rage disarm'd,
> O'er all below a solemn Quiet grown,
> Joys in th' inferiour World, and thinks it like her Own.

One may conjecture that these musings, arising so directly from her response to her physical surroundings, pertain to a vaguer and more sentimental religion than that which she expresses in her divine poems. A general knowledge of her work, however, will render this assumption dubious. Lady Winchilsea's poems are sometimes pre-romantic in the sense that they possess a fondness for nature, a keenness of eye and a simplicity of expression which will play a part in the Romantic Movement; but temperamentally she is much less of a sentimentalist than Parnell. Nevertheless it may be said of her, as was said of Parnell, that the great majority of her more emotional and lyrical poems are not only definitely religious but definitely Christian.

The above remark can hardly be applied to the poems of Lady Mary Chudleigh (1656-1710).[55] Many of them bear indirectly on religion, but her one definitely "divine" poem is *The Song of the Three Children*

---

[55] Since her *Poems on Several Occasions* appeared in 1703, when she was forty-seven years old, she is definitely a seventeenth-century writer. But many if not most of the poems were written during the retirement which speedily followed her unhappy marriage in 1685, and she may be regarded as one of the links which connect the seventeenth and eighteenth centuries.

Paraphrased. From a literary viewpoint this pseudo-Pindaric ode is unremarkable, but it deserves attention because the author interprets the original in the light of contemporary science. The nature of the additions and the spirit in which she works are made clear in the preface: "In Paraphrasing that part of the Hymn which mentions the Stars, I have made use of the Cartesian Hypothesis, that the Fixt Stars are Suns, and each the Center of a Vortex; which I am willing to believe, because it gives me a noble and sublime Idea of the Universe, and makes it appear infinitely larger, fuller, more magnificent, and every way worthier of its great Artificer." So immense a universe, she also feels, has the desirable effect of abasing human pride. Burnet is cited as her authority for "supposing the Face of the Ante-deluvian Earth to be smooth, regular and uniform."

She tempers her scientific enthusiasm by meekly averring that "if anything in that part of the Poem which mentions the Creation of the World is thought to be contradictory to the received Principles of Philosophy, or the Mosaical Account of the Creation, I shall readily acknowledge my error." Women, she interjects with a touch of that feminist acrimony which characterizes the seventeenth-century learned lady, "are kept strangers to all ingenious and useful studies," and hence she may have erred through ignorance.

She is all the more anxious not to give offense because she honors the priesthood, and considers that "the Church of England was never blest with a more learned, Orthodox, and Ingenious Clergy than now." This anchor thrown out to windward, she indulges in two pages of latitudinarian *clichés:* extremes should be avoided, inessentials should not be stressed, internal religion is more important than external, and so on to the conclusion: "'Tis not Talking, but Living well, not the being of this or that Denomination, or of this or that Sect or Party, that will make them [people] eternally happy; but the being exactly conformable to those divine Rules which are prescrib'd in the Holy Scriptures."

Elsewhere in Marissa's effusions, however, there is not much science, nor much interest in external nature, nor much that is quite identifiable as Christianity. She appears as a stoical, epicurean, sentimental Platonist. It is not my fault if the combination is incongruous. In the general preface to her *Poems on Several Occasions,* she assures us that "'tis impossible to be happy without making Reason the Standard of all

our Thoughts, Words, and Actions," and that our woes would disappear
if we learned to "contract our Desires."

It follows that "the way to be truly easie, to be always serene, to have
our Passions under a due Government . . . is to retire into our selves."
But in order to retire into ourselves, Lady Chudleigh frequently reminds
us, we must retire from the world:

> Those few who dare be good, must live alone,
> To all Mankind, except themselves, unknown;
> From a mad World, to some obscure Recess
> They must retire to purchase Happiness.[56]

What sort of happiness is thus purchased? "Books," she says in *The
Resolution,* "are the best Companions I can find." Among her favorite
authors are Burnet, Stillingfleet, and Tillotson—all good latitudinarians.
Norris, Platonist as well as latitudinarian, she particularly cherishes:

> Plato reviv'd, we in his writings find,
> His sentiments are there, but more refin'd.

Though she admires Lucretius as a poet, she considers it

> Strange that a Man of such a Strength of Thought,
> Could think a World was to Perfection brought
> Without Assistance from the Pow'rs above,
> From the best Source of Wisdom, and of Love!

Nevertheless she recoils from the verge of Christianity to voice approval
of the Lucretian ethics, which convinces her "that happiness in Virtue
lies." Above all, it banishes her dread of death:

> The shocking Prospect of a future State,
> Does in our Souls an anxious Fear create;
>
> .   .   .   .
>
> But were we by enlightned Reason led,
> Were false Opinions banish'd from the Mind,
> And we to the strict Search of Truth inclin'd,
> We sure should meet it with as much Delight
> As the cool Pleasures of a silent Night,
> And to our Graves with Chearfulness should run,
> Pleas'd that our tedious Task of Life were done.

This seems to imply utter disbelief in immortality, but Marissa had better not be pinned down too closely.

[56] *To Eugenia.*

Despite brief moments of dalliance with Seneca or Lucretius, the presiding genius of Lady Chudleigh's retreat is Plato. She longs to be among those happy ones who,

> . . . in some obscure Recess,
> . . . could with silent Joy think all their hours away,
> And still think on, till the confining Clay
> Fall off, and nothing's left behind
> Of drossy Earth, nothing to clog the Mind,
> Or hinder its Ascent to those bright Forms above,
> Those glorious Beings whose exalted Sense
> Transcends the highest Flights of human Wit;
> Who with Seraphick Ardor fir'd,
> And with a Passion more intense
> Than mortal Beauty e'er inspir'd;
> With all th' endearing Ecstasies of Love,
> Will to their blest Society again
> The long lost Wanderers admit,
> Where freed from all their former Pain,
> And cleans'd from ev'ry Stain,
> They bask with Pleasure in eternal Day,
> And grow as pure, and as refin'd as they.

This extremely sentimental *amor intellectualis* is not to be enjoyed in utter loneliness, for Lady Chudleigh's solitude is a special kind of *solitude à deux*. Very unhappily married, she persistently indulges in pseudo-Platonic gush about female friendship, inviting Amystrea, Eugenia, Lucinda, and Clorissa to share her retirement.[57] Fortunately for her reputation, she wrote before the days of the psychoanalyst. Clorissa is assured that in "some belov'd Retreat,"

> . . . of a Thousand Sweets possest,
> We'll live in one another's Breast:
> When present, talk the flying Hours away,
> When absent, thus our tender Thoughts convey:
> And when, by the decrees of Fate,
> We're summon'd to a higher State,
> We'll meet again in the blest Realms of Light,
> And in each other there eternally delight.

The joys of the future life are simply those of female-friendship-in-retirement raised to a higher level—"Changed not in kind, but in degree,"

[57] See the poems addressed to these ladies.

as Browning puts it. *To Amystrea* gives a fascinating glimpse of a heaven in which sentimentalized Christianity, Plato, and the opera are mingled. Though a little too absurd to be perfectly typical of Lady Chudleigh, it may serve as a summary of the quality of her religion. Those "who in the dregs of life delight," she declares, must learn while on earth

> To wish for nothing but exchange of thoughts,
>   For intellectual joys,
>   And pleasures more refined
> Than earth can give, or can create.
> Let our vain sex be fond of glitt'ring toys,
> Of pompous titles, and affected noise,
> While we resolve a nobler path to tread,
>   And from tyrannick custom free,
> View the dark mansions of the mighty dead,
>   And all their close recesses see.
> Then from those awful shades retire,
>   And take a tour above,
> And there, the shining scenes admire,
>   The opera of eternal love;
> View the machines, on the blest actors gaze,
> Then in a holy transport, blest amaze,
> To the great Author our devotion raise,
> And let our wonder terminate in praise.

Lady Chudleigh doubtless considers herself a good Christian, but in her poems she is much more of a sentimentalist than either Parnell or Lady Winchilsea. In her we see a seventeenth-century gentlewoman, neglected by her husband, trying to find solace in retirement and reading. She has feelings which she perhaps too hastily identifies as spiritual, and she hankers to express them in verse. Intellectually, she accepts the cool, broad, sensible Christianity of Tillotson and admires the physico-theological speculations of Burnet. But they do not satisfy her emotions: there is no poetry in the former, and not much in the latter. Seneca and Lucretius appeal to her in certain moods, but their ideas will not express the vague upward surge of her heart. Her need, then, is satisfied by a latitudinarianism earlier than Tillotson's—that of the Cambridge Platonists. Their severer scientific and metaphysical speculations, their efforts to find a rational basis for Christianity, do not interest her. They are helpful, however, in seeming to provide a warrant for indulging in lofty nonsense about ideals. She greatly admires John Norris, and it seems probable that he is her chief guide into these mysteries. We have already observed that while Norris is a good Christian Platonist, his Platonism could easily part company from his Christianity and function as a separate religion.[58] This has happened, or almost happened, in the case of Lady Chudleigh. Apparently also she is influenced by the softer and more languishing Platonism of the courtly *précieuse* tradition, with its chatter about virtues and perfect friendships. From this blend of courtly and academic Platonisms she distills a religion of sentimental idealism. Marissa's operatic heaven is the goal of a faith which, without denying Christianity, almost wholly neglects it in favor of attitudes which she deems more poetical and exciting.

Students of the eighteenth century will probably credit Ambrose Philips (1674-1749) with some slight naturalistic and sentimental leanings. To judge from his *Epistle to the Earl of Dorset* he could also, on occasion, look at real objects with his own eyes. An ardently Whiggish member of the Addison circle, Philips was a Low Churchman, a worshipper of William of Orange, a hater of popery, and a somewhat priggish moralist. The evidence for these statements, however, must be sought chiefly in his periodical, *The Free-Thinker*.[59] His poems tell us almost nothing about his religious views and feelings. The ode *On the Death of the Right Honourable William Earl Cowper* contains some gloomy reflections on the vanity of mortal life and some trite remarks on the heavenly rewards of virtue, but with this exception there is nothing definite to report. Namby-Pamby's affection for rural simplicities and—not quite disinterestedly—for the children of prominent persons is too feeble to have any religious significance for him or for the reader. His Christianity has grown too dull and moralistic to have any grip upon his imagination, but no other spiritual force has taken its place. Philips is a mild sentimentalist who has not yet discovered the religion of sentiment.[60]

---

[58] *Vide supra*, p. 111.

[59] The title implies no heterodoxy. Philips and the group of divines who supported him in this moral-reform project were trying to purify the connotations which the term had acquired from such works as Collins' *Discourse of Freethinking*.

[60] I should have mentioned interest in balladry as one of his pre-romantic symptoms had not his editorship of *A Collection of Old Ballads* (1723) been almost conclusively disproved by Lillian De La Torre Bueno, "Was Ambrose Philips a Ballad Editor?" *Anglia*, LIX, 252-270.

It cannot be said that there is anything wildly romantic about the work of Thomas Tickell (1685-1740), another member of Cato's little senate. A keen-eyed diagnostician, however, may observe several telltale symptoms. At Oxford he was the intimate friend of Edward Young. He likes Chaucer and Spenser, and thinks of fairies in *Kensington Gardens*. *To a Lady Before Marriage* praises retirement and displays some feeling for nature. Elsewhere he speaks of solitary mourning as a "Sad luxury, to vulgar minds unknown." [61] *A Fragment on Hunting* is an early imitation of Virgil's *Georgics*. A well-known locus in the ballad-revival is *Colin and Lucy*. Although Goldsmith goes too far in asserting that "a strain of ballad-thinking" runs through all his work, he is not quite the typical Augustan. He is hardly an imaginative writer, but he has a pleasant vein of fancy. Even when he is most loyal to neoclassical conventions he tends to express feelings rather than merely to versify ideas. In *To the Earl of Warwick, On the Death of Mr. Addison* he succeeds in communicating the genuine emotion which has gripped him.

Tickell's father and grandfather were Anglican clergymen; but he left no divine poems behind him and not much in his secular poems is pertinent to our subject, although their general tone is that of a man who is friendly to good morals and probably to religion. His well-known attachment to Addison may lead one to exaggerate the fervor of his Whiggery. He was never, in fact, a strong party man, and some of his earlier poems show him hesitating between the two factions. Thus *A Poem on the Prospect of Peace* (1712) attempts simultaneously to praise the Whig heroes and support the Tory peace policy. At about the same time, with the Tories still in power, he penned some lines expressing sympathy for Charles I, "God's substitute below," and detestation of Cromwell.[62] This uncharacteristic poem is inscribed to George Clarke, a fellow of All Souls' and a Tory politician.[63]

But once George I is firmly on the throne, we find no further suggestions of Toryism in Tickell's poems. In 1717 he who had lamented the Royal Martyr now satirizes his descendants in *An Epistle from a Lady in England to a Gentleman at Avignon*. The "lady" asks her exiled Jacobite lover for the latest news of the Pretender's plans:

[61] *To the Earl of Warwick.*

[62] *Thoughts Occasioned by the Sight of an Original Picture of King Charles I, Taken at the Time of His Trial.*

[63] R. E. Tickell, *Thomas Tickell and the Eighteenth Century Poets*, p. 28.

> Say, for thou know'st I own his sacred line,
> The passive doctrine, and the right divine,
> Say, what new succours does the chief prepare?
> The strength of armies? or the force of prayer?
> Does he from Heaven or Earth his hopes derive?
> From saints departed, or from priests alive?
> Nor saints nor priests can Brunswick's troops withstand,
> And beads drop useless through the zealot's hand;
> Heaven to our vows may future kingdoms owe,
> But skill and courage win the crowns below.

The literature of the century presents many other instances in which hatred of Stuart popery leads good Protestant Whigs into basically irreligious attitudes.

This hard realism disappears when there is no ecclesiastical foe to be attacked. *To the Supposed Author of the Spectator* enthusiastically praises Addison's efforts to reform the age. Thanks to his essays, morals have improved,

> And the rash fool, who scorn'd the beaten road,
> Dares quake at thunder, and confess his God.

The thought of Addison, indeed, brings out all the religion that his admirer possesses. The famous elegy mingles piety with its praises of the dead. How, Tickell wonders, will Addison spend his time in heaven?

> Does he delight to hear bold seraphs tell
> How Michael battled, and the dragon fell;
> Or, mix'd with milder cherubim, to glow
> In hymns of love, not ill essay'd below?
> Or dost thou warn poor mortals left behind,
> A task well-suited to thy gentle mind?
> Oh! if sometimes thy spotless form descend:
> To me, thy aid, thou guardian genius, lend!

Observe the neat allusions to Addison's works: *The Campaign,* the divine "odes," and *Spectator.* But Tickell loved his friend, and the cleverness of the lines does not prove them insincere.

A more interesting passage in the same poem recalls his feelings at Addison's funeral in the Abbey:

> How silent did his old companions tread,
> By midnight lamps, the mansions of the dead,

Through breathing statues, then unheeded things,
Through rows of warriors, and through walks of kings!
What awe did the slow solemn knell inspire;
The pealing organ, and the pausing choir;
The duties by the lawn-rob'd prelate pay'd;
And the last words that dust to dust convey'd!

Quite evidently the occasion moved his emotions through his senses. At such moments there was a chance that religion might really get under his skin.

But Tickell is so plainly a poet of compromise and transition that it is difficult to generalize about him. Perhaps he should be called a man of some religious sensibility without a very clear sense of a God above and beyond his feelings, a Christian whose Christianity has lost most of its definiteness and hence most of its intensity. If we look back at him from later stages of this study, we may faintly discern in his work the germs of a tendency to seek religious satisfaction in non-religious forms of emotional experience.

My readers will readily identify John Hughes (1677-1720) as the author of a successful tragedy, *The Siege of Damascus*, the first eighteenth-century editor of Spenser, an occasional contributor to *Tatler, Spectator,* and *Guardian*, and the translator of the French source of Pope's *Eloisa to Abelard*. Not many, however, will be acquainted with his non-dramatic verse. The two volumes of *Poems on Several Occasions*, posthumously published by his brother-in-law William Duncombe in 1735, run the familiar gamut of neoclassical versifying, from *The House of Nassau. A Pindarick Ode* to *On a Peacock Finely Cut in Vellum by Molinda*. One's first impulse is to cast Hughes aside with the reflection that he is neither very good nor very bad.

Examined more closely, however, these poems display features of some historical significance. Though not a writer of real power, Hughes at least attempts to be emotional and imaginative more often than most poets of his generation. More obviously, he shows considerable skill and variety in the use of stanza-forms. Pindarics and lyrical measures of many different kinds greatly outnumber his poems in heroic couplets. His pindarics, too, are of the fluently melodious rather than of the shaggy and furious kind. Himself a violinist, he frequently writes for a musical setting—operas, pastoral masques, cantatas, love-songs, "odes for music." This marked peculiarity leads Duncombe to call him, boldly and absurdly, "our finest Lyrick Poet."

Hughes is also a lover of external nature. He tells a friend that poetry cannot be expected to flourish in the city, for it requires

> . . . warbling Birds, soft whisp'ring Breaths of Wind,
> And murmuring Streams.

He yearns to retire to those "Delightful Springs and Woods" which are the "blest Remains" of Eden's primal innocence.[64] Though he lacks the skill to make his sense-experiences come alive in words, one cannot doubt, after reading *Ode on the Spring, An Ode in the Park at Asted,* and *Barn-Elms,* that he looked at natural objects with close and happy attention.

Hughes is by no means a wit; he almost never indulges in epigram, satire, or burlesque. Though he strives for easy melodious elegance, and avoids ponderous moralizing, there is nothing in his work that Queen Victoria might not have read with approval. If his poems were subscribed for by Voltaire, they were also subscribed for by his old schoolfellow, Isaac Watts. Mrs. Rowe certifies him to be "really an author of genius and strict morals." [65] From November, 1713, to February, 1714, he collaborated with Blackmore in a moral-reform periodical, *The Lay Monk.*

Like Dennis, Watts, Blackmore, and many others, Hughes believes that poetry, though now sadly corrupted, is sacred in its origins and should be restored to its proper function of singing God's praises. In Eden

> Descending Angels, in harmonious Lays,
> Taught the first happy Pair their Maker's Praise.
> Such was the Sacred Art— We now deplore
> The Muse's Loss, since Eden is no more.
>
> .   .   .   .
>
> Yet to some Few, whose dazzling Virtues shone
> In Ages past, her heav'nly Charms were known.
> Hence learn'd the Bard, in lofty Strains to tell
> How patient Virtue triumph'd over Hell;

[64] *A Letter to a Friend in the Country.*
[65] *Miscellaneous Works . . . of Mrs. Elizabeth Rowe,* II, 168.

And hence the Chief, who led the chosen Race
Thro' parting Seas, derived his Songs of Praise:
She [the Muse] gave the rapturous Ode, whose ardent Lay
Sings Female Force, and vanquish'd Sisera;
She turn'd to pious Notes the Psalmist's Lyre,
And fill'd Isaiah's Breast with more than Pindar's Fire! [66]

The association of divine poetry with "rapturous odes" like those of
Pindar has become familiar to us. In his *Essay on Allegorical Poetry* he
declares: "I might here give Examples of this noble and antient kind of
Writing, out of the Books of Holy Writ, and especially the Jewish
Prophets, in which we find a Spirit of Poetry surprizingly sublime and
majestick: But these are obvious to every one's reading. The East seems
indeed to have been principally the Region of these figurative and em-
blematical Writings. Sir John Chardin in his Travels has given us a
Translation of modern Persian Poetry; which shews that there are traces
of the same Genius remaining among the present inhabitants of those
Countries." This suggestion of an historical and comparative view of
scriptural poetry is significant. Hughes would be startled by the notion
that the prophetic books are merely very interesting specimens of ori-
ental poetry, but his own remarks contain the germ of such an interpretation.

This writer of love-songs, cantatas, and loyal eulogies seldom attempts
to apply the religious conception of poetry to his own work. When he
does so, one generally suspects that he has merely seized upon an opportunity to write an ode. *The Ecstasy,* a highly pindaric vision of earth
from heaven, freely paraphrases Casimir's *E rebus humanis Excessus,*
"from which it is plain," as Hughes observes, "that Cowley likewise took
the first Hint of his Ode call'd the Ecstasy." [67] Toward the end of the
poem, however, Hughes becomes entirely original. His visionary sees "a
pointed Flame" rising from earth and ranging about among the planets:

'Tis Newton's Soul, that daily travels here
In search of Knowledge for Mankind below.

The poet begs "the great Columbus of the skies" to be his guide through
the mazes of the universe:

---

[66] *On Divine Poetry.*
[67] For a version of Casimir's ode by John Norris, *vide supra,* p. 110. Hughes is doubtless
familiar with Norris's poem as well as Casimir's.

Here let me, thy Companion, stray,
From Orb to Orb, and now behold
Unnumber'd Suns, all Seas of molten Gold;
And trace each Comet's wand'ring Way,
And now descry Light's Fountain-Head,
And measure its descending Speed;
Or learn how Sun-born Colours rise
In Rays distinct, and in the Skies
Blended in yellow Radiance flow,
Or stain the fleecy Cloud, or streak the watry Bow.

The Ecstasy was first published in 1720. We do not know when it was written, but even this date is extremely early for such lines as have been quoted. By this time Newton had become the great source of physico-theological arguments, but very few other poets, if any, had responded to his discoveries in so lyrical and imaginative a strain.

Another effort at sublimity is *An Ode to the Creator of the World. Occasion'd by the Fragments of Orpheus.* Parts of it are borrowed from Norris's *On the Creation.* After several stanzas of inflation, the poet attains a glimpse of the Throne of Glory only to be struck dumb with awe:

Then, Muse, th' adventrous Flight forbear!
These Mystick Scenes thou canst no farther trace;
Hope may some boundless Future Bliss embrace,
But *What,* or *When,* or *How,* or *Where,*
Are Mazes all, which Fancy runs in vain;
Nor can the narrow Cells of human Brain
The vast immeasurable Thoughts contain.

To a slight extent Hughes's fondness for nature is combined with religious feeling in *A Thought in a Garden* which, he obligingly tells us, was written in 1704. This poem, with its four-stressed couplets, its nature-feeling, and its retirement-for-contemplation theme, is a very early imitation of Milton's octosyllabics.[68] But for Hughes the term "contemplation" has lost its technically Christian meaning and has become merely a half-moral, half-sensuous reverie of the fancy. The conclusion, the most serious part of the poem, does extract a little sermon from the landscape:

[68] R. D. Havens, in *The Influence of Milton on English Poetry,* p. 669, places it fifth in a chronological list of poems influenced by *L'Allegro* or *Il Penseroso.* One of the four earlier poems, a paraphrase from Horace, is by Hughes himself.

For see, where beauteous Thames does glide
Serene, but with a fruitful Tide;
Free from Extremes of Ebb and Flow,
Not swell'd too high, nor sunk too low:
Such let my Life's smooth Current be,
Till, from Time's narrow Shore set free,
It mingle with th' Eternal Sea;
And, there enlarg'd, shall be no more
That trifling Thing it was before.

Thus the river of Denham's *Cooper's Hill,* "Strong without rage, without o'erflowing full," will transcend its trim restrictions in the after-life. But there is nothing very definitely Christian in this hope of ultimate escape and expansion. Compared to Parnell's *Hymn to Contentment,* a poem of the same general type, the religious element in *A Thought in a Garden* is thin and hazy.

Hughes came of a Wiltshire family of prosperous and cultivated puritans, but his clerical grandfather was ejected from his living as a nonconformist in 1662, and his father's modest station was that of a clerk in the Hand-in-Hand Fire Office. The poet was educated, with Isaac Watts and William Duncombe, at Thomas Rowe's nonconformist academy in Little Britain. Naturally he was a stout Whig, and in some of his patriotic odes he combines the political and the ecclesiastical views of his party.[69] Once he appears as a satirist of Tories and High Churchmen: *Hudibras Imitated* (1710) is almost unique in employing Butler's verse-form and general manner as weapons on the Whig side. His closest literary friends were Addison, Steele, and Nicholas Rowe. He was on friendly terms, however, with equally Whiggish but more definitely pietistic writers such as Isaac Watts, Elizabeth Rowe, and Sir Richard Blackmore.

Such a man might easily have become a dissenting preacher and divine poet like Watts, or a semi-professional improver of mankind like Blackmore. But with the partial exception of *The Lay Monk,* he chose instead the career of a definitely secular dramatist, poet, and man of letters. His importance for us lies in the fact that no other poet of the 1700-1720 period is at the same time so rich in pre-romantic symptoms, so unmistakably puritan in background, and so lacking in poetic response to specifically Christian ideas. A probable explanation is that Hughes, like so many other dissenters of his time, was attracted by the vague breadth

[69] Cf. *The House of Nassau* and *The Triumph of Peace.*

of latitudinarianism. One of his friends not hitherto mentioned was Bishop Hoadly, another descendant of puritans, with whom he conducted a long correspondence. Hughes was a Christian; but since his actual beliefs were too colorless and sensible to be stimulating to his imagination, his poetry and his Christianity are much less closely related than in Parnell or Lady Winchilsea. His work shows what may happen when puritanism grows secular, soft, and nebulous.

On February 24, 1717, William Duncombe wrote a pious-sounding letter to Hughes, his brother-in-law, telling of the desperate illness of "our unfortunate Friend," Henry Needler (1690-1718).[70] He urges Hughes to edit Needler's papers and memorialize his virtues. But Hughes did not undertake this task, and in 1724 Duncombe performed it himself by publishing *The Works of Mr. Henry Needler. Consisting of Original Poems, Translations, Essays, and Letters.* According to Duncombe's preface, Needler was born in Surrey in 1690, and received some education at a private school. "In 1708, he accepted a small place in a Publick Office,[71] where he continu'd the Remainder of his Days." Thanks to "a Gentleman of Taste, who furnish'd him with proper Books," he gave himself a good classical and scientific education in his spare moments. Mathematics was his greatest delight. Those studies, however, gave him "a violent Pain in his Head" which grew worse and worse. A youth who had "even in his Constitution a strong Tincture of Melancholy," he finally went mad and died of a "fever" in 1718 at the age of twenty-nine. "Mr. Needler's whole life," says Duncombe, "was influenc'd by Principles of sincere unaffected Piety and Virtue; And as his Morals were unblemish'd, so he was full of the Hopes of a blessed Immortality. On all proper Occasions, he was a strenuous Advocate for universal Toleration and Forbearance in Matters of Religion." To one familiar with the jargon of the age, the last sentence means that Needler was either a dissenter, like his friends Hughes and Duncombe, or a distinctly "low" Anglican.

Since Needler's ideas have occasioned a dispute among the learned, some attention may be devoted to the "Essays and Letters" which compose about two-thirds of the works.[72] He discourses *On the Excellency*

---

[70] *The Works of Mr. Henry Needler* (1728), pp. vi-xi.   [71] The Admiralty.
[72] Poems or fragments of poems are inserted in some of the essays and letters.

of *Divine Contemplation,* by which he means meditation on the Divine Attributes rather than contemplation in the strict sense. "The Soul thirsts," he says, "for an Infinite Good, nor can anything less fully satisfy its Desires." That this infinite good is revealed in the harmony of creation is the theme of an essay *On the Beauty of the Universe.* Here Needler finds proof of the existence of a benevolent God in "those innumerable gay Appearances, or delightful Spectacles, which are scatter'd through all the Scenes of the visible Creation."

Among the letters, the titles *In Praise of the Country* and *The Benefits of Retirement* speak for themselves. Needler's scientific interests appear in the latter part of his letter *Against false Humility. And of the Improvements in Philosophy by means of the Microscope and Telescope.* Of the microscope he says: "How many beautiful and surprizing Works of the All-wise Creator, had for ever lain conceal'd in their own Minuteness, if this had not discover'd them to us."

On the true Cause of Natural Effects argues "that 'tis God only, who is the true Author of all the Changes that happen in Nature; or that all those regular Effects, which we observe to be produced therein, ought to be immediately attributed to him, as the true *Anima Mundi* or *Active Principle* of Nature." The hint of familiarity with Cambridge Platonism suggested by the term *Anima Mundi* becomes much broader in *A Character of Mr. Norris's Theory of the Ideal World.* Here, at times with almost rapturous enthusiasm, he asserts that John Norris's Platonico-Christian view is true, useful in support of religion, and above all beautiful. "How Noble and Rational a Notion does it give to us of the Beatifick Vision, which it makes to consist in a clear Intellectual View of that Eternal Mind, who comprehends all Truth in his Omniform Essence; in whom the uncreated Ideas of all things, eternally shine forth with an unclouded Splendor." Coleridge would have liked Needler very much.

As for Needler's poems,[73] they sometimes represent a more conventional type of religious experience than the essays and letters. There are three Scripture-paraphrases, a poem *On the Prodigies, which attended our Blessed Saviour's Crucifixion,* a pious *Ejaculation,* and *A Hymn in Affliction. To Sir Richard Blackmore, On His Poem, entitled, Creation* hails the physician-poet as the conqueror of Lucretius. The temperature

[73] He is by no means exclusively a religious poet. Disregarding translations, about one half of his poems have some bearing on our subject.

of these pieces is a trifle warmer than the average for the period, but their content is in no way unusual.

We may more profitably dwell upon a few poems which reflect more closely, though still imperfectly, the ideas observed in his prose. The six lines comprising *On Arithmetic and Geometry* express that mathematico-Platonic transcendentalism which flourished in the early days of the new science but which he probably draws from the Cambridge school:

> Hail heav'nly Pair! by whose conspiring Aid
> The beauteous Fabrick of the World was made!
> Led on by You, audacious Men forget
> The narrow Bounds by envious Nature set;
> To yon' bright Mansions soar with happy Flight,
> Survey the Starry Realms, and range thro' Worlds of Light!

This is in the vein of the essay *On the Excellency of Divine Contemplation,* where he writes: "The Grandeur and Magnificence of an Infinite Object affect it [the mind] with an ineffable Complacency.... Thus we find that those Theorems in Geometry, which have a Relation to Infinite, afford the greatest Delight and Satisfaction to curious Minds."

But for Needler this idea is less often a means of escaping from the phenomenal world than a means of seeing that world in the light of a universal beauty. The gusto with which physical details are rendered in *A Description of a Summer-Night in the Country* shows that he loves "the beauteous fabric." When he lies stretched on the grass beneath an oak, he feels a kinship with the Druids:

> Diviner Thoughts enrich my Brain,
> And lift me to a loftier Strain;
> Thus Mona's Bards receiv'd of old
> The Secrets they the People told,
> Whilst whisp'ring Genii of the Air
> Inspir'd the Truths, they did declare.[74]

Not merely the pagan but the Christian can learn the truths of religion from the vernal wood. *A Poem in blank Verse, proving the Being of a God from the Works of Creation* was also, Needler tells us, composed "as I sat under a Tree in a Meadow." [75] It rather clumsily versifies the teleological arguments of his own essay *On the Beauty of the Universe.*

[74] *Written under an Oak.*
[75] The poem appears in a letter written August 16, 1711.

"All things are full of Thee!" cries the poet in *A Vernal Hymn, in Praise of the Creator*. But things are full of God only as a mirror is full of the objects which it reflects. The thought is both Christian and Platonic:

> As yon' clear Lake the pendent Image shows,
> Of ev'ry Flow'r that on its Border grows,
> So, in the fair Creation's Glass, we find
> A faint Reflection of th' Eternal Mind.

He believes that God's

> ...Vital Pow'r, diffus'd from Pole to Pole,
> Inspires and animates this ample Whole.

But as if to reject any pantheistic implications latent in this thought, he immediately adds:

> If Thou [God] were absent, the Material Mass
> Wou'd without Motion lie in boundless Space.
> The Sun, arrested in his Spiral Way
> No longer wou'd dispense alternate Day;
>
> .   .   .   .
>
> Whate'er, thro' false Philosophy is thought
> To be by *Chance* or *Parent-Nature* wrought,
> From Thee alone proceeds.[76]

A writer of the 1700-1720 period whose religious feelings were stirred both by mathematical infinity and by external nature could not, for all his obscurity, long escape the eye of the modern scholar. In his paper on "Shaftesbury and the Ethical Poets in England, 1700-1760," [77] Professor C. A. Moore considers Needler as an example of the fact that there were a few obscure disciples of Shaftesbury among English poets even before Thomson. But Professor Herbert Drennon, in "Henry Needler and Shaftesbury," [78] contends that this poet "should be related, in the history of ideas, to the Newtonian divines and to poets like Sir Richard Blackmore rather than to the author of the *Characteristics*."

For the details of this debate the reader must consult the two articles. There can be no doubt, I think, that Moore states his thesis too broadly and mars it with unfortunate errors of fact, and that Drennon succeeds in puncturing it. But even the fortress of the victor is not impregnable.

[76] Cf. the letter *In Defense of the following Proposition: A Creature cannot continue to exist of itself, but will drop into Nothing, if not supported by the Divine Power*.
[77] *PMLA*, XXXI, 264-325.   [78] *PMLA*, XLVI, 1095-1106.

Unquestionably Needler admires Blackmore's *Creation*, but he seems to me a much more transcendental person than Blackmore both temperamentally and philosophically. Pure Newtonianism would not very richly satisfy Needler's hankering for the Platonic *mystery* of mathematics, for the wonder of infinitude, for a vision of the universe which is an aesthetic rather than merely a mechanical harmony. If he is "related to poets like Sir Richard Blackmore," he is also, and not less closely, related to later poets like Akenside, Henry Brooke, John Gilbert Cooper, and James Harris. Why should he not be *both* Newtonian *and* Shaftesburyian? Literary historians sometimes demand too rigorous a logical consistency of the muddled young men about whom they write.

Needler has ideas and feelings which are *like* those of Shaftesbury. In annotating his friend's works, Duncombe draws parallels—not all of them superficial—between the two. As Drennon observes, Needler was delighted with a copy of *The Moralists*, or with a passage transcribed from it, which Duncombe sent him in 1711. There is additional evidence, unnoticed by either Moore or Drennon, that Needler was pretty well acquainted with Shaftesbury's work and favorably impressed by his religious ideas.[79] Professor Moore did not prove that Needler was directly influenced by Shaftesbury, and it is probably impossible to do so. He could easily have shown, however, that Needler was influenced by a type of thought which also influenced Shaftesbury. We have observed, as has Drennon in his article, that the poet was an admirer of John Norris. Now Norris, the direct heir of the Cambridge Platonists, can hardly be called an orthodox Newtonian. His Platonic enthusiasm for the infinite and for the finite as a reflection of the infinite enters into Shaftesbury and into Needler. Whereupon we warmly debate the question of Needler's indebtedness to Shaftesbury.

Henry Needler had more religion in him than most men of his time. Along with unusually warm aspirations toward the supernatural he had an unusually warm love for the natural. These feelings were inadequately satisfied by the dull, broad, unenthusiastic Protestantism in which he had been reared. It was too vague to stir him through concrete images and too sensible to transport him to the skies. This religion he never repudiates, and indeed he sometimes tries to extract poetry from it, but

[79] Cf. *Philological Quarterly*, XIV, 176.

consciously or subconsciously he goes beyond its boundaries in search of an Infinite Perfection reflected in the beauty and order of the finite world. Newtonian science often provides him with a way of externalizing and justifying the piety with which he regards nature. But Newtonianism in itself is too cool and rationalistic to meet the needs of a spirit haunted by a desire to unite the abstract and the concrete. His favorite sciences are pure rather than applied—arithmetic and geometry, interpreted in a pre-Newtonian and more or less transcendental way. He is, in a word, essentially a Neo-Platonist. It is probable that he is influenced by Shaftesbury, but reasonably certain that he draws, largely through Norris, upon the tradition of Cambridge Platonism to which Shaftesbury himself owed so much. For all his Platonism, Needler does not cease to be a Christian; but the moorings of his Christianity are loose: his personal religion, to an extent which he himself probably failed to realize, is independent of Christian doctrine.

Of eleven poets studied in this chapter, one (Lady Chudleigh) was born between 1650 and 1659; one (Lady Winchilsea), between 1660 and 1669; three (Parnell, Philips, Hughes), between 1670 and 1679; five (Fenton, Pack, Croxall, Gay, Tickell), between 1680 and 1689; and one (Needler), in 1690. Since Parnell's birth year was 1679, only four of the eleven entered the world before that date. This group is therefore a trifle later than any yet examined, its closest rival in this respect being the middle-classicists of Chapter IV. Furthermore, the careers of six of these poets run well beyond 1720, and Needler died before his time. On the other hand, the early dates of Lady Chudleigh, Lady Winchilsea, and John Hughes show that the tendencies represented by these poets are firmly linked with the past as well as with the future.

The political leanings of the group are decidedly Whiggish. No more than four of the eleven are Tories, and of these only Lady Winchilsea and Fenton are earnest ones. The Whigs are all Low Churchmen or dissenters. Of the Tories, Parnell (with reservations) and Lady Winchilsea are "high" in both a religious and a political sense, while the altitude of Fenton and Gay is merely a matter of party affiliation.

These poets are interesting to the general literary historian chiefly because they are, considering their dates, unusually rich in tendencies which are later to characterize the Romantic Movement.[80] The special purposes of this study, however, demand that we consider the relation between the pre-romanticism of these poets and their religion.

Ambrose Philips, Tickell, Hughes, and Needler form a fairly homogeneous sub-group which could easily have been included with the middle-classicists of Chapter IV. They are all Whigs. Philips and Tickell are Low Churchmen; Hughes and perhaps Needler are nonconformists. The first three are prominent members of the Addison circle, and Needler is indirectly related to the same coterie through his friend Hughes. Philips and Tickell to a slight extent, Hughes and Needler to a much greater extent, foretoken the rise of a religion of feeling which germinates in the broad and wavering Protestantism of their tradition, but which will eventually lose almost all contact with Christianity. Needler is especially significant for his combination of naturalistic and Neo-Platonic enthusiasms.

Although these men are certainly feelers, none of them explicitly preaches the full gospel of sentimentalism. Plainly, however, they would agree with the latitudinarian views expressed by the Whig controversialists of Chapter II—views which imply Defoe's identification of nature with reason and of reason with conscience. Their favorite theological pabulum, too, would be those latitudinarian sermons in which Professor Crane has found so many sentimental symptoms.[81]

Lady Winchilsea and Parnell stand on a different footing, for their religious feelings are inseparable from their clear and definite Churchmanship. The former is hardly a sentimentalist at all; the latter is a sentimental person whose emotions are still satisfied by orthodox Christianity. The Countess, born in 1661, may be considered a legacy from the seventeenth century. As for Parnell, the Catholic element in his imagination is hard to account for. It is obvious, however, that the eighteenth century will increasingly discourage such religious feeling as his. Even in the Queen Anne period High Churchmanship has lost most of its spiritual vitality, and in the Age of Walpole it will stand for little more than a disgruntled political conservatism. One cannot long continue to derive poetic inspiration from a Church which has turned her back on poetry.

[80] This is not true in any important respect of Fenton or Pack, who serve chiefly as a means of leading up to Croxall.

[81] R. S. Crane, "Suggestions Toward a Genealogy of the 'Man of Feeling.'" ELH, I, 205-230.

Parnell is, after all, the heir of the puritan tradition, and the influence of Addison is already at work in him. In a later generation a poet of his temperament would inevitably be drawn into the stream which descends from seventeenth-century puritanism to men like Hughes and Needler.

It will be remembered that the Whig controversial writers of Chapter II include several free-thinking, free-living, and not at all religious characters like Maynwaring, De Breval, and Amhurst. There are Tory equivalents in Tom Brown and Ned Ward, but at long last Whiggery proves the more appropriate home for such men. Liberty and toleration are slogans attractive to those who desire a great deal of the former and need a great deal of the latter.

In the present chapter this type is represented by Fenton, Pack, and Croxall, who have been called "libertine sentimentalists." Fenton is a Tory, but Pack and Croxall, in whom the tendencies of the group are much more fully developed, are latitudinarian Whigs. The somewhat tender sensuality of these writers betokens a compromise between the polished wit of the aristocratic tradition and the nascent sensibility of middle-classicism. In Restoration days Pack and Croxall would probably have been Epicureans, but the breadth of eighteenth-century Whiggery has furnished them a rationalization more in keeping with the spirit of the times.

The traits observed in these men will continue to appear throughout the century. The type is of course an unstable one. To the extent that the libertine sentimentalist is a *libertine,* he will react against that moral earnestness which is part of the puritan heritage of pre-romanticism. The feeling heart on which he relies for guidance is not the feeling heart of Richardson; it is more like Fielding's, and still more like Sterne's. But to the extent that the libertine sentimentalist is a *sentimentalist,* he will gravitate toward the Philips-Tickell-Hughes-Needler tradition. This fact is clearly illustrated by Samuel Croxall—emphatically a libertine sentimentalist but also a latitudinarian cleric whose writings are rich in pre-romantic symptoms and who concludes his career with a hymn to the God of nature.

John Gay is a wit with a strong tinge of libertine sentimentalism. His Toryism is not at all deep or organic. He was reared in a bourgeois Whiggish atmosphere, in his more serious moments he feels the influence of Addison and Steele, and when his work is of any religious or pre-romantic significance it betrays its kinship with the Philips-Tickell-Hughes-Needler group.

Lady Chudleigh is a latitudinarian Whig who reads Stillingfleet and Tillotson with intellectual satisfaction and who dabbles in Cartesian science, but whose poetry is inspired by a Neo-Platonism in which the Christian element almost disappears in a ferment of muddled emotions. The earliest poet treated in this chapter, she comes nearest to expressing a non-Christian religion of feeling. But Lady Chudleigh's pseudo-Platonic sentimentalism will prove too ethereal and highfalutin for a bourgeois society which, with all its emotionalism, has a solid respect for the tangible and the useful. Her illusions about the infinite, to be potent in eighteenth-century thought, must be combined with illusions about the finite. In other words Shaftesbury, or the type of thought represented by Shaftesbury, must be seized upon and used by middle-classical Whigs who, though gradually losing their Christianity, continue to have warm religious feelings. Henry Needler has already begun to blend religious Newtonianism with a Platonism resembling Lady Chudleigh's.

Thus the balance of power and the key to the future lies in the hands of such men as Ambrose Philips, Tickell, Hughes, and Needler. These writers are closely akin to the Whig controversial poets of Chapter II and to the middle-classicists of Chapter IV, whose thought and feeling in turn relate them with the Low Church and nonconformist divine poets of Chapter III. The main trend of our subject, apparently, moves from puritanism through latitudinarianism to sentimentalism.

PART TWO: 1720–1740

Chapter VI

NEITHER CHRISTIAN NOR VERY SENTIMENTAL

THE POETS TO BE CONSIDERED IN THIS SECOND PART OF OUR STUDY FLOURISHED chiefly between 1720 and 1740, though in several cases their careers began before 1720. The period included some able prose writings in defense of Christianity against deism, but it is generally admitted that at this time the emotional and imaginative aspects of Christianity receded to a lower level than at any other period in English history. On the other hand, it is in the 1720's that sentimentalism and its supporting literary tendencies begin to grow and multiply. The relation between these phenomena may become clearer as we proceed, but we must begin by examining them separately. Hence the present chapter gathers up a handful of writers whose poems reveal no Christianity and at most only a faint suggestion of sentimentalism.

We must not assume that none of these writers is a Christian. The Reverend Tipping Silvester (1700-1768),[1] for example, wrote copiously in prose on devotional and theological subjects. He appears in this chapter merely because his poems are never religious in subject or feeling. Almost all of his original pieces—there are some translations from the Latin—are trivial bits of occasional verse. More substantial is *The Microscope,* translated from the *Musae Anglicanae,* an enthusiastic description of the marvels revealed not only by the miscroscope but also by the telescope. But even here, where a physico-theological note would be expected, religion is absent. This clergyman's feeble impulse to scribble verses seems quite unrelated to his Christianity.

Though Henry Fielding (1707-1754)[2] was no lover of the "unco' guid,"

---

[1] Son of a London linen draper. He was educated at Pembroke College, Oxford, where he became a fellow in 1724. In 1736 he became Vicar of Shabbington.

[2] Almost all of his poems appeared in the *Miscellanies* of 1743, and some of them were written as early as 1728. Hence his inclusion in the 1720-1740 period.

he considered himself a sound common-sense Christian. At the close of his life he was preparing an elaborate refutation of Bolingbroke.[3] But this is not the place for a discussion of the great novelist's moral and religious ideas: they are not adequately represented in the verses which he dashed off with careless haste. Though less casual and gay than most of his poems, the ethical epistles *Of True Greatness* and *Of Good-Nature* do not look beyond the limits of a classical humanism. "True greatness," we are told, "lies but in the noble mind"; for a perfect example we are referred to Bubb Dodington. In the latter poem, the description of "the glorious lust of doing good" as the flower of virtue has a faintly Shaftesburyian ring, reminding us that if Fielding had not been a great wit and a great hater of cant he would have been a rather sentimental person.

Had Fielding's old enemy, Colley Cibber (1671-1757)[4] fully expressed himself in verse we should probably find a rather negative latitudinarianism verging on deism and tinged with the mood of the sentimental libertine. His poems, however, provide no basis for a study of his real feelings. The sneering *Rhapsody upon the Marvelous* identifies the sublime with the unintelligible in a way implicitly antagonistic to the contemporary theory of divine poetry. In his earliest poetic attempt, *A Poem, on the Death of . . . Queen Mary* (1695), he dutifully lauds the piety of his pious heroine. Several of the laureate odes make vapid allusion to Providence. Thus on New Year's Day, 1731, he addresses the happy Britons:

> Your Plenty to the Skies you owe;
> Peace is your Monarch's Care;
> Thus Bounteous Jove, and George below,
> Divided Empire share.

This is a fair sample of Cibber in his piously patriotic vein.

In 1722 Matthew Concanen (1701-1749), later to achieve somewhat malodorous fame as a partisan scribber on the ministerial side, favored the polite world with *Poems on Several Occasions*. The work of a very

---

[3] See the *Fragment of a Comment on Lord Bolingbroke's Essays,* which enlists the easy banter of Shaftesbury in the Christian cause.

[4] His verse dribbled all the way from 1695 to the 1750's, but since he was appointed poet laureate in 1730 it seemed proper to assign him to this period.

young man, they are chiefly flattering eulogies, gallant compliments to the ladies, and humorous "occasionals." Like Croxall, he thinks Jacob's wrestling with the angel a fitting subject for *double-entendre*.[5] On the whole, however, the volume is harmless enough, but it never strikes a religious note except in offering consolation at the close of a pastoral elegy.[6] He may not be serious in telling Lord Tyrawley that he seldom prays,[7] but his poems provide no reason for disbelieving him.

The light society verse of the Earl of Chesterfield (1694-1773) reveals nothing of his Bolingbrokian deism, his Horatian ethics, his distaste for vulgarly noisy expressions both of piety and of disbelief, or his view that religion "must be allowed to be a collateral security, at least, for virtue." [8] One finds merely a few jocularly gallant allusions to scriptural incidents and theological doctrines, not all as fit for quotation as these concluding stanzas of a *Song:*

> You say, that love's a crime, content:
> Yet this allow you must,
> More joy's in Heav'n if one repent
> Than over ninety just.
>
> Sin then, dear girl, for Heaven's sake,
> Repent and be forgiven;
> Bless me, and by repentance make
> A holiday in Heaven.[9]

Such trifles neither warrant any indignant outcries against Chesterfield nor strongly support recent attempts to wash him whiter than snow.

If *The Economy of Human Life* (1750) may be regarded as a sort of prose-poem, and if it is the work of Chesterfield, our treatment of the Earl should be revised. This precursor of Tupper's *Proverbial Philosophy* is ascribed to Chesterfield in the *D. N. B.*,[10] but there is no real evidence for the attribution.[11] Mr. Roger Coxon observes that Maty and Horace

---

[5] *On Struggling for a Kiss—An Ode.*
[6] *Meliora's Tears for Thyrsis: A Pastoral, Lamenting the Death of the Late Lord Southwell.* Meliora is informed that his lordship has gone to heaven.
[7] *To the Right Honourable Charles Lord Tyrawley.*
[8] Quoted by Bonamy Dobrée, *The Letters of . . . Chesterfield,* I, 212.
[9] See also *Verses Written in a Lady's Sherlock Upon Death* and *On Miss Eleanor Ambrose.*
[10] Articles on Chesterfield and Dodsley.
[11] Three notes in *Notes and Queries,* 1st. ser., X, 8, 74, 318, are wholly inconclusive.

Walpole say nothing about the book, and that its view of woman is much higher than that expressed in Chesterfield's letters. "We find it impossible to believe," says Coxon, "that he could have written anything so un-original in substance and conventional in manner." [12] It might be more pertinent to ask whether his lordship could have written such balderdash as the following: "The butcher relenteth not at the bleating of the lamb; neither is the heart of the cruel moved with distress. But the tears of the compassionate are sweeter than dew-drops falling from roses on the bosom of the spring." From beginning to end the *Economy* reeks with a sentimentality which Chesterfield would have scorned. In my next volume it will be hesitantly assigned to Robert Dodsley.

The poems of another nobleman, Thomas Catesby Paget, Baron Paget (d. 1742) [13] provide a more reliable index of his mind. Most of them, to be sure, are trivial imitations of Prior's epigrams and familiar epistles, "compos'd for the Noble Author's own Amusement in the Country, during the Intervals of bad Weather, in Hunting-seasons;" [14] but at least two of them are of some intellectual interest.

An Epistle to Mr. P—— [15] imitates the form and mood of Prior's *Alma* or *Epistle to Fleetwood Shepard*. Mental life, says Paget, needs the clash of disagreement no less than the body needs exercise;

> And happy 'tis, that Church and State
> Yield endless Matter of Debate;
> And nothing e'er was yet so plain,
> But may be argued o'er again.
> Thus Arians, Sectaries, Socinians,
> Are Football-players of Opinions.

But we must not suppose that any solid truth will emerge from these mental contests. The history of England since the days of Charles I moves in a futile circle:

---

[12] *Chesterfield and His Critics*, p. 220.

[13] Son of the Earl of Uxbridge; M.P. for Staffordshire; gentleman of the bedchamber to George II both before and after his accession.

[14] *Advertisement* of *Miscellanies in Prose and Verse*, 1741, a volume privately printed for a few friends.

[15] So in *Miscellanies*, but the title of the poem as separately published in 1737 is *An Epistle to Mr. Pope, in Anti-heroics*.

> Both sides leave morals in the Lurch,
> And make Religion's grave Pretence,
> A Cloak for want of common Sense:
> 'Till tir'd of Plund'ring, Canting, Praying,
> Each Party still their Friends betraying;
> Call home the murder'd Father's Son,
> And end just where they first begun;
> There, for a while, stock-still remain;
> 'Till the old Game begins again.
> What to infer from all these Rumbles,
> These Follies, Skirmishes, and Jumbles,
> But that Mankind a little varies,
> Just from Vagaries to Vagaries.[16]

This frivolous gentlemanly cynicism is supported by something approaching a philosophy in Paget's most substantial poem, *An Essay on Human Life*. First published in 1734, it went through four editions. The poem is an imitation of the less optimistic side of the *Essay on Man* written under the influence of Prior's sceptical determinism. Pleasure, we are told, is illusory:

> Sad State of Nature, doom'd to fruitless pain;
> Something to wish and want, but never gain:
> Restless we live, and disappointed die,
> Unhappy, tho' we know not how nor why.

"Reason," on which we vainly rely as a guide through life's perplexities, is but another name for "impulse." Every man is swayed by a "ruling passion," and those passions are all reducible to "Self-Love." We act as our temperaments compel us to act:

> Virtue or Wisdom but the vain Pretence,
> These may direct, but Passions influence.
> Presumptuous Man! why dost thou boast Free-Will,
> By Constitution doom'd to Good or Ill?

The staggering modern discovery of the difference between "real" and "apparent" reasons is an old story to Paget, who knows that "Opinion is but Int'rest in Disguise." We cloak our base motives in noble words:

---

[16] Similar views are expressed in *A Kind of Dialogue in Hudibrasticks,* an imitation of Prior's *Alma.*

> Wisely the Springs of Action we conceal,
> Thus Sordidness is Prudence; Fury, Zeal;
> Ambition makes the Publick Good her Care,
> And Hypocrites, the Masks of Saintship wear.
> Inur'd to Falshood, we ourselves deceive,
> Oft what we wish, we fancy we believe,
> We call that Judgment which is only Will,
> And as we act, we learn to argue ill.

Paget's destructive psychology, though second-hand, is keen and search-ing. The logical conclusion of such ideas would be a nihilism like that of Hume, but in the latter part of the poem the author tries to be more cheerful and affirmative. He cannot, however, escape the trap which he himself has set. For a moment he argues that though all is folly, opposite follies may

> . . . combine,
> And jointly carry out Heav'n's great Design;

but he makes nothing of this notion, perhaps because he remembers having denied the possibility of any "great Design" in writing, a few lines above, "By Chance we live, and act, now right, now wrong." At last he recommends to man, hitherto described as the puppet of the passions, the voluntary cultivation of stoical virtue:

> Virtue alone, unchangeable and wise,
> Secure, above the Reach of Fortune lies:
> Tho' doom'd to Meanness, Poverty or Scorn,
> Whilst Fools and Tyrants are to Empire born:
> Blest in an humble, but a peaceful State,
> She feels no Envy, and she fears no Hate:
> With Stoick Calmness views Life's empty Round,
> Where Good is sparing sown, but Ills abound.

He has already called virtue "the vain Pretence," but that was eight pages earlier.

Two separately published anonymous poems of this period deserve some attention. *Of Active and Retired Life, an Epistle* (1735) finds much to be said for both modes of existence. But he who seeks retirement must be free from cynicism, melancholy, and bigotry. The serene, urbanely culti-vated retreat of Portio is contrasted with

> ...*Umbra's* gloomy Scene,
> Estrang'd from all the chearful Ways of Men!
> There Superstition works her baneful Pow'r,
> And darkens all the melancholy Hour.
> Unnumber'd Fears corrode and haunt his Breast,
> With all that Whim or Ing'rance can suggest.
> In vain for him kind Nature pours her Sweets;
> The visionary Saint no Joy admits,
> But seeks with pious Spleen fantastick Woes,
> And for Heav'n's sake Heav'n's offer'd good foregoes.

The author prefers a humanistic-classical retirement which by 1735 had become rather unfashionable. He believes in a cheerful, sensible God, and he associates the melancholy sort of retirement with superstition and morbid enthusiasm.

It was obviously a deist who wrote *Of Superstition: An Epistle to a Friend* (1734), for he asserts that reason demands belief in a Supreme Being who has implanted eternal and immutable moral principles in every breast, and that to obey those precepts is to be religious:

> Our Minds, of true Morality, comprize
> The Rules—and there, all true Religion lyes.

This doctrine is the very core of sentimentalism, and if the author had devoted to it more than a few lines of his eighteen-page poem he would belong in another chapter. He concerns himself almost wholly, however, with a destructive assault on "superstition"—that is, on organized religion in general and Christianity in particular.

The epistle expresses the familiar views of negative deism. Creeds are shams invented to cheat the gullible. Prayer is a futile attempt to tell God our needs, which he knows better than we, or to change his unchanging ordinances—

> As if the Rules his Wisdom has approv'd,
> Cou'd be, by our Impertinence, remov'd!

Religion has been made a cloak for "Inhumanity and Fraud." Doctrines and forms of worship vary with time and place, but those who hold the majority opinion in a given locality think themselves possessed of absolute truth and persecute those who disagree with them. England, to be sure, boasts her hard-won "Liberty of Action, and of Thought";

but this means merely that every Briton has his own absurd notions, and is as sure of their truth as if he were the Pope:

> Without Direction, his sagacious Mind
> Can judge, and leave enquiring Thought behind;
> Of Mysteries can, uninstructed, preach;
> And All, beside Himself, divinely teach.

Like Defoe,[17] the author is distressed by the fact that when men exercise the right of consulting their own bosoms, they find a good many different things. Indeed, considering the universality of the pure principles of deism, his faith in their ultimate triumph is surprisingly weak:

> My Friend! what can we do? with stubborn Will
> Fools are persisting in their Errors still;
> In vain false Adoration we reprove,
> And false Opinion labour to remove;
> With Falsehood's Lust the shallow Rabble burns,
> And at Conviction obstinately spurns.

But he consoles himself by remembering that in their own day Socrates and Columbus were ridiculed. Such is the fate of "The most-deserving Wits in ev'ry Age."

We have seen that *Of Superstition,* though chiefly destructive in tenor, pays brief and superficial tribute to the religion of the heart. It becomes increasingly difficult for Englishmen seriously to attack Christianity in verse without offering some form of sentimentalism as a substitute. Even in this chapter the more significant writers have their quasi-religious enthusiasms. To some slight extent this is true of Richard Glover (1712-1785).[18]

In 1728, when only sixteen years of age, Glover contributed some lines in memory of Newton to Henry Pemberton's *View of Sir Isaac Newton's Philosophy.* Here the lad's religion seems to be that broad rationalistic Christianity which finds in nature as explained by science the most satisfying revelation of divine power and goodness. God owes much to Newton, for it was he

---

[17] *Vide supra,* p. 70
[18] His literary career began in 1728, and all his important poems except *Athenaid* were published before 1740.

> ... who first th' Almighty's works display'd,
> And smooth'd that mirror, in whose polish'd face
> The great Creator now conspicuous shines.

This sort of religion easily slides over into the sentimental-naturalistic deism of Thomson, whom he is quite evidently trying to imitate. A passage in praise of scenery, solitude, and contemplation is symptomatic. But Glover was not to follow his more famous friend along the path of nature-poetry, though he did follow him in his political thinking. On growing up Glover engaged in the Hamburg trade, like his merchant father, and became a figure in city politics. Warmly anti-ministerial, he was well regarded by Lyttelton and the rest of the "Patriots." The personal religious views of his maturity are unknown to me, but as the friend of Thomson, Mallett, and Armstrong he was probably either a very broad latitudinarian or a deist. His moral character was high, and he is reported to have led the life of a Greek philosopher. At least he attempted to unite the probity of a good London merchant with those Spartan virtues which he celebrates in *Leonidas*.

Except for the juvenile effusion on Newton, the poems of this bourgeois Neo-Hellenist contain little that can be called religious. *London: or, The Progress of Commerce,* in the usual "Whig panegyric"[19] vein, bases a sort of jingoistic idealism on trade. His sometimes not ignobly frigid epics, *Leonidas* and *Athenaid,* eschew all supernatural machinery—following, we may imagine, not only Lucan's precedent but his personal taste. Of both poems the theme is patriotism, and the former in particular was joyfully hailed by the supporters of Prince Frederick. His Newtonianism lost or no longer vocal, Glover attaches a slight degree of religious feeling to the ideals of the merchant, of the Cobhamite "patriot," and of the ancient Greek. His spirit, however, is so cold and rationalistic that he can hardly be labelled a sentimentalist.

The spiritual history of John Bancks (1709-1751) may be reconstructed from *D. N. B.* with the help of his two collections of verse. His humble father died when John was very young, and he was reared in poverty by his grandfather, a provincial tailor. Still a mere lad, on his grandfather's death he worked as a farm hand. He had had very little school-

---

[19] C. A. Moore, "Whig Panegyric Verse, 1700-1760. A Phase of Sentimentalism," *PMLA,* XLI, 362-401.

ing, and knew not how to satisfy his thirst for knowledge. Following
the loftiest model known to him, he began to write verses:

> With Quarles in Hand, (I though a noble choice)
> On Rural Themes I try'd my feeble voice;
> The meanest Fancies now were taught to chime,
> And Cows, and Horses, Subjects were for Rhime.[20]

His taste was improved, however, by the guidance of a gentleman
named Williams; and an uncle managed to send him to a nonconformist
academy at Reading. The principal was one Peter Belbin, a Baptist
preacher of "leathern Lungs, and Brazen Throat" who

> Had got the Knack to draw Respect
> From Folks of feeble Intellect.[21]

The youth was eager to fit himself for the dissenting ministry; but the
pompous Belbin—envying, if we may believe Bancks, his pupil's piety
and good parts—snubbed him cruelly, sneered at his ambitions, and reported him as a dullard. This treatment knocked all the piety out of him.

On the strength of Belbin's adverse reports, his uncle removed him from
school and apprenticed him to a weaver in Reading. Soon, however, an
accident of some sort incapacitated him for this trade, and, using a small
legacy which had come to him, he went to London and set up a bookstall
in Spitalfields.

Such was the young man who in 1730, emboldened by Queen Caroline's favors to Stephen Duck the poetical thresher, published *The
Weaver's Miscellany: Or, Poems on several Subjects. By John Bancks, now
a poor Weaver in Spittle-Fields.*[22] Most, if not all of the poems in this
volume were written before he had determined to learn the ways of the
world. They are as crude as would be expected. Though utterly harmless,
they convey no hint of religion except for *A Resolution,* which announces

---

[20] *The Introduction*—the versified preface of *The Weaver's Miscellany,* 1730. Cows and
horses do not figure in this, his first collection. Perhaps he thought his very earliest efforts
too "low" for print. The *D.N.B.* article does not mention Bancks's agricultural experience,
but he is quite explicit about it. It is possible, however, that he is inventing a circumstance
which would make the reader associate him with the fortunate Stephen Duck.

[21] *Saying and Doing are Two Things.* See also *Balaam's Pedigree.* Belbin later conformed
and took Anglican orders.

[22] Apparently he never worked at weaving after he came to London; but Duck's example
leads him to capitalize his former humble employment.

the curious plan of writing divine poetry as a temporary substitute for love. He had, in fact, composed a few divine poems at Reading, but did not print them in 1730. Two of them—an earnestly clumsy "irregular ode" on *Eternity* and a vapid *Hymn to the Christian Sabbath*—were to appear eight years later in his second collection.

By 1738 the lowly, ignorant, serious John Bancks has undergone a transformation. It is a new man who now smirks at the reader in two handsome subscription volumes, "Adorned with Sculptures, and Illustrated with Notes"—*Miscellaneous Works, in Verse and Prose.* He is still a bad poet, but eight years have wrought an amazing improvement in his knowledge and technical finish. Not a word of his having been a poetical weaver: he now aspires to write like a witty gentleman.[23]

The *Miscellaneous Works* are not without traces of the earlier Bancks. The two divine poems noted above are thrown in to satisfy a friend. There are also one or two Scripture-paraphrases, and compliments to Young and Lillo as moral guides.[24] But such poems must have been written several years before. The main trend of the collection is definitely anti-religious. It is full of smut, often combined with sneers at the clergy and other pious folk, who are hypocrites by definition. He defends his bawdy tales by insisting that "It is not necessary an Author should be either vicious himself, or an encourager of Vice in others, because he describes the Gallantries and Intrigues of the Sexes with less Reserve than many of his Brethren. On the contrary, by so doing, he renders That ridiculous, which Others make only criminal, and has therefore a better Chance of succeeding against it." The disingenuousness of this apology will be clear to anyone who will glance at the poems.

The theme of *Love atones for little Crimes* is that

> A Priest may strictly keep his Embers,[25]
> Yet never curb his Carnal Members.
> These tend by Nature to their Goal,
> As the touch'd Needle to the Pole:
> And shall we damn a human Creature,
> For *being*—what he *is* by Nature?

[23] At this time he is a bookseller's journeyman.

[24] *To Dr. Young, On Reading some of his Works* [namely *The Last Day* and *Love of Fame; Night Thoughts* has not yet been written], and *Of Tragedy; and the Comparison of Public and Private Characters. To Mr. Lillo.*

[25] That is, observe abstinence on the Ember Days in the calendar of the Church.

Then—to make use of his footnote—he "proceeds here to support the main Point by the Examples of Paul, Joseph, Solomon, and David, all of whom are proved to have had carnal Inclinations. Now upon the Supposition that all such Inclinations are sinful in themselves, it is argued, that the Necessity must atone for the Guilt, otherwise neither the Persons here mentioned, nor any others, could have deserved the Reputation of being Saints." Why then should we resist the promptings of nature?

Is such unsavory nonsense, of which many other examples could be given, related to any definable religious viewpoint? In *The Author's Picture; A Fourth Epistle to Mr. Pope* the following passage indicates that Bancks would have called himself a deist:

> His Thoughts and Principles religious,
> Are neither intricate nor tedious:
> Founded on Maxims free and rational;
> More universal than mere national.
> In Life, not scrupulous, nor vicious;
> In Mind, not brave, nor superstitious;
> Myst'ries he leaves to Men of Learning,
> And future Things to Faith's Discerning.
> Unwarp'd by Rev'rence, or Contempt,
> From Priests, and theirs, he lives exempt.
> For dreading Fury, Fire, and Treason,
> He trusts them only when they reason:
> And when from Myst'ry they descend,
> The Priest is swallow'd in the Friend.
> Yet then, and always, he prefers
> His own weak Reas'ning—ev'n to theirs.

Of course he is a great hater of bigotry,[26] and a warm admirer of Voltaire.[27]

Bancks believes that he has embodied the philosophy of Voltaire in his own epistle *To Mr. Mitchell*.[28] He is now, he confides, employed on a piece of religious hackwork; hence he jokingly poses as too orthodox to be corresponding with so tolerantly sceptical a fellow as Mitchell.[29] But

---

[26] *Of Bigotry: To Sylvanus Urban.*

[27] *Mons. Voltaire to the Marchioness du Ch——.* A translation of the poem in which Voltaire dedicates his *Elements of the Newtonian Philosophy* to the Marquise du Châtelet.

[28] This is Joseph Mitchell, a deist of the sentimental-libertine sort whose poems will be dealt with in a later chapter.

[29] The hackwork alluded to is probably a *Life of Christ*, which the *D.N.B.* article on Bancks mentions as his next publication after the *Miscellaneous Works*.

Bancks has no intention of deserting the muses for "that wither'd Matron, Mother Church." The tedious job will soon be done with:

> The Time's at Hand when I, as oft before,
> Shall act the Zealot less, the Poet more;
> Of Forms and Creeds be loos'd from the Controul,
> Abridg'd of Income, but enlarg'd in Soul;
> That Day shall strike out all my native Fire,
> To turn the Tale or sweep the sprightly Lyre.
> Then leaving the Pursuit of mystic Themes,
> To court plain Reason, Stranger to Extremes,
> I'll judge of Nature's Works by Nature's Laws;
> Admire not blindly, but explore the Cause.

This declaration introduces a eulogy of those "Fathers of Science," those "Illustrious Souls, who Custom dar'd assail," Euclid and Archimedes:

> Immortal Newton on your Thoughts refin'd,
> And caught the Sense of the Creator's Mind.

The Newtonian spirit has now been extended from science into theology, which like astronomy was once a jumble of "Pomp and Miracles":

> At length some Few, the Newtons of the Mind,
> Heav'd off that huge Incumbrance of Mankind,
> The Cant of Words, and Pedantry of Rules,
> That monstrous Plenitude, contriv'd in Schools:
> Found the true Path, by Prophets, Patriarchs trod,
> A spacious Orbit, verging still to God.

Bancks thinks of religion as an intellectual system not identical with that of physical science, but parallel to it and built upon the same divine gravitational plan:

> One Pow'r impels, retains, directs our Race,
> Like that which holds yon' Planets in their Place.
> As those, attracted, round their Center move,
> Religion draws, by her Attraction, Love;
> Draws to that One, amid the Passions' Strife,
> The Source, the Center, and th' Abyss of Life;
> One who, immense, all Beings shall absorb;
> Like Stars, impinging on their central Orb.

> Thro' Nature, thus, two Principles we find;
> The Chain of Matter, and the Chain of Mind.
> Keep These in View; lo! instant disappear
> Unmanly Wonder, superstitious Fear.
> How calm the Breast! the Vulgar how unlike,
> Whom Notions, Dreams, Appearances can strike!
> Who swallow Systems with submissive Thought,
> And bow to Miracles God never wrought!
>
> .   .   .   .
>
> To gape and stare were always for the Crowd;
> But these are Hints we must not give aloud.

This poem has been dwelt upon as our first illustration of the fact that Newton's discoveries can as readily be used by the deist as by the physico-theological Christian Rationalist. Bancks's deism is too negative and too much a rationalization of his libertinism to give him any religious satisfaction. The slight germ of sentimentalism which it contains, however, draws some nourishment from the ideals of the masonic lodge. *Over the Orders of a Friendly Society* reads:

> United thus by voluntary Laws,
> A common Stock supports a common Cause,
> Of Heart beneficent, in Friendship true,
> The social Virtues dictate all we do.
> Our rising Fund advances various Ends:
> Hence on the needy Sick our Help descends;
> Hence decent Obsequies adorn the Dead;
> And timely Comfort lifts the Widow's Head.

In more passionately lyrical vein, *Of Masonry: An Ode* begins:

> Genius of Masonry! descend,
> In mystic Numbers while We sing:
> Enlarge Our Souls; the Craft defend;
> And hither all Thy Influence bring.
> With social Thoughts our Bosoms fill,
> And give Thy Turn to ev'ry Will! [30]

Our pious young dissenting weaver has become a libertine in imagination if not in fact, a purveyor of anti-clerical bawdry, and an extremely nega-

---

[30] Bancks is mentioned in the section on "Freemasonry" in J. H. Harder, *Some Tendencies of Sentiment and Ethics,* pp. 294-296, with a few other references to masonic poets of the eighteenth century. The connection between masonry and deism is obvious.

tive deist; but as a good mason he cherishes a beneficent heart full of social virtues.

Another freemason—judging from *A Prologue, Designed to be spoke by a Youth of Twelve Years of Age before the Free Masons*—was John Winstanley (1678?-1750).[31] He is a versifier in the witty-genteel tradition whose poems are chiefly epigrams and light occasional pieces modelled on Prior or Swift. He is usually thin and trivial, and sometimes indecorous. The judgment of *D. N. B.* that his verse "is often amusing and clever" strikes me as overenthusiastic. Except for some conventional praise of retirement in *A Rural Ode,* he betrays no pre-romantic symptoms.

Almost nothing in Winstanley's poems bears upon religion. Politically at least he is a friend of the Church of England and an opponent of occasional conformity, for he proposes *A Toast* to

> He that owns with his Heart, and helps with his Hand,
> The Church that's establish'd by the Laws of the Land,
> Conforming for Conscience, and not on Occasion,
> Not eluding the Laws by a knavish Evasion.

Nevertheless—probably at a later date—he makes *The Man of True Worth* describe himself as one who follows "Cool Reason" and avoids all extremes: "I'm not High Church, nor Low Church, nor Tory, nor Whig." All such differences are reconciled in the ethical creed of the latitudinarian:

> When we shall all at God's just Bar appear,
> Think you, he'll ask us, of what *Church* we are?
> No! no! let then this foolish Diff'rence rest,
> They're of the truest *Church,* that live the Best.[32]

It is not very easy to imagine that Winstanley himself belonged to this Church, but we had better give him the benefit of the doubt.

[31] An Irishman of whose career very little is known. On the title-page of his *Poems* he describes himself as an M.A. and a fellow of Trinity College, Dublin, but according to *D.N.B.* his name does not appear in Todd's *List of Graduates.* His poems indicate that he was acquainted with Swift, whom he admires and sometimes imitates. *Poems Written Occasionally* appeared in 1742. Since he was then past sixty, it is probable that much of his verse was composed in the 1700-1720 period. The volume is "Interspers'd" with poems by other "Ingenious Hands," but the pieces not written by Winstanley are assigned to their proper authors.

[32] *On high, and low Church Parties.* The same view is expressed in *A serious Thought.*

The results of this chapter may be briefly summarized. Out of eight writers for whom the facts are available, four were born between 1700 and 1709—Silvester, Fielding, Concanen, and Bancks. Glover, whose career began at an unusually early age, was born in 1712. Cibber was born in 1671, Winstanley probably in 1678, and Chesterfield in 1694. Five of the eight, then, are wholly the children of the eighteenth century. The writers here studied resemble those of Chapter I in that their political views seem not to be an important factor in their attitude toward religion. Indifference or hostility to religion apparently cuts across partisan lines.

As regards social stratification, four out of nine poets are of the upper class, four are bourgeois, and one is a proletarian; but they all, like the poets of Chapter I, strive to maintain the aristocratic, neoclassical, non-romantic tradition. Even between 1700 and 1720, however, that tradition is on the wane, and in the 1720-1740 period it dwindles markedly. Many aristocrats and would-be aristocrats continued to toy with the pen, and doubtless their poems were often non-religious or anti-religious; but a smaller proportion of their work found its way into print than in the preceding period. Literature in the Age of Walpole was fast becoming less a polite pastime than a business to be regarded with that earnestness which all commercial activity inspires in the heart of the bourgeois. The bookseller was supplanting Maecenas, and the person of quality usually shrank from competition with Grub Street.

The group considered in this chapter is a small one, and only two or three of its members are of much intellectual interest. At this time a man who wished to undertake a serious criticism of religion would probably contribute in prose to the Deistic Controversy. Except for the faintly sentimental leanings occasionally revealed, the poetry here examined displays no pre-romantic symptoms. Judged even by its own standards, it is never very good and sometimes very bad. Poetry demands a faith of some sort, and these are simply not believing men. Fielding and Chesterfield of course are eminent in prose, but with the doubtful exception of Glover there is not a single well-known eighteenth-century poet on the list. Further search would reveal other writers eligible for inclusion, but none whose names would add prestige to the group. The non-religious poets of Chapter I were more numerous and included more names of importance. Perhaps we may infer that disbelief, like Christianity, is steadily losing its power to stimulate poetic activity. It should be remembered, however, that admission to the present chapter has been doubly restricted: the poets must not write as Christians, and they must not be so sentimental as to deserve to be called sentimentalists. We shall find as we continue that the smallness and insignificance of the group here presented are partly signs of the growth of sentimentalism.

The only writers of this chapter whose attitude toward religious problems deserves any careful attention may be classified under two heads. Fielding, Paget, and Glover express classical, more or less stoical, principles of ethics. John Bancks and the unknown who wrote *Of Superstition,* on the other hand, express a deistic viewpoint. Paget's recommendation of virtue is a futile evasion of the nihilistic consequences of his own psychology, but Glover's attempt to unite the patriotism of ancient Sparta with that of the Prince of Wales's faction has dimly sentimental implications. Fielding's views in *Of Good-Nature* are a trifle too soft to be Senecan, but would not be repudiated by Shaftesbury or Hutcheson. The deism expressed in *Of Superstition* and in the later poems of Bancks is almost wholly negative and destructive. Nevertheless the anonymous foe of priestcraft believes that the light of religion shines in every heart, and Bancks associates masonry with warm benevolent impulses. Thus the evidence, though meagre, suggests that both stoicism and deism, when tinged with the slightest degree of positive religious feeling, point in the direction of sentimentalism.

Chapter VII

DIVINE POETS

ALTHOUGH THE POETRY OF POLITICO-ECCLESIASTICAL CONTROVERSY BY NO means disappears in the 1720-1740 period, it greatly diminishes because of the increasing secularization of political thought and because of reluctance to disturb the peace of Whiggery by reviving issues which had aroused so much bitterness during the reign of Anne. Verse of this type, furthermore, displays less and less of the quasi-religious conviction which in the earlier period sometimes entitled it to our attention: it illustrates the history of church politics but not the history of religious feeling. For these reasons no separate chapter of Part II will be devoted to the controversialists. Instead we shall pass at once to the divine poets of the second generation. The present chapter includes definitely Christian writers who specialize in sacred poetry and whose thought is unaffected, or at most very slightly affected, by sentimentalism.

Beyond the Scottish border, the stern creed of Calvin was still a vital force. At the beginning of the century the fervor of Scotch Presbyterians was warm and intense compared to that of English Nonconformists. Some complaints were heard of increasing worldliness and indifference, but the secularization and rationalization of life had progressed much less rapidly in Scotland than in England. In 1696 Gabriel Semple declared in the Assembly of the Kirk: "I was witness to the old times before the Restoration, and to the times under the persecution, and I never saw so much of the spirit poured out as I have since the Revolution." [1]

The Kirk retained its grasp on the social life of its people. In Edinburgh assemblies for dancing were prohibited until 1710, and theatres of course were out of the question. On the Sabbath one might neither saunter nor walk fast in the streets. A reaction, especially among the young men of

[1] Quoted by G. M. Trevelyan, *England under Queen Anne*, II, 203n.

the universities, was inevitable. "No wonder 'Hell-Fire Clubs' and 'Sulphur Clubs' met surreptitiously to flout the Kirk in ways more questionable than the drama and the dance." [2]

Gradually, too, the spirit of theological liberalism began to stir in circles not at all inclined to play with brimstone. There arose a younger generation of Presbyterian divines who called themselves "Moderates." In England they would have been bigots, but in Scotland they were latitudinarians. They aimed to preserve a rational balance between Presbyterianism and the trend of the modern world, to uphold the *Institutions* without encouraging fanaticism, enthusiasm, or antinomianism. Bitterly opposed to them were the "Evangelicals," old-fashioned free-grace Calvinists unspotted by the world.

The Act of Union encouraged the growth of liberalism by breaking down Scotland's insularity and exclusiveness. By 1720 the Moderates were in control of the General Assembly, which regulated the actions of the Presbytery. Their views, formerly suspect, were now official; and like good liberals they made the most of their power once they had it. One of the sharpest thorns in their flesh was Ralph Erskine (1685-1752). The son of a Presbyterian minister in Northumberland who had been ejected in 1662, he studied theology at Edinburgh and was ordained in 1711. The theme constantly stressed in his poems as well as in his theological writings and in his preaching was salvation by faith alone. Grace was an absolute, unconditional promise to the elect. The "legal doctrine" of a covenant of good works between God and man was anathema. To the Moderates these perfectly orthodox Calvinistic views were repugnant as running counter to the ethical utilitarianism of the age—or, to translate their objections into theological terms, Erskine was a dangerous antinomian. In 1721 he was arraigned before the Synod of Fife. After a long series of disputes he and some Evangelical supporters seceded from the Kirk of Scotland in 1737. [3]

---

[2] *Ibid.*, p. 198.

[3] Four years earlier his unpoetical brother Ebenezer, whom Ralph had converted to evangelical principles, had seceded on similar grounds. The "Secession Church," of which Ebenezer Erskine was the founder and of which Ralph Erskine now became a main pillar, itself soon split into two factions, which at last joined in 1847 to become the United Presbyterian Church. The history of the Erskine brothers reminds one of recent events in America, where Dr. Machen, the Presbyterian fundamentalist, was forced into schism by the dominant unorthodox party in his denomination. The conducting of heresy trials by heretics is a curious feature of modern religious life.

The formidable body of sacred verse bequeathed by Ralph Erskine to an ungrateful posterity may be examined by running through the sections which comprise the Aberdeen, 1858, edition of his *Poetical Works*. *Gospel Sonnets,*[4] his best-known production, was first published as *Gospel Canticles* in 1720. It reached a twenty-fifth edition in 1797, and was several times reprinted in the nineteenth century.[5]

The "sonnets" were popular not because they were poetical—they are far from that—but because the common folk of Scotland cherished them as a versified compendium of theology. Erskine's devotion to free grace appears again and again:

> Though *works* of *righteousness* I store,
> Yet *righteousness* of *works* abhor;
> For righteousness without a flaw,
> Is *righteousness without the law*.[6]

In more emotional flights he likes to portray the saved human soul as the Bride of God:

> O happy soul, Jehovah's bride,
> The Lamb's beloved spouse;
> Strong consolation's flowing tide,
> Thy husband thee allows.
>
> .   .   .   .
>
> Though hellish smoke thy beauties stain,
> And sin deforms thee quite:
> Thy surety's merit makes thee clean,
> Thy husband's beauty white.
>
> Thy pray'rs and tears, nor pure nor good,
> But vile and loathsome seem,
> Yet gain, by dipping in his blood,
> Thy husband's high esteem.[7]

Sensitive to the charge of antinomianism, he permits his interlocutor in a dialogue to object:

---

[4] They are of course not sonnets in the technical sense. In Scotland the term was often applied to any sort of poem other than narrative.

[5] The latest edition known to me is Glasgow, 1870.

[6] *The Believer's Riddle.*   [7] *The Believer's Jointure.*

> Mayn't some from hence take latitude
> And room their lusts to please?
> If Christ do all, then very good,
> Let us take carnal ease.

But the reply, though not altogether satisfying, is vigorous:

> Christ will in flaming vengeance come,
>   With fury in his face,
> To damn his foes that dare presume,
> And thus abuse his grace.[8]

Erskine would insist that his creed is firmly grounded upon right reason, but for him reason is more than seeing and inferring: at its highest, it is itself a form of faith:

> Strange contradictions me befall,
>   I can't believe unless I see;
> Yet never can believe at all,
>   Till once I shut the seeing eye.
>
> When sight of sweet experience
>   Can give my faith no helping hand,
> The sight of sound intelligence
>   Will give it ample ground to stand.

In preferring the closed eye of faith to the open eye of worldly reason, Erskine is at war with the ruling spirit of his age.

In the *Poetical Works, Gospel Sonnets* is followed by *A Paraphrase, or Large Explicatory Poem, upon the Song of Solomon, Wherein the Mutual Love of Christ and His Church, Contained in that Old Testament Song, Is Imitated in the Language of the New Testament, and Adapted to the Gospel Dispensation.*[9] The preface indicates that Erskine had submitted this paraphrase to Isaac Watts, who suggested a few revisions without reading the whole work. If even Watts did not finish it, I need feel no shame in confessing my own weakness. The title, though self-explanatory, inadequately suggests the crushing dullness of this attempt to rewrite *Canticles* in terms of free-grace Calvinism. There are two prefaces, addressed respectively to the "Curious" and to the "Serious" reader. The

---

[8] *The Believer's Principles.*

[9] First published in 1736. Though less popular than *Gospel Sonnets,* it went through several editions.

former is given fair warning that the subject is not "the Fair Circassian,[10] but the Fair Christian, and his infinitely fairer Head and Husband Jesus Christ." To the Serious Reader he says that the *Song of Songs* "has been greatly profaned by impure writers, who have used, or rather abused their poetical arts, to the gratifying of carnal minds....I have, therefore, endeavoured in this Paraphrase, so to open the import of every metaphor, as to secure it from being perverted and abused to wanton passions.... The composure upon every text is such, as I think, without great violence done to it, can never be applied to any lovers inferior to that glorious Bridegroom, the Lamb of God; and *the Bride, the Lamb's wife,* as the church is designed, Rev. XXI, 9."

Nothing surely could be less provocative, or for that matter less elevating, than the ninety-three pages of hymn-stanzas which compose this paraphrase. A very favorable specimen is his rendering of "His mouth is most sweet; yea, he is altogether lovely:"

> Lo! his blest mouth that once did taste
> The bitter gall for me,
> With charms divinely sweet is grac'd,
> Unto the last degree.

> Grace pour'd into his life, alway
> Does thence so sweetly run;
> They share the Father's grace for ay
> Who do but kiss the Son.

The next section of *Poetical Works* consists of *Scripture Songs*—two hundred and twelve pages of hymns for congregational use which were first collected and published in 1754, two years after the author's death. These crude dogmatic commentaries or paraphrases on passages of Scripture need not detain us.

The concluding section, *Miscellaneous Poems,* is devoted chiefly to a group of three "Funeral Poems on the Death of Some Eminent Persons," all of them Presbyterian ministers. These not very lugubrious elegies praise the theological purity of the departed, all of whom believed in free grace and abhorred "the legal doctrine." It was from such men, who died in ripe old age during the author's young manhood, that he derived his creed and his spiritual temper.

---

[10] A disapproving glance at Croxall's voluptuous paraphrase. *Vide supra,* p. 225.

As a religious poet Erskine is contemptible, but as an historical phenomenon he is noteworthy. He reminds us that during a period when strict Calvinism was at ebb tide in England the theology of the Covenanters was preserved in Scotland. His thought links the Calvinism of the seventeenth century with the Calvinism of the English Evangelical Movement. In 1741 he corresponded with Whitefield, and persuaded him to visit the saints in Scotland.[11] Another famous Evangelical, James Hervey of the sentimentally pious *Meditations,* admired *Gospel Sonnets* and kept it "constantly on his table."[12]

We do not know whether Jean Adam (1710-1765) ever sat at the feet of Ralph Erskine, but they would certainly have approved of each other. The orphan daughter of a Renfrewshire shipmaster, she became housekeeper and governess for Mr. Turner, minister of Greenock. His library gave her the little education she possessed. In 1734 her *Miscellany Poems* were printed in Glasgow at the expense of Mrs. Drummond of Greenock. Shortly thereafter Miss Adam opened a girls' school at Crawfordbridge, but failing to make a financial success of this venture she became a hawker and ended her days in a Glasgow poorhouse.

Except for a wistful little speculation as to the actuality of the phoenix, all of Jean Adam's poems are "divine."[13] She insists, indeed that

> 'Tis no Arcadia nor Elysian Field
> I sing, which cannot solid Pleasures yield.
>
> . . . . .
>
> On Helicon I scorn to spend a Breath,
> Since Zion's King deliver'd me from Death.
> To Him the Tribute of my Praise is due,
> And should I have a lower End in View?[14]

Like Erskine, she disapproves of Croxall's *Fair Circassian,* averring that

---

[11] The Secession Church at first greatly admired Whitefield and urged him to confine his ministry to them, "the Lord's people"; but Whitefield replied that "the devil's people" had greater need of his message. Thereafter the Seceders grew cooler toward Whitefield, and Erskine found his revival in Lanarkshire tainted with enthusiasm. (See *D.N.B.* articles on Ebenezer Erskine and Ralph Erskine.) The essential kinship between the Secession Church and Whitefield's Calvinistic Methodism is nevertheless clear.

[12] "Life of Ralph Erskine," by "The Rev. Mr. Brown of Whitburn," *Poetical Works,* p. xxvi.

[13] *The Song of the Mariner's Wife* ("There's nae luck about the house") has sometimes been attributed to her, but not on reliable authority.

[14] *The Grateful Muse.*

He who lays wanton Wit in Wisdom's Place,
Erects a Trophie to his own Disgrace. [15]

The quality of her work is guaranteed in a preface by Archibald Crau-
ford, apparently one of her sponsors. " 'Tis expected," he says, "the measures will be found to be just, the Grammar good, and the Phrases,
Allusions and Figures, will not be found disagreeable to the best English
Poets, that have written within Seventy Years last past." Even with this
chronological reservation the praise is excessive. One can say that she
responds a little more warmly than Erskine to the same doctrines. Her
faith makes her wish to sing; she would like to write religious poetry
if she could. But she lacks the gift, and her education has been just sufficient to destroy the graces of nature without imparting the graces of art.
The absurdity of her more ambitious flights may be seen in the opening
couplet of the pindaric ode *On Fortitude:*

Thou useful, ornamental virtue Fortitude,
Thou may be stil'd a Star of greatest Magnitude.

But when she is content to write simple, hymnlike verses, the sincerity of
her spirit combines with our knowledge of her personal handicaps to give
us a sort of respect for her work. She is at her best in *The Privilege Of
Saints:*

I was the Object of his Care,
   Ere ever I was born;
He wrote his Wisdom on my Frame,
   When first it took a Form:
Yet more amazing is the Love
   That he has shown for me,
By the Provision he has made
   From all Eternity.

From our viewpoint, the least negligible feature of Jean's thought is
her strong sense of the inadequacy of merely natural revelation. It is not
enough that divine goodness is everywhere displayed in the physical
universe:

Implicit Nature speaks her Lord
   Both powerful, wise, and good;
Creating Pow'r, preserving Care,
   Were seen since Nature stood:

[15] *On the prophane Author of the Circassian.*

> But what can Nature teach to Man
>   Of free electing Grace,
> Which was conceal'd, till Time was full
>   Within the Prophet's Glass.[16]

Nor can natural moral strength unaided by grace be relied upon in the struggle with sin. When one fault has been suppressed, seven more grow in its place.[17] On the other hand,

> When by the Strength of Grace I strive
>   To overcome a Sin;
> When from a Motive pure and just,
>   I plot the Death of one:
> It is not one I overcome,
>   But seven more that fall;
> As he, who keeps the Law in one
>   Commandment, keeps it all.[18]

This dependence on a transcendent supernatural power is thoroughly unsentimental. But Miss Adam does not believe that the natural passions should be stifled: rather they are to be guided by a reason which in turn is sanctified by religion:

> Hail hallow'd Passion, humane Nature's Glory,
> How dazling are thy Rays in sacred Story!
> The crown of nat'ral Passion is the Reason,
> A holy Thorn that's green in every Season:
> The Crown of humane Reason is Religion.[19]

The sequence, passion—reason—religion, is an ascending one. Unlike some of her contemporaries, this poet never seems tempted to invert it into the descending sequence, religion—reason—passion.

Some degree of literary self-consciousness on Jean's part is shown by her long series of poems in blank verse on the fall of Adam. They do not, however, remotely suggest the diction or movement of *Paradise Lost:* emulation of Milton is hinted only by the lack of rhyme and by the subject. Taken as a unit, the series forms a roughly continuous narrative mingled with theological reflections. Not without spiritual energy is *A Triumph sung by Eve* just after the passing of divine sentence upon Satan, Eve, and Adam:

[16] *On Redemption.* The same idea is expressed in *On Creation.*
[17] *The Discord of the Vices.*   [18] *The Harmony of the Graces.*
[19] *The Origin and End of Passions.*

> Avaunt Dispair, fly from the humane Breast,
> Heaven never meant it for a Nest
> For such a bird as thee;
>
>   . . . .
>
> Lift up thy Snares, and get thee hence away,
> Tho' in my Nature be as many Stains
> As there are Drops of Blood within my Veins
> The hallow'd Streams, that do from Mercy flow,
> Will turn the redest Crimson white like Snow.

Here and elsewhere, the glory of salvation is a much more prominent feature of Jean Adàm's Calvinism than the dread of damnation. For her as for Erskine, the great theme is "grace abounding to the chief of sinners."

The series concludes with sedate *Reflections on the Fall,* the imagery being appropriate for a shipmaster's daughter:

> Thus was the costly ship Humanity
> Both built and launch'd into the Sea of Time,
> And rigg'd and mann'd and laden to the Brim
> With as much value of intrinsic worth
> As would have been an everlasting Fund,
> To keep the Royal Navy in Repair.

Poor little pious Martha, striving so hard and so vainly to be a Mary! One begins by laughing at her, but leaves her with a kind of pitiful affection.

Returning southward to England, we find nonconformity represented by the voice of the Reverend Hubert Stogdon (1692-1728).[20] He followed his father in becoming a Presbyterian minister,[21] but like so many English Presbyterians he soon acquired more or less Arian views. A somewhat restless seeker after truth, he later took up the doctrine of baptism by immergence and from 1724 to the year of his death ministered to a congregation of Paedobaptists at Trowbridge in Wiltshire. A few youthful love-verses in Stogdon's *Poems and Letters* (1729) give his editor, the

---

[20] His poems appeared in the year following his death. Some, perhaps many, of them were written earlier than 1720, but since he was only twenty-eight in that year it seems best to place him in the 1720-1740 period.

[21] His maternal grandfather, Francis Hubert, was also a nonconformist minister—of what sect I do not know.

Reverend Nicholas Billingsley, some uneasiness. In his preface he pleads
that "What ever Genius the Author might have had for compositions of
the gay kind, he has given full proof that he well knew how to check and
controul it." Even the love-poems are rich in what Professor Babbitt used
to call "the inner check." Lucia proving unkind, Stogdon delivers a *Farewell to Love* in which he dedicates himself to the praise of divine, not of
earthly, beauty:

> I'm weary of th' enchanted ground,
>   This false deluding mystery;
> I've danc'd with fairies in a round
>   Enough already; set me free.
>
> .   .   .   .
>
> I'll think thy former perjuries o'er,
>   Thus—thus I'll break your cursed spell;
> Now you shall pain and please no more,
>   BARBAROUS BEAUTY NOW FAREWELL.
>
> .   .   .   .
>
> Now to the world I'll tell and prove
>   What worthless things these beauties be.
> Now if I ever die for love,
>   It shall be, Lord, for love of thee.

After this not very convincing outburst he devotes himself entirely to
sacred poetry.

Stogdon finds it a not unpleasant duty to remind the thoughtless crowd
that death and judgment are imminent realities. When he hears a passing-
bell, he warns an ancestor of Young's Lorenzo:

> Hark! my gay friend, that solemn toll
> Speaks the departure of a soul:
> 'Tis gone, that's all we know, but where
> Or how the unbodied ghost does fare
>
> In that mysterious world, God knows,
> And God alone, to whom it goes:
> To whom departing souls return,
> To know their doom to shine, or burn.[22]

---

[22] *The Unknown World, occasioned by the hearing a passing Peal.*

Grimly he "improves" *The Death of nine Persons suffocated in a Coal-Mine:*

> Yet think not, they who felt that day
> Were sinners more than you:
> But learn what chaff you are, learn what
> A jealous God can do.
>
> Ye living men, whom mercy spar'd,
> In trembling praise conspire:
> Fear him, who bears the dreadful name
> GOD A CONSUMING FIRE.

But although his sense of "grace abounding" is much less hearty than that of Erskine or Jean Adam, he does not forget the truth expressed in the title, *God not implacable, or Despair no Virtue.* "The Lamb's heartblood" can wash away the blackest sins. And on subjects like *The Death of a Child* he can show tenderness:

> How sweet was the surprize!
> (The thought th' imagination warms,)
> When Angels bid the infant joy,
> And claspt him in their arms!

Such a poem as *The Appeal* suggests that Stogdon enjoys the analysis of his own emotions:

> My God, and am I not sincere?
> Here feel my throbbing heart:
> O how it panteth to draw near,
> And see thee as thou art!
>
> .   .   .   .   .
>
> If I but hear thy name, I start;
> Oh what must be thy face?
> If I but say, "Think, Oh my heart,
> The joys of his embrace";
>
> I gush and feel my mass of blood
> Like boiling billows roll,
> And something swift as lightning wou'd
> Shoot thro' my very soul.

Here one feels some confusion between contemplation of God and contemplation of self.

Like Young almost twenty years later, Stogdon prefers a nocturnal setting for his despairs and raptures:

> Thro' groves of bliss I seem to stray;
> And in the thickest gloom of night.
> I shine in everlasting day,
> And blaze with intellectual light.
>
> While half the world dream, start, and sleep;
> And half cheat, fight, curse, rave, and groan;
> Then I my silent jubilee keep,
> And hold my festival alone.[23]

Observe the scornful glance at the rest of mankind. Love of God and love
of nocturnal solitude set Stogdon apart from

> ... those who know no other bliss
> Than this poor dying life can give.

The same sense of superiority is strong in *Spirits in Prison*:

> Souls that are conscious of their birth
> And think how spirits live,
> Feel daily somewhat worse than death,
> Or stupid souls conceive.

He is by no means envious of those "stupid souls" who are unable to
attain the distinction of his suffering.

Since in all this a comparison between Stogdon and Edward Young
continues to suggest itself, we turn with curiosity to *Some Thoughts on
reading Dr. Young's Poem on the Last Day, in a Letter to Mrs. R——e.*[24]
It begins with praise of retirement, a theme dear to his pious correspondent:

> There are sweet seasons, when the mind puts on
> More serious thoughts, and loves to be alone:
> Collects herself, and proves the happy mean
> 'Twixt gloom and laughter, vanity and spleen:
> Calls in her salient airs, abates her fires,
> Leaves to th' unthinking herd their vain desires,
> Looks round, and smiles, and sighs, and so retires.

Again we see that such moods are not for the spiritually vulgar.

---

[23] *Welcome Evening.*
[24] Dated 1718 in *Poems and Letters.* "Mrs. R——e" is probably Elizabeth Singer Rowe.

This smiling-sighing retirement, of course, can be enjoyed only in the country. Stogdon takes a soft pleasure in the scene:

> Kind Heav'n has blest me with a dear retreat,
> Too tender for description, yet too great:
> So soft the shade, so reverend the grove,
> One must be all religion, or all love;
> Here bending alders bending alders greet,
> Obsequious branches mingle as they meet,
>
> . . . .
>
> While gently the young curling tendrils play,
> Whisper, and nod, and beckon all the day.
> 'Tis here a solemn arch corrects the rays,
> Screens off the gaudy lustre, and allays,
> And sweetly tempers the fierce noon-day blaze.
> Such shades, methinks, e'en consecrate the ground,
> And cast an awful sanctity around.

Even more noteworthy, perhaps, than the association of scenery with sanctity is the line, "One must be all religion, or all love." "Il faut l'amour ou la religion pour goûter la nature," writes Mme. de Staël. But remembering that Mrs. Rowe had been a fine woman in her day, we need not make too much of the point.

Suddenly Stogdon recollects himself and attacks his main theme:

> Where am I rov'd? I only meant to say,
> Here I read Young, and thought on the last day.

His high but not quite unreserved praise of Young's poem is of no importance for us, though I cannot refrain from quoting two couplets:

> When a strong impulse threats the Poet's brain,
> How warily he checks the obedient rein!
> The stagg'ring muse he tenderly unloads,
> And gently breathes her in cool episodes.

Young has done well, but Judgment Day is after all too tremendous a theme for a single poet. There should be a great coöperative poem on the subject. Addison, for example, might describe "The grand tribunal blazing in the air," while the actual account of divine judgment and its consequences should be assigned to an even greater poet:

> Watts would describe the rapture, and despair;
> And tell, what thoughts and shrieks will echo there.

This poem enables us to string the names of Stogdon, Mrs. Rowe (probably), Young, Addison, and Watts on a single thread. It also presents an arresting picture of a Presbyterian-Arian-Paedobaptist minister enjoying *The Last Day,* far from "th' unthinking herd," in an arbor whose shade gives him feelings of sanctity—or it is love? Remembering that the religion of Stogdon's father was precisely that of Erskine's father, we see that our poet has come a long way. His creed has begun to wobble and crack a little, and the fissures have been puttied with sensibility. Though stern, he has unexpected soft spots. He can enjoy his own piety as a sort of emotional treat. He is melancholy, and feels supercilious toward more cheerful and stupid people who lack the taste for nocturnal solitude. He writes not only to edify, but to exploit his personality. Though not a good poet, he is deliberately literary: he tries for effects, and sometimes achieves them.

I have written myself into a view of Stogdon which would justify his inclusion among the sentimentalists of a later chapter. On the whole, however, this borderline figure may as well remain where he is. Viewed in relation to the total body of his verse, his sentimentalism is less obtrusive than it appears in this discussion; for no notice has here been taken of a large number of poems which reflect a wholly conventional Protestantism. Compared to many of his contemporaries he can hardly be called a sentimentalist, though compared to more faithful exemplars of his own religious tradition he predicts the deliquescence of nonconformity.

Leaving the dissenters, we seek out divine poets within the Establishment. An excellent example of the sterile and querulous High Churchmanship of the period is seen in Samuel Wesley the younger (1691-1739), who remains loyal to his father's now unfashionable principles.

The clerical schoolmaster's credentials for admission to this chapter are dubious, for at least a third of the pieces in *Poems on Several Occasions* (1736) are secular. In translations, satires, tales, "songs," and occasional trifles he proves himself a distinctly good neoclassical verseman; it is not surprising that his wit was esteemed by men of the sort who scorned his brother's enthusiasm. Not included in this volume are still livelier pieces—politically rash or morally indecorous—which were currently attributed to him. In his preface he "hopes no body who knows him thinks him capable of Undutifulness to his Earthly Sovereign, or of

Treason against the King of Kings: and whatever Ludicrous Copies may be attributed to him by common Fame, if they do not transgress those Bounds, how severe soever upon particular Crimes, he neither owns nor disowns them; Fear was made for the Guilty only." [25] This is noble, but slightly shrill.

Wesley would insist, however, that it is quite possible to be a man of the world and a sound Christian at the same time. He composed a large amount of divine poetry, and probably did so with complete sincerity. On one point he parts company with the neoclassicists, for he strongly opposes the use of pagan machinery, decoration, and allusion by modern writers. In his mind pagan art and pagan morals are closely associated. He grows warm on this theme in *Advice to One who was about to Write, To avoid the Immoralities of the Antient and Modern Poets.* Consonantly with his own advice, he substitutes Christian for pagan machinery when he reworks an allegory by Addison into *The Battle of the Sexes.*[26] In his preface to this poem he insists that the ancient deities, being no longer believed in, no longer "contribute to the Marvellous in Poetry," and indeed "transgress all Bounds of Probability." From this appeal to two antipodal literary standards, he shifts to moral and religious objections: "Yet the Majority of Modern Poets stand up stiffly for an indefeasible Right to their old Heathenism; and some of them seem by their Writings to take in the *Agenda,* as well as the *Credenda,* of that No-Religion; and to be Pagans in Practice, as well as Belief."

It is not, he urges, "impracticable to be a compleat Poet upon a Christian Scheme; if any one thinks so, let him read *Paradise Lost.*" Or, we may suggest, let him read Wesley's own *Wedding-Song* as an attempt to provide a definitely Christian epithalamium. The second stanza addresses, not Hymen, but God the Father:

> If e'er thy forming Hand has giv'n
> Woman, latest Work of Heav'n,
> With social dear domestic Joys,
> Height'ning lonely Paradise;

---

[25] He also says that a few of the poems in this 412-page volume are the work of another hand. Possibly one of his brothers? In any case the reader must allow for a slight margin of error in this discussion.

[26] Addison's essay is *Guardian* No. 152.

> If e'er thy kind paternal Care
>   Join'd and bless'd the wedded Pair,
> In spotless Bonds ordain'd to be
>   Emblems of thy Church and Thee;
> If e'er thy mightier Love decreed
>   Life from Jesu, Woman's Seed,
> The Loss of Eden to retrieve,
>   Sprung from Mary, second Eve;
> If e'er thy Work has endless Rest
>   Shadow'd by the Nuptial Feast;
> Heav'n, our last Wish and farthest Aim,
>   Mystick Marriage of the Lamb!
> Show'r thine Influence from on high,
>   Author of the Nuptial Tye;
> Show'r thy Graces, holy Dove,
>   God of Peace, and God of Love!

Wesley is also the Christian rather than the neoclassical wit in opposing that even more dangerous paganism which finds in natural virtue a sufficient guide for human conduct. Up to its conclusion, *On Happiness* deals tritely with a trite neoclassical theme. Where is happiness to be found? Not in fame nor in obscurity, and so on. Where then? "Only in virtue," most of Wesley's contemporaries would answer. But for Wesley, as later for Dr. Johnson, the answer is, "only in piety." Similarly, in the allegory of *The Battle of the Sexes*, Modesty and Honor can do nothing against Lust until Religion comes to their aid.

As we should expect, then, Wesley tilts at the unbelieving philosophies of the age. Buckingham's old lines in praise of Hobbes [27] arouse his indignation and suggest a contrast between Hobbes and another philosopher:

> Not thus his matchless Wisdom Bacon show'd,
> He found in all Things, and he own'd, a God.
> As farther learn'd, still readier to adore;
> And still the more he knew, believ'd the more. [28]

Verulam would have lifted a cynical eyebrow at such praise. The lines show how, thanks to Bacon's discreet separation of science and religion, eighteenth-century Christians could welcome the new science while rejecting with horror the philosophy of Hobbes.

[27] *Vide supra,* p. 3.
[28] *On Mr. Hobbes. Occasioned by a Copy of Verses written by the Earl of Musgrave.*

Like even the highest of High Churchmen in his day, Wesley is a
stout foe of Rome; but he thinks her chiefly dangerous because her
superstitious excesses are likely to breed complete unbelief in those outside her fold. "Upon his going to travel," Sir Herbert Powell is warned
not to lose his religion while in Italy:

> Mother of Errors Rome we well may call,
> Parent of too much Faith,—and none at all:
> Where lying Miracles, and Monkish Dreams,
> Fright thoughtless Fools to contrary Extremes:
> Who their twelve Articles of Faith give o'er,
> Because the Trental Creed has twenty-four:
> And count the Flames of Hell a fabled Story,
> Because they see the Frauds of Purgatory.
> In vain you boast from Popery you are free,
> If ting'd with unbelief in Italy.[29]

In his desire to find a middle ground between believing too much
and believing too little, Wesley becomes rather nagging and negative.
He is excessively conscious of living in a world full of wicked Whigs,
Papists, Dissenters, Latitudinarians, Arians, Socinians, Deists, and Athe-
ists. A great disapprover, he has a curious habit of voicing his dislikes in
poems which are ostensibly eulogies of men whom he admires. *The
Parish Priest* describes Wesley's father as the perfect High Churchman,
"True to his Oath, his Order, and his God." Though he refused the
Declaration of Indulgence in the reign of James, he did not let his
fear of Rome plunge him into heresy:

> When favour'd Sects o'erspread Britannia's Plains,
> Like Frogs thick-swarming after Summer's Rains;
> Against far diff'rent Foes alike prepar'd,
> No wild Disputer found him off his Guard.
> Nor those who following late Socinus' Plan,
> Degraded God Incarnate to a Man;
> Nor those, who wrestling Texts with greater slight,
> With Heav'n, as taught by elder Arius, fight;
> Reasoners, who no Absurdity can see
> In a new-made dependent Deity.

.   .   .   .   .

---

[29] *To Sir Herbert Powell, Bart.* Powell is also warned, in a manner recalling Roger
Ascham, not to copy Italian vices. England is bad enough, but she has never produced an
Aretino.

No Colours false deceiv'd his wary Eye,
Nor lukewarm Peace, nor Atheist Liberty.
Scripture and Fathers guide his Footsteps right;
For Truth is one, but Error infinite.

Because

He show'd the Pow'r of Kings, the Mitre's Sway,
Which Earth can neither give nor take away,

he was accused by latitudinarians and dissenters of being a "Friend to Papal and Despotick Pow'r." Here his son lashes out at the Low Church bishops of the reigns of William and Anne and at their patrons, the Whig bosses.

Wesley describes his father as so little a friend of tyranny as to be sympathetic toward all human suffering. At Christmas, Easter, and Whitsunday, the good priest fed the poor at his own table, his children waiting on their humble guests. "There was not a Dissenter or Papist in his parish," says a footnote. Had there not been a few such priests, sound both in doctrine and in practise,

Whose slighted but effectual Piety
Stood like a Mound unshaken, to repress
Th' o'erbearing Floods of prosp'rous Wickedness;
The Christian Faith had left Britannia's Coast,
Her lamp extinguish'd, and her Gospel lost.

Another member of this loyal band was the divine whose virtues inspired *To the Memory of the Reverend Dr. South*.[30] He was no less severe against "courtly Revellers" than against "Rebel Saintship." We need him sadly in these unbalanced days when

Some all their Anger pour on Rome alone,
Plant all their Batt'ries at the Papal Throne;
In Sects of Deists they no Harm can see,
All Danger is compris'd in Popery.
While others freely Schismaticks will blame,
The Zeal of Scots, or Sects of Amsterdam;
Forgetting Rome, so plain in Scripture shown,
That Bellarmine confess'd Her Babylon.
Not thus, O South, thy well-weigh'd Censures flew,
Severe as Fate, but as impartial too.

[30] Robert South (1634-1716), well-known preacher and controversial writer of the High Church party.

To the Memory of the Right Reverend Francis Gastrell [31] expresses much the same ideas as the poems on Wesley's father and on Dr. South. The only noteworthy variant is a passage in praise of the loyalty of the Oxford colleges, "True to the Mitred Head, and Scepter'd Hand." In a line of some merit Gastrell is said to exemplify "The calm still Wonder of a Life well-spent."

Though Wesley is narrowly partisan in matters ecclesiastical, he can pay a tribute to the Christian goodness of a dead Quakeress.[32] Again, however, one feels that she is praised chiefly in order to rebuke the shortcomings of others. Her piety was not

> . . . cast in furious Pharisaic Mould,
> The Puritannick Shibboleth of old;
> That seem'd all Mirth as Sin to disavow,
> No formal Frowning sunk her even Brow,
> As if each Look display'd its Owner's Fate,
> And all that smil'd were seal'd for Reprobate;
> As awkward Sow'rness were a sign of Grace,
> And sure Election blest an ugly Face.

Whatever her theological deficiencies on earth, she now

> . . . rests secure from Dangers and from Dread,
> Where Unbelief dare never lift its Head;
> Where none the Sacred Gospel dare disown,
> Nor fav'rite Clarke the Son of God dethrone.
>
> .   .   .   .
>
> Now the True Church in Purity She owns,
> Nor starts at Bishop-Angels on their Thrones;
> The one Communion void of Fault descries,
> The Film for ever vanish'd from her Eyes.

Wesley's theology is too rigid to permit any dalliance with the cult of sentiment, and his literary practise too neoclassical to encourage the hope of finding in his work any of the more superficial pre-romantic tendencies. *The Prisons Opened* warmly supports James Oglethorpe's efforts to improve conditions in the jails, but without suggesting a sentimental philosophy. The standards implied are those of Christian charity and ordinary human decency.

---

[31] 1662-1725. He became Bishop of Chester in 1714. A High Churchman who attacked Sherlock's views on the Trinity.
[32] *On the Death of a Friend, a Dissenter from the Church of England.*

In *The Battle of the Sexes* Wesley imitates Spenser's allegorical manner in a pseudo-Spenserian stanza of ten lines, $ababcdcde^5e^6$. As we have seen, he shares his father's admiration for Milton as a sacred poet; but he very amusingly burlesques the employment of Miltonic blank verse in sentimentally didactic descriptive poetry by writing *The Descriptive. A Miltonick, After the Manner of the Moderns.* When his friend Oglethorpe invites him into the country he replies:

> Did Fortune answer to my Mind,
> My Wishes to my Love,
> No need of Invitations kind
> To lead me to the Grove,
> Where Nature's Works I might admire,
> Free from the City's Crowd,
> And from the Art of Man retire
> To view the Art of God.[33]

But after reading *The Descriptive* we are sure that Wesley's enjoyment of nature would be very different from Thomson's. He is either a strictly orthodox Churchman or a wit—never a sentimentalist.

Wesley's poems furnish a clear, energetic, and somewhat acidulous statement of his religious position. But do his beliefs kindle his imagination and make him wish to sing? They do so only infrequently, and never with results that command hearty admiration. In sacred poetry as in Churchmanship, he is his father's son. The four hymns on the three persons of the Trinity and on the Triune God say the proper things about their subjects, like the official odes of a poet laureate. *On the Passion of Our Saviour* has somewhat more personal vitality:

> See streaming from th' accursed Tree
> His all-atoning Blood!
> Is this the Infinite? 'Tis he!
> My Saviour and my God.
>
> For Me these Pangs his Soul assail,
> For Me the Death is born!
> My Sin gave Sharpness to the Nail,
> And pointed ev'ry Thorn.

His epitaphs are not rich in feeling, but exploit his neoclassical gift for epigrammatic expression. Generally one feels that they are fabri-

[33] *An Ode to James Oglethorpe, Esq.*

cated to convey a warning to the living. It is probably an imaginary dead
infant who is addressed in the words,

> When the Arch-Angel's Trump shall sound,
> And Souls and Bodies join,
> What Crouds will wish, their Lives below
> Had been so short as thine.

"A witty Fair" instructs her sisters from the tomb:

> Reader, should any curious stay,
> To ask my luckless Name,
> Tell them, the Grave that hides my Clay,
> Conceals me from my Shame.

> Tell them, I mourn'd for Guilt of Sin
> More than for Pleasure spent:
> Tell them, whate'er my Morn had been,
> My Noon was Penitent.

His Scripture-paraphrases, most of which take the form of pindaric
odes, are very workmanlike specimens of their kind, never absurd and
never exciting. Wesley's religious lyrics, in short, deserve little more than
cool recognition of their unillumined competence. He is a versifier of
opinions, not a singer; a man whose religion is sincere but not imaginative; an eighteenth-century wit who thinks it sensible to be a Christian
and proper to compose Christian poetry. His collected secular pieces
are not offensive, but they are hardly the work of a devoted priest. Wesley's High Churchmanship—so different from Bishop Ken's—is dry,
negative, and joyless. It could be lifted above the level of disgruntled
Toryism only by a Catholic ardor which Wesley would have detested.
Richer in politico-ecclesiastical grudges than in spiritual passion, he derives little happiness or beauty from the faith which he champions.

A High Churchman of a different sort was the humble printer
Thomas Gent (1693-1778).[34] Students of provincial printing, of chapbook literature, and of Yorkshire antiquities have taken some interest
in him, but he has never been considered from the viewpoint of our
subject. His autobiography[35] relates with engaging simplicity the life

[34] His publications extend from 1724 to 1772, but he was most active and prosperous
within the 1720-1740 period.
[35] *The Life of Mr. Thomas Gent, Printer, of York; Written by Himself.* London, 1832.

story of a manly, intelligent, pious craftsman. He was born in Ireland, but his father hailed from Staffordshire. From the beginning of his apprenticeship at about the age of twelve to his death at the age of eighty-five, he busied himself with types and ink. He worked in London as journeyman and master printer up to 1724, but in that year established himself at York. From his presses he issued a large number of his own compositions—historical, legendary or pious matter with a quaint chapbook flavor, generally embellished with crude woodcuts, and addressed to simple folk like himself. His verse is almost entirely religious. Not quite all of it is known to me, but since he loved to repeat himself the following samples will be sufficient.

Gent avers that he was only eighteen when he wrote *Divine Justice and Mercy displayed. Set forth in the unhappy Birth, wicked Life, and miserable End of that deceitful Apostle, Judas Iscariot.* He admits, however, that the poem was "improved" before he finally published it in 1772. Using as authorities "Eusebius, Josephus, Orosius, Sozomenes, etc.," he pieces together the strange old legend of Judas—"How," to quote the title-page, "his Parents, enclosing him in a little Chest, threw him into the Sea; where he was found by a King on the coast of *Iscariot,* who called him by that Name. His Advancement to be a Privy-Counseller; and how he unfortunately killed the King's Son. He flies to Joppa; and, unknowingly, slew his own Father; for which he was forced to abscond a second Time. Returning a Year after, he married his Mother; who knew him to be her Child.... And lastly, seeming to repent of his wicked Actions, he followed our blessed Saviour, and became one of his Apostles; but after betray'd him into the Hands of the chief Priests; and then, miserably hanging himself, his Bowels dropt out of his Belly." The poem is written in awkward heroic couplets, but both the matter and the author's viewpoint are completely and unaffectedly medieval. The simple printer never dreamed of taking part in a "romantic revival."

In 1724, Gent published his *Divine Entertainments: Or, Penitential Desires, Sighs and Groans of the Wounded Soul. In Two Books, Adorned with Suitable Cuts.* This pietistic emblem-book need not be dwelt upon, for it closely imitates Hermann Hugo's *Pia Desideria* with the help of Edmund Arwaker's seventeenth-century translation.[36] One

[36] *Vide supra,* p. 77.

need only observe the continuance among the common people of a tradition which the eighteenth century is sometimes supposed to have obliterated. Another publication which may be passed by as not sufficiently original for our notice is a paraphrase of *Job* entitled *The Pattern of Piety: Or, Trials of Patience* (1734).

I can assign no date to *The History of the Life and Miracles of our Blessed Saviour, Jesus Christ*. It narrates the life of our Lord in quatrains which, for all their crudity, sometimes have an artless charm:

> Alas! sweet Child! was there no other,
> No better Place to lay thy Head?
> No softer Bed for thy dear Mother,
> But both obscurely here be laid!

As an appendix there is a series of stanzas on the lives and sufferings of the apostles. St. Matthew's ministry is recorded thus:

> Thro' Persia and throughout the Parthian Lands,
> He preach'd the Gospel of our Blessed Lord;
> At Nuddabar, near Ethiopian Strands,
> He fell a Martyr for the Holy Word.
> The horrid People cast him in a Flame,
> Which not consuming his most precious Life,
> Quite thro' his bleeding Heart a Halbert came,
> And thus he left this World of Care and Strife.

Characteristically, in each case Gent gives the date of the apostle's festival.

This book concludes with a prose prayer, *The Soul's Expostulation with our Blessed Saviour Jesus Christ,* part of which must be quoted to show the unusual quality of Gent's religious feeling: "My Soul, which is espoused by Faith, and endowed with Spirit, thou, O Jesus! who has dignify'd with thy Image, and redeemed by thy Blood, must surely inspire her to love thee, by whom she is so much beloved. With exceeding great Devotion, most ardent Affection and Fervour she desires to receive Thee. How may she obtain a Union with Thee, O Lord, to find thee alone, to open her whole heart to thee as she desires. Truly, thou art Her Beloved, the Choice among Thousands, in whom she taketh Pleasure to dwell all the Days of her Life. How do's she love to remember Thee in that Blessed Sacrament, thou thy self hast instituted."

This completely Catholic prayer is probably drawn from some manual of devotions, but it is surprising that an eighteenth-century Englishman should even have transcribed it.

Still more curious is a publication of 1743, *The Holy Life and Death of St. Winifred; and Other Religious Persons. Wherein is set forth the Glory of North-Wales, thro' the powerful Virtue of Holy-Well in Flintshire.... With pious Annotations from the Holy Scriptures, and Early Writers of the Church, concerning the Judgments and Mercies of Almighty God.... Also proper Cuts to distinguish particular Passages relating to the cruel Sufferings of our Blessed Saviour, who died for Our Sake; and those precious bleeding Victims of both Sexes sacrificed for their Love to Him; with other mournful and instructive Remarks never published by any Writer of the Life of this noble and celebrated Virgin.* On dedicating this book to the Reverend John Standish, an Anglican clergyman, Gent says: "Think it not strange, dear Sir, in me, who was, like You, brought up in the orthodox Faith of the establish'd Church, that I have thus endeavour'd to treat of a Virgin Martyr, renown'd from Antiquity, for being esteem'd the Patroness of Wales; when I tell you, That, in my Journeys twice thro' that Country...I met with such courteous Usage from the kind Inhabitants, heard so many wonderful Things credibly reported of that once most charming Lady, and the surprizing salutary Effects that flow with the Streams of her celebrated Spring; I was resolv'd to shew my Gratitude and Fidelity." He recognizes that the miraculous rescuscitation of the saint after she had been decapitated may be distasteful to some readers, but suggests that an allegorical interpretation of the incident "might be made to soften the severest Censure." That task, however, he will leave to his readers. "They may kindly say, That the lovely Subject of my Pen is nothing but what is agreeable to several of my innocent Flights; that something of the *miranda* is necessary to render a Book acceptable."

The Life of St. Winifred is divided into five sections each prefixed by a jingle giving the argument, like the head-notes in the *Faerie Queene*. At the end of each section the moral is relentlessly pointed. The woodcuts are amusingly crude, and the verse-form of the main body of the poem, *ababcc*[5], adds to the unconsciously archaic effect. In the following passage the heathen prince Caradoc slays Winifred, who has withstood his advances:

> Die then, quoth he, thou most obdurate Maid!
> Then, as to Heav'n most piteously she cry'd,
> With such a Force he struck his glittring Blade,
> That quickly did her milk-white Neck divide.
> Low fell the Body! down he threw the Head!
> Whilst sanguine Streams like trickling Rills did spread.
>
> As by Christ's Sufferings, tho' supernal Call,
> We learn to bear Affliction's bitter Stings;
> So her Example, truly virginal,
> Should make us slight all temporary Things:
> For if to Heav'n we stedfast prove in Love,
> We shall be bless'd on Earth, and crown'd Above.

Later, after an enthusiastic account of the miraculous virtues of St. Winifred's Well, Gent observes that

> The Catholicks, unshaken in their Belief,
> With flowing Tears for tender Mercy cry:
> They think the Saint, who gives to all Relief,
> Will pray for *Them* to the Bless'd Trinity.
> The Litanies, exhibited, reveal
> That Love and Pow'r, they own, to pray, and heal.

At this point a footnote "exhibits," in English, a thoroughly Catholic *Litany of St. Winifred,* followed by two prayers invoking her intercession and by a *Hymn of S. Wenefride.* Gent does not argue for the invocation of saints; but he is surprisingly friendly toward such devotions —much friendlier than the narrative itself demands. He goes on:

> And sure, whatever Happiness can be
> In Heav'n, or Earth, all wish for to acquire.
> We are like Pilgrims to Eternity,
> And might be lost, or in our Journey tire,
> Thro' Sin's foul Burden, if we sought not Aid
> From Christ, as they do by this shining Maid.
>
> 'Tis scarce deny'd, that Heav'n hears ev'ry Pray'r,
> And Hymn that's offer'd, tho' it be to Saints;
> So we may learn, from Signs and Tokens clear,
> By sudden Cures in many sad Complaints!
> And may not Joy, like *good* Enthusiasm, range
> O'er boundless Scenes for such a rapturous Change?

And if we can but gain an happy End;
If God is with our Off'rings satisfy'd:
What matters, much, how, or by whom, we send;
Since Pray'rs conjoined thro' Christ are not deny'd:
For when strong Faith and Love in Woes appear,
No Sigh's unheard, nor drops in vain one Tear.

To this Yorkshire printer, who believes in *"good* Enthusiasm," "the communion of saints" is not a wholly meaningless phrase.

The copious notes repeatedly refer, always with reverent approval, to other saints and martyrs. The Scriptures are freely quoted not only in English but in Latin. Among his authorities we note such names as Plato (quoted in Latin), Pliny, Eusebius, Orosius, Cyprian, Augustine, Bonaventura, Juan of Osma, Giraldus Cambrensis, Bede, Thomas à Kempis, Camden, and Bishop Ken. That he knew all of these writers at first hand is doubtful, but it is remarkable that he knows anything of them at all. One wonders how he acquired his rich though disorderly stock of theological, hagiological, and legendary lore. Few clergymen of his day could compare with him in this respect.[37]

The same sort of learning abundantly appears in a work of his old age, *The Most Delectable, Scriptural, and Pious History of the Famous and Magnificent Great Eastern Window ... in St. Peter's Cathedral, York* (1762). The plan is to describe and annotate the window, pane by pane, in the utmost detail. A thin trickle of verse struggles through towering banks of notes showing wide miscellaneous knowledge of theology, church architecture, and ecclesiastical history. Here and elsewhere, Gent reveals himself as thoroughly Church-minded.

This writer has been allowed to speak for himself rather copiously as the only means of communicating his curious flavor. Unquestionably he is something of a puzzle. Mr. Charles A. Federer, in his Introduction to the First Series of *Yorkshire Chap-Books,* explains that the lower and lower-middle classes, especially in rural districts, had the subconscious sympathy of the underprivileged for outlaws, especially those who gave to the poor what they stole from the rich. Hence the popularity of chapbook lives of Robin Hood and Dick Turpin. Such fare was chiefly for men. The women, and of course some of the men, would

[37] Gent produced a similar work in prose, *Piety Display'd: In the Holy Life and Death of the Antient and Celebrated St. Robert, Hermit, at Knaresborough.*

want something more edifying. Poor people are especially anxious to believe "that present suffering entitles to commensurate recompense in the life to come." They were glad, therefore, to buy from the chapman lives of saints and especially of holy women, canonized or uncanonized. In such narratives are found "the same idea of redress of social inequalities, which underlies the conventional character of the outlaw, reappearing clothed in the monkish garb of the saint who on the one hand resists and punishes the wicked in high places, and on the other ministers to the wants of the poor, heals their diseases, and assures them of divine favour. This will account for the striking, and yet natural circumstance, that in a post-reformation period, such chapbooks as the 'Life of Saint Winifred' or the 'Life of Saint Robert of Knaresborough,' written by such a staunch anti-papist as Thomas Gent, saw the light in the strait-laced city of York."

Mr. Federer's explanation is helpful. To a considerable extent, no doubt, Gent was catering to an appetite for democratic marvels and martyrdoms. But this fact will hardly account for the genuine religious feeling which pervades his writings. He not only gave his public what *they* wanted, but what *he* wanted. It is impossible to read his work without recognizing that he was a devout Catholic whose religious feelings were inseparable from his sense of membership in Holy Church.

For his age, Gent is unusual for his sacramentalism. A prayer illustrating this fact has already been cited. In *Divine Justice and Mercy displayed* he says that after our Lord's death not all of those who had followed Him during His lifetime grasped the full meaning of the Eucharist:

> Eating his Flesh, and drinking of his Blood,
> Were Mysteries, by them not understood.
> That Life eternal was here justly meant;
> Because Life-giving Father had him sent:
> And as he liv'd by them, so those that eat
> Should even live, thro' that cœlestial Meat.

In *Divine Entertainments* he cries to Jesus,

> Let me be nourish'd by thy Blood,
> And fed with Sacramental Food.

Such passages were not calculated to satisfy any Robin Hood complex in his public, and the same may be said of the extremely Catholic litanies, prayers and hymns with which he embellishes *The Life of St. Winifred*. It is possible that Thomas Gent was a crypto-Romanist engaged in propaganda. This hypothesis, however, is not supported by any conclusive evidence. For a time he worked in London under Francis Clifton, a Roman Catholic printer,[38] but there is nothing to prove that he was influenced by this contact. When he speaks of "the learned Hermannus Hugo, of the order of the Holy Jesus" [39] one feels that this is, for eighteenth-century England, a strangely respectful way of referring to a Jesuit. The point, however, is very slight. On the whole the likeliest supposition is that Gent was an extreme High Churchman who, for reasons now hidden from us, retained to an unusual degree that seventeenth-century type of Anglo-Catholicism which in his own day had almost vanished. Several clues point in this direction. He was a sufficiently strong Tory to have been suspected of printing Jacobite libels.[40] In *Divine Justice and Mercy displayed,* after quoting "Father, forgive them," he cites analogous instances of sublime charity:

> Thus did the Proto-Martyr, Stephen, dye!
> Fill'd with the Holy Ghost! Who did he spy
> But God and Jesus? Lay not this to them,
> From Murd'rers sprung, of old Jerusalem.
> King Charles the First, how worthily display'd;
> A Transcript, fair; because, like Him, he pray'd.
> Read but the Icon— There the Royal Mind,
> As well as Person, set forth, *true,* you'll find.

In the versified preface to *The Life of St. Winifred* he mentions King Edmund as

> . . . high-prais'd by God-like Kenn [*sic*],
> The most seraphic of all mortal men,

and a footnote refers to the nonjuring bishop's epic on the Saxon martyr.[41]

His autobiography expresses the utmost reverence for that "holy prelate," Bishop Wilson of Sodor and Man, who carried the simon-pure Anglo-Catholic tradition well into the eighteenth century.[42] Probably, then, he means exactly what he says when he concludes *Piety Dis-*

---

[38] *The Life of Mr. Thomas Gent,* p. 85.   [39] *Ibid.,* p. 143.
[40] The charge is denied, *Ibid.,* p. 141, but at least there can be no doubt of his Toryism.
[41] *Vide supra,* p. 101.   [42] *Op. cit.,* pp. 42-43.

play'd [43] with the words: "And, whilst we seriously ponder upon these Things, may we be incited to beseech Almighty God, that the Members of Christ's Holy Catholic Church, now militant on Earth (particularly that pure Part of it established in this Kingdom) may, hereafter, through the Merits of our dear Redeemer, reign triumphantly with Him in Heaven." It is significant that one must exhume an obscure printer of chapbooks in order to illustrate the survival of this type of Churchmanship in the mid-eighteenth century.

I am familiar with no Low Churchman of the period who specialized in the writing of divine poetry. Disregarding ecclesiastical classifications, therefore, let me expand the scanty materials of this chapter with notes on two separately published religious poems.

Thomas Hobson's [44] *Christianity the Light of the Moral World* did not appear until 1745, but the author states that it was written more than eight years earlier, "only as a Christmas-exercise." Though Hobson accepts the common view that the essence of religion is moral conduct, he is one of those who would insist upon the necessity, for sound ethics, of the Christian revelation. In his Introduction he declares that "The most compleat rule of action that can possibly be collected from mere pagan philosophy, would be but a perplexed and undigested composition of inconsistent opinions and ineffectual precepts. The revelation of Christ was intended to remove these uncertainties, to rectify these errors, and supply these defects of unassisted reason.... The design of the following poem is to represent this great difference between the discoveries of *reason,* and those that are made by *revelation,* in a more obvious view."

This scheme is carried out in Miltonic blank verse which is not without a tumid kind of eloquence. The poem is an argument, but at least the argument is supported by emotion. Before the fall, Adam knew the will of God:

> Thrice happy man! in this transcendent light
> Of native reason, clear and unobscured
> By vapours foul, as that eternal source
> Of undiminish'd brightness, whence it flowed!

[43] His prose life of St. Robert of Knaresborough.
[44] Not in *D.N.B.* He styles himself "M. A. of Queen's College, Oxford." No other writings by him are listed in the British Museum Catalogue.

> No tongue can speak, no thoughtful heart conceive,
> With what transporting joy his raptur'd eye
> View'd all creation.

But through Adam's sin men lost the clear guiding vision of divinity.

> ... Hence various fancies form'd
> As various Gods. This deified a dance
> Of antic interfering atoms.[45] This
> The dull material system call'd his God; [46]
>
> .   .   .   .
>
> While some, with sceptic doubt, believ'd in none,
> Or, half-believing, impiously deny'd
> His providential eye.[47]

Amidst this intellectual din the clear voice of truth could not be heard:

> The philosophic wit, the deep-read sage,
> Immortal sons of *Reason,* ne'er could form
> A plan of *Moral Wisdom* just and true.

If happiness grounded on virtue is the goal of life, its attainment demands "A clearer light than best-taught reason lends." That "light of the moral world" is Christianity. After some rather cloudy oratory on the moral benefits of the Christian faith Hobson concludes:

> Let reason soar, when mounted on the wings
> Of meek-ey'd Faith; and, unpresuming, wait
> Till heaven evolves the mazy-winding folds
> Of God's eternal will.—How bright the scene,
> How just the plan, when each mysterious law
> Unveil'd shall shine! How big the swelling joy,
> When truth in tides shall flow upon the soul,
> And faith, complete, be swallow'd in fruition!
> When, full-reveal'd, the filial Light Himself
> Shall pour upon thee one immortal day!

The Magi. An Eclogue is printed with *Christianity* as a sort of lyrical pendant to that longer and more rhetorical poem, for here in the manger lies "the light of the moral world." The three kings offer their gifts, adore the Babe, and sing his praises in lines like these:

---

[45] "Democritus, Epicurus," reads Hobson's note.
[46] "Seneca and the Stoics"—Hobson.
[47] "Academics, Epicureans, and others"—Hobson.

Smile, sacred infant, smile! thy fragrant breast
Excells the odours of the spicy east!
The burnish'd gold is dross before thy eye;
Thou God of sweetness, God of purity!

.   .   .   .

Hail, Lord of nature, hail! to Thee belong
My song, my life—I give my life, my song:
Live in thy light, confess thy day divine,
Adore thy love, and freely give thee mine!

The Magi at least attempts an emotional response to the scene at the manger. Hobson is neither a genius nor a bungler. He seems to have rather strong religious feelings of an optimistic, expansive kind. His mood, though not his creed, is like Thomson's: he wants a religion of "swelling joy."

The same comment would apply to Samuel Codrington,[48] who published *The Beatific Vision: a Poem* in 1735. The Dedication to one Mrs. Stephens indicates that she has lost her husband, and that Codrington has lost an uncle who had been a close friend of Mr. Stephens. They should be thought of as happy in heaven. "To see Jesus, as he is, is the Perfection of their State; to see him on the Cross, of our's." And so the purpose of the poem is to console the bereaved woman by describing to her "the beatific vision" now enjoyed by her husband's spirit.

Thou Source of Love's unfathomable Deep,
Jesus, the pleasing Lustre of whose Eye
Kindles to Glory all the Realm of Day,
Forgive, and be propitious to my Song.

Something like Dennis's theory of poetico-religious enthusiasm combines with belief in the superiority of nature to art in Codrington's soaring ambition:

Could I but speak the Dictates of my Soul,
Or write in language suited to my Thoughts,
I'd glory to despise the Poet's Art;
Yet raise my Song above the Critick's View,
To lively Transports of a raptur'd Mind,

[48] Not in *D.N.B.* No other work of his is listed in the British Museum Catalogue.

Whose Spirit rises high above the Sphere
Of mortal Charms, exulting to ascend,
And meet his Smiles; thus, in his dear Embrace
Entwin'd, to rival Angels in their Bliss.

The full glory of God is revealed to us, not in the visible universe, but in the person of Jesus. If our earthly knowledge of Him is so wondrous, what must be the experience of beholding Him face to face in heaven! We are afraid to think of it, afraid to send our minds out across "the infinite Unknown." Nothing daunted, however, Codrington proceeds to imagine the Saviour

...amid Seraphic Throng,
Myriads of Angels that around him wait,
Swift to perform his Messages of Love;
Near they approach, with pleasurable Haste,
Their Sight enlarg'd, and fix a stedfast Eye
On the transcending Glory of his Throne,
Compos'd of pure unwasting Particles,
Its congruous Beauty mixt with Art divine,
In nice Proportion as the Builder's Mind;
Seated thereon in Majesty and Grace,
Joy in his Eyes, and Rapture on his Lips,
His Hand stretch'd forth full of Immortal Crowns,
Pond'rous in Glory as their Souls can bear.

These are hardly the "lively Transports of a raptur'd Mind." Up to this point Codrington has managed his blank verse competently and imbued it with some dignity of feeling, but the vision itself is a sad failure. Codrington is not a writer who should venture to speak of things unspeakable. It is something, however, that a man of this period should even attempt a "beatific vision," and something that he should wish to console Mrs. Stephens, not by reasoning at her, but by painting a picture of her dead husband's bliss.

The group discussed in this chapter is so small that statistics concerning its members are not of much significance. We may as well note, however, that three out of five poets—I have no facts for Hobson and Codrington—were born between 1691 and 1693 inclusive. Erskine, the oldest, was born in 1685; Jean Adam, the youngest, in 1710. The group is therefore a trifle earlier than that studied in the preceding chapter. Furthermore, Erskine, Stogdon, Wesley, and Gent had written a good deal before 1720. The three clerical poets, Erskine, Stogdon, and Wesley, are all sons of clergymen; the lay poets, Jean Adam and Thomas Gent, are humble folk. Hobson, however, is an Oxford M. A., and Codrington is probably a man of some culture.

When these writers are compared with those treated in Chapter III, it becomes apparent that as we pass from the 1700-1720 period to the 1720-1740 period the crop of divine poets becomes smaller in quantity and poorer in quality. In the latter period neither Nonconformity nor Anglicanism produces a single religious poet of any consequence. The earlier period, though barren, was not so barren as this. But since a good deal of sacred verse was written by the poets to be treated in the following chapters no further generalizations will be offered at this point.

Chapter VIII

NON-SENTIMENTAL CHRISTIANS

IN TURNING FROM THE EARLIER TO THE LATER OF THE TWO PERIODS COVERED by this study, we have seen what happens to the non-religious wit, and what happens to the specialist in divine poetry. But what are the fortunes of that large and rather miscellaneous group who were described in Chapter IV as "middle-classicists"? In the 1720-1740 period, generally speaking, the more emotional and imaginative examples of this type will considerably develop those sentimental traits which they displayed more obscurely in the earlier period. The duller and more conventional middle-classicists, on the other hand, will be slower to move in this direction. Let us deal first with these less interesting cases by examining certain poets who reveal various degrees of favorable response to Christianity but without marked sentimental or pre-romantic tendencies. They may roughly be arranged in a descending scale of piety, and five women may be allowed to lead the procession.

Elizabeth Tollett (1694-1754) [1] was much esteemed for her learning. "Besides great Skill in Music, and Drawing, she spoke fluently and correctly the Latin, Italian, and French Languages, and well understood History, Poetry, and the Mathematicks." [2] Isaac Newton, as a friend of the family, was interested in her mental progress.

About two-thirds of her poems pertain to religion. The other pieces include a good many classical translations (chiefly from Horace), pastorals and pastoral songs, and epigrams. *Anne Boleyn to Henry VIII,* featured on her title-page, is an imitation of *Eloisa to Abelard.* There are a few familiar epistles and little "occasionals," but on the whole she is

---

[1] Daughter of George Tollett, Commissioner of the Navy under William III and Anne. He superintended her education and left her a tidy fortune. Her *Poems on Several Occasions* were published the year after her death. Only a few of them can be dated, but it seems probable that, as a bluestocking of twenty-six, she was writing verse at least as early as 1720.

[2] Anonymous preface of *Poems on Several Occasions.*

unusually free from the "among-us-girls" prattle so much beloved by the versifying women of the century. She seldom writes unless she has something to say, and she says it with a clear, dry competence. She is very much herself when she declares that Horace is a better remedy for the spleen than woodland solitude.[3]

Miss Tollett's love of the classics blends with her religion. In Latin verse she paraphrases three psalms, a portion of *Job*, and Book V, Chapter VIII of *De Imitatione Christi*. Cicero imparts to her the precepts of that natural religion of reason which supports the Christian revelation:

> I read great Tully's Page, and wond'ring find
> The heav'nly Doctrine of th' immortal Mind;
> An Axiom first by Parent Nature taught,
> An inborn Truth, which proves itself by Thought.[4]

Conveniently, too, Cicero assures her that if this "inborn Truth" should happen not to be a truth at all, the error is at least a salutary one. In that case,

> Wilful I err, and with Delight I find
> The kind Delusion fortify My Mind.

For if the soul perishes with the body, no "philosophizing Ghosts" can reproach her for credulity;

> But if wise Nature's Dictates can prevail,
> And weighty Reason turn the doubtful Scale,
> The sure Decrees of heav'nly Justice wait
> A permanent Award, and future State.[5]

The scientific side of this bluestocking's education, however, is more importantly related to her religious ideas than the humanistic side. *On the Death of Sir Isaac Newton,* apparently written on the night of his funeral, shows great admiration for his achievements: "Bacon and Boyle thy Triumphs but fore-run." Fully accepting both the new science and Christianity, she confronts the resultant difficulties pluckily if not very profoundly. *Hypatia* is summoned from the shades to defend woman's right to consider the inscrutable mysteries of life:

> Whether that Spirit which o'er all presides
> Infus'd thro' all its equal Motions guides,

---

[3] *An Epistle.*   [4] *To my Brother at St. John's College in Cambridge.*
[5] *Occasioned by a Passage in Tully de Senectute, relating to the Immortality of the Soul, Si in hoc erro libenter erro, etc.*

> Or from the whole distinct, himself, unseen,
> Conducts and regulates the vast Machine,
> Let Heav'n decide; by Reason's finite View
> To judge the Diff'rence, wou'd the Doubt renew:
> Yet she [woman] aspires that Being to explore,
> The Source of all, and wond'ring to adore.

At the end of this poem we find a note: "If in this little Piece the Doubts concerning the Supreme Being be thought exceptionable ... it must be considered that I was to adapt my Notions to the Character of an Heathen and a Platonist, who is supposed to deliver them." But a disciple of Newton might find it equally difficult to believe in a personal God transcending the universal machine.

Not that Elizabeth Tollett is seriously beset by doubts. *On the Origin of the World* derides the doctrine of chance as mere nonsense. The orderly Newtonian system must have been planned and set in motion by some great orderly Mind. Defiantly she asks the sceptic whether the *Iliad*

> From the result of scatter'd Letters rose.
> If not, cou'd Chance the noblest Work produce
> For various Beauties, and for aptest Use?

The universe then, must be the work of an Homer:

> Reason exhausted with the long Dispute,
> And Passion to assert, or to confute,
> May all their Systems in a Word confine,
> 'Tis all the Fabric of a Pow'r Divine.

That this Power is none other than the God of Christianity is assumed as self-evident, for she continues:

> Then to the Book return, whence we receive
> All we are bound to practise or believe:
> Nor is the Book of Nature writ more fair
> Than is her Origin recorded there.

Thus Newtonian nature and the Scriptures preach the same gospel. The Book of Nature, however, is to be read with analytical reason, while the Bible is to be read with childlike faith:

> Of sceptic Sophistry thy Mind divest,
> And heav'nly Truth shall beam upon thy Breast;

> But not with such do these Inquiry sute,
> Whose Wit is doubting, Science to dispute.[6]
> God, rob'd in Pow'r rebellious Pride o'erthrows,
> But on the humble Heart his Grace bestows.

Precisely to the extent that it refutes the doctrine of chance, Newtonian science may provide arguments for determinism. In *Against Chance and Fate*, the poet finds the latter a more difficult obstacle than the former. "Consult the native Dictates of thy Soul" is her advice to those who wish to be sure of free will, though she also advances the familiar ethical objections against fatalism. But beyond the truths of which rational introspection can convince us lie such mysteries as the Trinity and "How we from Adam's Crime derive a Stain":

> Then, feeble Reason! thy Pursuit must cease:
> Implore the God of Knowledge, Truth, and Peace,
> To teach that Rebel Folly we call Wit,
> That 'tis her noblest Conquest to submit.

The intellectual Miss Tollett has an almost Tennysonian readiness to abandon reason whenever it threatens to make her uncomfortable.

To combat a feeling in others, and perhaps in herself, that man cuts a rather sorry figure as a part of Newtonian nature, she writes *The Microcosm, asserting the Dignity of Man*. According to a headnote it was suggested by Henry Baker's *The Universe*,[7] which she finds, though otherwise admirable, too grudging in its estimate of humanity's importance in the scheme of things. Man's study of nature should begin at home, for he himself is a little universe full of marvels. Some of these he shares with the brutes, but his reason could never have arisen from irrational nature: it can only be the gift of God.

Man may well feel insignificant when he contemplates the heavens, but

> Be that confess'd; we own his Care the more,
> Who taught to find those Worlds unknown before.

In other words astronomy is the work of astronomers in whose minds God has implanted the noble desire to understand the world that he has made:

---

[6] This awkward couplet may be rendered, "But heavenly truth cannot be attained by the inquiries of those for whom wit is a matter of doubting, and science a matter of negation."

[7] *Vide infra*, p. 464.

The very Doubt of all these wondrous Things,
From that high Monitor within thee springs.
Daughter of Heav'n, my Soul! for such thou art,
Not of material Elements a Part,
On this fair Scene thy present Sense employ;
But raise thy nobler Hope to future Joy.
Tho' Heav'n shall vanish, and the Stars shall fall,
And rolling flames dissolve this earthy Ball,
The Just in happy Mansions shall remain,
While Worlds shall perish, and revive again.

In these concluding lines she leaps from the nature of Newtonianism to the super-nature of Christianity.

Being capable of saying almost in the same breath that reason is man's glory and that man must be ready to throw reason overboard in order to achieve faith, Miss Tollett has no difficulty in considering herself an orthodox Christian. Her temperament is far from ardent, but besides the poems already cited she wrote a surprising amount of non-argumentative religious verse. Most of it, to be sure, consists of paraphrases. Besides the Latin exercises already mentioned, she renders in English thirty-two psalms, two or three other portions of the Bible including the Lord's Prayer, and the Nicene Creed. Most of her paraphrases are in heroic couplets and merely attempt to render the sense of the original as faithfully as the form will permit. Sometimes, however, she goes against her nature and endeavors to be lyrical. *Susanna: Or Innocence Preserv'd. A Musical Drama* turns the famous apocryphal story into a feeble little opera.

Very few of her original poems betoken a personal religious feeling. *My own Epitaph* expresses the assurance that the dispersed atoms of her body will be reassembled at the Day of Judgment. *Hymn to the Paraclete* [8] begs the Holy Spirit to descend into her heart and make His temple there. Neither of these poems radiates much warmth, but the irregular ode entitled *Ecce Homo* is a really fervent meditation on the crucified Christ.

Wretch! can'st thou think on this, and yet not feel
The thorny Wreath, the biting Steel,
Which pierc'd his Hands and Feet, and gor'd his tender Side!
For thee he bled, for thee he dy'd:
All this for ruin'd Man he bore,
And open'd heav'nly Mercy's boundless Store.

8. Dated "At Whitsuntide, 1723."

> Can'st thou, by him redeem'd, deny
> For him to bleed, for him to dy?
> O thou who singly can'st for all suffice!
> Our reconciling Priest! our spotless Sacrifice!
> Thou, the great Father's co-eternal Son!
> Whose ever-during Being with no Time begun.
> Propitious God! thy gracious Aid impart
> To crucify this sinful Heart,
> Transfix'd, like thine, with sympathizing Smart.
> Forbid it, Lord! that I untouch'd should be
> With Suff'rings from myself transferr'd on Thee.

As poetry these lines arouse no admiration, but they show that Elizabeth Tollett had her moments of spiritual ardor. Her feelings, however, are not deep or rich, and she seldom allows them full play. She aspires to be a thinker rather than a feeler, and so turns to science for the materials of a thoroughly rational religion. But Newton can give her only the religion of nature, and in her heart she wants Christianity. Hence her ultimate reliance is a quite unscientific faith which somehow lacks both the beauty of logic and the beauty of passion.

The less convoluted brains of Sarah Dixon [9] were untroubled by questions of fate and free will. Some of her friends cut paper flowers or arranged seashells, but Sarah's gift was for writing thin, pleasant, careless verses—pastorals with a personal application, stuff about female friendship, recondite little jokes which can never sparkle again. In her more serious moments, however, she often turned to religious subjects. Her efforts in divine poetry were doubtless encouraged by the Reverend John Bunce, Vicar of St. Stephens, near Canterbury, who "corrected" her verses before publication. Needless to say, she paraphrased two or three psalms. Once her ambitions soared to the height of a long narrative poem on *The Prophet Jonah,* but she left off just where the sailors throw him overboard.

Miss Dixon is a Tory: in *On the XXXth of January* [10] she not only

[9] Not in *D.N.B.* In her verses one sees her as a spinster who lived in or near Canterbury among a prosperous and cultivated though not aristocratic group of friends. *Poems on Several Occasions* was brought out by subscription at Canterbury in 1740. In the British Museum copy (11632.bb.35) several poems have been written in on the inside covers and fly-leaves by an unknown contemporary who gives facts showing them to be by Miss Dixon. I have drawn on these as well as on the printed poems.

[10] The feast of King Charles the Martyr.

hails Charles I as "the Christian Hero perfected" but implies a contrast between his ideals and those of the present:

> Reflect, O Britain, on thy *Native* Crimes;
> In all thy Boast of Peace and Plenty, bring
> To thy Remembrance, thy Martyr'd King.
> Then fell the Saint, the Patriot, and the Prince;
> Victim to Honour, and to Innocence:
> Erase our Annals, or our Griefs renew,
> Give to his Memory, at least, its Due.

The Royal Martyr, she thinks, represents values more important than Whiggish "peace and plenty."

That her political High Churchmanship includes a slight Anglo-Catholic element is perhaps indicated by a couplet in her paraphrase of the Twenty-third Psalm:

> In Deserts wide thou shalt my Table spread,
> And feed my Soul with Eucharistic Bread.

But more substantial evidence is provided by *The Ruins of St. Austin's, Canterbury*.[11] With very few exceptions, eighteenth-century poems on such topics dabble in Gothicism and melancholy but either ignore or condemn "monkish superstitions." Seldom do we find so friendly a view of monastic life as Miss Dixon's:

> If to relinquish all that we call good,
> The things delectable to flesh and blood,
> The wealth, the pow'r, the pleasure and the ease,
> To lead a recluse life like one of these,
> In watching, fasting, penitence and tears,
> Forgetful of the world, but in their pray'rs,
> Can promise Heav'n, and gain a hope secure;
> What coward heart, but would as much endure?
> That rugged, thorny, salutary way,
> Points the bright prospect of eternal day:

[11] Printed in the *Kentish Gazette* for June 30, 1774, and inserted in the British Museum copy of *Poems on Several Occasions*, with a note, by the person who copied in the manuscript poems. It was probably he who sent this poem to the *Kentish Gazette* in 1774, *à propos* of that paper's having printed "an extract from Mr. Grose's antiquities, relating to the Monastery of St. Augustine." He says that it was written by Miss Dixon "after she was seventy-three years old"; but since we do not know the year of her birth, this gives no clue to the date of the poem. It was probably written long after 1740, for nothing in *Poems on Several Occasions* suggests that she is more than middle-aged.

> Exulting there, no monumental pride
> Needs to declare how well they liv'd and died:
> With Mother Earth they now incorporate lie;
> A fate attendant on each Passer-by.
> Tread gently, stranger, o'er their ashes tread,
> And think that here rests many a holy head.

Consonantly with such views the author is an admirer of Bishop
Ken, whom she imitates in her *Hymn for Morning* and *An Evening
Hymn*. She is thoroughly Arminian in her view of Christ's sacrifice as
a triumph over sin and death which may be shared by all who believe in

> The just, the merciful, the good,
> Who shed for all his precious blood.[12]

In *To Psyche* she calms her disquieted soul with the assurance of divine
mercy:

> The Tide of Life runs swiftly on;
> Nor needs the Influence of the Moon,
>   Press'd onwards by our Cares;
>   No mortal Force
>   Can stop the rapid Course,
>   Nor bid come back the long neglected Years.
> Yet Peace, my Soul; the God of Peace still lives;
>   Essential Mercy and essential Power
>   Can every conscious Penitent restore;
> We sorrow, he forgives.

At times, then, Sarah Dixon is a happily devout Anglican. But she
provides rather thin soil for the seed, and easily relapses into the confidential inanities which her friends admired. She betrays a spiritual
weakness, too, by using religion for the exploitation of non-religious feelings. One fears that *Reflections on the Sight of a Vault* was written to
stimulate gooseflesh rather than awe, and that *To Strephon* is as spurious
in its piety as *Eloisa to Abelard*:

> Why, from the Airy, Witty and the Fair,
> Was I the choice of one so insincere?
>   .   .   .
>
> Fond Heart! false Strephon!—but the Conflict's o're;
> You can betray, nor I believe, no more.

[12] *A Penitential Thought.* See also *The Sacrifice* and *On the Resurrection and Ascension
of our Blessed Lord.*

> Forgive Us, Heaven! tho' never, never here,
> We meet again, may We be Angels there:
> There, may my faithful Passion find Reward;
> Your Guilt be pardon'd, and my Prayers be heard.[13]

We may add that Miss Dixon twice pays superficial respect to rural retirement and once imitates Lady Winchilsea in complimenting a nightingale.[14] But although she has a tinge of sentimentalism, the tendency is by no means strong in her. Nothing is strong enough in her to be very important.

Mrs. Jane Brereton (1685-1740) was born of Welsh parents named Hughes. In 1711 she married Thomas Brereton, scion of an old Chester family. His father, Major Brereton, had been reared a Roman Catholic and even designed for the priesthood but had left the Church in his youth. Thomas, a wild fellow, soon squandered the "considerable Fortune in Money" which he had inherited from his father. Despite these trials Jane "was the most affectionate and dutiful Wife, and always behaved with good Humour, Patience, and Submission. This might afford a large Field for displaying her Virtues. But as it can't be done, without casting a Cloud on Mr. Brereton, those who stand in the same relation to both, chuse to have it omitted, believing there is enough to give Lustre to her Character, without making another's a Foil to it."

In 1721, however, she could bear her husband no longer, and leaving him in London she retired to North Wales with her children. When in the following year she learned that he had been drowned "she fell into violent faintings . . .; tho' she was perfectly free from any Kind of Fits, till this unhappy Accident." Her widowhood was distinguished for piety and good works. The souls not only of her children but of her servants were her constant care. "She was extremely devout and observant of all religious Duties. . . . She was a true Member of the Church of England, but had great Charity for all those of different Persuasions," and followed the dissenters in being a strict Sabbatarian. She liked music and sometimes played cards, though not well. In her opinion not all stageplays need be suppressed merely because some of them are so wicked. As the end drew near "she rejoyc'd at every Symptom of approaching Death,

---

[13] Several of her poems refer to this faithless Strephon, whose actuality must remain problematical.

[14] See *To Silvio, Retirement,* and *The Nightingale*.

and was all Resignation.... Her Distemper was the Gravel." Her poetical name was Melissa.

I have been quoting from the anonymous *Account of the Life of Mrs. Brereton* prefixed to her posthumous *Poems on Several Occasions*. Her verses justify the forebodings aroused by the crude and barely literate memoir, for they portray a dull, vulgar, bungling woman. Somewhat more than a quarter of the poems are religious. In several of them her Low Churchmanship is indistinguishable from the more repellent type of nonconformity. The eternity of hell-torment is a congenial theme.[15] Her favorite source of inspiration, however, is the death of friends, and she seldom fails to improve such occasions with a warning to the survivors:

> ... How peaceful she resigns,
> Her Faith still rising, as her Strength declines!
> With fervent Longings she desires to be
> From this frail, sinful Tabernacle free,
> O dear Redeemer, and to rest with Thee!
> Her Pray'rs are heard,—the pious Soul is fled!
> Oh! may we all that now lament the Dead,
> Prepare to meet our own approaching Dooms!
> Unknown the Hour, at which the Master comes.[16]

The following lines represent her method of consoling a bereaved mother:

> 'Tis thus unerring Wisdom thinks it best,
> To prove that Here, we should not fix our Rest.
> He grieves not willingly the human Race;
> Afflictions oft are Tenders of his Grace:
> In Mercy he corrects, and wou'd controul
> The darling Sin that most besets the Soul.
> Our God a holy Jealousy avows,
> And of no Creature rival Love allows:
> If aught on Earth too ardently we prize,
> The much-lov'd Blessings vanish from our Eyes.[17]

This seems the wrong time to remind a friend of what Isaac Watts calls "the hazard of loving the creatures."

But although in much of her work Mrs. Brereton appears to have the gloom of Christianity without its joy, she elsewhere displays a quite

---

[15] *Thoughts on Life, Death, Judgment, Heaven, and Hell.*
[16] *A Thought, Occasioned by being present at the Death of a Friend; May 28, 1720.*
[17] *To Mrs. Whitmore on the Death of her Son.* Dated 1731.

different attitude. An ardent Whig, she has the "commerce-liberty-virtue-religion" complex of her party. As early as 1716 we find her substituting George I for Augustus in an imitation of *The 5ᵗʰ Ode of the 4ᵗʰ Book of Horace:*

> Our publick Fears we now resign,
>   And our domestick Care renew:
> The Merchant plows the briny Flood
>   To fetch us rich Brocades;
> And Carolina, great and good,
>   To virtuous Life persuades.
>
> . . . . .
>
> To Thee [George I] our purest Wishes flow,
>   To Thee our grateful Songs are due;
> Religion, Liberty, we owe
>   To great Nassau, and greater You!
> Long, long may your our Isle adorn,
>   While all confess your gentle Sway;
> These are our Toilet Vows each Morn,
>   And these each Ev'ning crown our Tea.

After Caroline became queen she decorated her "hermitage" in Richmond Park with images of the chief saints of latitudinarianism. To these and to their royal disciple Mrs. Brereton devotes her poem *On the Bustoes in the Royal Hermitage. Written in the Year 1733.* The following roll call is historically valuable:

> Reason, that Emanation of the Mind,
> Breaks forth in Locke; diffusive, and refin'd.
> Wisdom, and Piety, their Beams unite
> To shine in Boyle with strong convictive Light;
>
> . . . . .
>
> Newton th' Allwise Creator's Works explores,
> Sublimely on the Wings of Knowledge, soars;
> Th' establish'd Order of each Orb unfolds,
> And th' omnipresent God, in all, beholds:
> If to the dark Abyss, a bright Abode
> He points; the View still terminates in God.
> The moral Duties Woolaston [*sic*] displays;
> On Nature's Laws the firm Foundation lays.
> In Clarke the Christian Purity appears,
> Reveal'd Religion he divinely clears

From Mists of Error, Vapours of blind Zeal,
Which oft her Heav'n-born Beauties would conceal.

Jane Brereton considers herself a broadly rational Christian. In one of
the letters printed with her poems she grants that Mrs. Rowe "had a fine
Genius," but objects to "the Air of Enthusiasm in her Letters." [18]
She prizes the sermons of Dr. Carter [19] as being clear, cool, and sensible,
and sends them to her daughter with the commendation:

> No fiery Flashes, here, of zealous Rage
> No fumes of Bigotry obscure the Page;
> No wild enthusiast Flights pervert the Text;
> Nor is the Sense by sceptic Doubts perplext.
> But Reason's Pow'r is seen in clearest Light,
> And Gospel Truth appears divinely bright.[20]

On the other hand, she finds William Law's *Christian Perfection* far too
"rigid." [21]

It is curious that Mrs. Brereton can sometimes be a strict hell-fire
Protestant and sometimes pay her "toilet vows" to Locke, Newton,
Clarke, and Wollaston. Part I of this study has shown that Low Church
Anglicanism and nonconformity tend gradually to collapse into latitudinarianism. In Melissa's poems, however, one finds two extremes with no
hint of a transition from one to the other. The author's life provides a
credible explanation. Jane Hughes, obviously not a lady, seems to have
been reared in an atmosphere of gloomy and vulgar evangelical piety.
Probably this influence never quite disappears from her work, though we
may suppose it to be stronger in her earlier poems. The author, however,
married somewhat above her station and came into contact with other
social levels and other ways of thinking. Her biographer reports that she
was acquainted with many ladies of quality. In 1734 and 1735 we find
her a member of an incredibly silly coterie who conducted a humorous
correspondence in verse through the pages of the *Gentleman's Magazine*.[22] Whoever Fidelia, Astrophil, Pastora, Mrs. Manage, and Captain

---

[18] That is, in Elizabeth Rowe's prose work, *Friendship in Death, in Twenty Letters from
the Dead to the Living.*

[19] This is probably Nicholas Carter, D.D., who published *Seventeen Sermons* in 1738.

[20] *Verses to her Daughter. With Dr. Carter's Sermons.*

[21] *Written in Mr. Law's Treatise on Christian Perfection; being the Gift of Mrs.
Myddelton.*

[22] See pp. 215-303 of *Poems on Several Occasions.* The volume was published by Cave.

Fido may be, they are not solemn evangelicals. If not gentlefolk they at least have genteel aspirations, and their religious views were probably broader than those which shadowed Mrs. Brereton's youth. Perhaps her ideas were changed by association with such persons; perhaps she merely found it socially desirable to cultivate their viewpoint. In either case she learned to praise calm reason and scorn "vapours of blind zeal." When her poems were brought together for publication after her death the two strata of her development were combined between the covers of the volume.[23]

Many readers will remember Mary Barber (1690?-1757) as an example of Dean Swift's kindness to individual specimens of the genus Yahoo. The volume of her verses which he too charitably recommended to the Earl of Orrery contains almost nothing on specifically religious subjects but is pervaded by an atmosphere of pious morality.[24]

In her preface she assures the reader that she wrote "chiefly to form the Minds of my Children," and in *A True Tale* she describes herself as

> A Mother, who vast Pleasure finds
> In modelling her Children's Minds;
> With whom, in exquisite Delight,
> She passes many a Winter's Night;
> Mingles in every Play, to find
> What Byass Nature gives the Mind;
> Resolving thence to take her Aim,
> To guide them to the Realms of Fame;
> And wisely make those Realms their Way,
> To Regions of eternal Day;
> Each boist'rous Passion to controul,
> And early humanize the Soul.

The story-hour material which she uses to further these aims is drawn not only from the Bible but from Addison, Pope, and Gay. To her delight her son particularly loves Gay's *Fables* and bursts into tears on learning that so great a benefactor of mankind has been so meagerly rewarded.

[23] Unexpectedly, Mrs. Brereton is the author of *The Dream. In Imitation of some Parts of Chaucer's Second and Third Book of Fame.* Fame's judgment of the aspirants is modernized, high praise being given to Milton and Newton. I may add that she feebly hankers for rural solitude in the very early *Verses on the Loss of a Friend,* written in 1709. Otherwise her work is about as unromantic as possible.

[24] This hardly applies, of course, to the rather numerous light occasional pieces.

Another pedagogic device is that of putting edifying verses into her son's mouth. Thus when a chum has neglected him during an illness he is supposed to say:

> I little thought, that honest Dick
> Would slight me so, when I was sick.

> . . . . .

> Says my Mamma, who loves to make
> Reflections, for her Children's Sake,
> You see how Mortal Friendship ends—
> My Child, secure Cœlestial Friends;
> Make Heav'n your chief, your early Care;
> You'll meet no Disappointment there.[25]

When the lad receives a Bible she makes him exclaim:

> Welcome, thou sacred, solemn Guest,
> Who com'st to guide me to the Blest.
> O Fountain of eternal Truth,
> Thou gracious Guardian of my Youth!
> True Wisdom to my Soul dispense,
> That I may learn thy Will from hence.[26]

A mother eager to lead her children along the path of religion and virtue but handicapped by being the wife of a Dublin tailor might be pardoned for expecting some favors from the great. Mrs. Barber never doubted that the world owed her a better living than her husband could provide, for it was axiomatic that

> Poets, who write to mend the Mind,
> A Royal Recompense shou'd find.[27]

So far as I know no royal bounty came her way, but she had no reason to complain of the kindness of others.

The perfect mother began her career of poetical mendicancy in a manner both Christian and adroit: she asked a favor, not for herself, but for someone else. One Mrs. Gordon, widow of an army officer, was so impoverished that the bailiffs were at her heels. Her son was going blind, and there was no money for a doctor. All her friends had deserted her—

---

[25] *Written for my Son in his Sickness, to one of his School-Fellows.*

[26] *Written for my Son, in a Bible which was presented to him.* See also *A Letter written for my Son to a young Gentleman, who was sent to be educated at the Jesuits' College in Flanders.*

[27] *A True Tale.*

all except Mrs. Barber. In 1724 the benevolent ventriloquist addressed to
Lady Carteret, wife of the Lord Lieutenant of Ireland, *The Widow Gordon's Petition*. Speaking through her friend's lips, she makes the widow
describe her sufferings and incidentally flatter Lady Carteret:

> You, Madam, are the Wretch's last Resort.
> Eternal King! if Here in vain I cry
> Where shall the Fatherless, and Widow fly?

If Lady Carteret helps her, she will stand with her two children before
the throne on the Last Day and pray the Saviour

> That she, who made the Fatherless her Care,
> The Fulness of Cœlestial Joys may share;
> That She a Crown of Glory may receive,
> Who snatch'd me from Destruction and the Grave.

The *Petition* was sent through Thomas Tickell, then secretary to the
lords justices in Ireland, with a letter requesting his good offices and
ending with a poem written in Mrs. Barber's own person:

> Eternal King, is there one Hour,
>   To make me greatly bless'd!
> When shall I have it in my Pow'r
>   To succour the Distress'd?
>
> In vain, alas! my Heart o'erflows
>   With useless Tenderness;
> Why must I feel Another's Woes,
>   And cannot make them less? [28]

Unlike the *Petition,* the affecting letter to Tickell was not anonymous.
The Carterets did something for Mrs. Gordon, but they were less impressed by her woes than by the goodness of Mrs. Barber, who, herself
a poor woman, craved only the joy of helping the unfortunate. Such
benevolence could not be hid under a bushel. She soon met Swift, and
largely through him became acquainted with a wide circle of literary
folk and persons of quality—Pope, Gay, Arbuthnot, Ambrose Philips,
Tonson, the Boyles, the Temples, the Duchess of Queensberry, and many
others.

Her technique is further displayed in *Occasion'd by reading the Memoirs*

[28] *Written in the Conclusion of a Letter to Mr. Tickell, entreating him to recommend the
Widow Gordon's Petition.*

of *Anne of Austria, written by Madam de Motteville. Inscrib'd to the Right Honourable the Countess of Hertford.* The aim of the poem is to flatter the notably pious—and generous—Countess and to display the poet's own Christian goodness. The memoirs, she says, show that God punishes the sins of the wicked;

> Yet the short-sighted Atheist dares advance,
> These wondrous Changes are the Work of Chance;
> Not so this pious, penetrating Dame [Mme. de Motteville],
> Who to the sacred Fountain trac'd the Stream:
> Like lovely *Hertford,* who her Hours employs,
> To form her Mind for never-fading Joys.

Lady Hertford is remarkable for having preserved her faith amidst the distractions of court life. In this respect Mrs. Barber is more fortunate:

> I, who am destin'd to a low Estate,
> Free from the Vanities that vex the Great;
> Blest with a Happiness to Courts unknown;
> For I, thank Heav'n, may call my Hours my own:
> O may I pass those Hours in such a Way,
> As may prepare me for the last, great Day!

But one feels that the author would not be unwilling to risk those worldly perils over which the Countess has triumphed.

Another noble, rich, pious, and charitable family were the Thanets of Hothfield. To ingratiate herself with that clan and with the prince of contemporary poets she writes *To Mr. Pope: Intreating him to write Verses to the Memory of Thomas, late Earl of Thanet:*

> Shall for the Man of Ross thy Lyre be strung,
> And sleeps illustrious Thanet yet unsung?

The poem shows that although Mrs. Barber sets a high value on benevolence she believes that true charity cannot exist without piety. Love of God is no less needful than love of neighbor. Hence, despite her sentimental strain, she is by no means a simon-pure sentimentalist. She emphasizes the fact that Thanet's goodness did not depend "on Morality alone":

> Devotion's heav'nly Flame inspir'd his Breast;
> Still in the Temple were his Vows address'd:
> Tho' he in Virtue's Paths, delighted, trod,
> Studious to please, and imitate his God;

> The hallow'd Altar, grateful, he survey'd,
> And there his lowly Adoration paid.

In this respect his character is a rebuke to those free-thinking moralists who suppose it possible to be virtuous without supernatural religion:

> Ye vain Pretenders to superior Sense,
> Ye Empty Boasters of Beneficence,
> Who in the Scorner's Seat, exulting, sit,
> And vaunt your impious Raillery for Wit,
> The Gospel-Rule defective you pretend,
> When you the social Duties recommend:
> In Thanet see them heighten'd and refin'd;
> In Thanet see the Friend of human Kind;
> Heighten'd by Faith, see ev'ry Virtue's Force;
> By Faith, their surest Sanction, noblest Source.

These ideas would be welcomed by the Thanets, but there is no reason to suppose that the author does not mean what she is saying.

It was seldom that Mrs. Barber refused a week-end invitation, but in lines *Written from Dublin, to a Lady in the Country* she regrets that she cannot

> Delighted, thro' your Pastures roam,
> Or see the Kine come lowing home;
> Whose od'rous Breaths a Joy impart,
> That sooths the Sense, and glads the Heart;
> With Pleasure view the frothing Pails,
> And silent hear the creaking Rails;
> See whistling Hinds attend their Ploughs,
> Who never hear of broken Vows;
>
> .   .   .   .
>
> Thus thro' the Day, delighted, run;
> Then raptur'd view the setting Sun;
> The rich, diffusive God behold,
> On distant Mountains pouring Gold,
> Gilding the beauteous, rising Spire,
> While Crystal Windows glow with Fire.

After this pleasant bit of realistic pastoralism she goes on to say that when the sun had set the moon and the stars would inspire her with more than sensuous delight:

> Thence to the higher Heav'ns I soar,
> And the great Architect adore;

> Behold what Worlds are hung in Air,
> And view Ten Thousand Empires there;
> Then prostrate to Jehovah fall,
> Who into Being spake them all.

This rising scale of associations from frothing milk-pails to the Newtonian Jehovah is psychologically interesting. But Mrs. Barber so buxomly adapts herself to the tastes of her genteel correspondents that we must hesitate to call her a very ardent worshipper of Nature and Nature's God. Having contracted a dislike for this woman, I have probably been too hard on her. It would be rash to condemn her religion as spurious merely because it was profitable. The eighteenth century would probably regard her as an edifying example of the rewards of virtue. She may also, as we have seen, be credited with at least a theoretical understanding of the difference between morality and religion.

Mary Jones [29] is perhaps as religious as any of the four women hitherto considered, but she does not often deal with serious subjects. Her verses were written chiefly to amuse a little circle of feminine friends, and one imagines that they succeeded in doing so. She has a quick, direct, humorous, Fanny Burneyish sort of mind which makes even her confidential chatter pleasant enough.

The Story of Jacob and Rachel attempted, a narrative poem rather than a paraphrase, is out of her line: she tries to be impressive, and fails. Occasionally, however, a note of apparently genuine religious feeling is struck in poems arising from her personal relationships. In *Birth-Day* she wishes a friend

> Health and joy, long life and peace.
> Pray we next, for Poets may
> Sure, as well as Prose-Folks, pray—
> And as this Day rolls around,
> May you still be perfect found:
> Still, in Virtue's noble race,
> Pressing for the foremost place;
> Scorning all that's low, or lewd,
> Daring to be great and good:

[29] Not in *D.N.B.* She lived at Oxford, where her *Miscellanies in Prose and Verse* were published in 1750, but had friends at court as well as in academic circles. Since her verse impresses one as the work of a woman who has reached or is approaching middle age, I have conjecturally placed her *floruit* toward the close of the 1720-1740 period.

> Till your race of life is done,
> And the glorious meed your own;
> Such as Angels now receive,
> Such as Heav'n alone can give.

On the death of Miss Clayton, with whom she had often giggled in verse, she expresses the pious hope:

> Yet if thy friendship lives beyond the dust,
> Where all things else in peace and silence lie,
> I'll seek thee there, among the Good and Just,
> 'Mong those who living wisely—learnt to die.
>
> .   .   .   .
>
> A little while, and lo! I lay me down,
> To land in silence on that peaceful shore,
> Where never billows beat, or tyrants frown,
> Where we shall meet again, to part no more.[30]

Miss Jones's few substantial poems reflect the influence of Pope's *Moral Essays*. They are not, however, mere imitations: within limits imposed by her environment she has herself observed the characters of men and women. That she is interested in the contemporary psychology of sensation and association may be inferred from *In Memory of the Rt. Hon. Lord Aubrey Beauclerk, who was slain at Carthagena*:

> The active mind, ascending by degrees,
> Its various ties, relations, duties sees:
> Examines parts, thence rising to the whole,
> Sees the connexion, chain, and spring of soul;
> Th' eternal source! from whose pervading ray
> We caught the flame, and kindled into day.
> Hence the collected truths coercive rise,
> Oblige as nat'ral, or as moral ties.
> Son, brother, country, friend, demand our care;
> The common bounty all partake, must share.
> Hence virtue in its source, and in its end,
> To God as relative, to Man as friend.

To anyone who objected that God plays no very important part in this ethical system, the Christian disciple of Locke [31] would respond that the

---

[30] *Verses to the Memory of Miss Clayton*. Observe the elegiac stanza. James Hammond's popular *Love Elegies*, published in 1743, encouraged the use of this old pattern for tender and mournful themes.

[31] This poem is dated 1743—six years earlier than Hartley's *Observations on Man*.

Alpha and Omega of the associative process is a Supreme Being whose gospel is one of activity and service.

Lord Beauclerk can die for his country, but Mary Jones is a mere woman. Although usually cheerful and often gay, she is sometimes bored and restless. She has a better mind than many of the dons who come to tea, but what is there for her to do with it? Also, despite her praise of female friendship, some of the letters printed with her poems do not suggest much enthusiasm for spinsterhood. "In vain do we Female Philosophers preach up the Necessity and Usefulness of Marriage, when those who ought to have been our Help-mates are under a Vow of Celibacy. So that were we never so desirous of changing this Solitary State of Life (to which we Virgins of Oxford are more peculiarly call'd) 'tis to no purpose to think of it, unless the present Parliament in their great Wisdom (as we hear they intend it) shall graciously take our Cases into Consideration, and allow our Fellows of Colleges to marry." Of course she will not permit herself to be serious: "As to the Passion of Love, 'tis a pretty Amusement, I grant you, for the Heart; but when once it gets up into the Head, 'tis bitter bad.... 'Tis well, if among our Sex it goes off in Rhyming; for if once we can settle ourselves to write about it, I reckon the Danger is over."

But this danger, and the danger of a less definable restriction of mind and spirit, are not to be escaped so easily. There are times when the Oxford Virgin can share the mood of Prior's *Alma:*

> O Charlot! when alone we sit,
> Laughing at all our own (no) wit,
> You wisely with your Cat at play,
> I reading Swift, and spilling tea;
> How would it please my ravish'd ear,
> To hear you, from your easy chair,
> With look serene, and brow uncurl'd
> Cry out, "A—— for all the world!"
> But you, a slave to too much breeding,
> And I, a fool, with too much reading,
> Follow the hive, as bees their drone,
> Without one purpose of our own:
> Till tir'd with blund'ring and mistaking,
> We die sad fools of others' making.[32]

[32] *Epistle, from Fern-Hill.*

The true remedy, however, is not defiance of the hive but submission to its dictates. In the Popean epistle *Of Desire* she sketches various "characters" of men and women whose desires are unworthy or inordinate, and concludes that the really happy man "has but few wishes, and enjoys them all."

Pain, according to the moral essay *Of Patience,* depends "not upon outward accidents, but upon different degrees of sensibility." For one who wishes to contract his desires, then, sensibility is a curse: "Touch but a Genius, and he smarts all o'er." The "downright Ass," on the contrary, is exempt from pain:

> O envy'd creature! who nor feels nor fears,
> Who all things suffers, all things bravely bears.
> Whom neither Hope, or Fear, or Shame can move,
> Nor kindling mounts to Rage, or melts to Love.
> His pleasures always equal, flowing, full,
> For ever patient and for ever dull.[33]

But Miss Jones scorns the ass, and she is not truly satisfied with her own prescription for happiness. She knows, too, that it is futile to reason about these matters. If suffering depends on sensibility, sensibility in turn depends on the physical constitution of the individual:

> Did ever axioms sooth the nervous ill?
> Or syllogisms pay the doctor's bill?
> Too, much, I fear, of reason's aid we boast,
> Where most 'tis wanted, there it fails us most.
> 'Tis not the soldier's reason makes him bear
> Th' inclement season, and the toilsome war;
> 'Tis not the nice deduction of the squire,
> That keeps him well and warm without a fire:
> The mind does little; 'tis the body here,
> That is, in strictness, the philosopher.

In the long run, then, suffering and irrational beings must fall back upon faith. The "Contents" of *Patience* reads in part: "This life a state of probation; and therefore requires a considerable mixture of affliction, or natural evil, to try and ascertain our virtue.... Afflictions therefore permitted for our real good; and the right use of them to teach us resignation to That Being, who will compensate our sufferings here with an eternity of happiness hereafter."

[33] Observe the parody of the famous passage in Denham's *Cooper's Hill.*

And so this witty, bored, and wistful spinster will skate as lightly as possible over life's surface. In moments when the ice cracks she will suppress desire and cultivate patience, clinging to a sincere but not very ardent belief in Providence and the life of the world to come.

The first man to be considered in this chapter is strangely inconsistent in his religious views. Alexander Nicol,[34] the son of "a poor mechanic," was left fatherless at the age of six. He had only a few months of schooling, and for a time led the life of a packman.[35] He gradually educated himself, however, and became a teacher of English at Abernyte in Perthshire.

Part I of *Poems on Several Subjects* consists of secular and chiefly "Comical" pieces, many of them in Scots dialect—tales, familiar epistles, occasionals, and song-lyrics. Though in itself this work is trivial, it is not uninteresting as a minor link in the chain connecting Allan Ramsay —to whom he addresses a eulogistic epistle—and Robert Burns.

The atmosphere of the second part of the volume is totally different. If Part I was written by Sandy, Part II was written by Alexander, for it consists entirely of religious poems in what the author supposes to be standard English. The warm earthy humanity of the "comical" verses gives place to a strain of gloomy, canting doggerel:

> I am corrupt in every part;
> My words, my thoughts and ways;
> My pow'rs, performances, and heart,
> Full of corruption lyes.
>
> Is not my nature and my will
> All enmity within?
> I'm forward unto evil still;
> My heart's a sink of sin.

A special section of Part II is entitled "A Bundle of Flowers for Children: Being Verses on the most remarkable Men and Women mentioned in the Bible." From this spiritual bouquet may be culled the verses on Absalom:

[34] *D.N.B.* says "fl. 1739-1766." But *Poems on Several Subjects, Both Comical and Serious,* 1766, merely combines and reprints two volumes both of which were issued separately in 1739: *Nature without Art: or Nature's Progress in Poetry, being a Collection of Miscellaneous Poems,* and *Nature's Progress in Poetry, being a Collection of Serious Poems.* Thus all of his verse was in print before 1740.

[35] *An Account of the Author,* a biographical epistle in verse addressed to the Countess of Strathmore in 1727.

> Absalom for beauty did excel,
> Yet he against his father did rebel,
> For which he was in battle overthrown,
> And doubtless unto hell the wretch is gone.
> So beauty is no sign of goodness, sure;
> Fair Helen was but an adult'rous whore.

More ambitious is *The Child's Companion; In A Natural Dialogue Betwixt a Child and One of Riper Years,* designed to give instruction on free grace and predestination. The child grants that God is good to the elect, but what about the others?

> But still something appears to me
> That's cruel and unkind,
> Concerning these poor miscreants
> That he hath left behind:
> Can love and goodness pleasure take
> Those creatures to torment,
> For ever to eternity,
> And not at all relent?

The "Companion" explains that

> Though God is good and merciful, yet he
> Is also just, and therefore cannot be
> Said to be cruel, though he never had
> Sav'd one of all the human race he made.

Since we all deserve damnation, it is very indulgent of God to save *any* of us. "But why," pleads the child,

> ... might not Almighty God,
> By his infinite pow'r
> Establish man, when he was made,
> From sin and death secure?

The answer is conclusive:

> Because 'twas not according to his will;
> For what he pleases that he does fulfil:
> Besides, his glorious attributes had not
> Been so display'd, nor he such praise had got.

Puzzled, we return to Part I, where on closer scrutiny we find several poems which imply a conception of religion rather different from that expressed in Part II. One is *A Poem, showing the Original, Antiquity, Beauty, and Glory of Masonry.* Nicol asserts that God was the first mason, for He surely deserves "the title of a Master Builder's name." Other members of what might be called the Old Testament Lodge are Noah, who built an altar after the ark settled on Ararat, and Moses, who "hew'd and squar'd two tables fair of stone."

The conflict between congregation and patron in parochial government and the worldly ambitions of ministers are satirized in *The honest Country-man's Meditation, as he was humming it over alone in Words at Resting-time.* Quite without the Calvinistic rigor of Part II is *The Author's Wish,* one of the many poems inspired by Pomfret's *Choice.* Nicol desires

> A healthy body, and a conscience clear;
>
> .   .   .   .
>
> My choice of books, and nought but read to do.
> In winter-time a piece fat beef to tottle;
> And now and then with friends a hearty bottle.
> A cleanly house; a warm clear canty fire;
> Clean linens, and my garments all entire.
> A warm soft bed; a virtuous spouse, and kind;
> Some pocket-money; these can please my mind.
> When death approaches, not to dwine, but die;
> And, after death, bless'd with felicitie.
> These are my wishes; and I crave no more:
> If Heaven grant them, Goodness I'll adore.

This little bargain with God should not be taken too seriously, but it certainly lacks the note of free-grace theology.

That note is even more strikingly absent from *An Account of the Author,* which he addressed to the Countess of Strathmore in 1727. It includes the following *confessio fidei:*

> As for opinions, I confess
> I never upon them laid stress;
> Sometimes a Whig, sometimes a Tory,
> But seldom steadfast in one story.
> The reason is, I'm not yet fix'd,
> So my religion is but mix'd;

> Yet, most of all, I do incline
> The old Episcopalian line;
>
> .   .   .   .
>
> Th' essential parts of my opinion,
> Is not in any sect's dominion;
> Nor will I e'er be tied to think,
> That in one spring I ought to drink.
> In Christendom we all affect
> The Christian name, in some respect;
> Yet, to our shame, and our derision,
> We're full of schisms and division.

After mentioning several sects he continues:

> To follow which I cannot tell,
> Therefore I bid them all farewell;
> Because I know, that faith and love
> The sphere is wherein I should move;
> For sure, without true charity
> None can enjoy felicity.
> But charity, now at this day,
> She is oblig'd to fly away;
> Instead of which, envy and hate,
> Contempt, resentment, and debate,
> Is most in each society.
> This makes me all these sects deny.
> 'Tis not in word, as I do read,
> But Christians must be so in deed;
> So, Madam, this is all my creed.

From the "Serious Poems" of Part II we should take Nicol to be a strict Presbyterian. Here, however, he says that he is more of an Episcopalian than anything else, but that on the whole he wishes to be considered a non-sectarian lover of mankind. Not enough of Nicol's poems can be dated to enable us to trace his mental history. We may guess, however, that he moved from Calvinism to a rather extreme latitudinarianism. It is conceivable that he moved in the opposite direction, but considering his personal background and the trend of the age the former supposition is much more probable. In that case the career of this poetical packman would resemble that of John Bancks the poetical weaver.[36] But it may also be significant that the packman become a schoolteacher. In Scotland education and religion were so closely intertwined that the "Seri-

[36] *Vide supra*, p. 276.

ous Poems," many of which are intended for children, may have been motivated partly by anxiety to fulfil the obligations of a pedagogue. The real man, we feel, is not Alexander, but Sandy, a humorous and convivial Scot whose religion "is but mix'd."

The intrinsically worthless poems of the Reverend Edward Cobden, D.D. (1684-1764),[37] Archdeacon of London, deserve attention as the work of a representative Anglican cleric. Of a total of ninety-six pieces in *Poems on Several Occasions* (1748), only about fifteen have any bearing on religion, and vapid occasional prattle composes over half the volume. Except for a nasty hudibrastic epistle on the jakes the secular poems are inoffensive, but their tone is anything but clerical. He is forever paying gallant compliments to the ladies. There are no pre-romantic symptoms other than an outburst in *On the intended Marriage of the Prince of Orange with the Princess Royal. An Imitation of Horace's Ode on Pindar,* where the English poet's sublimity is substituted for the Greek's:

> Milton is like a flood, whose tide,
> Swell'd with tempestuous deluge, roars,
> Which from some lofty mountain's side
> Resistless foams, and knows no shores.

Cobden's own poetry, however, is never in spate.

The Archdeacon reserves a separate compartment of his mind for a reasonable and conventional piety. Needless to say, he is no enthusiast. In *On the Bishop of London's Book of Devotion* he writes:

> Those, who the Force of true Religion feel,
> With Understanding temper still their Zeal.
> When Faith and Reason friendly Forces join,
> They storm with Violence the Throne divine.
> With Fragrance sweet the warm Oblations rise,
> And in their Saviour's Censer, pierce the Skies.

Cobden's zeal is so plentifully tempered with judgment that from his poems alone one can hardly tell whether he is high or low. When Lady

---

[37] B.A. Trinity, Oxford; M.A. Kings, Cambridge; B.D. and (1723) D.D., Oxford. Chaplain to Bishop Gibson, through whose lasting favor he received not only a plurality of livings but prebends at Lincoln and later at St. Paul's Cathedral. He held a royal chaplaincy, became Archdeacon of London in 1742, and was elected president of Sion College in 1751. He published a number of sermons. I have not seen *An Essay Tending to Promote Religion* (1755), which is partly in prose and partly in verse.

Betty Spelman shows him a lock of Charles the First's hair, he expresses indignation at the regicides and exclaims:

> O may these Relicks of the Royal Hair,
> By you preserv'd with such peculiar Care,
> Still in your noble Family descend
> From Hand to Hand, till all Succession end!
> Till they're demanded at the last great Day,
> And ev'ry Hair be chang'd into a Ray.[38]

His loyalty to the house of Hanover, on the other hand, is immaculate.[39] *An Ode on the Year 1715* describes the "Providential tokens" and "wonders" attending the accession of "illustrious Brunswick": the defeat of the Jacobites; a solar eclipse, at which "Toland begins to fear a God"; a "light-night"; meteors; unusual cold and snow. These are likened to the tokens vouchsafed the Israelites as they left Egypt under the leadership of Moses, who is thus the prototype of George I. The author's career spanned not only the first but also the second Jacobite uprising: in 1745 he wrote *A Religious Ode, occasioned by the present Rebellion*. George II is lauded as the champion of Protestantism, and the notes accuse the Papists of cruelty, obscurantism, and superstition.

A versifying cleric should write a few hymns, and these Cobden accordingly produces in a dutiful but unexciting manner: *On the Creation, Before the Sacrament, On Easter Day*. These are "divine odes" of the Addisonian type rather than congregational hymns. He shows more feeling in *Upon the Opening of his Chapel, on Nov. 24, 1720:*

> Seraphic Love, and purest Zeal,
>   This happy pious Season [40] claims,
> Submissive while our bodies kneel,
>   Our Souls should mount in holy Flames."

The chapel is compared to a redeemed Eden:

> See, here we taste the Tree of Life,
> Which Paradise scarce saw, and lost.

---

[38] *To the Honourable Lady Spelman, upon Her Showing a Lock of King Charles the First's Hair*. In the closing couplet the reminiscence of *The Rape of the Lock* is probably unintentional.

[39] The seeming inconsistency is explained by the fact that Cobden was a satellite of Bishop Gibson, who held moderately "high" views but was nevertheless Walpole's chief ecclesiastical ally.

[40] The Advent season, very seldom mentioned in the Anglican poetry of the century.

> We taste it in the sacred Word,
> In Symbols of almighty Love,
> Forbidden by no flaming Sword
> What Bliss or Knowledge may improve.

Recovery from smallpox, too, can inspire in him a warm though ungainly gratitude:

> When all *within*, inflam'd with Pains,
> Was melted like the flowing Stream;
> And all *without*, deform'd with Stains,
> Was curdled, like the turning Cream:

> I in that gloomy Hour my Trust
> In his almighty Arm repos'd,
> That can restore the moulder'd Dust,
> Which Urns for Ages have enclos'd.[41]

Except on such unusual occasions, however, Cobden's religion is a matter of common-sense ethics. Heaven is the place for spiritual joys; the earth is the place for right conduct and its reward in an easy conscience. *Moral Reflections* ends with the stanzas:

> To taste of Blessings yet complete
> No Mortal is by Heav'n allow'd:
> The sweetest Pleasure here's a Cheat,
> The brightest Beauty but a Cloud.

> Reflections, which from Virtue flow,
> From gen'rous Deeds and pious Love,
> Are the best Shadows here below
> Of solid Bliss in Realms above.

One feels the implication that on this side of the grave "love your neighbor" is more important than "love God."

These and similar "sacred" performances, be it remembered, form only a small part of a volume which might otherwise have been written by any secular fribble of the period. To express surprise at this fact would betray a want of historical sense. Archdeacon Cobden is a normal specimen of eighteenth-century Anglicanism, and only a disreputable enthusiast would cavil at his lack of ardor. I know of no reason to charge him with insincerity or with slackness in the performance of his duties. Nevertheless, *Poems on Several Occasions* is not the work of a spiritually

[41] *After a Recovery from the Small Pox.*

gifted man. The most Christian thing about it is that it was printed for the benefit of his curate's widow.

In this procession of nonentities the modest figure of the Reverend Christopher Pitt ·(1699-1748)[42] assumes almost majestic proportions. His translations of the *Aeneid* and of Vida's *De Arte Poetica* were highly esteemed. Even in his own day, however, no one regarded his original poems as important. They are few in number, negligible in matter, and frigidly competent in style. Completely unromantic, he imitates Spenser only in a silly piece of nastiness about the chamber pot.

Generally, however, he is solid and sober; and he shows a few signs of the Christianity which he undoubtedly possessed. His poems include nine Scripture-paraphrases—one of them, a version of *Psalm CXXXIX,* in Miltonic blank verse. He also translates a very fervent Greek ode on *Christ's Passion,* but the fervor must be credited to the original author, "Mr. Masters, formerly of New College." *On the Art of Preaching* is a studied imitation of Horace's *Art of Poetry.* The preacher, like the poet, should maintain consistency of tone, should adapt his sermon to the occasion, and so on:

> Still to your hearers all your sermons sort;
> Who'd preach against corruption at the court?
> Against church-power at Visitations bawl,
> Or talk about damnation at Whitehall?

In these poems Pitt is still the translator and imitator. His strictly original work contains almost nothing for us. The fact that the Prince of Wales' bride is a descendant of Frederick, Elector of Saxony, who championed Luther, provides a chance to inject a bit of loyal Protestantism into *On the Marriage of Frederick Prince of Wales, and Princess Augusta of Saxe-Gotha.*[43]

A Poem on the Death of the Late Earl Stanhope illustrates a difficulty felt by eighteenth-century Christians who were anxious to accept the new

[42] The son of a reputable physician of Blandford. Educated at Winchester and New College, he received his M.A. in 1724. In 1722 he became Rector of Pimperne, Dorsetshire, and passed the remainder of his days in that rural parish. His *Poems and Translations* appeared in 1727, but a man born in 1699 can hardly have written much poetry during the 1700-1720 period.

[43] Pitt was a "Patriot." His *Epistle to Edward Young* expresses admiration not only for Young but for Bubb Dodington.

astronomy without abandoning the traditional imagery of their faith. Leaving the earth, Stanhope's soul speeds through the skies and

> Sees where the planetary worlds advance,
> Orb above orb, and lead the starry dance.
> Nor rests she there, but, with a bolder flight,
> Explores the undiscover'd realms of light,
> Where the fix'd orbs to deck the spangled pole,
> In state around their gaudy axles roll.
> Thence his aspiring course in triumph steers,
> Beyond the golden circles of the spheres;
> Into the Heaven of Heavens, the seat divine,
> Where Nature never drew her mighty line.
> A region that excludes all time and place,
> And shuts creation from th' unbounded space.

Thus in order to reach the Christian heaven the soul must go beyond the limits of Newtonian nature.

According to Dr. Johnson, an excellent judge of such matters, Pitt became a worthy priest—"reverenced for his virtue, and beloved for the softness of his temper and the easiness of his manners." He seems to have been a quiet, shyly benevolent man. But the spiritual side of his character is not reflected in his poetry. Soon after he took orders, indeed, his efforts to write original verse of any sort came to an end.

George Jeffreys (1678-1755) [44] is a respectably mediocre exemplar of the genteel classical tradition which was his birthright. In translations, epistles, compliments, "songs," and epigrams he is neither offensively pompous nor a mere fribble. Though worldly, he is never offensive. For a man of his type, he seems rather well disposed toward religion. In the

[44] His father was a gentleman of Northamptonshire; his mother, a sister of James Brydges, Lord Chandos. He had a rather distinguished academic career at Cambridge, but vacated his Trinity fellowship rather than take orders. He was admitted to the bar but never practised, was for three years secretary to the Bishop of Derry, and had a post in the customs house. Most of his life, however, was spent as a retainer of the Dukes of Chandos. His tragedies, *Edwin* (1724) and *Merope* (1731), and his translation of Vida's *Chess* are remembered. Since his earliest verses were written before the death of William III he should perhaps have been placed in Part I. But he published nothing before 1724, and his dramas and all his poems of any importance for us are later than 1720. Hence although his "age-group" and his "floruit" do not agree, he may nevertheless be called a poet of the 1720-1740 period.

preface of his *Miscellanies in Verse and Prose* (1754) he praises Sir John Davies' "Poem on the Immortality of the Soul" [45] and Isaac Hawkins Browne's *De Animi Immortalitate*.[46]

A few of his epigrams deal with sacred themes. *On the Resurrection* concludes:

> The Fabric Samson shook, and fell beneath;
> Here shakes the World at its Creator's Death:
> Convulsions Earth, for his Reception, rend,
> And Angels at his empty Tomb attend:
> Thus to each Truth is Testimony giv'n;
> Earth owns his Death; his Resurrection, Heav'n.

His contemporaries would not have felt, as we do, that this is a little too crisply ingenious for the subject.

Though he admires Pope, Jeffreys can criticize his philosophy:

> The fam'd Essays on Man in this agree,
> That so things are, and therefore so should be:
> The proof inverted would be stronger far;
> So they should be, and therefore so they are [47]

These lines seem to imply a Christian viewpoint.

With this writer, even epitaphs are epigrams. One written on a deceased clergyman begins, "Still, like his Saviour, known by breaking bread." No sacramental allusion is intended, however, for the next line runs, "The Rich he entertain'd, the Needy fed." *The Death of Monimia* inspires a lyrical rather than a witty response. Our tears cannot restore her to us,

> Yet, oh! could we dare
> To learn of the Fair,
> A Saint in devotion, a Martyr in pain;
> We might see her once more
> As bright as before,
> An Angel in glory, and know her again.

Here a verse-pattern commonly found in humorous songs invades a more elevated sphere.

That Jeffreys is capable of a more or less sentimental exploitation of religious feeling is seen in his narrative poem, *Father Francis and Sister*

---

[45] This of course is *Nosce Teipsum*.
[46] *Vide infra*, p. 474.   [47] *On the Essays on Man*.

Constance.[48] Constantia loves Theodosius, but her father favors a wealthier suitor. Theodosius goes away in despair and writes that he is about to kill himself. Constantia then vows to marry nobody, becomes very melancholy, finds solace in religion, and enters a convent as a novice. To her confessor, Father Francis, she tells her sad story. Alas, Father Francis is none other than Theodosius! He does not at once reveal his identity, but discloses the truth by a letter after Constantia has taken the veil. Unable to see each other, the lovers correspond pathetically for ten years. When at last he succumbs to the plague she dies on the same day and joins him in the tomb. All this is related very stagily, with pseudo-pious and pseudo-passionate speeches in the manner of Pope's *Eloisa.*

The Triumph of Truth. An Oratorio was written about 1750. Jeffreys declares that it was never intended for public performance or even for a musical setting. The work might be described as the libretto of a closet-opera rather than of an oratorio, for the dramatic element is fairly elaborate. It is based upon the familiar story of Zerubbabel and his praise of truth as mightiest of all things in the *First Book of Esdras.* In Jeffreys' hands, the deeply religious Jew who awakens the better nature of Darius becomes an eighteenth-century latitudinarian, a precursor of Lessing's Nathan. Mingled with his broad commonplaces about toleration and virtue is a bit of Platonism:

> ...Woman sure is strong;
> But Truth is stronger. The Divine Ideas,
> Eternal as the Mind in which they dwell,
> Are Truth; the standard, counter-part, and source,
> Of all created Things.[49]

Judging from the spurious religiosity of *Father Francis and Sister Constance* and the flabby breadth of *The Triumph of Truth,* Jeffreys might have been a sentimentalist had he belonged to a softer generation. Both poems, it may be noted, come late in his career. But as a gentleman born in 1678 he is restrained by cooler, harder trends of thought. The Christianity of which he approves means little to him, but he has not therefore become a disciple of the cult of feeling. He may be summed up in a

[48] Published in 1736 with his translation of Vida's *Chess.* It is, as Jeffreys states, "enlarg'd" from Addison's story in *Spectator* No. 164. He also asserts in his preface that Pope read the poem and suggested alterations.

[49] Here one is reminded not only of *Nathan der Weise* but of Ahasuerus, the Platonic Wandering Jew, enlightening the Sultan in Shelley's *Hellas.*

SENTIMENTAL

pensée drawn from his *Miscellaneous Thoughts, in Prose:* "A man must beware of straining piety to a pitch he cannot maintain throughout: 'tis like beginning a tune too high: he must take it a note or two lower, or give disgust before he comes to the end of it, by downright squeaking." George Jeffreys never cracks on the top note, for he never tries to reach it.

"Correctly cold, and regularly low" are the poems of William Hay (1695-1755).[50] None of them displays any spiritual feeling. That he took some interest in religion, however, is suggested by the fact that he translated Isaac Hawkins Browne's popular *De Animi Immortalitate.*[51]

Although Hay's biographer credits him with being "perhaps the first to ornament cornfields with walks and plantations,"[52] his topographical poem *Mount Caburn* is free from naturalistic or sentimental hankerings. The prospect includes two ruined abbeys which suggest severe reflections on monasticism:

> In this recess the hooded friar lay,
> Dissolved in ease, and slumb'ring life away:
> Luxurious far'd, his mattins duly said,
> Sang o'er the dead, and on the living prey'd:
> The supple layman treated as he pleas'd,
> Tortur'd with penance, or with pardon eas'd;
> To poverty the gates of Heav'n were barr'd,
> But for the rich to enter was not hard;
> Brokers in sin did their assistance lend;
> Who paid the monks could never God offend.
>
> .   .   .   .
>
> Unlearn'd, and skill'd in pious frauds alone,
> They gave us Heav'n to make the earth their own.

These abuses have given place to the blessings of latitudinarianism. In a prose essay entitled *Religio Philosophi*,[53] Hays shows a hearty distaste for ecclesiastical authority and for tradition, priests, ceremonies, and "mysteries." The Bible contains all of Christianity. Christ taught only a

---

[50] A country gentleman of Sussex who gave good service as a magistrate. Although deformed he represented Seaford in Parliament from 1734 until his death. He was a Whig and a supporter of Walpole, under whose ministry he was a commissioner for victualling the navy and later keeper of records in the Tower of London. He wrote *Remarks on Laws relating to the Poor* (1751) and twice vainly introduced a poor-relief bill in the House of Commons.

[51] *Vide infra*, p. 474.   [52] *The Works of William Hay, Esq.*, I, viii.
[53] First published in 1753.

few simple principles of conduct, and beyond these we should not go in formulating a creed. Furthermore, Christ's "commission extends only to our Planet, and to the present race of mankind." He is the saviour of all *men* but not of all the "rational creatures" who may inhabit other planets. These ideas are not poetically inspiring to Hay, for he never expresses them in verse.

The Spleen, that witty and at the same time rather imaginative poem, establishes Matthew Green (1696-1737) as the ablest writer to appear in this chapter. His other poems are few and of small intrinsic value, but some of them contribute to an understanding of his spiritual history.

Green came of a dissenting family much respected among the saints for its strictness. As he grew up he reacted against the rigidity of his early environment, but did not abandon Christianity entirely. If we may accept evidence provided by *The Seeker,* he sampled various doctrinal viewpoints:

> When I first came to London, I rambled about
> From sermon to sermon, took a slice and went out.

His adherence was solicited by "a lech'rous old friar," a formal non-con," and "a jolly church parson." Of these a Quaker finally told him that

> Dominion and wealth are the aim of all three,
> Though about ways and means they may all disagree;
> Then prithee be wise, go the quakers' by-way,
> 'Tis plain, without turnpikes, so nothing to pay.

Although Green never became a Quaker, there was a time when he had much admiration for that sect. *On Barclay's Apology for the Quakers* is sympathetic:

> These sheets primeval doctrines yield.
> Where revelation is reveal'd;
> Soul-phlegm from literal feeding bred,
> Systems lethargic to the head
> They purge, and yield a diet thin,
> That turns to gospel-chyle within.
> Truth sublimate may here be seen
> Extracted from the parts terrene.

If these physiological images have a tinge of burlesque, one cannot doubt the earnestness of the lines:

Place, me, O Heav'n, in some retreat;
There let the serious death-watch beat,
There let me self in silence shun,
To feel thy will, which should be done.
Then comes the spirit to our hut,
When fast the senses' doors are shut;
For so divine and pure a guest
The emptiest rooms are furnish'd best.
O Contemplation! air serene!
From damps of sense, and fogs of spleen!
Pure mount of thought! thrice holy ground,
Where grace, when waited for, is found.
Here 'tis the soul feels sudden youth,
And meets, exulting, virgin Truth;
Here, like a breeze of gentlest kind,
Impulses rustle through the mind;
Here shines that light with glowing face,
The fuse divine, that kindles grace;
Which, if we trim our lamps, will last,
'Till darkness be by dying past.

These lines are hardly inspired; but we had better be grateful for them, for they give out as pure a strain of religious lyricism as can be heard during the 1720-1740 period. After reading them one cannot say that Green was attracted merely by the negative side of Quakerism. Plainly, at one stage in his career he could feel something of the poetry of religion.

The passage just quoted suggests how readily, in the absence of any firm belief in the divine reality of the Inner Light, "retreat" and "contemplation" might lose all Christian significance and collapse into a loose pre-romantic reverie where "impulses rustle through the mind." Green's development, however, is not from semi-Quakerism to sentimentalism. On the contrary, other tendencies in the *Zeitgeist* draw him toward a witty, tough-minded, and rather cynical worldliness. In his chief poem this former friend of Quakers can write:

I never am at meeting seen,
Meeting, that region of the Spleen;
The broken heart, the busy friend,
The inward call, on Spleen depend.

Laughter is of course a sovereign remedy for the spleen, and among objects of laughter are

A strict dissenter saying grace,
A lect'rer preaching for a place,
Folks, things prophetic to dispense,
Making the past the future tense,
The popish dubbing of a priest.

He laughs also at the Society for the Propagation of the Gospel in Foreign Parts, preferring to

... keep my pence
From spoiling Indian innocence.

Green stands firmly in the tradition of Burton when he associates melancholy with superstition and enthusiasm:

Th' enthusiast's hope, and raptures wild,
Have never yet my reason foil'd.
His springy soul dilates like air,
When free from weight of ambient care,
And, hush'd in meditation deep,
Slides into dreams, as when asleep;

. . . .

Then, fond of new discoveries grown,
Proves a Columbus of her own,
Disdains the narrow bounds of place,
And through the wilds of endless space,
Borne up on metaphysic wings,
Chases light forms and shadowy things,
And in the vague excursion caught,
Brings home some rare exotic thought.
The melancholy man such dreams,
As brightest evidence, esteems;
Fain would he see some distant scene
Suggested by his restless Spleen,
And Fancy's telescope applies
With tinctur'd glass to cheat his eyes.

To all such absurdities Green applies the test of "plain common-sense." Freed from the "legendary fears" of his childhood, he refuses to be hoodwinked into superstition by any form of ecclesiastical authority. If he has not quite become a deist, he has at least reached the furthest boundary of a cool and negative latitudinarianism. The little flame of poetic belief which burned for a moment in the lines on Barclay's *Apology* has subsided. Perhaps it has not utterly disappeared. Even now he can be moved by the mystery of divinity:

> To thee, Creator uncreate,
> O Entium Ens! divinely great!—
> Hold, Muse, nor melting pinions try,
> Nor near the blaze of glory fly,
> Nor straining break thy feeble bow,
> Unfeather'd arrows far to throw:
> Thro' fields unknown nor madly stray,
> Where no ideas mark the way.
> With tender eyes and colours faint,
> And trembling hands forbear to paint.
> Who features veil'd by light can hit?
> Where can, what has no outline sit?

But the inscrutability of God is made an excuse for setting Him aside:

> My soul, the vain attempt forego,
> Thyself, the fitter subject, know.
> He wisely shuns the bold extreme,
> Who soon lays by th' unequal theme,
> Nor runs, with wisdom's Syrens caught,
> On quicksands swall'wing shipwreck'd thought;
> But, conscious of his distance, gives
> Mute praise, and humble negatives.

Thus, mutely and negatively praising a God "who can't be cruel or unjust," Green steers the ship of his mind:

> At helm I make my reason sit,
> My crew of passions all submit.
>
> .   .   .   .
>
> Though pleas'd to see the dolphins play,
> I mind my compass and my way,
> With store sufficient for relief,
> And wisely still prepar'd to reef,
> Nor wanting the dispersive bowl
> Of cloudy weather in the soul,
> I make, (may Heav'n propitious send
> Such wind and weather to the end)
> Neither becalm'd, nor over-blown,
> Life's voyage to the world unknown.

The remaining poets of this group provide only one poem apiece. The Reverend John Dart (d. 1730)[54] was a clerical antiquarian with a great enthusiasm for Chaucer. Besides contributing a life of that poet to the Urry edition of 1721, he wrote *A Poem on Chaucer and his Writings* and modernized the apocryphal *Complaint of the Black Knight*. His only production of concern to us, however, is *Westminster Abbey*.[55] This might pedantically be described as an "interior loco-descriptive poem," for it mingles description, history, and reflection in a way which reminds one of the topographical pieces of the period. The goddess Contemplation, by this time usually the genius of rural shades, is brought into the Abbey and invoked more or less Miltonically:

> Sweet Contemplation, Daughter of the Skies,
> Still lifting to thy native Realms thine Eyes,
> Hither immortal Goddess! heavenly bright!
> With Look as fix'd as Silver Cynthia's Light,
> And Pace as sober, entring in a Cloud;
> So thy fair Face with decent Covering shrow'd;
> Thy Neck and Breast in Linnen pure as Snow
> Confine, and let th' unsully'd *Stola* flow;
> O'er all be Folds of thickest Sable laid,
> And let the Cypress cast a decent Shade.
> While I to thy much favour'd Haunts retire,
> The long resounding Isle, and hallow'd Choir;
> Attend, and lead, where pensive I essay
> To press thy Footings thro' the cloyster'd Way.

Despite this literary affectation, religious feelings are aroused in Dart by the hallowed beauty of the edifice and the solemn tones of the music, for he continues:

> Seiz'd with religious Awe, here let me roam,
> View the low Chapel and the high rear'd Dome;
> Here let me every solemn Beauty trace,
> And make my Mind the Picture of the Place.
> With lifted Eye the figur'd Roof behold,
> Rich with Intaglio, and bestreak'd with Gold:

---

[54] Abandoned law for the priesthood and in 1728 became perpetual curate of Yately in Hampshire. His works, including a translation of Tibullus, appeared between 1718 and 1726.

[55] Prefixed to his prose work in two imposing folio volumes, *Westmonasterium. Or The History and Antiquities of the Abbey Church of St. Peters Westminster*, 1726.

> While the loud Choir alternate Chant around,
> While the loud pealing Organ's deeper Sound
> With something more than mortal strikes the Ear,
> Lifts Souls to Heaven, or brings its Angels here.

The inference that Dart is a High Churchman is not inevitable, but one is not surprised to find him lauding Atterbury and lamenting the fate of the Abbey under the Commonwealth,

> When nothing sacred 'scap'd th' outrageous Force,
> Nor awful Temples stop'd their wasteful Course;

> . . . . .

> Thy [the Abbey's] rev'rend Priests were forced to quite the Place,
> To hot-brain'd Zealots, a destructive Race.
> Religion then sunk down her decent Head,
> And wild Disorder triumph'd in her Stead:
> Till Heaven with pitying Eye survey'd the Land,
> Drew back his Arm, and stop'd his angry Hand;
> Restor'd to just Command the Regal Train,
> And calm Religion reassum'd her Reign.

The association of sectarian enthusiasm and political radicalism is a typically Tory attitude.

Although the poem is written in heroic couplets, the author's classicism is less orthodox than his Anglicanism. In describing the Poets' Corner he not only praises Chaucer and Spenser but dwells at greater length on Cowley as "th' inspir'd Nine's peculiar Care." Admiration for Cowley's pindaric vein mingles with High Churchmanship in a passage on "the tuneful Prelate," Bishop Sprat,

> Who round the sacred Mitre wreath'd the Bays;
> His Bosom warm'd with more than common Fire,
> Array'd in holy Lawn he boldly struck the Lyre.

Such tastes, considered along with the pseudo-Miltonic invocation, point toward a sentimental quality in Dart which might be more obvious if he furnished a larger body of material for analysis.

Most of Dart's contemporaries found "calm Religion" less easily in ancient abbeys than in the Newtonian universe. Passing from the 1700-1720 to the 1720-1740 period, the reader has noted the increased importance of science as a factor in religious thought. The death of Newton in 1727 was the signal for a volley of physico-theological poems. Some of these are too sentimental, or too non-Christian, or both, to be treated in the present chapter; but three of them may here be examined.

Unlike John Dart, the Reverend Richard Collins [56] is a Whig and a latitudinarian. He admires Walpole, believes that Hoadly's arguments

> ... must all convince
> Who love their God, their Country or their Prince,

and detests Hoadly's arch-enemy, Snape. He declares that he wrote *Nature Display'd* (1727) to popularize "the Notions of the ancient and modern Philosophers," [57] and to apply them "to their proper Use, the promoting of Religion."

In accordance with this aim we find a few remarks on providential ingenuities and a more or less Cartesian proof of the existence of God. On the whole, however, there is so little religion in the eighty-two pages of *Nature Display'd* that one suspects Collins of wishing merely to versify miscellaneous notes on the circulation of the blood, the rainbow, bees, volcanoes, and other objects of scientific curiosity. The poem lacks any unifying principle and is so incoherently arranged as almost to suggest a lack of mental balance.

Though Collins occasionally refers to Newton, he is more interested in botany and physiology than in mathematics, physics, or astronomy. His favorite topic, however, is what would now be called physiological psychology. He observes the close relations between body and mind, and stresses with almost Pavlovian zest the influence of the former upon the latter:

> Sometimes the Body, by Digestion bad,
> Wants Nourishment, and then the Soul is sad.
>
> .   .   .   .
>
> And now the truest cause of Groans to tell,
> They are but Air, the Lungs oppress'd expel.
>
> .   .   .   .
>
> Blame not Lucretius, if his Thoughts are bad,
> But blame Lucilia, who first made him mad.

Lucretius, however, can be defended on other grounds, for he has been misinterpreted by later ages:

[56] Not in *D.N.B.* He was Rector of Crayford in Kent.
[57] He chiefly means *natural* philosophers.

> An Epicure, is always mark'd, to be,
> A Glutton, Drunkard, or a Debauchee;
> Yet, Epicurus, rightly understood,
> Who Pleasure makes to be the greatest Good,
> Of Pleasure, surely, had the truest Tast,
> For, he was ever Temperate, ever Chast.

Nature Display'd is so muddle-headed and ineptly written that we may be grateful to Collins for his failure to carry out the threat expressed in these concluding lines:

> Let this, on Nature be the first Essay,
> The next, shall Arts, and Sciences, display,
> Here, I propose through the whole Course to run,
> Of peopled Earth, and Nations first begun;
> Of Languages, the Progress, and the Source,
> Their Difference, Analogie, and Force.
> Of Governments, Religions, Customs, Laws;
> The different Nature, and the different Cause.
> And, when the Muse, with Labour has explain'd,
> What in the World's most distant Parts contain'd:
> To what concerns us most will, fitly, come,
> And show the State of all things here at Home.
> Nature's chief Master-piece completes the Scheme.
> Thus will immortal WALPOLE be my Theme.
>
> .   .   .   .
>
> His Greatness true, his active Virtues show,
> None can receive the Good, he can bestow.
> What Angry, would-be Statesmen say's a Sham,
> For Walpole has refin'd on Walsingham;
> Who found the Way, at once, to humble Spain;
> Eliza lik'd him,—and he Grac'd her Reign.[58]

Even allowing for the eulogistic conventions of the age, this will justify our dismissing the reverend author with contempt.

No feeling, contemptuous or otherwise, is aroused by *The Copernican System, A Poem* (1728). The author, Samuel Edwards,[59] addresses the

---

[58] At the risk of confusing the reader I have preserved Collins's insane punctuation because it conveys something of the quality of his mind.

[59] Not in *D.N.B.* On his title-page he styles himself: "Samuel Edwards, A.B. of Trinity College, Cambridge; And one of His Majesty's Scholars on the Royal Foundation of Modern History and Languages."

reader: "As to the Style of this Poem, I wish it were an Imitation of the Sacred Milton, whose every Work is Praise! Concerning Copernicus, his Labours can speak him best; but I beg leave to acquaint the Reader that he was born in Germany.[60] How are we indebted to that Empire, to which we owe the best of Kings, and so great a Philosopher, who laid the Foundations of the amazing Structures of the never enough to be admir'd Sir Isaac Newton!"

In spring, says Edwards, it is pleasant

> ... to rove
> On Banks of Cam, or Isis, fam'd in Song,
> To meditate the Great Creator's Praise;
> Who in his Works so manifest is seen,
> As far as Nature can her Author paint.

These lines, and a brief allusion to that final day when the Copernican system shall be liquidated, represent the sum total of the religious element in the poem.

The young author's motives, in fact, are neither religious nor scientific: he is merely trying to write a sort of celestial blank-verse *Georgic* and to pay handsome compliments to Newton and George II. His treatment of the subject is decorative rather than didactic; he gives little real information, but dresses up a few elementary facts in pompous, would-be Miltonic verbiage.

Highly regarded by Newton himself, the Reverend John Theophilus Desaguliers (1683-1744) was one of the leading physicists of his day. His father, a Huguenot pastor, fled with him to England on the revocation of the Edict of Nantes. After graduating from Oxford the son took Anglican orders; but the summit of his ecclesiastical career was his appointment as chaplain to that egregious libertine Prince Frederick, and his only published work in theology was a Thanksgiving sermon preached before George I in 1716. He was an enthusiastic freemason.[61]

But neither the Church nor the lodge was allowed to interfere with his scientific studies. He was a prominent fellow of the Royal Society, and according to *D.N.B.* "is said to have been the first to deliver learned lec-

---

[60] Copernicus was of course a Pole; but he was born at Thorn in *Prussian* Poland, where his father, a native of Cracow, had settled as a trader.

[61] In 1732 he published *The Constitutions of the Free-Masons.*

tures to general audiences." Besides inventing several machines, he published ten scientific treatises, chiefly on physics and its practical applications. He was also one of the pioneer investigators of electricity.

Desaguliers' only poem is *The Newtonian System of the World, The Best Model of Government: An Allegorical Poem* (1728). In his preface he states that he has written primarily for the King and Queen, but more especially for the latter. "I was resolv'd to endeavour at something that might at once show my Zeal and Loyalty, and at the same Time divert Her most Gracious Majesty with my first Poetical Experiment, as I have had the great Honour of entertaining Her with Philosophical ones. The following Poem was wrote last Summer, and intended to be publish'd on the Day of the Coronation"; but he withheld it in order to add explanatory notes, "though they were not necessary to those Great Persons, for whom my Poem was chiefly design'd." The dedication to the Earl of Ilay lays down the axiom that the best form of government must be that which agrees most closely with "the Natural Government of our System, according to the Laws settled by the All-wise and Almighty Architect of the Universe." His poem will show that English parliamentarianism meets this requirement.

In clear, smooth, undistinguished verse, and with the scorn of the true experimentalist for hypothetical speculations, Desaguliers brings the history of astronomy down to Descartes. The Frenchman's "Physical Romance," accepted in his native land, was rejected in England,

> For the bold Britons, who all Tyrants hate,
> In Sciences as well as in the State,
> Examin'd with experimental Eyes,
> The Vortices of the Cartesian Skies,
> Which try'd by Facts and mathematick Test,
> Their inconsistent Principles confess'd,
> And jarring Motions hast'ning to inactive Rest.
> But Newton the unparallel'd, whose Name
> No Time will wear out of the Book of Fame,
> Cœlestial Science has promoted more,
> Than all the Sages that have shone before.
> Nature, compell'd, his piercing Mind obeys,
> And gladly shows him all her secret Ways;
> 'Gainst Mathematicks she has no Defence,
> And yields t'experimental Consequence.

His tow'ring Genius, from its certain Cause,
Ev'ry Appearance, a priori draws,
And shews th' Almighty Architect's unalter'd Laws.

According to these laws the sun is a limited monarch who governs the Newtonian system exactly as George II governs England:

Like Ministers attending ev'ry Glance,
Six Worlds sweep round his [the sun's] Throne in Mystick Dance.
He turns their Motion from its devious Course,
And bends their Orbits by Attractive Force;
His Pow'r coerc'd by Laws, still leaves them free,
Directs, but not Destroys, their Liberty;
Tho' fast and slow, yet regular they move,
(Projectile Force restrain'd by mutual Love,)
And reigning thus with limited Command,
He holds a lasting Sceptre in his Hand.

Although written chiefly to amuse the philosophic Caroline, the poem doubtless represents the author's personal views. They are different from those of his Huguenot father. God is referred to in the dedication and once or twice in the text as the "Almighty Architect," but He plays no essential part in the allegorical scheme. It would have been kinder to make Him the real George II of the universe, with the sun as Prime Minister. At any rate the inference is clear that God, no less than the sun, is restricted by the system of checks and balances which He has devised for the government of the worlds. Newtonianism has transformed the Almighty into a limited monarch endowed with all the symbolic dignity and all the actual futility of the king of England.

So many of these writers are unknown to fame that we have dates for only nine out of fifteen. Jeffreys, whose long career flowered tardily, was born in 1678. Three were born between 1680 and 1689, and five between 1690 and 1699. Thus the group closely corresponds to the divine poets of the preceding chapter but is slightly older than the non-religious poets of Chapter VI.

The social status of twelve of the fifteen can be ascertained. Jeffreys is definitely an aristocrat, and Hay a country gentleman. Miss Tollett and Miss Jones are hardly aristocrats but are "well connected." Alexander Nicol is of humble birth. The remaining seven are of the middle class, though some of them belong to the upper levels of that deep stratum. A large majority of the fifteen appear to be Whigs. Furthermore, with the trifling exceptions of John Dart and Miss Dixon, none but Whigs bring their politics into their poetry: Brereton, Pitt, Hay, Collins, Edwards, Desaguliers. Pitt and presumably Desaguliers (as chaplain to Prince Frederick) are Whig "Patriots"; Collins and Hay are "Walpole" Whigs. Neither social class nor political party, however, is a very important factor, since the group as a whole fully accepts the eighteenth-century compromise. Jeffreys, Pitt, and Green make some attempt to carry on the aristocratic tradition; all the others are "middle-classicists."

One-third of the fifteen are Anglican clergymen, and one-third are women. The women are considerably more pious than the parsons—a situation which will not surprise the modern Episcopalian. The list contains no genuine dissenters. Green moves from nonconformity through Quakerish sympathies to an almost deistic latitudinarianism. Desaguliers, born at La Rochelle of Huguenot parentage, becomes an Anglican cleric whose real creed is the Newtonian system. Alexander Nicol apparently begins as a strict Presbyterian and ends as a latitudinarian with vague Episcopalian preferences. Mrs. Brereton swings from a rather evangelical Anglicanism to the cult of Locke, Clarke, and Wollaston. This trend from dissent or "low" Anglicanism to latitudinarianism, paralleled by the history of John Bancks in Chapter VI,[62] is a marked feature of the period. A related tendency is the influence of Newtonian science as seen in the work of Miss Tollett, Collins, Edwards, Desaguliers, and to a less extent in that of Pitt, Mrs. Brereton, and Mrs. Barber. By this time Newtonianism is a much stronger factor in Christian Rationalism than ancient philosophy, though Miss Tollett draws upon Cicero to some extent. Hay is a disciple of Hoadly; Mrs. Barber, Miss Jones, Cobden, and Jeffreys are colorless. Alone among the fifteen, Miss Dixon and John Dart stand as feeble representatives of High Churchmanship. Through the whole group runs a preference for a calm, rational, and practical religion.

These poets are of slight interest to a student of sentimental and preromantic trends. In this respect they are about on a par with the less noteworthy of the middle-classicists of Chapter IV. Measured against an imaginary ideal of pure neoclassicism the exceptions noted in the foregoing pages and a few similar points which the reader has been spared would assume some importance, but measured against the real facts of

[62] *Vide supra*, pp. 273 ff.

literary history they are insignificant. Sentimental tendencies appear only sporadically in these poets without any apparent organic relation to the main body of their work.

Considering the scale of this study the group is rather large, but its members are almost as obscure as those of the preceding chapter. Nor can we say that it contains any neglected geniuses. Miss Tollett is at least aware of the existence of intellectual problems; and Miss Jones, though no poet, is a very nice woman. Pitt can translate, and Jeffreys can write smooth couplets. In his own non-poetical field, Desaguliers is an able man. Green is a wit who might have been something of a poet. Further than this the most indulgent charity cannot go.

The currents of the age have swept these feeble writers into a Sargasso Sea of compromise where the ancient "nothing too much" has come to mean "nothing in particular." Taken in the lump, they are neither keenly intellectual nor warmly emotional; neither elegantly aristocratic nor heartily bourgeois; neither vital believers nor vital sceptics. They would all [63] call themselves Christians, but none of them seems moved for more than a fleeting moment by a positive and joyous faith. When they think about religion their ideas are muddled; when they feel about it, their emotions are tame, flat, and chilled by dread of enthusiasm. In short they are a dull crew of Laodiceans, and one leaves them with a sigh of relief.

[63] With the possible exception of Green in his final stage.

Chapter IX

SENTIMENTALISM—MILD CASES

TO A GREATER OR LESS EXTENT, ALL THE POETS WHO REMAIN TO BE CONSIDERED illustrate the growth of sentimentalism and its attendant pre-romantic tendencies. The present chapter will deal with "mild cases"—writers who are not of major importance for our study but whose viewpoint deserves to be recorded. Chapter X will be devoted to "severer cases"—writers who represent more strikingly the growth of a new religion of feeling. In Chapter XI, Pope and Thomson will receive separate treatment as the two outstanding poets of the period.

Except for the very popular *Love Elegies,* the only surviving poem by James Hammond (1710-1742)[1] is a *Prologue to Lillo's Elmeric* which asserts that Lillo "knew no art, no rule." The sixteen *Elegies* are Tibullus-and-water. They include no religious element nor anything of pre-romantic significance other than a flavor of spurious emotionalism and a dash of melancholy.

Another specialist in the joys and sorrows of lovers is Martha Fowke.[2] Her *Epistles of Clio and Strephon* are described on the title-page as "a Collection of Letters that passed between an English Lady, and an English Gentleman in France, who took an affection to each other, by reading accidentally one another's Occasional Compositions, both in prose and verse." Miss Fowke is probably, though not quite certainly, responsible for both sides of the correspondence. Strephon, though very pure, noble, and full of sensibility, is sometimes so gross as to entertain the hope of being Clio's husband. Clio, on the contrary, is all for Platonic love.[3] Gently she rebuffs her correspondent:

[1] Educated at Westminster; equerry to Prince Frederick, 1733; M.P. for Truro, 1741-1742. A member of the Thomson circle.

[2] A friend of Hill, Thomson, Mallet, and Dyer. She married a Mr. Sansome (possibly the Strephon of her epistles?) and died in 1736.

[3] The third edition, 1732, was entitled *The Platonic Lovers.*

> But with my praises I should chidings join,
> Thy Body is inform'd of our design.
> Did I not tell thee it a share would claim,
> And strive to damp our everlasting flame?
>
> .   .   .   .
>
> Thou art not an *Intire Angel* yet,
> But hast a little of the *Serpent's* wit:
> A day will come, thou wilt be all refin'd,
> Thy *Body* as immortal as thy *Mind*.

Add to this feeble survival of seventeenth-century courtly Platonism the moral views of *Spectator,* a little mawkishness, and a little melancholy, and you have the ingredients of the *Epistles*. Clio and Strephon sometimes exchange conventionally pious remarks, but religion plays no real part in their feelings and their sentimentalism is too specialized to demand our closer scrutiny.

Imbedded in the second volume of William Pattison's *Poetical Works* (1728)[4] are a few poems by one "Mr. Roche" of Kings College, Cambridge. Their quality is such that the young author might well be allowed to remain in oblivion had he not written an *Ode to Melancholy* which mingles the mildly pensive and horrific types. Scenery like that of a Salvator Rosa landscape arouses in him a faint religious feeling, for he says that

> Lofty Trees in Arches meeting,
> Echoes hollow Blasts repeating,
> Cliffs in crumbling Ruins bending,
> Streams from distant Rocks descending,
> Allay the Passions, heavenly Thoughts supply,
> And charm each Sense with wild Variety.

A more striking thought expressed in the same poem is that the pleasures of melancholy retirement were enjoyed by Christ. The poet addresses the spirit of Solitude:

> Thy calm Delights the Godhead deign'd to prove;
> When for our Sake (O unexampled Love!)
> To die for us, he left his Throne above.
> Oft, from the noisy Populace retir'd,
> On Mountain-Tops his Prayers to Heaven aspir'd;

[4] *Vide infra,* p. 438.

Oft o'er unhospitable Wilds he stray'd,
At rending Winds, and Thunder undismay'd;
The Lightning shone around his sacred Hair,
Like Meteors, with an inoffensive Glare:
In Adoration Winds their Voices raise,
And Thunder in rude Accents spoke his Praise.

Mr. Roche is a pious youth, but his pre-romantic feelings bid fair to transform our Lord into an eighteenth-century man of sensibility.

In 1739 the Reverend James Miller (1706-1744)[5] addressed to a young friend the first of two epistles on *The Art of Life. In Imitation of Horace's Art of Poetry*.[6] Except for a brief compliment to Handel on his "sacred Strains" this poem about how to live completely ignores religion. Most of the advice, though morally inoffensive, is worldly common sense. Despite the restraining influence of Horace, however, the poem has a few soft spots. Miller is a benevolist who urges the youth to cultivate

Love interesting, gen'rous, unconfin'd,
That Social Chain which links us to the Kind;
Illumines all we do, and all we speak,
Beams in the Eye, and smiles upon the Cheek,
Employs each Hand, engages ev'ry Heart
To act the Parent's, Friend's, or Patron's Part;
Shines like the Sun impartial o'er the whole,
With Rays attractive joining Soul to Soul.

The first line of this passage contains an early use of "interesting" as meaning "provocative of sensibility."

The pleasure of helping the unfortunate is most intense when the object of our charity freely displays the sorrow with which we are to sympathize:

If then you'd make me Partner in your Woe,
With unfeign'd Anguish first your Tears must flow,
Then your Misfortunes melt my pitying Breast,
And sympathetick Sorrows stand confess'd.

Thus while the art of life excludes religion it includes social loving and social weeping. Since Miller was a clergyman one must recognize the

5 A lecturer at Trinity Chapel, Conduit Street, London, who wrote plays in order to enlarge his income.

6 The second epistle is not in the British Museum; perhaps it was never published. In "Epistle the First" the English poem is printed on the left-hand pages opposite the Latin passages which Miller has imitated.

possibility that he intended to rise to the religious level in the second epistle, but nothing in the first encourages this conjecture.

Although chiefly a man of the theatre, Benjamin Victor (d. 1778)[7] wrote a considerable amount of verse—elegies, epigrams, occasionals, loyal odes, and bootlicking epistles. Something drew him toward men who had sentimental leanings: he associated with Colley Cibber, Steele, Aaron Hill, Dyer, Mallet, and Thomson,[8] and was an admirer of Young. In an epistle *To Sir William Brewer* he begs his muse to attune herself to the beauties of the baronet's garden:

> Sweet let thy verse from unforc'd nature flow,
> Yet strongly marked let the full figures glow;
> As when drawn clouds unveil the blushing sky,
> And Heav'n burns broad with a vermillion dye,
> While thro' the grovy tracks, cool zephyrs pass,
> To fan the silver streams, and sweep the grass.

How happy would Victor be in a cottage near Sir William's "heav'nly umbrage"! There, "stretch'd in sweet leisure on the silent ground," he would read Milton, Dryden, Shakespeare, "wild Spenser," and "familiar Jonson";

> But Waller's numbers most my heart shall move,
> For the prevailing passion there, is love.

This is the proper approach to a noble amateur of gardening. Elsewhere, however, Victor cultivates neither the retirement theme nor any other definitely pre-romantic tendency. His slight sentimentalism vents itself only in boosting Walpole and the Whig civilization which that "happy patriot" [9] has created:

> Hibernia sees with grateful eyes,
> Her arts, and industry arise;
> Our looms! our parts! our wealth display!
> And thus we breathe the grateful lay.

---

[7] Barber, tradesman, linendraper, theatrical manager, stage historian, pamphleteer, and poet-laureate of Ireland. His absurd odes for royal birthdays continue until 1776, but his most nearly serious efforts in poetry belong to the 1720's and 1730's.

[8] In a long footnote to *On Returning the Manuscript Poem, call'd Winter, to the Author, Mr. James Thomson* he credits himself and Mallet with having persuaded the bookseller Millar to buy Thomson's poem.

[9] *On the Arrival of His Royal Highness Prince Frederick.* See also *On the Death of Sir Richard Steele* and the dedication of *The Levee-Haunter.*

From the religious viewpoint Victor is a complete blank. He says nothing either for or against Christianity, and seems to rely on no other source of spiritual strength.

Josiah Relph (1712-1743) was the son of a humble Cumberland "statesman," but received a good education at the Appleby Free School. After taking orders he became perpetual curate of his native parish of Sebergham, where he labored with great devotion among his rude parishioners until his death at the age of thirty-one.

The poems of this rustic young priest who lived so close to nature and to God might be expected to provide material of some value, but they do nothing of the sort. Most of his poems are short, jocular occasional pieces, not in the least offensive but not markedly pious or even much concerned with morals. He paraphrases two psalms, and he writes a not very mordant *Epigram. On the Author of a Late Sermon against Episcopacy.* But he is more like himself in another *Epigram* which defends Lollius against those who are shocked at his sleeping in church:

> But I think Lollius keeps the sabbath best;
> For why, he makes it still a day of rest.

This native of the Wordsworth country is by no means strikingly preromantic. He displays, to be sure, a mildly pleasant vein of unpretentious lyricism. His pastorals in the Cumberland dialect, for which he is still dimly remembered, would furnish more convincing evidence of his affection for nature were they not so obviously imitations of Gay's *Shepherd's Week:* the dialect, one fears, makes them seem more genuine than they are. Yet Relph is not without a tinge of sentimentalism. He desires to live like "a little pleasing riv'let" running "in a vale thro' silent groves." [10] In *The Boy and the Birds* he decries cruelty to animals, insisting that even the hawk "never for diversion kills." And he displays plenty of sensibility in *Occasion'd by a little Miss's bursting out into tears upon reading the Ballad of The Babes in the Wood:*

> Sweet softness! still O still retain
> This social heart, this sense humane.
> Still kindly for the wretched bleed,
> And no returns of pity need. [11]

[10] *The Wish.*   [11] In a footnote Relph alludes to Addison's praise of this ballad.

Had he possessed more sophistication and more leisure to indulge such tender moods, Relph might well have developed a severer case of sentimentalism.

Leonard Welsted (1688-1747),[12] translator of Longinus and enemy of Pope, is pre-romantic only in critical theory. He insists that "the soul of good writing, is not to be come at through mechanick Laws; the main graces, and the cardinal beauties of this charming art, lie too retired within the bosom of Nature, and are of too fine and subtle an essence, to fall under the discussion of Pedants, Commentators, or trading Criticks.... These beauties, in a word, are rather to be felt, than described." Not that he would banish reason from the realm of poetry. On the contrary, he proceeds to draw a distinction which is weighty in its implications not only for criticism but for religion: "It is certain, everything depends upon reason, and must be guided by it; but it is as certain, that reason operates differently when it has different things for its object. Poetical reason is not the same as mathematical reason.... The care to be had, in judging of things of this nature, is to try them by those tests that are proper to themselves, and not by such as are proper only to other knowledges." The *je ne sais quoi* conception of poetry is not unknown in Welsted's day, but its association with a relativistic view of reason is unusual. Welsted also agrees with his Longinus that "no one ... can be a sublime Writer, who has not a sublimity and nobleness of soul."

These ideas are expressed in *A Dissertation concerning the Perfection of the English Language, the State of Poetry, etc.,* appended to his *Epistles, Odes, etc. written on Various Subjects,* 1724. But as for his poems, neither those included in this volume nor those composed later in his career are at all prophetic of the Romantic Movement. Indeed, he is somewhat more loyal to the seventeenth-century aristocratic tradition than most of his contemporaries, unconsciously illustrating his own statement that since Milton

> ... in verse few wonders have been wrought,
> And our smooth cadence flows devoid of thought.[13]

Rather exceptional is *The Picture of a fine April Morning* (1719), which contains some pleasantly fresh images of nature.

[12] His *Apple-Pye* was printed as early as 1704, but he did not become steadily productive until about 1718 and a large majority of his poems fall within the 1720-1740 period.
[13] *An Epistle to His Grace the Duke of Chandos.*

Although a clergyman's son, Welsted gives us no divine poetry and has little to say about religion. It is significant that his critical *Dissertation* does not reflect the influence of the Dennis-Watts-Blackmore theory of sacred verse. Like Rag Smith, however, he was impressed by the piety of John Philips. In 1710 he dedicated to Bolingbroke a poem in honor of the dead poet, ironically marvelling at the spectacle of a writer who remained a zealous Christian in times when religion is a standing jest to polite wits

> Whose maxims are, to live by Nature's rule,
> That the poor Parson is the Statesman's tool;
> That Priesthood then began to flourish most,
> And find increase, though at the people's cost,
> When subtle laws and politicians found,
> Mankind by laws restrain'd, by conscience bound,
> Themselves in more security might reign,
> And Priests perceiv'd that "Godliness was gain."

Bolingbroke was fond of Philips, but he was himself a libertine champion of "Nature's rule," and, from political motives, an advocate of laws restraining liberty of conscience. To address such a poem to him was either stupid or hypocritical.

The year 1710 was a propitious season in which to write poems in praise of Tory poets and address them to Tory statesmen.[14] Matters were different in 1714, when Welsted published *An Epistle to Mr. Steele, on the King's Accession to the Crown*. Here he is all for Protestantism, liberty, commerce, and Hanover:

> Refulgent Rome from her proud height shall stoop,
> And see her long-neglected honours droop:
> The worship'd image shall neglected stand,
> And boast in vain the work of Raphael's hand.

Dissenters no longer stand in dread of Tory oppression. What is even more important, business will improve:

> Not long Religious Rage mankind shall tear,
> Nor wasting Zeal her bloody standard rear.
> Commerce again prepares to lift its head,
> Again to flourish, and its bounds to spread;

. . . . .

[14] In 1709 Welsted had inscribed to Harley *A Poem occasioned by the late famous Victory of Oudenarde*.

I see disclos'd Augusta's future state:
Lo! her proud fleets admire their costly freight:
Her busy mart th' adventuring world employs:
Confusion greatly splendid! welcome noise!
Thames, swell'd with wealth, his envious banks o'erflows,
Seeks other shores, and a new empire knows.

The easy transition from toleration to commerce is thoroughly Whiggish. Hereafter Welsted supports the dominant party and holds minor official posts.

Further insight into Welsted's religious views is furnished by *An Epistle to the late Dr. Garth, Occasioned by the Death of the Duke of Marlborough*. The dead physician is urged to welcome the general to a heaven which is half pagan and half Whiggishly latitudinarian. The spirit of Dr. Garth is addressed:

On flowery beds, meseems, I see thee lie,
While young immortal maids pass smiling by;
Close at thy feet while rivulets flow of wine,
And Sappho slights her Phaon to be thine.

This, of course, because Garth took a leading part in the 1717 translation of the *Metamorphoses*. But heaven is also populated by champions of civil and religious liberty, for Garth is told that

There men, who liv'd upright like thee reside;
There the brave legion, that for Freedom dy'd;
Whoe'er in arts polite divinely wrought;
And pious Priests, that Hoadly's doctrines taught;
And they, who virtue, sunk in ills sustain'd;
And Bards inspir'd, and Kings like George that reign'd.

Marlborough, Garth, Houris and Hoadly! The hodge-podge makes us wonder whether a heaven of any sort is more than a rhetorical device for Welsted.

From such passages his ecclesiastical viewpoint may be inferred. He had reason to be grateful to Hoadly, for it was probably through the bishop's influence that he was promoted from an extraordinary to an ordinary clerkship in the Ordnance Office. John Nichols, in his "Brief Memoirs of the Author and his Family," quotes a letter in which Welsted calls Hoadly his "great Patron" and thanks him for many favors.[15]

Nichols also declares that despite Pope's attacks "our author does not

15 *The Works, in Verse and Prose, of Leonard Welsted, Esq.* (1787), xi and *n*.

appear to have been a mean poet: he had certainly from nature a good genius; but, after he came to town, became a votary to pleasure; and the applauses of his friends, which taught him to over-value his talents, perhaps slackened his diligence, and by making him trust solely to nature, neglect the assistance of art." This suggests that his critical heterodoxy may have been partly a rationalization of his laziness and self-esteem. But Nichols adds disapprovingly that "a gentleman now living recollects hearing of Welsted's fame as a chess-player at the Temple coffee-house." Such evidence will hardly convict the poet of violent libertinism, and Pope's "Flow, Welsted, flow, like thine inspirer, beer" was written by an enemy.

Nevertheless in the life and writings of Welsted one observes the going-to-seed of a promising, spoiled, conceited youth whose character lacked any solid ethical or religious center. Apparently he never abandoned a Hoadleian sort of Christianity: it did not oppress him sufficiently to be worth shaking off. In 1736 a piece of prose hackwork, *The Scheme and Conduct of Providence, from the Creation to the Coming of Messiah,* expresses conventionally proper views. But he puts more zest into his last poem, *The Summum Bonum; or Wisest Philosophy,* 1741. The theme of this Horatian epistle is that we should enjoy life and let the mad world run its course:

> Haste, Sall, the oranges and arrack bring;
> Fetch me the water from Castalia's spring:
> Since nought with reason may impede our bliss,
> Let's every grief and every care dismiss:
> All my Hephestion has that's worth possessing:
> Then seize the swift-wing'd hour and fleeting blessing.

The very similar *Weltanschauung* of Hildebrand Jacob (1693-1739)[16] is expressed in the stanza:

> To Venus, Bacchus, and the Nine
> Our future Moments we'll resign,
>   Sincerer Pleasures can we prove?
> Glory, and Riches we disdain,
> While, with the Muses, and Champagne,
>   We fill the intervals of Love.[17]

[16] Son of a baronet; brother of Giles Jacob of *Poetical Register* fame; father of Sir Hildebrand Jacob the eminent Hebrew scholar.
[17] *Ode I. To Cloë.*

This gentlemanly fribble continues the tradition of sentimental libertinism which we observed in Part I. His work combines inanity, nastiness, and superficial tenderness.

Jacob's amateurish little prose essay on *How the Mind is rais'd to the Sublime* regards Milton as a great example of sublimity and pays respect to "that Kind of *Enthusiasm*, which Aristotle, and Longinus mention, as necessary to succeed in poetry."[18] His own verse, however, is very far from enthusiastic; indeed one of his few merits as a poet is that he almost never pretends to be anything but what he is. A friend who urges him to write on weighty subjects receives the answer:

> My Friend, I never cou'd take Pains,
> Still sporting in light, idle Strains;
> I'm stranger to all state Affairs,
> And leave Ambition to my Heirs.[19]

As for satire, how can he hope to reform mankind when Horace, Pope, and Young have failed? And even if he were able to write with the power of these great ones,

> I still, well meaning Friend, have thought
> This Preaching never worth a Groat,
> One might as well lay down, and sleep;
> The Roots are fix'd, the Stains lye deep.
> I judge from all I've seen, or read
> Of Mortals now Alive or Dead,
> That Vanities were still the same,
> And Man had still this Itch to blame.[20]

When pre-romantic tendencies appear in Jacob's work they are colored by his frivolous temperament. His *L'Allegro* is less an imitation of Milton than an Anacreontic defiance of all serious thought. *Occasion'd by Phoebe's consenting* opens with a tender strain of sentimental naturalism:

> Look down, ye Monarchs, and behold
> A Treasure, richer far than Gold,
> A Nymph, thrown out in Nature's Pride,
> Form'd in her perfect Mould,
> And bred up, artless, by the green Wood side,
> Whose Heart can ne'er be bought, or sold,
> Who shines, without the help of Gems
> Far brighter than your Diadems.

[18] *Works*, p. 421.   [19] *Epistle IV. To B. B. Esq.*
[20] *Epistle III, Reasons for not writing Satire. To R. D. Esq.*

But immediately he adds:

> With her, remote from anxious Strife,
> On Banks of Flowers I repose,
> And joke, and kiss, and quaff, and doze,
> And lead an idle, lazy, happy life.

In Jacob's hands too, that child of nature, the Noble Savage, becomes a sceptical wit. An Indian demands of a Jesuit missionary:

> Why I, who ever have been free,
> And whom you Lord of all declare
> On Earth, in Water, and in Air,
> Shou'd yet be forc'd to take a Wife
> For better, and for worse; for Life;
> Keep all the children, she provides;
> Renouncing all the Sex besides?
> The Father, staring in his Face,
> My Son, you yet are void of Grace:
> The Devil baffles all I say.
> The Savage sneer'd, and ran away.[21]

I have not seen *The Progress of Religion,* which was published two years later than the *Works* of 1735, but cannot suppose that it would do much to invalidate the statement that there is no religious feeling in Jacob's poems. *Chiron to Achilles,* a conventional didactic epistle to a youth who has just come of age, preaches the golden mean without once hinting that man belongs, as Young puts it, to a "sky-born, sky-guided, sky-returning race."

Against the fear of death Jacob fortifies himself with the proud thought that he has had a good time:

> What sudden Damp invades my Heart?
> O Death! who can thy Pow'r withstand?
> No matter! I embrace the Dart,
> Prepar'd, to follow thy Command;
> For I have liv'd! each Hour employ'd!
> Thou canst not take, what I've enjoy'd.[22]

In short, Hildebrand Jacob, having filled the intervals of love with the muses and champagne, is quite the captain of his soul. He has burned always with a gemlike flame.

[21] *The Indian. Tale VII.*   [22] *Ode III. To Death.*

The long and tortuous career of James Ralph (1705?-1762) cannot here be described in any detail. It may be remembered that he was a merchant's clerk in Philadelphia when Benjamin Franklin became his friend and turned him from Christianity to deism. When this pair of virtuous apprentices departed for London, Ralph left his wife and child behind. In London he took as mistress a milliner to whom Franklin vainly made advances during Ralph's absence as a village schoolteacher in Berkshire. Ralph, who had been sponging on his friend, made Franklin's perfidy the excuse for cancelling all debts to him.

In 1728, no longer Franklin's comrade, Ralph is a shabby hack-writer in London. That year saw the publication of *Night,* his best-known poem, and the publication of the first *Dunciad.* Eager for glory, he was prompt to attack Pope on behalf of Grub Street; hence in the second edition of the *Dunciad* the public was told that Ralph "makes *night* hideous" by baying at the moon.[23]

The poems of this shady, ambiguous, rather clever man are almost destitute of religious thought or feeling. Pre-romanticism is more in evidence; but his work, though sometimes effective, is so histrionic in manner that one doubts his sincerity. Like Richard Savage, whom he resembles both as a man and as a poet, he likes to indulge in lofty mouthings about virtue, truth, love, liberty, the public good, and universal benevolence.

Night may conveniently be described in the words of an authority on the type which it represents: "It really anticipates the completed *Seasons* [having been published in 1728], since its four divisions follow the parts of the year. The Thomsonian influence is plain. . . . *Night* is an episodic descriptive poem in blank verse. Its method is a free-hand copying of Thomson and Vergil, supplemented by original observation. . . . Ralph is usually imitative, but he has zest and energy. The eagerness with which he seizes upon Thomson's nature description, his humanitarianism, his sensibility, indicates a volatile nature full of enthusiasm. Ralph does not make as much of the ideas of natural revelation of the divine as do Thomson, Mallet, and Savage; there is, however, in Book III an interesting

---

[23] Besides publishing several poems, Ralph tried unsuccessfully to write for the stage. He was long active as an anti-ministerial pamphleteer and journalist until the Pelham ministry bought him off. His *History of England during the Reigns of King William, Queen Anne, and King George I,* 1744-1746, is regarded as a work of some merit.

celebration of the wonders of the stars, worlds which reveal the Creator of the universe." [24]

Ralph's other poems are not rewarding. *The Muses' Address to the King* (1728) is at least noteworthy as a technical innovation: it is a *rhymeless* irregular ode running to forty-one pages. *Zeuma: Or the Love of Liberty* makes the Spanish invasion of Chile the vehicle for sentimental primitivism. The Indians before the coming of the Spaniards are embodiments of "Innocence and Joy." Zeuma, the Indian king who holds out against the invaders for three books of blank verse, has the liberty-loving ideals of a sound anti-ministerial Whig.

In a curious poem entitled *The Tempest: Or, The Terrors of Death* (1727) young Lycus devotes about sixteen pages to what sounds like a tame and feeble version of Blair's *The Grave*. Death levels all pretensions and disappoints all hopes. But death also ends the woes of life, and heavenly joys wait beyond the grave. Some time after these musings, Lycus wearies of the solitary, contemplative life which has nourished such thoughts and embarks on a sea-voyage. A storm arises, and is lavishly described. Lycus is drowned, but before the waters close over his head he poignantly experiences those "terrors of death" which his dry-land moralizing had so easily dismissed. This poem is the only overt expression of Ralph's contempt for orthodox religious belief.

The verses of Stephen Duck (1705-1756), "the thresher-poet," recalls Johnson's comparison of the preaching woman and the dancing dog. They were not done well, but it was surprising that they were done at all. To this surprise he owed the patronage of Queen Caroline and the condescending interest of Joseph Spence and other literary folk.

Duck's tardy entrance into priesthood was probably an anchor thrown out to windward at a time when he was ceasing to be an object of curiosity. From the first, however, he seems to have been a modest, worthy, sensibly pious man. Whatever the cause of his suicidal end, it was not the normal consequence of the rest of his life. His modern biographer assures us that "there is ample testimony to the effect that Duck was a useful parish priest, and performed his duties conscientiously." [25] Nothing

---

[24] D. L. Durling, *Georgic Tradition in English Poetry*, pp. 127-128.
[25] Rose Mary Davis, *Stephen Duck, the Thresher-Poet*, p. 105.

in his poems causes one to regard him as disqualified for the holy office. He says of them: "I don't think them good, and better judges will doubtless think worse of them than I do. Only this, I believe, I may say of them,. that, if they have nothing to delight those who may chance to read them, they have nothing to give modesty a blush; if nothing to entertain and improve the mind, they have nothing to debauch and corrupt it." [26] For him morality and religion go hand in hand, and he often tilts against the unbeliever. Here are the *Proper Ingredients to Make a Sceptic:*

> A little learning, twenty grains of sense,
> Join'd with a double share of ignorance;
> Infuse a little wit into the scull,
> Which never fails to make a mighty fool;
> Two drams of faith, a tun of doubting next;
> Let all be with the dregs of reason mixt:
> When, in his mind, these jarring seeds are sown,
> He'll censure all things, but approve of none.

In another poem the Thames provides a crushing argument against the infidel:

> Say Atheists, since you own, by Nature's laws,
> There's no effect produc'd without a cause;
> Why should the restless stream run to and fro,
> And, with alternate motion, ebb and flow;
> Did not some Being, of superior force,
> Rule the wild waves, and regulate their course? [27]

Thus although Stephen is no zealot, he is plainly on the side of the angels. One may take almost at face value his lines *To a Gentleman, who requested a Copy of Verses from the Author,* where he declares his longing to write sacred poetry, especially a great work on the life, death, and resurrection of Christ;

> But now I must omit Messiah's praise,
> Lest I degrade him with unworthy lays;
> My fate compels me silent to remain,
> For want of learning to improve my strain.

His only poem classifiable as "divine" is *The Shunamite,* which relates the story of Elisha's resuscitation of the Shunammite woman's son.[28] It is remarkable neither from a religious nor from a literary viewpoint;

[26] Preface of *Poems on Several Occasions,* 1736.   [28] II Kings; iv, 8-37.
[27] *On Richmond Park, and the Royal Gardens.*

but Duck tells the tale with reverence and with more simplicity than his sense of inferiority usually permits. He himself had toiled in the fields beneath the blazing sun. In "An Account of the Author" prefixed to *Poems on Several Occasions,* Joseph Spence gives several facts concerning *The Shunamite,* which he justly considers Duck's most successful effort. The device of making the woman tell the story herself was suggested by Prior's *Solomon.* The poem was originally composed in blank verse, but, "upon reading it over, he found his language was not sublime enough for it; and...therefore he was forced to write all over again, and turn it into rhyme." The concluding chorus was suggested by the rejoicing of the angels after the creation in Milton's epic. "What first gave him a higher taste of poetry than he had been us'd to," says Spence, "was Milton's *Paradise Lost....* Stephen read it over twice or thrice with a dictionary before he could understand the language of it thoroughly."

Unlike Burns, the thresher-poet was not wise enough to write like him-self. Even in *The Thresher's Labour,* one of his earliest poems, he spoils his first-hand material and obscures his basically realistic view of it with classical affectations which he supposes to be literary. In later productions he adapts himself to certain aspects of the sentimental mode. *Avaro and Amanda* versifies the tenderly primitivistic story of Inkle and Yarico.[29] In *A Description of a Journey to Marlborough, Bath, Portsmouth, etc.* he describes himself as "pleas'd with the silent horror of the grove." *On Richmond Park, and The Royal Gardens* belongs to the softer type of loco-descriptive poem. Here he pays his respects to scenery, retirement, and "pensive contemplation"; but he prefers a trim and orderly landscape:

> Not so attractive lately shone the plain,
> A gloomy waste, not worth the Muse's strain;
>
> . . . . .
>
> Till Royal George, and heav'nly Caroline,
> Bid Nature in harmonious lustre shine;
> The sacred *Fiat* through the Chaos rung,
> And symmetry from wild disorder sprung.[30]

[29] The fact is not observed by L. M. Price, who gives a very exhaustive treatment of this once-famous tale of an Indian maiden and her faithless white lover in his *Inkle and Yarico Album.*

[30] The same naïve blasphemy appears in his dedication of *Poems on Several Occasions* to Queen Caroline: "It was your generosity which brought me out of obscurity, and still condescends to protect me; like the Supreme Being, who continually supports the meanest creature, which his goodness has produced."

But neither the religion nor the sentimentalism of Duck is of much importance. He gives us all that could be expected of him: soberly unimaginative Christianity combined with some eagerness to make the proper poetical remarks about nature.

The author of *The Chase* would be surprised to learn that his keen eye for the things he loved and his slight but not contemptible poetic gift had won for his sportsman's Georgic a place in the history of the Romantic Movement. William Somerville (1692-1742) was a country squire, magistrate, and fox-hunter who liked to write verses. Oxford, his Alma Mater, had left him comparatively untouched. His muse sticks close to the earth, and can express herself with hearty coarseness. Both in and out of his cups he is a good fellow, but no one would describe him as rich in the gifts of the spirit. Nevertheless, being opposed to outlandish notions in religion as in everything else, he cleaves to the traditional faith of an Englishman. He says of his favorite chair:

> Here on my yielding down I sit secure;
> And patiently, what Heaven has sent, endure;
> From all the futile cares of business free;
> Nor fond of life, but yet content to be:
> Here mark the fleeting hours; regret the past;
> And seriously prepare to meet the last.[31]

In *The Chase,* the immortality of the soul provides a religious justification of hunting:

> ... The soul
> Of man alone, that particle divine,
> Escapes the wreck of worlds, when all things fail.
> Hence the great distance 'twixt the beasts that perish,
> And God's bright image, man's immortal race.
> The brute creation are his property,
> Subservient to his will, and for him made.

But his theology must have been somewhat naïve, for the short epistle *To the Author of the Essay on Man* shows that he regarded Pope as a great teacher of Christian truth.

Somerville is never more completely the country squire than in his detestation of dissenting "fanatics." In Canto III of *Hobbinol,* Tabitha,

[31] *Address to His Elbow-Chair.*

one of the contestants in the women's footrace, "carries weight" because
she was got with child by a student at a nonconformist academy in nearby
Tewkesbury, where

> ... Gamaliel sage,
> Of Cameronian brood, with ruling rod
> Trains up his babes of grace, instructed well
> In all the gainful discipline of prayer;
> To point the holy leer, by just degrees
> To close the twinkling eye, t' expand the palms,
> To expose the whites, and with the sightless ball
> To glare upon the crowd.

A tale called *The Devil Outwitted* contrasts the jollity of a sensible vicar
with the sourness of

> ... some hide-bound folk, who chase
> Each merry smile from their dull face,
> And think pride zeal, ill-nature grace.

Obviously an admirer of *Hudibras,* Somerville recalls with whimsical
approval

> ... those blest days of jubilee,
> When pious Charles set England free
> From canting and hypocrisy;
> Most graciously to all restoring
> Their ancient privilege of whoring.[32]

The general trend of Somerville's work justifies the suspicion that on
the infrequent occasions when he voices sentimental or pre-romantic ideas
he has his eye on Thomson or on his friend Shenstone. The ideas are
there, however, and fairness demands that they be recorded. He assures
a benevolent physician that

> Full well thy soul can understand
> The poor man's call is God's command;
> No frail, no transient good, his fee;
> But Heaven, and bless'd eternity.
> Nor are thy labours here in vain,
> The pleasure over-pays the pain.
> True happiness (if understood)
> Consists alone, in doing good.[33]

---

[32] *The Night-Walker Reclaim'd.* See also *The Happy Lunatic,* an unsavory joke on a
"saint," and *An Epistle to Allan Ramsay,* where he gibes at the Presbyterians.
[33] *To Dr. Mackenzie.*

When the same doctor is found "reading mathematics," he is reminded of the uselessness of learning:

> Vain our pursuits of knowledge, vain our care,
> The cost of labour we may justly spare.
> Death from this coarse alloy refines the mind,
> Leaves us at large t' expatiate unconfin'd;
> All science opens to our wondering eyes,
> And the good man is in a moment wise.[34]

The death of an honest farmer, perhaps one of the squire's own tenants, suggests the reflection that

> In Cottages and homely cells,
> True piety neglected dwells:
> Till call'd to Heaven, her native seat,
> Where the good man alone is great:
> 'Tis then this humble dust shall rise,
> And view his Judge with joyful eyes;
> While haughty tyrants shrink afraid,
> And call the mountains to their aid.[35]

In all these cases one feels a slight tendency to sentimentalize traditionally religious attitudes.

Almost at the end of *The Chase,* Somerville voices a desire to plumb the depths of nature and

> ...with judgment read
> Th' expanded volume, and submiss adore
> That great creative Will, who at a word
> Spoke forth the wondrous scene.

But if his soul is too gross and earthy to follow "where Newton leads the way," he will be content to live a serene, obscure, retired life. The passage would be more impressive had not Thomson earlier expressed the same alternative aspirations in very similar language. In the last six lines of his poem Somerville drops these literary notions and prays for enough health to enable him to keep on with his fox-hunting. There, no doubt, speaks the real man.

The notorious Lætitia Pilkington (1712-1750) should perhaps have been assigned to the preceding chapter, but although in life she parted from

[34] *To Dr. M——, Reading Mathematics.*   [35] *Epitaph upon Hugh Lumber, Husbandman.*

her husband the pair of rogues may as well be embalmed together in this history. The traces of sentimentalism in Lætitia's verse are very slight. *The Petition of the Birds to Mr. Pilkington, On his Return from Shooting* begins on a humanitarian note but at once becomes a complimentary conceit. Pilkington should spare the birds, for he himself is birdlike: he possesses the chastity of the dove, the courage of the eagle, and so on.

Delville, the Seat of the Rev. Dr. Delany [36] is an "inspiring" spectacle of "Nature improv'd, and rais'd by art." Its owner is addressed:

> Here nature's beauties you explore,
> And searching her mysterious store,
> Through all her operations find
> The image of the sov'reign mind,
> And in each insect, plant and flow'r,
> Contemplate the creating pow'r.

But the benevolent Delany is not content to serve God merely in the contemplative life:

> Nor is thy love of him alone
> In fruitless speculation shewn;
> Through life you happily exert,
> The christian virtues of your heart;
> To give new schemes of culture birth
> And bless and beautify the earth;
> To raise th' afflicted from despair,
> And make the friendless wretch thy care:
> To thee the highest bliss is given,
> A soul to praise, and copy heav'n.

It is well to remember that Delany was the author's patron.

The hope of profiting from a compliment may also play its part in *To the Reverend Dr. Hales.* The famous physiologist and inventor is eulogized as a

> ... holy sage! whose comprehensive mind
> Not to this narrow spot of earth confin'd,
> Thro' num'rous worlds can nature's laws explore,
> Where none but Newton ever trod before;
> And, guided by philosophy divine,
> See thro' his works th' Almighty Maker shine.

[36] Patrick Delany, D.D. (1685?-1768), friend of Swift and fortunate husband of Mary Granville Pendarves. In 1744 he became Dean of Down through his wife's influence.

History has little to say of Stephen Hales as a divine, but Lætitia thinks
him a great interpreter not only of nature but also of Holy Writ. When
he expounds the Bible,

> In radiant colours truth array'd we see,
> Confess her charms, and guided up by thee,
> Soaring sublime, on contemplation's wings,
> The fountain seek, whence truth eternal springs.
> Fain would I wake the consecrated lyre,
> And sing the sentiments thou didst inspire!
> But find my strength unequal to a theme,
> Which asks a Milton's, or a Seraph's flame!

Readers of Mrs. Pilkington's diary may smile at these lines, forgetting
that imagination is imagination. To judge from her poems she is decidedly more pious than her clerical spouse, for she often expresses religious
feeling in a way which conveys no hint of insincerity. At a time of distress she consoles her husband with a glimpse of "a better world,"

> Where calumny no more shall wound,
>   Nor faithless friends destroy,
> Where innocence and truth are crown'd
>   With never-fading joy.[37]

Lætitia shows some originality in treating the faculty of *Memory* from
a religious viewpoint:

> Nor love, nor holy friendship, without thee,
> Could ever of the least duration be;
> Nor gratitude, nor truth, nor piety.
>
> .   .   .   .
>
> Lord, let me so this wond'rous gift employ,
> It may a fountain be of endless joy,
> Which time, nor accident, may ne'er destroy.
>
> Still let my faithful Memory impart,
> And deep engrave it on my grateful heart,
> How just, and good, and excellent thou art.

Although Mrs. Pilkington was a person who could rather easily convince herself of the rightness of her motives, memory can hardly have
proved a fountain of joy for her. Perhaps her religion was merely a

---

[37] *Consolatory Verses to her Husband.* Other distinctly pious poems are *Sorrow, Expostulation. Written in Distress,* and *To his Grace the Lord Archbishop of York.*

spurious vehicle for sentimental feelings; perhaps she was a genuinely believing sinner. We only know that she cried, "Pardon the soul that sues to be forgiven." [38] and that as death approached she wrote:

> My Lord, my Saviour, and my God,
> I bow to thy correcting rod;
> Nor will I murmur or complain,
> Tho' ev'ry limb be fill'd with pain;
> Tho' my weak tongue its aid denies,
> And day-light wounds my wretched eyes. [39]

Lætitia's husband, the Reverend Matthew Pilkington (fl. 1733), was a coxcomb, a rogue, and a bad poet. Besides miscellaneous trifles he wrote translations and imitations—chiefly of Anacreon, Horace, and Martial, short love-pastorals, and stuff about the inability of Cupid to distinguish between Venus and the Countess of Kildare.

He believes that he would achieve higher things in poetry were he not immured in hurried, noisy Dublin, for

> ...the gay Sons of Phœbus love
> The silent, thick-embow'ring Grove,
> To lye beside the limpid Spring,
> And hear the wood-born Warblers sing,
> To wander o'er sequester'd Scenes,
> Or tread the Flow'r-enammel'd Plains,
> Or near a Cowslip'd Bank reclin'd
> To catch the Fragrance from the Wind,
> Of Noise and Crowds, and Cares afraid,
> High rapt in Solitude and Shade. [40]

The same aspiration is expressed in *Happiness,* where, weary of seeking the favor of the great, he longs for "the calm, uncrowded rural Scene." The conclusion that the sole origin and end of happiness is God is apparently meant to arise from the sylvan contemplation celebrated earlier in the poem, but Pilkington is too incoherent and clumsy to make the point clear. Another hint of his religion may be gleaned from his longest and most formal poem, *The Progress of Musick in Ireland:*

> Musick and Love the savage World refin'd,
> Reform'd the Manners, while they rais'd the Mind,
> Gave Man a Foretaste of the Joys above;
> For what is Heav'n but Harmony and Love?

[38] *Sorrow.*   [39] *Written on her Death-Bed.*   [40] *To Lycidas in the Country.*

The evidence is slight, and the witness's character is shabby. One can only report that Pilkington thinks, or pretends to think, of cots and grots as favorable to poetry and religion, and that he has tender notions about heaven.

Some will remember the Whig pamphleteer and journalist Thomas Cooke (1703-1756) as the translator of Hesiod, others as the victim, with Burnet and Oldmixon, of a famous couplet in the *Dunciad,* and perhaps others as the author of some fantastic *Proposals for Perfecting the English Language.*[41] Although his poems include four Scripture-paraphrases, he is so lacking in religious feeling that one would never suppose him to be the son of a Muggletonian innkeeper. He brands as "Enthusiastic Fools" those who would give up all for the glory of God:

> What? Give up all, give all I have, ye say:
> To follow what, give all I have away?
> 'Tis not the Cry of God, nor Nature's Cry:
> Is Mankind dearer to myself than I?
> Dearest to me the nearest are in Life;
> Dear are my children, dear my blameless Wife.[42]

If Cooke had been the rich young man in the Gospel, he would have gone away arguing.

His latitudinarianism is further evidenced by his view of Samuel Clarke as

> The just Asserter of th' almighty Cause,
> Who trac'd thro Nature God's unerring Laws.

Clarke has recently departed to a heaven where the highest places are reserved for

> Priests who like Hoadley [*sic*] sacred Truths maintain,
> Who strive by Reason to convince their Foes,
> Who with a Christian Meekness Rage oppose.[43]

The philosopher's soul is pictured as straying through heaven's "enamel'd Mead, or vocal Grove," conversing with the shades of Locke, Newton,

---

[41] He advocated such forms as "writed," "begined," and "reasonabel."

[42] *Rhapsody on Virtue and Pleasure.*

[43] *Epistle the Fifth, To the right honourable Thomas Earl of Pembroke, occasioned by the Death of Dr. Samuel Clarke.* Dated November, 1729. See also *Epistle the Sixth, To the Right Reverend Dr. Benjamin Hoadley* [*sic*].

Tillotson, and Shaftesbury. Evidently Cooke feels no difficulty in considering Shaftesbury a soundly rational Christian.

The pre-romantic symptoms in Cooke's verse are just strong enough to save him from the limbo of the preceding chapter. That he edited Marvell's works in 1726 is perhaps some indication of non-classical tastes, and his friendship with Tickell, Ambrose Philips, Welsted, Steele, and Dennis suggests a preference for Whigs of the warm-hearted variety. A footnote in his *Rhapsody on Virtue and Pleasure* pays tribute to those natives of St. Kilda who are later to be praised on much the same grounds in Collins's Highland ode: "The few inhabitants, as they are by Nature separated from the World, and consequently know Nothing of the Arts of Luxury and Gain, are an innocent People. They have no money among them, but deal in Exchange of Commoditys. Here is an Epitomy of the World as painted by the Poets in its State of Infancy and Innocence!" In harmony with these remarks are two conventional pieces in praise of rural solitude, *On Retirement* and *On the Same*.

But despite the primitivistic footnote on the Hebrideans, "back to nature" is by no means the main theme of the *Rhapsody on Virtue and Pleasure*. The poet aims, on the contrary, to show that the only true happiness lies in the active employment of virtue in the service of humanity. "Sweet are the Pleasures of the bounteous Soul!" And though innocent poverty may be a great blessing on St. Kilda, *London* reeks with that Whiggish glorification of commercial progress which Professor Moore rightly describes as an aspect of sentimentalism.[44]

"Hesiod" Cooke is not an interesting writer, but his case is satisfyingly clear. The Muggletonian boy grows up to be an admirer of Clarke, of Hoadly, and even of Shaftesbury. Then the latitudinarian, finding no emotional values in his desiccated Christianity, dabbles weakly in an inconsistent mixture of benevolism, sentimental primitivism, and idealized commercialism.

The vapid prattle of the Reverend James Delacour [45] is almost completely barren of ideas. *On the Prospect of Poetry,* however, seems to

[44] C. A. Moore, "Whig Panegyric Verse, 1700-1760: A Phase of Sentimentalism." *PMLA.,* XLI, 362-401.

[45] Not in *D.N.B.* An A.M. of Trinity College, Dublin, he was a clergyman in Ireland. His *Poems* were published at Cork in 1778. This is apparently a first edition; but *Abelard to Eloisa,* his most ambitious effort, was written in 1729, and none of the fairly numerous pieces which can be dated from internal evidence belongs later than 1748. His volume

imply a preference for the soft and luscious. He sets a high value on descriptive verse, and gives a peculiar twist to a hoary critical dogma when he advises:

> ... Let nature be your guide,
> Rise in the spring, or in the river glide;
> In every line consult her as you run,
> And let her Naiads roll the river on.

As might be expected of a writer for whom "follow Nature" means "describe scenery," Delacour holds that "Thomson is another name for nature now." [46]

But Delacour lacks the power to put his critical notions into practise. Though he often refers to external nature with mawkish approval he never seriously tries to render its qualities in verse. Similarly he avoids philosophical problems although he declares that Plato, "a worthy heathen with a Christian mind," is to philosophy what Dr. Delany, "greatest of Divines," is to theology.[47]

This poet waxes very tender on the subject of love. His Popean epistle, *Abelard to Eloisa,* ignores the conflict between religion and passion in Abelard's breast; one would hardly suspect that this lackadaisical lover is a monk at all. In *To a Lady With Mrs. Rowe's Letters from the Dead to the Living, stil'd Friendship in Death,* Delacour responds almost wholly to the amatory aspect of these sentimentally pious effusions:

> Where cou'd she find so ravishing a theme?
> She saw it sure in some delightful dream,
> When heav'nly music lull'd her pow'rs to rest,
> And only love lay waking in her breast:
> When virtue's self descended from the sky,
> To paint Elysium on her closing eye,
> To prompt with visions the romantic maid,
> On beds of lilies languishingly laid.

In conclusion he hints that, in a spoony sort of heaven, he would enjoy a little "friendship in death" with the fair one to whom his poem is addressed.

impresses one as the work of a young man. My conjecture is that he wrote little after taking orders, but was led by the vanity or the penury of old age to publish a collection of the verse which he had written chiefly in much earlier years.

[46] *To Mr. Thomson, On His Seasons.* Thomson repaid this staggering compliment by hailing Delacour as the pride of Hibernia in *To Mr. James Delacour, on his Prospect of Poetry.*

[47] *On the Prospect of Poetry.* For Delany, *vide supra,* p. 379.

The Reverend James Delacour likes to cock his eye at a fine painting, but religious pictures do not give him religious feelings. He writes *To Mr. Weaver, Portrait-painter from Bath on his exquisite Madona* [*sic*]:

> This pensive posture see, spectators call
> To view devotion fervent, warm, to all;
> A Titian's manner, join'd to Lely's art,
> Maratti's style, with hand upon her heart:
> There Contemplation speaks in thought profound,
> With flaxen hair, her eyes upon the ground,
> Which seems to say in meditation mute,
> Praxiteles with Weaver can't dispute!
>
> .   .   .   .
>
> Where modesty is painted in the face,
> A matron's meekness, and religion's grace:
> Those lips discourse, as elegance might say,
> And oh how soft, how rubicund they pray!

By some miracle of grace Delacour may have become a worthy priest. Considering him as a poet, however, one must say that a weak emotionalism supplants religion in his work even when he deals with subjects of spiritual import.

> A Churchman and Dissenter
> Had once an odd adventure,
> And grew exceeding hot.
> They made a mighty pother
> And railed at one another
> About they knew not what.
>
> But when they came to cooling,
> And leave off party fooling,
> They found they'd been to blame;
> Like Christian and like brother
> They look'd at one another,
> For each man meant the same.[48]

Thus easily does Henry Carey (1687?-1743)[49] brush aside theological cobwebs. He belonged to the Whig group that frequented Button's Coffee

[48] *The Union of Parties.*

[49] Since his *Poems on Several Occasions* first appeared in 1713, Carey might have received treatment in Part I. But this slender volume, published when he was a very young man, contains few of his best and most characteristic poems; and it seemed desirable to assign the author of *Chrononhotonthologos* (1734) and *The Dragon of Wantley* (1737) to the 1720-1740 period.

House, but like some other members of his party he assumes a bland indifference toward political disputes:

> If my friend be an honest lad
> I never ask his religion:
> Distinctions make us all mad,
> And ought to be had in derision;
> They Christen us Tories and Whigs,
> When the best of 'em both is an evil.
> But we'll be no party prigs;
> Let such godfathers go to the devil.[50]

Some will admire as broadly sensible this distaste for ecclesiastical and political "distinctions"; others will find in it a sentimental impulse to assert that vitally different viewpoints "mean the same." I incline to the latter interpretation. In any case this amiable, careless, innocently Bohemian man of song had no liking for harsh analysis. His ideal may be symbolized by the band of jolly fellows who, forgetting all their differences, touch glasses and sing:

> Then let us drink, and never shrink,
> For I'll tell you the reason why.
> 'Tis a great sin to leave a house
> Till we've drunk the cellar dry.[51]

In the memoir prefixed to his edition of Carey's poems, Mr. Frederick T. Wood casts no light on the poet's religious opinions. Probably there was little to be told. It is plain, however, that Carey's desire to like everything and everybody did not extend to the followers of Wesley: *The Methodist Parson* is an early example of a satirical type which later becomes very common:

> What signifies learning and going to school,
> When the rabble's so ready to follow a fool?
> A fool did I say? No, his pardon I crave;
> He cannot be a fool, but he may be a knave.

These canting preachers, he sneers, are merely out for money;

> But let them alone, and they'll dwindle away,
> As they rose of themselves, of themselves they'll decay;
> At first they astonish, at last they're a joke,
> For they burst forth in flames, and they vanish in smoke.

Carey is an excellent song-writer, but a poor prophet.

[50] *A Ballad on the Times.* See also *Carey's Wish.*   [51] *A Bacchanalian's Song.*

Nowhere, however, do Carey's poems betray an anti-religious or libertine outlook. Though sometimes a trifle broad, he is never seriously offensive. On occasion he can even step forth as a "divine" poet, for his verse includes a few conventionally pious hymns and epitaphs. His fondness for nature is tinged with some religious feeling in *A Pastoral Eclogue on the Divine Power of God,* which was "Spoken by two Young Ladies in the Habits of Shepherdesses, at an Entertainment Performed at Mrs. Carey's School by Several of her Scholars." Seraphina and Dodona praise God in such lines as:

> That sacred pow'r whose boundless essence rolls
> Far, far above the skies, as far beyond the poles,
> He gives a verdant tincture to the fields,
> And all these various dyes which nature yields:
> He fills the bank with violets, and bestows
> A fragrant odour to the blushing rose:
> By Him our tender lambs are taught to bleat;
> He gives the motion to their nimble feet.

Himself an accomplished musician, he is reminded of celestial harmonies by the strains of Handel:

> For when, absorb'd in elemental flame,
> This world shall vanish, musick shall exist.
> Then thy sweet strains, to native skies returning,
> Shall breathe in songs of seraphims and angels,
> Commixt and lost in harmony eternal,
> That fills all Heaven.[52]

Like many other men of his type, Carey is sometimes a champion of good morals. Perhaps he knows from unhappy experience *The Effects of Gaming:*

> A curse on cards, a curse on dice,
> A curse on gaming, wretched vice!
> It wastes our time, it wastes our wealth,
> And is the modish way of stealth.

Less disinterested, one imagines, is *A Satire on the Luxury and Effeminacy of the Age,* for it chiefly attacks that Italian opera which was so inimical to his own livelihood:

---

[52] *The Laurel Grove, or The Poet's Tribute to Musick and Merit, and First to Mr. George Frederick Handel.*

> When words instruct and music cheers the mind,
> Then is the art of service to mankind;
> But when a castrate wretch of monstrous size
> Squeaks out a treble, shrill as infant's cries,
> I curse the unintelligible ass,
> Who may, for aught I know, be singing Mass.[53]

Here a surprising amount of sexual, national, religious, and professional prejudice is compressed into six lines.

One can hardly describe as "pre-romantic" this writer of light satirical squibs, songs, cantatas, ballad operas, and dramatic burlesques. His lyricism, however, is not without historical significance. His songs are true songs, for they possess great variety of rhythm and stanza form, are genuinely popular in atmosphere, and though usually gay and trivial sometimes display a playful tenderness or even a deeper sort of feeling. His frequent praise of the country and of rustic artlessness is not wholly a pastoral pose; his affection for simple city folk like *The Happy Butchers' Wives* and *Sally Sweatbread,* though whimsical, is strong and true. One remembers that his sportive father was a gentleman but that his nameless mother was probably not a lady. He refers to his famous *Ballad of Sally in Our Alley* as "this little sketch of nature." At least three times he uses the retirement theme.[54]

But this was not enough romanticism to support a man whose Christianity was nebulous and who had found no other rock that was higher than he. When his daughter Rachel died he was struck to the heart:

> Oh! lead me where my darling lies,
>   Cold as the marble stone;
> I will recall her with my cries,
>   And wake her with my moan.

But she cannot rise from her "bed of clay."

> Since then, my love, my heart's delight,
>   Thou can'st not come to me,
> Rather than want thy pleasing sight
>   I'll dig my way to thee.[55]

---

[53] See also the more amusing but less printable *Sorrowful Lamentation for the Loss of A Man and No Man,* a gibe at Senesino.
[54] *The Retirement, Mrs. Stuart's Retirement, The Happy Rustics.*
[55] *The Distress'd Father, or The Author's Tears Over His Dear Daughter Rachel.*

At this time his despair found no vent in action; but later, on the day when his infant son Charles died, the merry author of *Namby-Pamby* hanged himself.[56]

Almost the antithesis of Carey is Moses Browne (1704-1787), a man of conventional but slightly sentimentalized piety whose later career merges with the Evangelical Movement. The son of a pen-cutter, he owed his modest place in the literary world to the friendship of Edward Cave. For some years he was the star contributor of verse to the *Gentleman's Magazine* and bore away several of its cash prizes. Encouraged by James Hervey he took orders and became curate to the noted evangelical in 1753. Later Lord Dartmouth, of whom Cowper said with amazement that he "wears a coronet, and prays," presented him to the now famous living of Olney. He became non-resident in 1763 because, as the father of thirteen children, he needed the additional funds provided by the chaplaincy of Morden College. John Newton acted as his curate at Olney during his absence. Browne published several sermons and a translation of Zimmermann's *The Excellency of the Knowledge of Jesus Christ,* which went through three editions. In politics he was a pro-Walpole Whig.

The pre-romantic traits discernible in Browne's poems may be listed as follows: admiration for Milton, with frequent use of Miltonic blank verse and one attempt to imitate Lycidas; [57] familiarity with Spenser, Donne, Herbert, and Izaak Walton; [58] admiration for Thomson; close and affectionate observation of external nature; desire for rural retreat; humanitarianism; a serious view of love; graveyardism and spookery; fondness for old castles which inspire pensive melancholy. But these are mere flecks of ore painfully extracted from large heaps of slag which in general are far from romantic. The only deposit of any richness is *Piscatory Eclogues*. Published in 1729 when the author was only twenty-five, this ichthyeutic is not without glimmerings of imagination. But as Browne grew older the hand of dullness let the curtain fall, and his slight preromantic hankerings almost wholly disappeared.

---

[56] In his memoir Mr. F. T. Wood supposes that the only possible explanation of the death of father and child on the same day is that Carey went mad, killed his son, and then committed suicide; but surely it is quite as probable that he found the child dead and killed himself in his grief, as he had been tempted to do on Rachel's death.

[57] *Renock's Despair,* No. V of *Piscatory Eclogues.*

[58] Besides repeatedly referring to Walton in *Piscatory Eclogues,* he edited *The Compleat Angler* with notes in 1750.

This sketch of Browne is based on *Poems on Various Subjects*, printed for him by Cave in 1739, fourteen years before he took orders.[59] Even in this volume, however, the future curate of James Hervey is plainly revealed. In his preface he particularly recommends to the reader's attention the section of "Poems Moral and Divine." Although such themes are sadly neglected by English poets, "we have yet...a Spencer, and Herbert, a Milton, and Waller; and those present living ornaments, our Pope, our Young, and Watts to boast. It is with pleasure too that I can here remember the late resolves of the great and good Mr. Addison, which were, to have devoted the last remains of his useful life in applications to religious poetry. Happy should I be in a reward more satisfying than the brightest fame, might I be successful, in any small degree, to rescue the age from its present degenerate taste, to preserve them from being poisoned by the many favourite Authors of the Unclean, the Infidel, and factious class, and to excite in prejudiced minds a relish to innocent entertainment, and works purely intended for the improvement of sobriety, reason, and virtue."

He provides his antidote for the poisons of the age in such poems as *The Consumate State of Man* (on the "Four Last Things"); *The Christian Hero; The Divine Attributes; Melancholy Thoughts Under a Pressing Affliction* (the death of a child); *The Power and Presence of God; Verses on the Death of a dear and most lov'd Wife; Trust in a Redeemer, A Divine Dialogue* (between Christ and a Penitent); *Renovation, a Hymn;* and *To the Rev. Dr. William Harris, occasion'd by his excellent Sermons, entitled Funeral Discourses.* But my reader has already suffered so much that I shrink from adding to his burdens a detailed account of Browne's divine poems. Suffice it to say that in their emphasis on personal redemption through the sacrifice of the Cross they strike an evangelical note at a time when the Evangelical Movement had hardly begun to stir. This fact, however, does not imply that Browne is a genuine pioneer: he is merely one of several links between men like Watts and men like Hervey. Although Browne has evangelical opinions, he seems to lack evangelical feelings. His religious poems are dull, heavy, cold, and clumsy.

Some attention, however, must be devoted to Browne's *Essay on the Universe*. It first appeared in the 1739 volume, but in his dedication to the

---

[59] He seldom wrote verse after 1739, but in 1749 he published *Sunday Thoughts, a Poem* and in 1756 a loco-descriptive piece entitled *Percy Lodge.*

generous, pious, and pre-romantic Countess of Hertford the author says that he has worked on it fitfully for ten years. His purpose is to give mankind "an easy, and at the same time magnificent, conception of the amazing *Theory of the Universe,* improveable to a virtuous and religious end. The best and wisest use of philosophy is to direct it to such attainable purposes, in preparing the mind with raised and enlarged apprehensions of the great and wonderful Creator: When it does this, it is a rational and noble entertainment.... Nature, or Creation, is the Book of God, a kind of other written Revelation."

Thus the *Essay* is a definitely Christian physico-theological poem quite without any Neo-Platonic or Shaftesburyian talk about universal harmony. Browne's spirit is like that of Blackmore in *Creation,* for he uses the argument from design to abash those unbelievers who,

> ...mad with pride, and slaves to pagan night,
> Attempt to cloud the heavenly Christian light,
> Affect dark systems of the sceptic schools,
> And sit degraded in the form of fools.

On peering through the microscope we are moved to exclaim:

> What kingdoms of the numerous insect kind
> On one small leaf commodious dwelling find!
> Perhaps on this mean spot the little powers
> View rivers, hills, and fields—a world like ours.

When we gaze at the heavens through the telescope, again we behold a revelation of the divine plan. The great astronomers have explained the mainspring of the system:

> Sagacious Kepler, still advancing, saw
> Th' elliptic motion, nature's plainest law,
> That universal acts thro' every part:
> This laid the basis of Newtonian art.
> Newton! vast mind! whose piercing pow'rs apply'd
> The secret cause of motion first descry'd;
> Found *Gravitation* was the primal spring,
> That wheel'd the planets round their central King;
> Mysterious impulse! that more clear to know
> Exceeds the finite reach of art below.

Browne's footnotes show that he has read a good deal of scientific literature—so much, indeed, that his knowledge sometimes makes it difficult for him to reconcile the God of Nature with the God of Scripture. To how much of the universe, for example, does *Genesis* apply? Were the other planetary systems

> Form'd when the world at first existence gain'd?
> And to one final period all ordain'd?
> Or, since wide space they independent fill,
> Apart created, and creating still?
> Do scriptures clear, the aw'd assent oppose?
> They chiefly *our* original disclose.
> Do they assert, ere we in being came,
> God ne'er was own'd by the Creator's name?
> Where then were Angels, elder race to man?
> Who fell seduc'd, perhaps, ere he began:
> Do they assert prolific pow'r at rest
> Shall in no future instance shine confest?

Browne adds in a note that "The more judicious have thought the Creation recorded by Moses, principally, was confined in its view to the several productions we observe in our visible and solar system."

But by Browne's day the belief that the planets of our own and of other solar systems were inhabited had become a familiar corollary of the doctrine of the plurality of worlds, and it was not regarded as hostile to Christian orthodoxy.[60] In such a poem as the *Essay,* however, the idea that the divine creative fecundity may even now be in operation provides an interesting hint that the uniformitarian view of the universe is giving place to a diversitarian view.[61] Such ideas do not trouble the poet's faith: he concludes with a "Hymn of Praise" to the God who is both the redeemer of man and the artificer of the Newtonian system:

> Hail, infinite Creator! with thy praise
> The Muse began, with Thee shall end my lays.
> These are thy works, blest architect divine!
> This earth, and all this beauteous offspring thine.
> Thy breath first bid inactive matter move,
> And strait with life the genial atoms strove,
> Producing animal, and plant, and flow'r,
> Concurrent proof of wisdom and of pow'r.

With Browne's *Essay* may be grouped *The Beauties of the Universe, A Poem. By a Gentleman of the Navy* (1732). The initials "R. G." ap-

---

[60] See A. O. Lovejoy, *The Great Chain of Being,* pp. 124-135 *passim.*

[61] The importance of this change is fully discussed in the closing chapters of Lovejoy's work.

pended to the dedication are those of Robert Gambol.[62] According to his preface he was inspired to attempt this task by an "essay" on the same subject by Henry Needler, "an ingenious Gentleman of my Acquaintance, who died some Years ago."[63] But the more striking qualities of Needler's work—his Neo-Platonism and his emotional view of geometry and natural science—are quite absent from Gambol's *Beauties*. His poem is in the conventionally Newtonian tradition of Derham's *Physico-Theology*.

Gambol desires to prove that nothing in nature can be the result of chance. For him "beauty" means teleological design—not Shaftesbury's universal harmony but, as footnote-references to Scripture attest, the providential ingenuity of the Christian God. He has much less technical knowledge than Moses Browne, and seems to care little about natural science except as a general buttress for his edifying theme. In his notes he occasionally refers to popular scientific works, but the poem itself is vaguely rhetorical. Few passages are so specific as the following:

> If with the microscope you aid the eye,
> Worlds within worlds, in miniature you'll spy;
>
> .   .   .   .
>
> Drop on thy glass one speck of quick'ning spawn,
> While scaly broods of life are in the dawn,
> You'll find a flood, and fish in wanton play,
> More faintly moving as it dries away!
> Who thus will the all-wise Creator trace,
> The works of wisdom never can disgrace.

The thesis that Gambol is a sentimentalist must not be urged too warmly. One can, however, distinguish him from the completely non-sentimental Christian Newtonians of the preceding chapter by his tendency to blur, soften, and prettify the harsh outlines of his scientific material. As a means of confuting the unbeliever he prefers the beauty of women to the intricacies of the digestive system:

> Her form how beauteous! what Angelic Grace
> Dwells in each Feature of her lovely Face!
>
> .   .   .   .

[62] Not in *D.N.B.*

[63] For all one can tell, the "essay" might have been Needler's prose treatise *On the Beauty of the Universe* or his *Poem in blank verse, proving the Being of God from the Works of Creation*. Needler was a clerk in the Navy Office, and Gambol was "a Gentleman of the Navy"—which may mean that he held a similar post.

Who streak'd her Breast with azure Veins, or bid
The Channels open to a crimson Tide?
Who form'd the Streams that nourish her fair Fruit
With gradual Growth from Principles minute?
Say, Atheist, say, who did this Piece design,
Or made the Fair one in such lustre shine,
That you, ev'n you, who nought beside adore,
Yet here confess the Maker's gracious Pow'r.

The following lines, too, are not exactly rich in intellectual austerity:

Who paints the orange with that lovely hue,
Yellows the lemon, dyes the plum with blue,
Reddens the cherry, and the apple streaks,
And gives those blushes to the peach's cheeks?
Sure none but He, who kindly hath decreed,
While he supplies to humankind the need,
Their food shall be as pleasing to the sight,
As it is grateful to the appetite.

This very tender teleology is quite in the vein of Saint-Pierre's *Études de la Nature*.

Unlike the more orthodox Browne and Gambol, the anonymous author of *Order, a Poem* has been impressed by Shaftesbury's analogy between aesthetic and ethical harmony.[64] "To follow Nature," he declares, "is to follow God," for nature is the universe as regulated by the divine decree, " 'Thro' all my Works be Order's Laws obey'd.' " Without many technical details, the poet displays the rule of order in the sun, moon, stars, and finally in the earth. Here, however, there is one tragic exception in that

... Man, sole Rebel of this nether World,
From this to that Extravagancy hurl'd,
From Order's flow'ry Path perversely strays,
And wanders on in Error's fatal Maze;
And spite of Nature, and in Reason's spite,
Pursues wrong Measures, conscious of the Right.

This departure from the ordered norm of nature is the source of all human ills.

But like so many of his contemporaries, this writer is a primitivist who

---

[64] For a discussion of this theme see M. F. Libby, "The Influence of the Idea of Esthetic Proportion upon Shaftesbury's Ethics," *American Journal of Psychology*, XII, 458-491.

believes in progress.[65] The passage just quoted would seem to imply a stage in human history when man was the obedient child of Order: he can hardly have been created a rebel. We learn, however, that "our rustick Fathers" were

> A lawless, cruel, and ignoble Crowd.
> Charm'd by no Reason, by no Law confin'd,
> Nor Truth nor Beauty moved their savage Mind.

> . . . . .

> But Order rose, the beauteous Child of Jove,
> Parent of Pleasure, Harmony and Love;
> Smiling she rose, and Discord took its Flight,
> The Savages grow mild, the Rude polite.

The results—all of them regarded with warm approval—are peace, plenty, laws, marriage, social ties, cities, states, patriotism, arts and sciences, navigation and commerce, sculpture, painting, and architecture—of which the pinnacle is Castle Howard, seat of the Earl of Carlisle, to whom the poem is dedicated.

Unruffled by the fact that man has both fallen and risen, the author sweeps on to a stoical-sounding conclusion:

> Restrain thy Passions, call thy Reason in,
> And quell the fierce exulting Foe within;
> To Order's Standard be thy Acts confin'd,
> Let Order rule the Sallies of thy Mind:
> With prudent Care thy lesser World command,
> As moves the greater by th' Almighty's Hand:
> As shifts no Star, but by his Sov'reign Sway,
> So follow thou, as Order points the Way;
> From this Foundation sure to climb to Bliss,
> For none can err who strictly move by This;
> A Truth the Laws of Nature still proclaim,
> For Happiness and Order are the same.

In this poem God is actually little more than a personification of that order of which He is theoretically the creator. The author, to be sure, is more responsive to the non-sentimental side of Shaftesbury's ethics than most of his contemporaries who dealt with similar themes. His strong emphasis on measure and restraint makes it impossible to regard him as

[65] A paradox fully treated in Lois B. Whitney, *Primitivism and the Idea of Progress in English Popular Literature of the Eighteenth Century.*

a champion of mere expansiveness. At bottom, however, his system of "Sweet Symmetry," of "Pleasure, Harmony, and Love," is a much softer thing than the ascetic rationalism which he tries to deduce from it.

From these "universe-poems" we turn to George Lyttelton, first Baron Lyttelton (1709-1773). The statement that he became more orthodox and less sentimental with advancing years need not imply that he was at any time either wildly romantic or ardently pious. During the 1720-1740 period he seems to have regarded formal creeds with cool aristocratic in-difference but without eagerness to "écraser l'infâme." Free from any tinge of libertine mockery, his verse rather often appeals from the Church to what he imagines to be a loftier moral standard:

> To error mild, to vice alone severe,
> Seek not to spread the law of love by fear.
> The priest, who plagues the world, can never mend.
> No foe to man was e'er to God a friend:
> Let reason and let virtue truth maintain,
> All force but theirs is impious, weak, and vain.[66]

As we should expect of a supporter of the Prince of Wales, Lyttelton's favorite virtue is patriotism. From love of country, however, his ideals readily expand to a more general love of mankind:

> Happy is He, and He alone, who knows
> His Heart's uneasy discord to compose;
> In gen'rous love of others' good to find
> The sweetest pleasures of the social mind;
> To bound his wishes in their proper sphere,
> To nourish pleasing hope, and conquer anxious fear:
> This was the wisdom ancient sages taught,
> This was the sov'reign good they justly sought;
> This to no place or climate is confin'd,
> But the free native produce of the mind.

These lines, somewhat incongruously addressed To my Lord Hervey, combine the stoicism of "ancient sages" with a more sentimental view of the joys of benevolence. Herein they are characteristic of "the good Lord Lyttelton." Both in his life and in his writings he retained much of the balanced, unenthusiastic Augustan spirit; but he was also in some degree a Man of Feeling. Though an important figure in political affairs,

[66] To the Reverend Dr. Ayscough.

he never ceased to be an unworldly, absent-minded, and awkward benevolist. Sharp-witted people like Hervey, Chesterfield, Horace Walpole and Smollett were inclined to sneer at him; but Thomson was his protégé, Joseph Warton his domestic chaplain, and Glover, James Hammond, and Shenstone his close friends.

In his poems, though not strikingly pre-romantic, Lyttelton is hardly an orthodox neoclassicist. *Blenheim* is written in Miltonic blank verse and includes a reverent tribute to Chaucer. His conception of love is unusually earnest and idealistic. He likes external nature, and has some ability to describe it.[67] In the familiar *Monody* his memories of his dead wife are closely associated with the scenes amidst which she moved:

> O shades of Hagley, where is now your boast?
>   Your bright inhabitant is lost.
> You she prefer'd to all the gay resorts
> Where female vanity might wish to shine,
> The pomp of cities, and the pride of courts.
> Her modest beauties shun'd the public eye:
>   To your sequester'd dales
>   And flow'r-embroider'd vales
> From an admiring world she chose to fly;
> With Nature there retir'd, and Nature's God,
>   The silent paths of wisdom trod,
> And banish'd every passion from her breast,
>   But those, the gentlest and the best,
> Whose holy flames with energy divine
> The virtuous heart enliven and improve,
> The conjugal, and maternal love.

Lyttelton himself seems not to have been an ardent worshipper of "Nature's God," but he highly values the sort of retirement which crowns a career of public service:

> Not him I praise, who from the world retir'd,
> By no enlivening generous passion fir'd,
> On flow'ry couches slumbers life away,
> And gently bids his active pow'rs decay;
> Who fears bright Glory's awful face to see,
> And shuns renown as much as infamy.
> But blest is he, who, exercis'd in cares,
> To private leisure public virtue bears;

[67] For evidence on these points see *Blenheim, The Progress of Love,* and *A Monody.*

Who tranquil ends the race he nobly run,
And decks repose with trophies Labour won.[68]

But when his beloved wife died in 1747, Lyttelton found small comfort in reason, virtue, patriotism, and benevolence. Perhaps a longing for more powerful aid influenced the feelings with which, in the same year, he read Gilbert West's *Observations on the Resurrection.* But in her dissertation on *The Good Lord Lyttelton,* Miss Rose Mary Davis has upset the tradition that he was converted by West's treatise. For several years he had been carrying on a friendly correspondence with Philip Doddridge, the eminent nonconformist divine; he had been turning more and more toward Christian orthodoxy; his own *Observations on the Conversion and Apostleship of St. Paul,* though published four months after his wife's death, was written the year before that event.

No doubt, however, his personal tragedy made Lyttelton's religious feelings deeper and more urgent. For the remainder of his life he was a sensible, sober, mildly evangelical Christian. He persuaded himself that his treatise on St. Paul had converted Thomson, and after the poet's death he set about preparing an edition of his friend's poems in which every unorthodox passage was to be revised or deleted. Patrick Murdoch, the "little, round, fat, oily, man of God," had the honesty and good taste to dissuade his lordship from carrying out this plan.[69]

The piety of Lyttelton's later years, however, is not reflected in his verse: he ceased to be a poet and began to be a Christian almost simultaneously. The fact is not much to be lamented, for to judge from the treatise on St. Paul his religion was not of the poetically inspiring sort.

Pope's translation of the *Odyssey* has preserved the name of William Broome (1689-1745) [70] with that of Elijah Fenton. Broome was the son of a poor Cheshire farmer, but through his own industry and the kindness of others he obtained a good education at Eton and Cambridge and became a sound Greek scholar. As a clergyman he achieved ease rather than eminence. He held very comfortable livings, married a rich widow, and lived well to the end of his days.

[68] *To Mr. Poyntz.*

[69] Léon Morel, *James Thomson: sa vie et ses œuvres,* pp. 156-157, 181-182.

[70] He was writing verse at least as early as 1710 and ceased to be productive after 1728, when his quarrel with Pope deprived him of his chief inspiration and source of criticism. Most of his poems, however, group themselves about the beginning of the 1720-1740 period.

His smooth, correct, rather elegant verses are slightly above the average level of accomplishment for his period.[71] At first glance they seem better than they really are: on further acquaintance one sees that most of them are clever imitations—usually of Pope, fairly often of Waller and Prior, sometimes of Butler. From such models his work derives an aristocratic tone, though his natural temperament is middle-classical.

Divine poetry composes only a small proportion of this clergyman's writings. Of his original religious poems—there are two or three paraphrases—the majority brood sombrely upon death. In the *Epistle to ... Fenton,* his treatment of the *memento mori* theme is perhaps more classical than Christian:

> Unhallow'd feet o'er awful Tully tread,
> And Hyde and Plato join the vulgar dead;
> And all the glorious aims that can employ
> The soul of mortals, must with Hanmer die:
> O Compton, when this breath we once resign,
> My dust shall be as eloquent as thine.

More in the mood of Edward Young is *A Poem on Death,* where a vision of the horrors of dissolution is interrupted by an angel who observes that, considering the ills of mortal life, death is a great blessing.

Broome thinks of death even when congratulating a handsome little boy on his third birthday:

> Pass a few days and all those beauties fly!
> Pass a few years, and thou alas! shalt die! [72]

The same edifying but unattractive habit appears in his lines *To Belinda, On her Sickness, and Recovery:*

> Brighter from her disease she shines,
> As fire the precious gold refines.
> Thus when the silent grave becomes
> Pregnant with life, as fruitful wombs,
> When the wide seas, and spacious earth,
> Resign us to our second birth;
> Our moulder'd frame rebuilt assumes
> New beauty, and for ever blooms;
> And crown'd with youth's immortal pride,
> We angels rise, who mortals dy'd.

[71] In *To Mr. A. Pope, who corrected my Verses,* Browne implies that Pope gave him a substantial amount of help, but he may be exaggerating his obligation.

[72] *On the Birth-Day of a Gentleman when three Years old.*

It is more pious than gallant to assure a lady, "Madam, you are prettier than ever since your illness, but on the Day of Judgment you will look vastly better." Beneath the elegance of the literary tradition which Broome eagerly adopts, there remains a stratum of lower-class Protestant feeling.

The poet is too devoted an admirer of Pope and Waller to give free play to this tendency. Sometimes, however, he satisfies his submerged emotionalism by dabbling a little in the pre-romantic. *The Complaint* is an imitation of *Eloisa to Abelard* with a slight touch of the eighteenth-century "mad song":

> Gods! what soft words, what sweet delusive wiles
> He boasts! and oh! those dear undoing smiles!
> Pleas'd with our ruin, to his arms we run,
> To be undone by him, who would not be undone?
> Alas! I rave! ye swelling torrents roul
> Your wat'ry tribute o'er my love-sick soul!
> To cool my heart, your waves, ye oceans, bear!
> Oh! vain are all your waves, for love is there!

Although in working on the *Odyssey* Broome showed a remarkable knack at writing Popean couplets, he preferred Miltonic blank verse as a medium for translating Homer, and his poems include two passages from the *Iliad* "In the Stile of Milton." In dedicating *Poems on Several Occasions* to Townshend he quotes Thomson's *Seasons* to illustrate the pleasures which his lordship must be enjoying in his retirement. Broome himself is not an ardent nature-lover, but as early as 1710 he provided a striking exception to this statement in *A Poem On the Seat of War in Flanders, Chiefly with Relation to the Sieges: With the Praise of Peace and Retirement.* The first part is a battle-piece like Addison's *Campaign,* but the second part shifts to country contentment, vegetarianism, and mildly melancholy contemplation:

> Here grant me, Heav'n, to end my peaceful days,
> And steal myself from life by slow decays;
> Draw health from food the temp'rate garden yields,
> From fruit, or herb, the bounty of the fields;
> Nor let the loaded table groan beneath
> Slain animals, the horrid feast of death:
> With age unknown to pain or sorrow blest,
> To the dark grave retiring as to rest;

Ye gloomy grots! ye awful solemn cells,
Where holy thoughtful Contemplation dwells,
Guard me from splendid cares and tiresome state,
That pompous misery of being great!

. . . . .

Come thou chaste maid, here let me ever stray,
While the calm hours steal unperceiv'd away.

For such a poem 1710 is an early date. Perhaps Broome's subservience to
Pope, which at this time had not yet begun, later checked the development of the sentimentalism which here plainly suggests itself.

However this may be, only one other poem of Broome's has equal
interest for the student of pre-romantic trends. *Melancholy, an Ode* was
occasioned by the death of his five-year-old daughter in 1723. Without a
word of religious sorrow or hope, the bereaved priest banishes Mirth and
invokes Melancholy:

Adieu vain Mirth, and noisy joys!
Ye gay desires, deluding toys!
Thou thoughtful Melancholy deign
To hide me in thy pensive train!

. . . .

Come, blissful Mourner, wisely sad,
In sorrow's garb, in sable clad,
Henceforth, thou care, my hours employ!
Sorrow, be thou henceforth my joy!

. . . .

By tombs where sullen spirits stalk,
Familiar with the dead I walk;
While to my sighs and groans by turns,
From graves the midnight echo mourns.

Open thy marble jaws, O Tomb!
Thou Earth conceal me in thy Womb!
And you, ye Worms, this Frame confound,
Ye Brother Reptiles of the Ground.

O life, frail offspring of a day!
'Tis puff'd with one short gasp away!
Swift as the short-liv'd flow'r it flies,
It springs, it blooms, it fades, it dies.

. . . .

> Come then, O friend of virtuous woe,
> With solemn pace, demure, and slow:
> Lo! sad and serious, I pursue
> Thy steps—adieu, vain world, adieu!

In these stanzas the sombre piety which was noted elsewhere in Broome has become secular, literary, and sentimental. It would be unfair to say that he saw in Anne's death only an opportunity for aping *Il Penseroso:* an imitative writer may be compelled to express his most genuine feelings in an imitative form. Nevertheless the poem leaves us with a slightly horrified wonder.

The poems of John Whaley (d. 1745),[73] though harmless enough, are decidedly of this world. He sets up as a polite wit whose favorite model is Prior. Barring a few Scripture-paraphrases none of his work is "divine," and *A Thought on Gaming* is one of a very few pieces of moral didacticism.

This poet, however, has a softer side which does not exclude a dubious kind of piety. Like James Delacour,[74] Whaley fancies himself as a connoisseur of art. *An Essay on Painting* and *A Journey to Houghton, the Seat of the Right Hon. Robert Walpole* would be of much interest to a student of eighteenth-century aesthetics. About half of the latter poem consists of a description of Walpole's pictures, many of which are of course religious. Whaley pauses before Rubens' "Mary Magdalene Anointing the Feet of Christ":

> See! the proud Rabbins at the sumptuous Board,
> Frown on the Wretch who kneels before her Lord,
> And the rich Unguent, in Devotion meet,
> Pours, mixt with Tears, on her Redeemer's Feet;
> In vain with Hypocritic Rage they glow,
> While Mercy smooths the Heav'nly Stranger's Brow;
> He the true Penitent with Ease descries,
> Sees the Heart speaking in the melting Eyes,
> Bids ev'ry Tear with full Effect to stream,
> And from his Vengeance all her Sins redeem.

---

[73] *D.N.B.* devotes no separate article to Whaley, but gives a few facts about him in the article on his friend Sneyd Davies. He was the private tutor of Horace Walpole, a fellow of King's College, Cambridge, and a lover of the bottle.

[74] *Vide supra,* p. 385.

Whaley's response to the work is only a trifle more spiritual than Delacour's would have been; but "the Heart speaking in the melting Eyes" of a fine woman appeals to his sensibility and the rage of the Pharisees tickles his latitudinarianism. When he passes on to Parmegiano's "Christ Laid in the Sepulchre" he is the true critic:

> What striking Attitudes! what strong Relief!
> We see, we wonder at, we feel the Grief.

Whaley, who can praise Tillotson, Pope, and Parnell as great moral teachers,[75] would have found excessive "enthusiasm" in the devotion which originally inspired such paintings. Charles I, rendered by Van Dyck, is dismissed with charity:

> Peace to his Soul! howe'er 'gainst Right he fought,
> Be in his dreadful Doom his Sin forgot.

But there can be no forgiveness for

> Laud and the Queen, whose fatal conduct shew,
> What bigot Zeal, and headstrong Pride cou'd do.

Kneller's portrait of William III, on the other hand, must bring joy to every Protestant and patriot. Observe the hero's

> ... fierce determin'd Eye,
> Freedom to save, or in her Cause to die;
> As when on Boyne's important Banks he stood,
> And, as his deeds surpriz'd the swelling Flood,
> All torn and mangled false Religion fled,
> And crush'd Oppression snarl'd beneath his Tread.

Worldly Cambridge don, admirer of Walpole, latitudinarian Whig— the type, as we have seen before, is subject to sentimentalism. Whaley's is a mild case, but the virus is at work in him. In *An Epistle to——, Written by Moon-Light,* the scene suggests thoughts of heaven blended with vague forebodings of his sweetheart's death. He hopes he may die first, for life without her would be insupportable. This jumble of love, death, heaven, and moonshine reveals him at his tenderest.

Whaley occasionally shows a fondness for "simple" nature. In the *Essay on Painting,* to be sure, he lauds the Renaissance masters because in dissipating the "Cimmerian night" of the Gothic age they

[75] *To a Lady with Parnell's Poems.*

> Preserv'd each Charm that careless Nature taught,
> And banish'd from their Breast her ev'ry Fault.

Nevertheless he insists that craftsmanship is worthless without genius:

> 'Tis Nature in the Breast implants the Ray,
> Art only feeds, and wakes it into Day.

The work of Correggio shows

> How far the Force of Nature cou'd prevail.

.   .   .   .

> Untutor'd Beauties fill'd his happy Heart,
> His Breast the only Source of all his Art.

Similarly in *Kew Gardens* he is pleased when, looking beyond "the nice Path, and regulated Shade," he glimpses the untrimmed fields in the distance:

> Delighted erst we prais'd the force of Art,
> But Nature's stronger Charms now vanquish all our Heart.

Not content with disliking geometrical flower-beds, he dislikes geometry itself. For a fellow of Cambridge, these *Verses Wrote Extempore in the first Leaf of Euclid's Elements* are treasonable:

> Let Souls that in a lower Circle move,
> What they affirm with nice Exactness prove;
> What plodding Euclid says let others hear,
> The Soul Poetick knows a higher Sphere.

.   .   .   .

> I envy not the Man whose skill can show,
> If conically true the Firr-Trees grow;
> Who from a gay Parterre no Joy receives,
> But what the Box in Angles rising gives:
> Who looks on Paint with geometrick Eyes,
> And nought, but well-rang'd Perspective, can prize.

Whaley's work does not indicate that his "Soul Poetick" was at home in very lofty regions, but as an imitator of Prior who weakly hankers to be something quite different he is a good clinical specimen.

Like his friend Whaley, Sneyd Davies (1709-1769) was a fellow of King's College, Cambridge, a stoutly Protestant Whig, a foe of enthusiasm, and an admirer of Walpole.[76] His verse presents much the same combination of trivial wit and feeble sentimentalism as Whaley's, but is slightly more poetic, pious, and pre-romantic.

A clergyman and the son of a clergyman, Davies wrote a few Scripture-paraphrases and a few original divine poems. Of the latter *The Nativity*, in Miltonic blank verse, is probably the most successful. He is especially responsive to the gentleness and humility of Jesus, speaking with some scorn of the prophets as

> Fond! to believe his Presence shou'd avail
> Their Spleen and Hebrew Gall; with angry Bolt
> Smiting the blasted Foe.—He gracious came
> With Balm upon his healing Wings; he came
> Not to destroy, but lift the World to Heav'n.
>
> . . . . . .
>
> ...Nor Tokens none
> Of Grandeur: Hymning Angels sung the Tale,
> In Heav'nly Chorus, over Bethlem's Field:
> Sung it to lowly Shepherds, as they lay
> Tending their fleecy Charge: They listen'd glad,
> And from their Hovels drank immortal Strains.

Another blank-verse piece, entitled *A Night Thought,* warns the reader that Time

> To the Thatch'd Hovel, to the Trophied Arch
> Levels alike his undiscerning Scythe;
> And Death, wide-sweeping, no Distinction owes
> To the crown'd Villain. All alike in Hell.
> Caligula and Chartres, seated both
> On burning Couches in the fiery Hall.

These lines, plainly indebted to Young, are traditionally Christian; but the heaven described in the passage immediately following is a curious place

> ...Where brightest in her Robe of Sky
> Sits *Virtue* under Shade of Palm; with look
> Serene, but stern.

The blessed spirits "nearest her Throne" are those of such men as Epaminondas, Marcus Aurelius, Nerva—in short,

[76] For the last three points see *Verses, Wrote on the 2d of February. In Memory of King Henry VI.*

> All the choice Few, Union of Great and Good;
> Poor Epictetus, with his Free-born Soul:
> More's chearful Wisdom, Boyle with study wan,
> Beneficent, and meek; th' Athenian Sage,
> And Indian, in abstruse Discourse sublime
> Of the first Good.

This free mingling of pagans and Christians and the intrusion into heaven of a goddess named "Virtue" suggest that Davies' theology was comfortably broad. In this connection it may be noted that he collaborated with Timothy Thomas in translating the *Essay on Man* into Latin verse.

As the *Rhapsody to Milton* indicates, Davies is an admirer of *Paradise Lost* and a champion of blank verse. An unusually large proportion of his poems employ this form. Another pre-romantic trend must in some degree be represented by *Caractacus,* a poem which I have not seen. *A Voyage to Tinterne Abbey in Monmouthshire from Whitminster in Glocestershire* includes a bit of Gothicism, a bit of nature-description, and a bit of pensive melancholy. Referring to the abbey he says:

> Enter with Reverence her hallow'd Gate,
> And trace the glorious Relicks of her State;
> The meeting Arches, Pillar'd Walks admire,
> Or musing hearken to the silenc'd Choir.
> Encircling Groves diffuse a solemn Grace,
> And dimly fill th' Historic Window's Place;
> While pitying Shrubs on the bare Summit try
> To give the roofless Pile a Canopy.
> Here, O my Friends, along the mossy Dome
> In pleasurable Sadness let me roam.

But Davies' sentimentalism appears more plainly in the conflict between the gospel of inactivity and the gospel of activity. *D.N.B.* observes that this country parson was a simple, unworldly lover of retirement but that he was also extremely lazy. *Vacuna,* a pleasantly whimsical panegyric in honor of the Goddess of Indolence, is not to be taken seriously, but *To the Hon. and Rev.*—— is written in earnest. As a youth, says Davies, he had plenty of ambition until fortune placed him

> Amid the gloomy Scene of Fir and Yew,
> On Poppy Ground, where Morpheus strew'd the Bed:
> Obscurity her Curtain round me drew,
> And Siren Sloth a dull Quietus sung.

Sithence no Fairy Sights, no quick'ning Ray,
Nor stir of Pulse, nor Objects to entice
Abroad the Spirits; but the Cloyster'd Heart
Sits squat at Home, like Pagod in a Nitch
Demure; ...

. . . .

And prating Sanhedrins, and drumming Wars,
Affect no more than Stories told to Bed
Lethargic, which at Intervals the Sick
Hears and forgets, and wakes to doze again.
Instead of Converse and Variety,
The same trite Round, the same stale silent Scene;
Such are thy Comforts, *blessed Solitude.*

To be sure, the life he leads is peaceful and innocent, but that is not
enough:

Meads lowing, Tune of Birds, and Lapse of Streams,
And saunter with a Book and warbling Muse
In Praise of Hawthorns.—Life's whole Business this?
Is it to bask i' th' Sun? If so, a Snail
Were happy crawling on a Southern Wall.

The confluence of Edward Young and Robert Browning is quite startling.

Indolence, in short, is a curse: the happy peasant is happy only because
he works. Davies feels that his correspondent is burdened with his own
darling vice, and urges him to shake it off:

Bestir, and answer your Creation's End.
Think we that Man with Vig'rous Pow'r endow'd,
And room to stretch, was destin'd to sit still?
Sluggards are Nature's Rebels, slight her Laws,

. . . .

Riches and Fame are Industry's Reward.

. . . .

Think of (Reflection's stab!) the pitying Friend,
With Shoulder shrug'd, and sorry. Think that Time
Has golden Minutes, if discreetly seiz'd:
And if some sad Example indolent
To warn and scare be wanting, think of me.[77]

[77] Davies cannot be accused of imitating Thomson's *Castle of Indolence* in this poem. It
appeared in 1745, three years before Thomson expressed the same view of the same problem. It is possible, indeed, that Thomson's second canto owes something to Davies. "Bestir,

For once, a piece of moral advice was acted upon. The recipient of this epistle was Frederic Cornwallis,[78] who, promptly bestirring himself, became Bishop of Lichfield and later Archbishop of Canterbury. As he rose, he dragged his lazy mentor along behind him; for through his favor Davies became successively a chaplain to the king, Master of St. John's Hospital, a prebendary of Lichfield, and Archdeacon of Derby. At Lichfield he cut a figure among the local literati. In early youth, Anna Seward looked up to him as a saint,[79] but this is probably not an example of the unerring intuitiveness of childhood.

Despite the fact that his father was a well-known dissenting minister in Ireland, Samuel Boyse (1708-1749) led a sordid, drunken, sponging, bailiff-dodging life which ended in a pauper's grave. So low did he sink that his wife became a harlot without his opposition and perhaps even with his connivance. He suffered many pangs of remorse, and seemed to have taken a turn toward reformation a few months before his death; but he was drunk when at last he was run over by a coach. "Such," says Alexander Chalmers, "was the life of a man whose writings . . . are uniformly in favor of virtue, remarkable for justness of sentiment on every subject in which the moral character is concerned, and not infrequently for the loftiness and dignity which mark the effusions of a pure and independent mind." [80]

This judgment, though pompously delivered, is true to the facts. Perhaps too many of Boyse's poems were written to get money out of somebody, but on the whole they impress one as the work of a man who had strong religious convictions. The warning given the passer-by in *The Author's Epitaph* was rendered more, not less, sincere by the author's knowledge of his own shortcomings:

> Think as you walk, what treacherous ground you tread!
> The mother-earth, that mixes now with me,
> Next moment may reclaim its share in thee!

. . . . .

and answer your Creation's End" sounds exactly like the Knight of Arts and Industry. *Vide infra,* p. 532.

[78] The fact is established by a MS note in the British Museum copy (11631. d. 60) of Whaley's *A Collection of Original Poems and Translations* (1745), where Davies' poem appears. Cornwallis and Davies had been schoolmates at Eton.

[79] *D.N.B.,* art. "Sneyd Davies."

[80] *The Works of the English Poets,* XIV, 522.

Like bubbles on the stream of time we pass,
Swell, burst, and mingle with the common mass!
Then, oh reflect! ere fate unheeded come,
And snatch this lesson from the vocal tomb!
Known in thy conduct, fix'd upon thy mind,
"The love of God, and welfare of mankind."

The Deity (1739), Boyse's most ambitious and most successful production, stands high among the divine poems of the period. It is a treatise in heroic couplets on the attributes of God, which are listed as Eternity, Unity, Spirituality, Omnipresence, Immutability, Omnipotence, Wisdom, Providence, Goodness, Rectitude, and Glory. As happens in much of the apologetic literature of the age, Boyse often defends religion by means of a non-religious kind of reason. But although the poem is heavy with rationalistic argument and shrill with eagerness to confute the infidel, it is not written merely in cold blood. Boyse feels very deeply the sublimity of his theme. The following attack on atheism will illustrate the interfusion of rhetorical and imaginative elements:

Should we, deceived by Errour's sceptic glass,
Admit the thought absurd—that nothing was!
Thence would this wild, this false conclusion flow,
That nothing rais'd this beauteous all below!
When from disclosing darkness splendour breaks,
Associate atoms move, and matter speaks,
When non-existence bursts its close disguise,
How blind are mortals—not to own the skies!

. . . . .

Could nothing link the universal chain?
No, 'tis impossible, absurd, and vain!

. . . . .

In him from whom existence boundless flows,
Let humble faith its sacred trust repose:
Assur'd on his eternity depend,
"Eternal Father! and eternal Friend!"
Within that mystic circle safety seek,
No time can lessen, and no force can break;
And, lost in adoration, breathe his praise,
High Rock of ages, ancient Sire of days!

Perhaps Young's attempt to combine the spirit of debate and the spirit of song in *Night Thoughts* owed something to Boyse's example.

In establishing the omnipotence of God, Boyse assumes the familiar position that "Reveal'd in nature Nature's Author reigns." The Deity is no less omnipresent than omnipotent, for He is

> ... th' Eternal, all informing Soul,
> Whose sight pervades, whose Knowledge fills the whole.

The immanent God does not cease to be transcendent: Boyse is not a pantheist, but a panentheist:

> In his [God's] wide grasp, and comprehensive eye,
> Immediate worlds on worlds unnumber'd lie:
> Systems enclos'd in his perception roll,
> Whose all-informing mind directs the whole:
> Lodg'd in his grasp, their certain ways they know;
> Plac'd in that sight from whence can nothing go.

The phrase "enclos'd in his perception" reflects Newton's idea that God is everywhere present in space because space may be thought of as God's sensorium.[81]

But despite his emphasis on the natural revelation Boyse well knows that God is beyond nature, beyond science, beyond all human reason:

> By what bright images shall be defin'd
> The mystic nature of th' eternal Mind!
> Or how shall thought the dazzling height explore,
> Where all that reason can—is to adore!
>
> .   .   .   .   .
>
> Him would in vain material semblance feign,
> Or figur'd shrines the boundless God contain;
> Object of faith! he shuns the view of sense,
> Lost in the blaze of sightless excellence!

This feeling of the unknowableness of God clashes with Boyse's confidence in his own ability to describe Him. A little poem entitled *The Only Wish. Fiat Voluntas Tua!* condemns on anti-intellectualistic grounds the whole purpose of the longer work:

> Let others, vainly curious in the schools,
> Judge of their maker;—by their narrow rules
> Thy essence and thy attributes define;
> To love, to serve, to worship thee be mine!

[81] See E. A. Burtt, *The Metaphysical Foundations of Modern Physical Science*, p. 257.

Far from being deistic or even latitudinarian, the thought of *The Deity* is very definitely Christian. Although Goodness, God's "fairest" attribute, is attested by "smiling Nature," it appears most fully in Christ's redemptive sacrifice:

> O strong effect of unexampled love!
> View him descend the heav'nly throne above;
> Patient the ills of mortal life endure,
> Calm, though revil'd, and innocent, though poor!
> Uncertain his abode, and coarse his food,
> His life one fair continued scene of good;
> For us sustain the wrath to man decreed,
> The victim of eternal justice bleed!
> Look! to the cross the Lord of life is tied,
> They pierce his hands, and wound his sacred side;
> See God expires! our forfeit to atone,
> While Nature trembles at his parting groan!

But the God of perfect love is also the God of perfect justice. On Judgment Day men must answer for their sinful use of that supreme blessing, free will, and some must expect an eternity of fiery torment.

Why the religion apparently so firmly grasped by Boyse in mind, heart, and imagination had so little effect upon his life is an unanswerable question. Neither this nor any other faith guided his steps. I include him in this chapter because of a perhaps fallacious opinion that very religious people who behave very irreligiously are liable to be sentimentalists at bottom. His poems do not, however, provide much specific evidence for this view. One of a few exceptions is *Friendship, an Ode,* the conclusion of which is rather soft and messy:

> When all of art and all of nature dies,
>   When the dissolving Sun shall veil his head;
> Friendship, victorious, shall adorn the skies,
>   Shall shine, when all their fading pomp is fled.
>
> Thence wide shall beam, benevolent, her ray
>   To worlds philosophy has never guess'd:
> Gild with diffusive light the realms of day,
>   And yield eternal pleasure to the blest.

Boyse is neither very rich nor wholly lacking in those pre-romantic traits which are commonly regarded as outward signs of the sentimental spirit. *Retirement, The Triumphs of Nature,* and *Nature* are loco-descriptive pieces, all—rather suspiciously—addressed to noblemen at whose country seats he has been, or would like to be, entertained. *Nature* has some fairly vivid descriptive touches, but on the whole he is not much inclined to look at things with his own eyes. Nevertheless he expresses enthusiasm for scenes

> Where nothing nice or regular has part,
> But all is nature, undisguis'd with art;

and he has mastered the stock phrases of the retirement theme:

> Nature, thou pow'r divinely fair and young,
> Like the Great Being from whose word thou sprung!
> Unwearied still, the blessings I explore,
> Which o'er the earth thy hands incessant pour:
> And while I view thy works with fond delight,
> Wealth and ambition vanish from my sight.[82]

In his epistle *To ... Lord Kinnaird* he decries the cruelty of hunting and even of fishing, and yearns for a return of that Golden Age when bloodshed was unknown and

> ... through the happy grove, serene and mild,
> Man walk'd with man,—and all creation smil'd!

A lover of Chaucer, Boyse modernized the *Squire's Tale* and *Cook's Tale*. *The Olive: An Heroic Ode* purports to be written "In the Stanza of Spenser," but the pattern is $ababcdcde^5e^6$—the ten-line stanza of Prior's *Ode humbly inscrib'd to the Queen* which Boyse declares to be his model. One of several psalm-paraphrases, *Part of Psalm XLII* is "In Imitation of the Style of Spenser." The form is $ababcc^5$, and the style suggests Spenser only in the use of a few queer spellings.

But the pre-romantic qualities of Boyse seem less genuinely a part of him than the Christian fervor of *The Deity*. Perhaps this "idle, selfish, dishonest, wretched man," [83] as Southey calls him, was too much the Christian to find any deep satisfaction in sentimentalism, and too much the sentimentalist to be able to live the religion of which he wrote so earnestly.

Another strangely flawed character is that of the Scotch poet Joseph Mitchell (1684-1738). He will be treated at some length not because his work possesses any intrinsic merit but because it offers an unusual oppor-

---

[82] *Nature.*   [83] *Specimens of the Later English Poets,* II, 130.

tunity for studying the spiritual biography of one kind of eighteenth-century man.

Mitchell is now remembered, if at all, only as a disreputable toady of Sir Robert Walpole's. *D.N.B.* preserves Cibber's judgment of him as "vicious and dishonest" and "governed by every gust of irregular appetite," but makes no mention of his pious beginnings.[84] His original ambition was to be become a Presbyterian minister, and for two years the stonemason's son studied theology at Edinburgh University. He liked secular literature, however, and aspired to be a poet as well as a parson. With Allan Ramsay he belonged to the Athenian Society, a group of lively and "broad" young men who were growing restive under the austerity of the Kirk. Probably he shared Ramsay's desire to establish the theatre in Scotland; at least he says that "the Presbytery of Edinburgh ... refused him their Testimony and Licence, because he had read and recommended Dramatic Poetry, and would not believe and pronounce the Stage to be in itself absolutely unlawful, and an Abomination in the Eyes of the Lord." [85] There may of course have been stronger though less specific reasons for rejecting him.

His ecclesiastical ambitions thwarted, Mitchell embarked on the sea of letters. It was several years, however, before he lost the impress of his early training. More or less pious poetry was all that he knew how to write, and despite the blow from the Presbytery he continued to write it. *Lugubres Cantus,* his first collection of verse, was occasioned by the death of his brother John on January 5, 1719. It was published in the spring of the same year under the auspices of the Athenian Society, but in London. By this time Mitchell had established himself in the metropolis.

Part I of *Lugubres Cantus* is by Mitchell, Part II by John Calender.[86] One need not suppose that the whole volume of two hundred pages was written between January 5 and May 7, when John Hume of the Athenian Society signed the preface. Doubtless the authors added a few pieces directly inspired by John's death to a larger body of more or less lugubriously religious and moral poems which they had composed at various times.

---

[84] The facts which follow are plainly stated in his poems or in notes appended to them.

[85] Footnote to *The Shoe-Heel.*

[86] Calender's work, which is of the same general nature and of about the same quality as Mitchell's, will not be discussed. His *Epistle to Robert Blair* shows that he was a close friend of the famous graveyardist.

In the poems referring to the personal tragedy a self-conscious desire to exploit an affecting situation mingles with apparently genuine sorrow and desire for spiritual solace. Hume's preface commends as especially "passionate" Mitchell's *Epistle to Mr. John Calender*, his collaborator. Soaring with his muse, the poet seems to see his brother in heaven:

> Array'd in Robes of heav'nly Light and State,
> How near he stands to the Almighty's Seat!
> Eternal Transports of consummate Joy,
> Of Love, and Wonder are his dear Employ.
>
> .   .   .   .
>
> Dear Calendar! You long as well as I,
> To look below you on this Earth and Sky.
> Your Spirit chides low Nature's lazy Wheels,
> And longs to mount the everlasting Hills;
> To climb with Pleasure the celestial Road
> That leads to John, your Saviour, and your God.
> 'Tis but a while we must of Sorrows taste,
> To make us value more a heav'nly Feast.
> 'Ere long we shall transcend the vaulted Sky,
> And, like free'd Larks, sing Joyful as we fly.

Most of the more general religious poems are on such sombre themes as *The Woes of Life* and *Thoughts on Death and Judgment*. Rather exceptional is *The Panting Soul*, which begins:

> When, O my God, my Soul surveys
>   The Wonders of thy Grace,
> And glimpses the celestial Rays
>   Of thy refulgent Face,
> Transported to an Ecstasy
>   Of Gratitude and Love,
> I spurn the Bliss beneath the Sky,
>   And pant for Joys above.

The only poem of any pre-romantic significance is *The Lark*, a lyrical retirement-piece ending with a personal religious aspiration. "Inspir'd by Nature," the bird shows the wisdom of shunning urban life to seek happiness "In humble huts and rural Bow'rs."

> And thou, my Soul, with Little blest,
> Secure and in a close Retreat,
>   By Wit and Virtue render'd sweet,
>   Enjoy a pleasing Rest.

> In Solitude retir'd from Noise
> As on a Bay, behold below,
> And pity those who grasp at Joys,
> Or please themselves with shining Toys
>   That soon to Ruin go.
> Employ thy self on a sublimer Theme,
>   And, in thy lov'd Obscurity,
> Ne'er grasp at Honour, Glory, and at Fame;
> Nor court the World to keep alive your Name.
>   But fit thy self to fly;
> And, like the Lark, from thine obscure Abode,
> When Death shall ease you of your mortal Load,
>   Transcend the chrystal Sky,
> And there enjoy at once thy Brother and thy God.

Here the supercilious detachment of Lucretius strangely combines with sentimental naturalism and with Christian belief in the life everlasting.

Mitchell was still chiefly a divine poet when in 1720 he published *Jonah. A Poem*, retelling the story with a good deal of pious and rhetorical embroidery. The poem is addressed to Isaac Watts, who appears to have rendered Mitchell some service. "One reason of publishing this Poem," the author declares, "is, because so few modern Authors employ their pens in divine composures; which, of all others, best deserve to be attempted and read." He hopes that his work "may raise an emulation amongst our young Poets" to write on sacred themes. In calling this dedication "ironic" the author of the *D.N.B.* article on Mitchell too hastily assumes that this writer was *always* a scalawag. Dedication, preface, and text are, on the contrary, entirely serious.[87]

But in 1729, when Mitchell published *Poems on Several Occasions*, he was no longer a religious poet or a religious man. John Bancks, whose spiritual history followed exactly the same course, could now regard him as a fellow-sceptic.[88] After several years of shabbiness he was enjoying a brief period of affluence.[89] Sir Robert Walpole and the Earl of Stair had

---

[87] *Lugubres Cantus* contains a laudatory *Ode to the Reverend Mr. Isaac Watts.* The hymn-writer, always quick to encourage other divine poets, later interested himself in the publication of Blair's *The Grave;* and Blair was a friend of John Calender, Mitchell's collaborator. Perhaps Watts was similarly useful in connection with *Lugubres Cantus,* and this may be the service for which he is thanked in the dedication of *Jonah.*

[88] *Vide supra,* p. 276.

[89] Mrs. Sizer, widow of a prosperous country squire, unexpectedly left Mitchell a substantial legacy on her death in 1727. See the decorously gleeful *Ode Occasion'd by the Last Will and Death of Madam Sizer.*

shown him favors. Among the subscribers to these two rather elegant volumes were Lord Bathurst, Pope, Handel, Dyer, and Aaron Hill, while Walpole himself took six copies of the large-paper edition. Why should he write about Jonah any longer?

By no means all of the poems in this collection, however, represent Mitchell as he was in 1729. One of them, *An Ode on the Power of Musick,* may have been written as early as 1710. Several others, if not composed in his Presbyterian youth, must be regarded as literary survivals of a religiosity which is no longer an influence in his life. Although in this collection the only strictly "divine" poems are a few Scripture-paraphrases, he regrets that his old friend Allan Ramsay is so seldom "grave":

> Religious Verse from such a popular Pen,
> Might, more than Preaching, tame ungovern'd Men.[90]

To Aaron Hill he appropriately dedicates an ode entitled *The Muse's Original,* declaring that poetry, though now sadly debauched, was once the voice of religious passion:

> Priests were Themselves the Poets then,
> And *felt* the Pow'r they preach'd to Men.

When Moses sang he was inspired by "a divine Enthusiast's Fury":

> The God within beat strong his widen'd Heart,
> Celestial Raptures thro' his Spirits thrill'd,
> And his Verse flam'd with Fire, unknown to Art.

In Hill, greatest of modern poets, the spirit of Moses is restored:

> Sure, in thy Breast, the ancient Hebrew Fire
>   Reviv'd, glows hot, and blazes forth!
> How strong, how fierce, the Flames aspire,
>   Of thy interior Worth,
> When burning Worlds thou set'st before our Eyes,
> And draw'st tremendous Judgment from the Skies!
>   O bear me on thy Seraph Wing,
> And teach my weak, obsequious Muse to sing.
> To Thee I owe the little Art I boast;
> Thy Heat first melted my co-genial Frost.
>   Preserve the Sparks thy Breath did fan,
> And, by thy Likeness, form me into true poetic Man.

[90] *To Mr. Allan Ramsay.*

The Dennis-Blackmore-Watts theory of divine poetry, we see, is beginning to become a cult of untrammeled genius.

Similar views appear in Mitchell's *Ode on the Power of Musick*, which expands the idea of creative harmony with which Dryden begins his famous poem. It was music that first brought order out of chaos. The "New-born Earth" was "The Work, the Effect of Harmony, its wondrous off-spring." God's creative *fiat* was melodious—"The Voice was tuneful as his Love":

> At Musick's sweet prevailing Call,
> Thro' boundless Realms of Space,
> The Atoms danc'd, obsequious, all,
> And, to compose this wond'rous Ball,
> In order took their Place.

Man is the little masterpiece of the melodious universe:

> He boasts a pure, a tuneful Soul,
> That rivals the Celestial Throng,
> And can ev'n Savage Beasts controul
> With his enchanting Song.
> Tho' diff'rent Passions struggle in his Mind,
> Where Love and Hatred, Hope and Fear are join'd;
> All, by a secret Guidance, tend
> To one harmonious End.

"Music," cries Mitchell, "religious Thoughts inspires" and fosters poetic genius like that of Aaron Hill. Hence the madness of the art is a divine madness:

> Others may *that* Distraction call,
> Which Musick raises in the Breast,—
> To me, 'tis Ecstasy and Triumph all,
> The Foretastes of the Raptures of the Blest.
> Who knows not this when Handel plays,
> And Senesino sings?
> Our Souls learn Rapture from their Lays,
> While rival'd Angels shew amaze,
> And drop their Golden Wings.

I cannot corroborate Mitchell's assertion that this ode was first published in 1710. In any case the admiring reference to Aaron Hill, whom he cannot have met by that date, suggests that the poem underwent revision. The text of the poem as it appeared separately in 1721 is identical with that of the 1729 collection. But if *The Power of Musick* existed in any form by 1710 it is plain that Mitchell's earlier piety was tinged with a kind of aesthetico-religious enthusiasm. His admiration for Watts and Hill, both of whom possess the same outlook, is thus easy to understand.

Utterly discordant with such vaguely noble feelings is the unfinished *Memorial to Virtue*. The author reminds Virtue that he has long been her faithful servant but has only starved for his pains:

> I wou'd not leave Thee, wou'd'st thou Victuals give;
> But flowry Speeches cannot make me live.
>
> •   •   •   •
>
> Better to shun the Learning of thy School,
> Than starve in Life, and die a knowing Fool.

The date of this poem is unknown, but we may guess that it was written about 1724. In that year, at any rate, he produced his humorously brazen epistle, *The Sine-Cure: A Poetical Petition to the Right Honourable Robert Walpole, Esq; for the Government of Duck-Island, in St. James's Park.* Thereafter practically all his poems other than trivial occasional pieces are impudent begging letters addressed to Walpole, Earl Stair, Craggs, or Richard Steele. Truly he says of himself that

> Money and Credit, Place, or Pension, now,
> Is all the Shrine to which I humbly bow.[91]

In this final stage he likes to sneer at pious zeal. He assures Walpole that if he is made Secretary of State for Scotland he will "rid the Kirk of Bigotry and Cant." [92] *Miss Charlotte at Church* tells how a four-year-old child sees a white-sheeted female penitent in the church porch and is given the reason. On entering the church she sees the parson in his white surplice and infers that he has sinned in the same way.

His personal clash with the Kirk is several times alluded to. He thinks of himself as a gay genius whose flame was almost extinguished by the bigots of Edinburgh:

> By Custom's Influence, from a sprightly Wit,
> I sunk below the Zenith of a Cit.
> And had I not, with fond Ambition fir'd,
> Travel'd to see what blindly I admir'd,

[91] *To Sir Richard Steel* [sic].
[92] *The Promotion.* See also *The Alternative*, where he gibes at the preachers of the Kirk.

> Still at Edina, with religious Qualms,
> I Texts had snivel'd, and Sol-fa-a'd the Psalms.[93]

In *The Shoe-Heel,* an inferior imitation of *The Splendid Shilling,* he says that nowadays patrons are generous to poets as rarely

> As priests to Parish Poor distribute Alms;
> Or Presbytery fair Testimonials gives
> To free-born Genius, and Wit enslav'd.
> Tremendous Zeal of Kirk-men, blindly urg'd
> Against Heav'n's Gift, and Providence Supreme!
> Such I experienc'd, in my youthful Days,
> Where Love of Poesy was deem'd a Crime,
> By blind Prosaick Leaders of the Blind.

His scorn of religion is not confined to the Kirk. *Catholick Brass; or the Power of Impudence* [94] asserts that

> Sage Austin, Origen, Aquinas, Scot,
> Ambrose and Gregory, were on Brass begot.
> To Brass, the modern Hammond, Eachard, Mead,
> Burnet and Bentley owe their being read.
> Thou Atterbury, thou Sacheverell, know'st
> How much to holy Impudence thou ow'st.
> 'Twas that, which gave your Schemes and Conduct Birth,
> And stock'd with rev'rend Lumber, half the Earth.

The Mitchell of these later poems is not always gay and careless. Bitterly he congratulates a still-born infant:

> Thrice happy Child, exempt from Breath,
> From Birth, from Being, and from Death;
> Since Life is but one common Care,
> And Man was made to mourn and fear! [95]

He who once aspired to join his brother in heaven now writes these hopeless *Verses on the Death of Mr. S——:*

> Strong as he was, and healthy as the best,
> How soon he fell! to hungry Worms a Guest!

[93] *To Sir Richard Steel* [*sic*].

[94] A panegyric on "brass" (impudent affrontery) as the key to success in every walk of life. "Catholick" is used in the sense of "universal," for although the satire includes Romanist theologians it is not confined to them nor even to clerics in general.

[95] *Epitaph for the Tomb of an Infant, miscarried before it had received the Breath of Life.*

> Yet He, from Vices and from Follies free,
> Had more to plead, and less to fear than we.
> We may a while enjoy the transient Light—
> With him, alas! 'tis ever, ever Night!

Yet there are times when the notion that he is a genius gives him a pseudo-religious thrill. Apparently he retains belief in that form of immortality which he too boldly claims in *Poetic Faith*:

> Let Time, Oblivion, and Disgrace,
> Conspire my Memory to raze;
> Let all that is, and will be, join;
> Let Earth and Hell their Pow'rs combine;
> By Stair and Walpole's Favour crown'd,
> My Classick Muse shall shine renown'd,
> When Bards, pro Tempore so fam'd,
> With all their Works, are dead and damn'd!

Certain facts concerning these poets may now be assembled. Dates of birth and death are available for seventeen of the twenty-five. One (Mitchell) was born in 1684; five were born between 1687 and 1699; eleven between 1700 and 1712. Thus the group is the latest of those which have been examined, especially since most of the eight for whom dates are lacking were probably born after 1700.[96] The sentimental and preromantic tendencies exhibited in greatly varying degree by these writers point forward into the heart of the century.

Only ten of the total number reveal their political affiliations in their verse, but of these all are either "Walpole" or "Patriot" Whigs. If any of the remaining fifteen are Tories they say nothing to indicate the fact. We know that Carey is a Whig despite his assumed indifference to such matters.

In twenty-one cases out of twenty-five the social origin of the author can be determined. One is a nobleman; three others are gentlemen born; ten are of the middle class; six are plebeians. Carey, the twenty-first, occupies a special position because of his bar sinister. Five of the six plebeians—Duck, Cooke, Browne, Mitchell, and Broome—of course ascended to the middle-class level in the course of their careers, but this hardly applies to the humble pastor Josiah Relph. Obviously the bourgeois and

---

[96] Victor, for example, lived until 1778; and Delacour's poems appeared, not posthumously, in the same year.

sub-bourgeois element is strong—distinctly stronger than in any other group thus far considered.

Eight of the poets are clergymen—all Anglican; fourteen are laymen; one is a woman; for two I have no information. Two of the clerics, Duck and Browne, entered the Church rather late in life. Two of the laymen, Welsted and Boyse, were the sons of clerical fathers; and the same may be true of a few others for whom genealogical facts are lacking. The clerical element is therefore rather strong; but since the parsons and sons of parsons are neither more pious (except for Browne and Boyse) nor more pre-romantic than the general run of the group the importance ascribed to this factor in Herbert Schöffler's *Protestantismus und Literatur* may be somewhat exaggerated.

In any case the group, while including some estimable men, does not as a whole exhale the odor of sanctity. The two Pilkingtons, Boyse, and Mitchell are very unsavory; and the characters of Welsted, Jacob, Ralph, Whaley, and Davies are far from admirable. Poor Carey is the sort of man whom one likes but does not wish to imitate. The degree of positive correlation between religious living and religious writing shown by this group is significantly low. Except for the tediously edifying Browne, the most pious of all these poets are Boyse and Lætitia Pilkington. On the other hand Welsted, Jacob, and sometimes Carey approach that "sentimental libertine" type which has earlier been described. Mitchell cuts across the two classifications, beginning as a divine poet and ending as a sentimental libertine.

Although none of the twenty-five poets can be called a writer of real excellence, the average level of intelligence, imaginativeness, and technical skill rises distinctly higher than that of the preceding chapter. For a mixture of historical and critical reasons Carey, Lyttelton, Broome, Boyse, Welsted, Ralph, Hammond, Duck, and Cooke would be included in any detailed survey of eighteenth-century poetry.

But the religious verse produced by this group is extremely scanty and feeble—inferior in quality to the secular verse. The cause is not far to seek: few of these writers hold the Christian religion in a form that could be expected to stimulate a poetic response. The unfortunate Boyse stands out from the rest as a divine poet of some merit. He, his fellow-sinner Lætitia Pilkington, and the Mitchell of *Lugubres Cantus* are the only members of the group who respond to Christian faith emotionally and imaginatively. The sober evangelical Moses Browne writes many divine poems, but they lack wings. Hammond, Miller and Relph (both clerics), Victor, and Martha Fowke provide no reliable indication of their religious views. A tendency to blur and soften the severe outlines of Christianity appears in Roche, Matthew Pilkington, and Delacour, of whom the last two are clergymen. Duck is a faithful but plodding believer, and Somerville's religion is that of a conservative squire who hates dissenters. The rather grim plebeian piety of Broome is almost wholly submerged by a mixture of neoclassical and sentimental affectations. Browne's *Essay on the Universe* and Gambol's *Beauties of the Universe* are unexciting specimens of orthodox Newtonianism. Various shades of latitudinarian indifference are seen in Welsted, Cooke, Whaley, Davies, and Carey; but Welsted is sometimes more sceptical than this term usually implies, while Carey and Davies, on the other hand, have their moments of Christian feeling.

Although a few of these writers came of nonconformist stock, all those who can be called Christians at all may, with the exception of Boyse, be classified as nominal Anglicans. Their Churchmanship, however, is in no way distinguishable from a broad, flat, loose nonconformity. If the Catholic aspect of Anglicanism has not wholly vanished from their minds, it remains only as a superstition to be attacked by loyal Whigs.

The Christian phase of Lyttelton's life is not represented in his poetry, which preaches a set of classical-Whiggish ideals and virtues. Such vague nobility has no appeal for Jacob or the later Mitchell. Those frivolous mockers, with whom Ralph might also be included, appear to have no definite beliefs, but if they must be pigeonholed they may as well be called destructive deists. The only serious expression of formulated non-Christian religious belief is given by the anonymous poem *Order,* an unusually hardheaded example of the Shaftesbury type of deism.

A few of these men go through significant changes. Broome, the clerical son of a poor farmer, remains orthodox but loses most of his gloomy zeal. Mitchell moves from earnest Presbyterianism to disbelief in everything but the cult of genius. Boyse follows his dissenting father in belief but not in action. Cooke, the son of a Muggletonian innkeeper, becomes a latitudinarian. The latitudinarianism of Welsted acquires a slight libertine or epicurean tinge. Contrary trends are exhibited by the converted Lyttelton and by Moses Browne, who, though always pious, becomes more definitely evangelical with the passing years.

What conclusion can be drawn from this medley of religious viewpoints? Plainly, no great battle is being fought. We find some sneering scepticism, some indifference, and much vague incertitude, but no bold, organized, intelligent assault upon the traditional faith. That faith, however, has lost or is losing its hold on the imagination of a large majority of these poets. Yet with few exceptions they are not natural unbelievers: they are mostly the sort of men whose feelings urge them to believe in *something*. When Christianity and poetic imagination have parted company, what beliefs will nourish the poet's art? Without definitely answering this question, the present chapter has given a few hints which must be developed in the sequel.

Chapter X

SENTIMENTALISM—SEVERER CASES

THE FIGURES NOW TO PASS IN REVIEW BEFORE US ARE DISTINGUISHED FROM those of the preceding chapter by no clean-cut differentia, but the reader may agree that they present more striking examples of the religion of the feeling heart.

The researches of J. W. Draper [1] have shown that the type of eighteenth-century melancholy known as "graveyardism" descends from the more funereal side of seventeenth-century puritanism. No link in this chain is more familiar than *The Grave*.[2] Robert Blair (1699-1746) came honestly by his piety, for his father and grandfather were Presbyterian divines. He himself studied theology and was licensed to preach in 1718. Until 1730, however, he lived in Edinburgh as an unemployed probationer. A man of independent means who delighted in reading the Elizabethans, he felt no very strong urge to shoulder the cares of a pastorate. In 1731, however, he was ordained to the living of Athelstaneford in East Lothian.

Before leaving Edinburgh he had partly sketched out the plan for *The Grave*,[3] and he slowly completed the poem at Athelstaneford. By 1742 he had begun to seek for means of getting it into print. Both Watts and Doddridge were eager that it should be published.

In a letter expressing the hope that the poem will not be found "unbecoming my profession as a minister of the gospel," he reminds Doddridge that "in order to make it more generally liked, I was obliged sometimes to

---

[1] *The Funeral Elegy and the Rise of English Romanticism.*

[2] Though not published until 1743, the poem had been planned at least ten years earlier and most of it had been written by 1740.

[3] H. Schöffler, who makes much of the fact that the first half of *The Grave* is literary and the second half pious, ascribes the difference to Blair's having begun the poem in Edinburgh before his ordination. (*Protestantismus und Literatur*, p. 36.) Apparently, however, nothing more than a tentative "argument" existed before the poet went to Athelstaneford. It should also be remembered that in the Kirk "ordination" implies appointment to a particular parish. Blair was a licensed preacher as early as 1718, and the entire poem is the work of a cleric.

go cross to my own inclination, well knowing that whatever poem is written upon a serious argument, must, upon that very account, lie under peculiar disadvantages: and therefore proper arts must be used to make such a piece go down with a licentious age which cares for none of these things." [4]

These "proper arts" are concentrated in the first half of the poem, which is almost wholly destitute of religious thought or feeling. Here he aims merely to stir our emotions by describing the omnipotence of Death the Leveller and the physical terrors of the grave. But almost exactly halfway through the poem, when the reader has been pleasantly saddened and horrified but not in the least elevated by "sculls and coffins, epitaphs and worms," the lurking evangelist leaps upon his prey:

> Sure 'tis a serious thing to die! my soul!
> What a strange moment must it be, when near
> Thy journey's end, thou hast the gulf in view!
> That awful gulf, no mortal e'er repass'd
> To tell what's doing on the other side.
> Nature runs back, and shudders at the sight,
> And every life-string bleeds at thought of parting;
> For part they must; body and soul must part:
> Fond couple! link'd more close than wedded pair.
> This wings its way to its Almighty Source,
> The witness of its actions, now its judge;
> That drops into the dark and noisome Grave,
> Like a disabled pitcher of no use.

Thereafter, despite one or two macabre touches, the poem is menacingly pious up to a hopeful conclusion which declares that the Son of God has conquered the tomb, that only through the grave can we come to Him in glory, and that death holds no terrors for the virtuous Christian.

Blair would assert, probably with entire sincerity, that the first part of *The Grave* was designed to make the second "go down with a licentious age." A few years later he must have observed that Young had employed a similar means of baiting his hook. Not only Watts and Doddridge but James Hervey regarded *The Grave* as a work of edification. Yet one cannot read the poem without feeling that the melancholy and horror, both qualitatively and quantitatively, are out of all proportion to the religious element. This Presbyterian minister enjoys morbid gloom not only as an

[4] Quoted from *Letters to and from Dr. Doddridge* (1790) by Alexander Chalmers, *The Works of the English Poets*, XV, 62.

evangelistic device but in and for itself as an emotional indulgence. Only in this respect can he be called a sentimentalist.

A significant feature of the work is the transposition of Calvinistic graveyardism into an Elizabethan key. Blair is steeped in the mood of *Hamlet* and in the more lurid atmosphere of Webster's tragedies:

> Why this ado in earthing up a carcase
> That's fallen into disgrace, and in the nostril
> Smells horrible?
>
> Methinks I see thee with thy head low laid,
> Whilst, surfeited upon thy damask cheek,
> The high-fed worm, in lazy volumes roll'd,
> Riots unscar'd.
>
> Oh! how his eyes stand out, and stare full ghastly!
> While the distemper's rank and deadly venom
> Shoots like a burning arrow 'cross his bowels,
> And drinks his marrow up.[5]

In short, although Blair doubtless intended to write a religious poem, in his hands the spirit of the old funeral elegies becomes highly self-conscious and literary, and begins to detach itself from those pious fears and hopes in which it originated.

Mary Chandler (1687-1745) was the daughter of a dissenting minister, and so far as I know she herself never became an Anglican. A friend of Elizabeth Rowe and of Mary Barber, she resembles the latter in the success with which she attached herself to such personages as Lady Russell and the Duchess of Somerset. She remained a spinster all her life, and kept a shop in Bath.

Her verse has some of the advantages and all the disadvantages of a natural, careless facility. It was chiefly for non-literary reasons that her only substantial work, *A Description of Bath*, went through eight editions. Her other poems are short pieces addressed, she says, "only to the small circle of my Acquaintance, and those of my Superiours, to whom I have the Honour to appear in a favourable Light." Many of them are versified bread-and-butter letters.

What she would like others to think of her appears in *My Own Epitaph*:

[5] These are three of several passages aptly chosen to illustrate the same point by Eleanor Sickels, *The Gloomy Egoist*, pp. 32-33.

She loved the whole Species, but some had distinguish'd;
But Time, and much Thought, had all Passion extinguish'd.
Tho' not fond of her Station, content with her Lot;
A Favour receiv'd she had never forgot.
She rejoic'd in the Good that her Neighbour possess'd;
And Piety, Purity, Truth she profess'd.
She liv'd in much Peace, but ne'er courted Pleasure.
Her Book, and her Pen, had her Moments of Leisure.
Pleas'd with Life, fond of Health, yet fearless of Death;
Believing she lost not her Soul with her Breath.

My Wish, inspired by Pomfret's *Choice,* gives much the same impression. Her ideal is a golden mediocrity supported by an unexciting but solid religious faith. She wants health, peace, friendship, freedom from care, dry soil and temperate climate, about £100 a year free of encumbrances, a cosy house "above a Hut, below a Seat." This dwelling must be embowered in trees, and she must hear the sound of streams rushing down a hillside into a river visible from her window. Her neighbors would include an "honest Farmer" and a "friendly Cleric." She would write letters or read "some useful Book" beside a "purling Brook." Here also she would write poetry, avoiding both indecent themes and unattainably sublime ones such as "Great George."

External nature, we see, plays some part in this vision of snugness. Miss Chandler regards scenery as both poetically and spiritually inspiring. After visiting a prosperous friend's estate she writes:

Romantic Views these Prospects yield,
    That feed poetic Fire;
Each broken Rock, and Cave, and Field,
    And Hill, and Vale, inspire.

These various, gay, delightful Scenes
    Like Paradise appear;
Serene as ev'ning Sky my Soul,
    And hush'd is ev'ry Care.

. . . . .

The happy Genius of the Place
    Inspires with softest Joys;
And Contemplation, pure as Light,
    My raptur'd Soul employs.[6]

[6] *To Mrs. Jacob, On her Seat call'd The Rocks, in Gloucestershire.* See also *To the Reverend Dr. S——. An Invitation to a Morning-Walk in the Spring.*

She remembers, however, the utter dependence of nature upon the supernatural. In *A Description of Bath* she accepts Burnet's idea of the continuous decadence of the earth, insisting only that it is "lovely in Decay, and green in Age." She continues, still following Burnet:

> Wisdom immense contriv'd the wondrous Ball,
> And Form sprung Forth, obedient to his Call.
> He fix'd her Date, and bade the Planet run
> Her annual Race around the central Sun:
> He bade the Seasons, Days, and Nights return,
> Till the pent Fires, which at the Centre burn,
> Shall the whole Globe to one huge Cinder turn.
> Then, like a Phœnix, she again shall rise,
> And the new World be peopled from the Skies.
> Then Vice, and all her Train of Ills, shall cease,
> And Truth shall reign with Righteousness and Peace.

For all her love of rural retirement, furthermore, Miss Chandler is quick to champion the virtues of the active life. The beauty of *Mr. B——'s Garden* would be nothing without the goodness of its owners;

> But here true Happiness is understood,
> The noble manly Joy of doing Good;
> Here sterling Truth, calm Temperance, and Love,
> Lead from these pleasing Scenes to those above,
> To nobler Structures, built by Hands divine,
> Where Suns unclouded o'er the Prospect shine.

Like her friend Mrs. Barber, indeed, she is a connoisseur of benevolence. Dr. Oliver, who not only corrected her chief poem but cured her of a dangerous illness, receives her gratitude:

> Tho' neither Youth nor Beauty was my Friend,
> Nor Gold nor Fame could tempt; yet you attend.
> While soft Compassion languish'd in your Eyes,
> And gently breath'd in sympathetic Sighs,
> Pure Goodness wing'd your Feet, inspir'd your Tongue;
> Soft were your Accents, but your Reas'ning strong.
> Heav'n bade me live, and you prescrib'd the Way,
> To you, next Heav'n, my grateful Thanks I pay.[7]

She does not forget to thank God as well as the melting doctor, for in *On my Recovery* she cries,

[7] *To Dr. Oliver, who corrected my Bath Poem.*

> That Life, which thou hast longer spar'd,
> I would devote to Thee.
> O let thy Spirit be my Guard,
> Till I thy Face shall see!

In fact, although Miss Chandler is more of a sentimentalist than the women of Chapter VIII, she remains very definitely a Christian and a Protestant. Her father, the Reverend Henry Chandler, would like her description of Bath Abbey as

> The labour'd Work of superstitious Hands.
> When holy Craft supreme did guide the Helm,
> And Gothic Darkness overspread the Realm;
> The artful Priest amaz'd the gaping Croud,
> And sacred Truth was veil'd in mystic Cloud.

Her nonconformist parent might, however, be faintly perplexed by the tone of the lines which follow this fling at popery:

> Welcome, fair Liberty, and Light divine!
> Yet wider spread your Wings, and brighter shine;
> Dart livelier Beams on ev'ry British Soul,
> And scatter slavish Darkness to the Pole.[8]

He would more certainly be troubled by the cheerfulness with which his daughter concludes her lines *To Mrs. Moon*. Friendship, she avers, is

> ...pure as the ethereal Flame,
>   That lights the Lamps above;
> Pure, as the Infant's Thought, from Blame;
>   Or, as his Mother's Love.
>
>   .   .   .   .
>
> And thus, as swift-wing'd Time brings on
>   Death, nearer to our View;
> Tun'd to sweet Harmony our Souls,
>   We take a short Adieu;
>
> Till the last Trump's delightful Sound
>   Shall wake our Sleeping Clay:
> Then swift, to find our Fellow-souls,
>   As Light, we haste away.

Since the first line of the last stanza is something of a landmark in the history of religious feeling, we may observe that this poem is dated 1729.

[8] *A Description of Bath.*

Mary Chandler may be summed up as a sentimentalized nonconformist who reads serious books by the rippling stream, likes sighing, languishing physicians, and very differently from Blair thinks of Gabriel's trumpet as "delightful."

> How vainly through infinite Trouble and Strife,
> The many their Labours employ!
> Since all that is truly delightful in Life
> Is what All, if they will, may enjoy.[9]

Such is the bracing message of the Reverend Thomas Fitzgerald.[10] For him the cardinal virtues are cheerfulness and industry, and in two of his poems he addresses these abstractions almost as if they were independent deities. *Chearfulness,* we learn, dwells not with Avarice or Ambition, but only with her sister, Content. To the "tumultuous Joys" of banquets, balls, and hunt-meetings she prefers "the calm Transports of an honest Heart."

The truest source of content is the knowledge that one has served mankind in the active life. Hence *Industry* is hailed as

> Queen of all Virtues! for whate'er we call
> Godlike and Great, 'tis thou obtain'st it all.
>   .   .   .   .
> Inspir'd by thee to each superior Aim,
> We press with Ardour thro' the Paths of Fame
> Up to the sacred Top, and leave behind
> Th' inglorious Crowd, the Herd of Humankind.

The possessor of this virtue enjoys powers which in a later period might be called transcendental:

> No anxious Cares, no furious Lusts controul
> The free habitual Vigour of the Soul.
> Each Part, each Station gracefully we fill,
> And bend and shape our Fortune to our Will.

Industry will even banish the terrors of death by enabling us to look back upon a life well spent:

---

[9] *An Ode.*
[10] Not in *D.N.B.* Sir John Evelyn, his patron, presented him to the livings of Wotton and Abinger in Surrey. *Poems on Several Occasions* appeared in 1733. Judging from internal evidence, it is unlikely that much of his work was written before 1720.

> If useful we have pass'd through every Stage,
> And paid our Debt of Service to the Age;
> If still we've made our Duty our Delight,
> Nor hid our Master's Talent from our Sight,
> All's well; 'tis all by our own Heart approv'd,
> From hence we pass by God and Man belov'd;
> Cheerful we pass, to Heav'n's high Will resign'd,
> And leave a blessed Memory behind.[11]

Hence we reach heaven not through consciousness of sin, but through consciousness of active virtue. If we sincerely approve of ourselves, we may be sure that God approves of us. How different from the Calvinistic madman described in *Bedlam*—

> The Wild Enthusiast, that despairing sees
> Predestin'd Wrath, and Heav'n's severe Decrees.

Despite his glorification of industry, Fitzgerald persistently hankers after the joys of the pensive grove. He finds it hard to choose between the desirability of rushing into life and the desirability of shrinking away from it. *An Ode* declares that no rest or pleasure can be found in that "overgrown Prison," the town:

> From hence to the Country escaping away,
> Leave the Croud and the Bustle behind,
> And there you'll see liberal Nature display
> A thousand Delights to Mankind.[12]

Amid such rural scenes, free from ambition and avarice, he longs to spend his days in a manner quite inconsistent with the gospel of industry and service.

A witty colleague once remarked: "These people who say they want to write generally mean that they want to have written." Similarly one feels that for Fitzgerald the summit of human felicity would be, not the joy of industry, but the joy of remembering, in retired leisure, that he has been industrious. Sir John Evelyn delights in brief visits to the "rich romantic Scene" of his country estate, but his retired pleasures are heightened by the fact that most of his life is spent in active service:

[11] The same idea is expressed in *A Thought upon Death*.
[12] In *Spring* he expresses appreciation of external nature, but without looking at it very intently.

Blest is the Man without Offence,
From the plain Paths of Innocence,
    That never went astray;
And the next blest is he who mourns
His Errors, and repenting turns
    Back to the sacred Way.

But Oh! 'tis Bliss beyond compare
Such solid Joys as yours to share,
    Recalling still to Mind
An active Life from first to last,
In one perpetual Labour past
    To benefit Mankind.[13]

The happiest human being is the benevolist on a vacation from benevolence.

Writers in whom the retirement-impulse is strong are also likely to indulge in sentimental primitivism. In *Tomo Chachi: An Ode* he eulogizes an Indian chief whom General Oglethorpe had brought to England from Georgia: [14]

What Stranger's this? and from what Region far
    This wond'rous Form, majestic to behold?
Uncloath'd but arm'd offensive for the War,
    In hoary Age and wise Experience old;
His Limbs inur'd to Hardiness and Toil,
    His strong large Limbs what mighty Sinews grace,
Whilst Truth sincere, and artless Virtue smile
    In the expressive Features of his Face;
His bold free Aspect speaks his inward Mind,
Aw'd by no slavish Fear, from no vile Passion blind.

He reminds the poet of Cassibelanus or Caractacus. Such a man should not be called a savage, for he is

Ever by Reason's equal Dictates sway'd,
    Conscious of each great Impulse in the Soul,
And all his Words, and all his Actions weigh'd
    By unaffected Wisdom's just Controul.

The religious implications of the sachem's character are not stressed, but since he derives virtue and wisdom directly from nature he hardly seems to fit the Christian scheme of redemption.

[13] *To My Honoured Patron Sir John Evelyn, Bart.*
[14] For an account of Tomo-Chachi's visit, which took place in 1743, see B. H. Bissell, *The American Indian in English Literature of the Eighteenth Century*, pp. 63 ff.

In fact, although *Poems on Several Occasions* is much concerned with morality, it contains surprisingly little that can be called Christian.[15] In *The Freethinker* the clerical author pokes fun at young Clodio, who when drunk tries to show his parts by spouting "Rabbi Tindal's deep Discoveries." *The Muse's Complaint* inveighs against the licentiousness of modern poetry and drama, but unlike Dennis, Watts, and Blackmore, Fitzgerald does not regard poetry as essentially religious: when he recalls the past glories of the art he begins with Homer and says nothing about David. In his Scripture-paraphrases he turns part of *Psalm XXXVII* into a little sermon on his favorite virtues, and *Psalm CIV* into a feeble piece of nature-description.

His only substantial sacred poem is *Abraham and Isaac,* a narrative in heroic couplets. After the patriarch and his son have expressed their sorrowful submission to the divine command, an angel bids Abraham sheath his sword, praises his faithfulness, and reveals to him the future of his line to the time when

> ... Messiah's self shall rise,
> Sprung from thy Seed, descending from the Skies;
> Stupendous Union! Heav'n and Earth combin'd!
> Incarnate God, to rescue lost Mankind!
>
> .   .   .   .   .   .
>
> Mercy Divine Messiah shall bring down
> To sinful Man, and mighty in Renown
> Shall break Hell's Pow'r, and Death's tyrannic Chain,
> And end the long Reproach of Satan's Reign.

The theology of this amiable and cultivated clergyman was probably at least as orthodox as the age demanded. Nevertheless it is hard to feel that the Incarnation is of much more significance to him than industry, cheerfulness, rural retirement, and the natural virtues of Tomo-Chachi. The faith by which Fitzgerald actually lives is a complex of moral notions only vaguely related to Christianity or to any form of supernatural religion.

The leading authority on Allan Ramsay (1684?-1758) believes that modern students have exaggerated his pre-romanticism.[16] In such matters, of

[15] The volume includes a translation of the *Golden Verses of Pythagoras,* other classical translations chiefly from Theocritus and Martial, some original Latin verse, and a few short humorous occasional pieces. The poems discussed in the text, however, represent the foreground aspects of Fitzgerald's work.

[16] Burns Martin, *Allan Ramsay: a Study of His Life and Works,* pp. v-vi.

course, there can be no absolute standard of judgment. It is probably true that "although Ramsay had an interest in external nature and the idyllic dream, his distinctive contribution to literature has less to do with these than with the low life of the city and, to some extent, of the country." [17] The conventionally neoclassical element in Ramsay's work is also large. Nevertheless the literary historian cannot neglect his keen and loving eye for natural objects, the sentimental tinge which sometimes suffuses his realism, his contribution to the revival of the lyric, his emphasis on originality and on "simple" nature as opposed to art, his enthusiasm for ballad and folksong, for Middle Scots poetry, for Spenser and Chaucer. A writer of the 1720's who displays all of these traits as clearly as did Allan Ramsay must be allowed to retain his place in the annals of the Romantic Movement.

Ramsay's Jacobitism, chiefly the result of irritated nationalistic sentiment, did not prevent his being a Whig and a Presbyterian. "He was a pewholder," says Martin, "and many passages could be culled from his writings to show that he was a faithful, if conventional, believer." [18] The manuscript of *The Gentle Shepherd* concludes with the words, "All Glory be to God. Amen!" Martin finds "many Biblical allusions in Ramsay's writings. Without exception they refer to the Old Testament— striking evidence of the source of seventeenth- and eighteenth-century Presbyterianism." [19]

On the other hand, Ramsay disliked bigotry and enthusiasm. His biographer has seen unpublished poems which "show his contempt for Whitefield . . . and for the Marrow party within the Scottish fold." [20] He supported attempts to establish a theatre in Edinburgh, defended public assemblies for dancing, was looked at askance for the worldliness of his circulating library, and had a reputation for conviviality. A jolly, spontaneous, amiable fellow—certainly no tight-lipped precisian. His verse rather superficially bears witness that he has been reared in a Presbyterian environment, but though never anti-religious it is never moved by a spiritual impulse.

Ramsay's broad, easy, worldly Presbyterianism combines readily enough

---

[17] *Ibid.*, p. 69.   [18] *Ibid.*, p. 46.   [19] *Ibid.*, p. 59.

[20] *Ibid.*, p. 46. The "Marrow Men" were the members of the primitively Calvinistic Secession Kirk. *Vide supra*, p. 283. They derived this nickname from their admiration for Edward Fisher's compendium of Calvinistic theology, *The Marrow of Modern Divinity* (1645).

with approval of natural science. In *To Sir William Bennet* he scorns those "Plebeian souls" who neither appreciate poetry

> Nor through the microscope can take delight,
> T' observe the tusks and bristles of a mite;
> Nor by the lengthen'd tube learn to descry
> Those shining worlds which roll around the sky.

To the Royal Society of London he inscribes a memorial poem on Newton, who

> ... shunn'd the sophistry of words,
> Which only hatch contentious spite;
> His learning turn'd on what affords,
> By *demonstration*, most delight.[21]

He does not question the assumption that the religion of Newtonianism is the religion of the Bible. Indeed he appears to think that the solid facts of science will be useful in converting the heathen to Christianity, for he addresses the Royal Society:

> May from your Learned Band arise
> Newtons to shine thro' future times,
> And bring down knowledge from the skies,
> To plant on wild barbarian climes.
>
> 'Till nations few degrees from brutes,
> Be brought into each proper road,
> Which leads to wisdom's happiest fruits,
> To know their Saviour and their God.

So familiar a writer as Ramsay does not require further analysis. He illustrates a situation which we have already observed: commonsense Protestantism verging upon latitudinarianism; the obtaining of quasi-religious emotional satisfaction not through this dull and unimaginative Christianity, but through cultivation of sentimental naturalism and other pre-romantic tendencies.

Another Scot, William Hamilton of Bangour (1704-1754),[22] moved in higher circles than Ramsay but knew him well, admired his work, and

[21] *To the Memory of Sir Isaac Newton.*
[22] Well-born, well-to-do, and physically delicate, he lived in cultivated leisure until the rising of 1745, which he supported by his pen. On the defeat of the Jacobites he hid in the Highlands and later fled to France, but was allowed to return in 1749.

in 1724 contributed several pieces to *The Tea-Table Miscellany.* One of these contributions, *The Braes of Yarrow,* is a well-known landmark in the ballad-revival. Hamilton's *Contemplation* has been recognized as an example of the *Il Penseroso* tradition. In several poems he employs Miltonic blank verse. Once he imitates the style, but not the stanza, of Spenser,[23] and twice he paraphrases Shakespeare-passages in heroic couplets.[24] Not infrequently he endeavors to be seriously lyrical. His mock-heroic *Maid of Gallowshiels* provides some sympathetically realistic vignettes of Scots rural life in Ramsay's manner. *The Wish* is a retirement-piece with emphasis on the moral benefits of retreat.

But after reading Hamilton's poems in their entirety one cannot feel that he was moved by a strong romantic impulse. He has the gentleman's view of poetry as an elegant pastime, and he toys with various ways of writing none of which seem related to any emotional centre. He is more often neoclassical than pre-romantic, and in his amatory and eulogistic poems he tries to continue the tradition of Waller. In fact he is distinctly an old-fashioned man: much in his work that appears to be pre-romantic might more accurately be described as a seventeenth-century heritage which survived longer in Scotland than in England.

Hamilton's moral reputation is high, but apparently he was guided by a set of unanalyzed gentlemanly intuitions rather than by strong religious beliefs. As an upper-class Jacobite he was probably an Anglican, but he neither defends Episcopacy nor attacks Presbyterianism. In his fairly numerous epitaphs the consolation offered is generally rational and cool, or at most only conventionally Christian—the utterances of a versifying person of quality who knows how to say the proper thing. His one psalm-paraphrase is a mere exercise. In *A Soliloquy* he declares that the pleasures arising from beauty, poetry, and friendship are transitory, and that only faith in Providence can give true happiness. The theme of *A Serious Thought* is that we must live virtuously if we wish "perpetual bliss." Neither poem suggests any emotional response to Christianity.

Contemplation: or The Triumph of Love,[25] his Miltonic tribute to

[23] *On Seeing the Lady Montgomery Sit to Her Picture. In Imitation of Spencer's Style.* The imitation lies merely in a few archaisms.

[24] *A Soliloquy in Imitation of Hamlet* ("To be or not to be") and *King Lear's Speech to Edgar* ("Is man no more than this?")

[25] The sub-title applies only to the conclusion: even the pleasures of woodland contemplation will not permit him to forget Monimia. Though not published until 1747, the poem had been completed by 1739.

pensively melancholy retirement, has a sentimentally religious atmosphere which need not be taken very seriously but which is interestingly sympto-matic. Surrounded by the beauties of nature, Hamilton prepares his spirit for the approach of the goddess Contemplation. He invokes Faith, Hope, Charity, Friendship, Silence, and

> That aged venerable seer,
> With sorrowing pale, with watchings spare,
> Of pleasing yet dejected air,
> Him, heavenly Melancholy hight,
> Who flies the sons of false delight.

Another welcomed personification is "the decent nun, fair Peace of Mind," born of Innocence in the Garden of Eden.

But this unconscious parody of the technique of Christian meditation excludes that horrid thing, enthusiasm:

> But from these woods, O thou retire!
> Hood-wink'd Superstition dire;
> Zeal that clanks her iron bands,
> And bathes in blood her ruthless hands.

The reasonable devotee also banishes Hypocrisy, Malice, Anger, Rumour, Envy, Jealousy, Suspicion, Remorse, and—vainly, as the conclusion will show—the disturbing passion of Love:

> Thou hast no subject here, begone;
> Contemplation comes anon.

So much for *purificatio; illuminatio* and *contemplatio* now blend in a happy reverie:

> Above, below, and all around,
> Now nought but awful quiet's found,
> The feeling air forgets to move,
> No zephyr stirs the leafy grove,
> The gentlest murmur of the rill,
> Struck by the potent charm is still,
> Each passion in this troubled breast
> So toiling once lies hush'd to rest,
> Whate'er man's bustling race employs,
> His cares, his hopes, his fears, his joys,
> Ambition, pleasure, interest, fame,
> Each nothing of important name,
> Ye tyrants of this restless ball,
> This grove annihilates you all.

Oh power unseen, yet felt, appear!
Sure something more than nature's here.
Now on the flow'ring turf I lie,
My soul conversing with the sky.
Far lost in the bewild'ring dream
I wander o'er each lofty theme;
Tour on Inquiry's wings on high,
And soar the heights of Deity.

This hankering for an undefined "something more than nature," this soaring of "the heights of Deity" without a God, this contemplation without anything to contemplate, is not in the long run very satisfying even to Hamilton. The outcome of the mystic vision is that contemplation is all very well, but it cannot stifle his longing for the fair Monimia.

Christianity held no sway over the imagination of William Pattison (1706-1727), and his romanticism was too weak to provide a spiritual compensation. His story can be pieced together from his *Poetical Works* (1728) and from the memoir prefixed to them by an anonymous acquaintance. He was born at Peasemarsh, near Rye, in Sussex, the son of a prosperous farmer who rented "a considerable estate" from the Earl of Thanet. The Earl, attracted by the boy's superficial precocity, sent him to the Free School at Appleby on the River Eden in distant Northumberland.

As a schoolboy Pattison combined the natural sentimentalism of adolescence with pre-romantic tastes of a more self-conscious and literary kind. On the banks of the Eden he seemed to recognize those "romantick Representations and Paradisiacal Descriptions" which delighted him in Spenser. If he loved to fish in the river it was largely because of "that pleasant Gloom of Thought, which the Murmuring of the Stream naturally inspired him with." On these excursions he often wrote poetry, "and I [26] have heard him say, That many of his lines owed their smoothness and Harmony to these Streams. Here it was, he wrote that agreeable philosophical poem, *The Morning Contemplation.*"

Considering that the author was a lad of sixteen or seventeen, *The Morning Contemplation,* though not in the least "philosophical," deserves the epithet "agreeable." The mood of this retirement-piece in Miltonic

[26] Here the author of the memoir, who did not know Pattison in the Appleby days, quotes information supplied by an old schoolfellow of the poet.

octosyllabics resembles that of Dyer's *Country Walk*, which it antedates by two or three years. Pattison's sense-perceptions are less acute than Dyer's, but his enjoyment of nature is equally genuine. Neither here nor elsewhere in his work, however, does Pattison show a glimmer of religious feeling. For him, "contemplation" simply implies looking happily at rural scenery and making a few trite remarks about contentment, the evils of luxury, the futility of ambition, and so on. Even Hamilton's vague sense of "something more than nature" is absent.

A few other pieces in the *Poetical Works* were either written at Appleby or preserve memories of these early days. *A Harvest Scene* is a well-observed little sketch of an old farmer looking out over his fields. A childishly spooky ghost-ballad in anapaestic verse entitled *Song* would, if it had been written in the 1790's rather than in the 1720's, certainly be docketed as a bad imitation of Bürger.

The young poet hoped for election to a scholarship at Queen's College, Oxford, but "some Misunderstandings" arose between him and the governors of the school, and he was sent home in disgrace. Though the nature of his misconduct is unknown, some of his later poems suggest that his precocity was not confined to literary pursuits. His stern father was disgusted with him, and the benevolent and pious Earl apparently withdrew his patronage; but the indulgence of the boy's mother and some of her relations enabled him to enter Sidney-Sussex College, Cambridge, in 1724.

Here for a time he revelled in Spenser, Milton, and other great Cambridge poets of the past.[27] But his romantic impulses were not strong enough to withstand the worldliness of the university. Soon he set up for a wit, writing all sorts of little occasionals, bits of gallant flattery in imitation of Waller, familiar epistles and broad tales in imitation of Prior. His facetiousness is sometimes extremely nasty. His only serious efforts are translations of the *Heroïdes* and imitations of them—*Abelard to Eloisa, Rosamond to Henry, Yarico to Inkle*. Here his sentimentalism and his sexuality enter into an uneasy combination. Mr. Bell, his tutor, urged him to write divine poetry, but received an evasive answer.[28]

Mr. Bell grew increasingly indignant at Pattison's neglect of his academic obligations. The memoirist describes the tutor as very severe, but most of my readers will feel a lurking sympathy for the latter. Threatened with expulsion, Pattison withdrew from the University in 1724 and

[27] *To A Friend.*   [28] *An Apology to Mr. Bell.*

went to London. Here he continued his efforts, already begun at Cambridge, to secure subscribers for a volume of poems which was to consist of his translations and imitations of Ovid.[29] For a time he luxuriated in his new-found freedom. With a libertine swagger he tries to arouse the envy of his friend Roche: [30]

> While you, my dear, sit mop'd in College,
>
> .   .   .   .
>
> I make the present Day my own,
> And dedicate it to the Town:
> As how? why thus; here's just a Piece,
> And this is all my Pleasure's Price;
> With this I'll get politely drunk,
> With this I'll get some courtly Punk,
> Not one of your damn'd common Whores,
> That ply it at your Merchants' Doors;
> But one, ay, such a one! so fine!
> You Bards would call her some Divine—
> Some—but a Rapture here encroaches;
> Time spends—you Captain of the Coaches! [31]

But his mother's relations cut off his allowance, and before long he was eating husks. To this period belong a number of desperate begging letters in prose and verse. It was doubtless at this time, too, that he wrote the quatrain, *Ad Cælum:*

> Good Heaven! this Mystery of Life explain,
> Nor let me think I bear the Load in vain;
> Lest with the tedious Passage chearless grown,
> Urg'd by Despair I throw the Burden down.

Eusden the laureate, Walter Harte, and others were of some assistance to him. He began to do hackwork for Edmund Curll [32] and lodged in his house, but caught smallpox and was moved to a nursing home. Here he passed the crisis of the disease and seemed to be recovering. Some time before, he had written *An Epistle to His Majesty, King George II, On his Accession to the Throne*—a typical "Whig panegyric" full of peace and plenty, commerce and liberty. On July 10, 1727, probably through

---

[29] This apparently forms the second volume of the posthumous *Poetical Works* of 1728, which bears the separate title, *Cupid's Metamorphoses: or, Love in all Shapes.*

[30] *Vide supra,* p. 362.

[31] *To the Same.* [I.e., "Mr. Roche of King's College."]

[32] Curll published the *Poetical Works* by subscription.

Eusden's good offices, he was to have had the opportunity of presenting
this loyal effusion to the King in person. But on that day he "was taken
with a very violent delirious Fit" and perished. There is no proof that he
took his own life, but the language of the memoir at this point grows
vague and gingerly.

In happier days the boy had ended his *Morning Contemplation* with
the lines:

> But, Lo! the Clouds obscure the Sun,
> Swift Shadows o'er the Waters run!
> Trembling too, my Shadow flies,
> And by its very likeness dies.
> Hence learn, reflecting Pattison,
> How silent Fate still hurries on,
> How suddenly you must be gone!
> And as you now can tell no more,
> The Likeness that your Visage wore,
> On the Surface of the Flood,
> Where but now you gazing stood:
> So, as soon as you shall die,
> And resign Mortality,
> The delusive Breath of Fame,
> Shall forget your very Name.

It will hardly be necessary to produce the well-worn evidence for the
statement that the Welshman John Dyer (1701-1758) was a nature-poet
of considerable merit, a lover of rural retirement and pensive melancholy,
an imitator of Milton both in octosyllabics and blank verse, and a friend
of Aaron Hill, James Thomson, Richard Savage, and David Mallet. Somewhat less familiar is the fact that, like several of his contemporaries, he
could express enthusiasm not only for "simple" nature but for the completely contra-natural commercial civilization of his day. Book IV of *The
Fleece* is one long Miltonic boost for the woollen trade. *The Ruins of
Rome* couples commerce with liberty—a boon unknown to Italy. "But
those," he addresses Liberty,

> ... thy nobler Britons teach to rule,
> To check the ravage of tyrannic sway,
> To quell the proud, to spread the joys of peace,
> And various blessings of ingenious trade.
> Be these our arts; and ever may they guard,
> Ever defend thee with undaunted heart,

> Inestimable good! who giv'st us Truth,
> Whose hand upleads to light, divinest Truth!
> Array'd in ev'ry charm; whose hand benign
> Teaches unwearied Toil to clothe the fields,
> And on his various fruits inscribes the name
> Of Property.

Not merely liberty but religion is the sister of commerce. Trade, says Book II of *The Fleece,* sends men out

> O'er realms and seas. There in the solemn scene
> Infinite wonders glare before their eyes,
> Humiliating the mind enlarg'd; for they
> The clearest sense of Deity receive,
> Who view the widest prospect of his works,
> Ranging the globe with Trade through various climes.

This is an ingenious attempt to harmonize the cult of commercial bustle with the cult of "Nature and Nature's God."

It follows that this preacher of pensive retirement is also a preacher of vigorous action:

> Beast, bird, air, fire, the heavens, and rolling worlds
> All live by action: nothing lies at rest,
> But death and ruin: man is born to care;
> Fashion'd, improved, by labour. . . .
> . . . What simple Nature yields
> (And Nature does her part) are only rude
> Materials, cumbers on the thorny ground;
> 'Tis toil that makes them wealth.[33]

Such utterances clash violently with the escapism of *Grongar Hill,* where "Grass and flowers Quiet treads." Dyer is one of those eighteenth-century men who try to find ideal values sometimes by glorifying Whig civilization and sometimes by fleeing from it. *An Epistle to a Friend in Town* offers a rather unconvincing compromise. Dyer declares that he prefers to live "content in the shades,"

> Till Outrage arises, or Misery needs
> The swift, the intrepid avenger;
> Till sacred Religion or Liberty bleeds,
> Then mine be the deed and the danger.

[33] *The Fleece,* Book III.

But except in such crises, peaceful obscurity is best. Since life will so soon be over, the pursuit of "wealth and domain" is futile.

> Then glide on my moments, the few that I have,
> Smooth-shaded, and quiet, and even;
> While gently the body descends to the grave,
> And the spirit arises to heaven.

What he means by "sacred Religion" is hard to tell. The coupling of religion and liberty as if they were more or less synonymous is characteristic of the Whiggish and latitudinarian mind. Dyer's work is pervaded by a hazy religious feeling but seldom if ever strikes a definitely Christian note. He wrote no divine poetry, and when he took orders in 1740 he had composed all his major poems except *The Fleece*. According to Dr. Johnson his reasons for becoming a clergyman were "decline of health [34] and love of study." We may add that, having failed as a painter, he had just married a wife whom he would need to support by some other means. These motives are not discreditable, but they do not connote much spiritual ardor. The Protestantism displayed here and there in *The Ruins of Rome* is merely British distaste for popery.

In *Grongar Hill* "contemplation" has completely lost its Christian meaning to become a loose reverie in which enjoyment of scenery mingles with conventional moral reflections. His late poem *The Fleece* (1757) devotes part of its first book to praise of

> ... Nature, who in every change,
> In each variety, with wisdom works,
> And powers diversify'd of air and soil,
> Her rich materials.

Here Dyer is impressed by the way in which the instinctive impulses of all creatures not merely satisfy their own ends but coöperate in forming the harmony of the universe:

> Each strong affection of th' unconscious brute,
> Each bent, each passion of the smallest mite,
> Is wisely given; harmonious they perform
> The work of perfect reason, (blush, vain man!)
> And turn the wheels of Nature's vast machine.

[34] He had caught malaria while studying painting in Italy.

The hand of Providence is also seen in the fact that

> ... Every soil
> And clime, e'en every tree and herb, receives
> Its habitant peculiar: each to each,
> The Great Invisible, and each to all,
> Through earth, and sea, and air, harmonious suits.

Apparently, then, there is a "Great Invisible" above and beyond "Nature's vast machine," but the conception does not seem to be a living reality in Dyer's mind. He was aided in the composition of this poem by Mark Akenside, who, like other deists of the Shaftesbury type, makes much of universal harmony. It is not necessary, however, to label the Reverend John Dyer as a deist. He is simply a hazy latitudinarian who tries to satisfy his religious impulses with a jumble of scenery, retirement, melancholy, contemplation, liberty, "strive and thrive," and cosmic harmony.

The poems of Thomas Warton the elder (1688?-1745) were posthumously published in 1748 by his son Joseph, but it is difficult to say when they were written. Mr. Willoughby [35] is able to date only twelve of them—too small a proportion to be conclusive. He observes that "'A Farewell to Poetry' concerns Warton's departure from Oxford and his entrance upon pastoral duties. It was therefore probably written in 1723." One cannot be sure, however, whether it was written in 1723, when Warton became Vicar of Basingstoke and "ceased to reside regularly in Oxford," [36] or in 1728, when he finally abandoned his professorship of poetry. In any case these "farewells" sometimes resemble the "last appearances" of popular actors. Warton was not the man to let his pastoral duties absorb him completely. Of the twelve poems dated by Willoughby, however, one is as early as 1705 and several others were written before 1720. Since these pieces are fairly characteristic of his work, I should perhaps have assigned him to Part I; but I refrained from doing so lest I seem to exaggerate the pre-romantic qualities of the earlier period. In 1720 Warton was only thirty-two or thirty-three, and Willoughby shows that he continued to write verse until the year of his death. Hence it

[35] E. E. Willoughby, "The Chronology of the Poems of Thomas Warton the Elder," *J.E.G.P.*, XXX, 87-89.
[36] *D.N.B.*

13

seemed best to consider him here with a reminder that his career runs through both of the periods covered by this study.

The point derives its importance from the precursorial aspects of his work. To any readers who are unfamiliar with him he may be described as the literary as well as the biological parent of his more famous preromantic sons. He often sings of rural solitude, simplicity, and softly contemplative melancholy. He likes scenery, though he does not scrutinize it very closely. He is well saturated in Chaucer, Shakespeare, Spenser, and Milton, imitating Chaucer once, Spenser at least twice, and Milton repeatedly, both in octosyllabic couplets and blank verse. He paraphrases Old Norse and American Indian songs.

Considering Warton's chronological position, furthermore, these nonclassical traits are to an unusual extent dissociated from specifically Christian feeling. He is, to be sure, a moralist who can shake his head at his own fancies, insisting that "Virtue alone is Bliss compleat." [37] Several satirical poems lash the age in the half-solemn, half-witty manner of Young's *Love of Fame*.[38] At times, too, his moral interests blend with his sentimental naturalism, for he associates "simple" nature with virtues neglected by the polite world. The lady addressed in *On a May Morning* loves "rural Ease and Innocence"—unlike her sister in *Against Dress*, who is reminded that

> The studied Fopperies of Art
> No real Elegance impart,

and who is urged to observe

> How sweet the Lark and Nightingale
> Untaught and artless charm the Vale.[39]

Women are not the sole victims of Warton's didactic muse. Porus, *The Glutton*, is contrasted with the hermit

> Who in lone Caves, or near the rushy Flood
> With eager Appetite, at early Hours
> From maple Dish salubrious Herbs devours.

But Warton's primitivism never rises from the ethical to the religious level. Much as he loves the grove, he is not one of those who feel there

[37] *Ode.*
[38] *On Luxury, To a Friend on his Marriage, A Fragment of a Satire, Of the Universal Love of Pleasure.*
[39] See also *Verses Left on A Lady's Toilette.*

a supernatural *je ne sais quoi,* nor does he indulge in notions of universal harmony. In *Retirement,* to be sure,

> . . . Contemplation, Maid divine,
> Leans against some aged Pine;

but what she is contemplating remains a mystery.

Nevertheless Warton, a clergyman and the son of a clergyman, remains a Christian of sorts. He even provides a small amount of divine poetry. Two of several Scripture-paraphrases, *The Song of Judith* and *The XIIIth Chap. of Isaiah,* are cast in would-be Miltonic blank verse. The curious nature of another may be gathered from its title—*Hereafter in English Metre ensueth A Paraphrase on the Holie Book entituled Leviticus Chap. XI Vers. 13, etc. Fashioned after the Maniere of Maister Geoffrey Chaucer in his Assemblie of Foules.* This of course is merely a bit of whimsical antiquarianism.

An Elegy on an Infant offers the consolation that the child has been freed from the world's wickedness, which he now detachedly beholds from above. "Now let the Atheist tremble," begins *An Epistle to Dr. Young, upon his Poem on the Last Day.* Young receives high praise:

> O thou hast Pow'r the harden'd Heart to warm,
> To grieve, to raise, to terrify, to charm;
> To fix the Soul on God, to teach the Mind
> To know the Dignity of Human-kind;
> By stricter Rules well-govern'd Life to scan,
> And practise o'er the Angel in the Man.

Of the *Ode on the Passion* one can at least say that it was not written in cold blood. Very typical of Warton, however, is the fourth stanza, where he makes the Blessed Virgin speak the jargon of pre-romantic melancholy:

> Where can I lay my mournful Head?
> My Son, my King, my God is dead!
> To gloomy Deserts let me go,
> Among the horrid Rocks and Woods,
> The Caves, and pensive-falling Floods,
> Indulging Solitude and Woe! [40]

With this exception, it may be said that Warton's romantic poems are not Christian and that his Christian poems are not romantic. Tradition

---

[40] *Vide supra,* p. 362, for an ode by Roche which associates Christ with "contemplative" retirement.

represents him as a slothful, conceited, overbearing, incompetent, and boozy don—not a spiritual man even for his unspiritual age. The fact that he was a High Church Tory and indeed a Jacobite may seem to militate against any attempt to relate pre-romantic sentimentalism with the Low Church and Whig tradition. But Warton's High Churchmanship was never anything more than a matter of party politics. He was not always Tory, in fact, for in *To Mr. Addison* (1705) he speaks of *The Campaign* and of Marlborough in a way that would be possible only for a Whig. He turned Tory as the Tories rose to power. His convenient views gave him a snug birth in Tory Oxford, and as long as he retained his professorship he retained the appropriate ecclesiastical opinions. After such opinions ceased to be useful he became an adherent of Prince Frederick's party.

Warton's High Churchmanship, then, provides no important clue to an interpretation of his work. He is a conventional eighteenth-century clerical scholar with a marked streak of sentimentalism. Since his Christianity is drained of emotional value, he expresses his feelings through a complex of pre-romantic tendencies.

Past, present, and future are strangely blended in the character and work of Aaron Hill (1684-1750).[41] Many students have dismissed him as a fairy representative middle-classical [42] poet whose dullness is only slightly relieved by a tinge of eccentricity. Nevertheless he preserves, in the heart of the eighteenth century, much of that Cowleyesque bombast from which neoclassicism had turned in disgust. No writer of the 1720's cultivates the pseudo-Pindaric ode more assiduously or with a more ungainly effort at sublimity. Many of his slighter pieces, too, have a seventeenth-century flavor, as even their titles will suggest—*On a Bee, that was swallowed, by a Lady, in a Glass of Wine,* or *To a Lady, who put herself into a bad way, by taking Spirit of Nitre, by Spoon-fulls, instead of a few drops.* In the eighteenth century his numerous "projects," such as that for extracting a commercially profitable oil from beech-mast, seemed rather laughable; but a seventeenth-century virtuoso like Sir Kenelm Digby would have hailed him as a kindred spirit, and would have seen nothing

[41] He began to publish verse as early as 1707, but it was some years before he became regularly productive or achieved prominence in the literary world. In her dissertation, *Aaron Hill,* p. 153, Dorothy Brewster gives 1720-1728 as his floruit.

[42] The term would apply only to the qualities of his work, for he was of gentle birth.

outlandish in the names of his children—Urania, Astræa, Minerva, and Julius Caesar.

Precisely to the extent that he preserves more of the seventeenth century than most of his contemporaries he may from another viewpoint be regarded as one of the precursors of romanticism. Hill is a strong link in our historical chain. He imitates John Dennis in both the theory and the practise of poetry; but he is also the friend of Thomson, Dyer, Young, Richardson, Mallet, and Savage. Through much of his work runs a strain of turbid emotionalism, the result of his desire to exemplify a bardic and quasi-religious conception of poetry. He aspires to be *seriously* lyrical. Related to this aim is his interest in the poetry of primitive peoples [43] and in the popular songs of Scotland.[44] His view of love is preternaturally solemn: instead of treating with polite gallantry the situation underlying *To Celinda, complaining that her Harpsichord was out of Tune,* he bursts forth in an irregular ode quite staggering in its display of poetic fury. Hill is not without a taste for spookery.[45] He is genuinely fond of external nature, is not without ability to express sense-impressions, and appreciates the blessings of woodland retirement.[46] In *The Western Paradise* he longs for some exotic "uncurs'd Eden, still in nature's store."

Anyone who sees in these pre-romantic traits a sharp reaction against the spirit of puritanism should pause to consider that Aaron Hill is intensely puritanical in his moral views. He constantly talks about virtue, feels that he lives in a period of decadence, detests all frivolous trifling, and exhorts his fellow-poets to castigate and reform the times.[47] In all this he invites comparison with such moralists as Watts, Dennis, Blackmore, Defoe, Young, and Richardson. His pre-romanticism is the outgrowth of his puritanism.

Throughout most of his career Hill was a Christian. He produces more divine poetry than most writers of his period, and much of it expresses warm and genuine feeling. Miss Brewster agrees with H. G. Paul that his numerous Scripture-paraphrases were written in admiring emulation

---

[43] *Orra Moor,* a version of the well-known "Lapland Song." *Vide supra,* p. 208.

[44] *A Song. To the Tune of, I thy bonny Jocky* and *Ronald and Dorna; by a Highlander, to his Mistress. From a literal Translation of the Original.*

[45] *The Dream.*

[46] *The Choice, The Happy Man, The Reconciliation, The Dream, Solitude.*

[47] Such ideas are very common in Hill's work, but see especially *The Tears of the Muses, Answer to a scurrilous, obscene Poem, The Progress of Wit, Cleon to Lycidas,* and *Advice to the Poets.*

of those of John Dennis.[48] Hill's original religious poetry, however, is abundant. *Gideon* [49] is a tumescent Biblical epic in irregular-ode form, but subjects like *The Judgment-Day* are more congenial to his muse:

> Hark! the dissolving trumpet roars! thunders o'er thunders roll!
> A trembling angel sounds th' eternal call!
> Th' unbounded notes whirl higher and higher and rend my shiv'ring soul!
> Echoing from world to world, they burst o'er all:
> And gathering horrors, cold as death, in show'ry shadows fall;
> The conscious planets start to hear the sound,
>   And, from their orbits, bound,
>   Now, void of motion, and depriv'd of force,
> Th' arrested systems stop, at once, their course! [50]

Such passages are frequent in Hill's work. One may regard their extravagance as absurd, but in an age so lacking in passion and strangeness there is something to be said for a man who dares to be a little mad.

Hill certainly feels that the age lacks spiritual inebriation. He admires Handel for having regained the spirit of sacred music once possessed by David, and hopes that the composer's art may kindle the ardor of his hearers:

> Ne'er did religion's languid fire
> Burn fainter—never more require
> The aid of such a fam'd enliv'ner's care.
> Thy pow'r can force the stubborn heart, to feel,
> And rouse the luke-warm doubter into zeal.
>
>   .   .   .   .
>
> Teach us to pray, as David pray'd, before.[51]

And in an age when high-backed pews tempted to slumber, Hill can address the following lines *To the Preacher of an excellent Charity Sermon:*

> With rev'rend joy, my charm'd attention hung,
> To catch the musick of your truth-blest tongue.
> Spread, and dissolv'd, by mercy's moral heat,
> My heart, in sighs, exhal'd to seek your feet!

[48] H. G. Paul, *John Dennis*, p. 204n; Dorothy Brewster, *Aaron Hill*, pp. 164-165.

[49] According to Professor Brewster, *op. cit.*, p. 166, the manuscript as completed in 1724 runs to twelve books, but only three books were ever published. These appeared in 1749.

[50] *The Transport*, in the same aspiring mood, freely renders that ode of Casimir's which had earlier been imitated by Norris and Hughes. *Vide supra*, p. 109 and p. 251.

[51] *An Ode; on Occasion of Mr. Handel's great Te Deum, at the Feast of the Sons of the Clergy, on Feb. 1. 1732.*

> 'Twas far too mean a bliss, to look you thro',
> I wou'd have turn'd to air, and enter'd too!
> Still to have dwelt within you,—*pure,* like *you!*

Yet it is not unfair to say that Hill uses religious verse chiefly as an outlet for his craving to be expansive and sublime. His view of poetry reveals the real quality of his religious feeling. *The Creation,* a free Pindaric paraphrase of the first chapter of *Genesis,* has a preface, addressed to Pope, "concerning the sublimity of the ancient Hebrew Poetry." It agrees with Dennis' theory of religious enthusiasm as an essential element of great poetry. But in *Advice to the Poets* he draws from this theory the conception of poets as "prodigies" who "stretch existence, and awaken death." The true poet, he insists, is greater than king, hero, or philosopher. The "soft sons of rhyme" should rise to the high dignity of their vocation, scorn to imitate, and devote themselves to great themes.

Hill's passion for big feelings on big subjects is allied to his puritanical interest in reform. In *Cleon to Lycidas,*[52] after nagging at the evils of the age, he cries:

> Oh! for some hoarse Teutonic note, more stern,
> Than Runic bard, o'er hostile scalp, e'er sung,
> When Woden's hall resounded to his *clang!*
> Then shou'd satiric fervor, sharply strong,
> Roar, like the muses' bull, till the wak'd nine
> Concurred, in frightful consort; while intense,
> Up the steep cliffs of Pindus' pathless brow,
> Rumbling, I roll'd my tumbril theme along.

He urges his friend to be equally loud, rough, strong, and Nordic for the good of mankind:

> Up, from rhyme's poppy'd vale; ascend fame's hill:
> Soft to the soft: Thy theme be tempest— On.
> Write with a whirlwind's fury. Snatch the God,
> That thunders in blank verse, to ride thy storm.

If Carlyle had read Aaron Hill, he might have made him "the hero as poet."

To such a man, religion is valuable chiefly as a means of dilating his own personality. For Hill, creeds are much less important than inward feelings. In *The Excursion of Fancy* he brushes aside all theological mysteries:

[52] "Lycidas" is John Dyer.

> It is enough for us, that there must be
>   Ends in this, we cannot see!
>   And, since 'tis vain, to tug at fate,
>   With unavailing, human weight,
> Let us throw down this load of doubt, with which no race is won:
>   And, swift, to easier conquests, lighter, run,
>   The way, which reason is not bid to shun!
>   Let us, with never-ending courage, strive,
>   In spite of villainy, to thrive!
> And, from our resolution's spring, long streams of ·bliss derive!

That bliss is to be gained from courage, energy, and expansiveness is the essence of Hill's faith. Here Browning joins Carlyle as a parallel.

Hill has little use for enthusiasm except as a source of poetic sublimity. An admirer of Locke and Newton,[53] he likes a broad, rational, temperate Christianity. The antics of *The French Prophets* [54] arouse his indignation:

> Prophecy! no—'tis luxury of soul!
> No Cataracts, down religion's rivers, roll!
> Her streams, tho' deep, are ever smooth, and clear,
> And, from their bottoms, all things plain appear:
> On Superstition's sea, these vessels ride,
> Foul, with the dashings of the muddy tide.
>
> .   .   .   .   .
>
> With counterfeited shocks of soul, they swell,
> And, in forc'd sweats, convulsive falsehoods tell.
> To heights, like this, religion wou'd not fly;
> Ev'n zeal grows madness, when 'tis skrew'd too high.

This poet, then, is an enthusiast who distrusts enthusiasm. Despite the tumescent fervor of his divine odes, the only sort of Christianity in which his reason permits him to believe cannot lastingly satisfy his lust for vigor and boundlessness. We are not surprised, therefore, to find him dallying with deism toward the end of his career. In *Free Thoughts upon Faith: or the Religion of Reason* (1746) he seeks to draw some positive religious satisfaction from the familiar deistic negations. It is presumptuous of man,

---

[53] *To Miranda, after Marriage; With Mr. Lock's* [sic] *Treatise on Education* and *Epitaph on Sir Isaac Newton.*

[54] Members of the Camisard sect who fled to England after the Revocation of the Edict of Nantes. By 1706 they had gained some English adherents, not all of them among the poor and ignorant. The Prophets believed in the indwelling Holy Spirit, but specialized in prophetic trances, epileptic fits, the gift of tongues, and healing. In 1708 they were largely discredited by their failure to raise a dead man in Bunhill Fields. Shaftesbury's *Letter Concerning Enthusiasm* was inspired by their vagaries. They are the ancestors of the Shakers.

he declares, to speculate about the universe from the viewpoint of his own insignificant planet. Orthodoxy based on Revelation is hence a kind of blasphemy; he thinks—and here Tennyson joins Carlyle and Browning—that it is "more impious, to DECIDE, of God, than *doubt*." In Book IV of the poem this God of doubt is invoked as a muse:

> Giver of thought, oh, guide it.—Arm a mind,
> Tremblingly struck, to stem but one short glimpse,
> One distant, transient, momentary, flash
> Of thy keen light—and live!—oh!—far from *dream*
> To draw th' Almighty's deign'd approach too near—
> All, that my soul's touch'd sense aspires to tell
> Is—*that she dares not view thee*—thou, who know'st
> The muse's conscious rev'rence—aid her song.

Hill insists that Revelation is no more than man's term for "his own day-dreams, idoliz'd within." There can be no rational basis for dogmatic creeds. Miracles are superstitious fables. Many religions now dead could once appeal to a tradition older than that of Christianity. Papal infallibility is a mere assumption; noise is not proof. As for personal conviction, the Christian has no stronger assurance than the pagan who bows before his idols. Evidence drawn from the supposed influence of Christianity on morals is worthless, for there have been many bad Christians and many good heathen.

Now comes a shift from full speed astern to half speed ahead. We must believe in *something:* life cannot be a "fighting chaos." Spurning "fear's unworthy God," let us, then, believe in the Supreme Being's goodness, know Him in His works, and obey His laws. The order and the beauty of creation bespeak a loving Deity. The delightful variety of things rebukes the folly of a rigidly uniformitarian creed:

> ... Snuff this air:
> How numberless the scents, yet each distinct,
> Of every tree's known bloom;—Lean o'er these flow'rs—
> Lowliest, yet loveliest! Excellence, depress'd!
> Worth trod on by despisers! short-liv'd sweets!
> How oppositely soft, the streak-touch'd shades,
> That tinge their fragrant families!

Free Thoughts upon Faith concludes:

> Doubt all faiths, boldly, then—undoubting God,
> Appendant to no pride, mis-rob'd like zeal,

Hope all men bless'd alike—and injure none.
Grateful, I'll trace the fainter lights I find,
Un-envying other's blazing:—humbly, own
My aw'd conviction, of man's reachless power
To pierce omnipotence—and know it, near.
Let me, with distant rev'rence, pond'ring, dumb,
Dread arrogant decision; persecute
No fancied heresy—but clothing, calm,
Opinion's dazzled eye, bow darkly down
And hail th' unfathom'd vastness! Tho' the dusk
Thought fails to penetrate, revere what is,
Undaring to describe it. . . .

· · · ·

Peacefully patient, let me travel out
Life's unoffending journey. Mark, well-pleas'd,
New prospects, manners, tastes, beliefs, chang'd modes,
New systems— Every view, that sides my way,
Unprejudiced to any: till—at last
Death opening truth's barr'd gate, 'tis time, to see
God's meanings—in the light, his presence lends.

Since the Christianity of Newton, Locke, and Tillotson is cramping to Hill's emotional expansiveness, he must pass beyond its boundaries. Deism gives him more exciting things—mystery, vastness, variety, benevolence, and the feeling that man possesses a "reachless power to pierce omnipotence."

Hill's friend David Mallet (1705?-1765) edited Bolingbroke's posthumous works with entire approval of the views which they express. Hume describes his unsavory fellow-Scot as "a great declaimer in all the London coffee-houses against Christianity."[55] In poetry, however, his deism becomes less destructive and more affirmative and sentimental.

Mallet usually aspires to be a poet of witty rhetoric, but a few of his poems are rich in pre-romantic symptoms. *William and Margaret* and *Edwin and Emma* have their place in the annals of eighteenth-century balladry. *A Fragment,*[56] a Miltonic retirement-piece, contains some fresh descriptive touches. Rural solitude is associated with health, temperance, poetic imagination, and above all—thanks to Mallet's adherence to Prince Frederick—with liberty:

[55] Quoted in *D.N.B.*
[56] Despite its title, a substantial poem which seems to lack only a concluding flourish.

O Freedom! sovereign boon of heaven;
Great Charter, with our being given;
For which the patriot, and the sage,
Have plan'd, have bled thro' every age!
High privilege of human race,
Beyond a mortal monarch's grace:
Who could not give, nor can reclaim,
What but from God immediate came!

Except for this attempt to impart a supernatural *cachet* to the "Patriot" party the poem lacks any religious element.

The religion of nature, however, plays an important part in *The Excursion* (1728). The poem cannot be dismissed as a mere imitation of *The Seasons*. Friends since their student days at Edinburgh, Thomson and Mallet worked on these poems simultaneously, comparing notes and exchanging criticisms on an equal footing. Mallet's blank verse and his descriptive style probably owe much to Thomson; but while *The Seasons* is based on the *Georgics, The Excursion* is one of the numerous universe-poems of the century.

Mallet offers the following synopsis of his work: "*Canto I*. Invocation, addressed to Fancy. Subject proposed; a short excursive survey of the Earth and Heavens. The poem opens with a description of the face of nature in the different scenes of morning, sun-rise, noon with a thunderstorm, evening, night and a particular night-piece, with the character of a friend deceased. With the return of morning Fancy continues her excursion, first northward— A view of the arctic continent and the desarts of Tartary— From thence south-ward: a general prospect of the globe, followed by another of the mid-land part of Europe, suppose Italy. A city there upon the point of being swallowed up by an Earthquake: signs that usher it in: described in its causes and effects at length— *Eruption of a burning mountain,* happening at the same time and from the same causes, likewise described. *Canto II*. Contains, on the same plan, a survey of the solar system, and of the fixed stars."

After a not unsuccessful description of a sunset, Mallet pulls out the religious stop:

These scenes, where every Virtue, every Muse
Delighted range, serene the soul and lift,
Borne on devotion's wing beyond the pole,
To highest heaven her thought; to nature's God,

> First source of all things lovely, all things good,
> Eternal, infinite.

Such thoughts are inspired not only by the beauty but by the orderliness of the universe; for Mallet's enthusiasm for nature, like Thomson's, is partly aesthetic and partly scientific. In the starry heavens

> Ten thousand suns blaze forth, with each its train
> Of worlds dependent, all beneath the eye,
> And equal rule of one eternal Lord.
> To those bright climes, awakening all her powers,
> And spreading her unbounded wing, the Muse
> Ascending soars, on thro the fluid space,
> The buoyant atmosphere; whose vivid breath,
> Soul of all sublunary life, pervades
> The realms of Nature, to her inmost depths
> Diffus'd with quickening energy.

This energy is God's love, but it is also the law of gravitation:

> Simplicity divine! by this sole rule,
> The Maker's great establishment, these worlds
> Revolve harmonious, world attracting world
> With mutual love.

And of course it is Newton who has provided a rational explanation of Dante's "love that moves the sun and the other stars":

> This spring of motion, this hid power infus'd
> Thro universal nature, first was known
> To thee, great Newton! Britain's justest pride,
> The boast of human race; whose towering thought,
> In her amazing progress unconfin'd,
> From truth to truth ascending, gain'd the height
> Of science, whither mankind from afar
> Gaze up astonish'd.

Of equal interest to us is *Amyntor and Theodora*. This poem, incongruously addressed to Chesterfield, was published in 1747, but the author says that it "was orginally intended for the stage, and planned out, several years ago, into a regular tragedy." Aurelius, a high-souled Covenanter driven from Scotland after the Restoration, seeks refuge on the Hebridean island of St. Kilda. How Amyntor, the son of his chief oppressor, and Theodora, his own long-lost daughter, are later wrecked on the same island, and the pathetic situations ensuing, need not be dwelt upon.

In his preface Mallet bids us admire the virtues of the Hebrideans, "a race of people then the most uncorrupted in their manners, and consequently the least unhappy in their lives, of any, perhaps, on the face of the whole earth.... They live together, as in the greatest simplicity of heart, so in the most inviolable harmony and union of sentiments. They have neither silver nor gold; but barter among themselves for the few necessaries they may reciprocally want. To strangers they are extremely hospitable, and no less charitable to their own poor.... Both sexes have a genius to poetry."

In this primitivistic idyll Aurelius easily takes his place as a sort of patriarch. This persecuted Covenanter must at one time have cherished rather definite Christian convictions, but they have vanished by the time he reaches St. Kilda. There he becomes a vaguely benign hermit, loving the scenery, worshipping the Supreme Being through nature, and doing good to the natives. We see him on a headland at sunset contemplating nature's God through nature:

> ...Here, alone
> On earth's remotest verge, Aurelius breath'd
> The healthful gale, and felt the smiling scene
> With awe-mix'd pleasure, musing as he hung
> In silence o'er the billows hush'd beneath.

And at sunrise he utters the prayer of a nature-loving deist:

> ...O First and Best!
> Thy essence, tho from human sight and search,
> Tho from the climb of all created thought,
> Ineffably remov'd; yet man himself,
> Thy lowest child of reason, man may read
> Unbounded power, intelligence supreme,
> The maker's hand, on all his works imprest,
> In characters coëval with the sun,
> And with the sun to last; from world to world,
> From age to age, in every clime, disclos'd,
> Sole revelation thro all time the same.
> Hail universal Goodness! with full stream
> For ever flowing from beneath the throne
> Thro earth, air, sea, to all things that have life:
> From all that live on earth, in air and sea,
> The great community of nature's sons,
> To thee, first Father, ceaseless praise ascend!

The God thus addressed is the author not only of visible nature but of the great Whig ideals of liberty and reason. Laws chiefly exist, says Aurelius,

> ...one prime good to guard inviolate,
> Soul of all worth, and sum of human bliss,
> Fair Freedom, birth-right of all thinking kinds,
> Reason's great charter, from no king deriv'd,
> By none to be reclaim'd, man's right divine,
> Which God, who gave, indelible pronounc'd.

And at the close of the poem an old Hebridean, gifted with second sight, looks into the future and beholds King William coming to restore peace and freedom to Britain. Mallet's sentimental deism has grown from the soil of latitudinarian Whiggery.[57]

The unhappy Richard Savage (d. 1743) is so thoroughly false and histrionic that one can hardly hope to get at the centre of his nature. Often he vaguely praises religion along with such other abstractions as virtue, liberty, and patriotism, but he is neither a religious man nor a religious poet. "The reigning error of his life," says Dr. Johnson, "was, that he mistook the love for the practice of virtue, and was indeed not so much a good man, as the friend of goodness."

Savage's first effort in poetry, *The Battle of the Pamphlets*, was a satire directed against Bishop Hoadly. This fact, however, does not indicate that the author was a convinced High Churchman: he was merely exploiting the stir aroused by the Bangorian Controversy, and for some reason thought that more fame could be gained by attacking than by defending the latitudinarian bishop. Savage, indeed, had an ugly habit of writing on ecclesiastical disputes of which he knew nothing. Later in his career he contributed *The Progress of a Divine* to a quarrel between Edmund Gibson, Bishop of London, and the Arian divine, Thomas Rundle.[58] According to Dr. Johnson it describes the rise of "a profligate priest, by all the gradations of wickedness, from a poor curacy in the country to the highest preferments of the church ... and insinuates that this priest,

---

[57] I have not seen *The Transfiguration*, a Miltonic imitation first published posthumously in 1793, but written in college days. Even supposing that it is anything more than an academic exercise, it obviously represents a stage which Mallet soon left behind him. The unusual subject may in some measure reflect the fact that Mallet's father, a prosperous tenant-farmer, was a Roman Catholic.

[58] For Swift's defense of Rundle's eligibility for the bishopric of Derry, *vide supra*, p. 29.

thus accomplished, found at last a patron in the bishop of London. When he was asked, by one of his friends, on what pretence he could charge the bishop with such an action; he had no more to say than that he had only inverted the accusation; and that he thought it reasonable to believe, that he who obstructed the rise of a good man without reason, would for bad reasons promote the exaltation of a villain." [59] This unscrupulous performance led to a prosecution for obscenity, but Savage was acquitted on the plea that he had been obscene merely in the cause of virtue. For a time he planned to atone for this action by describing *The Progress of a Free-thinker,* intending, says Johnson, "to convert him from religion to infidelity, by all the modish sophistry used for that purpose." It is hard to agree with the Doctor that Savage's failure to perform this penance "is a real loss to mankind."

Probably such religious opinions as Savage possessed hovered on the border line between latitudinarianism and deism. Had he been an outright deist, Johnson would have been quick to point the moral. Savage describes his ideal clergyman in the lines:

> But Foster well this honest truth extends—
> Where mystery begins, religion ends.
>
> .   .   .
>
> Without craft, reverend; holy, without cant;
> Zealous for truth, without enthusiast rant.
> His faith, where no credulity is seen,
> 'Twixt infidel and bigot, marks the mean;
>
> .   .   .
>
> In him from Christian, moral light can shine;
> Not mad with mystery, but a sound divine;
> He wins the wise and good, with reason's lore;
> Then strikes the passions with pathetic power.[60]

Valuable as a religion like that of Foster might be as an antidote to bigotry and enthusiasm, it could not have been very stimulating to the emotional side of Savage's nature. Perhaps he found some spiritual satisfaction in freemasonry. At any rate he was an active and apparently a prominent member of the brotherhood, for he presided as Master when

[59] I have seen neither *The Battle of the Pamphlets* nor *The Progress of a Divine,* and depend on Johnson for my account of both poems.

[60] *Character of the Rev. James Foster,* a nonconformist divine whose chief work was *Discourses on all the Principal Branches of Natural Religion and Social Virtue,* 1749.

Thomson and Armstrong were initiated on September 13, 1736.[61] To some extent also he was able to extract quasi-religious values from the ideals of Whiggery. *Of Public Spirit in Regard to Public Works* lauds the civilization of Walpole:

> Thus public spirit, liberty, and peace,
> Carve, build, and plant, and give the land increase;
> From peasant hands imperial works arise,
> And British hence with Roman grandeur vies.

But Savage, to do him justice, is too intelligent to be taken in by his own rhetoric. The same poem, published in 1737, expresses alarm at what would now be called "technological unemployment":

> Such high perfection have our arts attain'd,
> That now few sons of toil our arts demand;
> Then to the public, to itself, we fear,
> E'en willing industry grows useless here;
> Are we too populous at length confess'd,
> From confluent strangers refug'd and redress'd?
> Has War so long withdrawn his barbarous train,
> That Peace o'erstocks us with the sons of men?
> So long has plague left pure the ambient air,
> That want must prey on those disease would spare?

The results of unemployment, over-population, and a lax immigration policy are prostitution, crime, and commercial trickery. Colonization is proposed as a remedy, but with this humane warning to the colonists:

> Do you the neighbouring blameless Indian aid,
> Culture what he neglects, not his invade,
> Dare not, oh dare not, with ambitious view,
> Force or demand subjection never due.
>
> .   .   .   .
>
> Why must I Afric's sable children see
> Vended for slaves, though form'd by nature free,
> The nameless tortures cruel minds invent,
> Those to subject, whom nature equal meant?

Humanitarianism is not the only pre-romantic tendency represented by Savage. A self-conscious egotist, he constantly exploits the probably fictitious tragedy of his life. Although he confines himself to the heroic couplet more consistently than most of his contemporaries, he handles

[61] G. C. Macaulay, *James Thomson*, p. 45.

the form almost as if it were blank verse, with frequent run-on lines and strong internal pauses in varied positions. When moved he expresses himself in a hectic, stage-tragedy style. He abounds in rather tawdry images and has almost no sense of construction. External nature—especially grandiose, terrific, or melancholy scenes which suggest landscapes by Salvator Rosa—greatly appeals to him. He often takes a solemn view of love and a quasi-religious view of modern science. Though of course he will flatter anyone as occasion demands, the poets whose work he most genuinely admires are all pre-romantic: Dyer, Hill, Young, Mallet, Thomson. Much of his verse was revised by Aaron Hill.

His sentimental side appears most clearly in *The Wanderer*. This poem was published in 1729, a year later than Mallet's *Excursion*.[62] From Mallet he borrows the idea of an "excursion" of the imagination through various scenes, combining this device—thanks to Pope—with the Abelard-ish story of a lovelorn hermit.

The descriptive elements of the poem exist chiefly for their own pictorial sake but are sometimes infused with a little Newtonian religion. Through the telescope

> ... the beams of the far-lengthen'd eye
> Measure known stars, and new remoter spy.
> Hence commerce many a shorten'd voyage steers,
> Shorten'd to months, the hazard once of years;
> Hence Halley's soul etherial flight essays;
> Instructive there, from orb to orb she strays;
> Sees round new countless suns, new systems roll!
> Sees God in all! and magnifies the whole!

Passages like the following, however, sentimentalize Shaftesbury rather than Newton:

> Beauty, who sways the heart, and charms the sight;
> Whose tongue is music, and whose smile delight;
> Whose brow is majesty; whose bosom peace;
> Who bade creation be, and chaos cease;
> Whose breath perfumes the spring; whose eye divine
> Kindles the sun, and gave its light to shine.

Savage makes no attempt to identify the religion of nature with Christianity. He apostrophizes the sun as an independent deity:

[62] G. C. Macaulay, *James Thomson*, pp. 235-236, rightly calls attention to the influence of Thomson on *The Wanderer*. Mallet's influence, however, is even more obvious.

> From Thee, bright, universal Power! began
> Instinct in brute, and generous love in man.

Canto I narrates the journey of "Contemplation" through various "rural scenes," ending in a Salvatorian mountain landscape where the poet, or his contemplative fancy personified as "the Wanderer," encounters a youngish hermit who receives him kindly. The chapel-cave is adorned with religious carvings which are described with the zest of a connoisseur:

> Meek martyrs smile in flames; gor'd champions groan!
> And muse-like cherubs tune their harps in stone!
> Next shadow'd light a rounding force bestows,
> Swells into life, and speaking action grows!
> Here pleasing, melancholy subjects find,
> To calm, amuse, exalt the pensive mind!
>
> .   .   .   .   .
>
> Such penitential Magdalene reveals;
> Loose-veil'd, in negligence of charm she kneels,
>
> .   .   .   .   .
>
> The sinful world in sorrowing eye she keeps,
> As o'er Jerusalem Messiah weeps.
> One hand her bosom smites; in one appears
> The lifted lawn, that drinks her falling tears.

The hermit, however, is strictly non-sectarian. His only religion is that of the tender heart, and these "pleasing, melancholy" decorations merely express his sensibility. He is, in fact, a bereaved lover rather than a penitent. In Canto II he tells how he has sought solitude in the vain endeavor to stifle his sorrow at the loss of his wife:

> Mid cloister'd solitary tombs I stray,
> Despair and horror lead the cheerless way!
>
> .   .   .   .   .
>
> Olympia!—my Olympia's lost! (I cry)
> Olympia's lost, the hollow vaults reply!
> Louder I make my lamentable moan;
> The swelling echoes learn like me to groan;
> The ghosts to scream, as through lone aisles they sweep;
> The shrines to shudder, and the saints to weep!

The indebtedness to *Eloisa to Abelard* is patent.

In Canto III the Wanderer parts from the hermit and indulges in reflections arising from the scenery. Canto IV describes a later excursion of wandering fancy. In another picturesque landscape, with a ruined aqueduct in the background, the hermit again appears. In Canto V the Wanderer and the hermit make a reflective-descriptive tour of the habitable globe. But it appears that the hermit has died since his first meeting with the Wanderer, and is now an angel in mortal guise. Hence he is able, in a way borrowed from Parnell's *The Hermit,* to clear up the Wanderer's perplexities:

> Were the whole known, that we uncouth suppose,
> Doubtless, would beauteous symmetry disclose.
>
> .   .   .   .
>
> Sword-law has often Europe's balance gain'd,
> And one red victory years of peace maintain'd.
> We pass through want to wealth, through dismal strife,
> To calm content, through death to endless life.

After some edifying remarks on knowing God through symmetrical and harmonious nature the angelic hermit vanishes.

Perhaps Savage meant all this in the moment of composition, but he seems a more honest man in the first part of *The Bastard.* There for one moment he sneers triumphantly at the whole smugly respectable world, appealing to a "nature" which has nothing whatever to do with universal harmony:

> Blest be the bastard's birth! through wondrous ways
> He shines eccentric, like a comet's blaze!
> No sickly fruit of faint compliance he!
> He! stamp'd in nature's mint of ecstasy!
>
> .   .   .   .
>
> Born to himself, by no possession led,
> In freedom foster'd, and by fortune fed;
> Nor guides, nor rules, his sovereign choice control,
> His body independent as his soul;
> Loos'd to the world's wide range—enjoin'd no aim,
> Prescrib'd no duty, and assign'd no name:
> Nature's unbounded son, he stands alone,
> His heart unbias'd, and his mind his own.

"Now, gods, stand up for bastards!" But this also is a form of play-acting. The rôle, though congenial, cannot long be maintained, and the poem ends in a warm bath of pathos.

Henry Baker, F.R.S. (1698-1774) [63] would wish to be remembered as student of natural history and as author of treatises on microscopy and other scientific subjects. In youth and early middle age, however, he invaded the realms of poetry. *Original Poems: Serious and Humorous* (1725) is not of much value for us, since it consists principally of slight occasional pieces, epigrams, gallant songs, and the like. There is a rather strong anacreontic element, with much stuff about panting bosoms and "dying" in the beloved's arms—a feeble, half-snickering, half-sentimental kind of nastiness.

Although there is no real poetry in him, he portrays himself in his preface as something of a natural genius: "As I scarce ever have intentionally sat down to write, but only copied the Ideas, I know not how arising, accidentally in my own Mind; as I have followed no Rules, nor at all consulted the Thoughts of Others upon the same Subjects, it is very probable, there may be less of Art, and more of Nature, than is usually found in Compositions of the like Sort." But despite this declaration his wood-notes wild are anything but rich in foretokenings of romanticism. *A Ballad,* in barefaced imitation of Nicholas Rowe, makes a betrayed maiden lament her fate "On the banks of a river so deep." *The Petition,* a retirement-piece in the neoclassical tradition of Pomfret's *Choice,* prays for "an happy mediocrity." This poem provides the only clear indication of Baker's religious viewpoint:

> May true Religion, that unerring Guide,
> Direct my Flight,
> To Heav'n aright,
> But let me lay its empty Forms aside.
> Health and sound Reason give me still,
> To judge unbiass'd what is Good or Ill.
> Obedient let my Passions be
> To all the Rules of strict Morality.

Elsewhere in the volume this anti-ecclesiastical religion of health, reason, and right conduct is not much in evidence. "Death," he once observes conventionally enough, "is the Road to everlasting Life" and "a Friend that sets the Wretched free." It opens doors leading in opposite directions

---

[63] The son of a chancery-clerk. He was apprenticed to a bookseller, but soon devised a method of teaching deaf-mutes and made a good living by it. He married Sophia, youngest daughter of Daniel Defoe.

—one for the virtuous and one for the wicked.[64] But in *A Serious Reflection on Human Life* he can portray the vanity of human wishes without offering any religious hope or consolation. The poem concludes:

> No Age, no State, unhappy Mortals know,
> Which is not full, and over-charg'd with Woe:
> Troubles from Life, as Sparks from Fire, 'rise;
> Man's born, knows Care, looks round, laments and dies.

Baker, however, is usually merrier than this. More in his proper vein is *The Spinning-Wheel,* a fabliau in the manner of Prior which deals with the sexual inadequacy of a parson.

All these poems are the work of a lively young bourgeois of twenty-seven who aspires to write like a witty gentleman. He appears as a much solider person when, some time later, he publishes *The Universe: A Poem Intended to Restrain the Pride of Man.*[65] Though still not a poet, Baker has gained in control over his medium; his scientific interests have developed greatly; his religious views, though even less orthodox than in *Original Poems,* have grown more serious and philosophical.

Baker interprets the Newtonian universe in the light of the venerable metaphor of the "Chain of Being."[66] The plenitude of this best of all possible systems is especially emphasized. Ours is not the only world that is crammed full of happy creatures:

> Nor can those other worlds, unknown by Thee,
> Less stor'd with Creatures, or with Beauty, be,
> For God is uniform in all his Ways,
> And everywhere his boundless Pow'r displays.

With a good deal of technical detail, the poet sets forth the wonders of astronomy and natural history as proofs of the existence of a wise and benignant God. There is no approach to pantheism: the dependence of nature upon a personal Divine Being is strongly urged. On the other hand, no attempt is made to identify this Being with the God of Christi-

---

[64] *Death.*

[65] The undated first edition of the poem is conjecturally assigned to 1727 in the British Museum Catalogue. Apparently, however, there is rather strong evidence that *The Universe* first appeared in 1734. See G. R. Potter, "Henry Baker, F.R.S.," *Modern Philology,* XXIX, 301-321. I may add that it seems unlikely that Baker could have written so substantial a poem as *The Universe* within two years after publishing the trivial volume of *Original Poems.*

[66] For an exhaustive and brilliant account of this tradition, see A. O. Lovejoy, *The Great Chain of Being.*

anity or to harmonize natural and supernatural revelation. The poem preaches an affirmative and constructive type of deism. Baker's deism is derived from Newton rather than from Shaftesbury: one observes no Neoplatonic tendency to regard the universe as the aesthetically harmonious product of divine creative imagination.

A particularly important feature of *The Universe* is implied by its subtitle—"a poem intended to restrain the pride of man." Baker scorns "the absurd Opinion, that all the Works of Providence we see around us, were created only for the Use of Man." In "the eternal Scale of Beings," man occupies first place "upon this Globe"; but this globe is quite insignificant in relation to "the grand Universe":

> Why did'st Thou murder yonder harmless Fly?—
> Because 'tis Good for Nothing, dost Thou cry.
> The same of Thee, tho' now so vain and gay
> As justly might superior Beings say.[67]

Thus Baker's aim, as he goes on to say in his prefatory address *To the Reader,* is "that, by considering the Grandeur of the Whole, Man might be made sensible of his own Littleness and Insignificance, except in the very Place he stands."

But in contemplating the universal grandeur man may achieve a higher and more unselfish joy, for he now grasps the true purposes of "the impartial Parent of the Universe. ... The primary Intent of the Almighty in the Existence of every Being must have been to make it happy, and the Relation in which it stands to every other Creature is only such as is most conducive towards the Felicity of the Whole. Every Individual was made principally for its own Sake, the meanest Insect as well as the proudest Monarch. We are all Fellow-Creatures":

> Eternal Goodness certainly design'd
> That ev'ry one, according to its kind,
> Should Happiness enjoy: for God, all-just,
> Could ne'er intend his Creature to be curs'd.
> When Life he gave, he meant that Life should be
> A State productive of Felicity.

These truths are drawn from nature as interpreted by reason:

> Hail, sacred Reason! glorious! and divine!
> Bulwark eternal of Religion's Shrine!

[67] The ultimate philosophical basis of Uncle Toby's great act of sensibility.

> Truth's firmest Friend! but Superstition's Foe!
> To whom our whole of Happiness we owe!

Since reason is granted to everyone, there is nothing mysterious about the divine plan. Baker assures God:

> Nor are thy Laws perplext, (as some have taught,
> With Vanity possess'd, and void of Thought,)
> But plain and easy. Thou, all-wise and good,
> Could'st ne'er command what can't be understood.

In short this "poem intended to restrain the pride of man" is beamingly optimistic. Baker's prosaic style suggests that his philosophy is more sentimental than his personal temperament, but the universe as he portrays it contains all the essentials of a full-fledged cult of feeling.

By his second marriage Robert Nugent (1702-1788) acquired the name of Craggs,[68] the parish of Gosfield in Essex, a seat in parliament for St. Mawes in Cornwall, and about 100,000 pounds. A third matrimonial investment was also profitable. He used his large fortune to gain political advancement, and used his political influence to get more money. "As for convictions in politics," says *D.N.B.*, "he had none; from the first he laid himself out for the highest bidder." Rewards other than monetary also came his way, for he became Viscount Clare, Baron Nugent, and later Earl Nugent, in the Irish peerage.

Nugent was reared a Roman Catholic, turned Protestant before he entered public life, and returned to Rome in old age. His memory is not fragrant, but there was nothing deeply sinister about him. He might have stepped from the pages of Smollett. Glover called him "a jovial and voluptuous Irishman, who had left Popery for the Protestant religion, money, and widows."[69] That Goldsmith granted him his friendship may be placed on the credit side of the account.

In 1739, when he published *Odes and Epistles,* his only collection of verse, Nugent was a financial backer of the Prince of Wales. *An Ode to William Pulteney* traces his development from mental slavery up to the pure truths of Frederick's party:

> Remote from Liberty and Truth,
> By Fortune's Crime, my early Youth

[68] He took the surname of his new wife, Anne Craggs.   [69] Quoted in *D.N.B.*

> Drank Error's poison'd Springs.
> Taught by dark Creeds and Mystic Law,
> Wrapt up in reverential Awe,
> I bow'd to Priests and Kings.

But soon the "friendly Star" of Hooker shed upon him a glow of reason which prepared him for the broad daylight of Locke. Thus he became a Protestant and a lover of liberty:

> Now warm'd with Noble Sidney's Page,
> I pant with all the Patriot's Rage,
> Now wrapt in Plato's Dream,
> With More and Harrington around
> I tread fair Freedom's magic Ground,
> And trace the flatt'ring Scheme.

In the present corrupt and venal age he hails Pulteney as a rare embodiment of these ideals.

"The "Patriot" creed again finds expression in *An Ode, to His Royal Highness,*[70] *on His Birthday:*

> Let Priests an hallow'd Bondage preach!
> Let School-men earth-born Godhead teach!
> Let Loyal Mad-Men rave!
> Wise Nature feels, she mocks their Rules,
> And Laws oppress'd, from diff'rent Schools,
> Unite the Free and Brave.

Against priestcraft and kingcraft Nugent opposes a nature whose spontaneous feelings release men from slavish rules. One of these rules, to judge from the second line of this stanza, is the doctrine of Christ's divinity.[71]

In a less lyrical and more argumentative tone, *An Epistle to the Right Honourable the Lord Viscount Cornbury* undertakes to show "that Justice fans the Flame of Social Love." Love of mankind is that virtue which

> Sublimes our Souls, and animates our Clay;
> Above low Self exalts our nobler Frame,
> And emulates that Heav'n, from whence it came.
> O would it never be confin'd to Place;
> But beam, extensive, as the Human Race;

[70] *Prince Frederick.*

[71] The line may possibly allude to the divine right of kings, but I do not see why this doctrine should be ascribed to "School-men."

> Be, as it was design'd, the World's great Soul,
> Connect its Parts and actuate the Whole.
> So each should think himself a Part alone,
> And, for a Nation's welfare, stake his own!
> Yet farther still, tho' dearest to the Breast,
> That Nation think but part of all the rest!

Implicitly, then, to love Prince Frederick is to love England, and to love England is to love the human race.

Vainly does the unbeliever strive to sunder morals and religion, for we read with some surprise that Christianity is the guarantor of social love:

> Proceed, ye Deists! blindfold Rage employ,
> And prove the sacred Truths ye would destroy,
> Prove Christian Faith the wisest rule to bind,
> In Chains of cordial Love our jarring Kind;
> And thence conclude it human, if ye can,
> The perfect Produce of imperfect Man.

Self-interest, this eminently self-interested poet continues, is not necessarily hostile to universal benevolence; but the firmest basis for the latter is justice—by which he means proportionateness, or harmony. Justice in this sense is the very groundwork of the universe, for it was "in all his Works the great Creator's guide." Creation is a "mimic World" copied by God from eternal intellectual types.

> The Types are real, since from them he drew
> The real Forms of whatso'er we view.
>
> .   .   .   .
>
> But Chance could never frame the vast Design,
> Where countless Parts in justest Order join.
> The Types eternal all Proportions teach,
> Greater or less, more or less perfect each;
> These ever present Power omniscient sees,
> On them he forms his ever made Decrees.
> Nor can he ever love what merits least,
> Man than an Angel, or than Man a Beast.
> Hence Reason, hence immortal Order springs:
> Knowledge and Love, that justly suit the Things.
> And thence th' unerring Rule of *Justice* flows,
> To act as Order prompts, and Reason shows.

Nugent says nothing to indicate that the types themselves are thoughts of the divine mind. Apparently God is just merely as drawing just copies from an absolute verity which conditions His activities. The association of social love with Platonic harmony suggests the influence of Shaftesbury, but such ideas were too pervasive to enable one to be sure of the fact. The *Ode to Pulteney* has shown that Plato entered into the complex of seventeenth-century liberal notions which Nugent espoused on leaving the Roman fold.

Primeval man shared the divine perception of the eternal truths:

> In the pure Splendor of substantial Light,
> The Beam divine of Reason bless'd his Sight;
> Seraphic Order in its Fount he view'd;
> Seeing, he lov'd; and loving, he pursu'd.

"But soon by Sin the sacred Union broke," and man lost contact with the Platonic types. Later generations vainly tried to compensate for the loss by using "the Force of human Prudence." The result was government, which culminates in monarchy. But monarchy generates evils which must be curbed by lovers of freedom like Cornbury or embodiments of the cosmic justice like Lord Chancellor Hardwick,

> ... whose righteous Seat,
> Gave to the Innocent a sure Retreat:
> Severely just, and piously humane,
> The Crime you punish, while you share the Pain:
> Tears, with the dreadful Words of Sentence flow,
> Nor can the rigid Judge the Man forego.

Lewis Carroll's Walrus was a man of feeling.

Thus in *Odes and Epistles* Nugent displays a religion compounded of uncurbed "natural" feeling, political liberalism, Platonism, and benevolism. But a Christianity of sorts continues to buttress these sentiments. In *An Epistle to the Right Honourable Earl of Chesterfield,* Nugent describes humanity's vain pursuit of happiness. But, he urges, there must be happiness somewhere—otherwise we should not strive for it so ardently:

> Bliss is ordain'd for All, since Heav'n intends,
> All Beings should attain their destin'd Ends.
>
> .   .   .   .   .
>
> There must be Pleasures past the Reach of Sense,
> Some nobler Source must Happiness dispense:

> Reason, arise! and vindicate thy Claim,
> Flash on our Minds the Joy-infusing Flame.

Responding to this invocation, Reason clears up the whole matter:

> Conspicuous now is Happiness display'd,
> 'Tis in possessing Him for whom we're made.
> For He alone all human Bliss completes,
> To Him alone th' expanding Bosom beats;
> Who fills each Faculty, each Pow'r can move,
> Exerts all Thought, and deep absorbs all Love.

>   .   .   .   .

> No sickly Tastes the heav'nly Rapture cloys,
> No weary'd Senses sink in whelming Joys;
> While, rais'd above low Matter's grosser Frame,
> Pure Spirit blazes in His purer Flame.

But the descent from this height is rapid. Since Pure Spirit wants us to lead good lives, it follows that "the greatly Virtuous are the greatly Blest"; and since to be virtuous is to refrain from excess, we fall back upon that "nothing too much" of which Chesterfield is the great exemplar.

The God toward whom Nugent here briefly aspires is not necessarily the God of Christianity, but the condemnation of deism in the *Epistle to Cornbury* implies that the author deems himself a Christian. After 1739, the date of *Odes and Epistles*, Nugent became absorbed in more profitable matters than poetry; but in 1774, an old man of seventy-two, he published *Faith. A Poem.* There is no clear indication that he has yet returned to Rome, but he is much more orthodox than in his Patriot days. In his preface he calls for a defensive alliance of "all who are ranged under the Banner of a Man-God, however they may differ in other points, whether of Doctrine or of Discipline: This will be no more than a just Compensation for the Prejudices drawn upon their Common Faith by that intolerant Rancour with which different Sects have persecuted each other. Of those Prejudices Infidelity hath not failed to take every unfair Advantage, and would conclude against the Law of Disinterestedness, Forgiveness, and universal Benevolence, because cruel and interested Men have acted in direct Opposition to its Spirit and Commands." Christians must unite to clear themselves of the charge that they do not believe in social love.

The formidable Argument of the poem seems to promise a thorough-going rebuttal of Epicureanism, materialism, and deism; but the text itself is a garrulous jumble of assertions—forty-four pages of the short trochaic couplets beloved by Namby-Pamby Philips. The following thrust at materialism is perhaps the best passage:

> If, as impious Teachers say,
> Souls are animated Clay;
> If, by chemick Pow'r refin'd,
> Matter, high-sublim'd to Mind,
> Rich with Wisdom, Foresight, Skill,
> Chuses, thinks, and moves at will;
> A new Essence thus supply'd,
> To the native Mass deny'd,
> Total Change—such alter'd State
> Who produces, must create:
> In the wond'rous Work imprest,
> The Creator shines confest;
> Still the Soul retains her Claim,
> Pure and animated Flame.

The argument that the emergence of mind from matter is a fact, but that this fact proves rather than disproves the existence of God, represents a rather advanced stage in apologetics.

Nugent is less telling, and more truly himself, when he argues that the millions, incapable of philosophy, need the moral guidance of the Christian faith. What if the reason of an Epictetus could deduce the precepts of natural religion?

> Be this boastful Claim allow'd!
> What avails it to the Crowd?
> What to them, the unknown Use
> Of Philosophy abstruse?
> Hard their Doom, if millions stray,
> While a Sophist finds his Way.
>
> .   .   .   .
>
> All that in fair Virtue charms,
> All in social Love that warms,
> All in Sympathy that glows,
> Melting at another's Woes,
> All that righteous Zeal should dare,
> All that bids sweet Mercy spare,

> All that in confided Trust
> Steels the never-yielding Just,
> These, confirm'd by Heav'n's Command,
> On a Base eternal stand.

These lines justify the assertion that even now Nugent is not primarily a Christian but rather a sentimental benevolist who has found in orthodoxy the best means of protecting his sentimentalism. Whether this consideration motivated his final return to Catholicism one cannot say. In any case this not very virtuous lover of the social virtues will soon accept the "dark Creeds and Mystic Law" which he spurned so heroically in the *Ode to Pulteney*.

The son of a clergyman, Isaac Hawkins Browne (1705-1760) was educated at Westminster and at Trinity College, Cambridge. Later he studied law and was admitted to the bar, but never practised the profession seriously. From 1744 to 1754 he sat in the Commons as a supporter of the Pelham ministry. Browne was noted for his wit, charm, and intemperance; but these are not the qualities suggested by one of his earliest poems, *Of Design and Beauty,* which was published anonymously in 1734. It has sometimes been listed among the more or less Shaftesburyian poems on universal harmony, and to that tradition it is certainly related. It differs from other examples of the type, however, in being a sort of philosophical *Ars Poetica*. Browne's specific critical opinions are interesting, but we must confine ourselves to the theory which underlies them.

Browne has read his Shaftesbury, his Addison, and his Longinus. In every art, he declares, "the soul of all beauty" is design, and beautiful design demands a combination of native genius and acquired skill:

> Truth of Design, which Nature's works impart,
> Alike extends to every work of art.
> To compass this, both skill and genius meet,
> Genius to bring materials, skill to fit;
> Where both conspire, is Beauty; which depends
> On the fair aptitude of means to ends.

Nature itself, as the above passage implies, is a great aesthetic design, and the artists's love of order is an impulse to imitate the orderliness of the universe.

True sublimity balances similarity and difference, harmony and discord, the circumstantial and the vast, in a pattern which is all the more beautiful for having attained

> The noblest purpose by the simplest means;
> More perfect, as more wide its branches shoot,
> While all are nourished by one common root.
> And such, if man Immensity could pierce,
> Such are the beauties of the Universe;
> The various movements of this great machine
> Are all directed by one Pow'r within;
> One Genius, as in human frame the soul,
> Rules, and pervades, and animates the whole.

The universe is the supreme work of art, and God is the supreme artist. Perfect beauty is therefore to be sought in the shaping intelligence of God, the source of all design.

If God's creation is a poem, it follows that the human poet is akin to divinity. The creative artist,

> ... not content the shallow shore to keep,
> Dauntless expatiates in the boundless deep,
> Ranging through earth, and air, and sea, and sky,
> Where'er the scatter'd seeds of Beauty lie;
> Surveys all Nature, and together brings
> The wide-dispers'd dependency of things.
> Hence those enlarg'd ideas which impart
> The common sympathies of art with art;
> Hence Order upon Order seems to rise
> A comely series, till it touch the skies.

Thus the poet does much the same work as God, and in much the same way. Read in its entirety, however, *Of Design and Beauty* is less romantic than this view would imply. Browne is restrained by his classical preference for neat patterns, measure, and balance. Nevertheless this son of a clergyman has, by the age of twenty-nine, acquired an aesthetic religion which seems independent of Christianity.

The earnest and indeed rather elevated spirit of this poem was not to be characteristic of Browne either as man or as writer. Only two years later he found his true vein in a series of clever parodies, the well-known *Pipe of Tobacco,* and thereafter devoted himself almost wholly to humorous trifles of a thoroughly unromantic kind.

The gout caused by his excessive drinking inspires one of his few serious poems, which declares that such maladies are meant to check "lawless appetite" and awaken man's better nature through dread of pain.[72] At another earnest moment, *On the Author's Birthday,*[73] Apollo scolds him for his frivolous verses:

> Oh! born for nobler ends, dare to be wise,
> 'Tis not e'en now too late, assert thy claim;
> Rugged the path, that leads up to the skies,
> But the fair guerdon is immortal fame.

The poet, however, heeded neither gout nor Apollo until 1754, when he published a long religious poem in Latin, *De Animi Immortalitate.* Since it lies well beyond the close of our period, and since we have elsewhere confined ourselves to English verse, we need not devote much attention to it. The poem certainly appealed to the taste of the age, however, for it was translated into English no less than five times—by William Hay, Richard Grey, John Cranwell, Soame Jenyns, and John Byrom. In Jenyns' translation, which is printed by Browne's son in the 1768 edition of his father's poems, a summarizing passage reads:

> Thus stands my argument.—The thinking soul
> Cannot terrestrial or material be,
> But claims by Nature immortality:
> God, who created it, can make it end,
> We question not; but cannot apprehend
> He will; because it is by him endued
> With strong ideas of all-perfect Good:
> With wond'rous pow'rs to know, and calculate
> Things too remote from this our earthly state,
> With sure presages of a life to come,
> All false and useless; if beyond the tomb
> Our beings cease: we therefore can't believe
> God either acts in vain, or can deceive.

The somewhat circular argument, then, is that a wise and loving God would never have planted in our minds the vision of immortal life if that vision did not correspond to the truth. Such thinking harmonizes readily with that of the "Common Sense" school, of which Jenyns was a member.

Although *Of Design and Beauty* is for us by far the most interesting

[72] *On a Fit of the Gout.*   [73] His thirty-sixth—the poem is dated 1741.

of Browne's poems, it obviously represents an early and transitory stage in his development. The earnest young Shaftesburyian aesthete soon becomes a careless wit, but ends his career as a defender of Christian doctrine.

The historical and intrinsic interest of the work of Henry Brooke (1703-1783) [74] has so often been observed by critics, and he has received such intelligent treatment at the hands of Miss Scurr,[75] that a good deal may here be taken for granted. Few will deny his pre-romanticism. He was a sentimental primitivist, a benevolent man of feeling, a lyricist, and a lover of nature, of olden times, and of distant places. His writings faithfully reflect his character. Contemporary reports agree in describing him as impulsive, innocent, tender-hearted, lovable, and slightly crack-brained.[76] As a schoolboy, he refused to disturb a mother bird on her nest; in manhood, he gave up his political career to please the timorous child whom he had married, and ruined himself financially by his generosity to the unfortunate. He was immensely learned in agriculture but could never make anything grow.

Brooke's religious ideas have received some attention from students. The son of an Irish clergyman, he had a warmly spiritual nature and never ceased to regard himself as an earnest Christian. He never took orders, but his simple neighbors revered him as a local saint. One Sunday, in the vicar's unexpected absence, he was prevailed upon to preach *extempore*. When the vicar arrived late, he found the congregation dissolved in tears.[77] There is no telling what Brooke may have said to them, for some of his notions were peculiar. He may have been talking Behmenism or Methodism, or he may no less probably have enunciated

> Great Nature's law, the law within the breast;
> Form'd by no art, and to no sect confin'd,
> But stamp'd by Heav'n upon th' unletter'd mind.[78]

[74] Most of his plays and both of his novels appeared later than 1740; but he began writing verse about 1728 and most of his non-dramatic poetry belongs to the 1720-1740 period.

[75] Helen Margaret Scurr, *Henry Brooke*. See also Lionel Stevenson, "Brooke's 'Universal Beauty' and Modern Thought," *PMLA.*, XLIII, 198-209; but the author of this interesting paper regards Brooke with an astonishment which would be tempered by greater familiarity with the type of thought which he represents.

[76] He became definitely insane toward the close of his life.

[77] Chalmers, *English Poets*, XVII, 334.   [78] Prologue to *Gustavus Vasa*.

Perhaps he melted his hearers with such words as these:

> Sweet as a field that vernal breezes fan,
> Sweet are emotions in the heart of man;
> Sweet are the tears of worth, the ties of kin,
> And all the home-bred charities within!
> When human feelings the warm breast inspire,
> When pity softens, and when passions fire;
> Then glows the mint of Nature, apt, refin'd,
> And virtue strikes her image on the mind.[79]

Passages illustrating Brooke's religion might be culled from a number of his lesser pieces, but it will be more profitable to confine ourselves to three long poems—*Universal Beauty* (1735), *Redemption* (1772), and *Conrade*. Of these the first deserves particular attention as being one of the most substantial philosophico-religious poems of the 1720-1740 period.

Brooke believes that the universe is the work of Mind, for the order and harmony of things could not have been produced by involuntary mechanism. It is even more inconceivable that human thought should have arisen from brute matter:

> Mysterious Thought! swift angel of the mind!
> How dost thou glow with just disdain, how scorn
> That thought should ever think thee earthly born?

In language suggestive of transcendentalism, man's thought is hailed as

> Thou who canst distance motion in thy flight,
> Wing with aspiring plume the wondrous height,
>
> .   .   .   .
>
> Throughout the universal system range,
> New form old systems, and new systems change;
> Through nature traffic on, from pole to pole,
> And stamp new worlds on thy dilated soul.

So divine a faculty bespeaks a divine origin. By means of "contemplation," the human mind pierces through "outward forms" and arrives at the "inward truth":

> The system one, One Maker stands confess'd,
> The Prime, the One, the Wondrous and the Bless'd;
> The One in various forms of Unity express'd!

[79] Prologue to *The Earl of Westmoreland*.

The One underlying the many is called "Almighty Architect," "Great Intellect," "Sovereign Geometrician," "Nature's God," and "Thou Voluntary Goodness." His attributes are truth, beauty, love:

> Essential truth! and beauty's charm! in course,
> Of boundless love the ever boundless source!
> Of boundless love, which would not, could not miss,
> To be the boundless source of boundless bliss!

In short this deity is

> The Eternal Spring, whence streaming bounty flows;
> The Eternal Light! whence ev'ry radiance glows;
> The Eternal Height of indetermin'd space!
> The Eternal Depth of condescending grace!
> Supreme! and Midst! and Principle! and End!
> The Eternal Father! and the Eternal Friend!
> The Eternal Love! who bounds in ev'ry breast;
> The Eternal Bliss! whence ev'ry creature's bless'd.

God's way are motivated by a benevolent fecundity of imagination. The universe is His "great poem," and He has thoroughly enjoyed writing it. He likes to create, and He likes to share His creative joy with rational beings of His own shaping. Brooke's view of the process of creation is thoroughly Platonic. Addressing the Deity, he declares that in the beginning

> All, all, things past—now present—yet to be,
> Great Intellect! were present all to thee;
> While thou sole infinite essential reign'd,
> And of finites the infinite contain'd,
> Ideal entities in One Supreme,
> Distinguish'd endless, yet with thee the same,
> Thy pow'r their essence, and thy will their claim.
> Whence—at thy word, worlds caught the potent sound,
> And into being leap'd this wondrous round.

Though full, richly variegated, and infinitely complex, the universe is a perfectly integrated and harmonious whole in which every creature enjoys the greatest possible amount of happiness appropriate to its position in the scale of being:

> Thrice happy all, and lords of wide domains,
> Celestial vales and elemental plains!.

> One is the flood which universal flows;
> And hence the reptile, hence the seraph glows;
> Still equal, though inequal, that and this;
> Since fulness bounds, and all are fill'd with bliss.

God is not inconsistent in loving both order and variety, for a complex system demonstrates his shaping power more triumphantly than a simple one. A footnote speaks of "that order, which the Supreme Self-Existence, to manifest his own power and goodness, has caused to flow through an infinite variety on the union of a few principles; which few principles are further and ultimately resolvable and united in him, the only Original, and Self Eternal Principle." Here is an interesting reconciliation of the uniformitarian and diversitarian trends of the century.

The bulk of the poem is a description of the beautiful interplay of variety and order in God's works. The factual background is Newtonian, but even when Brooke grapples most closely with scientific detail—and he sometimes becomes very technical indeed—his spirit is that of a man engaged in the contemplation of beauty. The following is a fair sample:

> Orb within orb in loving circlets turn,
> And central suns through every system burn;
> Revolving planets on their gods attend,
> And tow'rds each sun with awful reverence bend;
> Still tow'rds the lov'd enliv'ning beam they wheel,
> And pant, and tremble, like the amorous steel.
> They spring, they revel in the blaze of day,
> Bathe in the golden stream, and drink the orient ray.

Brooke has found a way of being both religiously and poetically stimulated by science.

The reader is never allowed to forget the real Unity which lies behind the phenomenal diversity. In studying nature we

> ... trace her maze of complicated schemes,
> Where differing parts identity compose,
> Yet endless how, from One! each varying essence flows;
> Each vegetable set in beds of bliss,
> Their sap exhaling from the Prime Abyss.

The main theme of the poem, then, is expressed in the lines:

> Thus Beauty, mimick'd in our humbler strains,
> Illustrious through the world's great poem reigns!

The One grows sundry by creative power;
The Eternal's found in each revolving hour;
The Immense appears in every point of space;
The Unchangeable in Nature's varying face;
The Invisible conspicuous to our mind;
And Deity in every atom shrin'd.

Such language savors of pantheism. But while it seems obvious that the summit of the religious feeling expressed in this poem would be the pantheistic thrill, Brooke clings to a belief in a God who is not less transcendent than immanent. He speaks reverently of "Nature" merely because she embodies a supernatural reality. Once indeed he refers to "substituted Nature," as if the system of natural laws were permitted to act as God's viceroy; but he never identifies Creator and creation,

For deep, indeed, the Eternal Founder lies,
And high above his work the Maker flies;
Yet infinite that work, beyond our soar;
Beyond what Clarkes can prove, or Newtons can explore!

In her dissertation Miss Scurr argues at some length that the ideas of *Universal Beauty* are deistic,[80] and from the viewpoint of a modern student of religious thought she is doubtless right. It is not probable, however, that Brooke thought of himself as a deist, or that his contemporaries necessarily regarded him in that light. Nothing in the poem is inconsistent with a very broad, soft, hazy type of Christian Rationalism. The Newtonian element would have been accepted as impeccably orthodox. As for the Platonism, we remember that Nugent, in his *Epistle to Cornbury,* combines very similar ideas with an attack on deism. Brooke probably considered himself a *Christian* Platonist, an heir of the Cambridge school, for he chooses as his motto the opening verses of St. John's Gospel. The element of pious teleology is strong: several passages challenge the sceptic to explain this or that marvel of nature. Furthermore, Brooke's devotion to his Platonic deity is warm, personal, and almost evangelistic. Far from preaching deism, he is endeavoring to support his conception of Christianity by means of a philosophy which, in its effort to be purely rational, abstains from any appeal to Christian revelation. The result is inevitably a deistic poem, but I do not believe that the author realized the fact.

[80] *Op. cit.,* pp. 25 ff.

Brooke never ceased to regard *Universal Beauty* as his best poem, and there is no reason to dispute his choice. It is, to be sure, loose in structure and redundant in style. Often his attempt to confine emotions of a quite Thomsonian expansiveness within the bounds of the heroic couplet gives unfortunate results. Despite his enthusiasm for nature, Brooke does not look at anything very closely: his poem is versified oratory. Much greater poets, too, would have found recalcitrant material in such topics as the circulation of the blood. But despite these faults *Universal Beauty* is a not unworthy expression of a lofty vision. From beginning to end it is intensely felt—a genuinely emotional response to important scientific, philosophical, and religious ideas.

Brooke's poem is related to a venerable intellectual tradition. In the early days of the new science, Copernicus, Galileo, and Kepler, like Giordano Bruno and Pico della Mirandola before them, regarded their geometrical universe as the thought of a divine mathematician who took a Pythagorean and Platonic interest in numerical proportion.[81] The subsequent growth of Baconian empiricism almost banished Plato from the new science, but not quite, for the older Renaissance view is preserved and developed by the Cambridge Platonists. It unites itself readily with a more or less pantheistic sort of deism, but can also be harmonized with Newtonian Christianity. By the time this complex of ideas reaches Shaftesbury the Platonico-Pythagorean conception of a universe based on mathematical proportionateness has broadened and softened into a more general notion of aesthetic harmony, and in this form it is ready to be used by Brooke.

We need not quarrel with Miss Scurr's contention that Brooke's ideas are derived from their clearest, most systematic, and most effective spokesman, the Earl of Shaftesbury, provided we share her doubt as to whether this influence is direct or indirect. Brooke began work on *Universal Beauty* in 1728, at a time when the literary luminaries of the Patriot party were eager to exploit his allegiance. Pope gave him the benefit of his advice, but we do not know how specific his suggestions were. If we banished from the *Essay on Man* the more negative side of Bolingbroke's thought, greatly enlarged the affirmative, sentimental, and Shaftesburyian aspect of the work, and added a strong infusion of Newtonianism, we

---

[81] E. A. Burtt, *The Metaphysical Foundations of Modern Physical Science*, pp. 41-42, 47-48, 57-58.

should have the same sort of poem as *Universal Beauty;* but on the other hand we should not have a poem that much resembled the *Essay on Man.*

It is more pertinent to observe that the second edition of the works of Henry Needler was published in 1728, and that three-quarters of Thomson's *Seasons* was in print when Brooke began his poem.[82] The fourth edition of Shaftesbury's *Characteristics* appeared in 1727, and the fifth in 1732. From any or all of these Brooke could have drawn the main doctrines of *Universal Beauty.* He is by no means, however, a mere imitator. Needler presents only a feeble sketch of ideas which Brooke is to develop more fully, systematically, and imaginatively. Thomson is at the same time less technically Newtonian and less Platonic than Brooke. *Universal Beauty* is especially noteworthy for the author's effort to combine Newtonianism and sentimentalized Platonism in a single view of the universe. The more purely Shaftesburyian poems of I. H. Browne, Akenside, Cooper, and Harris do not maintain this equilibrium; while Baker's *The Universe,* on the other hand, is almost wholly Newtonian.

No other work of religious importance was produced by Brooke during the 1720-1740 period. The mixture of Behmenism and Methodism in his novels, *The Fool of Quality* and *Juliet Grenville,* does not concern us. We may, however, glance briefly at the poem entitled *Redemption* (1772), which illustrates the spiritual temper of his old age. Brooke is now a disciple of William Law and consequently an admirer of Jacob Boehme. From them he draws the Manichaean conception of a struggle between the spirit of the fallen Adam and the spirit of Christ within the human breast:

> Thus the new offspring shall the old put on,
> Making a double manhood, two in one;
> Of diff'rent principles, of diff'rent sires,
> Conceptions, tastes, enjoyments, and desires:
> The one, as Earth, crude, grudging, grappling all
> To the dark centre of its craving ball;
> The other, as the Sun, benign and bright,
> A going forth on all in life and light.

Apart from this Behmenistic element the poem may be described as a sincerely felt though turgid and muddled treatment of the Incarnation as the means of redemption.

[82] If Mr. Potter is right in his contention that Baker's *The Universe* first appeared in 1734 (*vide supra,* p. 464n) it probably had no influence on Brooke's poem, which though not published until 1735 was begun in 1728. I. H. Browne's *Of Design and Beauty* was also published in 1734.

Thus in the course of his long life Brooke moved from the viewpoint of *Universal Beauty* to a somewhat mystical type of evangelicalism. Probably he never quite found a religious position which wholly satisfied the desires of his heart, for he was eminently one of those who always dream of something "behind the beyond." This yearning sighs out in the opening lines of *Conrade,* a curious Irish legendary tale which otherwise has no bearing on our subject: [83]

> What do I love—what is it that mine eyes
> Turn round in search of—that my soul longs after,
> But cannot quench her thirst?—'Tis beauty, Phelin!
> I see it wide beneath the arch of Heaven,
> When the stars peep upon their evening hour,
> And the Moon rises on the eastern wave,
> Hous'd in a cloud of gold!—I see it wide
> In Earth's autumnal teints of various landscape,
> When the first ray of morning tips the trees,
> And fires the distant rock! ...
>
>   .   .   .
>
> ... At my heart I feel
> Its potent grasp, I melt beneath the touch,
> When the tale pours upon my sense humane
> The woes of other times!—What art thou, Beauty?
> Thou art not colour, fancy, sound, nor form—
> These but the conduits are, whence the soul quaffs
> The liquor of its Heaven— Whate'er thou art,
> Nature, or Nature's spirit, thou art all
> I long for!—O descend upon my thoughts!
> To thine own music tune, thou power of grace,
> The cordage of my heart! fill every shape
> That rises to my dream, or wakes to vision;
> And touch the threads of every mental nerve
> With all thy sacred feelings!

In other days Brooke had regarded beauty, along with truth and love, as the attribute of a Platonic but definitely personal God who could be addressed as "The Eternal Father; and the Eternal Friend!" But here beauty is an object of loose reverie, a delicious something-or-other which may be called "Nature," or "Nature's spirit," or what you please. Remem-

[83] In her study of Brooke, Miss Scurr rightly laments her inability to date *Conrade.* If it is earlier than the Ossianic forgeries, which it closely resembles in content and spirit without any hint of actual imitation, Brooke's status as a pre-romanticist is greatly enhanced. Whatever its actual date may be, it must be assigned to a late stage in his career.

bering Masefield's familiar poem beginning "Be with me, Beauty," we may feel that *Conrade* represents an advanced stage in the deliquescence of religious emotion.

In summarizing the results of this chapter we have the years of birth and death for fourteen out of sixteen poets. Four were born between 1684 and 1689, and ten between 1698 and 1706. The gap between the two divisions is curious, but not significant. Evidently, however, one cannot say that the "severer cases" of sentimentalism are on an average later than the "milder cases" diagnosed in Chapter IX.

Socially and politically, our findings are much the same as in the preceding chapter. Three poets are of gentle and three of plebeian origin; the background of the others is, bourgeois. Hamilton and Warton are Tories; Savage is anything and nothing; the rest are explicitly or inferentially Whiggish.

Three of the poets are Anglican clergymen, and one is a Presbyterian minister. Of these four, two are the sons of clerical fathers. I know nothing of the Reverend Thomas Fitzgerald's parentage. Since Mary Chandler and three laymen are also children of the manse exactly half the group are clergy, or sons of clergy, or both—a larger proportion than in the preceding chapter. Nonconformity is also a slightly more important factor, for Blair and Ramsay are Presbyterians and Mary Chandler a dissenter of unknown denomination. Mallet and Baker (the latter at least in *The Universe*) are deists. Of Pattison's doctrinal background we are ignorant, but whatever it was it counted for nothing. Hamilton and Warton are "high" Anglicans, but their altitude is merely political. The remaining eight are very roughly classifiable as Anglican latitudinarians throughout the bulk of their careers. But Hill sometimes writes as a deist, Nugent wavers from Catholicism to extreme latitudinarianism and back to Catholicism, while Browne and Brooke are closer to deism of the Shaftesbury type in youth than in maturity. The fact that both Nugent and Mallet were reared as Roman Catholics is of some interest.

Just as the poets of Chapter IX are on the average more eminent, and deservedly so, than those of Chapter VIII, so are the poets of Chapter X more eminent than those of Chapter IX. At least ten of the sixteen are well known to all students of the eighteenth century. Obviously one cannot say that in the 1720-1740 period sentimental and pre-romantic traits are to be found only in a few obscure, unpopular writers. On the contrary there is high positive correlation, and probably some causal connection, between the sentimentalism of these writers and their contemporary prestige.

These poets, like those of Chapter IX, suggest that the sentimentalist is not necessarily either a bad man or a good one. Hamilton, Hill, and Brooke were of high moral worth; while Pattison, Mallet, Savage, and Nugent must be grouped near the opposite end of the scale. But except occasionally in Pattison and Savage one discerns no traces of a libertine viewpoint even in the least edifying members of the group. They may not be extremely virtuous, but they usually write as if they believed in virtue.[84] The more significant sentimentalists have a serious reverence for their own feelings.

To anatomize the sentimentalist in order to discover what breeds these soft hearts is a difficult task, for who can classify and label the quicksilver vagaries of human impulse? Nevertheless we now have fairly plentiful materials from which to abstract a generalized description of the type. The sentimentalist is normally a Whig and a bourgeois; in any case he almost always writes as one who has accepted the Whig and bourgeois standards of the age. In critical theory and literary practise he leans toward the pre-romantic. The familiar precursorial tendencies are much more abundant in his work than in that of non-sentimental writers.

As for religion, the *opinions* of the sentimentalist are usually latitudinarian. Newton, Locke, Tillotson, Clarke, Hoadly, Addison are the saints of his calendar. The Church as the Bride of Christ and the mother of all faithful souls means nothing to him. His beliefs simply represent a more or less advanced stage in the decay of Low-Church Anglicanism and Nonconformity. Sometimes, indeed, his latitudinarianism has left Christianity behind. Not infrequently the modern student would call him a deist, though he himself would usually repudiate that title.

But the sentimentalist is a feeler, and his feelings find scant satisfaction in the pallid, anti-enthusiastic, unimaginative Christianity which his reason has led him to adopt. When he attempts to respond poetically to this unpoetic faith, the results are either conventional, perfunctory, and frigid, or they suggest that he has used the trappings of Christianity as a means

---

[84] Most of I. H. Browne's verse is frivolous, but morally it is quite inoffensive. Baker is sometimes nasty, but not philosophically so.

of expressing emotions which are not essentially Christian. The religion of his heart is not the religion of his head.

How shall one describe the religion to which the heart of the sentimental poet most genuinely responds? He is never quite sure whether the good life consists in energetic expansiveness and benevolence or in retiring to the bosom of "simple" nature. Between these inconsistent viewpoints, however, one common denominator can be found: the idea that feeling is good because man is good. Both active service and solitary "contemplation" are outpourings of nature's pure impulses. The psychological root of sentimentalism is a sense of the beauty and rightness of the heart's affections. This feeling may be very strong or very weak, and it may exist alongside of views which are fundamentally inconsistent with it. But when we compare the 1720-1740 period with the 1700-1720 period the growth of sentimentalism is strikingly evident.

The difference between the two periods in this respect, however, is less emphatic than my segregation of the poets into two compartments is likely to suggest. Of poets with sentimental leanings who have been assigned to Part II, several began their careers before 1720. In a graphic representation of the subject the line would at no time approach the perpendicular, though it would begin to climb rather steeply near the division between our two periods.

By the end of the 1720-1740 period, sentimentalism has become not only more abundant but more self-conscious than during the 1700-1720 period. Even a feeler must think, if only to validate his feelings. The good heart must be established as part of a good universe, and the universes of Christian Rationalism and of merely destructive deism are insufficiently exciting for the purpose. Hence in Dyer, Hill, Mallet, Savage, Baker, Nugent, I. H. Browne, and Henry Brooke—to name only the clearest examples—the basic urge of sentimentalism is formulated into something like a creed. A more or less Platonic Divine Spirit has thought the universe into being by an act of creative imagination. "Nature" is the universe as permeated by this benign spirit. Since the deity is revealed only in nature and in that most godlike part of nature, the human breast, "Nature" and "God" are almost synonymous terms; but a careful sentimentalist prefers to speak of "Nature *and* Nature's God." The creation is a delightful spectacle not merely because it is an ordered whole nor because it is so richly variegated, but because its unity proliferates into diversity and its diversity reveals a unity. Nature was not made for man, for every creature has the right to seek its own ends and to live as abundantly as its position in the scale of being permits. Nevertheless man occupies a distinguished position in the universal harmony. His bosom teems with warmly benign impulses akin to those of his Maker. His conduct is regulated by an intuitive spiritual taste, a virtuoso's ability to appreciate the cosmic masterpiece, a creative urge not unlike that which moved the Almighty Poet to write "the world's great poem." The sense of inward divinity may be satisfied either by retired contemplation of the works of Nature's God or by expressing in the active life one's personal share of the divine benevolence.

Although not all men of feeling would subscribe to everything in the foregoing paragraph, this is the theoretical norm against which variants and imperfect cases can be measured. The creed may be espoused by a man who calls himself a Christian; but it is plainly a tender-minded form of deism—a religion in itself, quite independent of Christianity and essentially hostile to the traditional faith. Christianity preaches the redemption of sinful man through Incarnate God; but since the sentimentalist stands in no need of redemption the entire groundwork of Christianity is cut away, and the Saviour becomes irrelevant. Christianity therefore either disappears or survives merely as a body of unreal traditional rhetoric some parts of which may be applied to sentimental uses.

Sentimentalism, to be sure, includes something faintly analogous to the Christian doctrine of the Fall. In some inexplicable way, man has forgotten the pure lessons of reason and nature, and often plays a less gracious part in the universal harmony than do the flowers and the birds. The sightless chasm between theory and reality doubtless accounts for much of the melancholy which shadows the sentimentalist's optimism. But the return of reason, nature, harmony, and universal benevolence is to be accomplished by man without any prayer to be lifted up upon the rock that is higher than he. There is no positive disharmony between us and our Creator—only a lack of will to assert harmony. The trouble is not that we are sinners, but that we are insufficiently aware of our natural sinlessness.

Yet although sentimentalism is not only un-Christian but implicitly or explicitly anti-Christian, to describe it historically as a sharp reaction against the spirit of seventeenth-century Protestantism would be to distort the facts. We have seen Low-Church Anglicanism and Nonconformity breaking down into latitudinarianism, and latitudinarianism breaking down into deistic sentimentalism. What we have to interpret, then, is not the swing of a pendulum but the course of a stream. But before we undertake this task we must consider in relation to our subject the two chief poets of the first half of the eighteenth century.

Chapter XI

POPE AND THOMSON

THE FAMILIAR VIEW THAT POPE'S CATHOLICISM WAS MERELY NOMINÁL deserves careful scrutiny. It is possible to deny that there is anything "merely nominal" in the fact that from baptism to viaticum he was the child of Holy Church. That he was an erring child is of no theological significance, for all Catholics are sinners by definition. His moral deficiencies, the occasional indecency of his writings, his neglect of the special obligations and opportunities of the Catholic life—these blots cannot efface his name from the roll of the universal parish. It can further be argued, though perhaps not quite ingenuously, that Pope never explicitly denied any doctrine necessary to salvation; and even if one more frankly admits that he sometimes wrote heretically or blasphemously, one may still urge that final penitence and absolution qualified him for the ascent of Mount Purgatory.

But even for those Catholics who adhere most rigidly to an *ex opere operato* view of the sacramental process, something would depend upon the purity of "intention" with which Pope received the last ministrations of the Church. When the dying poet was asked by Hooke if he did not desire the services of a priest he answered, "I do not suppose that it is essential, but it will look right: I heartily thank you for putting me in mind of it." This is a somewhat absent-minded form of *bona mors*. Yet, feeble as he was, he got out of bed to receive the sacrament on his knees, and the priest was well satisfied with the spiritual condition of his penitent.[1] Further than this we need not inquire: our concern is with the man's work, not with the state of his soul.

Pope may, of course, have had other than strictly religious motives for clinging so stubbornly to a faith which entailed grave inconvenience to its English adherents and which gave his enemies special opportunities for satirical abuse. Early impressions continued to exert their subconscious in-

[1] George Paston, *Mr. Pope: His Life and Times*, II, 696.

fluence, and the longevity of his parents—especially of his mother—extended something of the atmosphere of his childhood into his maturity. As everyone knows, Pope's consideration for his parents' feelings was a main factor in his continued adherence to the Church. In the letter to Atterbury which provides the best evidence on this point, he writes as a good son rather than as a good Roman Catholic; for he uneasily tries to represent himself as a Catholic who is at the same time not a "Papist." [2]

Before the factor of filial loyalty had ceased to operate, Pope had become involved in such bitter quarrels that to abjure Catholicism would have furnished the dunces a deadly weapon. Pope, the misshapen little papist, beaten into submission by his foes! Rather than give them the chance to crow in that fashion, he would let them continue to abuse him for cleaving to a faith which he no longer warmly cherished. His status as a Catholic was not so completely disadvantageous as it has sometimes been represented: it helped him to maintain that pose of lonely, disinterested, non-partisan virtue which was valuable to him as a satirist.

Pope's loyalty to the unpopular Church, then, need not imply that a bright though hidden flame of Catholic devotion burned in his breast. On the other hand, we may doubt that he ever closed his mind to the possibility that the Catholic faith, interpreted very broadly and vaguely, might be true. His scepticism was of that weathercock kind which points neither to real belief nor to real disbelief. His impulse to sneer wittily at devotion never quite stifled an impulse to get down on his knees in worship of Something. Doubtless much of what the priests told him in his early years was nonsense, but he had better keep on the safe side.

Hence he is able to say in a well-known letter to Swift: "I am of the religion of Erasmus, a Catholic; so I live, so I shall die; and hope one day to meet you, Bishop Atterbury, the younger Craggs, Dr. Garth, Dean Berkeley, and Mr. Hutcheson in heaven." The only inference to be drawn from this list of names is that all good men, whatever their religious beliefs may be, are likely candidates for salvation. Erasmus, he thinks, would agree with this latitudinarian view; hence if Erasmus could call himself a Catholic, Pope may lay claim to the same comforting title. Here is a way of satisfying both men like Caryll and men like Swift.

2 *Ibid.*, p. 217. Neither Pope nor his High Church correspondent would recognize the existence of any other form of Catholicism than the Roman. It may be urged that Pope is showing the transmontane spirit which was rather strong among English Romanists of the eighteenth century, but this is not a sufficient explanation of the ambiguity of his viewpoint.

But it is not for his Catholicism that Pope values Erasmus. In the *Essay on Criticism* the great humanist is praised for having conquered the Gothic ignorance and superstition of the monks. He

> Stemm'd the wild torrent of a barb'rous age,
> And drove those holy Vandals off the stage.

Pope calls him "the glory of the Priesthood, and the shame," not because Erasmus in some respects sullied the holy calling to which in other respects he added lustre, but because his liberalism remained a standing rebuke to priestcraft. In the imitation of *The First Satire of the Second Book of Horace,* Pope describes himself as

> Papist or Protestant, or both between,
> Like good Erasmus in an honest Mean,
> In moderation placing all my glory,
> While Tories call me Whig, and Whigs a Tory.

Here Pope is paraphrasing a passage in which Horace confesses his own easy-going eclecticism, but the lines furnish some insight into the implications of "the religion of Erasmus."

When did Erasmus become for Pope the prime example of how to be a Catholic without believing in Catholicism? Plainly, at least as early as the *Essay on Criticism*. But we recall that the nominally Catholic Wycherley, one of the first of those sceptical wits who weaned Pope away from the pious atmosphere of Binfield, was an approving reader of *The Praise of Folly*.[3] Doubtless he relished other works of Erasmus, and he may have imparted his enthusiasm to the young poet.

Bolingbroke, a later but much more powerful anti-Christian influence in Pope's thought, was also an admirer of Erasmus. He often refers to the humanist and cites him in arguing against the Church. He knows that Pope shares this admiration, for after speaking of medieval saints' lives as "too nearly akin to heathenism" in their superstitious credulity he adds, addressing Pope: "Let not your zeal for the honor of saints, martyrs, and confessors make you think the expression too hard. I can quote you one much more hard from Erasmus, for whom you profess the same veneration that I have."[4]

The reference to Pope's "zeal" is surely a bit of raillery. In his posthumous works Bolingbroke often addresses Pope as a Catholic—good

---

[3] *Vide supra,* p. 9. [4] *Works,* III, 478.

evidence that the poet never, even in private converse with his deistic mentor, expressly denied the faith of his childhood. Unlike the foregoing passage, most of the instances consist of colorless phrases like "your church" or "some of your writers." There is no attempt at direct argument with Pope. Though the *Letters or Essays* and the *Fragments* persistently assail, often in the most offensive terms, ideas which are essential to Catholic religion,[5] St. John never seems to fear that his friend will be hurt or angered. His usual tone, on the contrary, implies confidence that the poet will agree with him. He knows that Pope's Catholicism amounts to very little. "Marchmont," he sneers, "will tell you that presbytery is *jure divino*. I shall tell you that episcopacy is so; and though you are not a very good papist, you will tell us that popery is so. Let us be candid, and confess that none of them are so."[6] Elsewhere, after remarks on the corruption of Christianity by ecclesiasticism, he turns to Pope: "I do not expect, on this occasion, from you the answer I should be sure to have from persons more orthodox, than I know you to be, in the faith of the pretended Catholic church. Such persons would insist on the authority of the church,"[7] etc.

There was little reason to expect that Pope would rise in defense of the Church. After reading Voltaire's *Henriade* he had written to St. John: "Do not smile when I add that I esteem him for that honest principled spirit of religion which shines through the whole, and from whence, unknown as I am to M. Voltaire, I conclude him at once a freethinker and a lover of quiet; no bigot, but yet no heretic."[8] In short Voltaire is "like good Erasmus in an honest mean," and Pope has no difficulty in recognizing him as a fellow-Catholic.

Bolingbroke, a bitter foe of religious mysteries, reminds Pope of "a passage you quoted to me once with great applause, from a sermon of Foster, and to this effect 'Where mystery begins, religion ends.'"[9] This idea, a commonplace of latitudinarianism and deism, necessarily implies an anti-clerical viewpoint. "George Paston" is rash in suggesting that John Dennis's treatise on *The Danger of Priestcraft to Religion and Government* "was probably one of the reasons why Pope attacked him" in the

---

[5] See *Works*, III, 247, 257-258, 376, 410-411, 482.   [6] *Ibid.*, IV, 51.
[7] *Ibid.*, III, 457.   [8] George Paston, *Mr. Pope*, I, 296.
[9] *Works*, III, 62. *Vide supra*, p. 458, for Savage's poem on Foster, which uses these identical words. I do not know whether they come verbatim from Foster, or whether Pope expressed an idea of Foster's in this line and imparted it to Savage.

Essay on Criticism.[10] That very poem derides the propagators of mystery, and when his boldness shocks his Catholic friends he retorts: "As to my writings, I pray to God they may never have other enemies than those they have met with—which are first, priests; secondly, women, who are the fools of priests; and thirdly, beaux and fops, who are the fools of women."[11] Pope was quite as alive to the dangers of priestcraft as either Dennis the Protestant or Bolingbroke the deist could desire. Passages like those in the *Essay on Criticism* appear elsewhere in his work, unbalanced by any praise of the Church or her consecrated servants.

Catholic laymen are seldom extreme prigs: they are, if anything, inclined to be too much at ease in Zion. Nevertheless it is not pleasant to remember that the notoriously foul-mouthed Tidcombe relished Pope's "pretty, atheistical jests"[12] or to read certain letters which speak of sacred things with careless mockery. The obscene parody of the First Psalm is more easily forgivable than Pope's attempt to deny having written it. Even more distasteful is the glee with which he tells Teresa Blount that in this matter he has "equivocated pretty genteelly. You may be confident," he adds, "it was not done without leave from my spiritual director."[13] One hardly knows whether or not to hope that the last sentence is a lie.

The poet who not only parodied the First Psalm but wrote *The Dying Christian to His Soul* was no cold-blooded hypocrite. He merely lacked any firm spiritual centre. To call him an aesthete may seem absurd, but it is difficult to find anything at the heart of the man except a boundless appetite for writing good verses. One might justly apply to him the words of Keats's letter: "No one word I ever utter can be taken for granted as an opinion growing out of my identical nature—how can it, when I have no nature." Himself intellectually and spiritually confused, this "chameleon poet" reflected in excellent couplets the confusion of his age. He told Atterbury that when he read works of theological controversy in his father's library as a boy he turned Papist or Protestant according to the last book he had examined. So he was to continue—

> Papist or Protestant, or both between,
> Like good Erasmus in an honest mean.

How much of the admired balance of the eighteenth century is a jumble of inconsistencies?

[10] *Op. cit.*, I, 46n.   [11] *Ibid.*, I, 97-98.   [12] *Ibid.*, p. 139.   [13] *Ibid.*, p. 187.

Furthermore, one psychological effect of Pope's physical deficiencies was a desire to win as many allies as possible. His constant effort to be all things to all men is easy to understand but very repugnant. Writing to Cromwell on April 10, 1710, he explains that he would have written sooner but for his unwillingness to speak of mundane things in Holy Week. "Besides," he continues, "our family would have been scandalised to see me write, who take it for granted I write nothing but ungodly verses; and they say here so many prayers that I can make but few poems; for in this matter of praying I am an occasional conformist. So, just as I am drunk or scandalous in town, according to my company, I am for the same reason grave or godly here." [14] He is, to be sure, not quite sober when he tells his fellow-Catholic, Patty Blount, "Every one values Mr. Pope, but every one for a different reason: one for his adherence to the Catholic faith, another for his neglect of Popish superstition; one for his grave behavior, another for his whimsicalness; Mr. Titcomb for his pretty, atheistical jests, Mr. Caryll for his moral and Christian sentiments." [15]

In a half-hearted defense of the authenticity of Pope's Catholicism, Miss Mary Segar relies chiefly on letters to Caryll in which Pope seems anxious that his Catholic friends should not be offended by certain passages in the *Essay on Criticism*.[16] But these equivocations merely reflect his desire that everyone should value Mr. Pope. The same ambiguity appears in his letter to Lord Harcourt concerning the prospect of testifying at Atterbury's trial: "I could almost wish I were asked if I am not a Papist. Would it be proper in such a case to reply, that I don't perfectly know the import of the word, and would not answer anything that might, for aught I know, be prejudicial to me during the Bill against such, which is impending.[17] But that if to be a Papist be to profess and hold many such tenets of faith as are ascribed to Papists, I am not a Papist; and if to be a Papist be to hold any that are averse to, or destructive of, the present Government, King, or Constitution, I am no Papist." [18] Pope saw nothing improperly evasive in this proposed answer. The religion of Erasmus, as he interpreted it, did not lead to the martyr's crown. It permitted him to

---

[14] *Ibid.*, p. 35.　　　　　[15] *Ibid.*, p. 139.

[16] "Some Notes on Pope's Religion," *Dublin Review*, CXC, 237-253.

[17] The bill proposed to raise £100,000 by a tax on Roman Catholics in addition to the double land-tax to which they were already liable.

[18] George Paston, *op. cit.*, I, 284.

change "A mighty maze of walks without a plan" into "A mighty maze, but not without a plan." He merely felt that he had polished a line.

Specifically Catholic "notes" are rare in Pope's poetry, though one could cull a few images and allusions which seem to reflect his early impressions. As for entire poems, we have the *Prayer of St. Francis Xavier,* a translation made at the request of a Romanist priest, and the juvenile *Paraphrase of Thos. à Kempis, l. III. c.2.* According to Spence he wrote a complete tragedy on the life of St. Genevieve at about the age of thirteen, but this is not extant.[19]

Christian poetry in a more general sense is slightly more abundant, though all of it could be omitted from his works without much damage to his artistic reputation. He comes closest to being a Christian poet during the years 1710-1713, the period in which he approached most closely the middle-classical viewpoint of Addison and Steele.[20] At this time the remnants of his Catholic rearing, his frustrated sexuality, and the emotionalism which was strong in his early years and which never wholly deserted him even when he later "stooped to truth," drew him in one direction; while the classical precepts of his first literary mentors and the scepticism of the wits drew him in another. To a writer who aspired to please everyone, the Addisonian position seemed a restful compromise.

Hence, at about this time, a cluster of poems which christianize the classics or classicize Christianity. *The Dying Christian* makes Hadrian a believer in the life of the world to come. The devout Mrs. Rowe is said to have repeated it on her deathbed. In *The Messiah,* Virgil joins Isaiah as a prophet of the Incarnation.[21] *Eloisa to Abelard* is a christianized Ovidian epistle. Pope's Catholic friends were troubled by parts of the *Essay on Criticism,* but both they and Addison must have liked the severe reference to the Socinians and the strong element of bourgeois morality which is here imposed upon the Horace-Vida-Boileau tradition. In *Windsor Forest*[22] the second happiest man is a lover of retirement who contemplates

[19] We may also note that Pope painted two Madonnas—one sent to the Carylls, and one destroyed as a failure—and a picture of St. John at prayer reported by Spence. (George Sherburn, *The Early Career of Alexander Pope,* pp. 102-103.)

[20] Pope's own social background, of course, was thoroughly bourgeois, though he was to achieve his greatest success as a continuator of the aristocratic tradition.

[21] For this of course there was good medieval precedent. In some measure the poem is doubtless related to Pope's Catholic background.

[22] The poem as finally completed shows him turning away from the Whigs, but its general character harmonizes with the other poems mentioned in this paragraph.

God's goodness as displayed in the Newtonian universe. This poem gives us the first glimpse of the system which is to form the groundwork of the *Essay on Man:*

> Here hills and vales, the woodland and the plain,
> Here earth and water seem to strive again;
> Not Chaos-like together crushd and bruis'd,
> But, as the world, harmoniously confus'd:
> Where order in variety we see,
> And where, tho' all things differ, all agree.

Pope's Christian poems greatly enhanced his prestige among "serious" eighteenth-century readers, but few modern students would accept them as powerful expressions of religious feeling. The eloquence of *The Messiah* is rather forced and showy; one can readily imagine, with Professor Sherburn, that it "was hastily executed in the design of pleasing Steele and perhaps such Catholics as had begun to regard Pope's gifts as heterodox if not ungodly." [23] About *Eloisa to Abelard* opinions differ. I consider the poem a very effective piece of claptrap, but Cazamian declares that "Never has Pope been nearer to true inspiration" than in this work.[24] Probably no one, however, would assert that its religious element exists for any other purpose than to add spice to the erotic situation. Yet for this very reason *Eloisa to Abelard* is something of a landmark: it is perhaps the earliest English poem in which the author exploits, wholly for non-religious and sensationalistic purposes, the religion which he professes. The adaptability of Christianity to the uses of literary sentimentalism has been discovered.[25]

As is well known, Pope's art moved in a counter-historical direction. The 1717 volume is not without hints of pre-romanticism.[26] But several years before its appearance he had deserted the Whig moralists for the Tory wits of the Scriblerus Club. Setting aside the *Essay on Man* for later discussion, one may say that the great satirical and didactic poet who emerges after the period of translating and editing is neither romantic nor Christian. Sometimes we find apparently genuine expressions of

---

[23] *The Early Career of Alexander Pope*, p. 97.

[24] Legouis and Cazamian, *History of English Literature*, p. 756.

[25] It is interesting to recall that the English version of the letters of Abelard and Heloise which provided Pope with his chief source was the work of the sentimentalized dissenter John Hughes, whose importance for our subject has been explained.

[26] See S. W. Stevenson, " 'Romantic' Tendencies in Pope," ELH, I, 126-155—an article that says all, if not rather more than all, that can justly be said in support of this statement.

reverence for that mysterious Power who gives men their ruling passions and who

> Bids seed-time, harvest, equal course maintain,
> Thro' reconciled extremes of drought and rain,
> Builds Life on Death, on Change Duration founds,
> And gives th' eternal wheels to know their rounds.[27]

Nevertheless, since allies are more important to him than ever, he continues to be all things to all men.

For the proper occasion he has the proper response. If his friends of the Patriot party want high-sounding talk about virtue and public service, they shall have it. If Warburton objects to "Nature well-known, no miracles remain," "miracles" shall be changed to "prodigies." To his Catholic friend Martha Blount he holds out the hope of "raptures in a life to come,"[28] While Newton's death inspires the epitaph which was to offend Dr. Johnson:

> Nature and Nature's Laws lay hid in Night:
> God said, *Let Newton be!* and all was Light.[29]

Putting his best foot forward in the *Epistle to Dr. Arbuthnot,* he describes himself in the line, "I pay my debts, believe, and say my pray'rs," and asks, with a pathos both sincere and calculated, "Have I no friend to serve, no soul to save?"

In the *Dunciad,* with Swift at his elbow, Pope adheres to a soundly conservative norm of religious opinion. The armor in which he attacks Grub Street must present no chink through which a *riposte* may be delivered.[30] The proper scorn of vulgar enthusiasm is expressed:

> So swells each wind-pipe; Ass intones to Ass;
> Harmonious twang! of leather, horn, and brass;
> Such as from lab'ring lungs th' Enthusiast blows,
> High Sound, attemper'd to the vocal nose;
> Or such as bellow from the deep Divine;
> There, Webster! peal'd thy voice, and Whitfield! thine.

[27] *Of the Use of Riches.* [28] *To Mrs. M. B. on her Birth-Day.*
[29] *Epitaph Intended for Sir Isaac Newton.*
[30] In the Advertisement prefixed to *Satires and Epistles of Horace Imitated,* Pope says that the freedom to be severe assumed by John Donne in his satires "seem'd a proof with what indignation and contempt a Christian may treat Vice or Folly, in ever so low, or ever so high a Station."

But even in his distaste for zeal Pope is not unduly zealous. For him, Bishop Hoadly is little better than a deist:

> Toland and Tindal, prompt at priests to jeer,
> Yet silent bow'd to *Christ's No kingdom here.*[31]

Yet any dunce who seizes upon this couplet as evidence of highflying Toryism must reckon with the poet's sneer at "the right divine of kings to govern wrong." If Pope disapproves of the sceptic Mandeville, he equally disapproves of Mandeville's mystical-evangelical-nonjuring opponent, William Law.

Although Pope approached deism more closely than any other definable religious viewpoint, in the *Dunciad* he condemns Toland, Tindal, and Woolston. In a speech of real solemnity, the ghost of Settle warns such unbelieving scribblers not to go too far:

> 'Tis yours a Bacon or a Locke to blame,
> A Newton's genius, or a Milton's flame:
> But oh! with One, immortal One dispense,
> The source of Newton's Light, of Bacon's Sense.
> Content, each Emanation of his fires
> That beams on earth, each Virtue he inspires,
> Each Art he prompts, each Charm he can create,
> Whate'er he gives, are giv'n for you to hate.
> Persist, by all divine in Man unaw'd,
> But, "Learn, ye Dunces! not to scorn your God." [32]

The conservatism of the *Dunciad* appears also in Book IV, where Samuel Clarke is made to describe his own "high Priori" rationalism as a philosophy leading to disbelief. The chief of the Intellectual School had a large following which included Queen Caroline; but Pope's attack upon him would please the orthodox, who accused this philosopher of Arianism. It would also please the Patriot party, for Clarke was ardently ministerial; and in particular it would please Bolingbroke, whose *Fragments* often refer to Clarke as an example of that hypothetical type of reasoning which he detested. Clarke concludes his speech by addressing Dullness:

> Oh hide the God still more! and make us see
> Such as Lucretius drew, a God like Thee;

[31] He alludes to Hoadly's controversial sermon on the text, "My kingdom is not of this world."

[32] The last line paraphrases *Aeneid*, VI, 619.

> Wrapt up in Self, a God without a Thought,
> Regardless of our merit or default.
> Or that bright Image to our fancy draw,
> Which Theocles in raptur'd vision saw,
> While thro' Poetic scenes the GENIUS roves,
> Or wanders wild in Academic Groves;
> That NATURE our Society adores,
> Where Tindal dictates, and Silenus snores.[33]

Pope's satire here grows aimless, for Clarke is certainly no disciple of Theocles in Shaftesbury's *Moralists*. One observes with interest, however, the attempt to represent the dunces as a set of Epicurean—deistic—pantheistic nature-worshippers, a "society," as Warburton's note on this passage suggests, like that for which Toland prepared his *Pantheisticon*. There must have been times when Pope read Shaftesbury with a good deal of approval, but no person so unorthodox is to be praised in the *Dunciad*.

Everyone remembers the genuinely poetic passion with which the satire concludes:

> See skulking Truth to her old cavern fled,
> Mountains of casuistry heap'd o'er her head!
> Philosophy, that lean'd on Heav'n before,
> Shrinks to her second cause, and is no more.
> Physic of Metaphysic begs defence,
> And Inspiration calls for aid on Sense!
> See Mystery to Mathematics fly!
> In vain! they gaze, turn giddy, rave, and die.
> Religion blushing veils her sacred fires,
> And unawares Morality expires.

Perhaps in these lines Pope is not merely satirizing the confusion of others, but is revolting against the confusion that existed in his own mind.

But Pope's only substantial effort to clarify the muddle of the age is itself a glaring example of how philosophy, in the eighteenth century, "shrinks to her second cause, and is no more." Detailed analysis of the *Essay on Man* would be a waste of time. Its ideas and its general intellectual background are known to all students of the period.[34] We must

---

[33] The Pope-Warburton note reminds us that Silenus figures as a drunken Epicurean in Virgil's sixth *Eclogue*.

[34] They will be still better known, however, if Mr. Maynard Mack publishes his Yale doctoral dissertation, which elaborately studies the poem in relation to the theological trends of the age. Students of Pope's thought are also greatly indebted to A. O. Lovejoy's *The*

ask, however, to what extent the *Essay* illustrates the breakdown of Christianity and the rise of sentimentalism.

No Catholic theologian would brand the *Essay on Man* as heretical merely because the author avoids the special language of Christianity. Pope was entirely free to use his natural reason in constructing a system of natural ethics, metaphysics, and religion provided that system did not conflict with the Christian faith. There, of course, is the rub. If Christianity implies the remaking of man through faith in the Incarnation, the atoning Sacrifice, and the Resurrection of Jesus Christ the Son of God, one must say that the *Essay* not merely ignores Christianity but is radically inconsistent with it. From this viewpoint the poem is obviously deistic. But if Christianity is merely another name for the two primary laws of natural religion—love of God and love of man—then Pope was entitled to plead that his poem inculcated the essentials of Christianity. He was not more than half disingenuous when he assured the anxious Caryll that his poem depended on the Gospel because it taught Christian love and charity. His mentor Bolingbroke represented himself as a Christian on grounds which amounted to saying that Christ was a good deist who preached the religion of nature. "Christianity," he writes, "is founded on the universal law of nature. I will not say that Christianity is a republication of it. But I will say that the Gospel teaches the great and fundamental principle of this law, universal benevolence." [35] This is really all that Christ taught, apart from a few puzzling remarks which had better be discounted as priestly corruptions of the simple message. "The theology contained in the gospel lies in a very narrow compass. It is marvellous indeed, but it is plain, and it is employed throughout to enforce natural religion. This seems to be the end, and revealed religion the means, both which it would have been for the honor of Christianity and for the good of mankind to have left so." [36] Now if the sole purpose of Christianity is "to enforce natural religion," who can say that the believer in natural religion is not a Christian?

This attitude was adopted by Bolingbroke merely as a weapon against metaphysics, theology, and ecclesiasticism; but it was held more sincerely by many latitudinarian Christians, both lay and clerical, who would have

Great Chain of Being, and to his two articles: "Optimism and Romanticism," *PMLA*, XLII, 921-945; and "Pride in Eighteenth Century Thought," *Modern Language Notes*, XXXVI, 31-37.

[35] *Works,* III, 396.   [36] *Ibid.,* IV, 286.

rejected with horror the imputation of deism. Such an interpretation of
Christianity agreed with Pope's native disposition to run with the hare
and hunt with the hounds. He could have defended his orthodoxy in a
syllogism: *"The Essay on Man* teaches that the universe is 'one close
system of benevolence.' This is precisely what Jesus taught. Hence the
Essay on Man teaches the pure and uncorrupted Christianity of Jesus."

The implied argument did not satisfy men like Caryll, Young, Walter
Harte, and Henry Brooke; but most readers missed the fallacy lurking
in the minor premise. To this day the notion that the poem is a manual
of piety has not quite vanished from simple minds. The rumor, carefully
nourished by the author, that the *Essay* had been written by an eminent
divine was at first widely accepted. The heterodoxy of the poem did not
pass unnoticed, but no formal attack was brought against it until it was
translated into French, a language in which writers are expected to say
what they mean. At first, in private conversation, Warburton had spoken
of the *Essay* with the utmost contempt. According to his friend Stukely
he wrote, and seriously considered publishing, a treatise "to prove it to be
atheism, spinosaism, deism, hobbism, fatalism, materialism, and what
not." [37] But after the publication of De Crousaz' *Examen* this lover of
controversial paradox defended the *Essay* in his *Vindication* as "a Justification of Providence against the impious Objections of Atheistical Men."
To cap the climax, when Bolingbroke's posthumous works appeared,
Pope's champion violently assailed them.

We should not condemn the poet without remembering that he wrote
in days when Warburton could be a bishop. It is idle to debate the question of Pope's sincerity, for in religion he had no settled convictions to
which one can say that he was true or false. The paramount consideration
was that everyone should value Mr. Pope. To Caryll he emphasized Christian charity, but the Richardsons "declared that he was well aware of the
deistic and fatalistic tendency of certain passages in his poem, which they
had often discussed with him." [38] Similarly Chesterfield reported that
Pope had often told him that he was a deist who believed in a future
state. When Henry Brooke pressed Pope for a definite statement of belief,
the answer was: "I sincerely worship God, believe in his revelations, re-
sign to his dispensations, love all his creatures, am in charity with all

[37] Quoted by A. W. Evans, *Warburton and the Warburtonians*, p. 72.
[38] George Paston, *op. cit.*, II, 483-484.

denominations of Christians, however violently they treat each other, and detest none so much as that profligate race who would loosen the bands of morality, either under the pretence of religion or freethinking. I hate no man as a man, but I hate vice in any man; I hate no sect, but I hate uncharitableness in any sect." This masterpiece of hedging is consonant with deism, but nothing in it clashes with a discreetly Bolingbrokian interpretation of "the religion of Erasmus."

Professor Sherburn has pointed out the significance of the plural "revelations" in this letter of December 1, 1739.[39] Even in a tight corner, Pope could not bring himself to assert that natural revelation is inadequate without the aid of supernatural revelation. In Epistle III of the *Essay* the growth of religion is described as a wholly natural process originating in reverence for the *paterfamilias*. As for the claims of one form of supernatural revelation against another, Pope did not believe that the Christian faith possesses absolute truth:

> For Modes of Faith let graceless zealots fight;
> He can't be wrong whose life is in the right:
> In Faith and Hope the world will disagree,
> But all Mankind's concern is Charity.

There is, then, no real distinction between religion and ethics. Creeds are unimportant and the hope of immortality is uncertain; but the essence of religion is human benevolence, and the truly religious man is

> Slave to no sect, who takes no private road,
> But looks through Nature up to Nature's God.

That such ideas should be expressed by a man who calls himself a Christian need occasion no astonishment. Thousands of twentieth-century liberal Christians would agree with him, and the eighteenth century is the soil from which their liberalism has burgeoned. But how Pope could hold these views and continue to profess the Catholic faith is not so easy to understand. The most charitable and indeed the most probable supposition is that Pope saw no essential difference between Catholicism and constructive deism. Universal benevolence, their common denominator, was all that mattered. "The rest is all but leather and prunella."

It is impossible to trace the steps by which Pope arrived at this absurd position. We know little about the temper of Roman Catholicism in

[39] *Selections from Alexander Pope*, p. 410.

eighteenth-century England. That Catholics were less inclined to compromise with the spirit of the age than other bodies of Christians is easy to believe; that they did not compromise at all is very unlikely. Professor Sherburn has shown that Binfield and the neighboring villages contained not only an unusual number of Romanists, but also an unusual number of nonconforming Protestants. "It seems fair to infer," he says, "that the region had a reputation for tolerance." [40] The boy received orthodox instruction in Catholic principles, but the opportunity to lead a fully Catholic life must have been restricted. Meanwhile the less formal education of the whole Binfield environment may have taught him the vaguer, but in the long run more influential, lesson that "he can't be wrong whose life is in the right." However this may be, from the very beginning of his literary career the Zeitgeist, as reflected in his own mind no less than in the minds of sceptical mentors and friends, drew him steadily [41] away from the beliefs of his childhood, until at last his Catholicism was so completely drained of intellectual and spiritual content that he could not see the dishonesty of calling himself a Catholic and at the same time writing the Essay on Man. There is no more striking illustration of what the first half of the eighteenth century did to Christianity.

To say that Christianity, Catholic or Protestant, played no real part in Pope's imagination is not to say that he was wholly devoid of religious feeling. Though assuredly he did not abound in the gifts of the spirit, he could on occasion rise above that natural reason which he usually regards as the only valid source of knowledge. Like most deists, he approaches pantheism when his religious impulse is strongest, as in those moving lines which begin, "All are but parts of one stupendous whole."

In fact Pope's religious emotions, such as they were, responded much more actively to the sentimental cult of cosmic and personal benevolism than to orthodox Christianity. The Chain of Being is described as a "chain of love" in which

> Nothing is foreign: Parts relate to whole;
> One all-extending, all-preserving Soul
> Connects each being, greatest with the least;
> Made Beast in aid of Man, and Man of Beast;
> All serv'd, all serving: nothing stands alone;
> The chain holds on, and where it ends, unknown.

[40] Early Career of Alexander Pope, p. 37.
[41] The influence of Addison and Steele was a deterrent, but only very briefly.

This is essentially the thought of Shelley's *Love's Philosophy*. In this "close system of benevolence," where "whatever is, is right," God loves downward into the universe and man loves upward toward God, his self-love becoming social love:

> God loves from Whole to Parts: but human soul
> Must rise from Individual to the Whole.
> Self-love but serves the virtuous mind to wake,
> As the small pebble stirs the peaceful lake.

These amiable truths can be grasped by "the good, untaught," in whose bosom the image of heaven is reflected with unruffled clarity. There is a strain of sentimental primitivism in Pope's thought. "The state of Nature," he declares in Epistle III, "was the reign of God." In the early stages in the process of civilization all was well so long as reason copied the creations of natural instinct, for instinct is

> Sure by quick Nature happiness to gain,
> Which heavier Reason labours at in vain;
> This too serves always, Reason never long;
> One must go right, the other may go wrong.

> .   .   .   .

> And Reason raise o'er instinct as you can,
> In this 'tis God directs, in that 'tis Man.

Gradually, however, reason forsook her loyalty to instinct, and man lost the virtues of that Golden Age "when Love was Liberty, and Nature Law." [42] Quite in the manner later to be described by Rousseau, the excessive activity of self-love brought corruption and injustice. The good poets and patriots who arose to combat these evils strove for a return to nature, "the World's great harmony," through restoring man's weakened sense of the identity of self-love and social love.

Rousseau is also foreshadowed in Epistle II, where a passage deals with the limitations and moral dangers of science. Here too he praises the ethical value of uncurbed "natural" feeling:

> As fruits, ungrateful to the planter's care,
> On savage stocks inserted, learn to bear;
> The surest Virtues thus from Passions shoot,
> Wild Nature's vigour working at the root.

[42] Epistle III, l.208. The same line, except for the tense of the verb, appears in *Eloisa to Abelard*, l.92.

In an even more obviously romantic spirit he writes,

> On life's vast ocean diversely we sail,
> Reason the card, but Passion is the gale;
> Nor God alone in the still calm we find,
> He mounts the storm, and walks upon the wind.

And since there is no fixed line between sentimental naturalism and sentimental transcendentalism, one is not surprised to read:

> This light and darkness in our chaos join'd,
> What shall divide? The God within the mind.

Thus by pulling out the right couplets we can represent the *Essay* as a thoroughly sentimental poem. Such an interpretation, however, would be absurdly lopsided. The negative, cynical, satirically realistic element in Pope's thought is very strong. Savagely he decries man's chief sin, the pride of intellect.[43] We are not permitted to raise our thoughts above our fixed place in the scale of being, and the assumption that that place is a lofty one is derided. This is assuredly not the best of all possible worlds from the viewpoint of human desire. The universe, Pope delights in reminding us, was not created for our special benefit. Unable to fathom the nature of God, we must be content with self-knowledge.

In the magnificent opening lines of Epistle II, man is invited to see himself as Pope sees him:

> Placed on this isthmus of a middle state,
> A Being darkly wise, and rudely great:
> With too much knowledge for the Sceptic side,
> With too much weakness for the Stoic's pride,
> He hangs between; in doubt to act, or rest;
> In doubt to deem himself a God, or Beast;
> In doubt his Mind or Body to prefer;
> Born but to die, and reas'ning but to err;
> Alike in ignorance, his reason such,
> Whether he thinks too little, or too much:
> Chaos of Thought and Passion, all confused;
> Still by himself abused, or disabused;
> Created half to rise, and half to fall;
> Great lord of all things, yet a prey to all;
> Sole judge of Truth, in endless error hurled:
> The glory, jest, and riddle of the world!

[43] For the background of this idea see A. O. Lovejoy, "Pride in Eighteenth Century Thought," *Modern Language Notes,* XXXVI, 31-37.

Such is the being who is to "know his own place" and live therein a life of rational happiness, the being who is to merge his self-love with social love and ultimately with universal benevolence! Christianity, as his friend Arbuthnot could have told him,[44] has an explanation of this paradox, but Pope has forgotten what it is. For him the dimly discerned superhuman is sometimes merely a means of sneering at a humanity which has no way of being lifted above itself. Even Newton, elsewhere honored by Pope in an epitaph of almost blasphemous reverence, is not exempt:

> Superior beings, when of late they saw
> A mortal man unfold all Nature's law,
> Admired such wisdom in an earthly shape,
> And shewed a Newton as we shew an Ape.

The most glaring inconsistencies of the *Essay on Man* result from the clash between sentimental and anti-sentimental elements. Not all of the contradictions are to be ascribed to Pope's lack of philosophic insight. Most of them were inherent in the half-latitudinarian, half-deistic cosmology and ethics of his day; some of them had been imbedded in the Chain of Being tradition since the Middle Ages. We should not, on the other hand, represent Pope as an empty-headed scribbler pulled hither by one source and thither by another. He was quite capable of thinking for himself and of becoming independently confused. Nor should we regard the *Essay* as the result of a struggle between the sentimentalism of Pope and the anti-sentimentalism of Bolingbroke. There was plenty of anti-sentimentalism in the former, and some—though not much—sentimentalism in the latter. The muddle of the Age of Pope was the muddle of Pope's own mind.

The description of the universal system in Epistle I depends upon the proposition that God, as a being of infinite wisdom and goodness, must have formed the best of all possible worlds. It follows, according to the Chain of Being tradition, that

> ...all must full or not coherent be,
> And all that rises, rise in due degree.

But these ideas can hardly be established by the grovelling empiricism to which man, forbidden to "think or act beyond mankind," is restricted. The optimism of this part of the poem is also vitiated by the fact that

[44] *Vide supra*, p. 167.

nothing that man thinks or does can have the slightest effect upon the operations of the stupendous whole; whereas the other three epistles are meaningless unless man possesses some degree of free will.

Epistle II brushes aside most of Epistle I by declaring that "The proper study of Mankind is Man." We learn that

> Two Principles in human nature reign;
> Self-love, to urge, and Reason, to restrain.

But the restraining function of reason is apparently very feeble, since "What Reason weaves, by Passion is undone." The chief impression arising from this section is that Man is the helpless slave of those "modes of self-love," the passions, and especially of the Ruling Passion:

> Reason itself but gives it edge and power;
> As Heaven's blest beam turns vinegar more sour.

This view agrees with the attack on pride in Epistle I, but is ruinous to the optimistic conclusion toward which Pope is struggling. In its context the argument that the passions, as expressions of "wild Nature's vigor," are the source of the virtues seems merely an attempt to make the best of a bad job. Since reason is the tool of passion the quite different idea announced later, that self-love and reason "join to some mysterious use," is unconvincing; and the suggestion that there is a "God within the mind" who can resolve this chaos vainly appeals to a conception of reason which the poem repeatedly denies.

On this bewildering psychological foundation Epistle III attempts to erect a structure of social ethics. The sentimental conclusion that

> ... God and Nature linked the gen'ral frame,
> And bade Self-love and Social be the same

is but ill prepared for by the very *un*sentimental passage beginning with line 269, where Pope states that the excesses of self-love have necessitated some degree of altruistic behavior:

> How shall he [man] keep, what, sleeping or awake,
> A weaker may surprise, a stranger take?
> His safety must his liberty restrain:
> All join to guard what each desires to gain.
> Forced into virtue thus by Self-defence,
> Even Kings learned justice and benevolence:
> Self-love forsook the path it first pursued,
> And found the private in the public good.

That man is sometimes "forced into virtue" in spite of himself does not mean that he has found his place in "one close system of benevolence," for one cannot be truly benevolent against one's own will. Hobbes and Mandeville cannot be enlisted in the cause of Shaftesbury.

Epistle IV is simply a moral essay on the trite theme that happiness lies only in virtue, which appears to be man's share of the universal benevolence that holds the Chain of Being together. Lines 361-372 eloquently express the thought that self-love stimulates "the virtuous mind" to broaden its scope until

> Wide and more wide, th' o'erflowings of the mind
> Take every creature in, of every kind;
> Earth smiles around, with boundless bounty blest,
> And Heaven beholds its image in his breast.

But this sentimental flourish is inconsistent with the cynical realism of Epistle II and with the more tough-minded parts of Epistle III. The effects of self-love on the mind which is *not* virtuous are not mentioned, and the passage says nothing more than that virtuous men are virtuous.

In short Pope cannot decide whether man is a naturally good, reasonable, and benevolent link in a "chain of love" or a stupid, selfish, and passionate fool in a world where "all subsists by elemental strife." Furthermore he has no religion sufficiently clear and powerful to guide him through the maze in which he is involved. The *Essay on Man* is therefore a very unsatisfying philosophical poem, but it is a remarkable example of the contemporary medley of sentimentalism and anti-sentimentalism as reflected in the eclectic mind of a great artist.

The timid Pope was distressed by the critical attitude of the more strictly orthodox toward the *Essay*. In an attempt to ingratiate himself with such readers he published, in June, 1738, *The Universal Prayer*. There can now be no doubt that this is a revision of a poem originally written about 1715.[45] Pope's aim is to paraphrase the Lord's Prayer in very broad and general terms to which neither the deist nor the Christian can object. He cannot here be accused of pantheism, for he reverently addresses a "Father of All" who is quite distinct from the creation. The third stanza avoids the fatalism that had been detected in the *Essay* by declaring that God, though

[45] See the second of George Sherburn's "Two Notes on the Essay on Man," *Philological Quarterly*, XII, 403.

> ...binding Nature fast in Fate,
> Left free the Human Will.

One finds also such edifying words as "conscience," "hell," "heaven," "grace," and "quickened by thy breath." But Pope resolutely avoids all specifically Christian doctrine, and all the implications of the poem are deistic. It is the prayer of universal Nature to Nature's God. Whether the "Great First Cause" is called "Jehovah, Jove, or Lord" is immaterial. The moral sense is more to be heeded than hope of reward of dread of punishment in a future life. There are—see the sixth stanza—other worlds than ours, and they are probably inhabited by rational beings to whom the Christian creed is irrelevant. Tolerance is enjoined because one sincere belief is as good as any other. God's temple, says Pope the Papist, is "all Space," and His altar is "Earth, Sea, Skies." That is to say, formal religious institutions are of little importance. The poet's contemporaries rightly nicknamed this poem "The Deist's Prayer."

Pope was quite incapable of defending himself against the onslaught of De Crousaz. Far from coming to his aid, Bolingbroke is said to have sneered at Pope behind his back for writing of matters beyond his comprehension. It is easy to imagine the poet's relief and gratitude when Warburton decided that there would be greater polemic glory in defending than in attacking him. With an eagerness only too self-revealing he assures the bishop: "You have made my system as clear as I ought to have done, and could not. It is indeed the same system as mine, but illustrated with a ray of your own....I know I meant just what you explain, but I did not explain my own meaning as well as you." [46]

Thereafter Pope's allusions to religious matters were sparing and cautious. His long-meditated scheme of a great "ethic work" in four parts was never completed. The third part was to have dealt with ecclesiastical and civil government, but, as he told Spence, "this was what chiefly stopped my going on. I could not have said what I would have said, without provoking every church on the face of the earth: and I did not care for living always in hot water." For a time he considered the possibility of expressing his ideas allegorically in the epic *Brutus,* but even this expedient seemed too rash. Since Pope's views on ecclesiastical government would almost certainly have been derived from Bolingbroke, his abandonment of this plan spares us the crowning bewilderment of be-

[46] *Works* (ed. Elwin and Courthope), IX, 203.

holding a professed Roman Catholic in the act of assailing the Church of Rome.

In the end, as we know, Pope granted that it would "look right" to make his peace with God. "The priest came out from him penetrated to the last degree with the spiritual state of mind in which he had found his penitent, resigned and wrapped up in the love of God and man." [47] In those last moments, did "love of God and man" mean the Catholic faith, or did it mean that universal benevolence which for Bolingbroke was the basis of natural theology and hence ultimately of Christianity? Since Pope had persuaded himself that there was no real difference between the two viewpoints, he could sincerely speak in a way that "looked right" to an eighteenth-century priest who was probably not inclined to treat the eminent poet with much rigor. Whether the dying thoughts of Pope looked right to God is beyond human guesswork. Bolingbroke was furious when he learned that Pope had called in a priest, but it was too late. His pupil had died in the religion of Erasmus. [48]

James Thomson must have been somewhat bewildered when, at the age of fifteen, he entered Edinburgh University to prepare himself for the study of theology. The transition from a rural grammar school to an urban university was difficult. Furthermore, he had been very humbly reared in a manse of the most rigid Calvinistic orthodoxy. His social background was not illustrious, for his paternal grandfather was a gardener, and in later years two of his own sisters established a millinery

---

[47] George Paston, op. cit., II, 696.

[48] Professor George Sherburn has suggested that I should consider the implications of the letter written by Pope to Louis Racine on September 1, 1742, in which he declares: "Upon the whole, I have the pleasure to answer you in the manner you most desire, a sincere avowal that my opinions are entirely different from those of Spinoza, or even of Leibnitz; but on the contrary conformable to those of M. Pascal and M. Fenelon: the latter of whom I would most readily imitate, in submitting all my opinions to the decision of the Church." (See E. Audra, L'Influence française dans l'œuvre de Pope, pp. 91 ff., and the facsimile of the letter used as a frontispiece.) Audra would see in these words "l'aveu le plus net de la tendance qu'eut Pope à retourner vers la religion où il avait été élevé. Au déclin de sa vie, sentant approcher l'heure où, a son tour, il allait affronter le Grand Peut-être, se préparait-il à rejoindre dans leur foi son père si respecté, sa mère si tendrement vénérée?" Perhaps. To me, however, it seems more probable that Pope, if pressed on this point, would argue that Pascal and Fénelon were at the same time good Catholics and preachers of the natural religion of universal benevolence, and that, as a believer in universal benevolence, he himself could claim to be a good Catholic. In the same letter this loyal son of the Church tells Racine that he is sending him a copy of Warburton's defense as evidence of his impeccable orthodoxy!

shop in Edinburgh with no sense of having come down in the world. The poet's father, the Reverend Thomas Thomson, was a Presbyterian minister of the old school—severe, narrow, even less likely to approve of worldly letters than the average member of his profession. Something of the atmosphere which pervaded the boy's early years is suggested by the fact that in 1716, the year after James entered Edinburgh, his father died as the result of an attempt to exorcize an evil spirit during an electrical storm. While he prayed over the possessed parishioner a ball of fire struck him on the head, and the fright was too much for him. For some time thereafter young Thomson was afraid of ghosts and demons, and refused to sleep alone at college.[49]

Influences of a somewhat different kind, to be sure, were exerted by his mother. Beatrix Trotter had stooped a little in marrying Thomas Thomson: she was the daughter of a petty laird, and on her mother's side was related to the prominent Home family. Affectionate, emotional, and full of sensibility, she was almost an enthusiast in her pious fervor. Doubtless she stimulated her son's imagination, and she may unwittingly have begun the sentimentalization of his religion. Even before his university days the boy had written a few timid verses. The rural scenes in which he grew up were pleasant, but they might not have inspired him to write had he not seen them partly through the eyes of Robert Riccaltoun. This early mentor had provided a rough model of the sort of poetry in which Thomson was to achieve his great success, and had shown him that poetry and piety were not irreconcilable.

Edinburgh was bewildering to Thomson not because it was wholly new, but because it so perplexingly combined the familiar and the novel. Officially, the Calvinism he had known at Southdean and Jedburgh still held sway over the city and the university. But a new spirit was in the air. After the Act of Union in 1707, cultural relations between England and Scotland rapidly grew much closer than they had been since before the Restoration. Newtonian science, latitudinarian theology, and polite literature swarmed over the border. A general secularity and rationalism of outlook was fermenting in the larger towns of the northern kingdom. In England, the transition from the Reformation to the Enlightenment was gradual; in Scotland, it was comparatively abrupt. The rapidity of

49 Léon Morel, *James Thomson: sa vie et ses œuvres*, pp. 23-24.

the change was stimulating to some young Scots, and demoralizing to others.

Tossed about in this flux of partly digested liberal ideas, Thomson's Calvinism soon began to lose its severity of outline. There is, however, no evidence that he cultivated the rather fashionable pose of libertinism. The worldly and frivolous tone of some of his Edinburgh letters is harmless enough. In the rakish Grotesque Club he did not shine, but he was well regarded in the soberer Athenian Society.[50] Though hardly an accomplished scholar, he did not neglect his work. Of the ancients only Virgil aroused his enthusiasm, but he did his duty as a classical student. He took a keener interest in the natural sciences, which were then more cultivated at Edinburgh than at Oxford or Cambridge. Before leaving Scotland, Thomson had already learned to regard the physical universe and its laws in a religious light. Instruction in mathematics and astronomy had an edifyingly theological quality, and in the divinity school physico-theology was enlisted in support of Christian revelation.[51] At Edinburgh, too, the youth developed his formative admiration for Shakespeare, Spenser, and Milton.

In 1719, having completed his general studies, Thomson became a student of divinity—so far as we know without reluctance. There is no obvious explanation of the fact that, five years later, he abandoned his ecclesiastical ambitions. The story that a professor criticized one of his discourses as more poetic than theological may be true, but this circumstance alone is not a sufficient cause. Probably his beliefs had gradually become more uncertain, his imagination more worldly, and his pen more active, until at last he decided to try his luck as a writer.

Before we follow him to London we shall glance at the poems of his student days. In general they exhibit the influence of secular literature and a broad and slightly soft type of religion upon a youth whose background is conventionally pious. Several of them are "divine," and even the secular pieces have a religious atmosphere. The rarity of definitely Calvinistic notes, however, is significant. Closest to the mood of his father is *A Complaint on the Miseries of Life,* where, alarmed by the wickedness

---

[50] *Ibid.,* p. 27.

[51] Herbert Drennon, "James Thomson's Contact with Newtonianism and His Interest in Natural Philosophy," *PMLA,* XLIX, 71-80.

of mortal existence, the young poet prays to be led untained through the world to heaven. In most of the other divine pieces the God of Calvin has begun to give way before the God of Nature. The nativity-eclogue *A Pastoral Bewixt David, Thirsis, and the Angel Gabriel* is more an exercise in pastoralism than a sacred poem; and *A Paraphrase of Psalm CIV* uses the original as a basis for descriptive embroidery.

In *Upon Happiness,* Thomson awkwardly combines traditional orthodoxy with a more rationalistic kind of religious thought. Like Henry Needler, he lies "underneath a spreading oak," [52] wondering why men are thwarted in their search for happiness:

> I reasoned thus—since the Creator, God,
> Who in eternal love has his abode,
> Hath blended with the essence of the soul
> An appetite as fixèd as the pole,
> That's always eager in pursuit of bliss,
> And always veering till it point to this,
> There is some object adequate to fill
> This boundless wish of our extended will.

Fatigued by these mental exertions he falls asleep. He dreams that he is standing on the mountain peak of Contemplation, from which vantage point he beholds the world where men vainly struggle for delusive joys. The libertine is assured that "virtue's pleasures never, never cloy," and is invited to join the poet on the mount of vision:

> You'll see that God, who, by his powerful call,
> From empty nothing drew this spacious all,
> Made beauteous order the rude mass control,
> And every part subservient to the whole.

This appears to be the God of Shaftesbury's *Moralists* or of the *Essay on Man.* But Thomson surprisingly continues:

> Here you'll behold upon the fatal tree
> The God of nature bleed, expire, and die,
> For such as 'gainst his holy laws rebel,
> And such as bid defiance to his hell.
> Through the dark gulf, here you may clearly pry
> 'Twixt narrow time and vast eternity;
> Behold the Godhead, just as well as good,
> And vengeance poured on tramplers on his blood;

---

[52] *Vide supra,* p. 256.

> But all the tears wiped from his people's eyes;
> And, for their entrance, cleave the parting skies.

The first couplet of this passage is impeccably orthodox: Christians believe that He who suffered on the cross is the creator and sustainer of the physical universe. But Thomson is already beginning to associate the phrase "God of nature" with ideas which, if pushed to their logical conclusion, would make the Incarnation irrelevant. The "nature" later to be hymned in *The Seasons* is already becoming not only the chief source of his poetic inspiration but the chief source of his religious beliefs. Witness *The Works and Wonders of Almighty Power*:

> How can I gaze upon yon sparkling vault,
> And view the planets rolling in their spheres,
> Yet be an atheist? Can I see those stars,
> And think of others far beyond my ken,
> Yet want conviction of creating power?
>
> . . . . .
>
> Here could I lie, in holy contemplation rapt,
> And pass with pleasure an eternal age!

This "contemplation" differs from that described in *Upon Happiness*. It has been shown that *The Works and Wonders of Almighty Power* is little more than a paraphrase of passages drawn from Shaftesbury's *The Moralists*.[53] Whatever else may be said of Shaftesbury's harmonious deity, he did not die for sinners "upon the fatal tree." It will not long be easy for Thomson to believe in a crucified Shaftesburyian "God of nature."

In his earlier as in his later days, Thomson was often glad to turn from these weighty matters to direct enjoyment of rural scenes. *Of a Country Life* is a pleasant descriptive piece combining the mood of the retirement tradition with the technique of the *Georgics*. "In these verses," says Robertson, "appears for the first time, scarcely recognizable, the

---

[53] Herbert Drennon, "The Source of James Thomson's 'The Works and Wonders of Almighty Power,'" *Modern Philology*, XXXII, 33-36. If we accept Aaron Hill's statement, cited in this article, we must conclude that Thomson wrote this poem just before his fifteenth birthday. Hill's statement was presumably based on information supplied by his friend Thomson. It is hard to believe, however, that a fourteen-year-old Scots grammar school graduate, the son of a primitive Calvinist minister, entered the university a disciple of Shaftesbury. Perhaps Hill misunderstood his informant, or perhaps his informant had followed Pope's habit of pushing back the dates of his first poems. But in this poem the absence of the sensuous concreteness with which Thomson would later have treated such a theme suggests an early date; and at the very least one must grant that Thomson knew and admired *The Moralists* soon after his Edinburgh studies had begun.

future author of The Seasons." [54] It would be more accurate to say that *The Seasons* will unite the half-realistic, half-sentimental sensuousness displayed in *Of a Country Life* with the philosophy of *The Works and Wonders of Almighty Power*.

We may imagine that when Thomson went to London toward the end of February, 1725, his mind was a jumble of rather broad and rationalistic Presbyterianism—its sterner elements perhaps subconsciously rather than consciously repudiated; Newtonian science and Newtonian physico-theology; the closely related but more Neoplatonic, aesthetic, and benevolistic philosophy of Shaftesbury; the common-sense ethical religion of Locke and Addison; enthusiasm for Shakespeare, Spenser, and Milton, and for the less purely classical aspects of Virgil; a warm affection for external nature; a sensuousness which sometimes bordered upon sensuality, and which was not unsupported by the contemporary spirit of negation. A strange medley, but one very characteristic of this age of flux. In London the remains of his Calvinism disappeared, and with them, apparently, went most of the essentials of Christianity. The process was doubtless gradual. In a letter of April 3, 1725, he refers to his chances of success in some project—probably a literary one—and adds, "Succeed or not, I firmly resolve to pursue divinity, as the only thing now I am fit for." Macaulay holds that "this is plainly inconsistent with the idea that he came up to London merely as a literary adventurer"; [55] but Morel more plausibly suggests that Thomson, finding it difficult at first to make his way in the literary world, briefly entertained the notion of taking orders in the Church of England. [56] The plan would not be inconsistent with complete lack of zeal and great latitude of belief.

As literary success approached, such intentions were cast aside. The mature Thomson must unquestionably be classified among the deists. To what extent he would have accepted this description, however, is less certain. While *The Seasons* does not depend upon Christianity, nothing in it is inconsistent with a rather extreme sentimental latitudinarianism; in spirit, the poem is less alien to Christianity than the *Essay on Man*. If Shaftesbury himself attended Church of England services as regularly as his health permitted and received Holy Communion three or four times

---

[54] *Complete Poetical Works of James Thomson* (ed. J. Logie Robertson), p. 497.
[55] G. C. Macaulay, *James Thomson*, p. 11.   [56] Léon Morel, *James Thomson*, p. 34.

a year,[57] Thomson need not have regarded himself as outside the Christian fold. So pious a woman as the Countess of Hertford would not have extended her patronage to a downright infidel. Her praise of Thomson was influential with her friend Mrs. Rowe, herself a lover of retirement who enjoyed "the charming solitude thro' which Mr. Thomson's muse leads the thoughts with a just and reasonable delight." [58] The fact that Thomson became a freemason in 1737 is inconclusive: eighteenth-century masons had marked deistic leanings, but many of them professed a broadly rationalistic Christianity. Inferences to be drawn from Lyttelton's efforts to convert him are much more significant, but one must remember that his lordship's conception of Christianity had become unusually strict. Probably Thomson's actual beliefs were vague and pliant. The amiable nebulosity of his utterances on religious matters would appeal to different people in different ways. The Arian divine, Dr. Rundle, could regard him as a sound disciple of Newton; [59] Lady Hertford, as a Christian benevolist; his friend Mallet, as a fellow-deist. Nor would Thomson be quick to deny any of these interpretations, though from the pious Lyttelton he apparently made no attempt to conceal the fact that he was not an orthodox Christian. The probability that his private conversation was less affirmatively religious than his poems implies no real hypocrisy: Thomson was a poet, and poetry requires a faith.

The Seasons was not, of course, written primarily to set forth a religious philosophy. Thomson's aim was to depict external nature in a manner which would combine realism of observation and inward sensibility without sacrificing that ideal of broadly generalized normality which classicism had imposed upon both poet and landscape-painter. For this purpose the best model would be Virgil's *Georgics,* and the best form in which to emulate that work would be the Miltonic blank verse already employed in the same *genre* by John Philips. With all its faults, *The Seasons* remains a work of art because the writer's motives were primarily aesthetic. "C'est en artiste et en poète qu'il contemple le monde," [60] says Morel.

[57] Shaftesbury, *Characteristics* (ed. J. M. Robertson), I, xxiii.
[58] *The Miscellaneous Works...of Mrs. Elizabeth Rowe,* II, 79. See also I, 162, and II, 54.
[59] Herbert Drennon, "James Thomson's Contact with Newtonianism and His Interest in Natural Philosophy," *PMLA,* XLIX, 75.
[60] *Op. cit.,* p. 403.

But a poet, no matter how pure an artist he may be, must have a cosmos to write in. Thomson's art demanded a universe that was large, warm, benevolent, and expansive, grandiose but elegant, variegated but composed. Often therefore he not merely sees and feels such a universe, but thinks about it and discusses it. His philosophy is interesting precisely because it is not a cool *a priori* fabrication, but a genuine outgrowth of his temperament. It is true that the germs of his sentimental patriotism and of his sense of a divine element in nature may be found in the *Georgics*,[61] but he makes them his own and greatly develops them. A man like Thomson feels first and considers the implications of his feeling later. Hence it is not surprising that many of the philosophical and religious reflections are either later additions or expansions of much briefer passages in earlier versions. There is no reason to say, with Morel, that these changes are merely concessions to the spirit of the times, or that they are "amplifications ajoutées au tableau de la nature, et ne font pas corps avec lui." [62] Thomson's philosophy agrees with several growing tendencies of the period not because of any concessions on his part, but because, when he thought, he thought as did his age. It would be hard to find a poet whose ideas are more organically related to his art.

Thomson's religion, in fact, is inseparable from his conception of poetry. In the preface to the second edition of *Winter* he declares that to scorn poetry, as many now do, "is affronting the universal taste of mankind, and declaring against what has charmed the listening world from Moses down to Milton. In fine, it is even declaring against the sublimest passages of the inspired writings themselves, and what seems to be the peculiar language of heaven.... Let poetry once more be restored to her ancient truth and purity; let her be inspired from heaven; and in return, let incense ascend thither." This is the spirit in which Watts, Blackmore, and Dennis recommend a revival of divine poetry. Such views would have been fostered by the influence of Aaron Hill, who from the first saw in Thomson a man who might exemplify the bardic ideal.

Completely in Hill's vein, the preface goes on: "Nothing can have a better influence towards the revival of poetry than the choosing of great and serious subjects, such as at once amuse the fancy,[63] enlighten the

---

[61] D. L. Durling, *Georgic Tradition in English Poetry*, pp. 46, 56.
[62] *Op. cit.*, pp. 255, 359.
[63] The phrase means, "put the fancy into a state of pensive musing.".

head, and warm the heart." As an example of lofty poetical ambition he quotes a quatrain from Hill's *The Judgment Day:*

> For me, suffice it to have taught my muse,
> The tuneful triflings of her tribe to shun;
> And raised her warmth such heavenly themes to choose,
> As, in past ages, the best garlands won.

But the phrase "heavenly subjects," which to Watts, Dennis, Blackmore, and in this poem even to Hill meant definitely Christian themes, is interpreted by Thomson with greater latitude. He immediately adds: "I know no subject more elevating, more amusing, more ready to awake the poetical enthusiasm, the philosophical reflection, than the works of Nature. Where can we meet with such variety, such beauty, such magnificence? All that enlarges and transports the soul? What more inspiring than a calm, wide survey of them?" Thus the old critical dictum, "To achieve sublimity, write about God," is transformed into, "To achieve sublimity, write about God's works." In two successive paragraphs he uses *Job* and the *Georgics* as great examples of nature-poetry.

The highest aim of the poet, then, is to communicate to the reader the enlargement, transport, poetical enthusiasm, and philosophical reflection which have been aroused in him by a calm, wide survey of the works of Nature. He is one who, as evening softly descends,

> ... lonely loves
> To seek the distant hills, and there converse
> With Nature; there to harmonize his heart,
> And in pathetic song to breathe around
> The harmony to others.

At such times he becomes

> ... lost in lonely musing, in a dream,
> Confused, of careless solitude, where mix
> Ten thousand wandering images of things,
> Soothe every gust of passion into peace—
> All but the swellings of the softened heart,
> That waken, not disturb, the tranquil mind.

The tranquillity of these moments, however, is deeply solemn, especially when the scene is "the midnight depth" of a grove. As Collins was to remember, Thomson liked to think of himself as a druid, a nature-inspired bard and seer:

> These are the haunts of meditation, these
> The scenes where ancient bards the inspiring breath
> Ecstatic, felt; and, from this world retired,
> Conversed with angels, and immortal forms,
> On gracious errands bent.

Even to the modern bard come heavenly messengers, commanding, "Of Nature sing with us, and Nature's God."

Thomson's angels are a little more than decorative personifications. As Mr. Potter has pointed out,[64] Thomson combined the Pythagorean doctrine of metempsychosis and the idea of the chain of being in a belief that a scale of spiritual evolution ascends from link to link of the universal chain. Hence he could easily credit the existence of beings who had once been men but who now occupied a position higher than man though lower than God. According to this idea man would ultimately become God, but Thomson did not press the thought so rigorously.

In Spring we find a most interesting attempt to describe poetico-religious meditation in psychological terms. The mind rises gently from a sense of well-being to mystical transport:

> ...Contentment walks
> The sunny glade, and feels an inward bliss
> Spring o'er his mind, beyond the power of kings
> To purchase. Pure serenity apace
> Produces thought, and contemplation still.
> By swift degrees the love of nature works,
> And warms the bosom; till at last, sublimed
> To rapture and enthusiastic heat,
> We feel the present Deity, and taste
> The joy of God to see a happy world!

Though not a mystic, Thomson at least believes in the possibility of mystically sharing God's joy through poetic imagination. Since divine joy is creative, the truly inspired poet is also a creative spirit:

> Come, Inspiration! from thy hermit seat,
> By mortal seldom found: may fancy dare,
> From thy fixed serious eye, and raptured glance
> Shot out surrounding Heaven, to steal one look
> Creative of the poet, every power
> Exalting to an ecstasy of soul.

[64] G. R. Potter, "James Thomson and the Evolution of Spirits," *Englische Studien*, LXI, 57-65.

Thomson is not without that sense of superiority which is one of the least ingratiating traits of the man of feeling. Like Damon in *Summer,* the true poet possesses

> A pure ingenuous elegance of soul,
> A delicate refinement, known to few.

But Thomson's benevolism would probably lead him to admit that the creative power of insight into the harmony of things, though much more fully developed in some persons than in others, is a universal human faculty.

There is nothing irrational about poetic ecstasy. The same truths are displayed to the eye of reason and to the eye of fancy,

> The first up-tracing, from the dreary void,
> The chain of causes and effects to Him,
> The world-producing Essence, who alone
> Possesses being; while the last receives
> The whole magnificence of heaven and earth,
> And every beauty, delicate or bold,
> Obvious or more remote, with lively sense,
> Diffusive printed on the rapid mind.

Fancy, one might say, is reason accelerated and intensified. But there is also the implication that fancy, as capable of rushing at once to the height of truth and grasping the whole in a single view, is a loftier faculty than the ability to trace causal relationships. Thomson is dimly groping toward Wordsworth's doctrine of imagination as

> ... but another name for absolute strength
> And clearest insight, amplitude of mind,
> And reason in her most exalted mood.

My readers will hardly require a detailed account of the truths revealed consecutively to Thomson's reason and simultaneously to his imagination. Abstractly, his universal system is much the same as that set forth in Epistle I of the *Essay on Man,* but the spirit in which he regards this system is very different from Pope's. The *Essay on Man* is the work of one who was born twelve years earlier than Thomson, and whose thought took form in a *milieu* very different from that of the younger poet. Not sceptical wits like Wycherley, Garth, and Walsh, but sentimentalists like Hill, Mallet, and Dyer, were Thomson's first important literary friends. Though Thomson reveres the coherence and unity of the creation, he dwells quite as much upon the "parts" of the "stupendous whole" as upon the "whole" itself, delighting in the rich diversity of concrete objects. He does not share Pope's gratitude that man's senses are no keener than they are. Gazing at flowers, he rejoices to see

> Infinite numbers, delicacies, smells,
> With hues on hues expression cannot paint,
> The breath of Nature, and her endless bloom.

Even the insects of summer are delightful as

> ... by myriads, forth at once,
> Swarming they pour; of all the varied hues
> Their beauty-beaming parent can disclose.
> Ten thousand forms! ten thousand different tribes!

Thomson's chain of being, therefore, has more diversity and less uniformity than Pope's. Then, too, the idea of spiritual evolution previously alluded to gives the system more fluidity and upsweep:

> ... I cannot go
> Where universal love not smiles around,
> Sustaining all yon orbs and all their suns;
> From seeming evil still educing good,
> And better thence again, and better still
> In infinite progression.

Every creature who lives worthily in its place in the scale of things may in a later incarnation of its spirit occupy a higher place.

At times, Thomson can rebuke intellectual pride very much in the manner of Pope. Since man is like a "critic-fly" on the dome of a huge building, how dare he presume to pass judgment upon the entire fabric? But such attempts to keep man in his place are very rare, and they are directed only at those who question the wisdom of the Supreme Being. Those who have faith in that wisdom are encouraged, rather than forbidden, to think beyond the merely human level. Thomson takes a more sanguine view than Pope of the power of science to penetrate the secrets of nature. Also, as we have seen, imagination frees its possessors from subjection to parts and enables them to grasp "the whole magnificence of heaven and earth." This godlike faculty gives man a very distinguished position, and Thomson does not abash him by reminding him of the innumerable higher links in the chain of being. To be sure, man has degenerated sadly since the Golden Age, when "reason and benevolence were law." Even now, however, he is not the helpless sport of the passions; even now,

> ... Man superior walks
> Amid the glad creation, musing praise,
> And looking lively gratitude.

In short this is the best of all possible worlds not only for the system in its entirety, but for man.

Thomson has none of that ironic realism which clashes so violently with Pope's attempt to identify self-love with social love. He is a genuinely optimistic lover of the whole species, eager to draw analogies between physical and ethical harmony. Universal benevolence acts in the moral as gravitation in the physical world. Unwavering is his belief that

> ... happiness and true philosophy
> Are of the social still and smiling kind.

God himself is so social and smiling that one is tempted to compare Him to the last glimpse of the Cheshire Cat in *Alice in Wonderland:* all of Him has faded away except the cosmic grin. In the "soft scenes" of spring "the smiling God is seen." His dearest joy is "to see a happy world." The great Parent of the insects is "beauty-beaming." "The wish of Nature" descends in showers that are

> ... lovely, gentle, kind,
> And full of every hope and every joy.

As part of the amiable creation of an amiable God, man himself is naturally amiable. It has been well observed that even the narrative episodes scattered through *The Seasons* are vehicles of social feeling, "all meant to inspire those sympathies and social virtues which are the essence of the 'inward harmony' of philosophers like Shaftesbury and Hutcheson." [65] Not that Thomson is blind to the cruelty, injustice, and wickedness of man: on such topics he can wax very indignant. These evils, however, are caused merely by man's forgetting his kinship with the harmony of things. If "the gay licentious crowd" ever paused to think of the sufferings of the less fortunate their natural benevolence would assert itself:

> The conscious heart of Charity would warm,
> And her wide wish Benevolence dilate;
> The social tear would rise, the social sigh;

[65] D. L. Durling, *Georgic Tradition in English Poetry*, p. 52.

> And, into clear perfection, gradual bliss,
> Refining still, the social passions work.

An indolent, sensuous Epicureanism partly vitiates not only Thomson's benevolism but his sense of the supernatural. Yet, though hardly a man of intense religious passion, he is moved by a diffused spiritual sensibility. Morel is only a little too flattering when he writes: "Quand, oublieux des subtilités métaphysiques où il lui arrive de se perdre, il se laisse entraîner à une effusion de piété, pour adorer la puissance suprême, force immanente et essence unique, ou au contraire Dieu créateur et Providence tutélaire, alors il trouve des accents d'une éloquence inflammée qui ne sont pas indignes de Milton." [66] Certainly Thomson is more deeply aware of God than Pope. More keenly responsive to the creation, he feels a livelier gratitude to the Creator. Hence, unlike Pope, he breaks out in

> ...hymns of holy wonder to that Power
> Whose wisdom shines as lovely on our minds
> As on our smiling eyes his servant-sun.

Such passages should make us hesitate to label Thomson, *sans phrase,* as a pantheist. Frequently, to be sure, he addresses personified Nature as a deity of independent power and conscious benevolence. But is this much more than a figure of speech? Thomson does not long forget that the sun is the "servant" of a higher Power. In *Summer* the orb, at first addressed almost as a god in itself, soon becomes a

> ...great *delegated* source
> Of light, and life, and grace, and joy below.[67]

And the poet immediately adds:

> How shall I then attempt to sing of Him,
> Who, Light Himself! in uncreated light
> Invested deep, dwells awfully retired
> From mortal eye, or angel's purer ken;
> Whose single smile has, from the first of time,
> Filled, overflowing, all those lamps of heaven;
>
> .   .   .   .   .   .
>
> But, should he hide his face, the astonished sun,
> And all the extinguished stars, would loosening reel
> Wide from their spheres, and chaos come again.

This surely is no mere deification of the system of nature.

[66] *Op. cit.,* p. 400.   [67] Italics mine.

Nor would it be accurate to say that Thomson is a pantheist harassed by an uneasy feeling that he should be something else. He asserts the transcendence of God as warmly as His immanence. And why not, since the God of Christians is both immanent and transcendent? If Thomson seems inconsistent on this point it is because he has almost wholly forgotten the Christian solution of this tremendous paradox, and has found no other solution. He believes in a mystery to which he has lost the clue.

Despite this handicap Thomson sincerely struggles to rise from worship of a Spirit *in* nature to worship of a Spirit *above* nature:

> Hail! Source of Being! Universal Soul
> Of heaven and earth! Essential Presence, hail!
> To thee I bend the knee; to thee my thoughts,
> Continual, climb; who, with a master-hand,
> Hast the great whole into perfection touched.

"Bend the knee" is not merely metaphorical. At times the Universal Soul of nature becomes an almighty *person* who may be addressed in the completely Addisonian prayer:

> Father of light and life! thou Good Supreme!
> O teach me what is good! teach me Thyself!
> Save me from folly, vanity, and vice,
> From every low pursuit, and feed my soul
> With knowledge, conscious peace, and virtue pure—
> Sacred, substantial, never-fading bliss!

In his more definitely personal and transcendent aspects, indeed, the God of Nature bears some resemblance to the God of Christianity. The concluding *Hymn* is at least a more recognizable paraphrase of *Psalm CXLVIII* than Pope's *Universal Prayer* is of the Lord's Prayer, and there is more than a graceful pastoral allusion in the assurance that

> ... the Great Shepherd reigns,
> And his unsuffering kingdom yet will come.

The same note is struck in the concluding passage of *Winter,* with its promise of "one unbounded Spring":

> 'Tis come, the glorious morn! the second birth
> Of heaven and earth! awakening Nature hears
> The new-creating word, and starts to life,
> In every heightened form, from pain and death
> For ever free.

But in Thomson this Christian hope, having lost its definitely Christian foundation, becomes merely a sentimental analogy drawn from the fact that spring follows winter, as in "modernist" Easter sermons. A few such passages are not sufficient to enable one to feel that Christianity enters at all deeply into Thomson's thoughts or feelings. Though he possesses a livelier sense of the supernatural than most of his contemporaries, he confines himself to the natural revelation. Hence despite his frequent assertion of belief in a transcendent God, the poem cannot but impress the reader as a pantheistic effusion. Deistic tenets combined wtih strong enthusiasm for external nature inevitably tend in the direction of pantheism. Since God is known only in His lovely works, those lovely works are likely to become the only God that really exists. In the *Hymn,* nature is exhorted to worship God, but it is hard not to feel that she is being exhorted to worship her own fair face. Consider the ambiguity of the opening lines, where Thomson says of the seasons:

> These, as they change, Almighty Father! these
> Are but the varied God. The rolling year
> Is full of thee.

These lines are not *explicitly* pantheistic: they simply assert that the seasons are varying manifestations of the "Almighty Father's" power, beauty, and love. But the lines are *implicitly* pantheistic because for Thomson "the rolling year" is not only full of God but is the sole basis of belief in Him. Thomson, however, ignores the logical implications of his sensibility. He believes in a God who

> ... ceaseless works alone, and yet alone
> Seems not to work,

although he has no rational ground for asserting God's aloneness. Had anyone demanded, "How can your thoughts climb from the natural to the supernatural when the supernatural has become submerged in the natural?" the whole system would have burst like a bubble. But few of Thomson's contemporaries were likely to ask that question, and he was not the man to plague himself with it.

For our purpose it is not essential that Thomson be forced either into a pigeonhole labelled "Shaftesbury" or into one labelled "Newton." Those interested in the problem may consult the articles by C. A. Moore and Herbert Drennon listed in the appendix of secondary sources. But above all they should read the anonymous critical note in *Philogical Quarterly*, XIV, 175-176, for an admirably just estimate of Drennon's "Newtonian" thesis. This scholar has clearly shown that Newton's influence on *The Seasons* is much stronger than Moore, with his excessive insistence upon Thomson's direct indebtedness to Shaftesbury, would lead us to expect. Even disregarding the evidence provided by the poem *To the Memory of Sir Isaac Newton*, no reader of *The Seasons* can deny that Newtonian thought plays an important part in Thomson's religious philosophy. For him, as we have seen, there is no conflict between imagination and scientific reason. The universe is rational through and through, and Sir Isaac is the great revealer of its rationality.

But there is no need to insist that since Thomson was a Newtonian he was not a Shaftesburyian. Before discovering that the juvenile piece *The Works and Wonders of Almighty Power* came straight from Shaftesbury, Drennon himself used the poem as evidence of Thomson's early interest in the sort of physico-theology which was drawn from Newton.[68] Any modern student would probably have agreed with him. The philosophies of Newton and Shaftesbury are not mutually exclusive, and they are freely blended in pre-romantic literature. Drennon grants—in a footnote—that "Thomson's rhapsodical treatment of the nature-theme" and "his praise of solitude as an abode of inspiration" may reflect the influence of Shaftesbury.[69] But to admit this is to admit a great deal, since Thomson's religion is expressed chiefly through a rhapsodical treatment of nature which, when most fervent, is inspired by solitary contemplation. Drennon greatly exaggerates the realism, objectivity, and scientific rationalism of the poem.

His interpretation leaves scant room for the interrelation of physical, aesthetic, and ethical harmony which is so vital to the thought of *The Seasons* or for the doctrine of cosmic benevolism which pervades it. Professor Bernbaum, in a useful summary, reminds us of Shaftesbury's belief "that the universe and all its creatures constitute a perfect harmony; and that Man, owing to his innate moral and aesthetic sense, needs no supernatural revelation of religious or ethical truth, because if he will discard the prejudices of tradition, he will instinctively, when face to face

[68] "James Thomson's Contact with Newtonianism and His Interest in Natural Philosophy," *PMLA*, XLIX, 73*n*.

[69] "Scientific Rationalism and James Thomson's Poetic Art," *Studies in Philology*, XXXI, 461*n*.

with Nature, recognize the Spirit which dwells therein,—and, correspondingly, when in the presence of a good deed he will recognize its morality. In other words, God and Nature are one, and Man is instinctively good, his cardinal virtue being the love of humanity, his true religion the love of Nature." [70] The creed as stated ignores Shaftesbury's tough-minded aspects, but it includes those softer ideas which the sentimentalists drew from him or from the general tradition of which he was the most eloquent and influential spokesman. These are so obviously foreground ideas of *The Seasons* that it seems almost perverse to deny that Thomson is even more significantly indebted to Shaftesbury than to Newton.

On May 21, 1747, Lyttelton, recently bereaved of his wife, wrote to Thomson: "My refuge and consolation is in philosophy—Christian philosophy, which I heartily wish you may be a disciple of as well as myself. Indeed, my dear friend, it is far above the Platonic." [71] Had the poet, in arguing with Lyttelton, championed the philosophy of Plato? The inference, though by no means inevitable, is tempting. Thomson's Platonism, one supposes, would be heavily tinged with the sentimentally Neoplatonic, aesthetic, quasi-pantheistic thought of Shaftesbury. If Thomson had attempted a strict formulation of the religious philosophy glimpsed in *The Seasons* we might have had a system much like that of Brooke's *Universal Beauty*—a system of Shaftesburyian Neoplatonism reinforced in its physical details by the results of Newtonian science.

The element of scientific rationalism in *The Seasons* is obscured and softened by the author's sensibility. The major inconsistency of the work is not, as in the *Essay on Man,* a clash between sentimentalism and anti-sentimentalism, but a clash between two types of sentimentalism—the contemplative and the active. Thomson loves pensive retirement and "simple" nature. His mind dwells much upon the Golden Age, rural and savage virtues, the blessings of ingenuous love, the cruelty of the huntsman, the evils generated by luxury and sophistication. But he is a perfect illustration of the thesis of Lois Whitney's *Primitivism and Progress,* for he is no less enthusiastic about organized government, patriotic service, the advance of science, material progress, commerce, industry, and all the shibboleths of bustling Whiggery. [72] Thomson is a clear case of that

---

[70] *English Poets of the Eighteenth Century* (ed. Ernest Bernbaum), p. xxiv.

[71] Quoted by G. C. Macaulay, *James Thomson,* p. 63.

[72] This inconsistency in Thomson is discussed by R. D. Havens, "Primitivism and the Idea of Progress in Thomson," *Studies in Philology,* XXIX, 41-52.

cleavage within the sentimental mind which was considered in the preceding chapter.[73] For him the problem of choosing between a back-to-nature type of contemplativeness and the life of action was urgent. Sensuous and indolent, he found it easy to set a high value upon meditative retirement in the bosom of "simple" nature.[74] But as a child of the Calvinistic manse, a Whig, a bourgeois, a man of the age of Locke, he was drawn toward the idealization of practical activity.

The link between these two types of sentimentalism, as has already been suggested, is the doctrine of a universal benevolence that fills both the heart of man and the heart of God. That "joy of God to see a happy world" which is revealed to the solitary in the grove is an active, creative, social passion, a divine lust to make the world beam with bliss. The psychology of benevolist contemplation may be traced through the following lines from *Autumn:*

> He comes! he comes! in every breeze the Power
> Of Philosophic Melancholy comes!
> His near approach the sudden-starting tear,
> The glowing cheek, the mild dejected air,
> The softened feature, and the beating heart,
> Pierced deep with many a virtuous pang, declare.
> O'er all the soul his sacred influence breathes;
> Inflames imagination; through the breast
> Infuses every tenderness; and far
> Beyond dim earth exalts the swelling thought.
> Ten thousand thousand fleet ideas, such
> As never mingled with the vulgar dream,
> Crowd fast into the mind's creative eye.
> As fast the correspondent passions rise,
> As varied, and as high—devotion raised
> To rapture, and divine astonishment;
> The love of nature unconfined, and, chief,
> Of human race; the large ambitious wish
> To make them blest; the sigh for suffering worth
> Lost in obscurity; the noble scorn
> Of tyrant pride, the fearless great resolve;
> The wonder which the dying patriot draws,

[73] *Vide supra,* p. 485.

[74] This implies no necessary relation between contemplativeness and indolence. But contemplativeness may be very tempting to a lazy man, especially in an age when the contemplative need not contemplate anything in particular.

> Inspiring glory through remotest time;
> The awakened throb for virtue and for fame;
> The sympathies of love and friendship dear,
> With all the social offspring of the heart.

These are the noblest fruits of meditative retirement. For Thomson's religion, neither philosophy nor melancholy is sufficient. They must be combined in Philosophic Melancholy—that blessed mood in which the philosopher-poet uses "the mind's creative eye." Thomson's belief in the power of the poetic spirit approaches a kind of transcendentalism. Long before Coleridge, he prizes the "shaping spirit of imagination." This is also Aaron Hill's doctrine,[75] and we know that it descends from the Dennis-Watts-Blackmore theory of sacred poetry. The divinity of divine poetry is being transferred from the subject-matter to the poet.

Apparently Thomson never forsook the religion of *The Seasons*. When Lyttelton wrote, "Thomson, I hope and believe, died a Christian," [76] the wish was probably father to the thought. In any case none of the poems suggests the likelihood of a conversion. But even before *The Seasons* have reached their final form he produces work which shows a shift of emphasis. We have repeatedly observed that the literary adherents of Prince Frederick loved to indulge in rhetoric about patriotism, public service, and political and religious liberty. When Thomson writes as a propagandist for this party, his active sentimentalism increases and his contemplative sentimentalism diminishes. He feels more and more the obligation to

> ...inhale
> That portion of divinity, that ray
> Of purest heaven, which lights the public soul
> Of patriots and of heroes.[77]

The most striking example of this trend from the private to the public soul is *Liberty,* published in 1735 and 1736 and dedicated to the Prince of Wales. The historical portions of the poem abound in ideas which were shared by latitudinarians and deists. The great civilization of Egypt decayed

> ...when mysterious Superstition came,
> And, with her Civil Sister [78] leagued, involved

[75] *Vide supra,* p. 450.   [76] Quoted by Morel, *op. cit.,* pp. 157n-158n.
[77] *Winter.*   [78] "Civil Tyranny," Thomson explains.

In studied darkness the desponding mind;
Then Tyrant Power the righteous scourge unloosed:
For yielded reason speaks the soul a slave.

In the Age of Pericles, on the contrary,

> ... Then stood untouched the solid base
> Of Liberty, the liberty of mind;
> For systems yet, and soul-enslaving creeds,
> Slept with the monsters of succeeding times.

Those monstrous times were of course the Catholic Middle Ages, when all was "Scholastic Discord," "cleric Pride," "holy Slander," "persecuting Zeal," "idiot Superstition," and "Ignorance." The modern Romans, who cling to these evils, are

> The slave of slaves, by superstition fooled,
> By vice unmanned and a licentious rule.

Their worship is hypocritical mummery:

> Mark how the temple glares, and artful dressed,
> Amusive, draws the superstitious train.

Little better than a papist was James I:

> ... lawless sway
> He, with his slavish Doctors, tried to rear
> On metaphysic, on enchanted ground,
> And all the mazy quibbles of the schools.

Thomson of course applauds the downfall of Charles I and James II, and hails with joy "the patriot of mankind ... Immortal Nassau."

This is all very familiar. The reader of this study will not be surprised to learn that a purer and more rational form of religion imparts her blessing to the virtues attendant upon Liberty:

> Nor be Religion, rational and free,
> Here passed in silence; whose enraptured eye
> Sees Heaven with earth connected, human things
> Linked to divine: who not from servile fear,
> By rites for some weak tyrant incense fit,
> The God of Love adores, but from a heart
> Effusing gladness, into pleasing awe
> That now astonished swells, now in a calm
> Of fearless confidence that smiles serene;
> That lives devotion, one continual hymn,

> And then most grateful, when Heaven's bounty most
> Is right enjoyed.

Thus easily can the cult of liberty, with its anti-clericalism and its Boling-brokian hatred of metaphysics and "mystery," take on a cheery tenderness.

This "rational and free" religion is that of *The Seasons,* but with increased emphasis upon the active virtues. Pythagoras, himself a scorner of tyrants,

> . . . first discerned the secret band of love,
> The kind attraction that to central suns
> Binds circling earths, and world with world unites.
> Instructed thence, he great ideas formed
> Of the whole-moving, all-informing God,
> The Sun of beings! beaming unconfined
> Light, life, and love, and ever active power—
> Whom nought can image, and who best approves
> The silent worship of the moral heart,
> That joys in bounteous Heaven and spreads the joy.

The strongly deistic implications of the last three lines should be noted. The thought of the whole passage—to return for a moment to the point at issue between Moore and Drennon—comprises but goes beyond the Newtonian viewpoint. Shaftesbury is closer than Newton to the Pythagorean-Platonic tradition of physico-ethical harmony on which these lines depend.

In Part V the Goddess of Liberty delivers a lecture on these matters. The noblest of all passions, she declares, is "devotion to the public." In acquiring this virtue one should not begin with self-scrutiny, for social love does not, as in Pope, broaden from the particular to the general. On the contrary, the mind must first soar to a love of the glorious whole, and this sentiment will then cast its beams upon specific objects of benevolence:

> An active flood of universal love
> Must swell the breast. First, in effusion wide,
> The restless spirit roves creation round,
> And seizes every being; stronger then
> It tends to life, whate'er the kindred search
> Of bliss allies; then, more collected still,
> It urges human kind; a passion grown,
> At last the central parent public calls
> Its utmost effort forth, awakes each sense,
> The comely, grand, and tender.

This roving of the spirit round the creation would of course be quite impossible for man as represented by Pope. It is made possible for Thomsonian man by his imaginative power. Perhaps Coleridge, also thinking about liberty, remembered Thomson when he wrote:

> Yes, while I stood and gazed, my temples bare,
> And shot my being through earth, sea, and air,
> Possessing all things with intensest love,
> O Liberty! my spirit felt thee there.[79]

But beneath these effusions of public soul Thomson continues to be torn by the conflicting claims of his temperament. In *The Castle of Indolence,* the conflict rises to the surface. When begun in 1735 or 1736, the poem was, as Murdoch explains, "a few detached stanzas in the way of raillery on himself, and on some of his friends, who would reproach him with indolence, while he thought them at least as indolent as himself. But he saw very soon that the subject deserved to be treated more seriously, and in a form fitted to convey one of the most important moral lessons." [80]

Canto I, the description of the castle and its inmates, retains a few traces of Thomson's original intention to write an intimate Spenserian burlesque. In a way more important for us, Thomson at times seems moved by a serious desire to champion free, gracious indolence as a harmless and even a good way of life. He has read not only Spenser but Rabelais, for his Bower of Bliss is very like the abbey where one does as one pleases—a place where, as he had written in *Liberty,* man, "joining bliss to virtue," may enjoy

> ...the glad ease
> Of Epicurus, seldom understood.

But Thomson's puritanism proves stronger than his Epicureanism. In the long run this lazy, carefree life leads to lethargy and melancholia, to gout, apoplexy, and other ills of intemperance. "When unpleasing grown," the inmates are pitilessly thrust into a dungeon beneath the castle.

In Canto II the castle is overthrown and its inhabitants reformed by the Knight of Arts and Industry, the complete personification of benevolent, Whiggish public service. The slaves of Indolence might also, one would suppose, have been redeemed by cultivating a more seriously contemplative attitude toward the beauties of creation, but such is not the theme of

---

[79] *France: An Ode.*

[80] *Complete Poetical Works of James Thomson* (ed. J. Logie Robertson), p. 306n.

the present poem. By this time Thomson seems to have decided, somewhat ruefully, to force himself into a thorough-going championship of the active life. From an aesthetic viewpoint Canto II ruins the poem, but the author would not wish us to ignore it.

Sir Industry's long harangue to the inmates opens with a bit of pantheism:

> What is the adored Supreme perfection? say!
> What, but eternal never-resting soul,
> Almighty power, and all-directing day,
> By whom each atom stirs, the planets roll,
> Who fills, surrounds, informs, and agitates the whole?

This cosmic soul-stuff is sentimentalized Protestant energy. We must seize upon it and make it our own. Faith in our ability to do so is supported by that doctrine of spiritual evolution which is dear to Thomson:

> Come, to the beaming God your hearts unfold!
> Draw from its fountain life! 'Tis thence alone
> We can excel. Up from unfeeling mould
> To seraphs burning round the Almighty's throne,
> Life rising still on life in higher tone
> Perfection forms, and with perfection bliss.

But perfection is not to be won without striving, for activity is its very essence. "Renown is not the child of indolent repose." Hard work is the surest prescription for happiness:

> Toil, and be glad! let Industry inspire
> Into your quickened limbs her buoyant breath!
> Who does not act is dead; absorpt entire
> In miry sloth, no pride, no joy he hath:
> O leaden-hearted men, to be in love with death!

Consider "the toiling swain ... perhaps the happiest of the sons of men." How he glows with health! How heartily he enjoys his food and the pleasures of "the pure nuptial bed!" "The losel is to him a miserable wight."

In *Summer,* Thomson had praised swimming as "the purest exercise of health," declaring that

> Even from the body's purity, the mind
> Receives a secret sympathetic aid.

In the same vein Sir Industry lauds "the vigorous joys of health." It is almost as if he were singing, with Browning's David:

> Oh, our manhood's prime vigor! No spirit feels waste,
> Not a muscle is stopped in its playing nor sinew unbraced.
>
> . . .
>
> How good is man's life, the mere living! How fit to employ
> All the heart and the soul and the senses for ever in joy! [81]

Sir Industry sees before him some "who wretched sigh for virtue, but despair." Can they hope to follow him to bliss along the path of public service and physical culture? What shall they do to be saved? Nothing simpler. They need only clench their fists and take a deep breath:

> Resolve! resolve! and to be men aspire!
> Exert that noblest privilege, alone
> Here to mankind indulged; control desire;
> Let godlike reason from her sovereign throne
> Speak the commanding word *I will!* and it is done!

The final appeal returns to the idea of spiritual evolution as a means of encouraging the former slaves of Indolence to believe in their inward divinity:

> Heirs of eternity, yborn to rise
> Through endless states of being, still more near
> To bliss approaching, and perfection clear—
> Can you renounce a fortune so sublime,
> Such glorious hopes, your backward steps to steer,
> And roll, with vilest brutes, through mud and slime?
> No, no!—your heaven-touched hearts disdain the sordid crime!

These are the authentic accents of Rabbi Ben Ezra: "A brute I might have been, but would not sink i' the scale." Students have rightly observed that *The Seasons* look forward to the romantic religion of nature. But another fact about Thomson is equally interesting. The cleavage in his sentimentalism is such that he is not only pre-romantic but pre-Victorian. *The Castle of Indolence* looks forward to a stage of nineteenth-century thought in which the religion of external nature, severely damaged by science, will prove less fortifying to the human spirit than a cult of manly, red-blooded, muddle-headed, altruistic striving and thriving and evolving.

[81] Browning, *Saul*.

In this precursorial quality, of course, Thomson is not unique. The same energy-worship abounds in Aaron Hill; its puritan origins are plainly seen in Isaac Watts; and it is implicit in the whole Whiggish attempt to extract ideal values from un-ideal activity. Both of Thomson's sentimentalisms, indeed, have been richly illustrated in the preceding chapters. He raises them to a higher pitch, brings them into more significant juxtaposition, and expresses them more skilfully than any of his contemporaries. He is the first man to derive poetry of enduring value from the new religion of feeling. For us, however, he is no less important as summarizing the main trend of our subject. He begins with strict Calvinistic puritanism. But he has a real poetic sensibility inseparable from feelings of inward goodness and power which he retains even after their Calvinistic basis—the doctrine of election—has crumbled. Hence he is drawn toward the sentimental rather than toward the rationalistic aspect of latitudinarianism. His religion steadily becomes broader, vaguer, softer, until the Scots divinity-student emerges as a sentimental deist with pantheistic hankerings.

Thus in the career of Thomson is compressed the history of the poetic response to religion in the first half of the eighteenth century. To show more precisely how and why this process took place is difficult, but the last chapter will make the attempt.

Chapter XII

PROTESTANTISM AND SENTIMENTALISM

IN ESSENTIAL RESPECTS SENTIMENTALISM DEPARTS FROM THE CHRISTIAN tradition, but the age-old elements of human nature from which it arises were given scope and encouragement by seventeenth-century Protestantism. This statement embodies no startling novelty. As early as 1857 the Reverend George Gilfillan ascribed the sombreness of much English poetry from Quarles to his own day, as contrasted with continental poetry of the same period, to "the greater depth with which the Protestant religion had ploughed itself into the British mind, during both the eighteenth and seventeenth centuries." [1] The close relation between Puritan gloom and the macabre and minatory type of eighteenth-century melancholy is now a commonplace of historical scholarship.[2] Often, also, the sentimentalist's milder, more pensive melancholy may represent a softened diffusion of the old grim mood.

A special aspect of this theme receives exhaustive treatment in J. W. Draper's *The Funeral Elegy and the Rise of English Romanticism*. The author sometimes gives the impression that melancholy and romanticism are almost synonymous, and that all the melancholy of the eighteenth century is traceable to the Puritan elegies. Nevertheless, responding to the broader implications of his subject, he offers some generalizations which would be highly significant if supported by material of ampler scope. He asserts that "in the seventeenth century the central fact of life to the average serious-minded citizen was Original Sin; in the nineteenth century, Original Genius—literary genius, artistic genius, the military and political genius perhaps, but especially the genius of modern big business." [3] The eighteenth century he sees as a transition from the former

---

[1] *The Poetical Works of Richard Crashaw and Quarles' Emblems* (Edinburgh, 1857), p. 194. I owe this reference to J. W. Draper, *The Funeral Elegy and the Rise of English Romanticism*, p. 21n.

[2] See A. L. Reed, *The Background of Gray's "Elegy,"* and E. M. Sickels, *The Gloomy Egoist*.

[3] *Op. cit.*, p. 314.

stage to the latter, the main factor in the change being "a great social movement" which "seems to consist mainly of the rise of the trading classes to wealth, their consequent return to artistic patronage and their re-interpretation of Protestantism on a Sentimental, instead of a Calvinistic, basis." [4] The puritan cultivated the sense of sin as a sign of "election." When his feelings of mingled depression and exaltation "were found to be not unpleasant, and were sedulously developed *ad hoc,* they became spurious and Sentimental." [5] Even when the puritan's creed "faded out to a Deistic haziness, the old attitude toward the excellence of emotionalism prevailed, and emotionalism, without religious or other adequate motive, can only be termed Sentimental." [6] Since the Christian Rationalism of the late seventeenth and early eighteenth century embodies this "fading" of puritanism into deism, it is pertinent to recall that R. S. Crane has found clear suggestions of the cult of benevolism in the utterances of latitudinarian divines. [7]

According to Professor Cazamian, the psychology of the puritan middle class largely motivates the course of modern English literature. In the seventeenth century it is this group "chez laquelle les ardeurs de la Renaissance se transpose de plus en plus dans le domaine de la foi and de la conduite." [8] In Restoration times its members retain much of their old sobriety and earnestness. Their piety, to be sure, has become less fervent, "mais déjà, chez elle, toutes les nuances du sentiment individuel se montrent; et plus bas, dans le peuple, les forces latentes du zèle puritain, découragées, comprimées, ne sont qu' assoupies; spontanément, elles se réveillent çà et là." [9] He instances the Quakers. In the eighteenth century the upper middle class accepted the standards of neoclassicism, but in accepting them impressed a puritan stamp upon them. "Elle conserve en elle le germe vivant du sentimentalisme, auquel elle ne pouvait renoncer sans périr, sans perdre le sens de sa continuité psychologique.... Ses tendances morales, d'ailleurs, sont inséparables de ses tendances émotives." [10]

The relationship between sentimentalism and romanticism cannot be

---

[4] *Ibid.,* p. 22.   [5] *Ibid.,* p. 152.   [6] *Ibid.,* p. 267.

[7] "Suggestions Toward a Genealogy of the 'Man of Feeling,'" *ELH,* I, 205-230.

[8] *L'Évolution psychologique et la littérature en Angleterre, 1660-1914,* p. 28.

[9] *Ibid.,* p. 64.

[10] *Ibid.,* pp. 86-87. Professor Cazamian expresses the same views in the *History of English Literature* which he wrote in collaboration with Legouis.

discussed in this volume, but most readers will concede their close kinship. Hence it is pertinent to remember the respects in which Vaughan, Traherne, and other seventeenth-century writers look forward to the great romantics. Dr. A. A. Perdeck has anticipated one of my main points in showing that the religious verse of the Queen Anne period preserves more of the non-classical qualities of seventeenth-century poetry than does the secular verse of that period.[11]

In the introduction to his collection of *Tracts on Liberty in the Puritan Revolution,* William Haller recognizes the romanticism of the puritan mystics. Of William Walwyn, for example, he writes: "He had ... effected for himself that transposition of Christian myth into romantic revolutionary images which held so much of significance for the future." [12]

The Methodist Revival has often been described as a sort of romantic movement in religion,[13] and Umphrey Lee has traced the history of "enthusiasm" from the Puritans to the Methodists.[14] The kinship between religious and literary enthusiasm throughout this historical curve has been shown by Sister M. Kevin Whelan, S.S.J.[15]

Herbert Schöffler's *Protestantismus und Literatur* treats the pre-romantic tendencies of eighteenth-century poetry as produced by the secularization of seventeenth-century Protestantism under the influence of the Enlightenment. The believing spirit of the seventeenth century and the reasoning spirit of the eighteenth flowed together in a compromise, each yielding something to the other. The clergy developed secular literary interests, while secular literature took over some of the clergy's traditional themes and moods. "Es handelt sich nicht um eine Wiederzurückdrängung des geistigen Lebens in das Puritanertum des 17ten Jahrhunderts, sondern um ein Erlösen des kirchlichen Denkens in das Gebiet des weltlichen Geistesleben hinein und um eine gegenseitige Durchdringung zweier Geistessphären, die vor der Aufklärung ein recht streng geschiedenes Sonderdasein nebeneinanderher nicht ohne gegenseitige Befehdung geführt haben." [16]

[11] *Theology in Augustan Literature.*

[12] *Op. cit.,* I, 40. No reader of Haller's more recent work, *The Rise of Puritanism,* can fail to be impressed by the way in which the more radical puritan thinkers anticipate the ideas of the romanticists.

[13] See especially F. C. Gill, *The Romantic Movement and Methodism.*

[14] *The Historical Backgrounds of Early Methodist Enthusiasm.*

[15] *Enthusiasm in English Poetry of the Eighteenth Century.*

[16] *Op. cit.,* p. 180.

The style of this passage may partly explain why this important study has received less attention than it deserves. Unfortunately the book has other faults which interfere with appreciation of its value. Schöffler's attempt to associate pre-romanticism with the work of clerics and sons of clerics narrows and warps his view of a very broad subject. His acquaintance with eighteenth-century poetry is not very rich or intimate, nor is he thoroughly at home in the history of English philosophical and religious thought. Since the trends which he sums up in the term *Aufklärung* were influencing both clergy and laity as early as the sixteenth century, his picture of two sharply contrasted intellectual spheres is over-simplified. In particular he makes the shift from the seventeenth to the eighteenth century much too abrupt by exaggerating the ascetic temper of seventeenth-century Anglicanism.

Although the books and articles mentioned in the foregoing paragraphs are not of such a nature as to make the present study a work of supererogation, they powerfully suggest, from one viewpoint or another, that eighteenth-century sentimentalism is the child of seventeenth-century Protestantism. One cannot say, however, that this idea has found a place among the generally received conclusions of scholarship, or that its implications for the history of modern literature have fully been recognized. Perhaps the present-day scholar is so little interested in religion that he shrinks from using a religious frame of reference. Perhaps there is an instinctive reluctance to accept an hypothesis which points to the conclusion that the romanticism of the 1780-1830 period is simply Protestant Christianity in a more or less delightfully phosphorescent state of decay. Or perhaps specialization is to blame. The "eighteenth-century man" is likely to have a much more realistic view of his own period than of the seventeenth century. When he contrasts the real eighteenth century with a highly simplified sketch of the seventeenth the continuity between the two periods is not fully apparent. Hence he tends to think in terms of reaction rather than of evolution and falls back upon that last resort of literary historians, the swinging pendulum. Though I am well aware that these remarks tempt my own nemesis I must, blending the material presented in this book with evidence drawn from sound authorities on the seventeenth century, make one more attempt to drive home a thesis which to me seems clearly demonstrable.

The marshalling of the arguments is a difficult task, for my case is more like a network than like a chain: every point is related to every other point. In the great majority of cases, as we have seen, the sentimentalists are either bourgeois Whigs or men who have readily accepted the standards of a bourgeois and Whiggish civilization. Now the intellectual and spiritual ancestors of these writers are seventeenth-century bourgeois Protestants with more or less strong puritan leanings. In studying the works of the sentimentalists we have repeatedly observed the breakdown of strict Protestantism into latitudinarianism, and sometimes the breakdown of latitudinarianism into deism. What happens in the imagination of these poets is simply what happens in the history of English religious thought from the Reformation to the period of our study. This trend, a definitely Protestant phenomenon, is much more strikingly evidenced by Low Churchmen and Dissenters than by Catholic-minded Anglicans. Many High Churchmen were affected by it, to be sure, but only at a sacrifice of principle. A Low Churchman who became a Christian Rationalist or a deist would merely be carrying his premises to their logical conclusion; an Anglo-Catholic who followed this path would be an apostate. The more closely we approach puritanism, the more we find ourselves in the main historical channel.

I have added much to the evidence adduced by Perdeck to show that in the 1700-1720 period the "romantic" elements of seventeenth-century poetry are preserved and transmitted to the pre-romanticists by divine poets or religiously-disposed secular poets. We have seen [17] that these transitional figures are mostly bourgeois or bourgeois-minded Whigs. In religious belief they vary from strict Protestantism to moderate latitudinarianism. With rare exceptions they are devoid of Catholic thought and feeling. These sacred poets and sober "middle-classical" secular poets look in two directions. Plainly, they are the heirs of Low Church Anglicanism or of Dissent. No less plainly, they are the immediate precursors of the sentimentalists.

The transition from original sin to original genius observed by Draper is already well advanced in the first half of the eighteenth century. Thomson and Hill provide a clear foretokening of the romantic conception of the poet as priest and seer, and of poetic imagination as a faculty akin to the divine creative power. This idea comes straight from the theory of sacred poetry championed by those pious survivors of the seventeenth cen-

[17] Especially in Chapters III, IV, and V.

tury, Dennis, Watts, and Blackmore. The tradition runs back to Milton and Cowley, from them to the sixteenth century, and thence to Plato. It is a Platonic-Renaissance doctrine preserved by learned puritans who wished to regard poetry in a religious light.[18]

The hypothesis now under consideration is entirely consistent with A. O. Lovejoy's account of the varying fortunes of *The Great Chain of Being*. In its original form, this cosmological metaphor implied "an absolutely rigid and static scheme of things."[19] But eighteenth-century writers begin to "temporalize" the chain of being, until it becomes a fluid, historical, progressive concept with a past and a present and a future.[20] The divine goodness and the good human life are now expressed in terms of variety and change rather than of uniformity and permanence. There arises "a new conception of value" implying *"no* finality, no ultimate perfection, no arrest of the outreach of the will. . . . Man is by nature insatiable, and it is the will of his Maker that he should be so."[21] Though for such a change there can be no one simple explanation, we may observe that it is in perfect agreement with the spirit of seventeenth-century Protestantism. The puritan developed ideals of individualism, liberty, and social change which could no more thrive in a static universe than in a static political and ecclesiastical system. It is not surprising that his descendents should have transformed the chain of being.

But Lovejoy, in an important article,[22] brings together deism and literary classicism as kindred manifestations of the old spirit of uniformity. Here a difficulty arises, for how can deism be hostile to diversity and insatiability and yet, as has been shown, friendly to the sentimentalism which embodies those ideals? The deists, one may reply, were much less logical than Professor Lovejoy. Undoubtedly deism in its early stages was mainly rationalistic, classical, and uniformitarian. But in rebelling against a faith which itself claimed to embody eternal and absolute truth, the deist was forced to preach the rights of diversity. He could not work his way back from Christianity to the religion of nature without arguing that different people, in different times and places, hold different beliefs. Deism became less and less a highbrow rationalistic revival of the religion of

---

[18] The idea is not preserved *solely* by puritans, for we find it in Bishop Ken. Nevertheless it is especially attractive to Low Churchmen and dissenters, and the decay of such Churchmanship as Ken's after 1688 makes it almost a monopoly of puritans and ex-puritans.

[19] *Op. cit.*, p. 242.   [20] *Ibid.*, pp. 244 ff.   [21] *Ibid.*, p. 250.

[22] "The Parallel of Deism and Classicism," *Modern Philology*, XXIX, 281-299.

Cicero, more and more an attempt to demolish the uniformitarian claims of Christianity. Such constructively religious aspects as it possessed during the eighteenth century had little to do with classicism and deductive rationalism. The affirmative element in eighteenth-century deism was provided by the large influx of recruits very different from Lord Herbert of Cherbury—bourgeois ex-puritans who had strayed beyond the dim boundaries of latitudinarianism. The idea of a static and uniform faith was no part of their tradition: their ancestors had fought that idea with might and main. Even when they adopted the old formulas about the universal religion of reason and nature they were merely rationalizing the sentimental desire to enjoy religious feelings without believing anything in particular.

The new science, of course, played its part in the transformation of the chain of being. In much of the sentimental poetry which we have examined, a religious view of the universe as interpreted by Newtonian science is strongly marked. Eighteenth-century nature poetry, says Rose Macaulay, "was the logical consequence of Natural Theology. The worship of the Deity through his works went hand in hand with semi-worship of those works for their own sake." [23] Taking a broader view, Basil Willey reminds us that "ever since the Renaissance the Creation had been steadily gaining in prestige as the 'art of God,' the universal divine Scripture which 'lies expans'd unto the eyes of all.' The emotion of the 'numinous,' formerly associated with supernature, had become attached to Nature itself; and by the end of the eighteenth century the divinity, the sacredness of nature was, to those affected by this tradition, almost a first datum of consciousness." [24] In the seventeenth century orthodox divines used the new science as a teleological weapon against the unbeliever. But gradually, in many minds, natural revelation became so clear and satisfying in itself that supernatural revelation seemed irrelevant if not utterly false. Thus Newtonianism, at first a means of defending Christianity, ultimately plays into the hands of deism, becoming a vehicle either for attacking the traditional faith or for championing a quasi-pantheistic religion of external nature.

The lower social and intellectual levels of puritanism, suspicious of worldly learning, did nothing to further the compromise between religion

[23] Rose Macaulay, *Some Religious Elements in English Literature*, p. 148.
[24] Basil Willey, *The Seventeenth Century Background*, p. 308.

and science. But the more cultivated and less bigoted puritans who desired to support their faith by solid reason furthered it more powerfully than any other group. Not until the era of puritan domination, indeed, did Bacon become a major influence. The puritans admired him as a utilitarian, a reformer, and a scientific rebel against that Aristotelian authority which they rejected in theology. His cautious separation of religion and science made it possible for them to accept his philosophy with no sense of spiritual peril.[25] Once they had thoroughly digested this philosophy, however, they were ready to engage in the latitudinarian harmonizing of science and Christianity.

But before science can contribute to the cult of sentiment, it must be steeped in the heart of the sentimentalist. The feelings in which he luxuriates are variable and inconsistent. He is very melancholy and very sanguine, very contemplative and very active. He preaches primitivism and progress, deterioration and perfectibility. Now he invokes the virtues of "simple" nature, now he is all for bustling public service in a commercial civilization. A strange medley, but did not the puritan display a very similar complex of traits? Since his criterion of religious truth was personal and inward, his feelings were profoundly significant to him and he was constantly taking the temperature of his soul. His mind, permeated by the fear of hell and the hope of heaven, wavered between gloom and gladness. There was much that impelled him to withdraw from the world. Man's heart was a cesspool; the paths of life were beset with Satan's snares. To keep themselves unspotted, the chosen few must shun the vast hordes of the unbelieving and the damned.

On the other hand, there was much that impelled the puritan toward vigorous and sanguine participation in the active life. There was a cause to be fought for, and there was a living to be made. To smite the Amalekites hip and thigh was plainly a religious duty, but to succeed in one's calling was no less obligatory. According to Reformation theology, the elected Christian need not struggle to win salvation, for he is saved already. His task is rather to glorify the God who has saved him by doing his duty in the state of life to which he has been called. As McGiffert says, "Freedom from the necessity of earning one's salvation by engaging in particular religious practices and performing works of special merit meant also the recognition of the sacredness of all callings, even the most secular

---

[25] R. F. Jones, *Ancients and Moderns*, pp. 77, 92.

and the most humble, and the possibility of serving God in worldly profession, business and trade as truly as in monastery and priesthood." [26] Since worldly success was one of the most reliable signs of election, the impulse to strive toward it and to associate spiritual values with the process as well as with the prize was very strong. Furthermore, since God called the individual to strive and thrive as an individual, not as a member of a universal holy coöperative society of believers, the struggle for practical success was highly competitive. Any restriction of the individual's rights to seek his own fortune in his own way—honest way, of course— would be completely un-Protestant. The seventeenth-century idea of leaving every man to his own judgment is, as Haller says, "a premonition of the doctrine of laissez faire." [27] Hence the nexus between Protestantism and capitalism which has been observed by such writers as Troeltsch, Weber, and Tawney.[28]

As early as the 1640's, Henry Robinson was urging in his pamphlets that religious intolerance is bad for trade.[29] This idea, blending with the general rationalistic pressure of the Enlightenment, helps to draw the practical puritan toward a latitudinarian vagueness of belief. His creed loses its color, but the profitable idea of successful work in one's calling persists, incongruously mingled with vestiges of more contemplative and melancholy puritan sentiments. The drive for self-aggrandizement must now acquire a quasi-religious sanction from ideals of patriotism and public service and from the attempt to identify self-love and social love, though at times there is a suggestion that vigorous activity for its own sweet sake is somehow spiritual. The energy-cult of the Knight of Arts and Industry is broken-down Calvinism.

Combined with the results of the new science, this emphasis upon practical individual activity often made the puritan a champion of the doctrine of progress rather than of deterioration. Whatever the formal articles of his creed might be, he found it hard to believe himself helpless and corrupt. God commanded him to succeed, and in order to succeed in a competitive civilization he must have faith in himself.

[26] A. C. McGiffert, *Protestant Thought before Kant*, p. 32. See also A. E. Sokol, "The Conception of a Calling in the German Literature of the Middle Ages," *PMLA*, L, 1-13.

[27] William Haller, *Tracts on Liberty in the Puritan Revolution*, I, 94.

[28] E. Troeltsch, *The Social Teachings of the Christian Churches;* M. Weber, *Protestant Ethics and the Spirit of Capitalism;* R. H. Tawney, *Religion and the Rise of Capitalism.*

[29] Haller, *op. cit.,* pp. 64 ff.

Faith in himself would be enforced by thinking well, not ill, of man in general. The original Reformation doctrine of total depravity was submerged in waves of individualism, utilitarianism, and social idealism. The Socinian trend which had become so strong by the beginning of the eighteenth century is not wholly rationalistic: it often implies a sentimental view of human nature. The Racovian Catechism of 1605, the first codified expression of Socinian principles, teaches the intellectual and moral sufficiency of man.[30] The mere humanity of Jesus is not the basis of this belief, but rather a corollary of it. He who thinks well enough of man—that is, of himself—may readily suppose with Milton that paradise has been regained for him, not by Incarnate God, but by "one greater man."

The wide spread of openly avowed Socinianism, of course, represents a late stage in the decay of Protestant theology. The official doctrines of the seventeenth century were either Arminian or Calvinistic. The Anglo-Catholics were Arminians. The Protestant-minded Anglicans and the larger and soberer bodies of dissenting puritans were Calvinists. The more irregular and enthusiastic sects were divided between the two viewpoints.

Although the medieval Church was strongly influenced by the Augustinian ideas which Calvin was to inherit, one may argue that the purest Catholic tradition is Arminian. God has predestined no human soul to damnation. He will forgive every repentant sinner, and rejoices to see the prodigal coming a long way off. Man is weak and prone to error, but not hopelessly corrupt and vile. He has that within him which can coöperate actively with grace once grace is bestowed. The Christian is saved not merely because Jesus is good, but because he himself may become good according to the measure of his faith in Jesus. Grace, if seized upon and used, gives him the power to behave in a manner pleasing to God. Faith and works, operating in harmonious union, may transform him into a being fit for salvation on his own Christ-given merits. The entire sacramental system of the Church would be meaningless without the support of these beliefs.

Restricting ourselves to consideration of secondary causes, we may agree with McGiffert's statement that Anglo-Catholic Arminianism "was not the fruit of liberalism or rationalism. It was due in part to hostility to Puritanism ... in part to paramount interest in the church and sacra-

[30] McGiffert, *op. cit.*, p. 109.

ments as means of grace. The significance of both seemed to be better conserved by a doctrine which left some share to man in working out his own salvation." [31] This type of Arminianism is inconsistent with the idea of total depravity, but not with that of human insufficiency. It is rational, but not rationalistic. It points toward the heart of Christianity rather than away from it.

But Arminian theology was not the exclusive possession of Anglo-Catholics. It appealed to many Protestants whose reason or whose feelings were shocked by the creed of Calvin. Without a firm setting in Catholic orthodoxy, Arminianism loses its equilibrium. Remove the conception of Holy Church and of the sacraments as real means of grace, blur the traditional images of mediation, over-emphasize human sufficiency and under-emphasize the human need of divine aid, let the transcendent Deity be felt less vividly than the Deity within us—and there arises an Arminianism which is little more than a restatement of the Pelagian heresy, and which points directly toward the cult of natural goodness and universal benevolence.

In seventeenth-century England, however, Protestantism was predominantly Calvinistic, and at first glance Calvinism and sentimentalism may seem to be the antipodes of religious feeling. The beliefs of the Calvinist were of course grim and threatening; as we have seen, he bequeathed his sombre soul-searching to the eighteenth century in the form of a painful-pleasing emotional indulgence. Nevertheless, the Calvinist was much less gloomy than the modern historian would be if *he* were a Calvinist. What Wakeman says of the sentimentalized Calvinism of the later eighteenth-century Evangelicals applies in large measure to their seventeenth-century forebears: "Basing their conception of religion, like Calvin, upon the total depravity of human nature, they used it to magnify the love of God in redemption, not to prove His justice in condemnation." [32] In other words the Calvinistic puritan, on the whole, made less of the thought that anybody might be damned than of the thought that anybody—even he—might be saved. If he experienced conversion—and he generally managed to do so—he had practically conclusive proof that he was one of the elect. In that case his struggle against sin was merely a healthful exercise, a game in which he was sure to be victorious. In the eyes of God he was

[31] *Ibid.*, p. 174.
[32] H. O. Wakeman, *An Introduction to the History of the Church of England*, p. 441.

whiter than snow, a seventeenth-century *schöne Seele*. He knew the truth, and the truth had made him free. Hence he could enjoy both the thrilling dramatic atmosphere of predestination and "the glorious liberty of the children of God." At the slight cost of a theoretical assertion of his utter worthlessness, he might obtain that great desire of the human heart, the sense of being strong, wise, and good.

As Professor Haller observes: "The concept of universal depravity, by leveling all superiority not of the spirit, enormously enhanced the self-respect of the ordinary man. If none were righteous, then one man was as good as another. God chose whom he would and the distinctions of this world counted for nothing. The concept of free grace still further heightened his confidence. If the only real aristocracy was the aristocracy created by God, then nothing really counted but character and inner worth.... If election were manifested not by outward conformity to an imposed law but by the struggle of the spirit within against the weakness and disobedience of the flesh, then any man might find reason for hope within his own breast. If all this was predestined, then there could be no fear concerning the issue of life's ordeal. 'If God be with us, who can be against us?' The triumph' of the saints was foreordained. Therefore nothing they could desire was impossible for them to attain. Heaven was theirs already, and if presently they demanded possession of the earth as well, that was no more than human." [33]

Under the rationalistic influences of the Enlightenment the Calvinist's formal beliefs decay more rapidly than his inward religious emotions. He loses most of his creed, but he retains, in a blurred and softened form, the emotions which his creed had both reflected and fostered. The God above him becomes more shadowy than the God within him, until at last he is left with the basic attitude of sentimentalism—a sense of inward virtue and freedom which must somehow find corroboration in the nature of the universe. Just enough brimstone remains to tinge his optimism with melancholy, just enough other-worldliness to make him shrink at times from the civilization which he has built. It is fitting that Jean-Jacques should have been reared in Geneva.

Thus Calvinism no less than Protestant Arminianism could slough down into the religion of feeling; indeed, the strong predominance of the former in seventeenth-century Protestant thought makes it more obvi-

[33] *The Rise of Puritanism*, pp. 89-90.

ously the ancestor of sentimentalism than the latter. But these theological distinctions are much less significant than the general sense of human freedom and power and of sure interior guidance which, in the seventeenth century, swayed men whose formal beliefs might be expressed in highly diverse ways.

This feeling was the inevitable consequence of the Reformation. It underlies the assertion of the right of private judgment in the interpretation of the Scriptures, the rejection of mediatorial agencies between the individual worshipper and his God, the revolt against authority and the demand for ecclesiastical and political reform, the emphasis upon the value of practical activity in this world, and the belief in the sufficiency of human reason stimulated by the new science. Much has been made of the fact that the English Renaissance was deeply affected by the spirit of the Reformation, but we sometimes forget how deeply the English Reformation was affected by the spirit of the Renaissance. Although the old "catastrophic" view of the Renaissance has been modified by more accurate historical understanding of the Middle Ages, "there does remain the fact of a great release, of a sudden quickening, of a renewed aggressiveness of the human spirit in its relations with its environment. . . . The consciousness of the goodness of man's life here and now burned hotly in the veins of the sixteenth century, and the awareness of his own limitless and immediate powers fired many a bold spirit to fresh conquest in every field of a gloriously opulent world." [34] In *every* field—that of religious experience was by no means excluded. In the seventeenth century, when the hot fires of the Renaissance were burning themselves out, it was the puritan rather than his more sophisticated contemporaries who preserved the sixteenth-century "faith in the essential amenableness of the world to the dreamer's desire." [35]

Thus the believer in total depravity was the champion of human goodness and power. By the beginning of the seventeenth century, says Miss White, "the principle of private judgment had certainly promoted theological speculation among the masses and had made the individual Christian lay hold vigorously upon the problems of his religion, but the authority which the Protestant rejected had not been replaced. Calvin strove vainly to replace the rejected authority of the Church, but the authority of the Bible privately interpreted rested ultimately upon the

[34] Helen C. White, *The Metaphysical Poets*, pp. 32-33. [35] *Ibid.*, p. 37.

belief that each enlightened Christian had within him a guide to enable him to take the Bible in the sense which the Holy Spirit intended it, in other words, the Inner Light." [36] It was theoretically possible to *assert,* but it became impossible genuinely to *feel,* that the possessor of this faculty was a vile and helpless worm. The substitution of original goodness for original sin within the Protestant mind was a natural result. Then when the sense of original goodness became so persistent as to make the transformation of sinful human nature through the Cross a meaningless legend, Protestantism quietly melted into sentimentalism.

This feeling of inward sufficiency and goodness was particularly intense among the more "enthusiastic" Separatist sects. The claim of their members to an immediate and private revelation is mocked by Samuel Butler, who describes the Inner Light as

> ...a dark lanthorn of the spirit,
> Which none see by, but those that bear it.

Yet although this jibe is not wholly unfair, the more enlightened sectarians—mystics like Walwyn, Saltmarsh, Everard, and Winstanley—believed that all men possess the Inner Light and that they could see by it if only they were aware of its abiding presence. It is no less a universal gift for being an individual one.

The Inner Light is the Holy Ghost illuminating the human heart. If the Presbyterians emphasized the first Person of the Trinity, and the Anglo-Catholics the second, the distinguishing mark of the sectarian enthusiast was his sense of intimacy with the third. Indeed, the Holy Spirit bade fair to absorb the other Persons of the Trinity. God the Father was a still small voice, and God the Son a sort of personification of the Christlike feelings inspired in man by the Paraclete. The old revelation of divinity in Jesus was less potent for sectarian psychology than the new revelation of divinity in the illumined human heart. Each believer could himself be a Word made flesh. Thus Henry Nicholas or Niclaes, the Westphalian founder of the Family of Love, was accused of teaching that Christ was not a man, but a state of inward spiritual perfection which man might attain.[37] Though perhaps not strictly accurate as regards

---

[36] *Ibid.,* p. 46.

[37] R. M. Jones, *Studies in Mystical Religion,* p. 144. Niclaes was born as early as 1501 or 1502, but in England the term "Familist" was applied, usually by unsympathetic observers, to enthusiasts of his general type from 1580 to 1708. Like several other so-called sects, the

Niclaes, the charge certainly describes an attitude which was to be wide-spread in the seventeenth century.

Most of the sects may be roughly classified as tending either toward the Seekers or toward the Ranters. To anticipate Carlyle's dichotomy of romantic temperaments, the former were puritan Wertherists and the latter were puritan Götzists. The term "Seeker" was applied to many loosely organized groups of mild, quietistic, earnestly spiritual people who refrained from making religious affirmations until the will of God should be revealed to them from within. Naturally enough, George Fox was able to lead many of them into the Quaker fold.

The Ranters, on the other hand, were boisterous fanatics. Extremely antinomian, they claimed to be personally infallible, above law and above sin. They relied so completely on the Inner Light that they scorned the Scriptures. Some of them even rejected belief in a personal God, preferring to deify Nature. Their real faith was pantheistic: one spirit pervaded and united everything. They loved to speak of the Light of Nature and of the Christ within men, but they regarded Christ merely "as a 'figure' or 'type' of the *true dispensation of the Spirit,* upon which they claimed to have entered." [38] As pantheists, they "declared that their actions were sanctified because a spark of divine essence was indwelling in each soul." [39] James Thomson's contemplative sentimentalism smacks of the Seeker; his active sentimentalism, of the Ranter.

Among several attempts to steer a middle course between the very hesitant and negative quietism of the Seekers and the rampant antinomianism of the Ranters, the most lastingly fruitful was that represented by the Quakers. Their tenets, centering about an almost exclusive reliance upon the Inner Light, need hardly be described here. Their significance in relation to our subject is expressed by a modern student in the words, "The greater share of the Friends reasoned that if God were indwelling, then man could not be hopelessly depraved and fallen. In this respect they anticipated certain aspects of the theory of man's essential goodness which Law and Rousseau embodied in their philosophies in the century following." [40] One may add that the doctrine of brotherly love emphasized by the Quakers as well as by other sects could, when detached from the

Familists hardly constituted a definite religious body. The term implies a viewpoint rather than a denomination.

[38] *Ibid.,* p. 469.　　[39] L. M. Wright, *The Literary Life of the Early Friends,* p. 19.
[40] *Ibid.,* pp. 33-34.

Christian creed, easily become transformed into the doctrine of universal benevolence.

The sectarian emphasis upon personal and immediate revelation, the Inner Light, the pantheistic union of man and nature in the dispensation of the all-pervading Holy Spirit, antinomian freedom, and brotherly love was merely the flowering, under specially favorable conditions, of a very old tradition. These ideas, appearing in various combinations and with different degrees of strength, have been traced by scholars like Rufus Jones and McGiffert downward from the *Timæus*. The intellectual and spiritual ancestors of the sectarians are Plato (Neoplatonically interpreted), Dionysius the Areopagite, John Scotus Erigena, the Waldensians, Beghards and Beguines, medieval pantheistic mystics like Amaury and Richard Rolle, groups like the Brethren of the New Spirit and the Friends of God, Merswin, Eckhart, Tauler, Suso, the unknown who wrote *Theologia Germanica,* Wyclif, the Lollards, the Anabaptists, the early Familists.

These individuals and groups can be lumped together only by ignoring distinctions which in other contexts would be essential. Nevertheless this tradition hands down to posterity a fairly unified and coherent religious message. God is a spirit of love and creative mental activity immanent in nature and in the heart of man. To become deeply aware of that spirit, to merge one's private share of the divine goodness with the goodness which pervades the universe, is to be wise, virtuous, and strong. Some of the precursors of the sectarians devote themselves mainly to attacking outward and institutional religion, while others are more constructively concerned with the enrichment of the inner spiritual life; but the results of their work are essentially the same.

When this proto-sentimentalism was expressed in violently heterodox terms, it was sharply curbed by the medieval Church; when it was expressed in language "recognizable as pious, though strangely colored"— to quote Carlyle's account of Coleridge's talk—it was usually tolerated. Albertus Magnus could not refrain from denouncing David of Dinant for teaching "that God, intelligence, and matter are identical in essence, and unite in a single substance." [41] But since the mystical experience was so intensely personal it was difficult, then as now, to pass judgment upon the orthodoxy of the fruits of contemplation. More often than not the irregular mystic was regarded with somewhat puzzled reverence as a man

[41] Quoted by R. M. Jones, *Studies in Mystical Religion*, p. 184.

obviously rich in the gifts of the spirit; if he did not openly flout the Church, he was let alone. The modern student, however, recognizes that this complex of religious feelings is quite foreign to Catholicism. For a mystic like David of Dinant the visible Church with its creeds, sacraments, and three-fold apostolic ministry was irrelevant to the higher spiritual life. It was at best a crutch for the weak and ignorant; the further one advanced on the path of inward perfection, the less the necessity for such aids. One who lived under the new dispensation of the Holy Spirit need not think much about the Cross.

Indeed, though proto-sentimentalism could be cultivated by men who regarded themselves as Christians, in its pure state it is not Christian at all. It generates ideas of human perfection which make the Incarnation and the Atonement meaningless; and it interfuses God, nature, and man in a pantheistic muddle. Hence it is that the feelings of natural goodness, inward illumination, and pantheistic union are quite capable of flourishing when Christianity no longer grips the imagination. In the long run the decay of Christianity encourages, not retards, the growth of the religion of sentiment.

As an expression of this type of thought, says Professor Haller, "the Puritan saga did not cherish the memory of Christ in the manger or on the cross, that is, of the lamb of God sacrificed in vicarious atonement for the sins of man. The mystic birth was the birth of the new man in men. The mystic passion was the crucifixion of the new man by the old, and the true propitiation was the sacrifice of the old to the new." [42] The same authority explains the lack of definitely Christian conviction in Milton's *Ode on the Morning of Christ's Nativity:* "The nativity and the passion have always been associated with the idea of atonement by the son of God for man's sin. But the young Puritan, full of the sense of his own power, felt in reality no sense of a redeemer outside his own breast. As his party, when it had the power, permitted little to be made of Christmas or Easter, he would later relegate the Christ child and the crucifixion to a subordinate place in his version of the [Christian] epic." [43]

The relations between proto-sentimentalism and Protestantism would be easier to express if it were at all possible to define the latter. Benn describes the Reformation as "a great religious revival, in which the sporadic mystical movements of the two preceding centuries were clari-

[42] *The Rise of Puritanism,* p. 151.   [43] *Ibid.,* p. 312.

fied, systematised, and united under a common standard. That standard was the Bible." [44] So far as the more enthusiastic sects are concerned this statement seems perfectly accurate, but it is not so obviously applicable to the theologies of Luther and Calvin. On the other hand, the main theme of McGiffert's *Protestant Thought before Kant* is the rise of a "modern" faith in human sufficiency which is neither Catholic nor Protestant, but which is permitted more scope for development by Protestant looseness of organization than by Catholic rigidity. To one who likes a very restricted conception of the term "Protestant" this idea has its attractions. But when we consider the argument that whatever in Protestantism is not "modern" in McGiffert's sense of the word is merely an exaggerated insistence upon certain aspects of the Catholic faith to the exclusion of other aspects, then we are inclined to think that the truly *protestant* elements of Protestantism are the age-old mystical impulses which Benn calls "medieval" and McGiffert calls "modern."

Beneath this quagmire of slippery terms lie a few solid facts about human nature. In any period the sentimentalist is a person in whom the feelings of self-sufficiency, self-assertion, self-expansion, self-aggrandizement, are strongly marked. Frequently, of course, he cultivates these impulses as a compensation for a still deeper sense of inferiority. Even when these impulses are genuine expressions of his nature, they are constantly being thwarted by hard facts which are ultimately all the harder for his efforts to deny them. Hence his uneasy vacillation between the extremes of irrational hope and irrational despair. Now Catholic orthodoxy rises like a wall against the sentimental impulses, curtly classifying them under the head of "pride." But Protestantism, though its formal doctrines seem at first even more hostile to the sentimental impulses than Catholicism, in the long run gives those impulses not only greater scope but positive encouragement. Some will explain this paradox by saying that Protestantism must in large measure be a rationalization of the sentimental spirit; others will warmly reject that explanation. The question eludes all possibility of proof.

One must also try to explain why the religion of the sentimentalist, whenever it rises to the mystical level, becomes a kind of pantheism.[45] Man and nature are the work of God. But belief in a transcendent per-

---

[44] A. W. Benn, *The History of English Rationalism in the Nineteenth Century*, I, 75.
[45] Some will say that *all* mysticism is pantheistic, but this I deny.

sonal God demands a deep sense of human inadequacy. The sentimentalist thinks too well of himself to have much of this feeling, or if he has it he is anxious to stifle and deny it. He is not likely to pray, "O lift me up upon the rock that is higher than I!" or "Lord, if thou wilt thou canst make me clean." His sense of a divinity within him being far stronger than his sense of a divinity above and beyond him, he emphasizes the immanence of God so much more strongly than His transcendence that the distinctions between *God and man* are blurred. Further, if God is immanent in the heart of man He is presumably immanent in all His works, and since this immanence is balanced by no clear images of transcendence, the distinctions between *God and nature* are blurred. Nature then becomes divine. It is easy for the sentimentalist to recognize the divinity of nature. Thinking well of himself, he is ready to think well of the world in which he lives: the setting should be worthy of the jewel. He is himself godlike—inspired by the love, wisdom, and imaginative power which constitute the spiritual reality of the universe. To say that man is full of God is to say that man is full of divinely-permeated nature, and to say that nature is full of God is to say that nature is full of man. Man is divine through nature, and nature is divine through him when, like Coleridge, he "shoots his being through earth, sea, and air, possessing all things with intensest love." Here, finally, the distinctions between *man and nature* are blurred.

Thus God, man, and nature are fused in "one stupendous whole." God is everything, and everything—but especially man—is God. This of course is an extreme position, but it is the extreme toward which fully developed sentimentalism steadily points. Not all pantheists, of course, are sentimentalists, but pantheism is the form which the mysticism of the sentimentalist most easily assumes. It must also be clear that the pantheistic leanings of sentimentalism would, in the seventeenth and eighteenth centuries, be greatly increased by the effort to absorb the new science into the fabric of religion. A person for whom the natural revelation has become all-important must choose between a barren rationalism and an implicit or explicit pantheism. Once this stage is reached, even non-sentimental forms of pantheism such as Spinoza's may be interpreted sentimentally, though the philosophy of Shaftesbury would be better suited to the purpose.

It should now be evident that the enthusiastic sects of the seventeenth century were the inheritors of a venerable religious tradition. Their more learned and cultivated members—far more numerous than is generally supposed—were aware of this heritage, well versed in the literature which embodied it, and cognizant of its continuations, in their own day, in Holland and other European countries. But how directly and powerfully did they transmit the heritage to later times? After the Restoration, and still more after the Revolution of 1688, the flame of sectarianism subsided. In the Queen Anne period it burned very low indeed. We hear of Muggletonians, and terms like "Familist" and "Seeker" continue to be applied, very vaguely, to dissenters who are regarded as fanatical. A more recent group, the Philadelphians, seems to embody much of the old spirit, but it soon runs to seed. There are Thomas Tryon and other scattered disciples of Boehme, admirers of the French Prophets, miscellaneous eccentrics. But most sects of the "ranting" type have gravitated toward the Particular Baptists, and most sects of the "seeking" type toward the Quakers. These two groups in turn have become sober, respectable, anxious to avoid the imputation of enthusiasm. So far as the direct influence of the seventeenth-century sects upon the eighteenth century is concerned, the most one can say is that they spread through certain sections of the middle class ideas which look forward to the religion of sentiment. Though for a time these ideas lost much of their force, they did not wholly disappear, and they rise again in an attenuated form with the rise of the bourgeois in the eighteenth century.

For us, however, the sects are chiefly significant not because of their direct influence, but because of the clarity and force with which they express tendencies which were widely though more obscurely pervasive among more temperate and conservative thinkers of the seventeenth century. They were simply the swiftest and most violent current in the general stream of thought.

In his *Exposition of the Thirty-Nine Articles* (1699), Bishop Gilbert Burnet explains that Article Seven, "Of the Old Testament," was originally framed to confute "an extravagant sort of enthusiasts" who carried antinomianism to the extent of rejecting the outward law in favor of "a new inward nature." [46] We have seen that, loyal to the tradition estab-

[46] Quoted by Umphrey Lee, *The Historical Backgrounds of Early Methodist Enthusiasm*, pp. 38-39.

lished by *Hudibras,* several satirists contemporary with Burnet associate enthusiasm with an appeal to a "nature" which exempts the dissenter from ordinary moral obligations. The universal love preached by mystics like John Saltmarsh, combined with the antinomian rejection of "legal" doctrine, was open to malicious exegesis—especially when transferred with great literalness from the realm of contemplation to that of everyday life. Though the sexual and Messianic aberrations arising from antinomianism have been much exaggerated, their existence cannot be ignored in any faithful picture of the seventeenth century.

Now an antinomianism supported by an appeal to the light of nature bears a kinship to the trend of philosophic libertinism which descends from Renaissance humanism. Their psychological common denominator is trust in one's inward impulses. Thus in the Queen Anne period wits who are strongly influenced by the libertine tradition are found satirizing enthusiasts who hold much the same fundamental philosophy. The differences between the two groups in culture, social status, and emotional temper must of course be recognized. One may also object that antinomian "nature" is the voice of God, while libertine "nature" is the voice of instinct. But this distinction collapses once instinct is deified. If the libertine is not a mere Satanist he is likely to justify his position by means of moral and quasi-religious notions about nature drawn from a muddle of Epicureanism and Stoicism. The antinomian in turn derives similar ideas of natural goodness from his pantheistic confusion of nature and God. This curious *rapprochement* explains the phenomenon which has been referred to in this study as "libertine" sentimentalism. In the eighteenth century the time-spirit draws men of pronounced libertine tendencies toward that sentimentalism which descends from their old enemies.

But if the lower levels of sectarianism included a good many unsavory eccentrics, the higher levels included plenty of earnest, high-minded, intellectually gifted men who were eager to establish a rational basis for their faith. They invoked, not "wild nature's vigor working at the root," but the soberer, more rationalistic ideal implied by the shibboleth, "nature and reason." In theology the Inner Light is the Holy Spirit; but in philosophy the Inner Light is that nature which is synonymous with reason—

Unerring nature, still divinely bright,
One clear, unchanged, and universal light.

In championing the Inner Light the chief spokesmen of the sects often preferred philosophical to theological terms. "For Walwyn," as Professor Haller tells us, "the rejection of belief in human depravity and the acceptance of natural goodness meant the assumption that nature had implanted reason in the breasts of common men." [47] Of *common* men—it is easy to see the transition from religious to civil liberty. In opposition to the idea of supernatural law working through Church and State there arises the idea of natural laws and natural rights within the breast of the free individual. Ecclesiastical and political tyranny was a sin against the Inner Light, against universal love, against the religion of reason and nature. "William Walwyn was convinced that love and reason were a law of nature which could not be abrogated with impunity. Lilburne, lawyer-like, must read the Law of Nature into Magna Charta. The task of turning the statement of the law of nature into a ringing declaration of the rights of man fell to Richard Overton." [48] Our eighteenth-century sentimental Whigs retain clear traces of this interweaving of religious, philosophical, and political liberalism.

It is theoretically true that the Inner Light, regarded as a concept of theology, is the Holy Ghost at work within the heart of man; but in the actual feelings of the sectarians the Inner Light is only very tenuously connected with that third Person of the Trinity "who proceedeth from the Father and the Son." For reasons which must now be apparent, it—the masculine pronoun would be inappropriate—is little more than a personification of the sentimental impulses. The more these impulses are rationalized in philosophical rather than in theological terms, the further they drift away from Christianity. At last the Inner Light ceases to be even nominally a Christian idea and becomes part of the sentimentalist's creed. It is then merely reason, nature, the moral sense, or whatever we please to call the voice with which we assure ourselves that we are particularly good parts of a good universe. The process is already far advanced when the latitudinarian Defoe equates nature, reason, and conscience; [49] and it has definitely taken place when the deist Toland invokes the natural reason which illumines the heart of every man. [50]

[47] William Haller, *Tracts on Liberty in the Puritan Revolution*, I, 62.
[48] *Ibid.*, p. 111.   [49] *Vide supra*, pp. 67, 68   [50] *Vide supra*, p. 92

In their appeal to reason the sectarian leaders were thoroughly in harmony with the age. The rationalistic temper of the seventeenth century is manifest on every social level and in almost every shade of belief. Not only Ranters and Levellers, but sober Presbyterians and Independents, "broad" Anglicans and broader deists, insisted that their beliefs accorded with nature and reason. Here Protestantism and the new science went hand in hand, for their spirit was in many ways the same. Descartes, in popularizing the idea of an infinitely extended universe with an infinite number of worlds, seemed at first to satisfy the desire for personal independence and expansiveness. To an extent beyond his own intentions, he aroused in his disciples "an exaltation of the value of individual experience, the importance of individual thought as the criterion of existence." [51] Here the rationalism of the ancients joins hands with that of the moderns, "for the first assumption of Descartes is precisely the Stoic faith in a beneficent God and an uncorrupted nature. A good God cannot deceive us, and our reason is from God; hence our reason is to be trusted." [52]

This is not to say that trust in reason was universal. The Anglo-Catholics, though convinced of the rationality of their position, clung to their belief in an absolute supernatural truth unconditioned by individual opinion; to the Church, the apostolic succession, and the sacraments; to the doctrines of divine right and non-resistance. Neither as Catholics nor as supporters of the Stuarts could they champion "reason and nature" in the same spirit as most of their contemporaries. Even at the Restoration, however, this type of Churchmanship never regained the status it had enjoyed before the Rebellion. After the secession of the Nonjurors, Anglo-Catholicism lost its distinctive religious character and became, with rare exceptions, the ecclesiastical expression of Toryism. In the long run it neither furthered nor effectively opposed the dominant trend of Protestant rationalism. As for those Anglicans who regarded themselves as Protestants, they were of course strongly affected by the puritan viewpoint. Within the general framework of Protestant thought and feeling no absolutely fixed lines of distinction can be drawn between the Low Churchman and the Presbyterian, between the Presbyterian and the Congre-

[51] Marjorie Nicolson, "The Early Stage of Cartesianism in England," *Studies in Philology*, XXVI, 371.

[52] T. O. Wedel, "On the Philosophical Background of *Gulliver's Travels*," *Studies in Philology*, XXIII, 448.

gationalist, or between the Congregationalist and the member of some Separatist sect.

The stream of rationalism was somewhat chilled by a current of scepticism—a scepticism directed not only against faith but against reason. Especially among the upper classes there were many irreligious Pyrrhonists, but in the seventeenth century they stand apart from the trend of our study. In the eighteenth century the libertinism which is often an element in their thought may, as has been suggested above, draw them toward the sentimental viewpoint. Conversely, when bourgeois writers adopt the literary standards of the aristocratic tradition, they are sometimes influenced by the ideas associated with that tradition—witness the mingling of hard-headed scepticism and extremely tender sentimentalism in the *Essay on Man*.

Scepticism is not necessarily hostile to religion. Professor Louis I. Bredvold, in *The Intellectual Milieu of John Dryden,* has shown that Roman Catholic controversialists of the time rather often attacked natural reason in order to make room for supernatural faith. But he finds that although fideistic arguments appear in Dryden's two major religious poems and occasionally in Anglican apologetics, they are never really popular in England. Perhaps their ambiguity is repugnant to the downright Saxon mind. Much more in evidence is a common-sense, middle-of-the-road scepticism which appears in a kind of positivism. When science raises questions embarrassing to the orthodox, when a harshly empirical philosophy threatens comfortable illusions, when enthusiasm grows indecently warm or when political radicalism clamors for innovation, reasonable men will hasten to point out the limitations of reason. Except in such exigencies, however, English Protestantism confidently takes its stand on the reasonableness of Christianity.

Even for seventeenth-century thinkers who would hotly have rejected the charge of enthusiasm, reason is a kind of Inner Light by which one may read the laws of nature. Those laws are eternal, unchanging, universal and uniform, easy to understand, plainly revealed to the natural reason possessed by all men. According to Miss Whitney "these five principles, stated with varying emphases and in diverse combinations, are fundamental not only to the rationalistic philosophy of the Enlightenment and the theology of the deists, but are found, with a slightly different genesis and with some modification, in the more mystical philosophy of the Cambridge Platonists." [53] She might have added that they are found also among the sects. "The 'inner light' of the Quakers," says Basil Willey, "ranks with the 'Reason' of the Platonists, the 'clear and distinct ideas' of Descartes, and the 'common notions' of Lord Herbert of Cherbury, as another of the inward attitudes by means of which the century was testing the legacies of antiquity and declaring its spiritual independence." [54]

At the other end of the theological scale, Hooker argues that besides the supernatural law revealed in the Scriptures one must take account of the natural law revealed to human reason. His arguments, designed to defend the Anglican ideal, could be used for quite different purposes. Lord Brooke's *Nature of Truth,* published in 1640, breathes the humanistic and Platonic spirit that one would expect from a cousin of Fulke Greville. But in the following year he champions the reason of the Platonic individualist against the prelatical position in *A Discourse opening the nature of that Episcopacie which is exercised in England.* Here, says Haller, "the courtly idealism of the Elizabethan aristocrat is transformed to the revolutionary doctrine of the law of reason, of the inner light, of the necessity for toleration." [55] Milton, also the heir of the Renaissance, basically agrees with Brooke when he writes in the *De Doctrina:* "Under the gospel we possess, as it were, a twofold Scripture: one external, which is the written word, and the other internal, which is the Holy Spirit, written in the hearts of believers, according to the promise of God. Hence, although the external ground which we possess for our belief at the present day in the written word is highly important, and in most instances, at least, prior in point of reception, that which is internal, and the peculiar possession of each believer, is far superior to all, namely, the Spirit himself." But the Holy Spirit is the light of natural reason. Herein Milton "is substantially at one with ... the Cambridge Platonists, whose attitude is summed up in the phrase of John Smith: 'To follow Reason is to follow God.' Reason ... was for the Platonists the ultimate source of authority in matters of faith; and the function of Scripture was to illuminate and confirm its dictates, never to contradict them." [56]

---

[53] Lois Whitney, *Primitivism and the Idea of Progress in English Popular Literature of the Eighteenth Century,* p. 10.
[54] *The Seventeenth Century Background,* p. 73.
[55] William Haller, *Tracts on Liberty in the Puritan Revolution,* I, 21.
[56] Willey, *op. cit.,* p. 72.

This very prevalent belief in reason as a universal intuitive faculty contributed to a sanguine view of humanity, for if man is naturally wise he must be naturally good. The doctrine of total depravity or even of human insufficiency could not long withstand the pressure of such ideas. The rationalistic view of the complete uniformity of the laws of nature may seem inconsistent with Protestant individualism. Occasionally a conflict between the two is apparent, but usually these viewpoints are harmonized by the fact that when the free individual uses his Inner Light he supposes that he has discovered the universal and immutable truth of things. If other men would only use *their* Inner Light properly, they would all be led to the same conclusions. The controversial temper of the seventeenth century encouraged the idea that the laws of nature consist of a few very clear and simple propositions. For the polemic writer, the truth is always as plain as a pikestaff. He is eager to show that his case agrees with reason and nature, and that it is self-evident to the man in the street. Hence the man in the street is constantly being assured, not that he is naturally weak and stupid, but that he is naturally competent and wise. Needless to say, however, there is no general agreement as to what these simple and obvious laws of nature are, and the universal light of reason leads different men to very different conclusions.

So diverse are these conclusions that it is rash to generalize as to what "reason" meant to the seventeenth century. One may, however, point out one important cleavage in regard to men's conception of this term. Is reason imparted from God directly to the mind of man? In that case it is itself a divine creative power capable of a bold imaginative dominance over external nature. Or is reason a faculty which God awakens in man chiefly through the rationality displayed in the creation? In that case reason, though still a precious faculty, is relatively passive. Its function is that of recognizing and responding to the stimuli presented to it by the senses. Both conceptions of reason run through the whole seventeenth century, but the former gradually gives way before the latter.

This change is closely related to changes in the spirit of science. The cosmological and astronomical speculations of the Renaissance reflected, and for a time powerfully fostered, a type of reason singularly free from that aridity and disenchantment which are usually implied by the term "rationalism." This reason was emotional, poetic, adventurous, and creative, permeated by Platonic idealism and by Neoplatonic visions of universal harmony and the identity of truth and beauty. Perfect thinking was geometrical thinking, but geometry was interpreted in a half-mystical Pythagorean-Platonic spirit which anticipated Novalis' "Mathematics is the life of the gods." There was a lofty transcendental scorn of the grubby work of the senses. This kind of reason richly satisfied the self-regarding and expansive impulses.

Soon, however, the world of objects to be observed, weighed, and measured began to assert its claims. Although the ideals of *pure* mathematics continued to be influential throughout the seventeenth century, they were increasingly affected by the ideals of *applied* mathematics. In the spirit of Francis Bacon, science turned more and more toward mechanics and the natural sciences. The reason associated with the experimental viewpoint was inevitably a tool to be used in the discovery of facts external to the mind and independent of its desires.

The educated puritan, as we have seen, was strongly attracted by Baconianism. It produced solidly useful results; it was hostile to tradition and dogmatic authority; it contributed at first to an illusion of creative mental activity. Then too, the idea of God's immanence in nature made physical science a branch of divinity—the study of natural theology. Did not all roads lead to God's footstool? There was no one to warn the puritan that the Inner Light and the microscope were not quite the same thing. The position of modern man in relation to nature is thus described by E. A. Burtt: "Just as it was thoroughly natural for medieval thinkers to view nature as subservient to man's knowledge, purpose, and destiny; so now it has become natural to view her as existing and operating in her own self-contained independence, and so far as man's ultimate relation to her is clear at all, to consider his knowledge and purpose somehow produced by her, and his destiny wholly dependent on her."[57] The seventeenth century carried man a long way toward this position. Championing the rights of individual personality, it gradually espoused a philosophy which would make personality insignificant; with loud cries of freedom, it placed men's necks beneath a heavier yoke than that of the Stuarts.

Descartes, mingling the older spirit of geometry with the newer spirit of physical science, at first encouraged feelings of individualism and self-sufficiency. Ultimately, however, his dualism greatly enhanced the prestige of matter as opposed to that of mind. Compared to the huge,

[57] E. A. Burtt, *The Metaphysical Foundations of Modern Physical Science*, pp. 10-11.

solid, mechanical world of extended objects in motion, the dubious little world of unextended, thinking spirits seemed thin, trivial, and visionary—little more than a pious relic of the past. "Cogito, ergo sum," of course; but having thus proved one's existence one discovered that human thought consisted of dutiful responses to a material, mechanical, non-spiritual, non-teleological, non-human world. Man became, in Santayana's phrase, "the clumsy conjunction of an automaton with a ghost."

The Cartesian dualism was roughly handled by Hobbes. He argued, that "all activity and change whatever are *motion;* now thinking in all its form is an activity, therefore thinking is a kind of motion. Mind is simply a name for the sum of an individual's thinking activities, is thus nothing but a series of motions in an animal organism." [58] In other words, mind is not a special substance distinct in kind from the rest of the universe. It is wholly corporeal, made up of atoms moving in accordance with laws of mechanics. These views are associated with a system of ethics which denies the altruistic impulses.

But the Inner Light was not to be snuffed out so easily. The repugnance with which Hobbes was regarded by a large majority of his contemporaries shows that the world was not yet ready for a thoroughgoing mechanistic philosophy. There were various avenues of escape from his conclusions. Dismayed by such impiety, even a very stout adherent of the natural revelation might appeal to orthodox Christian doctrines. One could invoke the older deductive rationalism against a philosophy which from that viewpoint seemed to deny the possibility of reason. Or, if one granted that Hobbes' philosophy was grounded on reason, one could either fall back upon a frank anti-intellectualism or posit some "higher" reason which would soar above his detestable notions without—a difficult point—incurring the perils of "enthusiasm." In the ethical sphere, of course, a doctrine of man's innate moral sense must arise to confute the Hobbesian picture of man as a selfish beast.[59] The spread of the idea of natural goodness owes much to the cynicism of its three savage enemies, Hobbes, Bayle, and Mandeville.

Of those who tried to accept the new science without surrendering the

[58] *Ibid.,* pp. 118-119.
[59] For facts showing the prevalence of the doctrine of natural benevolence in the seventeenth century, see a note by R. S. Crane in the bibliography, "English Literature, 1660-1800," *Philological Quarterly,* XI, 203-204. Professor Crane is trying to dissipate the impression that Shaftesbury is the sole source of this view for the eighteenth century.

Renaissance conception of reason as a divine creative faculty lodged within the human breast, the Cambridge Platonists are for us the most important group. It goes without saying that Henry More's thought is not identical with Cudworth's, nor Whichcote's with Culverwell's or Smith's, but they form at least a relatively homogeneous school. These lovers of God and reason were learned and spiritually gifted men who remained within the Anglican fold. Their mood of "sweetness and light," blending high cultivation and a broadly tolerant spirit with sincere devotion, suggests the Anglo-Catholicism of a Lancelot Andrewes. The bonds which connect them with an enlightened puritanism, however, are much stronger. In their indifference to the visible Church and their reliance upon individual reason as a guide to truth they are definitely Protestant.

These Platonists—or better, Neoplatonists—represent the seventeenth-century phase of a venerable Renaissance tradition which had flourished especially at Cambridge since the first confluence of humanism and the Reformation. The same tradition, through the puritans of Emmanuel College, strongly influenced the sects; but the Cambridge Platonists were not disposed to recognize the relationship. According to Rose Macaulay, they endeavored, "as Malebranche in France ... to combine reason, Cartesian methods of thought, Neo-Platonism, and Christian orthodoxy, and to evolve, in some sort, a new kind of religious viewpoint from the mixture." [60] That they did effect such a combination is true, but they probably did not do so with any deliberate desire to create "a new kind of religious viewpoint." Hobbes had repeated, in a more obviously subversive spirit, Bacon's assertion that reason and religion are two quite different things. The Cambridge school, on the contrary, held that true religion was rational and—an equally important point—that true reason was religious. Thus they advanced the old Renaissance-Platonic conception of reason. That this kind of reason could establish the truths of Christianity they had no doubt. The Christianity thus established, however, turned out to be a highly metaphysical affair, not hostile to the faith of the Scriptures, but essentially independent of that faith. Their Neoplatonic belief in a universal harmony revealed to the harmonious mind could readily detach itself from Christianity and continue to operate as an intellectualized expression of sentimentalism.

Henry More was a member of the Royal Society, and in general the

[60] *Some Religious Elements in English Literature*, p. 130.

Cambridge men were friendly to the experimental method. But they liked a slight flavor of magic in their science, and they resisted any restriction of reason within the limits of sense-perception. Eager to preserve God as a living force in nature and in the human mind, they were quick to sense the mechanistic implications of Cartesianism. Hobbes of course they detested; their Platonism was greatly stimulated by the need of defending the prerogatives of mind against his philosophy.

Desiring to accept as much of the new philosophy as possible, but suspicious of the growing tendency to ascribe reality only to the objective world of matter, the Platonists asserted the reality of spiritual substances. For Henry More no less than for Hobbes, it is inconceivable that anything could exist without extension, but the Platonist argues that extension need not be confined to matter. "For him, spirit too must be extended, though its other qualities are widely different from those of matter." Spirit can dilate and contract— "as full, as perfect, in a hair as heart," Pope was later to say. It has a sort of fourth dimension which More calls "essential spissitude"—the ability of a spiritual substance to fit into a large or a small space without any change in its own nature.[61]

The need of defending the reality of spirit without flouting the new science caused the Cambridge Platonists to revive the ancient idea of an *anima mundi,* or spirit of nature at work in the world.[62] Fearing that the Cartesian relegation of God to the function of prime mover separated Him so far from the world as to incur the perils of materialism, Cudworth, in his *True Intellectual System of the Universe,* seeks to bridge the gap by means of what he calls "Plastic Nature." This physico-spiritual mediating force is described by Tulloch as "a dull unconscious soul animating all things and working in all—a living yet blind power carrying out the purposes of the divine Architect, and insensibly clothing and making manifest the divine Mind." [63] Henry More, impelled by the same motives, also believed in this spirit of nature which imposes the perfect order and harmony of divine mind upon all creation. That he sometimes refers to it as "the universal soul of the world" [64] hints at the pantheistic

[61] Burtt, *op. cit.,* p. 129.

[62] "Revived" is hardly the word, for this conception had never wholly disappeared. For evidence of its survival in the sixteenth century and in the first half of the seventeenth, see Burtt, *op. cit.,* pp. 156-159.

[63] John Tulloch, *Rational Theology and Christian Philosophy in England in the Seventeenth Century,* II, 271.

[64] Burtt, *op. cit.,* p. 133.

implications of this theory. If God governs the world from which He is infinitely distant through Plastic Nature, then Plastic Nature is likely to take the place of God in the religious imagination. But More was never an avowed pantheist. For him, "this all-pervading order and harmony in the world itself implies the existence of an incorporeal substance of a yet higher order than the spirit of nature, a spiritual substance rational, purposive, supremely worthy of obedience and worship." [65] Brute matter *might* be able to move itself, but never in the orderly, harmonious, beautiful way in which it is moved by an unseen power. Hence there must be a wise and loving God who delegates the execution of His will to that humbler spiritual being, Plastic Nature.

But this God, though loftier than the spirit of nature, is much more shadowy. From the work of the spirit of nature He derives the only convincing evidence of His existence. Furthermore, if God is real He must, like all other real things, possess extension; and an extended divine substance must be extended throughout all space and time. In his later works, More closely approaches an identification of God with space. Thus the Cambridge Platonists' attempt to harmonize science and religion produced a Trinity not very closely related to that of the Creed—Space the Father, Plastic Nature the Son, Platonic Reason the Holy Ghost. The theory of the spirit of nature looks forward to the quasi-pantheism of our sentimental poets and through them to Wordsworth's "something far more deeply interfused."

The Cambridge Platonists are also interesting to us because their opposition to the ethics of Hobbes led them to emphasize the innate goodness of man. According to Tulloch, More asserts in the *Enchiridion Ethicum* that "the special seat of morality is in a certain 'boniform faculty,' by which we instinctively and absolutely desire what is best, and delight in it alone. It is the mind, not in the mere exercise of reason, but acting *ex sensu virtutis,* which brings us within the moral sphere. This is the highest and truly divine side of our being, corresponding to τò αγαθόν in the Platonic Deity. It is the side, moreover, which may be cultivated by all men. For all men are capable of the love of God and their neighbours, and this divine love is the highest form and best fruit of the 'boniform faculty.' At the same time, the intellectual and the divine are never to be separated. Morality is always agreeable to right reason, and in its nature,

[65] *Ibid.,* p. 136.

essence, and verity comes within its cognisance. Only it requires something more than reason—a certain divine instinct or special faculty of
good—to apprehend it in life, and realize it." [66] The reader need not be
reminded of the part which this idea is to play in the development of
sentimentalism.

The above quotation may suggest that the Platonists are not always
completely loyal in their championship of reason. The inconsistency, however, is more apparent than real. If reason is the communion of the human
soul with the Eternal Spirit, it is all-sufficient for the apprehension of
truth; but if it is the reason of Descartes—or worse, of Hobbes—it must
give place to something higher, a *Vernunft* which rises above mere
Verstand. Professor C. F. Harrold has noted that the Cambridge school,
in preserving a Platonic and Neoplatonic distinction between understanding and reason, foreshadows the viewpoint of later transcendental
philosophy. "Cudworth's reply to the scepticism of Hobbes," he remarks,
"has points of resemblance to Kant's reply to Hume; there is the attempt
... to construct a transcendental epistemology, which should base universal
truths, not on experience, which is incomplete, but upon the very laws
of reason itself as it determines experience." [67]

The members of the Cambridge school, one must repeat, exhibit plenty
of personal variations. Cudworth was soberer, more Aristotelian, and
more conventionally Christian than More. The latter is distinctly the
most mystical and Platonic of the group, and the most inclined to identify
the higher reason with divine illumination. His sweet, saintly nature included many eccentricities. He dabbled in prophetic interpretation and
Cabbalistic lore, had strange visions, and insisted that his flesh smelled of
violets. Endowed with a crotchety and ill-regulated though keen and
lively mind, he was not only mystical but superstitious: he believed in
ghosts, witches, and magic. This, it is not irrelevant to recall, is probably
the man who first used the adjective "romantic." In *The Immortality of
the Soul,* 1659, he writes: "I speak especially of that Imagination which is
most free, such as we use in Romantick Invention."

Henry More was a lover of free imagination. Although he wrote
against the enthusiasm of the sects, he identifies his own philosophy with
the enthusiasm of Plato and Plotinus when he says in *Enthusiasmus Tri-*

---

[66] Tulloch, *op. cit.,* II, 400-401.
[67] C. F. Harrold, *Carlyle and German Thought,* p. 123.

umphatus, "To such Enthusiasm as this, which is but the triumph of the Soul of man, inebriated, as it were, with the delicious sense of the divine life, that blessed Root and Originall of all holy wisedom and vertue, I must declare myself as much a friend, as I am to the vulgar, fanatical Enthusiasm a professed enemy." [68] But the differences between these enthusiasms are mainly differences of denominational loyalty, of metaphysical technique, of social status, of manner and tone of voice. In more essential respects the two forms of spiritual inebriation are closely akin. Both descend from the same Neoplatonic tradition; both emphasize "the triumph of the soul of man" in a sense which predicts, if it does not already announce, the transformation of Protestantism into sentimentalism.

We have observed the influence of Cambridge Platonism upon such poets as Norris of Bemerton, Lady Chudleigh, Henry Needler, and Henry Brooke. The obscurities of More's own *Philosophical Poems* of 1647 need not be grappled with.[69] We may, however, point to Thomas Traherne as an especially striking example of the Cambridge-Platonic spirit in seventeenth-century poetry.

The Church has always stood for the belief that grace comes to sinful man *from the outside,* that grace is God's love mediated to humanity through the sacramental Body of Christ. Denial or neglect of this principle is liable to cause confusion between God's grace and one's personal feelings of goodness, strength, and freedom. Uncurbed, these feelings may grow so strong as to obscure all necessity of redemption. Grace becomes not something that human nature needs, but something that human nature possesses. Different as they are in many respects, Donne, Crashaw, and Herbert are almost wholly free from this confusion. Since they are children of the Church their strong religious inwardness never becomes independent of outward grace, the gift of a transcendent God who has stooped to immanence. In no essential respect do they foretoken the romantic Wordsworth.[70] Vaughan, on the other hand, reminds us of

[68] Quoted by Umphrey Lee, *The Historical Backgrounds of Early Methodist Enthusiasm,* p. 85.

[69] It is interesting to note, however, that in the dedication of this volume he says that his Father has "tuned mine ears to Spenser's rhymes, entertaining us on winter nights, with that incomparable piece of his, *The Fairy Queen,* a Poem as richly fraught with divine Morality as Phansy." One thinks of Milton's "sage and serious Spenser."

[70] "Romantic" should be emphasized because the later, Anglican, Wordsworth displays points of kinship with Herbert.

Wordsworth precisely because he departs further from the Church ideal. A man of science and a Hermetist,[71] he thinks more of grace immanent in nature than of grace mediated to him across infinite distances by the Bride. His mysticism, even when expressed in Christian terms, has a pantheistic quality.

Traherne, though an Anglican priest, is still more Protestant and still more romantic. His intellectual background mingles puritanism and Cambridge Platonism. Hence in his most characteristic poems he substitutes Holy Ego for Holy Church. Free to interpret the Gospels in the light of his personal temperament, he finds that they authenticate his boundless self-sufficiency. They declare that in dying for him on the Cross, Christ has revealed Traherne's own supernal glory by revealing the essential divinity of the human soul:

> O Joy! O Wonder, and Delight!
> O Sacred Mysterie!
> My Soul a Spirit infinit!
> An Image of the Deitie,
> A pure Substantiall Light.
> That Being Greatest, which did Nothing seem!
> Why twas my All, I nothing did esteem
> But that alone. A Strange Mysterious Sphere!
> A Deep Abyss
> That sees and is
> The only Proper Place of Heavenly Bliss.
> To its Creator tis so near
> In Lov and Excellence
> In Life and Sence,
> In Greatness, Worth, and Nature; And so Dear;
> In it, without Hyperbole,
> The Son and friend of God we see.[72]

The son of God, Traherne looks about him with godlike eyes which transform earth into heaven. God's creation is his, since he himself is a divine spirit. In a sense he not only possesses but creates the natural world, for nature fulfils its purpose only to the extent that he beholds and uses it:

> That all things should be mine,
> This makes his Bounty most Divine.

[71] To discuss the Hermetic philosophy would lead us far afield, but its pantheistic implications are obvious.
[72] My Spirit.

But that they all more Rich should be,
And far more brightly shine,
As used by Me;
It ravisheth my Soul to see the End,
To which this Work so Wonderfull doth tend.[73]

Traherne's mood will not fully be regained by English poetry until the emergence of Blake, but in our sentimentalists it ferments and struggles for expression.

The Cambridge Platonists represent a less coolly rationalistic spirit than that which is to dominate the last quarter of the seventeenth century; but though in some respects they hark back to the Renaissance they also look forward into the future. John Norris is their disciple not only as poet but as philosopher. Important elements in their thought are passed down to Berkeley by such men as Norris and Cumberland.[74] Especially noteworthy for us, however, is the indebtedness of Shaftesbury to the Cambridge school. He edited Whichcote's sermons in 1698, and was thoroughly familiar with the work of More and Cudworth. If on the practical side his ethics is derived chiefly from the Stoics, the theoretical framework of his system is derived from the Cambridge Platonists. The fact is too familiar to require elucidation.

It is interesting, however, to recall that Shaftesbury's attitude toward enthusiasm is precisely that of Henry More. "Inspiration," he says, "is a *real* Feeling of the Divine Presence, and Enthusiasm a *false* one." [75] But inspiration may equally well be termed a true enthusiasm. The author of the sneering *Letter Concerning Enthusiasm* permits Theocles, in *The Moralists,* to call himself an enthusiast.[76] Vulgar sectarian enthusiasm is to be derided; a genteel Platonic-deistic-pantheistic enthusiasm is to be cultivated as the choicest mood of the virtuoso.

Shaftesbury's influence on the sentimental poets of the eighteenth century, though perhaps exaggerated by some students, was certainly strong. Scholars who have observed that the sentimentalists are both Shaftesburyian and bourgeois have been tempted to discover bourgeois elements

---

[73] *Amendment.*

[74] Berkeley is very different from the Cambridge thinkers, but the Platonic side of his philosophy owes much to them and his idealism is a more effective expression of their desire to resist materialism and affirm the primacy of mind.

[75] Quoted by Oliver Elton, "Reason and Enthusiasm in the Eighteenth Century," *Essays and Studies by Members of the English Association*, X, 134.

[76] *The Moralists* was originally entitled *The Sociable Enthusiast.*

in Shaftesbury himself. Cazamian, for example, observes that he brought into aristocratic and learned circles "des tendances qui risquaient de rester associées à une demi-vulgarité bourgeoise." [77] Mayo discerns in him "a certain middle-class 'soft-mindedness.' " [78] Seeking a source for the "emotional rhetoric" of Shaftesbury, Draper suggests that "its existence in the poetry, sermons, and devotional books of the dissenters and of the Whig Low Churchmen, followers of the former Lord Shaftesbury, [79] might well explain the adoption of it by the philosopher, and would certainly help to show why it was so rapidly taken up by the eighteenth century." [80] But there is nothing even "half" vulgar about Cambridge Platonism, "bourgeois" and "soft-minded" are not quite co-extensive, and it seems unlikely that the first Earl of Shaftesbury was deeply versed in the pious effusions of his more devout followers. A more probable explanation of the phenomenon which these suggestions attempt to clarify is that by about 1720, when Shaftesbury's influence began to manifest itself in poetry, the theological and social chasm between the Cambridge-Platonic and the sectarian types of enthusiasm had been closed by the blurring of Christian doctrine and by the rise of the middle class. The ex-puritan was anxious to repudiate the "fanaticism" of his forefathers, but he had inherited from them religious feelings which demanded satisfaction. He found what he wanted in Shaftesbury, an unusually sentimental aristocrat who had drawn from those learned and respectable despisers of the sects, the Cambridge Platonists, ideas essentially akin to those of sectarian enthusiasm.

Those who prefer to represent ideas as moving neatly from book to book may draw a line running from Plato and the Neoplatonists to the Platonists of the Renaissance, thence to the Cambridge Platonists, thence to Shaftesbury, and finally to our sentimental poets. But this graph would hardly do justice to the full complexity of the facts. It is safer to take one's stand on the crude observation that there have aways been many people who, whether from glandular or other causes, think, or desire to think, extremely well of themselves. The feeling of self-sufficiency is variously rationalized by different men in different ages; but its most characteristic religious expression, for reasons already explained, is a pantheistic mingling of God, man, and nature in a universal harmony of beauty,

---

[77] Louis Cazamian, *L'Évolution psychologique et la littérature en Angleterre*, p. 129.

[78] T. F. Mayo, *Epicurus in England*, p. 203.

[79] The philosopher's grandfather, who founded the Whig party.

[80] J. W. Draper, *The Funeral Elegy and the Rise of English Romanticism*, p. 203.

truth, and love. This form of religion may exist in a Catholic setting, but it can receive no positive support from orthodox Catholicism. Protestantism, however, not only allows it freedom to develop but lends it strong encouragement. Hence the religion of natural goodness and human sufficiency flourishes greatly in the sixteenth century and in at least the first half of the seventeenth.

But as the seventeenth century moves onward, science, at first the friend of the human spirit, begins to threaten man's wish to feel inwardly wise, good, free, and powerful. One side of the confrontation is seen in Hobbes, the other side in the Cambridge Platonists. The antagonism might have become acute had it not been for the spirit of compromise which appears in England with the Restoration and which becomes a dominant force with the Revolution of 1688. After more than a century of stirring but exhausting conflict among tremendous intellectual forces, Englishmen want peace and quiet. They frown upon whatever makes for controversy and oscillation. Monarchism and democracy, Cavalier and Puritan, aristocracy and bourgeoisie, agriculture and commerce, rationalism and empiricism, Epicureanism and Stoicism, utilitarian and altruistic ethics, supernatural religion and natural philosophy, Christianity and Deism, High Church and Low Church, Anglicanism and Dissent—these formerly discordant forces, strange bedfellows as they are, lie down together in comparative amity.

It was the Cambridge Platonists who were first called "Latitude-Men," but their religion is a soaring flame compared to the latitudinarianism which is the religious aspect of the compromise of 1688. This later form of latitudinarianism—the religion of Tillotson and Locke—preserved the outer shell of Christianity only by casting aside its poetic and imaginative elements in the name of "reason."

In the compromise of 1688, however, the most influential factor was the middle class, with its Whiggish and puritan background. The bourgeoisie did not rise to power without becoming much more temperate, unenthusiastic, genteel, and "classical" than their ancestors. They could not have dominated the compromise had they not accepted its spirit. Yet they did not tear from their hearts every vestige of the old puritan ardor. Latitudinarianism, as we know, did not exclude all stirrings of religious imagination. It had a positive as well as a negative aspect. It could be very soft and amiable, preaching universal benevolence as the core of this best of all possible worlds. Without zeal, but with a cheerful practicality, it brushed aside the ideas of sin and atonement, leaving a half-deistic Christianity of right conduct which encouraged man to think of himself as naturally good provided the thought inspired no indecorous heat. The prevalent idea that any sincere belief was as good as any other sincere belief left plenty of room for religious individualism. The constant emphasis on natural revelation would have amounted to a kind of nature-worship had it been possible to worship anything without incurring the charge of fanaticism. Reduced to common-sense, the Inner Light burned feebly; but it was not extinguished. Protestant self-sufficiency no longer leaps and runs, but it moves at a comfortable jog-trot over the flat and smiling fields of latitudinarianism.

The violent storms of the seventeenth century were not easily stilled. From the Restoration to the death of Queen Anne the trend toward compromise is shaken by contrary winds which sometimes threaten to overthrow it entirely. The old seventeenth-century conflicts continue to appear, though sporadically and with less intensity. With the accession of George I, however, complete equilibrium seems to have been achieved at last. The seventeenth century is dead, and the peace of the Augustans is at hand. But a very curious thing occurs. Hardly has the compromise become completely triumphant when it begins to break down—not from opposition, but from inward decay. Just as the water is about to freeze over, the ice begins to melt. The symptoms of sentimentalism, scanty and obscure in the 1700-1720 period, grow and multiply as soon as the completely unsentimental Walpole is firmly in the saddle. How is this paradox to be explained?

In the first place, the definite triumph of Whig civilization establishes the importance of the bourgeois ex-puritan both as a writer and as a member of the reading public. Having become the voice of England, he may express more freely than before not only the practical but also the sentimental side of his strangely divided temperament. In the second place, the compromise of 1688 had never genuinely represented the spiritual impulses of large sections of the English people. It was an essentially artificial attempt to reconcile conflicting tendencies which had recently torn the nation asunder. Intense religious feeling had caused the Civil War; hence the *display* of intense religious feeling must now be restrained for the common good. As long as the popish Stuarts remained a peril, as long as High Churchmen like Sacheverell continued their agitations, the danger of politico-religious strife was serious and the need for suppressing religious ardor correspondingly great. But after George I ascended the throne there was no longer any grave emergency. The dread of fanaticism, to be sure, had affected England so deeply that it remains a vital force even to this day; but comparatively at least it relaxed and diminished. Once a solid compromise had become possible there remained no particular need for it. Anxious suppression of feeling gave place to an easy-going looseness. There was no violent reaction in any direction, but both irreligious and religious men could now, within the comfortable framework of established Whiggery, say what they had to say without fear of bringing back the days of the Civil War. The floodgates which had held back religious feeling were slowly opened. Not much water was left in the stream, but what there was of it was free to trickle through.

The disruption of the compromise, however, was as gradual as had been its crystallization. The sentimental poets of the 1720-1740 period are still strongly influenced by its spirit. Their feelings are weak, uncertain, inconsistent. They hardly know what they want to express, and they have forgotten how to express it. In particular they are harassed by the fear that the practical Whiggish civilization which they have helped to create may be hostile to their desire for illusion. Nevertheless it is clear that the religion of sentiment is rising, and that it is rising from the ashes, never quite dead, of the fire of seventeenth-century puritanism.

One is not surprised to find that the religion which the sentimentalist is now relatively free to express is only nominally, and sometimes not even nominally, Christian. He inherits a tradition of natural goodness and self-sufficiency which is not essentially Christian at all. His melancholy is not Christian melancholy: it is merely the result of the clash between his illusions and the real facts of human nature. But herein he is by no means sundered from his seventeenth-century ancestors, for some of the most intense and vital religious feelings of the seventeenth century are alien to orthodox Christianity. His feelings are not so strong as those of his forebears because the dull latitudinarian compromise stands between him and them, but they are the same feelings. Then too, the emotions associated with the basic doctrines of Christianity have become so desiccated and unreal that a poet of religious temper can derive but little imaginative stimulation from them. One might almost say that the more emotional and imaginative a writer is, the less inspiration he can find in the religion of John Locke. Hence we find men whose *prose* religion is latitudinarian Christianity, but whose *poetic* religion is drawn from Shaftesbury. Head and heart begin to diverge in a way full of serious implications for the future. The only positive religious *feelings* are associated with the harmony of things, natural goodness, universal benevolence, the social tear, public service, contemplation of "Nature and Nature's God," and so on. These feelings constitute the faith of the sentimental poet. They had flourished, in a more intense and passionate form, under seventeenth-century Protestantism, but having no essential connection with Christianity they flourish equally well in a setting of deistic nature-worship. Sometimes the sentimental poet appears to think that he is a Christian, and sometimes not. It does not greatly matter.

This concluding chapter raises questions of some historical importance. If the thesis which I have defended is valid, it should be accepted and used; if invalid, someone should expose its fallacies. I shall merely add that students who prefer a sociological frame of reference should not regard their views and mine as mutually exclusive. The religious and the sociological interpretations are complementary: the rise of the middle class brings into prominence the religion of the middle class. The scholar whose personal motivation is religious rather than economic [81] will regard the religious interpretation as the more fundamental, while the economically motivated scholar will hold the opposite opinion. Which of the two approaches is the more fruitful in studying the history of poetry is a debatable question. To me it seems fairly obvious that poetry is more closely related to religion than to economics, but many will disagree. In any case neither frame of reference will be very profitable unless he who uses it recognizes the validity of the other.

The conclusions suggested by this book will assume added importance for readers who regard the Romantic Movement as a direct historical outgrowth of eighteenth-century sentimentalism. This is the almost unanimous opinion of scholars, and while the exact process of development

[81] Pending liquidation by the totalitarian state, I shall continue to assert that there *are* such persons.

needs further study the essential correctness of the view seems unquestionable. The terms "sentimentalism" and "romanticism" merely indicate different degrees of emotional intensity and aesthetic adequacy. In any period, the sentimentalist is a weak and uncertain romanticist. The sentimental poets of the eighteenth century are quite properly called "pre-romantic"—not only because they employ themes and forms which are to be used by Wordsworth and his contemporaries, but because, impelled by the same emotional drives, they have gropingly begun to cultivate the same type of religious experience as a means of satisfying those impulses.[82]

Since this study stops at about 1740, I have confined myself to the rise of sentimentalism without discussing its relationship to the Romantic Movement proper; but from time to time I have thought it appropriate to indicate the larger historical bearings of my theme by glancing forward to the romantics and even to the Victorians. These prophecies-after-the-fact, combined with the more substantial retrospect provided by this chapter, imply that the period discussed in this book is merely a brief stretch of a great river of religious imagination flowing down from the ancients to our own contemporaries.

In the next volume of this series the poetic expression of religious thought and feeling will be traced to about the year 1780—that is, to what is generally regarded as the beginning of the Romantic Period. The principal theme will be the continued rise of the religion of sentiment in the face of various obstacles, the slowly increasing freedom and power with which its ideals are realized and expressed. Some new factors, however, will claim our attention. We have seen that although poetic response to non-sentimental Christianity recedes to a very low ebb during the years covered by the present volume it never wholly disappears. Furthermore, although the general trend moves from Christianity to a more or less frankly deistic sentimentalism, a few poets of the 1720-1740 period reverse

[82] Students of comparative literature may ask whether, in view of the revival of Catholicism associated with the Romantic Movement in France and Germany, my thesis can be applied to any country but England. We have seen, however, that when sentimentalism reaches a certain point Christianity may become one more thing to be sentimental about. Is the romantic Catholicism of *Heinrich von Ofterdingen* and the *Génie du Christianisme* authentic, or does it merely add the glamor of mystery and tradition to an essentially non-Catholic kind of religious feeling? At some later time I should like to argue that, granting obvious differences of detail, the same interpretation applies with equal force to English, German, and French romanticism.

this trend, becoming more Christian and less sentimental as they grow older. By 1740 the long deistic controversy has almost spent itself, and the Evangelical Movement has begun to raise its head. The interrelations of sentimentalism, evangelicalism, and a renewed distrust of reason must be examined with some care. But that, the reader may be relieved to know, is another book.

Appendix I

PRIMARY SOURCES

THIS IS BY NO MEANS A BIBLIOGRAPHY OF THE POETS NAMED BELOW, BUT SIMPLY a list of the poetic material on which the study is based. Only enough of the title has been given to insure identification. Unless otherwise noted, place of publication is London. When a volume published anonymously is unquestionably the work of a particular author, it is entered under that author's name. Works of unknown authorship are listed under "Anon."

The following abbreviations are used: Chalmers = The Works of the English Poets. Ed. Alexander Chalmers. London, 1810. Sev. = Several. Var. = Various. Occ. = Occasions.

Adam, Jean [or Jean Adams, or Jane Adams]. Miscellany Poems. Glasgow, 1734.

Addison, Joseph. Miscellaneous Works. Ed. A. C. Guthkelch. Vol. I. 1914.

Amhurst, Nicholas. Poems on Sev. Occ. 1720.

—— Protestant Popery: or, the Convocation. 1718.

—— The Protestant Session. 1719.

—— The Resurrection. A Poem. Written by Mr. Addison. 1718. [Addison's Resurrectio Delineata Ad Altare Col. Magd. Oxon., with an English translation by Amhurst.]

Anon. Of Active and Retired Life, An Epistle. 1735.

Anon. Austin, and the Monks of Bangor. 1718.

Anon. An Epistle from an English Jesuit, to the Pope, Concerning Present Affairs of Europe. 1718.

Anon. A Muster-Roll of the B. of B[a]ng[o]r's Seconds. In a Collection of Poems, Panegyricks, Garlands and Characters: Composed in Honour of the B[ishop] of B[a]ng[o]r. 1720.

Anon. Order, A Poem. 1737.

Anon. Of Superstition: An Epistle to a Friend. 1734.

Anon. The Tower of Babel. An Anti-Heroic Poem. Humbly Dedicated to the B[isho]p of B[ango]r. 1718.

Arbuthnot, John, ΓΝΩΘΙΣΕ΄ΑΥΤΟΝ. Know Yourself In G. A. Aitken, The Life and Works of John Arbuthnot. Oxford, 1892.

Arwaker, Edmund. An Embassy from Heav'n: Or, The Ghost of Queen Mary. 1704.

—— Pia Desideria: Or, Divine Addresses, In Three Books.... Written in Latine by Herm. Hugo. Englished by Edmund Arwaker, M.A.

Baker, Henry. Original Poems: Serious and Humorous. 1725.
—— The Universe. A Poem Intended to Restrain the Pride of Man. n.d.
Bancks [or Banks], John. Miscellaneous Works, in Verse and Prose. 1738.
—— The Weavers Miscellany: Or, Poems on sev. Subjects. 1730.
Barber, Mary. Poems on Sev. Occ. 1734.
Blackmore, Richard. Creation. 1715.
—— Eliza. 1705.
—— The Nature of Man. 1711.
—— A New Version of the Psalms of David. 1721.
—— A Paraphrase on the Book of Job. 1700.
—— Prince Arthur. 1696.
—— Redemption. 1722.
—— A Satyr Against Wit. 1700.
Blair, Robert. The Grave. Chalmers, XV, 61ff.
Bockett, Richard. Fruits of Early Piety, Consisting of Several Christian Experiences, Meditations, and Admonitions.... The Third Edition. n.d. [British Museum Catalogue queries 1722 for this ed. The first edition must have appeared in 1721 or 1722.]
Boyse, Samuel. Poems. Chalmers, XIV, 516ff.
Brereton, Jane. Poems on Sev. Occ. 1744.
Breval, John Durant de. Miscellanies, Upon Sev. Subjects, Occasionally Written. By Mr. Joseph Gay [pseudonym]. 1719.
Brooke, Henry. Poems. Chalmers, XVII, 327ff.
Broome, William. Poems on Sev. Occ. 1739.
Brown, Thomas. Works. 1744.
Browne, Isaac Hawkins. Poems upon Var. Subjects. 1768.
Browne, Moses. Poems on Var. Subjects. 1739.
Browne, Simon. Hymns and Spiritual Songs. 1720.
Buckingham, Duke of. See Sheffield, John.

Carey, Henry. Poems. Ed. F. T. Wood. London, n.d. [1930.]
Catherall, Samuel. Cato Major, a poem upon the model of Tully's Essay. 1725.
—— An Essay on the Conflagration, in Blank Verse. Oxford, 1720.
Chandler, Mary. The Description of Bath. A Poem ... The Fourth Edition. To which are added, several Poems by the same Author. 1738.
Chesterfield, Philip Dormer Stanhope, fourth Earl of. Miscellaneous Works. 1777-1778.
Christian Poet, The. The Christian Poet, Or Divine Poems on the Four Last Things. 1735. [A miscellany of religious poems.]
Chudleigh, Lady Mary. Essays upon Sev. Subjects in Prose and Verse. 1710.
—— Poems on Sev. Occ. 1722.

Cibber, Colley. An Ode for His Majesty's Birth-Day, October 30, 1731.
—— An Ode to His Majesty, for the New-Year, 1730/31.
—— A Poem, on the Death of Our Late Soveraign Lady Queen Mary. 1695.
—— A Rhapsody upon the Marvellous: Arising from the First Odes of Horace and Pindar. 1751.
Cobb, Samuel. Bersaba: Or, The Love of David. 1695.
—— Poems on Sev. Occ. . . . To which is prefix'd A Discourse on Criticism, and the Liberty of Writing. 1710.
Cobden, Edward. Poems on Sev. Occ. 1748.
Codrington, Samuel. The Beatific Vision. 1735.
Collins, Richard. Nature Display'd. 1727.
Concanen, Matthew. Poems upon Sev. Occ. By the Author of The Match at Foot-Ball. Dublin, 1722.
Congreve, William. Poems. Chalmers, X, 269ff.
Cooke, Thomas. Mr. Cooke's Original Poems, with Imitations and Translations. 1742.
Croxall, Samuel. [For this poet I have used transcriptions of the whole body of his verse made by Louis C. Jones. See Appendix II for his M.A. essay on Croxall.]

Dart, John. Westmonasterium. Or The History and Antiquities of the Abbey Church of St. Peters Westminster. . . . To which is added, Westminster Abbey, A Poem, By the same Author. 1742.
Davies, Sneyd. [His poems are printed with those of John Whaley, q.v., in 1732 and 1745.]
Defoe, Daniel. The Double Welcome. A Poem to the Duke of Marlbro. 1705.
—— An Elegy on the Author of the True-Born-English-Man. With an Essay on the Late Storm. 1708.
—— A Hymn to the Mob. 1715.
—— A Hymn to Peace. 1709.
—— A Hymn to the Pillory. 1708.
—— Jure Divino. 1706.
—— More Reformation. 1703.
—— Reformation of Manners. 1702.
—— The True-Born English-Man. 1708.
Delacour [or De La Cour], James. Poems. Cork, 1778.
Dennis, John. Select Works. 1718.
Desaguliers, J. T. The Newtonian System of the World, The Best Model of Government: An Allegorical Poem. Westminster, 1728.
Divine Hymns and Poems. A Collection of Divine Hymns and Poems upon Sev. Occ.: By the E. of Roscommon, John Dryden, Esq; Mr. Dennis, Mr. Norris, Mrs. Kath. Phillips, Mrs. Singer, and others. The Third Edition. To which is added, I. Death's Vision, A Philosophical Sacred Poem. Writ at the Request of the late Mr. Locke. By Mr. Reynolds. II. God, the

Creator and Preserver. By the Reverend Mr. Daniel. With several others not in the Former Editions. 1719.

Dixon, Sarah. Poems on Sev. Occ. Canterbury, 1740.

Dodsley, Robert [probable author]. The Economy of Human Life. 1750.

Duck, Stephen. Poems on Sev. Occ. 1764.

Duke, Richard. Poems. Chalmers, XI, 209ff.

Dunton, John. The Pulpit-Fool. A Satyr. 1707.

—— The Second Part of the Pulpit-Fool. 1707. [This anonymous two-part satire is ascribed to Dunton in the British Museum Catalogue, but one could wish for more positive evidence.]

Dyer, John. Poems. Ed. Edward Thomas. 1903.

Edwards, Samuel. The Copernican System, A Poem. Cambridge, 1728.

Ellwood, Thomas. Davideis. 1712.

—— A Collection of Poems on Var. Subjects. n. d. [British Museum Catalogue queries 1730.]

Erskine, Ralph. Poetical Works. Aberdeen, 1858.

Eusden, Laurence. Original Poems and Translations. By Mr. Hill, Mr. Eusden, Mr. Broome, Dr. King, etc. 1714.

—— Verses at the Last Publick Commencement at Cambridge. 1714.

Evans, Abel. The Apparition. 1710.

—— Præ-Existence. A Poem in imitation of Milton. 1714. [Probably, but not certainly, by Evans.]

—— Vertumnus. 1713.

Farquhar, George. Complete Works. Ed. Charles Stonehill. 1930.

Fenton, Elijah. Poems. Chalmers, X, 386ff.

Fielding, Henry. Miscellanies and Poems. Ed. J. P. Browne, M.D. 1903.

Fitzgerald, Thomas. Poems on Sev. Occ. Published by his Grandson, the Reverend Thomas Wintour, A.M. Oxford, 1781.

Fowke, Martha. The Epistles of Clio and Strephon. 1729.

Gambol, Robert. The Beauties of the Universe. By a Gentleman of the Navy. 1732.

Garth, Samuel. Poems. Chalmers, IX, 417ff.

Gay, John. Poetical Works. Ed. G. C. Faber. 1926.

Gent, Thomas. The Contingencies, Vicissitudes and Changes of this Transitory Life. York, n.d. [1761.]

—— Divine Entertainments: Or, Penitential Desires, Sighs and Groans of the Wounded Soul. 1724.

—— The Most Delectable, Scriptural, and Pious History of the Famous and Magnificent great Eastern Window ... in St. Peter's Cathedral, York. [York] 1762.

—— The Pious and Poetical Works of Mr. Thomas Gent. Scarborough and York, 1734-1772.

Glanvill [or Glanvil], John. Poems: Consisting of Originals and Translations. 1725.

Glover, Richard. Leonidas, A Poem. 1737.

—— Poems. Chalmers, XVII, 3ff.

Granville, George, Lord Lansdowne. Genuine Works in Verse and Prose. 1736.

Green, Matthew. Poems. Chalmers, XV, 157ff.

—— The Spleen. Ed. W. H. Williams. 1936.

Halifax, Earl of. See Montagu, Charles.

Hamilton, William. Poems and Songs. Ed. James Paterson. Edinburgh, 1850.

Hammond, James. Poems. Chalmers, XI, 135ff.

Harrison, Thomas. Poems on Divine Subjects. 1719.

Hay, William. Works. 1794.

Hill, Aaron. Works. 1753.

Hobson, Thomas. Christianity the Light of the Moral World. 1745.

Hughes, John. Poems on Sev. Occ. 1735.

Jacob, Hildebrand. Works. 1735.

Jeffreys, George. Miscellanies in Verse and Prose. 1754.

Jones, Mary. Miscellanies in Prose and Verse. Oxford, 1750.

Keinton, Martha. A Poem. Gen. xlix. V. 23, 24, 25. The Archers have sorely grieved Him, etc. 1716.

Ken, Thomas. A Manual of Prayers for the Use of the Scholars of Winchester College, and all other Devout Christians. To which are added, Three Hymns for Morning, Evening, and Midnight. n.d. [British Museum Catalogue queries 1710.]

—— Works. Ed. William Hawkins. 1721.

Kennett, Basil. An Essay Towards a Paraphrase on the Psalms, In English Verse. To which is added A Paraphrase on the Third Chapter of the Revelations. 1706.

King, William, of Christ Church, Oxford. Original Works. 1776.

Lely, Richard. Poems and Translations on Sev. Occ. 1727.

Lyttelton, George, first Baron Lyttelton. Works. Dublin, 1775.

Mallet, David. Works. 1759.

Mandeville, Bernard. The Fable of The Bees. Ed. F. B. Kaye. Oxford, 1924.

—— Wishes to a Godson, With other Miscellany Poems. 1712.

Maynwaring [or Mainwaring], Arthur. Life and Posthumous Works. Ed. John Oldmixon. 1715.

Meston, William. Poetical Works. Edinburgh, 1767.

Miller, James. The Art of Life. In Imitation of Horace's Art of Poetry. Epistle the First. 1739.

Miscellanea Sacra: Or, Poems on Divine and Moral Subjects: Collected by N. Tate. 1698. [The second edition, enlarged, of "Vol. I" (1696) of what was to be an annual miscellany of divine poetry. No more was published.]

Mitchell, Joseph. Jonah. A Poem. 1720.

—— Lugubres Cantus. 1719. [Part II is by John Calender.]

—— Poems on Sev. Occ. 1729.

Monck [or Monk], Mary. Marinda. Poems and Translations upon Sev. Occ. 1716.

—— Poems by Eminent Ladies, II, 187-196. 1755.

Monitor, The. An Entire Set of The Monitors. [1712-1713. A periodical miscellany of divine and moral verse containing poems by Tate, Edmund Smith, and others.]

Montagu, Charles, first Earl of Halifax. Poems. Chalmers, IX, 329ff.

Montagu, Lady Mary Wortley. Works. 1803.

Morrice [or Morris], Bezaleel. Miscellanies or Amusements, in Verse and Prose. 1712.

Needler, Henry. Works. 1728.

Nicol, Alexander. Poems on Sev. Subjects, Both Comical and Serious. Edinburgh, 1766.

Norris, John. Poems. Ed. A. B. Grosart. Miscellanies of the Fuller Worthies Library, III, 147ff. 1871.

Nugent, Robert, Earl Nugent. Faith. A Poem. 1774.

—— Odes and Epistles. 1739.

Oldmixon, John. Poems on Sev. Occ., Written in imitation of the manner of Anacreon, With Other Poems, Letters, and Translations. 1696.

Pack, Richardson. Miscellaneous Works in Verse and Prose. Dublin, 1726.

—— Religion and Philosophy: A Tale. With Five Other Pieces. 1720.

Paget, Thomas Catesby, Baron Paget. Miscellanies in Prose and Verse. 1741.

Parnell, Thomas. Poetical Works. Ed. G. A. Aitken. 1894.

Pattison, William. Poetical Works. 1728.

Philips, Ambrose. Poems. Ed. M. G. Segar. The Percy Reprints, No. 14. Oxford, 1937.

Philips, John. Poems. Ed. M. G. Lloyd Thomas. Oxford, 1927.

—— Poems on Sev. Occ. 1720.

Pilkington, Laetitia. Poems by Eminent Ladies, II, 235ff. 1755.

Pilkington, Matthew. Poems on Sev. Occ. . . . To which is added, the Plague of Wealth. With several Poems not in the Dublin Edition. . . . Revised by the Reverend Dr. Swift. 1731.

Pitt, Christopher. Poems. Chalmers, XII, 363ff.

Pomfret, John. Poems. Chalmers, VIII, 307ff.

—— Poems upon Sev. Occ. . . . To which are added, His Remains. 1780.

Pope, Alexander. Selections from Alexander Pope. Ed. George Sherburn. New York, 1929.

—— Works. Edd. Whitwell Elwin and W. J. Courthope. 1871-1882.

Prior, Matthew. Poetical Works. Ed. R. B. Johnson. 1892.

—— Writings. Ed. A. R. Waller. Cambridge, 1905, 1907.

Ralph, James. Miscellaneous Poems. 1729.

Ramsay, Allan. Poems. Philadelphia, 1813.

—— Poems. Ed. J. L. Robertson. 1887.

Rawson, Mr. [probable author]. Sacred and Moral Poems. By a Cambridge Gentleman. 1716.

Relph, Josiah. A Miscellany of Poems. Glasgow, 1747.

Reynolds, John. Memoirs of the Life of the late Pious and Learned Mr. John Reynolds. . . . To which is Added, His View of Death: Or the Soul's Departure from the World. A Philosophical Sacred Poem. With a Copious Body of Explanatory Notes, And some Additional Composures, Never before printed. The Third Edition. 1735.

Roche, Mr., of King's College, Cambridge. [A few poems of his are included in Vol. II of the Poetical Works of William Pattison, q.v.]

Rowe, Elizabeth Singer. The History of Joseph. 1736.

—— Miscellaneous Works in Prose and Verse. 1739.

Rowe, Nicholas. Miscellaneous Works. 1733.

—— Poems. Chalmers, IX, 457ff.

Rowe, Thomas. Original Poems and Translations. [Vol. II, 245ff., of The Miscellaneous Works in Prose and Verse of Mrs. Elizabeth Rowe. 1739.]

Savage, Richard. Poetical Works. 1791.

Say, Samuel. Poems on Sev. Occ.: and Two Critical Essays, viz: The First, On The Harmony, Variety, and Power of Numbers, whether in Prose or Verse. The Second, On the Numbers of Paradise Lost. 1745.

Settle, Elkanah. Eusebia Triumphans. . . . The Hanover Succession to the Imperial Crown of England, An Heroic Poem. 1703.

—— An Heroick Poem on the Coronation of the High and Mighty Monarch, James II. Edinburgh, 1685.

—— A Pindaric Poem, On the Propagation of the Gospel in Foreign Parts. 1711. [Authorship uncertain.]

—— Rebellion Display'd: Or, Our Present Disturbances Set Forth in their True Light. 1715.

Sewell, George. A New Collection of Original Poems . . . By the Author of Sir Walter Raleigh. 1720.

—— Poems on Sev. Occ. 1719.

Sheffield, John, third Earl of Mulgrave, Duke of Buckingham and Normanby. Poems. Chalmers, X, 69ff.

Shippen, William. Faction Display'd. 1705.

—— Moderation Display'd. 1709.

Silvester, Tipping. Original Poems and Translations. 1733.

Smith, Edmund. Poems. Chalmers, IX, 165ff. [Other poems probably by Smith are in The Monitor, q.v.]

Somerville, William. Poems. Chalmers, XI, 147ff.

Specimens of the Later English Poets. Ed. Robert Southey. 1807.

Sprat, Thomas. Poems. Chalmers, IX, 309ff.

Stepney, George. Poems. Chalmers, VIII, 351ff.

Stogdon, Hubert. Poems and Letters. . . . Collected from His Original Papers. 1729.

Swift, Jonathan. Poems. Ed. W. E. Browning. 1910.

—— Poems. Ed. Harold Williams. Oxford, 1937. [My discussion of Swift in Chapters I and II had been written by the time this admirable edition appeared. I have checked my quotations with it to be sure of having made no significant textual errors and have drawn some information from its notes.]

Tate, Nahum. An Elegy on . . . His Grace, John [Tillotson], Late Lord Archbishop of Canterbury. 1695.

—— An Entire Set of The Monitors, Intended for the Promoting of Religion and Virtue, and Suppressing Vice and Immorality . . . Perform'd by Mr. Tate, Poet Laureat to Her Majesty, Mr. Smith, and Others. [1712-1713. Contains an uncertain number of poems by Tate.]

—— Funeral Poems. 1700.

—— Miscellanea Sacra: Or, Poems on Divine and Moral Subjects. Collected by N. Tate. 1698. [Contains poems by Tate.]

—— A New Version of the Psalms of David. [With Nicholas Brady.] 1696.

Thomson, James. Complete Poetical Works. Ed. J. L. Robertson. 1908.

Tickell, Thomas. Poems. Chalmers, XI, 97ff.

Toland, John. Clito: A Poem on the Force of Eloquence. 1700.

Tollett, Elizabeth. Poems on Sev. Occ. 1755.

Traherne, Thomas. Poetical Works. Ed. G. I. Wade. 1932.

Tunstall, William. A. Collection of Ballads, And some other Occasional Poems. . . . To which is added, Saint Cyprian's Discourse to Donatus. 1727.

Tutchin, John. A Congratulatory Poem to the Reverend Dr. John Tillotson. 1691.

—— The Foreigners. Part I. 1700.

—— An Heroick Poem upon the Late Expedition of His Majesty, To Rescue England from Popery, Tyranny, and Arbitrary Government. 1689.

—— Poems on Sev. Occ., with a Pastoral. To which is Added, a Discourse of Life. 1685.

Victor, Benjamin. Original Letters, Dramatic Pieces, and Poems. 1776.

Waldron, George. Compleat Works, in Verse and Prose. 1731.

Walsh, William. Poems. Chalmers, VIII, 399ff.

Ward, Edward. Hudibras Redivivus: Or, A Burlesque Poem on the Times. 1708.

—— Vulgus Britannicus: Or, The British Hudibras. 1711.

Warton, Thomas, the elder. Poems on Sev. Occ. Reproduced from the Edition of 1748. The Facsimile Text Society. New York, 1930.

Watts, Isaac. Horae Lyricae. Poems, Chiefly of the Lyric Kind. 1736.

—— Poems. Chalmers, XIII, 1ff.

Welsted, Leonard. Works, in Verse and Prose. Ed. John Nichols. 1787.

Wesley, Samuel, the elder. Elegies on the Queen and Archbishop. 1695.

—— An Epistle to a Friend Concerning Poetry. 1700.

—— The History of the Old and New Testament Attempted in Verse. Vols. I and II, 1704; Vol. III, 1715.

—— The Life of our Blessed Lord and Saviour Jesus Christ. 1693.

—— A Poem in Memory of Robert Nelson, Esquire. 1715.

Wesley, Samuel, the younger. Poems on Sev. Occ. 1736.

Whaley, John. A Collection of Original Poems and Translations. 1745.

—— A Collection of Poems. 1732.

Winchilsea, Ann Finch, Countess of. Poems. Ed. Myra Reynolds. University of Chicago Decennial Publications, Second Series, Vol. V. Chicago, 1903.

Winstanley, John. Poems Written Occasionally. Dublin, 1742.

Wren, John. The Country Life; Or An Invitation of the Soul to Retirement. Being a Poetical Soliloquy on Cant. vii. 11. 1717.

Wycherley, William. Complete Works. Ed. Montague Summers. 1924.

Yalden, Thomas. Poems. Chalmers, XI, 37ff.

Appendix II

SECONDARY SOURCES

A LIST OF WORKS, OTHER THAN EIGHTEENTH-CENTURY POEMS, WHICH HAVE BEEN cited in this study, together with certain books and articles which, though not expressly cited, have been directly or indirectly helpful.

Abbey, C. J., and J. H. Overton. The English Church in the Eighteenth Century. London, 1878.

Alderman, W. E. Bibliographical Evidence of the Vogue of Shaftesbury in the Eighteenth Century. Transactions of the Wisconsin Academy of Sciences, Arts, and Letters, XXI, 57-70.

—— Shaftesbury and the Doctrine of Benevolence in the Eighteenth Century. Transactions of the Wisconsin Academy of Sciences, Arts, and Letters, XXVI, 137-159.

—— Shaftesbury and the Doctrine of Moral Sense in the Eighteenth Century. PMLA, XLVI, 1087-1094.

—— Shaftesbury and the Doctrine of Optimism. Trans. of the Wisconsin Academy, etc., XXVIII, 297-305.

—— The Significance of Shaftesbury in English Speculation. PMLA, XXXVIII, 175-185.

Audra, E. L'Influence française dans l'œuvre de Pope. Paris, 1931.

Austin, E. M. The Ethics of the Cambridge Platonists. Philadelphia, 1935.

Barrett, W. P. Matthew Prior's "Alma." Modern Language Review, XXVII, 454-458.

Beach, J. W. The Concept of Nature in Nineteenth-Century English Poetry. New York, 1936.

Beattie, L. M. John Arbuthnot, Mathematician and Satirist. Cambridge (Mass.), 1935.

Benn, A. W. The History of English Rationalism in the Nineteenth Century. London, 1906.

Bernbaum, Ernest (ed.). English Poets of the Eighteenth Century. New York, 1918.

Bickley, Francis. The Life of Matthew Prior. London, 1914.

Bissell, B. H. The American Indian in English Literature of the Eighteenth Century. New Haven, 1927.

Bolingbroke, Henry St. John, Viscount. Works. Philadelphia, 1841.

Bonar, James. Moral Sense. London, 1930.

Bond, D. F. "Distrust" of Imagination in English Neo-Classicism. Philological Quarterly, XIV, 54-69.

Bond, R. P. English Burlesque Poetry, 1700-1750. Cambridge (Mass.), 1932.

Bredvold, L. I. The Intellectual Milieu of John Dryden. Ann Arbor, 1934.

Brewster, Dorothy, Aaron Hill. New York, 1913.

Burtt, E. A. The Metaphysical Foundations of Modern Physical Science. London, 1925.

Bury, J. B. The Idea of Progress; an Inquiry into Its Origin and Growth. London, 1920.

Cazamian, Louis. L'Évolution psychologique et la littérature en Angleterre, 1660-1914. Paris, 1920.

Clark, H. W. History of English Nonconformity. Vol. II. From the Reformation to the Close of the Nineteenth Century. London, 1913.

Closs, Karl. Jakob Böhmes Aufnahme in England. Archiv für das Studium der neueren Sprachen und Literaturen, CXLVIII, 18-27.

Coffin, C. M. John Donne and the New Philosophy. New York, 1937.

Coxon, Roger. Chesterfield and His Critics. London, 1925.

Crain, R. D. Richardson Pack. Notes and Queries, CLXX, 344.

Crane, R. S. Anglican Apologetics and the Idea of Progress, 1699-1745. Modern Philology, XXXI, 273-306, 349-382.

—— Suggestions toward a Genealogy of the "Man of Feeling." ELH, I, 205-230.

Creed, J. M., and J. S. Boys Smith (edd.). Religious Thought in the Eighteenth Century. Illustrated from Writers of the Period. Cambridge, 1934.

Cruickshank, A. H. Thomas Parnell, or What Was Wrong with the Eighteenth Century. Essays and Studies by Members of the English Association, VII, 57-81.

Crum, R. B. Scientific Thought in Poetry. New York, 1931.

Darnall, F. M. Swift's Belief in Immortality. Modern Language Notes, XLVII, 448-451.

—— Swift's Religion. Journal of English and Germanic Philology, XXX, 379-382.

Davis, Rose Mary. The Good Lord Lyttelton. [A Columbia doctoral dissertation which is shortly to be published.]

—— Stephen Duck, the Thresher-Poet. University of Maine Studies, 2d. ser., No. 8. Orono, Maine, 1926.

De la Torre Bueno, Lillian. Was Ambrose Philips a Ballad Editor? Anglia, LIX, 252-270.

De Maar, H. G. A History of Modern English Romanticism. Vol. I. Elizabethan and Modern Romanticism in the Eighteenth Century. London, 1924.

Dennis, John. The Age of Pope. London, 1909.

Dobrée, Bonamy. The Letters of ... Chesterfield. London, 1932.

Dottin, Paul. The Life and Strange Surprising Adventures of Daniel De Foe. New York, 1929.

Draper, J. W. The Funeral Elegy and the Rise of English Romanticism. New York, 1929.

Drennon, Herbert. Henry Needler and Shaftesbury, PMLA, XLVI, 1095-1106.

—— James Thomson's Contact with Newtonianism and His Interest in Natural Philosophy. PMLA, XLIX, 71-80. [For a valuable criticism of Drennon's contributions to the study of Newtonianism, see Philological Quarterly, XIV, 175-176.]

—— James Thomson's Ethical Theory and Scientific Rationalism. Philological Quarterly, XIV, 70-82.

—— Newtonianism: Its Method, Theology, and Metaphysics. Englische Studien, LXVIII, 397-409.

—— Scientific Rationalism and James Thomson's Poetic Art. Studies in Philology, XXXI, 453-471.

—— The Source of James Thomson's "The Works and Wonders of Almighty Power." Modern Philology, XXXII, 33-36.

Durham, W. H. (ed.) Critical Essays of the Eighteenth Century. New Haven, 1915.

Durling, D. L. Georgic Tradition in English Poetry. New York, 1935.

Elton, Oliver. Reason and Enthusiasm in the Eighteenth Century. Essays and Studies by Members of the English Association, X, 122-136.

Evans, A. W. Warburton and the Warburtonians. London, 1932.

Eves, C. K. Matthew Prior, Poet and Statesman. [A Columbia doctoral dissertation shortly to be published.]

Farley, F. E. Three "Lapland Songs." PMLA, XXI, 1-39.

Federer, C. A. (ed.) Yorkshire Chap-Books. First Series. London, 1889.

Gent, Thomas. The Life of Mr. Thomas Gent. Written by Himself. London, 1832.

Gilfillan, George (ed.) The Poetical Works of Richard Crashaw and Quarles' Emblems. Edinburgh, 1857.

Goodman, Paul. Neo-classicism, Platonism, and Romanticism. Journal of Philosophy, XXXI, 148-163.

Grierson, H. J. C. Cross Currents in English Literature of the Seventeenth Century. London, 1929.

Gulick, S. J., Jr. Jonathan Swift's "The Day of Judgment." PMLA, XLVIII, 850-855.

Haller, William. The Rise of Puritanism. New York, 1938.

—— (ed.) Tracts on Liberty in the Puritan Revolution, 1638-1647. Records of Civilization, No. XVIII. New York, 1934.

Handasyde, Elizabeth. Granville the Polite. London, 1933.

Harder, J. H. Observations on Some Tendencies of Sentiment and Ethics Chiefly in Minor Poetry and Essay in the Eighteenth Century until the Execution of Dr. W. Dodd in 1777. Amsterdam, 1933.

Harrold, C. F. Carlyle and German Thought. New Haven, 1934.

Havens, R. D. The Influence of Milton on English Poetry. Cambridge (Mass.), 1922.

—— Primitivism and the Idea of Progress in Thomson. Studies in Philology, XXIX, 41-52.

Howard, W. G. Good Taste and Conscience. PMLA, XXV, 486-497.

Hughes, H. S. Lady Winchilsea and Her Friends. London Mercury, XIX, 624-635.

Hunt, John. Religious Thought in England from the Reformation to the End of the Last Century. Vol. III. London, 1873.

Jeudwine, J. W. Religion, Commerce, Liberty, 1683-1793. London, 1925.

Johnson, Samuel. Lives of the English Poets. Ed. G. B. Hill. Oxford, 1905.

Jones, L. C. The Early Life and Poems of Samuel Croxall. [Unpublished Columbia M.A. essay.]

Jones, R. F. Ancients and Moderns. St. Louis, 1936.

Jones, R. M. Studies in Mystical Religion. London, 1909.

Kaye, F. B. (ed.) The Fable of the Bees, by Bernard Mandeville. Oxford, 1924.

Lamprecht, S. P. The Role of Descartes in Seventeenth Century England. New York, 1935.

Lecky, W. E. H. A History of England in the Eighteenth Century. London, 1878-1890.

—— History of the Rise and Influence of the Spirit of Rationalism in Europe. New York, 1866.

Lee, Umphrey. The Historical Backgrounds of Early Methodist Enthusiasm. New York, 1931.

Legouis, Émile, and Louis Cazamian. A History of English Literature. New York, 1929.

Leland, John. A View of the Principal Deistical Writers. London, 1757.

Libby, M. F. The Influence of the Idea of Esthetic Proportion upon Shaftesbury's Ethics. American Journal of Psychology, XII, 458-491.

Looten, C. La Pensée religieuse de Swift et ses antinomies. Paris, 1936.

Lovejoy, A. O. The Great Chain of Being. Cambridge (Mass.), 1936.

—— On the Discrimination of Romanticisms. PMLA, XXXIX, 229-253.

—— Optimism and Romanticism. PMLA, XLII, 921-945.

—— The Parallel of Deism and Classicism. Modern Philology, XXIX, 281-299.

—— Pride in Eighteenth Century Thought. Modern Language Notes, XXXVI, 31-37.

Macaulay, G. C. James Thomson. London, 1907.

Macaulay, Rose. Some Religious Elements in English Literature. New York, 1931.

McGiffert, A. C. Protestant Thought before Kant. New York, 1911.

Martin, Burns. Allan Ramsay, a Study of His Life and Works. Cambridge (Mass.), 1931.

Mayo, T. F. Epicurus in England (1650-1725). Dallas, Texas, 1934.

Milton, John. Works. Columbia Edition. Vols. X, XV. New York, 1931-1937.

Monk, S. H. The Sublime: a Study of Critical Theories in Eighteenth-Century England. New York, 1935.

Moore, C. A. Berkeley's Influence on Popular Literature. South Atlantic Quarterly, XIV, 263-278.

—— Did Leibniz Influence Pope's Essay on Man? Journal of English and Germanic Philology, XVI, 84-102.

—— John Dunton: Pietist and Impostor. Studies in Philology, XXII, 467-499.

—— The Return to Nature in the English Poetry of the Eighteenth Century. Studies in Philology, XIV, 243-291.

—— Shaftesbury and the Ethical Poets in England, 1700-1760. PMLA, XXXI, 264-325.

—— Whig Panegyric Verse, 1700-1760: a Phase of Sentimentalism. PMLA, XLI, 362-401.

More, P. E., and F. L. Cross (edd.) Anglicanism. London, 1935.

Morel, Léon. James Thomson: sa vie et ses œuvres. Paris, 1895.

Mossner, E. C. Bishop Butler and the Age of Reason. New York, 1936.

Nicolson, Marjorie. The Early Stage of Cartesianism in England. Studies in Philology, XXVI, 356-374.

Norris, John. A Collection of Miscellanies. London, 1706.

Paston, George [E. M. Symonds]. Lady Mary Wortley Montagu and Her Times. London and New York, 1907.

—— Mr. Pope: His Life and Times. London, 1909.

Paul, H. G. John Dennis: His Life and Criticism. New York, 1911.

Perdeck, A. A. Theology in Augustan Literature. Groningen, 1928.

Potter, G. R. Henry Baker, F.R.S. (1698-1774). Modern Philology, XXIX, 301-321.

—— James Thomson and the Evolution of Spirits. Englische Studien, LXI, 57-65.

Powicke, F. G. The Cambridge Platonists. London, 1926.

Price, L. M. Inkle and Yarico Album. Berkeley, California, 1937.

Reed, A. L. The Background of Gray's "Elegy." New York, 1924.

Reynolds, Myra. The Learned Lady in England, 1650-1760. Boston and New York, 1920.

Rich, G. B. Interpretations of Human Nature: a Study of Certain Late Seventeenth and Early Eighteenth Century British Attitudes toward Man's Nature and Capacities. New York, 1935.

Schöffler, Herbert. Protestantismus und Literatur: neue Wege zur Englischen Literatur des achtzehnten Jahrhunderts. Leipzig, 1922.

Scurr, H. M. Henry Brooke. Minneapolis, 1927.

Segar, Mary. Ambrose Philips. London Times Literary Supplement, December 7, 1933, 875.

—— Some Notes on Pope's Religion. Dublin Review, CXC, 237-253.

Shafer, Robert. Christianity and Naturalism. New Haven, 1926.

Shaftesbury, Anthony Ashley Cooper, 3d Earl of. Characteristics. Ed. J. M. Robertson. London, 1900.

Sherburn, George. The Early Career of Alexander Pope. New York, 1934.

—— (ed.) Selections from Alexander Pope. New York, 1929.

—— Two Notes on the Essay on Man. Philological Quarterly, XII, 402-403.

Sichel, Walter. Bolingbroke and His Times. Vol. I, London, 1901. Vol. II, New York, 1902.

Sickels, E. M. The Gloomy Egoist: Moods and Themes of Melancholy from Gray to Keats. New York, 1932.

Smith, Preserved. A History of Modern Culture. Vol. II: The Enlightenment, 1687-1776. New York, 1934.

Sokol, A. E. The Conception of a Calling in the German Literature of the Middle Ages. PMLA, L, 1-13.

Sprat, Thomas. The History of the Royal-Society of London. London, 1667.

Spurgeon, C. F. E. Mysticism in English Literature. Cambridge, 1913.

Stamm, R. G. Daniel Defoe: an Artist in the Puritan Tradition. Philological Quarterly, XV, 225-246.

Steele, F. M. Catholicism and English Literature in the Eighteenth Century. American Quarterly Review, XXXVI, 634-659.

Stephen, Leslie. English Literature and Society in the Eighteenth Century. New York, 1907.

—— History of English Thought in the Eighteenth Century. London, 1876.

Stevenson, Lionel. Brooke's Universal Beauty and Modern Thought. PMLA, XLIII, 198-209.

Stevenson, S. W. "Romantic" Tendencies in Pope. ELH, I, 126-155.

Sykes, Norman. Church and State in England in the Eighteenth Century. Cambridge, 1934.

Tawney, R. H. Religion and the Rise of Capitalism. New York, 1926.

Thompson, E. N. S. Mysticism in Seventeenth-Century English Literature. Studies in Philology, XVIII, 170-231.

Tickell, R. E. Thomas Tickell and the Eighteenth Century Poets. London, 1931.

Tiffany, E. A. Shaftesbury as Stoic. PMLA, XXXVIII, 642-684.

Trevelyan, G. M. England under Queen Anne. Vol. I, Blenheim. London, 1930. Vol. II, Ramillies and the Union with Scotland. London, 1932. Vol. III, The Peace and the Protestant Succession. London, 1934.

Troeltsch, Ernst. The Social Teachings of the Christian Churches. Tr. Olive Wyon. New York, 1931.

Tulloch, John. Rational Theology and Christian Philosophy in England in the Seventeenth Century. Edinburgh and London, 1874.

Vaughan, R. A. Hours with the Mystics. London, 1895.

Vincent, H. P. The Death of William Wycherley. Harvard Studies and Notes in Philology and Literature, XV, 219-242.

Wakeman, H. O. An Introduction to the History of the Church of England. Revised, with an additional chapter, by S. L. Ollard. London, 1914.

Weber, Max. Protestant Ethics and the Spirit of Capitalism. Tr. T. Parsons. New York, 1930.

Webster, C. M. The Satiric Background of the Attack on the Puritans in Swift's *A Tale of a Tub*. PMLA, L, 210-221.

—— Swift and Some Earlier Satirists of Puritan Enthusiasm. PMLA, XLVIII, 1141-1153.

Wedel, T. O. On the Philosophical Background of *Gulliver's Travels*. Studies in Philology, XXIII, 434-450.

Whelan, Sister M. Kevin, S.S.J. Enthusiasm in English Poetry of the Eighteenth Century. Washington, D. C., 1935.

White, H. C. The Metaphysical Poets: A Study in Religious Experience. New York, 1936.

Whitehead, A. N. Science and the Modern World. New York, 1926.

Whiting, G. W. Rowe's Debt to "Paradise Lost." Modern Philology, XXXII, 271-279.

Whitney, L. B. Primitivism and the Idea of Progress in English Popular Literature of the Eighteenth Century. Baltimore, 1934.

Willey, Basil. The Seventeenth Century Background. Studies in the Thought of the Age in Relation to Poetry and Religion. London, 1934.

Williams, G. G. The Beginnings of Nature Poetry in the Eighteenth Century. Studies in Philology, XXVII, 583-608.

Williamson, G. The Restoration Revolt against Enthusiasm. Studies in Philology, XXX, 571-603.

Willoughby, E. E. The Chronology of the Poems of Thomas Warton the Elder. Journal of English and Germanic Philology, XXX, 87-89.

Wright, L. M. The Literary Life of the Early Friends, 1650-1725. New York, 1932.

Wright, Thomas. Isaac Watts and Contemporary Hymn-Writers. The Lives of the British Hymn-Writers, Vol. III. London, 1914.

INDEX OF NAMES

See Index of Topics for: God; Holy Spirit; Jesus Christ; Mary, the Virgin.

Adam, 99, 289, 310, 311, 318, 481; *see also* Fall of Man *in* Index of Topics

Adam, Jean, 287-290, 292

Addison, Joseph, ix, 14, 52, 82, 87, 134, 202, 207, 208, 209, 210, 253, 295, 296, 327, 365, 400, 447, 472

leader of a circle, 121, 229, 246, 247, 260

moral and religious views of, 71, 179-183, 196, 201, 230, 231, 248, 261, 294, 390, 484, 494, 502, 514, 523

Aitken, G. A., 235

Akenside, Mark, 258, 444, 481

Amhurst, Nicholas, 85-87, 159, 224, 261

Anne, Queen, 4, 41, 42, 56, 63, 78, 79, 122, 177, 180, 185, 195, 225

Aquinas, Saint Thomas, 171, 419

Arbuthnot, John, 166-168, 228, 329, 505

Ariosto, 112, 207

Aristotle, 152, 187, 196, 198, 370, 542, 566

Armstrong, John, 273, 459

Arwaker, Edmund, 77-79, 90, 303

Asgill, John, 25

Athanasius, Saint, 83

Atterbury, Francis, 3, 84, 95, 106, 172, 353, 419, 489, 492, 493

Audra, E., 509

Augustine, Saint, 307, 419, 544

Babbitt, Irving, 291

Bacon, Francis, 152, 297, 316, 480, 497, 542, 561, 563

Baker, Henry, 318, 463-466, 481, 485

Bancks, John, 273-278, 339, 415

Barber, Mary, 327-332, 426

Barclay, Robert, 349, 350

Baxter, Richard, 78, 152

Bayle, Pierre, 562

Beattie, L. M., 166

Benn, A. W., 552

Bentley, Richard, 38, 419

Berkeley, 38, 108, 489, 569

Bernbaum, Ernest, 525

Beza, Theodore, 156

Bissell, B. H., 214, 432

Blackmore, Richard, vii, 8, 45, 71, 79, 131, 189-201, 206, 207, 209, 210, 214, 220, 227, 250, 253, 255, 257, 258, 391, 417, 433, 448, 516, 517, 528, 540

Blair, Robert, 373, 413, 415, 424-426, 430

Blake, William, 134, 222, 231, 569

Blount, Charles, 55

Bockett, Richard, 149-150

Boehme, Jacob, 475, 481, 554

Boileau-Despreaux, Nicolas, 131, 494

Bolingbroke, Viscount, 3, 7, 13, 14, 197, 229, 266, 267, 367, 453, 480, 490, 491, 492, 497, 499, 500, 501, 505, 508, 509, 530

Bond, R. P., 49, 237

Boyle, Robert, 38, 78, 152, 316, 325, 406

Boyse, Samuel, 408-412

Brady, Nicholas, 175, 193

Bredvold, L. I., 10, 558

Brereton, Jane, 323-327

Breval, John Durant de, 82-83, 261

Brewster, Dorothy, 447, 448, 449

Brooke, Henry, 258, 475-483, 485, 500, 526, 567

Brooke, Robert Greville, Lord, 559

Broome, William, 220, 398-402

Brown, Thomas, 43-45, 261

Browne, Isaac Hawkins, 345, 347, 472-475, 481, 485

Browne, Moses, 389-392, 393, 394

Browne, Simon, 140-141

Browning, Robert, 245, 407, 451, 452, 533

Buckingham, Duke of: *see* Sheffield, John

Burnet, Gilbert, 90, 382, 419, 554

Burnet, Thomas, 119, 120, 152, 183, 242, 243, 245, 428

Burns, Robert, 48, 336, 375

Burton, Richard, 240, 350

Burtt, E. A. 410, 480, 561, 564

Butler, Samuel, 11, 12, 45, 50, 53, 94, 121, 253, 269, 399, 548, 555

Byrom, John, 94, 474

Byron, Lord, 39, 167

Calamy, Edmund, 90

Calender, John, 413, 415

Calvin, John, 512, 544, 545, 552; see also Calvinism in Index of Topics
Carey, Henry, 385-388
Carlyle, Thomas, 167, 450, 451, 452, 549, 550
Caroline, Queen, 5, 208, 274, 325, 357, 358, 373, 375, 497
Caryll, John, 489, 493, 494, 499, 500
Case, A. E., 165
Casimir, 110, 211, 251, 449
Catherall, Samuel, 119-120, 135, 207
Catullus, 87, 222
Cave, Edward, 326, 389, 390
Cazamian, Louis, 189, 495, 536, 570
Chalmers, Alexander, 408
Chandler, Mary, 426-430
Charles I, 5, 12, 50, 52, 61, 66, 87, 88, 95, 101, 115, 162, 247, 309, 320, 341, 377, 403, 529
Charles II, 10, 122, 191
Chateaubriand, 167, 575
Chaucer, 13, 208, 220, 247, 327, 352, 353, 397, 412, 434, 445, 446
Chesterfield, Lord, 32, 166, 267-268, 397, 455, 469, 470, 500
Chudleigh, Lady Mary, 241-246, 262, 567
Chute, Francis, 82
Cibber, Colley, 266, 364, 413
Cicero, 22, 120, 316, 359, 399, 541
Clarke, Samuel, 29, 300, 325, 359, 382, 479, 484, 497, 498
Cobb, Samuel, 156-158, 163, 206, 207, 208
Cobden, Edward, 340-342
Codrington, Samuel, 312-313
Coleridge, Samuel Taylor, 205, 217, 255, 528, 531, 550, 553
Collier, Jeremy, 8, 56, 71, 89, 183
Collins, Anthony, 246
Collins, Richard, 354-355
Collins, William, 383, 517
Concanen, Matthew, 266-267
Congreve, William, 8
Cooke, Thomas, 382-383
Cooper, John Gilbert, 258, 481
Copernicus, 355, 356, 480
Corneille, Pierre, 131
Cornwallis, Frederic, 408
Cowley, Abraham, 13, 14, 78, 112, 131, 148, 151, 169, 188, 207, 251, 353, 447, 540
Cowper, William, 389
Coxon, Roger, 267, 268
Crain, R. D., 222
Crane, R. S., 261, 536, 562

Crashaw, Richard, 567
Creech, Thomas, 45
Cromwell, 87, 121, 247
Crousaz, Jean Pierre de, 500, 508
Croxall, Samuel, 225-227, 261, 267, 286, 287, 288
Cudworth, Ralph, 563, 564, 566, 569
Curll, Edmund, 82, 165, 440
Cyprian, Saint, 156, 307

Dante, 455
Dart, John, 352-353
Dartmouth, Lord, 389
David, 78, 81, 99, 148, 155, 156, 181, 251, 276, 449, 512
David of Dinant, 550, 551
Davies, Sir John, 345
Davies, Sneyd, 402, 404-408
Davis, Rose Mary, 373, 398
Defoe, Daniel, ix, 66-77, 272, 448, 463, 556
Delacour, James, 383-385, 402, 403
Delany, Patrick, 379, 384
De La Torre Bueno, Lillian, 246
De Maar, H. G., 225
Democritus, 311
Denham, John, 90, 253, 335
Dennis, John (eighteenth-century critic), 131, 183-189, 191, 192, 201, 206, 207, 209, 210, 229, 312, 383, 417, 433, 448, 449, 450, 491, 492, 516, 517, 528, 540
Dennis, John (modern scholar), 14
Derham, William, 152, 393
Desaguliers, John Theophilus, 356-358
Descartes, 152, 197, 242, 262, 354, 357, 557, 559, 561, 562, 563, 564, 566
De Staël, Madame, 294
Dixon, Sarah, 320-323
Dobrée, Bonamy, 267
Doddridge, Philip, 398, 424, 425
Dodington, George Bubb, 266, 343
Dodsley, Robert, 268
Donne, John, 389, 496, 567
Draper, J. W., 151, 202, 213, 424, 535, 539, 570
Drayton, Michael, 21, 208
Drennon, Herbert, 257, 258, 511, 513, 515, 524, 525, 526, 530
Dryden, John, 8, 10, 12, 21, 35, 44, 61, 66, 88, 115, 171, 180, 364, 417, 558
Duck, Stephen, 274, 373-376
Duke, Richard, 12, 20
Duncombe, William, 144, 145, 249, 253, 254, 258
Dunton, John, 88-90, 92, 134

Durling, D. L., 373, 516, 521
Dyer, John, 361, 364, 416, 439, 441-444, 448, 450, 460, 485, 519

Edmund, King, 101, 309
Edward VI, 79
Edwards, Samuel, 355-356
Elizabeth, Queen, 79, 195, 225
Ellwood, Thomas, 146-149, 209, 211
Elton, Oliver, 569
Emlyn, Thomas, 89
Epictetus, 7, 406, 471; see also Stoicism in Index of Topics
Epicurus, 36, 38, 55, 167, 196, 311, 355; see also Epicureanism in Index of Topics
Erasmus, 9, 489, 490, 491, 493, 501, 509
Erskine, Ebenezer, 283, 287
Erskine, Ralph, 283-287, 290, 292, 295
Euclid, 277, 404
Eusden, Laurence, 16, 440, 441
Evans, A. W., 500
Evans, Abel, 55-56, 168, 207, 212
Eve, 289, 297

Fairchild, H. N., 214
Farley, F. E., 208
Farquhar, 9, 20
Fénelon, 509
Fenton, Elijah, 220-221, 224, 227, 261, 398
Fielding, Henry, 222, 261, 265-266
Fitzgerald, Thomas, 430-433
Fontenelle, Bernard le Bovier de, 20
Foster, James, 458, 491
Fowke, Martha, 361-362
Franklin, Benjamin, 372
Frederick, Prince of Wales, 273, 356, 364, 396, 466, 467, 468; see also "Patriot" party in Index of Topics

Galileo, 480
Gambol, Robert, 393-394
Garth, Samuel, 14-15, 21, 79, 134, 165, 368, 489, 519
Gastrell, Francis, 300
Gay, John, 227-231, 261, 262, 327, 329, 365
Gent, Thomas, 302-310
George I, 43, 81, 84, 86, 158, 159, 164, 184, 185, 225, 325, 341, 368
George II, 29, 266, 341, 356, 357, 358, 427, 440
Gerhard, Johann, 163

Gibson, Edmund, 340, 341, 457
Gilfillan, George, 535
Glanvill, John, 17-20, 31
Glover, Richard, 272-273, 397, 466
Goldsmith, Oliver, 247, 466
Granville, Charles, Lord Lansdowne, 4-5, 20
Gray, Thomas, 15
Green, Matthew, 348-351
Gulick, Sidney L., Jr., 32

Hales, Stephen, 379, 380
Halifax, Earl of: see Montagu, Charles
Haller, William, xi, 122, 537, 543, 546, 551, 556, 559
Hamilton, William, 435-438
Hammond, James, 361, 397
Handasyde, Elizabeth, 4
Handel, George Frederick, 363, 387, 416, 417, 449
Harder, J. H., 278
Harley, Robert, 13, 164, 225, 367
Harris, James, 258, 481
Harrison, Thomas, 141-143, 210, 211
Harrold, C. F., 566
Harte, Walter, 440, 500
Havens, R. D., 168, 207, 252, 526
Hay, William, 347-348, 474
Herbert, George, 108, 151, 152, 208, 389, 390, 567
Herbert of Cherbury, Lord, 541, 559
Herrick, Robert, 21
Hertford, Countess of, 126, 208, 237, 330, 391, 515
Hervey, James, 287, 389, 390, 425
Hervey, John, Lord, 396, 397
Hill, Aaron, 189, 229, 361, 364, 416, 417, 418, 441, 447-453, 460, 485, 513, 516, 517, 519, 528, 534, 539
Hoadly, Benjamin, Bishop of Bangor, 42, 53, 83, 84, 85, 86, 87, 90, 106, 224, 254, 354, 359, 368, 369, 382, 457, 484, 497
Hobbes, Thomas, 3, 4, 19, 23, 37, 38, 51, 55, 65, 196, 237, 297, 500, 507, 562, 563, 564, 565, 566, 571
Hobson, Thomas, 310-312
Homer, 187, 195, 207, 433
Hooker, Richard, 467, 559
Horace, 144, 157, 158, 252, 267, 315, 316, 325, 340, 343, 363, 369, 370, 381, 490, 494
Hughes, John, 121, 128, 249-254, 260, 262, 449, 495

Hugo, Hermann, 77, 303, 309
Hume, David, 270, 453, ·566
Huntingdon, Countess of, 208
Hutcheson, Francis, 281, 489, 521

Isaiah, 251, 494

Jacob, Hildebrand, 369-371
James, Saint, 53
James I, 529
James II, 3, 5, 43, 44, 51, 61, 62, 75, 79,
    82, 96, 236, 529
Jeffreys, George, 344-347
Jenyns, Soame, 474
Johnson, R. B., 34
Johnson, Samuel, 3, 5, 163, 166, 173, 196,
    220, 297, 344, 373, 443, 457, 458,
    496
Jones, Mary, 332-335
Jones, R. F., 542
Jones, R. M., 548, 550
"Joseph Gay": see Breval

Kant, Immanuel, 566
Kaye, F. B., 23, 25
Keats, John, 205, 225, 492
Keinton, Martha, 81
Ken, Thomas, 95, 98-106, 109, 116, 134,
    208, 209, 237, 307, 309, 322, 540
Kennett, Basil, 116-117
Kepler, Johannes, 391, 480
King, William (1663-1712), 12-13, 20

La Fontaine, 238
Lansdowne, Lord: see Granville, Charles
Laud, William, 57, 60, 87, 88, 403
Law, William, 71, 84, 183, 326, 481, 497,
    549
Lecky, W. E. H., 41
Lee, Umphrey, 537, 554, 567
Leibnitz, G. W., 509
Lely, Richard, 162-163, 207
Lessing, Gotthold Ephraim, 346
Libby, M. F., 394
Lillo, George, 275, 361
Locke, John, 23, 108, 151, 152, 170, 179,
    180, 183, 197, 325, 333, 359, 382, 451,
    453, 467, 484, 497, 514, 527, 571,
    574
Longinus, 187, 366, 370, 472
Looten, C., 27
Lovejoy, A. O., 102, 217, 392, 464, 498,
    504, 540
Lucretius, 19, 35, 36, 55, 196, 197, 211,

243, 244, 245, 255, 354, 415, 497; see
    also Epicureanism in Index of Topics
Luther, Martin, 343, 552
Lyttelton, Lord, 273, 396-398, 515, 526,
    528

Macaulay, G. C., 459, 460, 514, 526
Macaulay, Rose, 541, 563
McGiffert, A. C., 542, 544, 550, 552
Mack, Maynard, xi, 498
Macpherson, James, 482
Malebranche, Nicolas, 108, 563
Mallet, David, 189, 273, 361, 364, 372, 441,
    448, 453-457, 460, 485, 515, 519
Mandeville, Bernard, 23-25, 183, 185, 497,
    507, 562
Marcus Aurelius, 405
Marlborough, Duke of, 13, 74, 77, 158, 195,
    225, 368, 447
Martial, 381, 433
Martin, Burns, 433, 434
Marvell, Andrew, 383
Mary II, 9, 51, 77, 113, 114, 170, 174, 266
Masefield, John, 483
Maynwaring, Arthur, 79-81, 261
Mayo, T. F., 35, 192, 196, 570
Meston, William, 50-52
Miller, James, 363
Milton, John, contemporary opinions of, 55,
    72, 112, 144, 162, 172, 220, 301, 327,
    340, 356, 364, 366, 370, 380, 390, 514,
    516
    influence of, 15, 61, 84, 119, 135, 138,
    161, 163, 168, 184, 187, 195, 207, 231,
    235, 252, 289, 301, 310, 343, 352, 356,
    370, 375, 377, 389, 397, 400, 401, 402,
    406, 436, 438, 441, 445, 446, 453, 511,
    515, 540
Mitchell, Joseph, 276, 412-420
Monck, Mary, 5-6, 20
Monk, S. H., 206
Montagu, Charles, Earl of Halifax, 3, 16,
    20, 38, 59
Montagu, Lady Mary Wortley, 6-8, 20, 21
Moore, C. A., 88, 90, 257, 258, 273, 383,
    524, 525, 526, 530
More, Henry, 108, 152, 563-567 passim,
    569
More, Paul Elmer, 104
More, Saint Thomas, 406, 467
Morel, Léon, 30, 510, 514, 515, 516, 522
Morrice, Bezaleel, 16-17, 20, 21
Moses, 99, 127, 242, 251, 341, 392, 416,
    516

Mossner, E. C., 88
Muggleton, Lodowick, 89; see also Muggletonians in Index of Topics
Murdoch, Patrick, 398, 531

Nayler, James, 89
Needler, Henry, 254-259, 260, 262, 393, 481, 512, 567
Nelson, Robert, 116
Newton, Isaac, 30, 38, 152, 183, 315, 317, 320, 353, 410, 453, 460, 465, 484, 515, 524
    contemporary allusions to, 251, 272, 277, 316, 325, 327, 354, 356, 357, 358, 378, 379, 382, 391, 435, 451, 455, 479, 496, 497, 505; see also Newtonianism in Index of Topics
Newton, John, 389
Niclaes, Henry, 548
Nicol, Alexander, 336-340
Nicolson, Marjorie, 557
Norris, John, 90, 106-112, 116, 131, 206, 209, 210, 211, 212, 243, 246, 251, 252, 255, 258, 449, 567, 569
Novalis, 561, 575
Nugent, Robert, 466-472, 479, 485

Oglethorpe, James, 300, 301, 432
Oldham, John, 10, 65
Oldmixon, John, 16, 20, 79, 80, 382
Ovid, 12, 16, 19, 220, 222, 226, 368, 439, 440, 494
Oxford, Lord: see Harley, Robert

Pack, Richardson, 221-224, 227, 261
Paget, Thomas Catesby, 268-270
Parnell, Thomas, 231-236, 241, 245, 253, 260, 261, 403, 462
Pascal, Blaise, 14, 117, 166, 168, 171, 504, 509
"Paston, George" [E. M. Symonds], 7, 220, 488, 491, 493, 500, 509
Pattison, William, 362, 438-441
Paul, Saint, 30, 276, 398
Paul, H. G., 188, 189, 210, 448
Percy, Thomas, 209
Perdeck, A. A., 537, 539
Peter, Saint, 101
Philips, Ambrose, 162, 196, 246, 260, 262, 329, 383, 471
Philips, John, 161-162, 178, 207, 210, 220, 367, 419, 515
Pilkington, Lætitia, 378-381
Pilkington, Matthew, 379, 381-382

Pindar, 145, 251, 340
Pitt, Christopher, 343-344
Plato, 111, 120, 205, 243, 244, 307, 384, 399, 467, 540, 570; see also Platonism and Neo-Platonism in Index of Topics
Pomfret, John, 142, 169-172, 211, 338, 427, 463
Pope, Alexander, 14, 15, 21, 30, 60, 134, 166, 168, 173, 189, 201, 208, 220, 228, 229, 249, 268, 329, 366, 368, 416, 450
    contemporary opinions of, 370, 372, 376, 390, 403
    influence of, 139, 269, 276, 315, 322, 327, 333, 335, 346, 383, 384, 398, 399, 400, 401, 406, 439, 460, 461, 480, 491
    religion of, 345, 403, 488-509, 512, 514, 519, 520, 522, 530, 531, 558
Potter, G. R., 464, 481, 518
Pretender, the: see Stuart, James Francis Edward
Price, L. M., 375
Prior, Matthew, 16, 23, 32-40, 72, 87, 134, 167, 212, 220, 225, 268, 269, 279, 334, 375, 399, 402, 404, 412, 439, 464
Pulteney, William, 466, 467, 469, 472
Pythagoras, 19, 433, 480, 518, 530, 561

Quarles, Francis, 77, 115, 274, 535

Rabelais, 222, 531
Racine, Jean, 131
Racine, Louis, 509
Ralph, James, 372-373
Ramsay, Allan, 336, 377, 413, 416, 433-435, 436
Rapin, René, 162
Rawson, Mr., 118
Reed, A. L., 535
Relph, Josiah, 365-366
Reynolds, John, 151-153, 208, 210
Reynolds, Myra, 5, 237
Riccaltoun, Robert, 510
Richardson, Samuel, 261, 448
Robertson, J. L., 513
Roche, Mr., of Kings College, 362-363, 440, 446
Rochester, Earl of, 65, 72
Rossetti, Dante Gabriel, 223
Rousseau, Jean-Jacques, 68, 503, 546, 549
Rowe, Elizabeth Singer, 128, 134-140, 155, 206, 207, 208, 209, 210, 212, 234, 237,

Rowe, Elizabeth Singer (*Continued*)
  250, 253, 293, 294, 295, 384, 426, 494,
  515
Rowe, Nicholas, 163-164, 208, 209, 214,
  253, 463
Rowe, Thomas, 134, 138, 140, 155
Rundle, Thomas, 29, 30, 457, 515

Sacheverell, Henry, 4, 13, 41, 48, 59, 75,
  79, 83, 84, 89, 96, 118, 183, 223,
  419, 573
Saint-Pierre, Bernardin de, 394
Saltmarsh, John, 548, 555
Sancroft, William, 57, 58, 60
Savage, Richard, 208, 372, 441, 448, 457-
  462, 485, 491
Say, Samuel, 144-146, 206, 207
Schöffler, Herbert, 168, 421, 424, 537, 538
Scurr, Helen M., 475, 479, 480, 482
Segar, Mary, 493
Seneca, 18, 244, 245, 311; *see also* Stoicism
  in Index of Topics
Settle, Elkanah, 61-64, 497
Sewell, George, 161, 164-165, 207, 208
Shaftesbury, Earl of, 23, 110, 190, 237, 393,
  422, 451, 465, 498, 507, 514, 562
  indebtedness of, to the Cambridge Pla-
    tonists, 108, 480, 569
  influence of, on eighteenth-century senti-
    mentalism, 257, 258, 259, 262, 266,
    383, 394, 395, 444, 460, 469, 472, 475,
    480, 481, 512, 513, 514, 521, 524, 525,
    526, 530, 553, 569, 570, 574
Shakespeare, 12, 21, 207, 208, 220, 364,
  426, 436, 445, 511, 514
Sharp, John, 30
Sheffield, John, Duke of Buckingham, 3-4,
  20, 297
Shelley, Percy Bysshe, 92, 205, 228, 503
Shenstone, William, 208, 377, 397
Sherburn, George, xi, 494, 495, 501, 502,
  507, 509
Sherlock, William, 44, 84, 120, 171, 267
Sherwood, Elizabeth, xi
Shippen, William, 60-61
Shirley, James, 5
Sichel, Walter, 3, 14, 42
Sickels, Eleanor, 426, 535
Sidney, Algernon, 78, 467
Silvester, Tipping, 265
Smart, Christopher, 239
Smith, Edmund, 161, 177, 178-179, 207,
  367
Smollett, Tobias, 397, 466

Sokol, A. E., 543
Solomon, 99, 138, 139, 225, 276, 285
Somerville, William, 376-378
South, Robert, 171, 299, 300
Southey, Robert, 12, 178, 412
Spence, Joseph, 373, 375, 494, 508
Spenser, Edmund, 112, 194, 195, 207, 208,
  225, 228, 247, 249, 301, 305, 343, 353,
  364, 389, 390, 412, 434, 436, 438, 439,
  445, 511, 514, 531, 567
Spinoza, Baruch, 55, 500, 509, 553
Sprat, Thomas, 13-14, 20, 353
Steele, Richard, 71, 121, 216, 229, 253, 261,
  364, 383, 418, 494, 495, 502
Stepney, George, 16
Sterne, Laurence, 261, 465
Stevenson, Lionel, 475
Stevenson, S. W., 495
Stillingfleet, Edward, 78, 243, 262
Stogdon, Hubert, 290-295
Stuart, James Francis Edward, "the Old
  Pretender," 26, 27, 42, 50, 52, 61, 63,
  95, 247; *see also* Jacobitism *in* Index of
  Topics
Surrey, Earl of, 208
Swift, Jonathan, ix, 7, 13, 23, 26-32, 57-60,
  228, 229, 231, 279, 327, 329, 334, 378,
  457, 489, 496

Tasso, 15, 86, 184, 187, 207
Tate, Nahum, 163, 174-178, 179, 193, 213
Tawney, R. H., 543
Temple, Sir William, 27
Tenison, Thomas, 90
Tennyson, 115, 318, 452
Thanet, Earl of, 330, 331, 438
Thomas à Kempis, 307, 316, 494
Thomson, James, 301, 372, 377, 378, 400,
  407, 454
  contemporary opinions of, 30, 209, 384,
    389, 460
  in personal relationships, 189, 208, 361,
    364, 397, 441, 448, 459, 515, 519,
    526, 528
  religion of, 194, 257, 273, 312, 455, 480,
    481, 509-534, 539, 549
Tibullus, 222, 352, 361
Tickell, R. E., 247
Tickell, Thomas, 247-249, 260, 262, 329,
  383
Tillotson, John, 42, 65, 79, 114, 175, 178,
  179, 183, 243, 245, 262, 382, 403,
  453, 484, 571
Tindal, Matthew, 55, 433, 497, 498

Toland, John, 7, 58, 61, 71, 88, 91-92, 157, 217, 237, 341, 497, 498, 556
Tollett, Elizabeth, 315-320
Traherne, Thomas, 537, 567, 568, 569
Trevelyan, G. M., 26, 41, 282
Troeltsch, E., 543
Tryon, Thomas, 554
Tulloch, John, 564, 565, 566
Tunstall, William, 155-156, 202
Tupper, Martin Farquhar, 267
Tutchin, John, 64-66

Vaughan, Henry, 108, 537, 567, 568
Victor, Benjamin, 364
Vida, 343, 494
Vincent, H. P., 10
Virgil, 15, 161, 187, 195, 207, 247, 343, 356, 372, 376, 389, 454, 494, 497, 498, 511, 513, 514, 515, 516, 517
Voltaire, 32, 250, 276, 491

Wakeman, H. O., 95, 545
Waldron, George, 158-161, 214
Waller, Edmund, 5, 20, 78, 222, 364, 390, 399, 400, 436, 439
Walpole, Horace, 268, 397, 402
Walpole, Robert, 280, 341, 347, 354, 355, 359, 364, 389, 402, 403, 413, 415, 416, 418, 420, 459, 572
Walsh, William, 15, 519
Walton, Izaak, 389
Walwyn, William, 537, 556
Warburton, William, 496, 498, 500, 508, 509
Ward, Edward, 45-49, 52, 261
Warton, Joseph, 397, 444
Warton, Thomas, the elder, 444-447
Watts, Isaac, 154, 207, 209, 210, 213, 294, 295, 390
    in connection with theory of divine poetry, 127-131, 140, 141, 142, 188, 189, 192, 206, 417, 418, 433, 516, 517, 528, 540
    in personal relationships, 134, 144, 151, 208, 250, 253, 285, 415, 424, 425

religion of, 120-134, 234, 324, 418, 448, 534
Weber, M., 543
Webster, John, 426
Wedel, T. O., 557
Welsted, Leonard, 366-369, 383
Wesley, John, 112, 116, 386
Wesley, Samuel, the elder, 112-116, 175, 207
Wesley, Samuel, the younger, 116, 295-302
West, Gilbert, 398
Whaley, John, 402-404
Whelan, Sister M. Kevin, 537
Whichcote, Benjamin, 563, 569
Whiston, William, 30, 83
White, Helen C., 547
Whitefield, George, 208, 287, 434, 496
Whiting, G. W., 163
Whitney, Lois B., 213, 395, 526, 558
Willey, Basil, 541, 559
William III, 17, 26, 51, 52, 57, 65, 66, 75, 77, 78, 79, 113, 170, 184, 189, 195, 246, 325, 403, 457, 529
Williams, Harold, 30, 32, 57
Willoughby, E. E., 444
Wilson, Thomas, 309
Winchilsea, Anne Finch, Countess of, 214, 236-241, 245, 260, 323
Winstanley, John, 279
Wollaston, William, 325, 359
Wood, F. T., 386, 389
Woolston, Thomas, 28, 497
Wordsworth, William, 33, 205, 235, 236, 241, 365, 567, 568, 575
Wright E. H., xi
Wright, L. M., 146, 549
Wright, Thomas, 126, 130, 138
Wycherley, William, 9-12, 222, 519

Yalden, Thomas, 172-174, 207, 212
Young, Edward, ix, 127, 170, 173, 201, 206, 213, 247, 275, 291, 293, 294, 295, 343, 364, 370, 371, 390, 399, 405, 407, 409, 425, 445, 446, 448, 460, 500

INDEX OF TOPICS

Activity, cult of, 9, 113, 185, 186, 270, 334, 397, 406, 407, 428, 430, 431, 442, 451, 485, 486, 526, 527, 530, 531, 532, 533, 542, 549

Altruism, 92, 396, 467, 506, 533, 562; see also Benevolism

Ancients and Moderns, quarrel of the, 192, 218

Angels, 78, 79, 98, 102, 111, 113, 119, 153, 168, 193, 195, 238, 292, 300, 313, 387, 392, 462, 518, 532

Anglicanism, 95, 98, 104, 154, 202, 203, 314, 322, 339, 340, 342, 359, 421, 422, 436, 483, 514, 538, 557, 558, 559, 563; see also Church of England

Anglo-Catholicism xi, 57, 88, 95, 98-106 passim, 154, 156, 234, 235, 260, 309, 310, 321, 489, 539, 540, 544, 545, 548, 557, 563; see also High Church; Nonjurors

Anima Mundi: see Nature, spirit of

Anticlericalism, 8, 9, 11, 14, 24, 28, 31, 65, 86, 87, 88, 96, 147, 183, 222, 223, 226, 228, 276, 347, 348, 367, 467, 490, 491, 492, 530

Anti-intellectualism, 8, 9, 171, 214, 311, 334, 378, 410, 471, 475, 479, 503, 504

Antinomianism, 48, 104, 130, 283, 284, 285, 549, 550, 554, 555

Anti-sentimentalism, 15, 25, 29, 240, 266, 301, 504, 505, 507

Apostles, the, 99, 101, 238, 304, 557

Arianism, 29, 30, 44, 83, 123, 200, 201, 268, 290, 298, 457, 497, 515

Arminianism, 33, 104, 234, 322, 544, 545, 546

Atheism, actual or imputed, 10, 34, 42, 44, 55, 65, 68, 100, 115, 119, 191, 196, 201, 238, 299, 311, 330, 374, 394, 409, 446, 492, 497, 500, 513

Atomism, 20, 35, 36, 166, 196, 198, 311

Atonement, 64, 104, 160, 284, 292, 301, 319, 411, 499, 551, 572; see also Redemption; Salvation

Authority, ecclesiastical, 26, 74, 82, 83, 86, 96, 97, 101, 343, 347, 350, 452, 467, 491, 499, 508, 509, 542, 547, 556, 557

Baconianism: see Reason, experimental; also Bacon in Index of Names

Ballads and folk-lyrics, 208, 209, 246, 247, 365, 434, 436, 439, 445, 448, 453, 463

Bangorian Controversy, 42, 53, 85, 457; see also Hoadly in Index of Names

Baptism, 25, 26, 89, 290, 488

Baptists, 83, 89, 143, 154, 554

Beauty, religiously regarded, 110, 111, 137, 255, 256, 313, 352, 353, 392, 393, 394, 395, 452, 455, 460, 472, 473, 476, 477, 478, 480, 482, 483, 512, 514, 517, 561, 570

Benevolence, universal, 467, 468, 470, 485, 486, 499-509 passim, 514, 520, 521, 525, 527, 530, 545, 550, 555, 556, 571, 574; see also Benevolism

Benevolism, 112, 144, 216, 266, 278, 328, 329, 331, 363, 377, 379, 396, 397, 427, 428, 432, 472, 475, 476, 485, 519, 521, 522, 536; see also Altruism; Benevolence, universal; Charity; Humanitarianism; Sensibility; Service; "Social"

Bible, the, and Protestantism, 83, 84, 86, 147, 547, 548, 552

use of, in poetry: New Testament, 107, 112, 113, 115, 116, 285, 303, 319, 405, 507, 523 (see also Jesus Christ, earthly life of); Old Testament (omitting many psalm-paraphrases), 41, 61, 81, 87, 115, 117, 141, 148, 179, 180, 183, 193, 194, 225, 232, 285, 304, 319, 320, 343, 346, 374, 375, 415, 433, 446, 449, 450, 492, 494, 512, 523 (see also Christian epic; Poetry, divine)

theological views and implications concerning, 30, 63, 64, 83, 100, 138, 139, 167, 200, 242, 251, 299, 300, 317, 328, 331, 342, 347, 380, 392, 393, 435, 516, 549, 559, 568

Bishops, 28, 30, 50, 53, 56, 57, 58, 64, 65, 72, 86, 87, 101, 106, 299, 300, 353, 365, 491, 500, 559

Blank verse, 135, 168, 209, 221, 372, 375, 450, 454, 460; *see also* Milton, influence of, *in* Index of Names

Blasphemy: *see* Compliments, blasphemous

Bourgeois: *see* Middle class

Calvinism, 33, 34, 36, 37, 38, 123, 125, 127, 129, 282, 285, 286, 290, 338, 339, 431, 509, 510, 511, 512, 513, 527, 534, 544, 545, 546; *see also* Antinomianism; Depravity, total; Election; Kirk of Scotland; "Legal" principles; Melancholy, related to Calvinism; Predestination; Presbyterianism

Cambridge Platonists, 108, 245, 256, 258, 259, 479, 480, 559, 563-567, 568, 569, 570, 571

Cambridge University, 172, 563

Capitalism, 442, 535, 542, 543; *see also* Commerce and industry

Cartesianism: *see* Descartes *in* Index of Names

Catholic religion: *see* Christianity

Catholicism, Anglican: *see* Anglo-Catholicism

Catholicism, Roman, 95, 101, 102, 104, 234, 483, 488-494 *passim*, 499, 501, 502, 509, 575
  associated with bigotry, superstition, priestcraft, papal authority, etc., 12, 13, 43, 44, 61, 63, 82, 84, 85, 86, 88, 92, 159, 164, 193, 195, 227, 248, 298, 299, 341, 347, 367, 429, 467, 490, 491, 529; *see also* Middle Ages; Monasticism
  associated with political despotism, 17, 55, 65, 82, 158, 164, 195, 529
  poets connected with, 3, 10, 14, 92, 156, 202, 309, 457, 466, 470, 483, 488, 490
  sympathetic allusions to, 27, 107, 306, 309, 321, 406, 509
  use of fideism in its apologetics, 10, 558

Chain of Being, 278, 333, 409, 464, 465, 473, 499, 502, 504, 505, 507, 518, 520, 540, 541; *see also* Diversitarianism; Plenitude; Uniformitarianism

Chance, philosophy of, 10, 35, 36, 38, 65, 125, 198, 224, 257, 270, 317, 318, 330, 393, 468

Charity, 24, 46, 56, 85, 102, 186, 299, 300, 330, 339, 345, 437, 449, 475, 499, 501, 521; *see also* Benevolism

Christian epic, 15, 112, 131, 148, 156, 184, 192, 449

Christian Rationalism: *see* Latitudinarianism

Christianity, 324, 325, 343, 345, 392, 405, 411, 412, 422, 445, 452, 468, 470, 475, 479, 488, 489, 495, 496, 501, 502, 505, 509, 543, 544, 575, 576; *see also* Anglicanism; Anglo-Catholicism; Catholicism, Roman; Jesus Christ; Protestantism
  decay of its emotional and imaginative aspects, 265, 302, 346, 360, 376, 383, 390, 398, 421, 423, 435, 438, 447, 451, 484, 571, 573, 574
  distinguished from sentimentalism, 219, 220, 232, 236, 240, 330, 331, 386, 429, 432, 443, 486, 499, 513, 523, 524, 535, 545, 548, 551, 552, 556, 567, 568, 571, 573
  emphasis of, on the supernatural, 319, 320, 331, 557, 567
  preserves romantic elements in poetry, 218, 219
  primitive, 53, 83, 100, 101, 102, 499, 500

Church of England, barren of emotion and imagination, 260
  blest in its clergy, 242
  Catholic, 102, 310
  conservative political institution, 20, 26, 29, 49, 55, 95, 96
  crippled by secession of Nonjurors, 106
  Erastian, 57, 58, 94, 95, 100
  friendly to new science, 38
  grounded on law, 185, 279
  lack of spiritual feeling toward, 20, 27, 43
  moderate, 43, 185, 376
  orthodox, 305
  Protestant, 54, 89, 96, 422, 484
  reasonable, 13
  respectable socially, 121
  shuns superstitious fears, 185
  the Tillotsonian ideal, 114
  withered matron, 277; *see also* Anglo-Catholicism; High Church; Low Church

Clergyman, the good, descriptions of, 24, 30, 57, 58, 90, 114, 144, 223, 224, 298, 299, 344, 345, 458

Clerical life, illustrations of, 11, 12, 16, 24, 27, 31, 33, 60, 72, 106, 120, 172, 225, 274, 343, 356, 365, 373, 398, 408, 443, 464, 500, 514; *see also* Clergyman, the good

Commerce and industry, glorification of, 96, 121, 160, 185, 186, 218, 273, 321, 325, 364, 367, 368, 383, 395, 440, 441, 442, 459, 526, 542; *see also* Capitalism

Common sense, 6, 10, 43, 54, 69, 75, 96, 169, 180, 190, 204, 269, 350, 363, 474, 514, 558, 572

Compliments, blasphemous, 4, 9, 16, 18, 62, 65, 77, 78, 79, 120, 180, 341, 375, 496, 505

Compromise, the eighteenth-century, 23, 38, 62, 96, 121, 122, 204, 249, 279, 282, 298, 347, 351, 358, 359, 360, 371, 458, 470, 491, 492, 494, 502, 571, 572, 573

Congregationalists: *see* Independents

Conscience, 7, 48, 68, 69, 70, 74, 76, 86, 97, 159, 165, 260, 338, 367, 508, 556; *see also* Inner Light; Moral sense; Natural goodness

Contemplation, 104, 109, 110, 143, 162, 181, 187, 191, 212, 230, 240, 252, 255, 273, 292, 349, 352, 375, 379, 380, 381, 385, 400, 401, 427, 436, 437, 438, 439, 443, 446, 461, 476, 486, 512, 513, 517, 518, 525, 526, 527, 542, 549, 574

Copernican system: *see* Copernicus *in* Index of Names

Creeds and dogmas, attitude toward, 54, 59, 67, 86, 102, 105, 117, 179, 271, 277, 319, 339, 348, 396, 450, 452, 467, 472, 488, 499, 501, 508, 528, 546

Crucifixion, 70, 75, 107, 113, 142, 178, 179, 255, 301, 319, 343, 446, 512, 551

Cynicism, 9, 15, 24, 26, 31, 34, 40, 231, 269, 270, 349, 370, 418, 504, 507, 562

Cyrenaicism: *see* Epicureanism

Damnation, 32, 150, 290, 337, 343, 545: *see also* Hell; Judgment Day

Day of Judgment: *see* Judgment Day

Declaration of Indulgence, 44, 298

Deism, 96, 197, 267, 372, 422, 465, 479, 483, 485, 499, 514, 557, 558, 574, 576
    attacked, 55, 71, 119, 153, 157, 196, 200, 201, 265, 299, 468, 470, 471, 497, 498, 500
    ideas of its champions, 19, 23, 90, 91, 92, 271, 272, 276, 281, 373, 444, 451, 452, 453, 456, 500, 501, 502, 508, 530, 540, 541
    related to neoclassicism, 540
    related to sentimentalism, 23, 209, 273, 453, 486, 524, 534

Depravity, total, 127, 129, 166, 284, 290,

336, 542, 544, 545, 547, 556, 560

Design, argument from: *see* Teleological arguments

Determinism, 36, 37, 38, 39, 40, 125, 166, 196, 198, 199, 200, 269, 318, 500, 506, 507

Disillusionment: *see* Melancholy of sceptical disillusionment

Dissent: *see* Nonconformity

Diversitarianism, 59, 110, 362, 392, 444, 452, 453, 477, 478, 485, 486, 495, 517, 520, 540

Divine right of kings, 46, 52, 66, 68, 69, 81, 86, 95, 248, 299, 300, 467, 497, 557

Druids, 15, 55, 256, 517

Easter, 239, 341, 551

Election, 129, 289, 300, 337, 534, 536, 542, 543, 545, 546; *see also* Predestination

Empiricism, 14, 16, 24, 96, 179, 480, 505, 558

Energy, cult of: *see* Activity, cult of

Enlightenment, 218, 510, 537, 538, 546, 558

Enthusiasm, 150, 183, 187, 188, 190, 204, 283, 360, 418, 510, 518, 537, 548, 554, 558, 562, 570
    in poetry, 99, 107, 187, 188, 193, 201, 205, 210, 217, 218, 312, 370, 416, 450, 517, 518
    in religion, reprehended or satirized, 10, 13, 22, 26, 55, 60, 96, 109, 114, 122, 218, 228, 271, 326, 340, 350, 382, 434, 437, 451, 458, 496
    true and false, distinguished, 192, 201, 306, 566, 567, 569

Epic, Christian: *see* Christian Epic

Epicureanism, 19, 35, 36, 37, 38, 171, 174, 191, 196, 197, 198, 201, 224, 242, 243, 261, 311, 355, 359, 369, 371, 471, 497, 498, 522, 531, 555

Episcopacy: *see* Bishops

Episcopalianism: *see* Church of England

Eroticism, religious, 77, 132, 137, 138, 139, 233, 234, 555

Eucharist, Holy, 4, 10, 26, 44, 49, 74, 76, 89, 104, 105, 133, 159, 165, 304, 308, 321, 341, 342, 488, 509, 514, 557

Evangelicalism, 208, 287, 326, 327, 359, 389, 390, 398, 482, 545, 576

Evil, problem of, 238, 337, 521

Evolution, spiritual, 518, 520, 532, 533

Faith, 13, 26, 32, 86, 102, 104, 114, 164, 165, 183, 204, 276, 280, 283, 317, 331,

Faith (Continued)
335, 409, 420, 437, 451, 458, 470, 501
Fall of man, 186, 191, 219, 289, 310, 311,
318, 341, 469, 486
Familists, 548, 550, 554
Fancy: see Imagination
Fatalism: see Determinism
Fathers, Church, 83, 100, 156, 299, 303, 307
Fideism, 10, 14, 33, 168, 199, 558
Freedom: see Liberty
Freemasonry, 278, 279, 338, 356, 458, 459,
515
Freethinking, 3, 38, 41, 87, 115, 237, 246,
331, 433, 458, 491, 501
Free will, 36, 38, 40, 167, 269, 318, 411,
471, 506, 508
French Prophets, the, 451, 554
Friends, Society of: see Quakerism
Friendship, 118, 138, 244, 246, 320, 328,
332, 333, 334, 380, 411, 436, 496, 528
Funeral elegies, 63, 90, 170, 213, 235, 286,
424, 426, 535

Genius, 28, 30, 128, 129, 158, 193, 205,
218, 335, 358, 404, 416-420 passim,
450, 463, 472, 473, 486, 497, 516, 517,
518, 528, 535, 568
God: see also Grace; Holy Spirit; Immanence; Jesus Christ; Nature, God of;
Providence; Revelation, natural; Revelation, supernatural; Transcendence;
Trinity, Holy
angry, 125, 292, 324, 512
answer, the only, to the riddles of nature,
197, 198
Architect, 331, 357, 358, 392, 477
Artificer, 242
attributes of, 27, 169, 255, 337, 390, 409
author of all natural processes, 255, 374
best of all possible worlds, formed the,
505
beyond human thought, 4, 39, 124, 252,
351, 410, 452, 453, 479, 504, 530
cheerful, 271
created universe by copying eternal types,
468
creates through an act of imagination,
110, 473, 477, 479, 485, 518
creates unceasingly, 392
Creator, 199, 229, 230, 255, 273 (and
frequently elsewhere)
deceives us never, 474
dwells within heart and mind, 92, 97,
217, 477, 504, 545, 553

father of mankind, 148, 167, 409, 456,
507
father of universe, 465, 496
fearsome, 7, 249
First Cause, 23, 62, 508, 564
forms of worship, uninterested in, 80, 238,
279
Freemason, the first, 338
Friday abstinence, uninterested in, 31
friend, the only perfect, 118, 409, 477
Geometrician, 477
good-natured, 10, 431, 521
Goodness, Truth, Beauty, 111, 145, 406,
456, 477, 520, 523
happiness, His wish for all His creatures,
8, 465, 518
happiness, only true source of, 470, 477
happiness, origin and end of, 381
hears our prayers, 181
Infinite Perfection, 259
insatiable, wants man to be, 540
Invisible, the Great, 444
just in punishment, 330, 337, 411, 512
King of kings, 111, 142, 296
His laws easily understood, 466
liberty, supports man's desire for, 69
limited monarch, 358
Love, 63, 111, 512, 529
loves the poor, 377
loving, 104, 126, 127, 152, 232, 243, 297,
337, 351, 411, 452, 486, 503
mechanic, celestial, 124
merciful, 101, 292, 322, 337, 351
Mind, Eternal, 157, 255, 257, 346, 410,
476, 477
His mind embraces the perfect ideas, 108
His mind includes the universe, 410, 477
name, answers to any, 508
nature, gives us the beauties of, 387
the One, 476, 478, 479, 497
order of nature, a personification of the,
395
Palladian churches, hard to find in, 183
of Peace, 297, 322
a poet, 14, 473, 477, 486
prayer, uninterested in, 18, 271, 530
purposeless never, 474
reasonable, 92, 271, 443
scorns stupid bigots, 32
Soul of the universe, 410, 502, 523, 532
source of being, 277, 317, 333, 409, 425,
478, 497, 519, 523, 530
space, identified with, 565
supports all His creatures, 375

Supreme Being, 271, 412, 452
surprised at His own handiwork, 173
tests us through adversity, 238, 324, 335
tithes, wants us to pay, 162
truth, gives us power to know, 474
variety, enjoys, 102
Whigs, fond of, 78, 79
Will, creative, 378
wisdom, source of, 243
works through natural laws, 68, 382
works through the passions as well as the reason, 504
Gothicism: see Horror-romanticism
Grace, 48, 67, 104, 105, 131, 147, 175, 234, 283, 284, 285, 286, 289, 290, 292, 300, 337, 349, 508, 544, 545, 546, 567, 568; see also Arminianism; Calvinism; "Legal" principles
Graveyardism: see Melancholy of graveyardism
Gravitation, 37, 38, 152, 277, 278, 391, 455, 521, 530

Hanover, House of, bulwark of Protestantism, 16, 62, 122, 157, 158, 159, 164, 225, 248, 341, 367
Happiness, 34, 69, 163, 167, 214, 243, 269, 330, 338, 427, 465, 477, 478, 532
depends on benevolism, 165, 377, 383, 428, 521
depends on religion, 297, 306, 311, 381, 469, 470, 494, 512, 523, 532
depends on virtue, 8, 335 395, 436, 445, 470, 507, 531
Harmony, universal, 8, 110, 219, 255, 258, 381, 393, 394, 395, 396, 417, 443, 444, 446, 455, 462, 468, 469, 472, 473, 476, 477, 480, 486, 495, 512, 519, 521, 525, 530, 561, 564, 565, 570, 574
Health, physical, 463, 532, 533
Heaven, traditional, 57, 92, 103, 125, 127, 164, 170, 240, 248, 312, 313, 344, 380, 414, 508
unusual varieties, 58, 77, 78, 79, 90, 110, 113, 137, 138, 165, 245, 368, 381, 382, 384, 403, 405, 406
Hell, 29, 32, 73, 90, 92, 120, 123, 125, 135, 170, 324, 405, 411, 433, 508, 512
Hermetism, 568
High Church views and policies, 3, 5, 13, 42, 44-61 passim, 95, 100, 121, 122, 173, 203, 237, 259, 260, 295-310 passim, 359, 447, 483, 489, 573; see also Anglo-Catholicism; Apostles; Arminianism; Authority, ecclesiastical; Bishops; Divine right of kings; Eucharist, Holy; Fathers, Church; Jacobitism; Non-resistance; Occasional Conformity; Ritual and ceremonial; Toryism
attacked, 15, 17, 42, 61-92 passim, 223, 224, 299, 497
Holy Spirit, 29, 72, 101, 123, 157, 309, 319, 349, 451, 548, 550, 551, 556, 559
Horror-romanticism, 321, 322, 389, 406, 425, 426, 439, 448
Huguenots, 82, 356, 358, 359
Humanitarianism, 46, 73, 165, 268, 347, 365, 372, 379, 389, 412, 459, 471, 475, 526; see also Benevolism; Charity; Sensibility; Service; "Social"
Hymnody, ix, 98, 131, 132, 140, 141
Hypocrisy, 10, 29, 59, 76, 86, 190, 224, 270, 275, 377, 402, 437, 529

Imagination, 13, 14, 35, 99, 180, 192, 203, 204, 205, 217, 249, 315, 409, 453, 454, 460, 510, 518, 519, 520, 525, 527, 531, 539, 560, 566, 574
Immanence, divine, 230, 316, 410, 473, 479, 518, 523, 524, 530, 546, 549, 550, 553, 561, 567, 568; see also Pantheism
Immortality, belief in, 6, 25, 128, 151, 163, 166, 223, 229, 239, 253, 308, 312, 313, 316, 318, 333, 345, 347, 376, 399, 414, 415, 427, 474, 494, 496, 500
scepticism concerning, 3, 5, 15, 18, 19, 243, 316, 373, 420, 501
Impiety and moral corruption of the age, 7, 10, 57, 58, 70, 71, 72, 73, 99, 119, 131, 177, 183, 189, 390, 448, 467; see also Reform
Incarnation, the, 70, 99, 102, 103, 232, 234, 433, 481, 486, 494, 499, 513, 548, 551
Independents, 50, 122, 123, 154, 557
Individualism, 96, 540, 543, 544, 547, 548, 556, 557, 559, 560, 561, 563, 572
Inner Light, the, 68, 69, 77, 89, 147, 148, 150, 171, 281, 349, 451, 486, 548, 549, 550, 551, 556, 558, 559, 560, 561, 562, 572
Intellectual School, 29, 497
Intuition, 221, 316, 318, 436, 519

Jacobitism, 4, 26, 50, 51, 52, 60, 61, 81, 82, 94, 160, 183, 247, 248, 309, 434, 435, 436, 447
Jesus Christ, earthly life of, 9, 18, 46, 57,

Jesus Christ (*Continued*)
    64, 75, 84, 103, 104, 112, 113, 176,
    188, 304, 311, 312, 362, 402, 403, 551;
    see also Crucifixion; Mary, the Virgin;
    Resurrection
theological views and implications, 62, 64,
    70, 75, 85, 95, 101, 102, 104, 105, 119,
    124, 127, 136, 142, 180, 200, 233, 284,
    286, 297, 304, 310, 312, 320, 345, 347,
    348, 369, 405, 425, 467, 470, 481, 499,
    500, 512, 513, 544, 548, 549, 551, 567,
    568; *see also* Atonement; Eucharist;
    Incarnation; Redemption; Salvation;
    Trinity, Holy
Jews, 59, 62, 70, 346
Judgment Day, 32, 103, 115, 119, 120, 126,
    131, 134, 135, 142, 161, 163, 169, 179,
    294, 319, 341, 411, 416, 428, 429, 446,
    449, 517

Kirk of Scotland, 282, 283, 413, 418, 419,
    424; *see also* Secession Church

Latitudinarianism, 29, 30, 53, 66, 69, 77,
    86, 111, 154, 159, 183, 185, 224, 279,
    325, 338, 339, 347, 348, 368, 422, 483,
    489, 499, 510, 571, 572; *see alos* Au-
    thority, ecclesiastical; Bishops; Compro-
    mise; Creeds and dogmas; Liberty;
    Moderation; Ritual and ceremonial;
    Sincerity; Superstition; Tolerance and
    toleration
lacking in emotional appeal, 245, 246,
    249, 254, 259, 383, 453, 484, 485
related to deism, 71, 78, 266, 350, 444,
    457, 458, 479, 484, 487, 491, 497, 501,
    505, 514, 528, 534, 539, 541
related to nonconformity and puritanism,
    69, 74, 84, 87, 89, 90, 122, 183, 189,
    253, 254, 262, 326, 359, 422, 435, 487,
    534, 539
related to sentimentalism, 216, 227, 242,
    260, 262, 346, 383, 435, 484, 487, 514,
    528, 534, 536, 571, 572, 574, 575
reprehended or satirized 42, 59, 60, 71,
    100, 102
"Legal" principles in theology, 127, 147,
    283, 284, 286, 555
Levellers, 122, 557
Libertinism, 3, 16, 18, 19, 25, 38, 44, 82,
    85, 174, 191, 197, 367, 440, 462, 511,
    512, 555; *see also* Sentimentalism, lib-
    ertine
Liberty, political and religious: *see also* Revolt

and atheism, 399
and Calvinism, 129, 546
and conscience, 367
and deism, 28, 91, 271
and latitudinarianism, 30, 368, 442, 443,
    529
and Nonconformity, 69, 75, 76, 80, 121
and "Patriot" party, 453, 454, 466, 469,
    528, 529
and Protestantism, 17, 84, 159, 164, 325,
    403, 429, 467
and puritanism, 540, 556
and science, 357
and sentimentalism, 372, 527, 530, 531
and Whiggery, 62, 66, 96, 155, 185, 186,
    261, 358, 440, 441, 457, 459
Loco-descriptive poetry: *see* Topographical
    poetry
Love, earthly, 6, 15, 17, 25, 137, 144, 145,
    150, 169, 214, 223, 225, 228, 267, 275,
    276, 291, 297, 323, 334, 371, 384, 389,
    397, 400, 403, 440, 448, 460, 495, 528,
    532
heavenly, 10, 85, 99, 104, 105, 106,
    109, 110, 111, 136, 137, 140, 142, 223,
    233, 234, 244, 286, 291, 292, 297, 304,
    313, 381, 384, 410, 414, 455, 530; *see
    also* Eroticism, religious
Low Church views and policies, 42, 61-92
    passim, 94, 160, 163, 178, 201, 544;
    see also Evangelicalism; Hanover, House
    of; Latitudinarianism; Methodism;
    Whiggery
attacked, 42, 44-61 *passim*, 299
related to latitudinarianism, 94, 183, 326,
    359, 484, 487, 539
related to nonconformity, 94, 121, 203,
    259, 260, 324, 359, 422, 484, 557
related to sentimentalism, 97, 262, 447
Lower classes, 48, 73, 75, 280, 304, 307,
    308, 336, 358, 400, 420, 483
Lyricism, serious, 193, 209, 228, 231, 232,
    237, 249, 250, 345, 349, 365, 388, 414,
    434, 436, 448, 475

Man of feeling: *see* Sensibility
Mary, the Virgin, 99, 102, 103, 107, 170,
    176, 178, 297, 304, 385, 446, 494
Materialism, 26, 37, 38, 153, 167, 198, 257,
    311, 354, 409, 471, 474, 476, 500, 561,
    562, 564; *see also* Atomism; Determin-
    ism; Mechanism
Mathematics, 23, 254, 256, 257, 258, 259,
    315, 357, 393, 404, 480, 498, 561

Mechanism, philosophy of, 19, 36, 38, 564; see also Determinism; Materialism

Medievalism, literary, 13, 21, 231, 234, 434, 445, 446, 453, 475

Melancholy, 212, 213, 218, 219, 240, 241, 247, 254, 321, 361, 390, 486, 542, 573
of enthusiasm, 270, 271, 349, 350, 431
of graveyardism, 212, 213, 231, 235, 389, 401, 424, 425, 426, 535
of pensive retirement, 136, 212, 231, 235, 362, 389, 400, 401, 406, 437, 441, 445, 446, 527, 535
of sceptical disillusionment, 7, 21, 35, 38, 173, 212
related to Calvinism, 38, 413, 414, 426, 431, 535, 542, 545, 546

Memento mori convention, 5, 163, 291, 324, 399, 405, 408, 441

Metaphysics, distaste for, 26, 27, 214, 350, 471, 497, 499, 530

Metempsychosis: see Transmigration of souls

Methodism, 287, 386, 475, 481, 537

Microscope, 162, 218, 255, 265, 391, 393, 435, 463, 561

Middle Ages, 86, 196, 303, 347, 429, 490, 505, 529, 544, 547, 561; see also Medievalism, literary

Middle class, 20, 33, 71, 96, 158, 171, 178, 183, 197, 201, 202, 203, 204, 205, 228, 231, 261, 262, 273, 280, 315, 326, 330, 358, 359, 420, 483, 484, 494, 509, 527, 536, 539, 541, 554, 558, 570, 571, 572, 574

Mind, the, 128, 129, 278, 333, 335, 354, 471, 474, 476, 504, 527, 561, 562, 564

Miracles, 28, 70, 125, 200, 277, 278, 298, 305, 452, 496

Missionary activities, 63, 64, 350, 371, 435

Mockery of piety and zeal: see Piety and zeal, satirized or sneered at

Moderation, 47, 61, 75, 79, 90, 93, 96, 101, 114, 175, 490

Monasticism, 11, 84, 92, 193, 321, 347, 490

Moral sense, 216, 271, 486, 508, 525, 556, 562, 565, 566; see also Conscience; Inner Light; Natural goodness

Morality, 4, 53, 297, 310, 311, 330, 331, 374, 452, 468, 471, 472, 498, 501, 530, 565; see also Virtue

Muggletonians 382, 554

Music, 27, 43, 106, 107, 141, 207, 249, 250, 363, 381, 387, 416, 417, 449

Mystery, religious: attitudes toward, 67, 83, 88, 96, 114, 124, 157, 179, 272, 276, 308, 347, 351, 450, 451, 458, 467, 472, 491, 492, 498, 530

Mysticism, 99, 110, 137, 140, 233, 438, 482, 518, 537, 548, 550, 551, 552, 553, 555, 566, 568

Mythology, classical, 5, 192, 193, 239, 296, 368, 381

Natural goodness of man, 69, 116, 166, 215, 216, 217, 219, 297, 417, 432, 485, 486, 507, 521, 534, 544-549 passim, 551, 554, 555, 556, 557, 560, 562, 565, 572, 574; see also Conscience; Inner Light; Moral sense

Natural religion: see Nature, religion of

Naturalism, sentimental, 8, 15, 217, 246, 273, 347, 365, 370, 415, 434, 445, 504, 526, 542; see also Nature and art; Primitivism; Rural life

Nature, and art, 112, 214, 301, 312, 336, 361, 364, 369, 370, 379, 403, 404, 412, 416, 432, 434, 445, 463, 475; see also Naturalism, sentimental; Primitivism
and reason, 13, 67, 68, 204, 260, 316, 394, 486, 541, 555, 556, 557, 560
god of, 161, 194, 261, 312, 317, 332, 391, 394, 397, 442, 454, 477, 485, 506, 508, 512, 513, 518, 523, 574; see also Revelation, natural
laws of, 10, 38, 46, 48, 62, 92, 159, 277, 325, 375, 377, 394, 395, 407, 475, 496, 499, 556, 558, 559, 560
plastic: see Nature, spirit of
religion of, 38, 70, 88, 123, 182, 200, 204, 316, 320, 454, 458, 460, 471, 499, 509, 540, 541, 561; see also Revelation, natural
rights of, 51, 69, 555, 556; see also Liberty; Revolt, spirit of political
"simple": see Naturalism, sentimental; Nature and art; Primitivism

Spirit of, 152, 255, 412, 438, 479, 482, 516, 526, 564, 565; see also Immanence; Pantheism

Nature (human), 206, 369, 492
as regarded by Christianity, 118, 126, 167, 289, 290, 327, 336, 425, 548, 552
regarded without religious or sentimental feeling, 24, 115, 269, 275, 367, 462

Nature (universal principles of virtue and right reason, lodged within the breast), 54, 67, 68, 69, 70, 97, 116, 171, 228, 382, 467, 474, 475, 476, 503, 549, 555, 556; see also Nature and reason

Nature (personified as a deity or monarch), 40, 68, 173, 174, 271, 522

Nature (scenery and natural objects), 21, 124, 136, 143, 147, 148, 181, 209, 210, 211, 225, 230, 231, 235, 236, 239, 240, 247, 250, 252, 256, 273, 294, 363, 366, 372, 375, 384, 389, 397, 412, 427, 434, 438, 439, 441, 445, 448, 453, 460, 475, 513, 514, 515, 517, 520; see also Rural life

Nature (state of happiness, innocence, and intuitive perception of truth), 69, 216, 370, 383, 388, 448, 503, 520; see also Naturalism, sentimental; Nature and reason; Primitivism

Nature (state of primitive strife and lawlessness), 51, 395

Nature (universe) as regarded by Christianity, 124, 125, 143, 194, 199, 210, 211, 218, 240, 288, 289, 301, 317, 378, 391, 411, 523, 553

  as regarded by contemporary science, with more or less admixture of religious feeling, 19, 67, 157, 272, 278, 344, 354, 357, 442, 454, 455, 496, 508; see also Newtonianism

  as regarded by sentimental religion, 161, 226, 229, 230, 332, 366, 394, 443, 456, 472, 479, 485, 498, 508, 513, 517, 518, 525, 526, 527, 533, 547, 568, 574

Necessity: see Determinism

Neoclassicism, 5, 21, 22, 117, 129, 131, 163, 189, 201, 202, 206, 209, 220, 232, 236, 295, 375, 434, 447, 473, 515, 536, 571

  an aristocratic tradition, 5, 9, 20, 33, 77, 93, 99, 202, 205, 222, 228, 231, 280, 344, 359, 366, 400, 436, 494, 558.

Neo-Platonism, 108, 110, 111, 154, 255, 262, 393, 479, 485, 514, 526, 550, 560, 561, 563-567 passim, 570; see also Cambridge Platonists; Platonism

Newtonianism, 38, 39, 124, 152, 182, 230, 252, 257, 258, 259, 262, 273, 317, 318, 319, 325, 332, 353-359 passim, 393, 422, 460, 464, 465, 478, 479, 480, 481, 495, 510, 514, 515, 524, 525, 526, 530, 541; see also Gravitation; Plurality of worlds; Revelation, natural; Science; Teleological arguments; also Newton in Index of Names

Nonconformity, 4, 32, 76, 120, 121, 122, 144, 154, 202, 203, 282-295 passim, 314, 422, 483, 502, 544, 557, 558; see also Enthusiasm; Independents; Latitu-

dinarianism; Low Church; Presbyterianism; Puritanism; Sects, Separatist

  attacked, 11, 13, 33, 44-61 passim, 121, 162, 228, 300, 353, 376, 377

  related to deism, 92, 359, 536

  related to sentimentalism, 430, 495

Nonjurors, 53, 57, 66, 79, 95, 98, 106, 156, 164, 236, 557

Non-resistance, 15, 61, 68, 75, 81, 95, 223, 248, 557

Obedience, passive: see Non-resistance

Occasional Conformity, 4, 58, 59, 60, 61, 74, 76, 80, 86, 91, 96, 122, 159, 279

Odes, pseudo-Pindaric, 8, 13, 27, 63, 108, 129, 132, 142, 156, 169, 209, 242, 249, 251, 288, 373, 447, 448, 449, 450

Optimism, 23, 312, 430, 431, 466, 477, 478, 486, 499, 503, 505, 506, 520, 521, 542, 546

Order: see Harmony universal; Uniformitarianism

Oxford University, 55, 85, 87, 300, 447

Painting and sculpture, 362, 385, 395, 402, 403, 404, 460, 461, 515

Pantheism, 92, 137, 210, 227, 257, 410, 479, 480, 498, 502, 507, 522, 523, 524, 526, 532, 534, 549-553 passim, 555, 564, 565, 568, 570; see also Nature, Spirit of

Passions, the, 327, 417, 463, 476, 503, 506; in relation to reason, 16, 114, 116, 126, 171, 186, 191, 194, 222, 242, 243, 269, 270, 335, 351, 395, 432, 506; see also Self-love

Pastoral poetry, 99, 134, 139, 162, 170, 180, 267, 365, 387, 512

"Patriot" party, 273, 343, 359, 420, 447, 453, 454, 466, 467, 480, 496, 497, 528

Patriotism, 266, 273, 364, 395, 396, 441, 457, 468, 516, 526, 527

Patristics: see Fathers, Church

Peace and war, 74, 96, 177, 185, 186, 247, 266, 321, 395, 400, 440, 441, 459, 462

Penitence and forgiveness, 100, 101, 127, 146, 181, 320, 322, 381, 390, 402, 488, 492, 509

Pessimism, 26, 168, 170, 173, 419, 464

Philadelphians, 89, 554

Piety and zeal, satirized or sneered at, 7, 10, 11, 226, 227, 228, 275, 331, 418, 419, 489, 492, 493; see also Wit

Platonism, 28, 108, 111, 130, 217, 242, 243, 246, 257, 317, 346, 361, 362, 468, 469,

Platonism (*Continued*)
477, 480, 481, 530, 540, 559; *see also*
Cambridge Platonists; Neo-Platonism
Plenitude of universe, 110, 277, 464, 478, 505
Plurality of worlds, 230, 252, 332, 348, 392, 393, 455, 460, 464, 478, 508
Poetry, corrupt state of, 16, 64, 72, 99, 130, 151, 177, 186, 190, 237, 250, 296, 390, 416, 433
divine, views concerning, 14, 17, 64, 99, 100, 112, 129, 130, 131, 140, 141, 154, 177, 182, 203, 204, 220, 232, 237, 250, 275, 287, 296, 374, 380, 390, 415, 417, 450, 517, 528, 539, 540; *see also* Christian epic
moral and religious nature and aims of, 16, 17, 64, 99, 112, 115, 118, 130, 141, 151, 175, 176, 177, 180, 184, 186-188, 191, 192, 194, 201, 204, 205, 206, 218, 229, 390, 416, 448, 450, 474, 516; *see also* Enthusiasm in poetry; Genius; Imagination; Sublimity
Positivism, 4, 7, 157, 351, 504, 506, 558
Pragmatism, 67, 96, 179, 451
Prayer, 11, 18, 26, 53, 181, 188, 232, 248, 267, 271, 304, 305, 306, 307, 362, 385, 449, 493, 496, 507, 508, 523
Preaching, 11, 42, 47, 90, 114, 175, 216, 260, 326, 343, 348, 449
Predestination, 34, 38, 40, 104, 123, 125, 127, 337, 431, 544, 546; *see also* Election
Pre-existence, 110, 168
Pre-romanticism, 21, 203, 205-262 *passim*, 280, 349, 359, 361-487 *passim*, 495, 509-534 *passim*, 538, 539, 575; *see also* Ballads and folk-lyrics; Blank verse; Horror-romanticism; Lyricism; Medievalism, literary; Melancholy; Nature; Romanticism; Sentimentalism
Presbyterianism, 17, 43, 50, 52, 59, 89, 122, 151, 154, 282, 283, 290, 299, 359, 377, 413, 434, 491, 510, 514, 548, 557; *see also* Calvinism; Kirk of Scotland
Primitivism, 7, 9, 31, 73, 213, 214, 215, 219, 350, 370, 371, 373, 375, 378, 383, 394, 395, 412, 432, 445, 448, 456, 459, 469, 475, 503, 526, 532, 542; *see also* Naturalism, sentimental; Nature and art; Rural life
Progress, 185, 206, 364, 368, 383, 395, 429, 459, 520, 522, 526, 540, 542
Protestantism, 53, 60, 69, 70, 84, 86, 90, 95, 104, 158, 159, 184, 194, 195, 203, 204, 218, 343, 429, 443, 539, 543, 551, 552, 563; *see also* Bible, the, and Protestantism; Calvinism; Capitalism; Hanover, House of; Individualism; Liberty; Low Church; Nonconformity; Puritanism; Reformation, Protestant
related to deism, latitudinarianism, and sentimentalism, xi, 97, 164, 248, 403, 534-576 *passim*.
Providence, 38, 196, 200, 229, 230, 237, 238, 240, 311, 341, 369, 436, 444, 500
Psalmody, ix, 41, 98, 140, 141, 175, 193
Psychology, contemporary viewpoints in, 170, 171, 188, 197, 269, 270, 333, 335, 354, 452, 506, 517, 518, 527, 528; *see also* Mind, the; Passions, the; Reason
Puritanism, moral and religious, 47, 69, 70, 71, 77, 134, 147, 176, 177, 178, 183, 193, 202, 218, 234, 261, 400, 424, 448, 531, 534, 536, 539, 551; *see also* Enthusiasm; Inner Light; Latitudinarianism; Nonconformity; Protestantism; Reform; Sects, Separatist
political and social, 41, 537, 540, 546, 547, 556; *see also* Liberty
related to Evangelicalism, 119, 123, 178, 537
related to sentimentalism, 254, 261, 262, 402, 448, 534-576 *passim*
Pyrrhonism: *see* Scepticism

Quakerism, 11, 89, 146-150 *passim*, 154, 211, 228, 300, 348, 349, 359, 536, 549, 550, 554, 559

Radicalism, political: *see* Revolt, spirit of political
Ranters, 122, 549, 554, 557
Rationalism, 23, 200, 201, 204, 218, 273, 282, 409, 479, 497, 510, 512, 514, 525, 526, 537, 540, 542, 544, 546, 547, 555-561 *passim*, 569
Reason, *see also* Anti-intellectualism; Common sense; Empiricism; Faith; Inner Light; Intuition; Mathematics; Metaphysics, distaste for; Mind; Nature and reason; Passions, the; Positivism; Pragmatism; Rationalism; Scepticism, Transcendentalism
avoids extremes, 277, 279
experimental, 277, 317, 357, 435, 519, 560, 561, 564, 566
faith, needs help of, to grasp religious

Reason (*Continued*)
 truths, 285, 310, 311, 317, 318, 340, 410
 gift of God, 318
 imagination, inferior to, 205, 519
 imagination, superior to, 13
 instinct, should follow, 503
 intuitive faculty, universal, 67, 68, 97, 171, 432, 451, 457, 468, 470, 520, 560
 a light within the soul, 68, 92, 260, 310, 469, 558, 559, 563
 morality, equivalent to, 190
 poetical reason not the same as mathematical, 566
 priestcraft, opposed to, 223
 religion, bulwark of, 465
 religion, the highest reason, 289, 563
 self-love, restrains, 506
 superstitious fears, dispels, 3, 18, 164, 243, 466
Rebellion of 1715, 50, 62, 341
Rebellion of 1745, 341, 435
Redemption, 64, 142, 181, 191, 194, 200, 289, 304, 320, 390, 476, 481, 486, 545; *see also* Atonement; Salvation
Reform, moral and religious, efforts toward, 56, 65, 70, 71, 72, 73, 115, 174, 177, 178, 180, 183, 188, 189, 190, 201, 204, 248, 250, 387, 390, 402, 445, 448, 449, 450, 494; *see also* Impiety and moral corruption of the age
Reformation, Protestant, 78, 104, 207, 510, 539, 542, 544, 547, 563
Religion, *see also* Christianity; Deism; Enthusiasm; Faith; God; Grace
 cheerful, 377, 521
 commerce and industry, favorable to, 442
 emotional and imaginative quality, lack of, 3, 204, 249
 forms, empty, averse to, 463
 greed, corrupted by, 46
 humble, the, at its best among, 378
 inhumanity and fraud, disguise for, 271
 internal, more important than external, 242
 joy as well as fear, includes, 146
 liberty, associated with, 91, 159, 325, 442, 443, 457, 529
 love, equivalent to, 10
 melancholy, marred by, 241
 morality, necessary for, 267, 297, 310, 311, 330, 331, 374, 468, 471, 472
 morality, not necessary for, 4, 53, 452

 not mysterious, 67, 179, 325, 458, 491
 politics, submerged in, 66
 priestcraft, distinguished from, 92
 reason and the passions, harmonizes, 186
 reasonable, 104, 183, 325, 340, 359, 396, 457, 529, 563
 service to mankind, consists of, 113
 shines in every heart, 281
 social stability, necessary for, 6, 26, 115
 virtuous conduct, equivalent to, 67, 163, 179, 271, 279, 310, 339, 342, 359, 374, 396, 501
 zeal, extravagant; should avoid, 340, 347, 353, 359, 451
Renaissance, 6, 22, 129, 130, 188, 196, 205, 217, 480, 536, 540, 541, 547, 555, 560, 561, 563, 569, 570
Restoration, 95, 191, 282, 510, 536, 554, 557, 571, 572
Resurrection, 5, 101, 161, 239, 322, 345, 398, 499
Retirement, Christian, 104, 136, 142, 143, 147, 148, 182, 210, 211, 218, 235, 240, 323, 349
 classical or humanistic, 9, 171, 172, 211, 270, 414, 415, 463
 sentimental, 15, 143, 211, 212, 224, 243, 244, 247, 252, 255, 273, 279, 293, 294, 327, 364, 375, 381, 383, 388, 389, 397, 400, 412, 431, 436, 437, 438, 439, 441, 442, 445, 446, 448, 453, 485, 494, 513, 515, 517, 525, 526, 527; *see also* Contemplation; Melancholy of pensive retirement
Retreat: *see* Retirement, Christian
Revelation, natural, 39, 114, 136, 137, 181, 197, 200, 210, 226, 255, 272, 288, 356, 372, 379, 391, 410, 452, 456, 460, 465, 478, 485, 501, 513, 524, 541, 559, 562, 572; *see also* Nature, God of; Nature, religion of; Newtonianism; Teleological arguments
 supernatural, 124, 125, 148, 191, 196, 200, 310, 311, 313, 316, 452, 465, 479, 499, 501, 525, 559
Revolt, spirit of political, 17, 52, 55, 56, 58, 61, 66, 69, 92, 537, 558
Revolution of 1688, 61, 121, 282, 554, 571
Ritual and ceremonial, 4, 18, 27, 43, 50, 53, 54, 58, 80, 87, 105, 141, 147, 159, 172, 239, 304, 347, 529
Roman Catholicism: *see* Catholicism, Roman
Romanticism, 21, 34, 129, 167, 205, 211, 213, 215, 217, 232, 499, 504, 533, 535,

Romanticism (*Continued*)
  536, 537, 538, 566, 567, 568, 574, 575;
  see also Pre-romanticism
Royal Society, 13, 38, 356, 435, 563
Rural life, 228, 246, 255, 274, 331, 338,
  365, 375, 388, 414, 434, 436, 439, 510

Sacraments: see Baptism; Eucharist
Saints, 58, 100, 103, 107, 248, 305, 306,
  307, 308, 325, 490, 494
Salvation, 26, 114, 283, 290, 322, 488, 499,
  542, 544, 545; *see also* Atonement; Redemption
Satire against piety and zeal: *see* Piety and
  zeal, satirized or sneered at
Scepticism, 7, 9, 10, 14, 26, 27, 33, 38, 39,
  40, 170, 171, 199, 223, 335, 452, 489,
  504, 514, 558, 576; *see also* Fideism
Schism Act, 74, 96, 159
Science, 199, 478, 480, 520, 526, 533, 541,
  542, 547, 561; *see also* Microscope;
  Nature (universe as regarded by contemporary science); Newtonianism;
  Royal Society; Telescope
  perilous to religion, 38, 40, 200, 201, 558,
    563, 564; *see also* Determinism; Mate-
    rialism; Mechanism
  related to deism, 20, 197, 278, 480
  related to latitudinarian and rationalistic
    trends in religion, 13, 38, 119, 120,
    144, 151, 152, 153, 154, 174, 201, 210,
    242, 272, 277, 278, 297, 316, 320, 392,
    393, 435, 460, 511, 557
Secession Church, 283, 287, 434
Sects, Separatist, 41, 47, 122, 268, 298, 299,
  544, 546-556, 559, 563, 570; *see also*
  Baptists; Enthusiasm; Familists; French
  Prophets; Levellers; Muggletonians;
  Philadelphians; Quakerism; Ranters;
  Seekers
Seekers, 549, 554
Self-love, 269, 467, 468, 503, 505, 506, 507,
  521, 562
Sensibility, 222, 261, 295, 329, 335, 363,
  372, 396, 403, 461, 469, 475, 476, 482,
  485, 510, 515, 519, 522, 524, 526, 527,
  534, 574
Sentiment, religion of, 219, 236, 246, 260,
  262, 272, 346, 424, 466, 485, 486, 534,
  542, 546, 551, 554, 573, 575
Sentimentalism, 8, 20, 163, 165, 215, 216,
  217, 219-262 *passim*, 265, 280, 281,
  282, 295, 315, 345, 353, 359, 361-487
  passim, 495, 499, 502, 503, 504, 505,

  507, 509-534 *passim; see also* Activity;
  Beauty; Benevolence, universal; Benevolism; Contemplation; Deism; Enthusiasm; Harmony, universal; Inner
  Light; Latitudinarianism; Liberty; Moral
  sense; Natural goodness; Naturalism,
  sentimental; Nature; Optimism; Patriotism; Pre-romanticism; Primitivism;
  Retirement, sentimental; Rural life;
  Sensibility; Sentiment, religion of; Service; Soul, the, sentimental implications;
  Whiggery
  libertine, 220-227 *passim*, 261, 266, 278,
    370, 371, 421, 484, 555, 558
  related to Protestantism, xi, 139, 260, 295,
    486, 487, 532, 534-576 *passim*
Sermons: *see* Preaching
Service, cult of, 9, 194, 333, 334, 372, 383,
  397, 409, 431, 432, 459, 496, 506, 528,
  530, 531, 533, 542, 574; *see also* Activity; Altruism; Benevolism; Humanitarianism; Patriotism
Sin, 26, 47, 69, 100, 114, 118, 123, 126,
  145, 146, 210, 219, 289, 301, 306, 318,
  320, 336, 469, 486, 488, 535, 536, 544,
  545, 548, 572; *see also* Depravity,
  total
Sincerity, 53, 54, 80, 221, 223, 292, 432,
  508, 572
"Social," contemporary use of the epithet,
  144, 165, 278, 331, 363, 365, 396, 458,
  467, 471, 506, 521, 528
Socinianism, 18, 42, 70, 89, 112, 123, 268,
  298, 494, 544
Solitude: *see* Retirement
Soul, 19, 35, 151, 152, 221, 354, 471
  sentimental implications, 107, 128, 159,
    165, 206, 223, 255, 278, 293, 318, 333,
    363, 366, 379, 383, 417, 430, 476, 517,
    519, 528, 532, 567, 568; *see also*
    Genius; Inner Light; Transcendental-
    ism
  traditionally Christian implications, 63, 99,
    109, 167, 211, 231, 241, 291, 304, 319,
    327, 376, 474, 496
Stage, disapproval of the, 11, 56, 115, 136,
  183, 190, 282, 413, 433, 434
Stoicism, 6, 7, 8, 19, 37, 120, 167, 191,
  242, 243, 270, 281, 311, 359, 395, 396,
  504, 555, 557, 569
Sublimity in poetry, 10, 64, 99, 129, 144,
  145, 169, 184, 187, 204, 206, 251, 266,
  294, 312, 340, 353, 366, 370, 375, 427,
  447, 450, 473, 517

Superstition, 3, 4, 12, 50, 55, 86, 91, 92, 114, 164, 183, 204, 223, 270, 278, 350, 437, 451, 510, 528, 529, 566

Teleological arguments, 38, 181, 197, 198, 199, 218, 256, 317, 354, 391, 393, 394, 464, 479, 541
Telescope, 218, 255, 265, 391, 435, 460
Test and Corporation Acts, 74
Tolerance and toleration, 42, 49, 59, 60, 76, 93, 94, 96, 121, 134, 159, 160, 163, 186, 254, 261, 299, 323, 346, 368, 385, 386, 453, 501, 502, 508, 559
Topographical poetry, 15, 347, 352, 375, 412
Toryism, 4, 5, 41, 44-61 passim, 93, 94, 96, 154, 162, 202, 203, 229, 259, 367, 447, 483, 557; see also High Church
attacked, 15, 61-92 passim, 158, 159, 225, 497
Transcendence, divine, 124, 148, 199, 200, 210, 229, 257, 289, 317, 344, 410, 444, 464, 479, 507, 522, 523, 524, 545, 546, 552, 553, 565, 567, 568
Transcendentalism, explicit or implicit, 14, 111, 127-130, 182, 183, 205, 217, 256, 258, 430, 453, 476, 504, 527, 528, 533, 534, 539, 540, 560, 561, 562, 563, 564, 566, 567, 568, 569; see also Genius; Imagination; Inner Light
Transmigration of souls, 19, 518, 520
Transubstantiation: see Eucharist, Holy
Trinity, Holy, 18, 30, 44, 98, 113, 123, 140, 159, 160, 170, 234, 301, 318, 548, 556, 565; see also Arianism; Socinianism
Truth, 27, 28, 57, 62, 76, 109, 171, 299, 316, 317, 346, 372, 380, 395, 432, 466, 476, 498, 504, 546, 559, 561

Uniformitarianism, 392, 452, 464, 478, 485, 486, 495, 519, 520, 540, 541, 558, 560

Union, Act of, 283, 510
Unitarianism: see Socinianism
Upper classes, 4, 5, 93, 201, 202, 246, 261, 280, 358, 420, 483, 570
indifferent or hostile to religion, 3, 6, 22, 29, 37, 72, 73, 81, 197, 221, 268, 269, 326, 327, 396
religious members of, 22, 118, 208, 209, 236, 237, 330, 389
Utilitarianism, 71, 180, 202, 262, 283, 527, 544, 561

Virtue, 8, 67, 92, 116, 155, 170, 185, 190, 231, 246, 266, 269, 270, 297, 311, 325, 330, 332, 333, 346, 372, 405, 406, 418, 432, 436, 445, 457, 471, 496, 506, 507, 512, 523, 531; see also Morality

Whiggery, 154, 163, 183, 185, 186, 201, 202, 203, 260, 321, 359, 483, 484, 539, 571, 572, 573; see also Compromise, the eighteenth-century; Sentimentalism; Utilitarianism
attacked, 44-61 passim, 96, 162, 299
economic and social ideals of, 73, 89, 273, 368, 442, 459, 526; see also Commerce and industry; Middle class; Progress
moral and religious ideals of, 45, 73, 61-92 passim, 93, 96, 97, 194, 195, 224, 234, 261, 262, 368, 386, 422, 443, 531, 534; see also Latitudinarianism
political and ecclesiastical ideals of, 15, 17, 61-92 passim, 95, 113, 158, 159, 160, 178, 259, 357, 358, 373, 386, 457, 556; see also Liberty; Low Church
Wit, 7, 12, 15, 29, 31, 64, 70, 73, 119, 166, 177, 190, 197, 214, 250, 261, 288, 302, 311, 315, 318, 331, 367, 374, 418, 439, 490, 494, 519; see also Piety and zeal, satirized or sneered at